Christoph Wille
Christian Koller

SAMS
Teach Yourself
ADO 2.5
in 21 Days

SAMS

A Division of Macmillan Computer Publishing
201 West 103rd St., Indianapolis, Indiana, 46290 USA

Sams Teach Yourself ADO 2.5 in 21 Days

Copyright ©2000 by Sams Publishing

International Standard Book Number: 0-672-31873-3

Library of Congress Catalog Card Number: 99-67449

Printed in the United States of America

First Printing: May, 2000

01   00   99   4   3   2   1

Trademarks

Warning and Disclaimer

ASSOCIATE PUBLISHER
Bradley Jones

ACQUISITIONS EDITOR
Danielle Bird

DEVELOPMENT EDITOR
Kevin Howard

MANAGING EDITOR
Charlotte Clapp

PROJECT EDITOR
Dawn Pearson

COPY EDITOR
Nancy Albright

INDEXER
Chris Barrick

PROOFREADER
Jill Mazurczyk

TECHNICAL EDITOR
Ken Cox

TEAM COORDINATOR
Meggo Barthlow

MEDIA DEVELOPER
Maggie Molloy

INTERIOR DESIGNER
Gary Adair

COVER DESIGNER
Aren Howell

COPYWRITER
Eric Brogert

PRODUCTION
Cyndi Davis-Hubler

Contents at a Glance

Contents

About the Authors

Christoph Wille, MCSE, MCSD, CNA, and MCP-IT, works as a network consultant and assists companies in planning and deploying Internet-connected networks. He also works as a programmer, specializing in Windows DNA. Christoph has authored or contributed to several books, including *Sams Teach Yourself Active Server Pages in 24 Hours, MCSE Training Guide: SQL Server 7 Administration, Sams Teach Yourself MCSE IIS4 in 14 Days,* and *Sams Teach Yourself MCSE TCP/IP in 14 Days.*

Visit his IIS and ASP resource site at `http://www.alphasierrapapa.com/iisdev/` for free articles and ASP component downloads. Christoph is recognized by Microsoft as Most Valuable Professional (MVP) for Active Server Pages.

Christian Koller is a programmer who specializes in employing database technologies in the classic client/server arena and in three-tier environments. His favorite tier technologies are Active Server Pages, Visual Basic, and SQL Server. Christian coauthored *Sams Teach Yourself Active Server Pages in 24 Hours* with Christoph Wille, in which he wrote the chapters about ADO.

Tell Us What You Think!

As the reader of this book, *you* are our most important critic and commentator. We value your opinion and want to know what we're doing right, what we could do better, what areas you'd like to see us publish in, and any other words of wisdom you're willing to pass our way.

As an Associate Publisher for Sams, I welcome your comments. You can fax, email, or write me directly to let me know what you did or didn't like about this book—as well as what we can do to make our books stronger.

Please note that I cannot help you with technical problems related to the topic of this book, and that due to the high volume of mail I receive, I might not be able to reply to every message.

When you write, please be sure to include this book's title and author as well as your name and phone or fax number. I will carefully review your comments and share them with the author and editors who worked on the book.

Fax: 317-581-4770
Email: adv_prog@mcp.com
Mail: Bradley Jones
        Associate Publisher
        Sams
        201 West 103rd Street
        Indianapolis, IN 46290 USA

Introduction

Welcome to *Sams Teach Yourself ADO 2.5 in 21 Days*. During the next three weeks you will learn many database tasks with ADO, such as retrieving data, working with transactions, creating scalable database applications, and securing and tuning databases. You have bought this book to come up to speed with ADO both quickly and thoroughly. Please take the time to read the next two sections to see where you want to concentrate your study.

Who Should Read This Book?

Sams Teach Yourself ADO 2.5 in 21 Days is targeted at programmers who use any kind of Visual Basic language derivative (VB, VBA, or VBScript) and want to access databases with ADO. Because this book is organized into weeks, beginners can start at ground zero in Week 1 and seasoned database programmers can join us in Week 2. If you are interested only in how to integrate with and optimize for COM+ and Web Services, you will find the most useful information in Week 3.

You should have at least intermediate knowledge of the Visual Basic programming constructs. A working knowledge of HTML will also help, but it isn't mandatory to follow the examples.

How This Book Is Organized

Each week covers different aspects of programming with ADO.

Week 1—The Basics of ADO and OLE DB

Week 1 starts by brushing up your SQL knowledge and introducing the Universal Data Access strategy and how ADO fits into it. You learn how to establish database connections and retrieve data. You acquire a firm foundation on recordset properties, which is further solidified when dealing with the process of inserting new data to a table.

The second half of the week begins with updating and deleting existing data. You then explore the intricacies of filtering and sorting resultsets, and also learn how to effectively deal with large recordsets. The week ends with SQL Server stored procedures, which enable you to strengthen your database applications.

Week 2—Advanced ADO

After mastering the basics, the first lesson of Week 2 prepares you for transaction processing. It is followed by an in-depth look at asynchronous database operations, which are necessary in distributed applications.

Two lessons are dedicated to analyzing businesses using Microsoft OLAP Services: one to get you started with the concepts and visual tools, and the other to train you on the MDX query language and how to employ ADO MD to retrieve data from your OLAP servers. You get in touch with the new Record and Stream objects of ADO 2.5 when accessing semistructured data.

Week 2 concludes with a database management lesson. You learn how to create new databases, modify database objects of existing ones, and finally, how to secure these objects against unauthorized use.

Week 3—Putting It All Together in Real Life

The final Week starts by taking you on a tour of COM+ and how your database applications can take advantage of its services. You also learn how to disconnect data from a database, remoting it as far as the Internet can take the data.

An important skill of today's database developers is to be able to encapsulate data access functionality in components. You acquire the necessary knowledge to get started with three-tier programming, which also encompasses Windows DNA. Because Web servers and database servers are under heavy loads when you deploy Windows DNA solutions, you discover various tuning and debugging tips for distributed environments—not to mention the usual dose of security management.

What You Will Need to Use This Book

Although many of the examples presented in this book also work on Windows NT 4, we use a lot of features that are available only on Windows 2000 Professional. Therefore, we strongly recommend that you work on a Windows 2000 machine when exploring the samples. For some of Week 3's tutorials you are required to have Internet Information Servicer 5 installed on your Windows 2000 machine.

Most of the examples in this book are written in Excel 2000; therefore, if you want to try them immediately, you have to install Excel on your machine. We tried to keep the source code as portable as possible so you can easily move it to Visual Basic or Active Server Pages. You'll also find examples that are entirely implemented in VB or ASP, especially in Week 3, which teaches interoperability.

Although it is not mandatory, we strongly recommend that you have SQL Server 7 installed on your machine for testing (MSDE is also sufficient). To follow the tutorials in Days 11 and 12 you need Microsoft OLAP Services (part of SQL Server 7, but not MSDE), and parts of Day 13 require you to have an Exchange 2000 installation.

WEEK 1

At A Glance

In the first week, you start by exploring what ADO is, how it is related to OLE DB, and what UDA can do for your database application. You then retrieve data, insert new data, and update and delete existing data. You explore the power of filters, sort recordsets without the help of the database engine, optimize your solution for large recordsets, and encapsulate data access logic in stored procedures.

- Day 1—You are introduced to ADO, OLE DB, and UDA. You learn how to use ADO in different scenarios and where to get the latest release for installation on various platforms.
- Day 2—You create code that enables you to retrieve data from a database. You explore the various ways of using the Recordset object to build solid code.
- Day 3—You acquire the necessary knowledge to build data-entry applications that can deal with error conditions that are typical in a three-tier or Web-enabled scenario.
- Day 4—You discover ways to modify or remove information that is stored in a database. You learn to complete these tasks in different ways.
- Day 5—You search and filter for information that is stored in a database table. You build code that can find records affected by specific database tasks or bookmark table data for later reuse.
- Day 6—You optimize your application for recordsets that possibly return thousands of result rows. You discover advanced techniques for searching and paging.
- Day 7—You tap the power of using SQL Server 7 stored procedures to add more speed and reliability to your solution. You update, delete, and insert data into the database using stored procedures.

1

2

3

4

5

6

7

DAY 1

Basic Knowledge About ADO

ActiveX Data Objects (ADO) exposes a set of compact objects that enable you to insert, delete, and update data as well as query a data source, access the resultset, or perform various operations, such as sorting against the resultset. You can easily manipulate various data sources even over enterprise networks or the Internet.

Using ADO makes it possible not only to retrieve data from several data sources, but there are also different ways to retrieve data, manage databases, create tables, and manipulate data. ADO uses methods and properties of ADO objects or SQL (Structured Query Language) statements executed by certain ADO methods to manipulate data sources.

ADO 2.5 is part of the Microsoft Data Access Components (MDAC) 2.5 package, which contains ADO and other components (such as database providers and database drivers) necessary to connect to various data sources.

Today, you learn the following basic knowledge about ADO, its use, and basic technologies:

- Introducing Universal Data Access (UDA)—UDA is a concept about accessing various data sources even over a company's intranet or the Internet. ADO is a key technology (besides other MDAC technologies) that enables UDA.

- Retrieving the latest ADO version—Where to get it and how to install it on a computer.

- Determining the installed ADO version—The Component Checker tool simply investigates the ADO installation on your machine.

- Installing Microsoft Platform SDK—Its documentation contains a huge amount of useful articles about ADO, databases (such as SQL Server and Microsoft Access), and other MDAC components.

- Investigating the ADO Programming Model—See the basic tasks necessary to use ADO for connecting to a data source. Discover the three main ADO component libraries: the ADO 2.5 core (ADO), ADO Extensions for Data Definition Language and Security (ADOX), and ADO Multidimensional (ADO MD).

Exploring ADO and Universal Data Access

ADO and its simple and flat object model provide an ease-of-use interface to access various data sources, even across enterprise networks or the Internet. Using ADO enables consistent and high-performance access to various data sources for manipulating all kinds of data stores and data content. ADO is a key technology of the UDA strategy.

 The idea behind *Universal Data Access* (UDA) is to provide efficient access to any kind of data across a network. The data is accessed where it is found, instead of storing it in a central data store.

MDAC contains the key technologies (ADO, OLE DB, and ODBC) that provide access to information across an enterprise in a simple manner.

ADO is language-independent, so you can use ADO with nearly any programming language—for instance, Visual Basic, Visual C++, VBScript (used in Internet Information Server, Internet Explorer, and Windows Scripting Host), Microsoft Visual J++, JScript, and Visual Basic for Applications (used in Microsoft Word, Excel, and Access).

ADO provides consistent access to various data sources, such as Microsoft SQL Server 7.0 or Microsoft Access 2000. Other data sources, such as text files or directory structures and file properties of a Windows 2000 file system, can be accessed using ADO 2.5. No matter which data source you access, you use the same ADO actions to add a dataset to a Microsoft SQL Server or Access 2000 database. The same ADO objects are used to access an ODBC data source, an Oracle database, or the information stored in an Indexing Service catalog.

NEW TERM *Indexing Service* is a base service of Windows NT and Windows 2000. It extracts contents from files and builds an indexed catalog to enable fast search operations to find files with certain content or with certain other properties. For querying the Indexing Service, you can use ADO objects in nearly any programming language to execute statements against the Indexing Service. You can perform querying, managing, or indexing tasks through ADO objects by executing statements written in Indexing Service Query Language Dialect (and Dialect 2), or in SQL.

Development needs are supported by ADO because the use of ADO objects is easy to learn and consistent for various data sources. When you have learned how to access an Access database using ADO, you have the skills to query a SQL Server or Oracle database through ADO.

ADO itself is a thin layer built on OLE DB, a technology designed to access various databases through defined interfaces.

NEW TERM *Object linking and embedding for databases* (OLE DB) is a set of interfaces used to access and manipulate data over an enterprise's network. It does not matter which type of data is accessed, OLE DB provides the database architecture to use for the application.

You can connect from OLE DB to ODBC (using an OLE DB provider for ODBC); therefore, you can access virtually any database because ODBC drivers are available for most modern databases.

NEW TERM *Open database connectivity* (ODBC) is a specification for a database interface, which is used to access various databases using database drivers. The ODBC interface that an ODBC driver exposes is database-independent. So every ODBC driver, whether the Access ODBC driver or the ODBC driver for text files, exposes the same functions to your application as long as the data store supports those functions. Virtually every database system in use can be accessed using ADO (with the underlying OLE DB interfaces) and the corresponding ODBC driver.

You can use ADO to access data on the same computer where the application is running. However, ADO provides all the requirements to access data across enterprise networks or the Internet. Applications can access a centrally located database server and even other workstations. Even Microsoft Internet Explorer 4.0 (or later) can make use of ADO in DHTML pages, so it is easy to build distributed information applications that access central data sources.

NEW TERM   *Dynamic Hypertext Markup Language* (DHTML) is an object- and event-based enhancement of the widespread HTML standard. It enables using objects, such as ADO objects and related events, in an Internet page. The only requirement to run a DHTML Internet page is to use Microsoft Internet Explorer 4.0 (or later) when calling an Internet page containing DHTML.

Remember, ADO enables you to access nearly any kind of data and information. It does not matter if the data is stored in a database, in a text file, or in a Microsoft Office document, for instance. Examples for databases that can be accessed using ADO are SQL Server, Microsoft Access, Oracle database, or IBM DB2 database server.

The connection between ADO, OLE DB, ODBC, and various data sources is shown in Figure 1.1.

FIGURE 1.1

The connection between ADO, OLE DB, ODBC, and data sources.

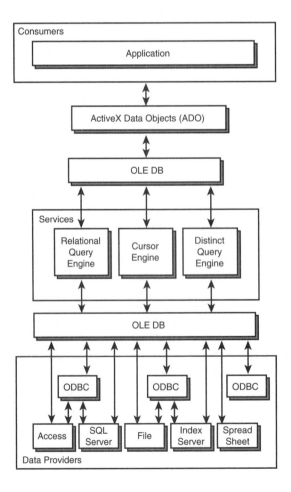

1

Imagine the process when a Visual Basic application wants to access a database or other data source. The application programmer uses various objects from the ADO object model in his Visual Basic source code to access and manipulate the data from the data.

The Visual Basic application is the data consumer that uses ADO as the interface to access the data source. ADO itself makes use of OLE DB technology (contained in OLE DB providers), which enables ADO to connect to various data sources. Commands and data are exchanged between the application (data consumer) and the database (data provider) using ADO and the OLE DB provider, making ADO and its underlying OLE DB technology the link between an application and a data source.

Although ADO provides the interface for the application, the OLE DB provider is the interface to the data source or database. Each data source or data store needs to be connected through a custom-made OLE DB provider. But no matter which OLE DB provider you have to employ, your application uses the same ADO objects for any kind of data source.

NEW TERM An *OLE DB provider* for a certain data source provides an OLE DB interface to the data source. Using the OLE DB provider enables ADO to access a data source. A database connection through OLE DB offers usually the best performance for an ADO connection.

Before discovering the characteristics and use of ADO and its object model, you see how to obtain and install the latest ADO version and the Microsoft Platform SDK. First find out how to determine the ADO version installed on a certain computer. The importance of the Platform SDK and its documentation to the ADO developer is pointed out in the next sections.

How to Obtain the Latest ADO Version

With the release of Windows 2000, MDAC 2.5 (containing ADO 2.5) is a part of the operating system's data access services. Although MDAC 2.5 is preinstalled on Windows 2000, check for updates and fixes to the components as part of the operating system's service packs. To install the latest version of MDAC on Windows 2000, you have to apply the latest Windows 2000 service pack to the operating system.

For other Windows operating systems, such as Windows 95/98 or Windows NT 4.0, you can obtain ADO 2.5 when installing MDAC 2.5 RTM from the Microsoft Web site `http://www.microsoft.com/data/`.

Because the ADO documentation is not part of Windows 2000 or the MDAC 2.5 RTM download, you also have to install the Microsoft Platform SDK to gain access to the documentation of MDAC and ADO 2.5 (and later).

To obtain the Microsoft Platform SDK, download it from the Microsoft Web site `http://msdn.microsoft.com/developer/sdk/platform.asp` and follow the instructions to download and install the Platform SDK on your computer.

Make sure you have Microsoft Internet Explorer 4.01 Service Pack 2 (or later), installed on the computer before installing Platform SDK; when you are using Windows 95/98 or Windows NT 4.0, you also have to download and install Windows Installer 1.1 (or later).

When running the Platform SDK setup program, choosing Custom Install option enables you to define which parts of the Platform SDK are installed.

Installing ADO 2.5

You can make sure that a certain ADO version is on a computer by installing the accordant MDAC on the machine. ADO 2.5 is contained in MDAC 2.5, for instance.

To install the latest MDAC on your machine, depending on the operating system, proceed as follows: For Windows 95, Windows 98, and Windows NT 4.0, download the latest available MDAC setup program (`_typ.exe`) from the Microsoft Web site at `http://www.microsoft.com/data/`.

 Note   MDAC 2.5 (or later) is available only for *x*86 machines. For Alpha computers, download the latest version of MDAC 2.1 (SP2).

In Windows 2000, MDAC 2.5 is an integral component of the operating system. Windows 2000 uses Windows File Protection (WFP) system (sometimes referred to as System File Protection, SFP) to protect system files from being overwritten by applications. Therefore, you cannot use the MDAC setup program; you have to apply a Windows 2000 service pack instead, which contains the latest MDAC version.

Running MDAC Setup Program

To DO: Installing MDAC on Your Machine

Run the MDAC setup program (`mdac_typ.exe`) using the following checklist:

1. Retrieve the new MDAC version. For Windows 95, Windows 98, and Windows NT 4.0, you have to download the MDAC setup program `mdac_typ.exe` from the Microsoft Web site at

   `http://www.microsoft.com/data/`

   For a Windows 2000 machine, obtain the latest service pack for Windows 2000.

▼   2. If you have Windows 95, make sure that you have DCOM95 installed on your machine, or download it at Microsoft Web site

`http://www.microsoft.com/com/resources/downloads.asp`

Most Windows 98 operating systems have DCOM98 automatically installed. When you need to download DCOM98, it can be retrieved from the Microsoft Web site.

3. Because MDAC 2.5 has dependencies to Microsoft Internet Explorer 4.01, make sure that Internet Explorer 4.01 (or later) is installed on your computer.

4. Before running `mdac_typ.exe`, shut down all Windows applications or Windows NT services using MDAC. For best results, close all user applications, including development tools and server applications, before running MDAC setup.

5. When installing on a Windows NT 4.0 machine, make sure that you are logged in as an Administrator.

6. Disable any antivirus software, disk security software, and memory-resident application running on your computer.

7. Ensure that you have at least 50MB free disk space to install MDAC. Note that MDAC installs files into the Program Files folder as well as into the system folder (`Windows\System` on Win 9*x*, or `WinNT\system32` on Win NT for default).

8. Make sure that a valid TEMP folder is defined and the TEMP drive has at minimum 50MB free. Determine the location of your TEMP folder by running SET in an MS-DOS prompt. The SET program lists environment variables, whereby the location of the TEMP folder is the value after the variables TEMP= or TMP=.

9. When installing MDAC on Windows 95, make sure that the MDAC installer is located on a mapped drive or locally on the computer.

10. If installing MDAC on a Terminal Server system, special steps are necessary. Please refer to the Microsoft Knowledge article Q216149, "How to Install ODBC or MDAC on Terminal Server." This article is also available at the following Microsoft Web site:

`http://support.microsoft.com/support/kb/articles/Q216/1/49.ASP`

11. Run the MDAC setup program `mdac_typ.exe` on your computer to install MDAC and ADO. When a message appears that DCOM95 or DCOM98 is not installed, obtain the DCOM95 or DCOM98 setup file (`dcom95.exe` or `dcom98.exe`), execute
▲   the file, and try to run the MDAC setup program again.

> When you install MDAC 2.5 (or later) on a computer running applications
> that access an SQL Server 6.5 database through the OLE DB Provider for SQL
> Server or the SQL Server ODBC Driver, and the catalog stored procedures
> installed on SQL Server 6.5 are not current, a warning message is raised
> when you access the SQL Server. You also might experience some serious
> problems, such as loss of schema information. To resolve this problem, you
> must install and run `instcat.sql` on SQL Server 6.5. The `instcat.sql` file
> comes with MDAC 2.5. The new catalog stored procedures of `instcat.sql`
> also are automatically installed when you apply SQL Server 6.5 Service Pack 5
> (or later) to the SQL Server machine.

If you want to install an older MDAC version over a newer one, you have to uninstall
MDAC from the computer. MDAC has no built-in uninstall feature, but you can use the
Component Checker tool to diagnose, reconfigure and uninstall MDAC. Component
Checker is described today in the section "Determining the Installed ADO Version with
Component Checker."

After installing a certain MDAC version on a machine, all ADO components, OLE DB
providers, and ODBC drivers of Microsoft products are updated. When you want to
update OLE DB providers and ODBC drivers from other vendors, you might have to
install them separately.

The MDAC setup program is also useful for redistributing MDAC with your application.
Please make sure that MDAC is installed only on machines with valid operating system
licenses (read the MDAC 2.5 End-User License Agreement—EULA)!

You can download MDAC packages as redistribution programs (`mdac_typ.exe`) for several MDAC versions from the Microsoft Internet site at
`http://www.microsoft.com/data/`.

Remember, when installing MDAC (2.0 and later) on Windows 95 or Windows 98, you
have to apply the DCOM95 or DCOM98 patch (`dcom95.exe` or `dcom98.exe`) prior to
running MDAC setup for MDAC versions 2.0 and later.

Checking Whether MDAC Is Installed Correctly

To check whether MDAC is installed correctly, the best you can do is to run applications
using ADO and MDAC. However, there are some short tests that can indicate whether
something went wrong during MDAC setup.

Check whether ODBC Administrator is working correctly. Open the Control Panel by
selecting Start button, Settings, Control Panel; double-click on the ODBC Data Sources
icon. Then try to create a new ODBC System DSN by performing the following steps:

1. Select the System DSN tab in the ODBC Data Source Administrator.
2. Click on the Add button to create a new System DSN.
3. Select Microsoft Access Driver (*.mdb) from the driver list and click on Finish.
4. Type CHECK in the Data Source Name box.
5. Click on the Create button in the Database section; the New Database window appears.
6. Type C:\CHECK.MDB in the Database Name field and click the OK button. A message appears that the Access database C:\CHECK.MDB was created successfully. Click OK in the message window.
7. Click OK in the Microsoft Access Setup window and close it.
8. In the Microsoft Data Source Administrator window, click OK to close the window.

When all steps are performed successfully, you can assume that the ODBC core files and ODBC Administrator are set up correctly.

To test whether ADO and RDS are installed correctly, use the Component Checker tool, which is described in the next section.

Determining the Installed ADO Version with Component Checker

To determine the currently installed ADO version on a machine, use the tool named Component Checker (ComCheck.exe). It enables you to check which ADO or MDAC version is currently installed on a machine. The tool is part of the Platform SDK and also can be downloaded separately from the Microsoft Internet site http://www.microsoft.com/Data/download.htm.

Only 32-bit and 64-bit operating systems (such as Windows 98, Windows Millennium, Windows NT 4.0, and Windows 2000) are supported.

The features of the Component Checker tool are

- Identifying the currently installed MDAC and ADO version on a computer.
- Identifying the files of the current MDAC version and showing reports about differences to major MDAC release versions.
- Allowing complete removal of a certain ADO version from a computer. Additionally, .dll conflicts and programs that reference a certain .dll are identified and listed.

The result after running Component Checker to identify the current MDAC/ADO version is shown in Figure 1.2.

FIGURE 1.2

Using the Component Checker tool.

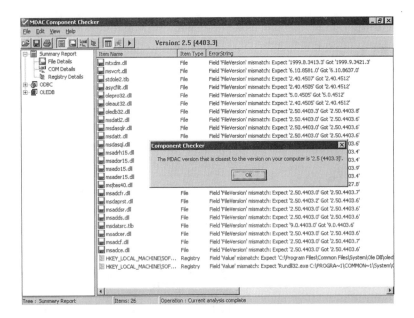

Installing Platform SDK Documentation

When you work with ADO 2.5, the Microsoft Platform SDK is essential to gain all the information about ADO 2.5 objects, their methods, properties, and events. There is an online version of the Platform SDK at the Microsoft MSDN library on the Web (http://msdn.microsoft.com/library/).

The Platform SDK is also available for download at the Microsoft Web site. Go to http://www.microsoft.com/downloads/, choose Platform SDK (and any windows operating system), search for the download and click on the Platform SDK link. (The download address is http://msdn.microsoft.com/developer/sdk/platform.asp.)

After you receive the Platform SDK, install it by running the setup file. When choosing Custom Installation in the setup menu, you can determine which parts of the SDK are installed on the computer and which are not.

In rare cases, it is possible that a developer tool or environment such as Visual C++ 6.0 will not be able to compile a project. The reason for this behavior is that the Platform SDK overwrites some files that are used for the MFC ActiveX components. Refer to the Microsoft Developer Network (MSDN), or to the MSDN Internet page at http://msdn.microsoft.com and search for the term Platform SDK to find articles about problems related to installing the Platform SDK.

After installing the Platform SDK, you have all the necessary information about ADO objects, ODBC drivers, and so on to successfully develop database applications using ADO.

To access the Platform SDK Documentation, select Start button, Programs, Microsoft Platform SDK, Platform SDK Documentation. The Microsoft Platform SDK documentation window appears (see Figure 1.3).

FIGURE 1.3

The Platform SDK documentation window.

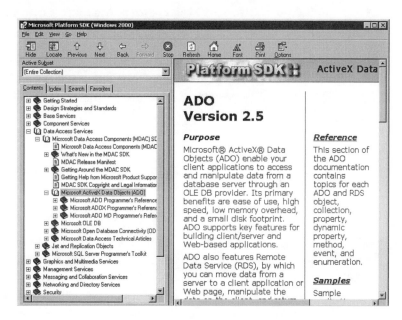

Tip

When the left pane with the Contents, Index, Search, and Favorites tabs does not appear in the documentation window, click the Show icon (upper-left corner of the toolbar).

Discovering the Characteristics of ADO

ADO allows you to access and update a database or other data source. The sequence of ADO activities necessary to execute a database action is called ADO programming model. The following section introduces the basic ADO activities and describes in common words how to perform database actions with ADO.

The ADO programming model is realized by using ADO objects. All ADO objects, their methods and properties are defined in the ADO object model. To use a certain ADO object in a programming language like Visual Basic, you have to use the corresponding

ADO component library. Most ADO 2.5 objects are contained in three component libraries: ADO core, ADOX (ADO Extensions for DLL and Security), and ADO MD (ADO Multidimensional).

Introducing the ADO Programming Model

A typical use of ADO when you execute a database action is as follows:

- Connect to a data source. This is even possible across networks or the Internet.
- Specify a statement or command to execute against the database.
- Execute the statement against the database.
- When the executed statement returns data rows from the data source, store the data rows in a so-called recordset. The recordset enables you to access the data returned from a database query.
- If appropriate, change the data of the recordset and update the data store with the changes.

Additionally, ADO provides the means to detect errors when connecting to a data source or retrieving data.

Especially for critical applications, ADO provides support for transactional processes.

NEW TERM   A *transactional process* (or *transaction*) is a set of statements whose changes are stored permanently only when all statements are executed successfully. Otherwise, the changes in the data store made by all statements in the transaction are canceled and the transaction fails. A typical example for a transaction in real life is when you have to ensure that on a buy both the money and the goods are exchanged. When a single operation—either handing over the money or the goods—fails, all other operations of the transaction also have to be canceled. Transactions are explained in detail on Day 8, "Enrolling in Transactions."

Describing the ADO Object Model

The object model of ADO is not strictly hierarchical, so you have several ways to realize certain data access needs using ADO.

ADO provides all the objects to gain access to a data source and to manage the resultsets returned from a database after the execution of a database query. Table 1.1 provides an ADO object summary.

TABLE 1.1 ADO Object Summary

Object	Description
Connection	Enables exchange of data between data source and application.
Recordset	Enables manipulation of data and navigation in resultsets retrieved from a data source.
Field	Embodies a recordset's or record's column. Fields are accessed through the Fields collection of the Recordset object.
Property	Allows access to a certain characteristic of an ADO object. Properties collections are associated with the Connection, Command, Recordset, and Field object.
Command	Embodies a statement that is executed against a data source.
Parameter	Enables you to access a command's parameter through the Parameters collection of the Command object.
Record	Embodies a row in a recordset, or a file or directory in a file system.
Stream	Represents the content of a file (or other binary stream).
Error	Embodies an error returned from a Connection object. Every Error can be accessed through the Errors collection of the Connection object.

For detailed information about the ADO programming model, refer to Microsoft Platform SDK. You can find the ADO Programming Model in Detail, as shown in Figure 1.4, and other and topics related to ADO in the Platform SDK documentation.

FIGURE 1.4

Platform SDK documentation with the Contents tree for ADO Programming Model.

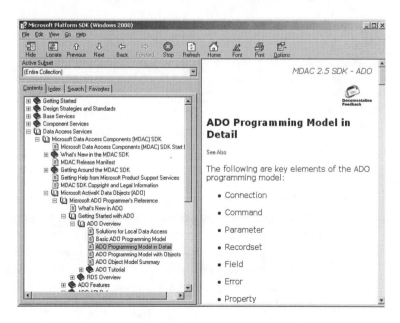

The most important key elements provided by ADO are as follows:

- A connection is used to gain access to a data source. It is the environment necessary to exchange data between your application and the data source. The target data source of the connection is specified in a connection string or a uniform resource locator (URL). A connection is embodied in ADO using the `Connection` object.

- The recordset is used to gain access to data returned from a data source query. The `Recordset` object enables reading all data from records (data rows) contained in the recordset (dataset). The `Recordset` object provides a recordset cursor, which points to the record (data row) actually in use in the recordset. You can move the recordset cursor forward or backward in the recordset to reference each record in the recordset. Furthermore, the `Recordset` object enables you to sort data or find certain information fast in a recordset.

- Fields are the entities that contain the information of a recordset. A recordset consists of one or more fields that contain data, such as first name, last name, birth date, or social security number.

- A `Command` object represents a predefined statement, often with various parameters. It can be executed against a data source using a `Connection` object. Using a command is especially useful for optimizing recurring database operations.

In Figure 1.5, you can see the relationship between `Connection`, `Recordset`, and `Field` objects.

FIGURE 1.5

The relationship between the `Connection`, `Recordset`, *and* `Field` *objects.*

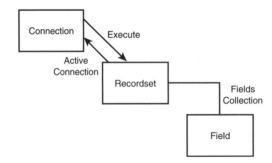

When you execute a statement against a database connection, the data source can return a resultset (as all employees of a company). This resultset (recordset) can be accessed through a `Recordset` object. The data of the records stored in the recordset can be accessed through the `Fields` collection of the `Recordset`. Each field contains information of the record (such as the first name, last name, or birth date of an employee).

An ADO *collection* comprises several ADO objects of the same kind. A `Recordset` object, for instance, contains the `Fields` collection, which consists of a certain number of `Field` objects. The number of objects in a collection can vary from case to case.

Take a look at Figure 1.6, which shows a schematic representation of a `Recordset` object.

FIGURE 1.6

A schematic representation of a Recordset *object.*

EmployeeID	LastName	FirstName	BirthDate
1	Davolio	Nancy	12/8/1948
2	Fuller	Andrew	2/19/1952
3	Leverling	Janet	8/30/1963
4	Peacock	Margaret	9/19/1937
5	Buchanan	Steven	3/4/1955
6	Suyama	Michael	7/2/1963
7	King	Robert	5/29/1960
8	Callahan	Laura	1/9/1958
9	Dodsworth	Anne	1/27/1966

The recordset of Figure 1.6 contains the data of 9 employees. Each recordset row (also referred to as a record) contains the data of one employee.

When you retrieve an ADO recordset, usually you can access the data of only one record until you move the recordset's cursor to another record.

More about the use of the `Recordset` object and other ADO objects is presented throughout the book and in Appendix D, "ADO Programming Quick-Reference."

Advantages of ADO for Programmers

ADO makes writing database applications easy and efficient. The flat object model of ADO decreases the amount and complexity of code a programmer has to write. For instance, using ADO makes it easy to connect to a data source, retrieve a recordset, and access data in the `Recordset` object. Other database access models, such as DAO (Data Access Objects) or RDO (Remote Data Objects), are highly hierarchical and therefore force programmers to go through all object steps from the top of the object model down to the recordset layer just to access some data from the recordset.

 Data Access Objects (DAO) is a programming interface to access and manipulate database objects. It was and still is commonly used to manipulate Microsoft Access databases.

 Remote Data Objects (RDO) offers a set of objects to manipulate database data. RDO is a predecessor to ADO. RDO is a thin object layer interface to the ODBC application interface, and ADO is an object layer built on the OLE DB interface.

ADO is designed for UDA, so you can access not only databases, but also all kinds of data sources as long as an OLE DB data provider exists. Programmers need only ADO to access databases, text files, data streams, properties of Windows 2000 directory structures, full-text index providers (such as Index Server), or any other kind of data source accessible through an OLE DB provider or an ODBC driver.

A programmer has to be familiar with only ADO to access various data sources.

ADO even enables you to access data sources through enterprise networks or the Internet. Using Microsoft Internet Explorer you have a simple but powerful data access client, which can be used to access ADO data sources using Active Server Pages (ASP) or Internet Information Server technology.

The ADO implementation allows disconnecting the data consumer and data provider between data access operations. With ADO it is no problem to design applications that connect to a database only during retrieving or updating information (see also Day 16, "Working with Disconnected Recordsets"). The database server's load is decreased especially when a high number of users are requesting database data simultaneously. This is the case for an Internet application, for example.

With ADO you can use efficient client-side cursor services that allow processing data locally without constant server requests. When your application accesses data across a network (intranet or Internet), fewer server requests also mean less network traffic, which is another example of how ADO helps to preserve database and network resources.

Using ADO you also can handle, manipulate, and store data in a Recordset object completely without any database connection and even without a database. Use ADO's built-in methods to sort, filter, or find certain data fast in a huge dataset that can be created and populated with or even without any data store. This special use of the ADO Recordset object is demonstrated and explained on Day 16.

Many development tools for programmers, such as Visual C++ 6.0 or Visual InterDev (for ASP programmers), support ADO and have features integrated to build database applications fast and efficiently.

Investigating the ADO Component Libraries

ADO in version 2.5 comprises three component (object) libraries:

- ADO 2.5 contains the core of the ADO technology. It enables database clients to access and manipulate data from a data source through an OLE DB provider. ADO also supports key features for building client/server and Web-based applications.
- ADOX (ADO Extensions 2.5 for Data Definition Language and Security) is an extension of the ADO objects and programming model. ADOX provides objects for schema creation and manipulation as well as for database security. Regardless of the inner structure of the data source, ADOX objects enable you to manipulate the

structure of various data sources using the same ADOX code (see Day 14, "Managing Your Database with ADOX").

- ADO MD (ADO Multidimensional 2.5) extends ADO with objects specific to manipulating multidimensional data. With ADO MD, you can use a metadata object called a `Cube` object, which consists of a structured set of related dimensions, hierarchies, levels, and members (see Day 11, "Analyzing Businesses With OLAP," and Day 12, "Building Applications with ADO MD").

To see the development and history of ADO and MDAC, the versions released, and their major features, refer to Appendix B, "Technologies, Features, and Release Packages of MDAC and ADO."

The Core of ADO 2.5

Because of the ADO history, the core of ADO 2.5 consists of three libraries. Each library has a programmatic identifier (ProgID) that is used to reference the library when you create an object contained in the respective library.

NEW TERM A *programmatic identifier* (ProgID) is a human-readable, universally unique identifier that names a COM component (such as ADO or ADOX). When you reference an ADO object, the name of the object, such as `ADODB.Recordset`, consists of the name of the ADO library (=`ProgID`), which can be `ADODB` or `ADOX`, and the name of the object in the library (such as `Recordset` or `Connection`).

NEW TERM The *Component Object Model* (COM) is a platform-independent and object-oriented system for creating interactive components. COM defines the nature of interfaces of COM objects so that applications or programming languages, such as Visual Basic or Visual C++, can create COM objects and interact with them using their COM interfaces:

- ADODB—Microsoft ActiveX Data Objects Library, which is contained in `msado15.dll`. It contains all core objects: `Connection`, `Recordset`, `Record`, `Command`, `Field`, and `Stream`.
- ADOR—ADO Recordset 2.5 Library (`msador15.dll`). ADOR 2.5 is a subset of ADO 2.5. It provides access to only the `Recordset` object (and related objects such as the `Field` and `Property` object). ADOR is used only in some special cases—for example, when you open a recordset directly in an Internet Explorer Web page. In all other cases, you should refer to ADODB when creating a `Recordset` object.
- RDS and RDSServer—Remote Data Services 2.5 Library (network client-side RDS, `msadco.dll`) and RDS Server 2.5 Library (network server-side RDS, `msadcf.dll`). Because ADO allows direct data access (from an application to a database), RDS enables you to access data sources through an intermediary, such

as Microsoft Internet Information Server (IIS). RDS and RDSServer provide the means to exchange data between the intermediary (IIS, for example) and the database client (Internet Explorer, for example).

The emphasis of the first week of this book is on the core of ADO 2.5 and related database subjects.

Based on core ADO and specific to the Microsoft Jet Database Engine (Access 2000) is Microsoft Jet and Replication objects 2.5 (JRO 2.5). JRO depends on an ADO Connection object to connect to an Access database. Use JRO to manage Access database replica sets, or to compact and secure Access databases.

ADO Extensions 2.5 for DDL and Security

Using ADOX it is easy to create structures and schemas in any data source. ADOX itself is a companion library to the core ADO objects that enables you to create, modify, and delete schema objects, such as database tables or database procedures. ADOX also contains security objects to maintain access permissions for database users.

ADOX itself provides a data source–independent object model. However, certain features of ADOX may not be supported for a certain data source, depending on the data provider (OLE DB provider or ODBC driver) used for connecting.

In-depth information about ADOX is provided on Day 14.

ADO Multidimensional 2.5

Similar to ADO 2.5, ADO MD 2.5 (ADO Multidimensional) uses an underlying OLE DB provider to access data. The provider must be a dimensional data provider, as defined by the OLE DB for OLAP specification.

 OLE DB for OLAP (Online Analytical Processing) providers enable you to access multidimensional data stores. OLAP is used for sophisticated data analysis by creating and managing summary data retrieved from various data sources.

To specify the creation of multidimensional objects, the OLE DB provider for OLAP executes multidimensional expressions (MDX) embedded in SQL syntax.

OLAP and ADO MD are discussed in-depth on Day 11 and Day 12.

Summary

Today introduced you to the nature of ADO—its uses, characteristics, basic objects, and components.

1

ADO enables access to various data sources even across networks. It uses the basic technologies of OLE DB and ODBC that provide the low-level interfaces for connecting to data sources and to applications. The ADO programming model is simple but powerful, because it provides all the objects necessary to connect to nearly every data source available in connection with Microsoft Windows.

You can find the syntax of all ADO objects, their methods, properties, events, and collections, as well as useful articles associated with ADO and databases (such as the SQL Server 7.0 database system) in the Microsoft Platform SDK documentation.

An advanced and powerful tool for examining the installed ADO version on a machine is the Component Checker tool, which is available for download at the Microsoft Web site.

Because ADO provides a simple-to-use, yet powerful object model, it is easy to use ADO in various programming languages.

For in-depth information about the use of ADO in Visual Basic, VBA (for Microsoft Office applications), and VBScript (as for Active Server Pages on Internet Information Server) refer to Appendix D.

Q&A

Q **There is so much information today, I'll never remember each detail. Is all this knowledge necessary to master ADO 2.5?**

A Today, you explored a lot of information. The goal of presenting all the issues and terms you learned today is to give you a feeling for technologies such as ADO, OLE DB, and ODBC, and for various terms used in conjunction with ADO.

Q **Today, I looked at several interesting technologies, but for an experienced programmer, most topics are treated only on the surface. Where can I find in-depth information about OLE DB, ODBC, or ADO for a Visual C++ developer?**

A First, the Platform SDK documentation contains many examples and information about the inner structure, defined interfaces, and implementation of OLE DB for Visual C++ developers. For more in-depth information about certain topics or problems—especially with technology from Microsoft—consult the Microsoft Developer Network (MSDN) Library or search on Microsoft's Web site for problem solutions.

Workshop

The quiz questions and exercises are provided for your further understanding. See Appendix A, "Answers," for the answers.

Quiz

1. What do you have to consider when you want to install a newer MDAC than version 2.5 on a Windows 2000 machine?

2. After you download MDAC 2.5 from the Microsoft Web site you also want to get information about the newest features of ADO 2.5, the syntax of all ADO objects, and the use of various OLE DB providers. What documentation contains all the information you search for?

3. You want to find out which ADO version is installed on a Windows 98 machine. What tool can you use that tells you the MDAC and ADO version, as well as the version numbers of all MDAC files installed?

4. Name the basic technologies that are contained in the Microsoft Data Access Components (MDAC) 2.5.

DAY 2

Retrieving Data Using ADO

ADO is the standard interface from Microsoft used to retrieve data from different data sources. You can use it from any programming language through its object model.

The tremendous advantage of ADO is its universal usage. Using the basic ADO objects, you perform similar tasks whether you are programming a Visual Basic application that retrieves data from a SQL Server database, or a C++ object that retrieves data from the Exchange message store. ADO and its flat object model provide a simple but, nevertheless, powerful way to manipulate data from nearly every data source. Because ADO does not have a very strict hierarchical object concept, there are many possible ways to use ADO objects for special tasks.

Today, you will learn the following:

- How to retrieve data using ADO
- The advantages of using the ADO library in a VBA project

- How to establish connections to different data sources
- How to open a Recordset
- How to navigate through a Recordset
- How to prepare a Recordset for special purposes
- How to retrieve multiple Recordsets using one `Recordset` object

Retrieving Data in a Simple Example

To give you an idea how to get a Recordset using ADO, I have prepared a simple example in Listing 2.1.

This listing can be used in any Visual Basic environment such as Visual Basic, Visual Basic for Applications (Word, Excel, Access), or VBScript (Active Server Pages, Windows Scripting Host).

LISTING 2.1 Retrieving Employee Data from the Northwind Database

```
1: Set conn = CreateObject("ADODB.Connection")
2:
3: conn.Open "DSN=MyNorthwind;UID=sa;PWD="
4: strSQL = "SELECT EmployeeID, LastName, FirstName "
5: strSQL = strSQL & "FROM Employees "
6: strSQL = strSQL & "WHERE EmployeeID < 5 "
7:
8: Set rs = conn.Execute(strSQL)
9:
10: Do While (Not (rs.EOF))
11:     strResult = rs("EmployeeID") & " : "
12:     strResult = strResult & rs("LastName") & " "
13:     strResult = strResult & rs("FirstName")
14:     Output strResult
15:     rs.MoveNext
16: Loop
17: rs.Close
18: conn.Close
19:
20: Set rs = Nothing
21: Set conn = Nothing
```

ANALYSIS Listing 2.1 opens a connection using the ODBC System DSN MyNorthwind to connect to the Access 2000 Northwind sample database. Next, it queries for all employees that have an `EmployeeID` smaller than five.

Note Before you can use the ODBC System DNS named MyNorthwind you must, of course, have created the DSN MyNorthwind. It must connect to the Northwind sample database of Microsoft Access 2000 or Microsoft SQL Server 7.0. I explained how to create a ODBC System DSN in Day 1.

A `Connection` object is created in line 1 and stored in the variable conn. This is done by simply using the `CreateObject` statement that creates a running instance of the ActiveX object `ADODB.Connection`, which is the standard connection used in ADO.

In line 3, a connection to the Northwind sample database is opened using the `Open` Method of the `Connection` object. The values of the UID (User ID) and PWD (Password) must be adjusted to allow connection to the Northwind database.

A SQL database query, which retrieves the employees' data, is stored in the variable `strSQL` in lines 4–6. The following SQL statement is used:

```
SELECT EmployeeID, LastName, FirstName FROM Employees WHERE EmployeeID < 5
```

This SELECT statement retrieves the IDs, last names, and first names of all employees whose ID number is less than five. To obtain a Recordset, which contains the resulting records from the SQL statement, the SQL statement is executed against the database using the `Execute` Method of the `Connection` object in line 8.

NEW TERM When you *execute a statement against a database,* you use some ADO method that passes the statement to a database provider, which represents the link between ADO and the database itself. The statement is *parsed* (translated into an executable form) and executed. When the statement delivers a recordset from the database, the database provider passes this recordset back to ADO.

After the SQL statement is executed, the resulting Recordset contains all records retrieved from the database and can be accessed through the `Recordset` object itself.

You can picture the Recordset as a collection of all records retrieved during the database query. In it, a cursor points to the active record that can be manipulated. You can perform some basic actions with a Recordset, such as reading the fields of the active record or moving the Recordset's cursor to navigate to other records.

When a Recordset is opened, the Recordset's cursor points to the first record. To move forward in a Recordset, you use the `MoveNext` method. How can you make sure that you have not already reached the last record? You can check whether the `EOF` property of the `Recordset` object returns TRUE. If that is the case, the Recordset pointer has moved beyond the last record.

2

In lines 10–16, the Do…Loop loop moves the cursor through all records, reads the record fields' values, and stores the values in the variable strResult. A field value can be read using the Fields collection of the Recordset.

The full statement to access a field's value is as follows:

```
strValue = Recordset.Fields("FieldName").Value
```

However, because the Value property of a field is the default property and the Fields collection is the default collection for the Recordset object, you can refer to the value of a certain field using the shorthand version, which looks like the following:

```
strValue = Recordset("FieldName")
```

When the Recordset is stored in the variable rs, the script can access the field value of the active record through expressions such as

```
rs("FieldName")
```

In line 14, the value of the string strResult, which contains the field values, is passed to the function Output. This function is not a specific Visual Basic command, but instead it is a placeholder for a self-written function that writes the result string to the user.

If you want to use the script as is, you can use one of the following functions in your application.

In Visual Basic or VBA (Visual Basic for Applications, used in Word, Access, Excel), the function Output can produce a message box displaying the string. When you use Excel, you can write every string that is passed to the function into a new row in a worksheet as shown in Listing 2.2

LISTING 2.2 Output Function for Use in Excel

```
1: Dim lngRow as Long
2: Function Output(strOut)
3:     lngRow = lngRow + 1
4:     Worksheets(1).Cells(lngRow, 1).Value = Replace(strOut, vbCrLf, vbLf)
5: End Function
```

ANALYSIS Line 1 must be at the top of the Visual Basic module. It defines the global variable lngRow which stored the current row position into which the value is written. With each call, the row position is increased by one in line 3. The argument of the function is passed to the variable strOut and written in line 4 to the current row.

In Active Server Pages (ASP) the function `Output` can be a function that writes the string to the client browser. The function `Output` for use in Active Server Pages (VBScript) is described in Listing 2.3.

LISTING 2.3 Output Function for Use in ASP

```
1: Function Output(strOut)
2:     Response.Write Replace(strOut, vbCrLf, "<BR>" & vbCrLf)
3:     Response.Write "<BR>" & vbCrLf
4: End Function
```

To continue with the analysis of the Do...Loop loop in lines 10–16, note that at the end of each loop the Recordset cursor is moved one record forward using the MoveNext method as shown in line 15. When the Recordset's cursor has moved beyond the last record, the EOF property of the Recordset returns TRUE and the Do...Loop loop terminates.

This is a simple example to demonstrate the basic procedures that can be performed by ADO. Of course, there are many more topics to come covering every aspect of ADO, including the usage of connections, navigation in Recordsets, special features in Visual Basic, and more.

ADO References in a VBA Project

Because ADO 2.5 offers new features (such as the Record and the Stream objects) and because of its universal usage, you will often use ADO 2.5 in Visual Basic for Applications (VBA). VBA is used in Microsoft Office 2000 and its applications Word, Excel, and Access. Therefore, this day will cover some special issues of ADO in VBA.

When you are working in VBA with an object library, such as the Microsoft ActiveX Data Objects 2.5 (ADO 2.5) Library, you must reference the object library in the application. Doing so will make development easier. You can use the features of the Object Browser, the Auto List Member, Auto Quick Info, or Syntax Check on ADO objects.

NEW TERM   An *Object Library*, or *Type Library*, is a container for all necessary information about the objects of a special library, their definitions, and what is necessary to create the objects.

To establish a reference to the ADO 2.5 type library in Excel you have to perform the following steps.

To Do: Establishing a Reference to ADO 2.5 in Excel

1. Open the Excel File to which you are adding the reference in Excel.

2. Go to the Visual Basic Editor. This can be achieved by using the key combination Alt+F11. Another way to open the VB Editor is to use the menu choosing Tools, Macro, Visual Basic Editor.

3. In the VB Editor, select Tools, References to establish a reference to an object library.

4. In the References window, you have to select the object library Microsoft ActiveX Data Objects 2.5 Library. Then click on the OK button.

Now the reference to the ADO 2.5 library is established, and you can use all ADO objects in the same way you use intrinsic VB objects.

You have gained many advantages. You can use automatic listing of properties and objects, the object browser, and syntax checking on ADO objects. Best of all, you can now use early binding (compile-time binding) of ADO objects to gain more speed for your application.

An example of early binding of the Connection object follows.

Instead of creating a Connection object using the CreateObject method and storing it in the variable conn using the Set statement, you can declare, create, and assign the Connection object in one step. The following line shows you how to declare a reference to the Connection object of the ADO library (using early binding).

```
Dim conn As New ADODB.Connection
```

The next lines have a similar function.

```
Dim conn as ADODB.Connection
Set conn = New ADODB.Connection
```

The only difference in the latter approach is that the declaration (Dim) is separated from the creation (Set). Although the previous creation only took one line, it is recommended that you use the two-line approach because it is faster. In the first approach, VB has the responsibility to create the object when it is first needed (time-consuming checks are added to your code). The two-line approach, however, enables you to control when to create the object. This releases VB from the order to check where the object is needed and to create the object before its first usage.

In contrast to early binding, you can also use late binding (runtime binding) when you explicitly want to use different types of objects in a certain variable. This practice is not really recommended.

An example of late binding when creating a `Connection` object follows:

```
Dim conn as Object
Set conn = CreateObject("ADODB.Connection")
```

In this case, you declare conn as a variable that contains a reference to any object. During the execution of the script, the variable conn is set to hold a reference to a `Connection` object.

Next, I will show you various ways to establish a connection to a data source.

Establishing a Database Connection

There are many ways to establish a connection to a database or another data source when you are using ADO. Each has advantages and disadvantages. All ways have one thing in common: The database connection is opened using the `Open` method of the `Connection` object after the `Connection` object is declared, created, and assigned to a variable.

The syntax for declaring, creating, and assigning a `Connection` object to the variable conn is described later in the day.

Visual Basic and VBA with a reference to the ADO 2.5 library is shown here:

```
Dim conn As New ADODB.Connection
```

Visual Basic and VBA without the reference to the ADO library is as follows:

```
Dim conn As Object
Set conn = CreateObject("ADODB.Connection")
```

VBScript (Active Server Pages, Windows Scripting Host) is

```
Dim conn
Set conn = CreateObject("ADODB.Connection")
```

The syntax for opening a connection is as follows:

```
conn.Open ConnectionString
```

If the username and password are not defined in the `ConnectionString`, you can provide them when opening the connection using a statement as follows:

```
conn.Open ConnectionString, UserName, Password
```

In the preceding description, conn is the variable that holds an instance of the `Connection` object.

Which `ConnectionString` you use depends on the kind of connection and the data source you want to access.

The `ConnectionString` specifies the type of connection and the data source, together with additional parameters specific to the connection that should be established.

The most important part of the `ConnectionString` is the provider. The provider defines which drivers or layers are used to access the data source. The default provider, which comes on duty when no provider is specified, is the OLE DB Provider for ODBC.

Using the OLE DB Provider for ODBC

Because ADO is a layer built on OLE DB, it is ideal when every data source exposes an OLE DB interface. If so, ADO can call directly into the data source. However, there are still many data sources that provide an ODBC interface only. This restricts them to being accessed through an ODBC driver.

ADO can access ODBC data sources using the OLE DB Provider for ODBC, which represents the connecting link between OLE DB, on which ADO is based, and any ODBC data source.

When you are using ADO to open a connection in your program, you are using a connection.open statement with a Connection String. The syntax is provided here.

```
connection.Open ConnectionString, UserID, Password, Options
```

The Connection String specifies the data source and additional parameters. In this case, these parameters are the User ID and Password.

ODBC Connection Through a DSN

When you want to establish a connection to an ODBC data source that is defined as DSN (Data Source Name) through the ODBC Administrator in the Windows Control Panel (and Administrative Tools in Windows 2000), the syntax of the Connection String is as follows:

```
"Provider=MSDASQL;DSN=dsnName;DATABASE=Database;UID=username;PWD=userPassword;"
```

MSDASQL is the name of the ODBC Provider, and it can be omitted because it is the default provider for ADO.

DSN-less ODBC Connection

If you want to establish a DSN-less ODBC connection without using a predefined DSN, you can use one of the Connection Strings described in the following paragraphs.

The general syntax for a DSN-less ODBC connection is as follows:

```
"PROVIDER=MSDASQL;DRIVER={driver};SERVER=Server;DATABASE=Database;
➥ UID=userName;PWD=userPassword;"
```

The most important advantage of a DSN-less connection is that you can use and access an ODBC data source without defining it in the ODBC Administrator—as long as the driver you want to use is installed on the computer.

Typical drivers you can use in DSN-less connections are described in Table 2.1.

TABLE 2.1   Drivers for DSN-less Connections

Data Source	Driver Name
Access	Microsoft Access Driver (*.mdb)
Excel	Microsoft Excel Driver (*.xls)
Text file	Microsoft Text Driver (*.txt; *.csv)
SQL Server	SQL Server

The connection string for a DSN-less ODBC connection to a SQL Server database looks like the following statement:

```
"Provider=MSDASQL;DRIVER={SQL Server};SERVER=Boyscout;DATABASE=Northwind;
➡ UID=sa;PWD=;"
```

When the SQL Server is the local machine, you can provide the name of the local machine as `ServerName` or the keyword (`local`). A DSN-less ODBC connection to the local machine is written as follows:

```
"Provider=MSDASQL;DRIVER={SQL Server};SERVER=(local);DATABASE=Northwind;
➡ UID=sa;PWD=;"
```

The connection string that can be used to connect to an Access database is shown here:

```
"Provider=MSDASQL;DRIVER={Microsoft Access Driver (*.mdb)};
➡ DBQ=C:\Northwind.mdb;UID=sa;PWD=;"
```

Note that you must specify the full database path and assign it to the keyword DBQ (instead of DATABASE).

Because there are many ODBC drivers available for a large number of data sources, you have to refer to the ADO documentation or the documentation of the ODBC driver to find the correct parameters to be used for a specific driver.

Using OLE DB Providers

OLE DB providers are available for the most important data sources, such as Microsoft Access and SQL Server, Oracle, Index Server, FrontPage, Internet Information Server (IIS), Web Folders, persistent recordsets, data on a remote machine, and Exchange Server Data.

Every provider needs a special syntax in the Connection String. The most important OLE DB providers are presented in the next section.

Because you have one layer less than you do when using an ODBC driver, the connection is more direct and, therefore, more efficient because you are using less overhead.

OLE DB Provider for Microsoft Jet/Access

The OLE DB Provider for Microsoft Jet provides the direct interface between ADO and a Microsoft Access database.

A Connection String using the Microsoft Jet 4.0 Provider (Access 2000 file format) that ships with ADO 2.5 is described here.

```
"Provider=Microsoft.Jet.OLEDB.4.0;Data Source=databaseName;
User ID=userName;Password=userPassword;"
```

For older Jet drivers the provider property must be adjusted.

Note

> There is a problem with the Jet 3.51 Provider, which is part of ADO 2.0. The Jet 3.51 Provider does not return the value of an Autonumber field when it inserts a new record. If you are dealing with tables that have their Primary Key defined using Autonumber columns, this problem prevents you from manipulating recently inserted records. It is not possible to delete or change the records until you re-open the Recordset.

NEW TERM An *Autonumber field* is a field whose value is determined by the database itself. For every new record, the database generates a new, unique number for this field. In SQL Server an Autonumber field is also called an Identity field.

OLE DB Provider for SQL Server

The Microsoft OLE DB Provider for SQL Server, which is named SQLOLEDB, allows direct access from ADO to a SQL Server database.

A typical connection string to access SQL Server through OLE DB is

```
"Provider=SQLOLEDB;Data Source=serverName;Initial Catalog=databaseName;
User ID=username;Password=userPassword;"
```

When the SQL Server is the local machine, you can provide the local machine's name or the keyword (local) as Data Source.

SQL Server can authenticate users in two ways: with a SQL Server login ID and password (as used previously), or through a Windows NT account. If your server is configured for the latter, you do not need to provide user ID and password—the NT account of the currently logged-in user is used to authenticate with SQL Server.

> **Caution**   If you use NT authentication from within a service such IIS, the service account is used to authenticate with SQL Server. You can very easily overlook this fact.

2

Other OLE DB Providers

For information about other OLE DB providers from Microsoft, please refer to the ADO documentation, which can be found in the Platform SDK for Windows 2000 under the topics Data Access Services, Microsoft Data Access Components (MDAC) SDK, Microsoft OLE DB, OLE DB Providers. For information about OLE DB providers from vendors other than Microsoft, contact the database or data source vendor.

Opening a Recordset

In Listing 2.3, you have already seen one method to open a Recordset. In it, the script is using the connection's Execute method. However, there are many more ways to obtain a Recordset; each has its advantages and disadvantages determined by usability, speed, and resource consumption.

The most useful ways to obtain a Recordset are described in the following sections.

Using the Execute Method

The Execute method of the Connection object can be used to obtain a Recordset very easily. All you need is a Connection object stored in a variable and a SQL statement that determines the Recordset retrieved from the database.

The usage of the Execute method is simple.

```
Set rs = conn.Execute(strSQL)
```

In this statement, conn is the Connection object, rs is the obtained Recordset, and strSQL is the executed SQL command.

To save resources and avoid unneeded records in the Recordset, you have to plan the SQL command wisely.

For instance, if you do not need all columns of a table, avoid a statement such as

```
SELECT * FROM Table
```

It is better to describe the necessary columns in the SELECT statement, as shown in the following example.

```
SELECT ProductName, UnitPrice FROM Products
```

Using this statement, you avoid dealing with the other eight columns of the table. This saves resources and enables better speed, especially when using lower-speed network connections to the database server.

The Recordset can also be restricted by using a WHERE clause in the SELECT statement. This also enables you to obtain only needed records.

For instance, if you need only the products with the UnitPrice from the Products table where the CategoryID has the value 1, you use a SELECT statement as follows.

```
SELECT ProductName, UnitPrice FROM Products WHERE CategoryID = 1
```

It is useful to define the Recordset you need using a SELECT statement when you do not want to get all data from the table. However, what if you need all data from a certain table?

In that case, you can use the Execute method of the Connection object, together with a special option instead of a SQL statement.

Given the fact that you want to retrieve all columns and records of a small table, you can use a statement with a special CommandType option. The option adCmdTableDirect can be used so that the database or the database driver does not need to parse a SQL statement. It only has to open the table. This results in a little more speed when you need all data from the table.

```
Set rs = conn.Execute(strTable, lngAffRec ,adCmdTableDirect)
```

The variable rs contains the returned Recordset, strTable contains the name of the accessed table, lngAffRec returns the number of records affected during the operation, and adCmdTableDirect is a ADO 2.5 constant, with the value 512.

> **Note**
>
> In Visual Basic and VBA, the ActiveX Data Objects Library provides the ADO constants. You can use these constants when there is a reference to ADO in your project.
>
> In Active Server Pages (VBScript), you have to define ADO constants or use their value, instead of the constant names. All ADO constants are defined in a file named adovbs.inc, which can be found on Windows 2000 in the directory <System Drive>:\Program Files\Common Files\System\ado. When you

use any ADO constant in your ASP page, just include the content of this file in your script using a server-side include directive with a reference to a copy of the adovbs.inc file.

Because the `Execute` method is often used to create and retrieve a Recordset in one step, you might want to create a Recordset, prepare its behavior, and then open it. This can be done using the `Recordset` object's `Open` method.

Using the `Open` Method of the `Recordset` Object

With the `Open` method of the `Recordset` object, you have much more control over the kind of Recordset you open than you have when you use the `Execute` method of the `Connection` object.

You can prepare Recordset options before opening the Recordset. This capability constitutes the main difference between this procedure and using the `Execute` method of the `Connection` object. The latter gives you a Recordset, but it also creates the `Recordset` object in the same step. You have no control over the `Recordset` object before it is opened.

The following example in Listing 2.4 demonstrates a typical use of the `Recordset.Open` method. Listing 2.4 retrieves data from the Shippers table of the Northwind database.

LISTING 2.4   Retrieving Shippers Data from Northwind Database

```
1: Dim conn As New ADODB.Connection
2: Dim rs As New ADODB.Recordset
3:
4: conn.Open "DSN=myNorthwind"
5:
6: strSQL = "SELECT ShipperID, CompanyName "
7: strSQL = strSQL & "FROM Shippers "
8:
9: rs.Source = strSQL
10: Set rs.ActiveConnection = conn
11: rs.CursorType = adOpenForwardOnly
12: rs.LockType = adLockReadOnly
13: rs.Open
14:
15: Do While (Not (rs.EOF))
16:     strResult = rs("ShipperID") & " : "
17:     strResult = strResult & rs("CompanyName") & " "
```

continues

LISTING 2.4 continued

```
18:    Output strResult
19: rs.MoveNext
20: Loop
21: rs.Close
22: conn.Close
23:
24: Set rs = Nothing
25: Set conn = Nothing
```

ANALYSIS In lines 1 and 2, the variables conn and rs are declared. A Connection object is created in line 1 and assigned to the variable conn, and a Recordset object is created in line 2 and assigned to the variable rs.

When you want to run this listing in VBScript (ASP for instance), you have to change lines 1 and 2 in this way:

```
1: Dim conn, rs
2: Set conn = CreateObject("ADODB.Connection")
3: Set rs = CreateObject("ADODB.Recordset")
```

You also have to include the file adovbs.inc, which provides the ADO constants used in lines 11 and 12, or you must insert the values of the ADO constants, instead of their names, in the script.

Line 4 opens a connection to the data source that is defined in the DSN name MyNorthwind. A DSN (Data Source Name) can be specified in the ODBC Administrator.

The SQL statement that is executed against the data source is specified in the lines 6–7 and assigned to the variable strSQL.

The lines 9–12 prepare the Recordset before it is opened in line 13.

In line 9, the Source property is set to the SQL statement that is to be executed. In line 10, the connection is assigned to the ActiveConnection property, thus binding the connection to the Recordset object.

Line 11 determines the cursor type of the Recordset. Every Recordset has a cursor that points to the active record. The cursor type provides information about how the cursor can be moved in the Recordset. When you set a Recordset's cursor type to adOpenForwardOnly, defining a Forward-Only Cursor, the cursor is limited to forward-only movement in the Recordset.

Of course, there are other cursor types that provide more flexible navigation through a `Recordset` object, so why should you choose such an inflexible cursor type? The overhead and the resources that ADO has to provide for more flexible cursor types are considerable. Saving resources becomes even more important when you use ADO in a multiuser application or when you have a slow network connection between your application and the data source. Other cursor types are explained in detail in the section "Preparing Recordset Options" later in this lesson.

Line 12 defines the lock type of the Recordset. To prevent two users from manipulating the same data at the same time with unpredictable results, a record is locked during editing.

When your script does not make any changes in the Recordset, you can use a lock type such as `adLockReadOnly`, which does not allow editing a record at all. It is important to specify the correct lock type for your needs because this saves ADO and database resources. Because the default lock type is `adLockReadOnly`, you can omit line 12.

After line 12 of the script, the Recordset is prepared to use a specific connection and execute a SQL statement. Also, the cursor type and lock type are determined according to your needs.

The next step, line 13, opens the Recordset using the following statement:

```
rs.Open
```

The syntax shown here is not the only use of the `Open` method. Instead of assigning parameters before opening the Recordset, you can assign them to the Recordset directly using the `Open` method. The general syntax for the `Open` method is

```
recordset.Open Source, ActiveConnection, CursorType, LockType, Options
```

`Source` can be something like a SQL statement or simply the name of a table to be opened.

`ActiveConnection` specifies which connection is used to open the Recordset. You can provide an open connection or a connection string as this parameter. When you use a connection definition provided by a connection string, ADO implicitly creates a new connection and opens it using the specified parameters in the connection string.

`CursorType` determines the type of cursor to use.

`LockType` determines the type of locking the provider should use when opening the `Recordset`.

All parameters are optional.

> **Tip**
>
> I recommend preparing the Recordset first and then opening it using the
> `Open` method. This helps readability, debugging, and maintaining the script.

When you want to open a whole table without using a SQL statement, which has to be
parsed by the provider, you can provide a table named The Recordset Source, similar to
that shown earlier using the `Execute` method of the `Connection` object. A simple example of opening a whole table using the `Open` method of the `Recordset` object is presented
in Listing 2.5. This listing retrieves all records from the Shippers table of the Northwind
database.

LISTING 2.5   Open the Shippers Table Without Using a SQL Statement

```
1: Dim rs As New ADODB.Recordset
2: rs.Open "Shippers", "DSN=MyNorthwind;UID=sa;PWD=", adOpenForwardOnly,
➥ adLockReadOnly, adCmdTableDirect
3: Do While Not rs.EOF
4:    ' Read the Records
5:    ' ...
6:    rs.MoveNext
7: Loop
8: rs.Close
9: Set rs = Nothing
```

ANALYSIS   Line 1 defines the variable `rs` as Recordset, creates a Recordset, and stores it in
the variable `rs`. In line 2, the Recordset is opened using the name of the table as
the first Recordset and `adCmdTableDirect` as the option parameter of the `Open` method.
In lines 3–7, the Recordset is used for reading its values or other tasks.

In Listing 2.5, the Recordset's source was a database.

However, the Recordset's source can also be a persisted Recordset.

NEW TERM   A *persisted Recordset* is a snapshot of a Recordset that has been saved in a file
using Extensible Markup Language (XML) or the Advanced Data TableGram
(ADTG) format.

When you want to open a persisted Recordset, the `Open` method can do the job.

> **Note**
>
> You can save a Recordsets as a persisted Recordset in a file using, for
> instance, the `Save` method of the `Recordset` object.

The next statement provides an example of how to retrieve a persisted Recordset using the `Open` method.

```
rs.Open "J:\recordset.xml", , , , adCmdFile
```

In this statement `rs` represents a Recordset, and the Source parameter is the file `"J:\recordset.xml"`, which contains the Recordset. The parameter `adCmdFile` specifies that the Recordset is retrieved from a file. Instead of a full path, such as `"J:\record-set.xml"`, you can also specify a relative path such as `"..\recordset.xml"` or a URL like `"http://server/directory/recordset.xml"`.

For further information about this topic consult the ADO 2.5 documentation.

Navigating Through a Recordset

You have seen that it is possible to navigate through a Recordset using the Recordset's `MoveNext` method. But this is only one of the four basic ways to navigate through a Recordset.

You not only can navigate forward in a Recordset using its `MoveNext` method, but you also can move backward using the `MovePrevious` method.

To jump to the first or the last record of a `Recordset` you can use the `MoveFirst` and `MoveLast` methods.

The `MoveNext` method moves the current record cursor one record forward. When the last record is reached, the Recordset's `EOF` (End of File) property is set to `TRUE`.

The `MovePrevious` method moves the record cursor one record backward. When the cursor is on the position of the first record and you use the `MovePrevious` method, the `BOF` (Beginning of File) property of the Recordset is set to `TRUE`.

If both the `EOF` and the `BOF` properties indicate `TRUE`, you have an empty Recordset.

A short example of using the `MovePrevious` method is provided in the listing that follows. If you want to read the last record of a Recordset (named `rs`) first and then move backward until you reach the first record, you can use a loop as shown in Listing 2.6. The Recordset must support moving the cursor backward to run Listing 2.6.

LISTING 2.6 Moving Backward in a Recordset

```
1: rs.MoveLast
2: While Not rs.BOF
3: ' Do something with the actual Record
```

continues

LISTING **2.6** continued

```
4:    ...
5: rs.MovePrevious
6: Wend
```

Tip

> In most cases, it is better to let the database do the correct sorting of your Recordset so that you only have to move forward in a Recordset. This can be done, for instance, using the keywords ORDER BY in a SQL statement. When the records are sorted in the correct order, it saves resources because you can use a Forward-Only Cursor.

Not all Recordsets support all basic navigation methods. It depends on how the Recordset is prepared before it is opened.

When you use a Forward-Only Cursor (CursorType property is not set or set to adOpenForwardOnly), the Recordset allows moving forward using MoveNext. When you call the MoveFirst method, the command that created the Recordset is re-executed so it can fetch the first record again. You cannot use the MoveLast method when using a Forward-Only Cursor because of the way the cursors are implemented in ADO. The Recordset must support backward movement when using MoveLast.

You cannot use the MovePrevious method together with a Forward-Only Cursor except when you cache some records in the memory using the CacheSize method, which specifies the number of cached records.

All other cursor types allow the four basic navigation methods: MoveNext, MovePrevious, MoveFirst, MoveLast.

More complex navigation in Recordsets can be done using *Bookmarks*, which are similar to dog-ears in a book. It is also possible to divide Recordsets into pages and jump between these pages much as you might leaf through a book. These techniques are explained in Day 6, "Working with Large Recordsets."

Reading Field Values

Generally speaking, a Recordset consists of Records, each of which has different Field values that contain the data of that specific Record. An example of a Recordset is shown in Figure 2.1.

FIGURE 2.1

A sample Recordset.

OrderID	CustomerID	EmployeeID	OrderDate	RequiredDate	ShippedDate	ShipVia	Freight
10248	VINET	5	7/4/1996	8/1/1996	7/16/1996	3	32.38
10249	TOMSP	6	7/5/1996	8/16/1996	7/10/1996	1	11.61
10250	HANAR	4	7/8/1996	8/5/1996	7/12/1996	2	65.83
10251	VICTE	3	7/8/1996	8/5/1996	7/15/1996	1	41.34
10252	SUPRD	4	7/9/1996	8/6/1996	7/11/1996	2	51.3
10253	HANAR	3	7/10/1996	7/24/1996	7/16/1996	2	58.17
10254	CHOPS	5	7/11/1996	8/8/1996	7/23/1996	2	22.98
10255	RICSU	9	7/12/1996	8/9/1996	7/15/1996	3	148.33
10256	WELLI	3	7/15/1996	8/12/1996	7/17/1996	2	13.97
10257	HILAA	4	7/16/1996	8/13/1996	7/22/1996	3	81.91
10258	ERNSH	1	7/17/1996	8/14/1996	7/23/1996	1	140.51
10259	CENTC	4	7/18/1996	8/15/1996	7/25/1996	3	3.25
10260	OTTIK	4	7/19/1996	8/16/1996	7/29/1996	1	55.09
10261	QUEDE	4	7/19/1996	8/16/1996	7/30/1996	2	3.05
10262	RATTC	8	7/22/1996	8/19/1996	7/25/1996	3	48.29
10263	ERNSH	9	7/23/1996	8/20/1996	7/31/1996	3	146.06
10264	FOLKO	6	7/24/1996	8/21/1996	8/23/1996	3	3.67
10265	BLONP	2	7/25/1996	8/22/1996	8/12/1996	1	55.28
10266	WARTH	3	7/26/1996	9/6/1996	7/31/1996	3	25.73
10267	FRANK	4	7/29/1996	8/26/1996	8/6/1996	1	208.58
10268	GROSR	8	7/30/1996	8/27/1996	8/2/1996	3	66.29
10269	WHITC	5	7/31/1996	8/14/1996	8/9/1996	1	4.56
10270	WARTH	1	8/1/1996	8/29/1996	8/2/1996	1	136.54
10271	SPLIR	6	8/1/1996	8/29/1996	8/30/1996	2	4.54
10272	RATTC	6	8/2/1996	8/30/1996	8/6/1996	2	98.03
10273	QUICK	3	8/5/1996	9/2/1996	8/12/1996	3	76.07

In the sample Recordset in Figure 2.1, each row represents a Record, and each Record consists of fields. All the records together represent the Recordset.

The Fields of the current Record of a Recordset can be accessed through the `Fields` Collection of the `Recordset` object as shown here.

```
FieldValue = Recordset.Fields("FieldName").Value
```

Because the `Value` property is the default property of the `Field` object and the `Fields` collection is the default value for the `Recordset` object, you can use the following short-cut to obtain the value of a certain field of the current record of the Recordset.

```
FieldValue = Recordset("FieldName")
```

When you deal with large text or binary data fields (BLOB for Binary Large Object), you also can use another way to retrieve data from these fields. Examples of large data fields are fields of the Access `Memo` data type or the SQL Server `Text` data type. A field of the `OLE Object` data type in Access or the `Image` data type in SQL Server are also examples of large binary data fields. The main difference between a BLOB field and other data fields is that the database does not store the data of the BLOB directly in the table because it contains such a large amount of data. Instead, the database stores a reference to the BLOB in the field so that you still can access the BLOB through the table field.

The value of a BLOB field can be retrieved the same way as you retrieve values of other fields. In addition, you can read chunks of a BLOB value using the `GetChunk` method as follows:

```
FieldValue = Recordset("FieldName").GetChunk(ChunkSize)
```

`FieldValue` is the value retrieved from the large text or binary field. `Recordset` is the name of the Recordset, `Fieldname` the name of the field from which you want to retrieve the value, and `ChunkSize` specifies the number of characters (or bytes of images) you want to retrieve from the field at once.

The property `ActualSize` enables you to read the size of a large text or binary field.

```
lngBytes = Recordset("FieldName").ActualSize
```

The property `ActualSize` always returns the number of bytes that are used to store the field value. When you have a field that contains a string, `ActualSize` returns the number of bytes that are used to store the string. In most cases, one byte is used to store one character so that the number of bytes returned from the `ActualSize` property equals the number of characters.

 Caution   Some database data types use two bytes to store one character. If you read the `ActualSize` property of a field that uses such a database datatype, you have to divide the number of bytes by two to get the number of characters. Examples for database data types that use two bytes per character are the SQL Server 7.0 data types `nchar`, `nvarchar`, and `ntext`. Such data types are called Unicode data types. Unicode encode is used to define a single encoding scheme for practically all characters used widely in the business world today. Unlike an encoding scheme (that uses one byte per character and can only represent 256 different characters), the Unicode scheme (that uses two bytes per character) can store 65,536 different characters.

When dealing with strings, `ActualSize` returns the number of characters—as long as you do not read the value of a Unicode field.

Using the `ActualSize` property, you can read the whole value of a BLOB at once as shown here:

```
TotalSize = Recordset("FieldName").ActualSize
FieldValue = Recordset("FieldName").GetChunk(TotalSize)
```

Caution   When dealing with Unicode characters you have to use the following code:
```
lngCharacters = Recordset("FieldName").ActualSize / 2
FieldValue = Recordset("FieldName").GetChunk(lngCharacters)
```

These two lines of code just read the value of the field the same way as the following line:

```
FieldValue = Recordset("FieldName")
```

The main usage of the method GetChunk is to read a value of a BLOB chunk by chunk. This is necessary when dealing with really large BLOBs, which can be multimegabyte monsters.

To read a BLOB chunk by chunk, 10,000 characters (or bytes when dealing with an image) at once, proceed as shown in Listing 2.7.

LISTING 2.7   Reading a BLOB Piece by Piece

```
1: lngPieceSize = 10000  ' Characters (or Bytes in an image)
2: lngActualSize = Recordset("FieldName").ActualSize
3: lngOffSet = 0
4: Do While lngOffset < lngActualSize
5:     varChunk = Recordset("FieldName").GetChunk(lngPieceSize)
6:     ' Do something with varChunk
7:     ...
8:     lngOffset = lngOffset + lngPieceSize
9: Loop
```

> **Caution**
>
> If the field with the name *Fieldname* contains Unicode characters, you have to divide the number of bytes returned by the ActualSize property by two to get the number of characters in line 2.
>
> ```
> 2: lngActualSize = Recordset("FieldName").ActualSize / 2
> ```
>
> When dealing with Unicode data, the GetChunk method (in line 5) always returns the same number of characters as specified in the argument for the GetChunk method.

ANALYSIS   Line 1 stores the number of characters (or bytes in images) that the script should retrieve at once. The actual size of the field value in characters (or bytes) is stored in the variable lngActualSize in line 2. (In the case that the field data is of some Unicode data type, you have to divide the ActualSize value by two to get the number of characters stored in the field.) In line 3, the offset, which indicates the position of the chunk that should be retrieved in the Do While loop, is set to zero. In lines 4–9, the loop retrieves and stores a chunk of the size lngPieceSize (in characters or bytes) from the field's value. During each processing of the loop, the offset is increased by the number of characters (or bytes) retrieved. The loop is performed as long as the offset is smaller than the whole size of the field's value.

Reading BLOBs in pieces is especially useful when you want to save resources in a multi-user environment. Imagine that 100 users are connected to your application, and every user wants to retrieve the value of a BLOB that contains 200KB data. If your application handles the whole BLOB at once, it uses up about 20MB of space to store all BLOBs for all users. However, if your application only handles 10KB of a BLOB at once for each user, it needs only about 1MB of memory.

Preparing Recordset Options

As shown previously, you can specify various properties of a Recordset. By doing this, you can obtain the type of Recordset you need to gain maximum speed without wasting resources of ADO or your database.

The cursor of a Recordset points to the current record and provides control to navigate in a Recordset. But the Recordset cursor also provides more functions as it controls the updatability of data and the visibility of changes made to the database by other users. To prepare a Recordset that best meets your needs, the most important Recordset properties are the following:

- CursorLocation: Determines the location of the cursor that allows access to the data in the active record of the Recordset
- CursorType: Specifies the type of cursor that is used for the Recordset
- LockType: Indicates the type of locking that is used on records during editing

All three Recordset properties are explained in detail in the next section.

Determining the Cursor Location

Let's see what provides the Recordset cursor. Is it provided by the data source (SQL Server, Access, Oracle) itself or the database provider (such as the OLE DB Provider for ODBC)?

As you have seen in Day 1, "Basic Knowledge About ADO," ADO is mainly a layer upon OLE DB, and OLE DB can make use of the Cursor Engine Service, which provides a cursor when needed. A cursor provided by ADO itself is an example of a client-side cursor. A server-side cursor, on the other hand, is a cursor provided directly by the database/data source or its driver. Both cursor locations, no matter if server-side or client-side, have their areas of application.

You can determine if you want to use a client-side or server-side cursor by setting the Recordset's CursorLocation property to an appropriate value before opening the Recordset. The default value for the CursorLocation property is adUseServer, which instructs ADO to use a server-side cursor. Therefore, every Recordset with no CursorLocation specified is a server-side cursor.

Server-side cursors are mainly used when you need to retrieve data using a forward-only cursor, thus enabling you to avoid using client resources. When you want to update a Recordset, you can do it faster through a server-side cursor.

Updating a Recordset is done when you retrieve the Recordset, change some of its values, and write the Recordset back to the database.

When you don't want to update a Recordset, using a client-side cursor, indicated by the CursorLocation value of adUseClient, provides more flexibility and features for scrolling through the Recordset. You can also, possibly, use a *Disconnected Recordset*—a Recordset that does not need a connection to the database during the whole period of its existence except when directly interacting with the database. (There is more about Disconnected Recordsets in Day 5, "Filtering and Sorting Resultsets"). Local or client-side cursors often provide more features than a driver or database-supplied server-side cursor does.

However, if you want to update your Recordset, often a server-side cursor will be a better choice. In this case, a client-side cursor has to make sure that changes in the client-side Recordset are also performed the same way in the underlying, server-side table. In this instance, the client-side cursor requires a remarkable amount of resources.

Also, when dealing with SQL Server 7.0, using a server-side cursor often improves performance and saves resources. Another advantage is that you can perform updates on records that do not include a primary key column, and no client-side cursor resources are needed at all.

When you have to make a decision about which cursor to use, base it on the action you want to perform on the Recordset, the provider, and the database you are using. For a special scenario refer to the ADO documentation of the Platform SDK of Windows 2000 or the documentation that ships with your development environment.

There are two possibilities to obtain a client-side Recordset. In Listing 2.8, you see the first possibility, which is to set the Recordset's CursorLocation to adUseClient before opening the Recordset.

LISTING 2.8 Using a Client-Side Cursor

```
 1: Dim conn As ADODB.Connection
 2: Dim rs As ADODB.Recordset
 3:
 4: Set conn = CreateObject("ADODB.Connection")
 5: Set rs = CreateObject("ADODB.Recordset")
 6:
 7: conn.Open "Provider=SQLOLEDB;Data Source=BoyScout;" & _
 8:     "Initial Catalog=Northwind;User ID=sa;Password=;"
 9:
10: rs.CursorType = adOpenStatic
11: rs.LockType = adLockReadOnly
12: rs.CursorLocation = adUseClient
13: Set rs.ActiveConnection = conn
14: rs.Source = "SELECT OrderID, ProductID FROM [Order Details]" & _
15:     "WHERE Quantity*UnitPrice > 9000"
16: rs.Open
17:
18: Do While Not rs.EOF
19:     Debug.Print rs(0) & " " & rs(1)
20:     rs.MoveNext
21: Loop
22:
23: rs.Close
24: conn.Close
25: Set rs = Nothing
26: Set conn = Nothing
```

Listing 2.8 was programmed in VBA for Excel. If you want to use the script in ASP (VBScript), you omit the declaration part in the Dim statements and be sure to declare the ADO constants or include the file adovbs.inc in your ASP page. In line 19, the values of the Recordset fields are written into Excel's Intermediate pane of the Microsoft Visual Basic Window. Just adapt this line to redirect the output to a place that fits your needs. In ASP, you can replace the Debug.Print statement with the Response.Write statement, for instance.

The variables conn and rs are declared in lines 1–2. conn is used to contain a Connection object and rs is used as a Recordset object.

In lines 7–8, a connection to the SQL Server Northwind database, which resides on the server named BoyScout, is opened using the OLE DB Provider for SQL Server. The cursor type is set to a *static* cursor using a *read-only lock* (these are explained later in this lesson). The client-side cursor is declared in line 12 by using a statement with the following syntax:

Recordset.CursorLocation = adUseClient

The Recordset's `ActiveConnection` property is set to the `Connection` object stored in the variable `conn` to specify the connection that the Recordset will use to connect to the database.

The SQL statement, which is executed to retrieve the Recordset's data, is defined in the lines 14–15 as follows:

```
SELECT OrderID, ProductID FROM [Order Details] WHERE Quantity*UnitPrice > 9000
```

This SQL statement selects the columns OrderID and ProductID of the records from the table Order Details where the product of Quantity and UnitPrice exceeds the value `9000`.

The prepared Recordset itself is opened in line 16 with the simple statement `rs.open`. Due to the assignment in line 12, this Recordset uses a client-side cursor.

The values of all records of the returned Recordset are processed in the `Do...Loop` loop in lines 18–21.

During each iteration of the `Do...Loop` loop, the Recordset cursor is moved to the record following the active record using the `Recordset` object's `MoveNext` method.

The `Debug.Print` statement in line 19 is specific to Visual Basic. However, the method to retrieve a `Field` value by specifying its index number rather than its name can be used in all languages. This is an ADO-specific feature. Note that the index is zero-based. Therefore, the value of the first column of the Recordset is retrieved using the index value zero, the second column uses the index number one, and so on. To retrieve the value of the first column, you can use a statement such as the following:

```
FirstColumn = Recordset(0)
```

When you specify the index number instead of the field's name, you gain some extra speed because ADO does not search for the column with that specific name.

Specifying the Cursor Type

A cursor is not only a cursor, just as a car is not only a car. There are cars with much power; some have four-wheel drive. Similarly, you can have four types of Recordset cursors. The four cursor types differ in the navigation possibilities and behavior when the Recordset's original data is being updated while the Recordset is in use.

The four cursor types are as follows:

- Forward-Only Cursor: This is the default cursor type. It only allows you to move forward in a Recordset using the `MoveNext` method. Calling the Recordset's `MoveFirst` method is allowed and results in the re-execution of the Recordset generating command.

- Static Cursor: This cursor allows you to navigate through the Recordset in any direction. You can use the methods `MoveFirst`, `MoveLast`, `MoveNext`, and `MovePrevious`. A static cursor is a snapshot of the data in the moment you received the Recordset. So if there are changes made to the underlying data by other users after you receive the Recordset, these changes are not visible to a Recordset with a static cursor.

- Keyset Cursor: This cursor allows you to navigate in any direction through the Recordset. Changes of other users in the data of the Recordset are visible, but any records added by other users to the database are not visible. For instance, you open a Recordset with a keyset cursor and retrieve all records of a product where the price is greater than 5. If another user has added a record with the price is greater than 5, this added record is not visible in your Recordset. Also, records deleted by other users still exist in the Recordset, but their data is not accessible any more.

- Dynamic Cursor: This cursor allows you to navigate forward and backward in a Recordset using the `MoveNext` and `MovePrevious` methods. A Recordset with a dynamic cursor reflects all changes done by other users. When other users change data of the underlying record source, all changes are visible in the Recordset. Therefore, the Recordset can shrink or grow while your script handles it. I recommend using a dynamic cursor only when it is necessary to handle data for which any changes should be available in real time. This cursor type uses up the highest amount of resources from both the server (database and database driver) and the client (the provider and the application).

Tip

> Be wise in the selection of the cursor type. Your selection can have a major impact on database speed, especially when multiple users access your application at the same time. Use a cursor that fits your needs. In most cases, a forward-only cursor will be adequate when you only want to have a snapshot of some data from a database. For more possibilities, you can use a static cursor to navigate through the Recordset, instead.

You can specify the type of cursor you want to use in a Recordset by setting the Recordset's `CursorType` property to one of the following values: `adOpenForwardOnly` (forward-only cursor), `adOpenStatic` (static cursor), `adOpenKeyset` (keyset cursor) and `adOpenDynamic` (dynamic cursor). Be aware that not every combination of `CursorType` and `CursorLocation` is useful or supported by the provider.

Tip

When you use a cursor type that is not supported by your provider, the provider uses another cursor type. You can determine the cursor type in use by reading the CursorType property of the Recordset after you open the Recordset.

A special cursor type is the firehose cursor used by the SQL Server database. This special cursor comes in handy when you connect to a SQL server using a server-side, forward-only, and read-only cursor. It is the default cursor you get when connecting to a SQL Server database. The firehose cursor is highly optimized for performance, and it maintains an open connection between SQL Server and the application until all data is streamed from the SQL Server to the application.

Not all data providers allow every type of cursor. Please consult the Platform SDK of Windows 2000 for detailed information about the provider you want to use in your script and the advantages of using a special CursorType, LockType, or CursorLocation for the task you want to execute against the database.

Note

You can find plenty of information about different providers in the Platform SDK of Windows 2000, especially when dealing with SQL Server 7.0.

Using Lock Types on Recordsets

Before opening a Recordset, you can specify what type of locking the provider should use when dealing with data updates.

The database or data source driver performs locking when data in a record is changed. This prevents different users from changing the same data at the same time. Such an occurrence can make the status of the record unpredictable.

There are different ways to lock data of a Recordset:

- Read-Only Locking: This is the default locking type. It is used as a cursor when no specific LockingType is defined. This is not really a lock, because you cannot change any data when using it. Specifying a read-only lock tells ADO that you will not change any data, and no specific lock has to be enforced.

- Optimistic Locking: This locking provides an exclusive lock only for the time ADO needs to execute the update of records. There are two options for optimistic locking. When you use optimistic locking together with the Recordset's Update method, which updates one row at a time, you use optimistic locking for single-row updates. This is indicated by a lock type of the value adLockOptimistic. However, when you choose optimistic locking together with multirow updates (or batch updates), using the Recordset's UpdateBatch method, this is indicated by the lock type adLockBatchOptimistic.

- Pessimistic Locking: This locking tells ADO to put a lock on any data row in the database that your application has changed in the Recordset from the moment you make the change until the changes are committed or rejected. When using this locking, you must have in mind that any pending change on a certain row prevents other users from accessing or even reading this row. This can lead to great problems, especially when using SQL Server version 6.5, because this database uses page locking rather than single-row locking. It locks a whole page of records from the moment one change in one row is made until the lock is neutralized by committing or rejecting the changes. Use pessimistic locking only when you really want to prevent other users from changing any data you have touched.

You can specify the type of lock you want to use for a Recordset by setting the appropriate value to its LockType property before opening the Recordset.

The four values that can be specified for the LockType property are as follows: adLockReadOnly (read-only locking), adLockOptimistic (optimistic locking for single-row updates), adLockBatchOptimistic (optimistic locking for multiple row updates), and adLockPessimistic (pessimistic locking).

 Note   Your database determines whether you can use other lock types directly on the database instead of using the locking types implemented by ADO. If you are using SQL Server 7.0, you can find information about special locking types in the Platform SDK of Windows 2000 and the SQL Server 7.0 documentation.

Retrieving Multiple Recordsets

When you specify a SQL statement such as

```
SELECT Column1 FROM Table1; SELECT Column2, Column3 FROM Table2
```

you have combined two SQL statements into a SQL compound statement.

When you execute this compound statement, you will retrieve the resulting Recordset of the first SQL statement, but the second SQL statement is not executed.

Note   You can use SQL compound statements against a SQL Server 7.0 database only when you are using a client-side cursor.

You can treat this Recordset as you would any other Recordset—navigate through it, read the field values, make updates, and so on.

However, when you want to execute the second SQL statement of the compound statement to retrieve the resulting Recordset, you must use the `NextRecordset` method of the first `Recordset` object to retrieve the resulting Recordset of the second SQL statement. This can be done as follows:

```
Set Recordset = Recordset.NextRecordset
```

The example in Listing 2.9 provides such a procedure.

LISTING 2.9   Retrieving Multiple Recordsets

```
 1: Dim conn As ADODB.Connection
 2: Dim rs As ADODB.Recordset
 3:
 4: Set conn = CreateObject("ADODB.Connection")
 5: Set rs = CreateObject("ADODB.Recordset")
 6:
 7: conn.Open "Provider=SQLOLEDB;Data Source=BoyScout;" & _
 8:    "Initial Catalog=Northwind;User ID=sa;Password=;"
 9:
10: rs.CursorType = adOpenStatic
11: rs.LockType = adLockBatchOptimistic
12: rs.CursorLocation = adUseClient
13: Set rs.ActiveConnection = conn
14: rs.Source = "SELECT CompanyName FROM Suppliers " & _
15:    "WHERE Country = 'USA';" & _
16:    "SELECT ShipName, ShippedDate FROM Orders " & _
17:    "WHERE ShipCountry = 'Austria' AND ShippedDate < '1/1/1997'"
18: rs.Open
19:
20: Do While Not rs.EOF
21:    Debug.Print rs("CompanyName")
22:    rs.MoveNext
23: Loop
24:
25: Set rs = rs.NextRecordset
26: Debug.Print "——"
27:
```

continues

LISTING 2.9   continued

```
28: Do While Not rs.EOF
29:    Debug.Print rs("ShipName") & ":" & rs("ShippedDate")
30:    rs.MoveNext
31: Loop
32:
33: rs.Close
34: conn.Close
35: Set rs = Nothing
36: Set conn = Nothing
```

ANALYSIS   The script defines and declares variables in line 1–5. A connection to the SQL Server database named Northwind is opened in line 7. The Recordset is prepared in lines 10–17. Line 17 contains the SQL compound statement that is to be executed. In line 18, the first SQL statement of the compound statement is executed. The resulting Recordset is returned and can be accessed through the variable rs. The loop in the lines 20–23 reads all values of the Recordset, which contains the result set of the first SQL statement. To gain access to the Recordset resulting from the second SQL statement, you have to perform the NextRecordset method. This returns the Recordset that contains the result of the following SQL statement, which, in this case, is the second SQL statement. Usually, you assign the second and all following Recordsets to the same Recordset variable because no more access to the first Recordset is available when another SQL statement is executed (as during the call of the NextRecordset method). The second loop gets all values from the second Recordset and writes them into the Debug window of Visual Basic. Because the script no longer needs any resources for the Recordset and the connection, it closes both the Recordset and the connection and frees their resources in lines 33–36.

There are few reasons for using compound SQL statements. But when you want to retrieve more than one Recordset from a stored procedure (running on SQL Server), you must use the NextRecordset method to gain access to all Recordsets. (More information about stored procedures is presented in Day 7, "Implementing Application Logic in Stored Procedures."

Getting the Number of Records in a Recordset

This section shows you how to retrieve the number of records returned from a data source and how to effectively limit the number of records returned from a data source.

When you open a Recordset, you often want to know how many records are in the Recordset.

The `RecordCount` property of the Recordset enables you to determine the number of records in the Recordset. However, some criteria must be met by the Recordset, if you want to use the `RecordCount` property.

When you open a Recordset and use the `RecordCount` property, you might retrieve the value -1, which indicates that no information about the number of records is available. This occurs when the default cursor type is the forward-only cursor, which does not support approximate positioning. Therefore, ADO cannot determine the number of records in the Recordset.

 Tip

> You can check if a Recordset supports approximate positioning using the Recordset's `Supports` method as shown in the following example.
>
> *blnSupports = Recordset.Supports(adApproxPosition)*

When you want to use the `RecordCount` method on a Recordset, you should use a Recordset with a static cursor or keyset cursor. Both cursors will return the correct number of records in the Recordset. When using `RecordCount` with a dynamic cursor, the data source determines if approximate positioning is supported. If so, `RecordCount` can be used to retrieve the number of records in the Recordset.

You might want to limit the number of records returned from the data source. This limitation can be enforced using the `MaxRecords` property of the Recordset.

In the following example, the number of records is limited to three because you are only interested in the first three records.

Listing 2.10 retrieves records from the SQL Server database named Northwind. It shows the three products that have the highest result when multiplying unit price and units in stock.

LISTING 2.10   Retrieving the First Three Records

```
1: Dim conn As ADODB.Connection
2: Dim rs As ADODB.Recordset
3:
4: Set conn = CreateObject("ADODB.Connection")
```

continues

LISTING **2.10**   continued

```
 5: Set rs = CreateObject("ADODB.Recordset")
 6:
 7: conn.Open "Provider=SQLOLEDB;Data Source=BoyScout;" & _
 8:      "Initial Catalog=Northwind;User ID=sa;Password=;"
 9:
10: rs.CursorType = adOpenStatic
11: rs.LockType = adLockReadOnly
12: rs.CursorLocation = adUseServer
13: rs.MaxRecords = 3
14: Set rs.ActiveConnection = conn
15: rs.Source = "SELECT ProductName, UnitsInStock,
➡ UnitPrice FROM Products " & _
16:      "ORDER BY UnitsInStock*UnitPrice DESC"
17: rs.Open
18:
19: Do While Not rs.EOF
20:    Debug.Print rs("ProductName") & ":" &
➡ (rs("UnitsInStock") * rs("UnitPrice"))
21:    rs.MoveNext
22: Loop
23:
24: rs.Close
25: conn.Close
26: Set rs = Nothing
27: Set conn = Nothing
```

The Connection and the Recordset are declared and created in lines 1–5. A connection is opened to the Northwind database, which is located on the SQL Server named BoyScout, in lines 7–8

The Recordset is prepared in lines 10–12 to be a read-only Recordset using a static, server-side cursor.

In line 13, the number of returned records is limited to 3 using the following statement:

Recordset.MaxRecords = 3

The open Connection is assigned as an active connection to the Recordset object in line 14. Lines 15 and 16 contain the SQL statement that is executed against the SQL Server Northwind database. A mathematical product of units in stock and unit price is calculated, and the products with the highest results of this calculation are received. The SQL statement itself uses the ORDER BY clause, together with the DESC(ending) keyword, to sort the records beginning from the product with the highest result when the number of units in stock are multiplied by unit prices. Because the number of records returned is restricted, the number of records retrieved when executing the SQL statement in line 17 is three. Only the first three records are available in the Recordset.

In the lines 19–22 the three records are returned to the user. The Recordset and the Connection are closed, and their resources released in lines 24–27.

Tip	When using SQL Server as a data source you also can use the TOP keyword in a SELECT statement to limit the number of returned records. The syntax of a SELECT statement that returns only the first three records is shown here.
	SELECT TOP 3 Columns FROM Table ...

Using Properties of Fields

Every record consists of fields, and each field is represented by a Field object. You can obtain information about a field by reading its properties. Table 2.2 provides an overview of the most important field properties.

TABLE 2.2 The Most Important Field Properties

Property Name	Description
Value	Field value (default property)
Name	Field name
Type	Data type of the field
ActualSize	Actual size of the field
DefinedSize	Size in characters or bytes in the field's definition
OriginalValue	Field value prior to changes
UnderlyingValue	Field's current value in database
Attributes	Field's characteristics

Additional properties—most of them dependent on the data source and data provider used—are accessible through the Properties Collection of the Field object.

Get the Field Name

The field's name can be obtained using the Name property of the Field object.

This is useful, for instance, when you loop through all fields of a Record as shown in Listing 2.11.

LISTING 2.11   Looping Through all Fields of a Record

```
1: For FieldIndex = 0 To rs.Fields.Count - 1
2:   Debug.Print rs.Fields(FieldIndex).Name & "=" & rs.Fields(FieldIndex).Value
3: Next
```

The script in Listing 2.11 loops through all fields. Each field is assigned a number, the Fieldindex. The first field of a record has index 0, the second field has index 1, third field has index 2, and so on. The number of fields in the Fields collection of a certain Recordset can be obtained using the collection's Count property. When there are four fields in the Recordset, the Recordset.Count returns the value 4. Therefore, the script in Listing 2.11 loops from 0 to the number of fields in the Fields collection minus one. Each field is referenced by its index number. The current index number during a certain loop is stored in the variable Fieldindex. To retrieve the name of a field with a certain Fieldindex number, use a statement such as the one shown here:

```
strFieldname = Recordset(Fieldindex).Name
```

Retrieving the Field Value

When you read the value from the field with the name "MyName", you can use a statement such as the following:

```
Value = Recordset("MyName")
```

This is the shortcut for the following statement:

```
Value = Recordset.Fields("MyName").Value
```

By using the first statement, you are reading the field's default property, which is the Value property that contains the value of the field.

You can also loop through the Fields collection using a For Each …Next loop. The script presented in Listing 2.12 performs the same job as Listing 2.11.

LISTING 2.12   Looping Through All Fields of a Record

```
1: For Each FieldItem In rs.Fields
2:   Debug.Print FieldItem.Name & " = " & FieldItem.Value
3: Next
```

When the script executes the loop, the FieldItem variable contains another member (Field) of the Fields collection. Therefore, you can retrieve the name of the current field in the loop using a statement as follows:

```
FieldName = FieldItem.Name
```

The value of the actual field in the loop can be retrieved reading the `Value` property of the variable `FieldItem`.

```
Fieldvalue = FieldItem.Value
```

Determining the Field's Data Type

You can determine the data type of a field by using the `Type` property of the `Field` object.

```
DataType = Recordset("FieldName").Type
```

The value stored in the variable `DataType` can be compared to values stored in the ADO data type constants, as shown in Table 2.3. It is possible to find the data type definition of a certain field. It depends on the way the field is defined, how you retrieved your Recordset, if the data type is defined in a table of a database, in a stored procedure, in the SQL statement, or another location.

TABLE 2.3 Mapping Data Types from Visual Basic to ADO

Visual Basic	ADO Constant	Data Length
Long	adInteger	4
Integer	adSmallInt	2
Byte	adTinyInt	1
Boolean	adBoolean	1
Double	adDouble	8
Single	adSingle	4
Currency	adCurrency	8
Date	adDate	8
String (normal)	adVarChar	variable
String (normal)	adVarWChar	variable
String (BLOB)	adLongVarChar	variable
String (BLOB)	adLongVarWChar	variable

Note

The ADO constants `adVarWChar` and `adLongVarWChar` are used for fields of Unicode data type. There is more about the use of Unicode data later in the book.

Getting the Actual Size of a Field

The actual size of a field describes how many bytes are used to store the field's value or how many characters are stored in the field. This is also true when the field is a large binary or text field (BLOB). You can obtain the actual size by reading the `ActualSize` property of a field.

Fields of certain data types, for instance `Integer`, `Currency`, or `Date`, always use the same number of bytes to store data, no matter which value is stored in the field. However, a field that stores a string value can have a variable actual size that depends on the length of the string stored in the field. The data lengths of the most important field types are shown in Table 2.3.

Imagine that you have retrieved a field from a SQL Server database. When this field is defined as a `VarChar(15)` field in the SQL Server database, SQL Server uses storage of variable length and a maximum of 15 characters, depending on the value that is actually stored in the field. The same is valid for a field in an Access database defined using the data type `Text`. The `ActualSize` property of a `VarChar` (SQL Server) or `Text` (Access) field returns the actual size of the field value in characters.

Getting the Defined Size of a Field

When a field's data type is defined, the size of the field is also defined. This is the maximum number of bytes or characters in a field that are used to store the field's value. The defined size can be obtained by using the field's `DefinedSize` property.

For most data types, the `DefinedSize` and the `ActualSize` property of a certain field return the same value. However, these two values differ when you are dealing with string fields of variable length or with large text or binary data fields (BLOBs).

Finding a Field's Value Prior to Changes

As you will see in Day 3, "Fail-Safe Inserting of Data," it is possible to retrieve a Recordset, change some of its values, and then write the Recordset back to the database. However, sometimes after you have made changes to the Recordset, it is useful to know the original value. In Figure 2.2, the first step retrieves a Recordset from the database, containing the value 8, which is the original value. In the second step, the value in the `Recordset` is changed to 4. However, you can get the value before any changes were made by using the `Field` object's `OriginalValue` property.

The usage of the `OriginalValue` property is explained in depth in Day 3.

The `OriginalValue` property is only guaranteed to work with a Recordset that can be updated. When you try to access the `OriginalValue` property of a read-only Recordset, you will receive an error. Special permutations of `LockType`, `CursorLocation`, and `CursorType` might also fail, depending on the provider or data source, when you access the `OriginalValue` property.

FIGURE 2.2

Original value and underlying value.

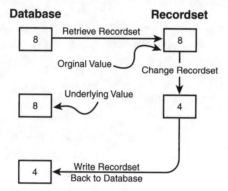

Retrieving the Current Database Value of a Field

A Recordset field has a corresponding field in the underlying database (see Figure 2.2).

You can retrieve the current value of the field in the underlying database using the field's `UnderlyingValue` property. Imagine that you have a Recordset that allows updates. You retrieve the Recordset, and while you are working with it, the value of a field of a certain record in the underlying table is changed. When you want to know if the data in a certain field is the same as its current value in the underlying database, you can use the `UnderlyingValue` property of that field to obtain the value in the underlying database. You can then compare that value against the current value in your Recordset.

Using the Field's `Attribute` Property

Although you can perform many actions on fields, such as updating their value, not every action is allowed on every field.

For instance when a field contains an `Autonumber` value, you are not allowed to change its value. Also you cannot assign a value to this field in a new record.

How can you determine whether a field has special attributes that do not allow certain actions such as updating a value, or if a field needs special treatment? (This is the case for large binary or text fields.)

You can find this information by taking a look at the definition of the field in the data source or by using the field's `Attributes` property.

The `Attributes` property contains a value that informs you about the attributes of a field, such as whether it can be updated, whether it contains a large binary value, or whether it is a primary key field.

All this information is encoded in the `Attributes` property.

ADO's most important field attributes are shown with their constants, their numeric values, and the information that each attribute provides in Table 2.4. The values are given in hexadecimal notation.

TABLE 2.4   ADO's Field Attribute Constants

ADO Constant	Value	Provided Information
adFldUpdatable	0x0004	You can write to the field.
adFldUnknownUpdatable	0x0008	The provider cannot determine if you can write to the field.
adFldFixed	0x0010	Contains fixed-length data.
adFldIsNullable	0x0020	The field accepts Null values
adFldMayBeNull	0x0040	The field can return Null.
adFldLong	0x0080	This is a long binary or text field.
adFldRowID	0x0100	This contains a persistent row identifier. Writing is forbidden.
adFldRowVersion	0x0200	Time or date stamp.
adFldKeyColumn	0x8000	This is (part of) the primary key.

You can use the `AppendChunk` and `GetChunk` methods to handle data of a special type with a field when it is indicated as a Long Binary or Text Field (`adFldLong`).

You can determine if a field has a certain attribute using a comparison as follows:

`(Recordset("Fieldname").Attributes And adConstant) > 0`

adConstant is a placeholder for the ADO's `Attributes` constant that you want to check for.

When the previous statement returns TRUE for a certain ADO constant, you can determine the field's behavior through the information related to the ADO constant.

Note

Sometimes a field is indicated as `adFldUnknownUpdatable`, even when it is updateable. Whether the field can be updated depends on how the `Recordset` is prepared using the Recordset's `LockType` property.

Reading the Field's `Properties` Collection

The field's `Properties` collection provides additional information about the field and its underlying column in the database.

To retrieve all properties, their names, and their values, you can make use of the script shown in Listing 2.13.

LISTING 2.13 Retrieving the Whole `Properties` Collection

```
1: For Each objProperty In Recordset("FieldName").Properties
2:_  Debug.Print objProperty.Name & "=" & objProperty.Value
3: Next
```

ANALYSIS The script is using the collection's `Name` and the `Value` properties to retrieve the name and the value of every item (property) in the `Properties` collection.

When you use different `CursorTypes`, `CursorLocations`, `LockTypes` or providers, the resulting `Properties` collection can differ.

Determining Connection Properties

When you are using your application in an unknown environment, it is especially important to retrieve specific connection properties and parameters. For instance, if you are using Active Server Pages on a provider's Web server, it is important to know which ADO version is installed or which methods are supported.

Retrieving the Name of the `Connection` Provider

The `Provider` property of a `Connection` object enables you to retrieve the name of the data provider used to establish the connection. Its usage is as simple, as shown here:

`strProvider = conn.Provider`

conn is the variable that contains the `Connection` object.

Finding the ADO Version Used

The ADO version number can be obtained using the `Version` property of the `Connection` object. You can use this property after the connection is opened to check what version of ADO is installed and used for the connection. This is important because every version of ADO supports different features, providers, objects, and so on.

To get an overview over differences in certain ADO versions refer to Appendix B, "Technologies, Features, and Release Packages of MDAC and ADO."

Reading the Connection's `Properties` Collection

To get common, in-depth information about a `Connection` object, its ADO version, and the underlying provider and database, you can read the values of the `Properties` collection.

Listing 2.14 returns all values from the `Properties` collection of a certain SQL Server connection.

LISTING **2.14**   Retrieving Connection Properties

```
1: Dim conn As ADODB.Connection
2: Set conn = CreateObject("ADODB.Connection")
3: conn.Open "Provider=SQLOLEDB;Data Source=BoyScout;" & _
4:    "Initial Catalog=Northwind;User ID=sa;Password=;"
5:
6: For Each Item In conn.Properties
7:    Debug.Print Item.Name & " : " & Item.Value
8: Next
9:
10: conn.Close
11: Set conn = Nothing
```

ANALYSIS   The script opens a connection in line 3. The example uses the Microsoft OLE DB Provider for SQL Server (`SQLOLEDB`) to connect to a SQL Server database.

The `For Each...Next` loop in lines 6–8 iterates over all properties in the `Properties` collection of the `Connection` object.

The output contains, among other things, the database name, the SQL Server version, the OLE DB Provider version or the username used to establish the connection, and the username alias in the database (which can be two different values for SQL Server databases).

Summary

In this lesson, you have learned the basic operations for using database data in your application.

You have examined what is necessary to open a connection, retrieve a Recordset from the database, and navigate through the Recordset. The possible choices when preparing a Recordset have been explained, as well as the procedures to limit the number of records in a Recordset. In the last part of this day, you have learned how to use properties of the field and the `Connection` object to retrieve some useful information about them.

Q&A

Q What kind of data can be accessed using ADO?

A You can access any data source that provides an OLE DB or ODBC interface. Many kinds of data are available. You can access text files, directories, different databases (SQL Server, Access, DB2, AS/400), Index Servers, Webfolders, and files served by Frontpage, Active Directories, and any other data source that can be accessed through an OLE DB or ODBC interface.

Workshop

The Workshop is designed to help you anticipate possible questions, review what you've learned, and get you thinking about how to put your knowledge into practice. The answers to the quiz are in Appendix A, "Quiz Answers."

Quiz

1. How can you determine how many records a Recordset contains?

2. When you have an open connection, how can you find out which ADO version is used?

3. Given the fact a data source has an OLE DB interface, how can it be accessed using ADO?

4. What are the four cursor types used in an ADO Recordset?

5. What characteristic does an empty Recordset have?

6. How can you find out if a certain field is allowed to contain NULL values?

Exercise

Not only the Connection and the Field objects have a Properties collection. The Recordset object also contains a Properties collection that can provide useful information about the Recordset. Open a Recordset to a data source of your choice using ADO and read all values from the Properties collection of both the Recordset and the Connection objects.

DAY **3**

Fail-Safe Inserting of Data

Objectives

In the previous day, you examined the ways to retrieve data from a database. The next database task, which is discussed today, is to insert data into a database. We also examine the ways to deal with errors that can be raised when ADO inserts data into a database. Such errors appear when you try to insert data that violates the table's definition (for example, inserting a string into an integer field), or when you violate other rules of the database (for instance, inserting data into an Autonumber field or using a value that is not allowed by foreign-key relationships).

There are different ways to insert data, depending on the demands of the application using ADO.

Today, you will learn the following:

- How to insert data into a database table
- How to deal with errors when using ADO

Inserting Data into a Table

Just as there are many ways to retrieve data from a database, you also have multiple ways to insert data into a database. In this chapter, you learn about the following topics:

- SQL INSERT statement: This statement can be used similarly to the SQL SELECT statement for inserting data. It cannot be used for inserting BLOB values into a database.

- Using the Recordset object's AddNew method: This method is used for adding a new record to a Recordset. The record is stored in the database by using the Recordset object's Update method.

- Dealing with BLOB fields: Special issues on how to insert BLOBs into a database are described in this day.

- Using stored procedures: The usage of stored procedures for data insert operations is mentioned; however, the programming techniques are dealt with in a later lesson.

- Usage of special field types: When inserting a new record into a table, you have to be aware of Autonumber fields, Timestamp fields, or other limitations that the table columns impose on the inserted data.

NEW TERM   A *Timestamp* field is a field in a database table that automatically contains the date and time of the creation or the last change in the data of the record.

Some special scenarios explained in this chapter are as follows:

- When you insert a new record into a table that has an Autonumber field, the database generates a value for this field. When ADO is inserting the new record, you can retrieve the Autonumber value. This is especially useful when you want to have an unequivocal reference to the inserted data for future use in your application.

- When inserting or changing data in a database field, you also have to be aware of any limitations, for instance, the maximum length of the data you can insert into a certain field or the correct data type. When you insert a new record into a table or change table data, some fields require a valid value, and others need no value at all.

- When your application tries to perform an illegal action using ADO, errors can be raised by ADO that result in runtime errors. If the provider returns an error or warning, this error can be accessed using the Connection object's Errors collection. The Errors collection contains error objects that provide information about the error, such as the error description and the error source.

All these scenarios are discussed at length today.

Usage of the INSERT statement

To add new data into a database table, you can use the `INSERT` statement, which is a SQL statement that can be executed against the database. You can use the `Execute` method of the `Connection` object to execute an `INSERT` statement.

The general syntax of the `INSERT` statement is as follows:

```
INSERT INTO Table (column_list) VALUES (values_list)
```

The `column list` is the list of table columns where the data values are inserted. The `values list` contains the data that is to be inserted into the table columns listed in the `column list`. A value can be the correct data type for the appropriate column, the keyword `NULL` (which stands for *No Value*), or the keyword `DEFAULT` when you want to insert the default value (which is contained in the table definition). An INSERT statement might read as follows:

```
INSERT INTO Employees     (LastName, FirstName) VALUES ('Hood', 'Robin')
```

If you want to insert a new record into the Employees table of the Northwind sample database (which ships with SQL Server 7.0 or Access 2000), you first have to take a look at the table definition, which is shown in Figure 3.1.

FIGURE 3.1

Definition of the Employees table.

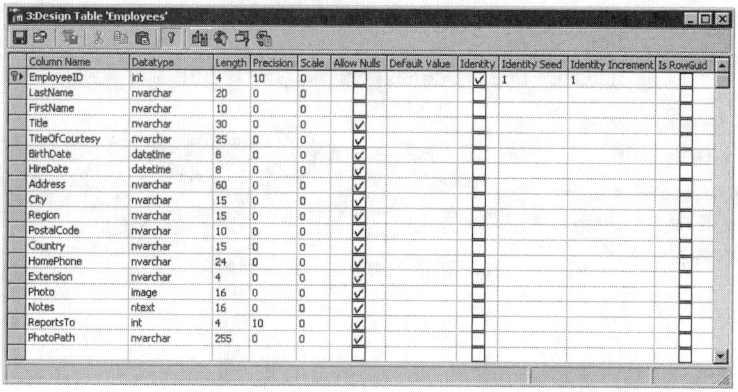

3:Design Table 'Employees'

Column Name	Datatype	Length	Precision	Scale	Allow Nulls	Default Value	Identity	Identity Seed	Identity Increment	Is RowGuid
EmployeeID	int	4	10	0	☐		✓	1	1	☐
LastName	nvarchar	20	0	0	☐		☐			☐
FirstName	nvarchar	10	0	0	☐		☐			☐
Title	nvarchar	30	0	0	✓		☐			☐
TitleOfCourtesy	nvarchar	25	0	0	✓		☐			☐
BirthDate	datetime	8	0	0	✓		☐			☐
HireDate	datetime	8	0	0	✓		☐			☐
Address	nvarchar	60	0	0	✓		☐			☐
City	nvarchar	15	0	0	✓		☐			☐
Region	nvarchar	15	0	0	✓		☐			☐
PostalCode	nvarchar	10	0	0	✓		☐			☐
Country	nvarchar	15	0	0	✓		☐			☐
HomePhone	nvarchar	24	0	0	✓		☐			☐
Extension	nvarchar	4	0	0	✓		☐			☐
Photo	image	16	0	0	✓		☐			☐
Notes	ntext	16	0	0	✓		☐			☐
ReportsTo	int	4	10	0	✓		☐			☐
PhotoPath	nvarchar	255	0	0	✓		☐			☐

In the table's definition you can see that three fields do not allow `NULL` values. These fields must contain a valid value after you have executed the `INSERT` statement. If they do not, the `INSERT` statement fails, and ADO raises an error.

The field EmployeeID is an Autonumber field because its `Identity` property is checked in the table definition. Its value is generated by the database for each new record.

Therefore, you cannot provide a value for this field. The second and the third fields that cannot contain NULL values are the LastName and Firstname fields. You have to provide valid strings for these fields when you insert a new record into the table. When inserting a new record into a table, you only can omit a field's value if the field in the table is allowed to contain a NULL value or a default value is defined for the field.

All other fields can be omitted safely when inserting data into the Employees table.

Of course, you have to take care that you insert data of the same or a similar data type, as defined in the table's definition. However, this rule is not that strict. As long as the data type you supplied can be converted implicitly by the database (or the database provider) into the correct data type, you're on the safe side. An example of implicit conversion occurs when you provide integer values and the database converts and stores them as decimal or string values.

To see a table's definition in SQL Server 7.0, perform the following steps:

To Do: Get a Table's Definition in SQL Server 7.0

1. Open the SQL Server Enterprise Manager, which can be found in the Microsoft SQL Server 7.0 program group.

2. In the console window, expand the SQL Server group that contains the SQL Server that maintains the database with the table you want to examine. Expand the correct SQL Server. Next expand the database folder of the SQL Server and, finally, the database that contains the table (see Figure 3.2).

FIGURE 3.2

The expanded tree in SQL Server Enterprise Manager.

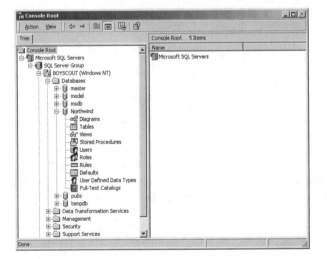

3. Select the Tables icon for the expanded database. All tables of the database appear in the right pane of the window.

4. Right click on the table whose definition you want to explore. Choose Design Table from the context menu.

5. The Design Table window appears. (It is very similar to Figure 3.1.) In this window, you can view and change the table's definition.

The table definition contains all the information about the construction of the table, the field types, and field properties. However, it does not contain information about referential integrity, such as Foreign Key relationships or SQL Server Triggers. Also, it does not inform you when a unique index is used on a column. This forces you to use unique values in each field of the column.

NEW TERM A *Trigger* in a SQL Server database is a defined action that is performed when a certain action takes place. For instance, an Insert Trigger of a table is performed each time you insert data into a table.

Note
When using a database other than SQL Server, you should refer to the user manual to find out how to display the table definition.

Another common database used with ADO is Microsoft Access. To get the table definition of an Access 2000 table, perform the following steps:

To Do: Get a Table's Definition in Access 2000

1. Open the Access 2000 database that contains the table.

2. Examine all tables that are defined in the database (Figure 3.3).

FIGURE 3.3

Tables defined in the Access 2000 Northwind database.

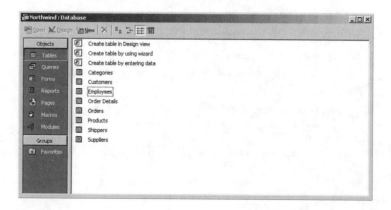

▼   3. Right click the table whose table definition you want to see and choose Design
          View.

        4. Access opens the table in Design View to see the table's definition (see Figure 3.4).

FIGURE 3.4

Access 2000 views the
table definition of the
Employees table.

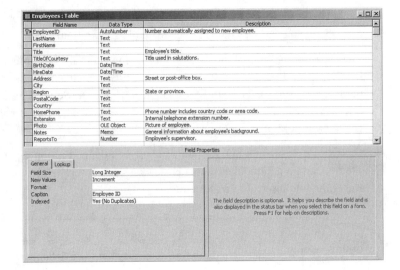

▲   5. To see the full definition of the data type of a certain field, move the cursor into
           that particular field.

The Design View of a table in Access 2000 provides valuable information. When you
want to pay attention to the exact definition of a specific field, you move the cursor into
the row of that field. Unique indices and foreign-key relationships are not shown in the
table definition, but you should know them so that you can use the table correctly, especially when inserting or changing data.

When you have all information about the table that you need, you can prepare a correct
INSERT statement to insert data into the table.

When you want to insert data into a database using an INSERT statement, you provide a
statement similar to the following one. The sample statement inserts data into the
Employees table.

```
INSERT INTO Employees
(LastName, FirstName, HireDate, Address, City, Region, PostalCode, Country)
VALUES
('Davis','Miles','10/10/1999','76 First Avenue','New York','NY','10011','USA')
```

This statement adds the new employee named `Miles Davis`, hired at `10/10/1999`, living in `76 First Avenue`, `10011 New York, NY, USA` to the Employees table of the SQL Server Northwind database.

Caution
| If you are inserting dates into a table using an `INSERT` statement, the way you provide the date depends on the database. |

In the SQL Server 7.0 database you can insert dates by using a valid date expression in a string. The following are examples:

`'12/31/2000'`

`'12/31/00'`

In the Access 2000 database, you can also use delimited strings or a date expression delimited by pound signs, as shown here:

`#12/31/2000#`

`#12/31/00#`

3

Caution
| The date format you have to provide (mm/dd/yyyy or dd.mm.yyyy, for example) depends on the locale settings for the database (SQL Server), or the server settings (Access). Most problems with dates arise out of these locale settings. |

Tip
| When you execute a SQL statement against a SQL Server database, and you want your date expression to be independent of all language settings, you can use a date escape clause such as `{ d 'yyyy-mm-dd'}`. This date escape clause is described in the SQL Server documentation (SQL Server Books Online) or the Windows 2000 Platform SDK under the title "Writing International Transact-SQL Statements."
For Access 2000 users there is no such workaround available. |

What about an `INSERT` statement that inserts a decimal number into a table? You can use an `INSERT` statement as shown in the following example.

```
INSERT INTO Table (Number) VALUES (3.14)
```

Once again, the regional settings of the computer on which your script is executed can be a problem. For example, the regional settings of the executing computer might use a comma (,) instead of a period (.) as decimal symbol. (This is done per default on a German operating system.)

For instance, when the variable lngNum contains the value 3.14, and the locale settings of your computer define a comma to display the decimal symbol, the following INSERT statement will fail:

```
lngNum = 3.14
strSQL = "INSERT INTO Table (Number) VALUES (" & lngNum & ")"
```

The resulting SQL statement is as follows:

```
INSERT INTO Table (Number) VALUES (3,14)
```

The reason for the problem is the comma between 3 and 14.

 Caution

> A comma in the VALUES list is used to separate values. The database provider expects a period as decimal sign. In the expression VALUES(3,14), the database provider assumes that there are two values provided in the VALUES list, which are 3 and 14. Because there is only one column specified in the column list, the execution of the SQL statement will fail and return an error.
>
> Therefore, when your application runs on a computer with regional settings that return a comma instead of a period as decimal sign, you have to replace the comma with a period.
>
> ```
> lngNum = 3.14
> strSQL = "INSERT INTO Table (Number) VALUES  " & _
>          " (" & Replace(lngNum, ",", ".")  & ")"
> ```

When you have created the (I hope) correct INSERT statement, the next step is to execute it against the database.

You can use the Connection object's Execute method to execute a SQL statement. Listing 3.1 provides an overview of how an INSERT statement is created and executed when using ADO. The purpose of Listing 3.1 is to insert a new employee into the Employees table of the SQL Server Northwind database. When you use the Access 2000 Northwind database instead, the script is the same, except for the connection string.

LISTING 3.1 Inserting a New Employee into the Employees Table Using an INSERT Statement

```
 1: Dim conn As ADODB.Connection
 2: Dim strLastName As String
 3: Dim dateHireDate As Date
 4: Dim strAddress As String
 5: Dim strCity As String
 6: Dim strRegion As String
 7: Dim strPostalCode As String
 8: Dim strCountry As String
 9:
10: Set conn = CreateObject("ADODB.Connection")
11:
12: conn.Open "Provider=SQLOLEDB;Data Source=BoyScout;" & _
13:     "Initial Catalog=Northwind;User ID=sa;Password=;"
14:
15: strLastName = "Davis"
16: strFirstName = "Miles"
17: dateHireDate = #10/10/1999#
18: strAddress = "176 First Avenue"
19: strCity = "New York"
20: strRegion = "NY"
21: strPostalCode = "10011"
22: strCountry = "USA"
23:
24: strSQL = "INSERT INTO Employees " & _
25:     "(LastName, FirstName, HireDate, Address, City, " & _
26:     "Region, PostalCode, Country) " & _
27:     "VALUES (" & _
28:     "'" & Replace(Left(strLastName, 20), "'", "''") & "'," & _
29:     "'" & Replace(Left(strFirstName, 10), "'", "''") & "'," & _
30:     "'" & dateHireDate & "'," & _
31:     "'" & Replace(Left(strAddress, 60) , "'", "''") & "'," & _
32:     "'" & Replace(Left(strCity, 15) , "'", "''") & "'," & _
33:     "'" & Replace(Left(strRegion, 15), "'", "''") & "'," & _
34:     "'" & Replace(Left(strPostalCode, 10), "'", "''") & "'," & _
35:     "'" & Replace(Left(strCountry, 15), "'", "''") & "')"
36:
37: conn.Execute strSQL
38:
39: conn.Close
40: Set conn = Nothing
```

ANALYSIS Let's examine the parts of the script in Listing 3.1. The variable declarations are done in lines 1–8, and the Connection object is created in line 10. The

3

connection to the SQL Server Northwind database is opened in line 12 using the OLE DB Provider for SQL Server (SQLOLEDB). All sample values of the new dataset are stored in variables in the lines 15–22. The SQL INSERT statement is built in the lines 24–35 and stored in the variable strSQL.

When you are inserting string data, you have to ensure that the length of the string does not exceed the maximum length for that field. For instance, you cannot store a string 25 characters long in a field that, because of the table definition in the database, can only hold 15 characters. When you try to do so, an error is raised by ADO.

In Listing 3.1 strings are cut to the maximum length allowed in the table fields by using the Visual Basic Left function. However, in a real world application, you should check if a value is valid for a certain field before you try to insert it into the database. This avoids errors caused by inserting a string with too many characters, values outside required ranges, or an invalid date into a table.

Another problem arises when you build a SQL statement that uses strings as values in a VALUES list of an INSERT statement or elsewhere in a SQL statement. Strings are delimited by apostrophes. When the delimited string itself contains an apostrophe, as in the following example, there is no way to distinguish between an apostrophe used as a string delimiter and an apostrophe used in the text. A sample containing an apostrophe follows:

```
'o'Conner'
```

Using such a value as a string in a SQL statement results in an error. The database provider assumes that the text ends with the second apostrophe. Therefore, you have to replace every apostrophe in the text of the string with two apostrophes. Two apostrophes together are not recognized as string delimiters, but as one apostrophe (in an apostrophe-delimited string). The correct version of the delimited string is shown here:

```
'o''Conner'
```

Tip

Every time you build a SQL statement that contains string values that are provided by Visual Basic variables, you have to make sure that each apostrophe is replaced by two apostrophes. This can be done using the Visual Basic Replace function as shown here.

```
strSure = Replace(strVariable, "'", "''")
```

Now we return to the script of Listing 3.1. After the SQL INSERT statement is built, the statement is executed against the database (in line 37) using the following Visual Basic command that finally inserts the new dataset into the Employees table:

```
conn.Execute strSQL
```

The variable conn contains the connection to the SQL Server Northwind database, and the variable strSQL contains the INSERT statement that includes all values of the new dataset.

After the INSERT statement is executed, the connection is closed, and the script frees its resources in the lines 39–40.

Note

> The code in Listing 3.1 does not contain error handling. When the execution of the INSERT statement fails, a runtime error occurs, and the script aborts its execution. The handling of such errors is described later in this day's lesson.

Do	Don't
Do use an INSERT statement to insert a new record. You do not need a Recordset object or Command object for inserting data into a database. Using an INSERT statement cuts processing time and memory requirements, and it avoids network traffic between the application and the database server.	**Don't** use an INSERT statement when you need a Recordset object to retrieve the value of an Autonumber field. Also, you cannot use an INSERT statement to write a value to a large binary field, because its value cannot be represented by a string.

To retrieve values of Autonumber fields, you insert a new record using the AddNew method of the Recordset object, which is described later in this chapter. When you are using a SQL Server database, you can use the @@IDENTITY function to retrieve the value of an Autonumber field as described in the following section.

Getting Autonumber Values from SQL Server

When you insert a new record into a database using the SQL INSERT statement and the new record in the table contains an Autonumber field, there is no simple way to find out which Autonumber value was created by the database for the new record. However, when you are using a SQL Server database, you can find out the last Identity value (Autonumber value) inserted in the database by the current connection. The SQL Server 7.0 function that allows you to retrieve the last Identity value generated for the current connection is called the @@IDENTITY function. You can use the @@IDENTITY function in a SELECT statement, as shown in the following example.

LISTING 3.2   Usage of the SQL Server's @@IDENTITY Function

```
 1: Dim conn As ADODB.Connection
 2: Dim rs As ADODB.Recordset
 3: Dim strProductName As String
 4: Dim lngProductID As Long
 5:
 6: Set conn = CreateObject("ADODB.Connection")
 7: Set rs = CreateObject("ADODB.Recordset")
 8: conn.Open "Provider=SQLOLEDB;Data Source=BoyScout;" & _
 9:     "Initial Catalog=Northwind;User ID=sa;Password=;"
10:
11: ' Insert New Product into Products Table
12: strProductName = "Punschkrapferl"
13: strSQL = "INSERT INTO Products (ProductName) VALUES " & _
14:     "('" & Replace(strProductName, "'", "''") & "')"
15: conn.Execute strSQL
16:
17: ' Get Identity Column Value
18: strGetID = "SELECT @@IDENTITY AS NewID"
19: Set rs = conn.Execute(strGetID)
20: If Not (IsNull(rs("NewID"))) Then
21:     lngProductID = rs("NewID")
22:     Debug.Print "Returned ProductID: " & lngProductID
23: Else
24:     Debug.Print "No value was returned..."
25: End If
26:
27: rs.Close
28: conn.Close
29: Set rs = Nothing
30: Set conn = Nothing
```

ANALYSIS The script opens a connection to the SQL Server Northwind database. In lines 12–15, a new product is inserted in the Products table. Because the Products table contains an Identity column, a value for this column is generated by the database for the inserted record. The script can retrieve the last generated Identity Value by using the @@IDENTITY function in a SELECT statement, as shown in the lines 18–25. The value of the @@IDENTITY function is stored in the Recordset rs in line 19. The script reads the

Identity Value from the Recordset in line 21. When no valid value is retrieved by the
@@IDENTITY function, the Recordset contains the value NULL.

When you add a record to a table in a SQL Server database, this action
might force a SQL Server Trigger to insert another record into another table.
If the other table contains an Identity column, the function @@IDENTITY contains the last generated Autonumber value, which is the value that the
Trigger inserts in the second table. To avoid this problem you should use a
Recordset and its AddNew method to write the new record into the table and
retrieve the generated Autonumber value.

Also when a Trigger inserts a record into a table that contains no Identity
column, the function @@IDENTITY returns NULL.

Using Recordset Object's AddNew Method

When you open a Recordset, you can add a new record to it using the AddNew method of
the Recordset object. This new record can be stored in the database by calling the
Update (or the related UpdateBatch) method of the Recordset object.

The following example will demonstrate the usage of the AddNew method to add new
datasets into a table.

The example assumes that you want to add a new territory into the Territories table of
the SQL Server Northwind database. Take a look at the table definition of the Territories
table as shown in Figure 3.5.

FIGURE 3.5

Definition of the
Territories table.

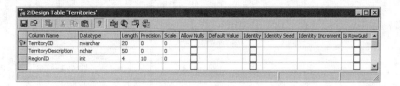

The Territories table contains three columns. The column TerritoryID is defined as the
Primary Key of the table, which is indicated by a little key symbol in Figure 3.5.
TerritoryDescription is a column that contains strings with a maximum of 50 characters.

RegionID is a Foreign Key column that contains the value of the related Primary Key
value in the Region table. The function of the RegionID in the Territories table is to
define how the Territories table and the Region table are related to each other. The table
definition of the Region table is shown in Figure 3.6

FIGURE 3.6

*Definition of the
Region table.*

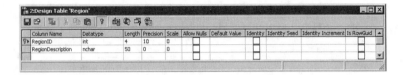

The Region table consists of two columns, the RegionID, which is an Primary Key field that is used to identify each dataset uniquely, and the RegionDescription, which contains a string with the maximum length of 50 characters. The values stored in the column RegionDescription are shown in Figure 3.7.

FIGURE 3.7

*Values in the Region
table.*

Each of these values is related to a record in the Territories table, and the relationship is defined through the RegionID. The relationship among the tables—Territories, Region, and Employees—is shown in Figure 3.8.

FIGURE 3.8

*The relationship
among the Territories,
Region, and Employees
tables.*

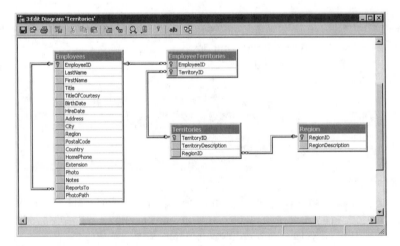

For now, you just need to know how the Territories table and the Region table are related to each other. The Primary Key RegionID column in the Territories table is the Foreign Key of the RegionID in the Region table. This Foreign Key relationship only allows you to insert values into the RegionID field in the Territories table that already exist in the

RegionID column of the Region table. When you try to insert another value, the database will recognize the Foreign Key violation, which is defined in the database, and raise an error.

When you want to insert a new record (or dataset) into the table Territories, the value in the field RegionID must be between 1 and 4 to refer to the corresponding RegionID of a region defined in the Region table (see values of the Region table in Figure 3.7). This fact is enforced by the Foreign Key relationship between the Territories and the Region table. A NULL value is not allowed in the column RegionID of the Territories table (see the table definition in Figure 3.5).

The value in the TerritoryID field must be unique in the TerritoryID column because it is defined as the Primary Key. It can contain any string up to a maximum length of 20 characters.

Listing 3.3 shows a simple example that inserts a new dataset (or record) into the Territories table using the Recordset's AddNew method.

LISTING 3.3   Inserting a New Territory into the Territories Table Using the AddNew Method

```
 1: Dim conn As ADODB.Connection
 2: Dim rs As ADODB.Recordset
 3:
 4: Dim strTerritoryID As String
 5: Dim strTerritoryDescription As String
 6: Dim lngRegionID As Long
 7:
 8: Set conn = CreateObject("ADODB.Connection")
 9: Set rs = CreateObject("ADODB.Recordset")
10: conn.Open "Provider=SQLOLEDB;Data Source=BoyScout;" & _
11:     "Initial Catalog=Northwind;User ID=sa;Password=;"
12:
13: strTerritoryID = "01234"
14: strTerritoryDescription = "Upperaustria"
15: lngRegionID = 3
16:
17: strSQL = "SELECT TerritoryID, TerritoryDescription, RegionID " & _
18:     "FROM Territories WHERE 0=1"
19:
20: Set rs.ActiveConnection = conn
21: rs.CursorLocation = adUseClient
22: rs.CursorType = adOpenStatic
23: rs.LockType = adLockOptimistic
24: rs.Source = strSQL
25:
```

continues

LISTING 3.3   continued

```
26: rs.Open
27:
28: rs.AddNew
29: rs("TerritoryID") = Left(strTerritoryID, 20)
30: rs("TerritoryDescription") = Left(strTerritoryDescription, 50)
31: rs("RegionID") = lngRegionID
32:
33: rs.Update
34: rs.Close
35: conn.Close
36: Set rs = Nothing
37: Set conn = Nothing
```

ANALYSIS   The script in Listing 3.3 prepares a Recordset to use in single-row update mode, which is specified by an optimistic lock. The prepared Recordset is opened with no records but, nevertheless, containing the definition of the fields TerritoryID and TerritoryDescription of the Territories table. The script adds a new record to this Recordset and specifies the values of this new record. The new record is written back to the database using the Recordset object's Update method.

The details of the script are as follows: Variables to hold the Connection object, the Recordset object and the values for the new record are declared in the lines 1–6. The Connection and the Recordset objects are created in lines 8 and 9. The script opens a connection to the SQL Server Northwind database, which contains the Territories table, in the line 10.

The values for the new record are stored in the variables strTerritoryID, strTerritoryDescription, and lngRegionID in lines 13–15.

Line 17 defines the SQL statement that is used to create the Recordset. The Recordset is necessary so you can add a new record to the database using the Recordset object's AddNew method. To avoid the overhead of retrieving unneeded records from the table, the SQL statement is defined as follows.

```
SELECT TerritoryID, TerritoryDescription, RegionID
FROM Territories
WHERE 0=1
```

This statement generates a Recordset that contains the correct references to the fields TerritoryID, TerritoryDescription, and RegionID of the Territories table.

To avoid returning any records, use a special WHERE clause in the SELECT statement.

```
... WHERE 0=1
```

Because no record can meet the requirement that zero equals one, no record is returned in the Recordset. The number of returned records is zero.

> **Note**
> You can also open a table using the table's name instead of using a SQL statement. However, because you cannot use a WHERE clause, this returns a Recordset that contains all records in the table. This is an unnecessary use of resources.

The Recordset is prepared in the lines 20–24. The connection, which the Recordset uses to connect to the database, is set to the connection stored in the variable conn. The cursor is set to be a client-side cursor, which has no further meaning in this script. The cursor type is set to a static cursor, and the lock type is set to optimistic lock to enable single-row updates of the Recordset. A Recordset must be updateable to add a new record to it. The SQL statement stored in the variable strSQL is assigned to the Recordset object's Source property, thus defining the SQL statement that is executed to populate the Recordset when opened.

Line 26 of the script opens the Recordset. After this line the variable rs contains a Recordset with the three fields of the Territories table, but no records stored in it. This is similar to an empty database table—all columns are defined but the table contains no data.

In line 28 the Recordset object's AddNew method adds a new record to the Recordset. Values are assigned to the fields of this new Recordset in the lines 29–31. The script uses Visual Basic's Left statement to makes sure that the strings are not longer than the maximum length that the table field can store in the database.

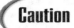

> **Caution**
> When assigning a value to a Recordset's field, make sure that the field value can be stored in the database. For instance, when you assign a string with more characters to a Recordset's field than the field's definition allows you to store, you will get an error.

The new Recordset is written to the database in line 33 using the Update method of the Recordset object.

In the lines 34–37 the Recordset and the Connection are closed and their resources freed by setting their variables to Nothing.

That's enough code details about this listing. What problems can arise when using the script? Because the field TerritoryID is a Primary Key, a unique value must be assigned to this field. When you execute the sample script twice without first erasing the added record or changing the value of the TerritoryID, the second pass will raise an error. The error message is shown in Figure 3.9, telling you that you tried to add two records with the same Primary Key value into the Territories table.

FIGURE 3.9

Error message when violating a Primary Key constraint.

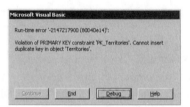

You can avoid such problems when you add error handling into your script. If you want to handle errors like the Primary Key violation in Listing 3.3 you can replace line 33 with the following code:

LISTING 3.4 Error Handling for Listing 3.3

```
 1: ...
 2: Dim lngObjectErrNum As Long
 3: On Error Resume Next
 4:
 5: rs.Update
 6:
 7: If Err.Number <> 0 Then
 8:     lngObjectErrNum = Err.Number - vbObjectError
 9:     Select Case lngObjectErrNum
10:         Case 3604
11:             Debug.Print "Unique Column Violation."
12:         Case Else
13:             Debug.Print "Error occurred."
14:     End Select
15: End If
16:...
```

ANALYSIS The On Error Resume Next statement prevents Visual Basic from stopping the execution of the script and raising an error message when an error occurs. In line 5, the Recordset is written to the database. In line 7, the script checks whether an error occurred and invokes error handling in the lines 8–14. When the SQL Server detects an invalid operation, such as inserting a duplicate value in a Primary Key column, it hands over the SQL Server-specific error number and the error message to ADO. The SQL Server-specific error number is stored in the variable `lngObjectErrNum` in line 8. The error number for inserting a duplicate value into a UNIQUE column (for instance a Primary Key column) is `3604` as described in the SQL Server documentation.

> **Note**
>
> When you add the value of the Visual Basic `vbObjectError` constant (`-2147221504`) to the SQL Server error number `3604`, you get the error number (`-2147217900`) as supplied by the Visual Basic `Err` object. This is the same value as shown in the error message in Figure 3.9.

Your application can perform the appropriate action when you provide reasonable error handling based on the error numbers you get from the `Err` object's `Number` property.

3

Retrieving an `Autonumber` Value

When you insert a new record (or dataset) into a table that contains an Autonumber field, you might want to know which value was assigned to this Autonumber field during the insert operation of the dataset into the table.

> **Note**
>
> In SQL Server an Autonumber Column is referred to as an Identity Column.

Provided that the Recordset is well prepared, you can retrieve the value of the Autonumber field from the corresponding field in the Recordset. To make it clear how the mechanism works, the sample script in Listing 3.5 performs this task. Listing 3.5 inserts a new record into the Products table of the SQL Server Northwind database and returns the `ProductID` that is generated by the database for the new record. Take a look at the definition of the Products table in Figure 3.10.

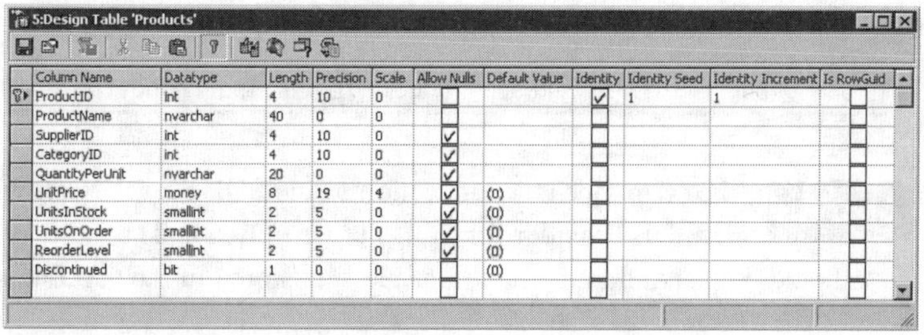

5:Design Table 'Products'

Column Name	Datatype	Length	Precision	Scale	Allow Nulls	Default Value	Identity	Identity Seed	Identity Increment	Is RowGuid
ProductID	int	4	10	0			✓	1	1	
ProductName	nvarchar	40	0	0						
SupplierID	int	4	10	0	✓					
CategoryID	int	4	10	0	✓					
QuantityPerUnit	nvarchar	20	0	0	✓					
UnitPrice	money	8	19	4	✓	(0)				
UnitsInStock	smallint	2	5	0	✓	(0)				
UnitsOnOrder	smallint	2	5	0	✓	(0)				
ReorderLevel	smallint	2	5	0	✓	(0)				
Discontinued	bit	1	0	0		(0)				

FIGURE 3.10

Table definition of the Products table.

The Primary Key column named ProductID is an Autonumber field. This indicates that, for every new record, a new and unique long integer number is generated and stored in the ProductID field of the new record. The only required value when inserting a record in the Products table is the value for the ProductName field.

LISTING 3.5 Inserting a New Product into the Products Table and Retrieving Its Autonumber Value

```
 1: Dim conn As ADODB.Connection
 2: Dim rs As ADODB.Recordset
 3: Dim strProductName As String
 4: Dim lngProductID As Long
 5:
 6: Set conn = CreateObject("ADODB.Connection")
 7: Set rs = CreateObject("ADODB.Recordset")
 8: conn.Open "Provider=SQLOLEDB;Data Source=BoyScout;" & _
 9:    "Initial Catalog=Northwind;User ID=sa;Password=;"
10:
11: strProductName = "Sacher Torte"
12:
13: strSQL = "SELECT ProductID, ProductName " & _
14:    "FROM Products WHERE 0=1"
15:
16: Set rs.ActiveConnection = conn
17: rs.CursorLocation = adUseClient
18: rs.CursorType = adOpenKeyset
19: rs.LockType = adLockOptimistic
20: rs.Source = strSQL
21: rs.Open
22:
23: rs.AddNew
24: rs("ProductName") = Left(strProductName, 40)
25: rs.Update
26: lngProductID = rs("ProductID")
27:
28: rs.Close
29: conn.Close
30: Set rs = Nothing
31: Set conn = Nothing
32:
33: Debug.Print "Returned ProductID: " & lngProductID
```

ANALYSIS The script opens a connection to the SQL Server Northwind database using the OLE DB Provider for SQL Server in line 8. The name of the product, which should be inserted in the table Products, is stored in the variable strProductName in line

11. The SQL statement, which returns a Recordset that consists of the columns ProductID and ProductName, is defined in the lines 13–14 and stored in the variable strSQL. The Recordset returned by this SQL statement will contain no records because the WHERE clause does not fit for any record in the table. The Recordset is prepared in lines 16–20.

Because the SQLOLEDB provider is used, and the Autonumber column—which is the ProductID column—is defined as Primary Key (and, therefore, uses a database index automatically), you can use a Recordset with client-cursor and optimistic lock type to retrieve the value of the Autonumber field. However, you can also use a server-side cursor to retrieve the value of the Autonumber field.

Tip

Not every combination of target database, provider, cursor location, cursor type, lock type, and indexed or non-indexed Autonumber column enables you to retrieve the value of the Autonumber field when you insert a new record into a certain database table.

Please refer to Table 3.1 to find a combination that allows you to retrieve an Autonumber value.

3

I need to make some remarks about Table 3.1: The Provider column specifies the OLE DB provider to use. The Target column specifies the target database system. The Index column specifies whether the Autonumber column in the database table must have an index or not. The Cursor Location column stands for the Recordset cursor location. The Cursor Type column describes the Recordset cursor type used. The Lock Type column specifies the necessary lock type of the Recordset object.

The following abbreviations are used in Table 3.1:

- *ODBC*: OLE DB Provider for ODBC, used with an ODBC driver for Access or SQL Server
- *Jet 4.0*: OLE DB Provider for Microsoft Jet 4.0 (Microsoft.Jet.OLEDB.4.0)
- *SQLOLEDB*: OLE DB Provider for SQL Server
- *Access*: Access 97 or Access 2000
- *SQL Server*: SQL Server 7.0 or SQL Server 6.5
- *Opt/Pes*: Optimistic or Pessimistic lock type (adLockOptimistic or adLockPessimistic)

TABLE 3.1   Conditions for Retrieving Autonumber Values

Provider	Target	Index	Cursor Location	Cursor Type	Lock Type
ODBC	SQL 7.0	Yes	Server	Keyset	Opt/Pes
		Yes	Client	All	Opt/Pes
		No	Client	All	Opt/Pes
	SQL 6.5	Yes	Server	Keyset	Opt/Pes
	Access	Yes	Server	Keyset	Opt/Pes
		No	Server	Keyset	Opt/Pes
SQLOLEDB	SQL Server	Yes	Server	Keyset	Opt/Pes
		Yes	Client	All	Opt/Pes
		No	Client	All	Opt/Pes
Jet 4.0	Access 2000	Yes	Server	All	All
		Yes	Client	All	Opt/Pes
		No	Server	All	All
		No	Client	All	Opt/Pes
	Access 97	Yes	Server	All	All
		No	Server	All	All

Now back to the script of Listing 3.5. The Recordset is opened in line 21, and the new record is inserted into the Products table of the database. As the conditions are met to retrieve the Autonumber value from the column ProductID (refer to Table 3.1), you can retrieve the value of the Autonumber field's ProductID by reading its value from the Recordset field named ProductID, as shown in line 26.

The script closes the `Recordset` and the `Connection` objects and frees their resources in the lines 28–31. Finally the retrieved Autonumber value, which is in fact the ProductID value, is printed in line 33.

Handling Large Binary or Text Fields

A Large Binary or Text field, often referred to as a *BLOB* (Binary Large Object), is a database field that, in fact, does not directly contain data but a reference or pointer to the data. Therefore, you can use two special methods to read data from or write data to a BLOB field of a database.

Reading BLOB Values

Basic tasks for reading of BLOB values were described already in Day 2. Here is a more in-depth description of how to read BLOB values.

When you want to retrieve the value of a usual database field you might use a statement such as the following:

```
Value = Recordset("FieldName")
```

However, if you want to retrieve data from a BLOB field, you can also use a statement similar to this one:

```
Value = Recordset("FieldName").GetChunk(ChunkSize)
```

In fact, you are using the GetChunk method of the Field object because the previous statement is a shortcut of the statement that follows.

```
Value = Recordset.Fields("FieldName").GetChunk(ChunkSize)
```

Using the GetChunk method, you can retrieve parts (or chunks) from a BLOB instead of retrieving the whole content of the BLOB at once. ChunkSize is the parameter of the GetChunk method that specifies how many characters (or bytes) you want to retrieve at once from the Field. To examine the usage of the GetChunk method, take a look at Listing 3.6.

The script in Listing 3.6 reads chunks of 500 characters from the field named CustomerDesc from the CustomerDemographics table until the whole value is read. For the definition of the CustomerDemographics table, see Figure 3.11.

FIGURE 3.11

Table definition of the CustomerDemographics table.

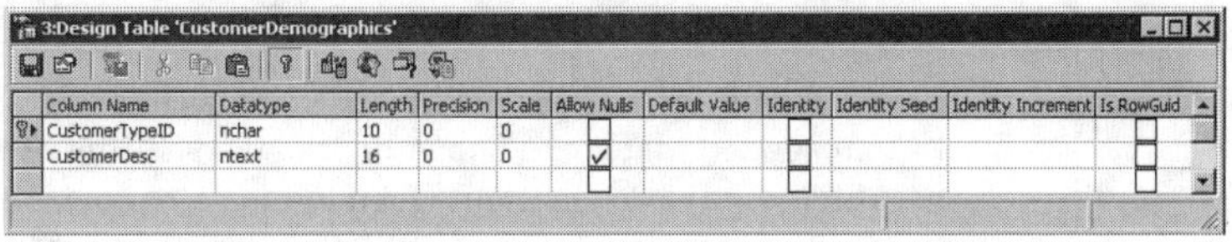

The CustomerDesc field is a BLOB field because it is defined as the SQL Server ntext data type. The data type ntext stands for a variable-length Unicode data field.

NEW TERM Using Unicode data, you can use any character that is defined by the Unicode standard, which includes all data defined in different character sets. Unicode provides an encoding schema for practically all characters used in business around the world. In SQL Server, the prefix n for the ntext data type stands for National (Unicode). In Access 2000 all character data (text and memo) are stored as Unicode data.

LISTING 3.6 Reading the Value of a BLOB Field Part by Part

```
1: ChunkSize = 500    ' characters
2: lngOffset = 0
3: lngBLOBSize = rs("CustomerDesc").ActualSize / 2
4: Do While lngOffset < lngBLOBSize
5:    varChunk = rs("CustomerDesc").GetChunk(ChunkSize)
6:    varBLOB = varBLOB & varChunk
7:    lngOffset = lngOffset + ChunkSize
8: Loop
```

 ANALYSIS Assume that Listing 3.6 is part of a larger program, and the Recordset named rs contains a Recordset that is connected to the CustomerDemographics table. The script reads the value of the field CustomerDesc in chunks of 500 characters and stores the whole value in the variable named varBLOB.

The actual size of the BLOB field is stored in the variable lngBLOBSize. As the BLOB field uses Unicode data you have to divide the actual size (in bytes) by two to get the number of characters. The Do...While loop retrieves chunks of the size (in characters) defined in the variable ChunkSize and stores them in the variable varChunk. Adding the chunks to the variable varBLOB sums up all chunks, so that this variable contains the whole value of the CustomerDesc Field when the loop has finished.

Every time you retrieve a chunk of a BLOB, the BLOB pointer is moved to the end of the chunk retrieved. Another call of the GetChunk method retrieves the chunk of data that comes after the last retrieved data chunk. Moving to another record or updating a record resets the BLOB pointer to the beginning of the BLOB field's data.

Note

When you can process a large BLOB's data chunk by chunk, it is strongly recommended that you do not store the whole value of the BLOB in a variable. This is especially important when writing a multiuser application (maybe a component or an Active Server Pages application) because the memory used is the size of the BLOB multiplied by the number of users accessing the application at the same time.

To retrieve the whole BLOB value at once you can use a statement that follows:

```
ActualSize = Recordset("FieldName").ActualSize
Value = Recordset("FieldName").GetChunk(ActualSize)
```

When the field uses Unicode data, you have to divide the actual size (in bytes) by two to get the size in characters, because the chunk size must be provided as the number of characters:

```
Characters = Recordset("FieldName").ActualSize / 2
Value = Recordset("FieldName").GetChunk(Characters)
```

Writing BLOB Values

The counterpart of reading BLOB values using the GetChunk method is writing BLOB values using the Field object's AppendChunk method. The AppendChunk method allows you to add data to a large text or binary field chunk by chunk.

The syntax of the AppendChunk method is as follows.

```
Recordset("FieldName").AppendChunk Data
```

The following example in Listing 3.7 inserts a new record in the Categories table of the SQL Server Northwind database. The definition of the Categories table is shown in Figure 3.12.

FIGURE 3.12

Table definition of the Categories table.

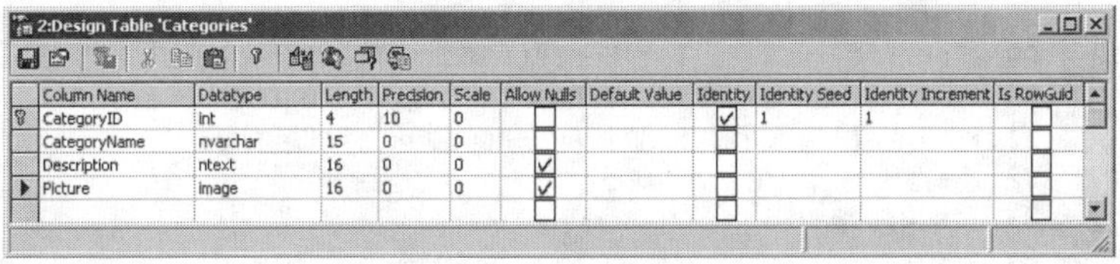

The table contains the four columns CategoryID, CategoryName, Description, and Picture. The Description column and the Picture column contain BLOBs. The Description field has the data type nText (Unicode Text).

Listing 3.7 provides an example of how to add data to a BLOB field chunk by chunk. A long description text is stored in a variable and then added—chunk by chunk—to the Description field of the new record.

LISTING 3.7 Adding a New BLOB Value to the Categories Table

```
 1: Dim conn As ADODB.Connection
 2: Dim rs As ADODB.Recordset
 3: Dim strCatName As String
 4: Dim strDesc As String
 5: Dim lngChunkSize As Long
 6:
 7: strCatName = "Gifts"
 8: strDesc = "Everything that can be used as a present " & _
 9:     "for a person or a company." & vbCrLf & _
10:     "From jewelries to a yacht, from cars to airplanes."
11: lngChunkSize = 10
```

continues

LISTING 3.7 continued

```
12:
13: Set conn = CreateObject("ADODB.Connection")
14: Set rs = CreateObject("ADODB.Recordset")
15: conn.Open "Provider=SQLOLEDB;Data Source=BoyScout;" & _
16:     "Initial Catalog=Northwind;User ID=sa;Password=;"
17:
18: strSQL = "SELECT CategoryID, CategoryName, Description " & _
19:     "FROM Categories"
20:
21: rs.CursorLocation = adUseServer
22: rs.CursorType = adOpenKeyset
23: rs.LockType = adLockOptimistic
24: rs.MaxRecords = 1
25: rs.Open strSQL, conn
26:
27: rs.AddNew
28: rs("CategoryName") = Left(strCatName, 15)
29: For lngI = 0 To Int(Len(strDesc) / lngChunkSize)
30:     strChunk = Mid(strDesc, (lngI * lngChunkSize) + 1, lngChunkSize)
31:     rs("Description").AppendChunk strChunk
32: Next
33: rs.Update
34:
35: rs.Close
36: conn.Close
37: Set rs = Nothing
38: Set conn = Nothing
```

ANALYSIS Listing 3.7 adds a new category to the Categories table. The name of the new category is Gifts, and the category description is

```
Everything that can be used as a present for a person or a company.
From jewelries to a yacht, from cars to airplanes.
```

The script stores the string for the category name and the description in the variables strCatName and strDesc in the lines 7–10. The length of each chunk for adding the new Description value to the Recordset field is defined in line 10 and stored in the variable lngChunkSize. Line 18 defines the SQL statement, which populates the Recordset, and stores it in the variable strSQL. The Recordset is prepared in the lines 21–24 to use a server-side, keyset cursor with optimistic locking. The optimistic locking type is used so that the script can add a new record to the Recordset and write the new record to the database. The number of records returned by the SQL statement is limited to one to save resources. This is done in line 24 using the MaxRecords property of the Recordset object. After the Recordset is opened in line 25, a new record is added to it in line 27 with the AddNew method. The category name of the record is stored in line 28. In lines

29–32, the value for the category description is added—chunk by chunk–to the Description field of the Recordset using the AppendChunk method. The new record is written to the database table in line 33.

> **Note**
>
> The example in Listing 3.7 demonstrates how to add a BLOB value, chunk by chunk, to a BLOB field. The variable strDesc is only used as a sample source for the value of the BLOB field. When the whole value for a BLOB field is already stored in a variable, you can append the whole value at once to the BLOB field:
>
> rs.("*FieldName*").AppendChunk *strValue*
>
> However, when your source for the value of the BLOB field is a file, a database BLOB field, a stream, or another source that delivers a BLOB value, chunk by chunk, it is often useful to manipulate data or add it to a field, chunk by chunk, to decrease memory usage.

When you want to manipulate bitmaps using GetChunk and AppendChunk, use the same techniques as shown in the preceding examples. For more information about the AppendChunk method refer to the ADO documentation.

Using a Stored Procedure to Insert Data

When you are using a SQL Server database, you also can use stored procedures to insert data into a database.

Using stored procedures is described in detail in Day 7, "Implementing Application Logic in Stored Procedures."

Dealing with Database Errors

A good application must meet certain criteria. It must handle problems, such as invalid user input, and it also must react to errors that arise out of database problems. The more complex an application gets and the more components are involved in an application, the higher the chance that some combination of circumstances violates explicit or implicit assumptions or rules.

No customer wants to use an application that crashes just because something occurred that the programmer did not plan for. When using ADO in your application, there are many sources of complications or errors. Whenever you perform a database query or insert data into a database, you have to pay attention to thousands of details. You must note things such as the use of correct data types or possible violations of database integrity. You must handle the possibility that you have forgotten something when plan-ning and programming your application.

What about an application that uses a SQL Server database that resides somewhere in the company's network? When you want to access data from the SQL Server, you must con-sider the possibility that the network might be down or the SQL Server might not be run-ning. When you insert data into a database, the new data might violate a Unique Key constraint or a Foreign Key relationship. Some data might not be optional when you are inserting a new record into a database.

So you see, even when you do a good job designing your application, choosing the best application layers, and designing the database correctly, your application can still face some unexpected problems.

When using ADO, you have to deal with two kinds of errors. There are ADO errors that generate runtime errors on one side, and there are provider errors that can be retrieved using the `Connection`'s `Errors` collection on the other side.

The `Errors` collection of the ADO `Connection` object allows you to retrieve warnings and errors that are returned from the database and the data provider, ODBC, OLE DB, or ADO.

Handling Visual Basic Errors

Usually, a program written in Visual Basic or VBScript ends its execution when an error occurs. In both Visual Basic and VBScript, you can use the following statement to tell your application to resume execution after an error is raised:

```
On Error Resume Next
```

This statement enables error handling after an error occurrs.

An `On Error Resume Next` statement becomes inactive when your application calls another procedure or function. To disable error handling, you can use the following state-ment:

```
On Error Goto 0
```

How can your application determine if an error occurred? The Visual Basic intrinsic `Err` object allows this and also determines what kind of error occurred. You can get the error message, the error source, or the error number from the `Err` object's properties. When an error occurs, the `Number` property of the `Err` object differs from 0. All ADO errors are exposed to the `Err` object.

Listing 3.8 shows the usage of the `On Error Resume Next` together with `Err` object to determine if an error occurred.

LISTING **3.8**   Error Handling with On Error Resume Next

```
 1: On Error Resume Next
 2: ...
 3: Err.Clear
 4: conn.Open "Provider=SQLOLEDB;Data Source=BoyScout;" & _
 5:    "Initial Catalog=Northwind;User ID=sa;Password=;"
 6:
 7: If Err.Number <> 0 Then
 8:    strErrNumber = Err.Number
 9:    strErrDescription = Err.Description
10:    strErrSource = Err.Source
11: ...
12: End If
13: ...
14: On Error Goto 0
```

ANALYSIS   Error handling is enabled using the On Error Resume Next statement in line 1. The Err object is cleared in line 3 to reset the Err object and to set its Number property to 0. This is necessary to ensure that no former error is trapped in line 7. Line 4 opens the connection to a SQL Server database. When the application cannot connect to the SQL Server database, an error is raised and the Number property of the Err object is set to a value that differs from 0. Line 7 checks whether an error has occurred. In lines 8–11, the error number, the error description, and the source of the error are stored in variables for further use. The script can, for instance, present a dialog to the user stating that no connection to the database can be established. The script can also present a detailed error message and perform other tasks, as well. In line 14, the error handling is disabled.

A more complex error handling is possible in Visual Basic procedures (but not in VBScript), using the following statement:

```
On Error Goto Label
```

The use of this statement in a procedure is as follows:

LISTING **3.9**   Error Handling with On Error Goto Label

```
 1: Sub Name()
 2: On Error Goto Label
 3: ' Procedure code goes here
 4: ...
 5:
 6: Exit Procedure
```

continues

LISTING 3.9 continued

```
 7: Label:
 8: ' Error handling code goes here
 9: ...
10: End Procedure
```

ANALYSIS The On Error Goto *Label* statement in line 2 enables error handling and forces the application to jump to the label named *Label* when an error occurs in the procedure. In the error-handling code, you can use the properties of the Err object to determine which error occurred. You can use the same mechanism in a function, too.

In contrast to using the Visual Basic Err object, you can use the Errors collection of the ADO Connection object for error handling. Only provider errors are exposed through the Errors collection, not the errors that have their origin in ADO itself. The Errors collection can contain warnings from the database about some effects of an ADO command that do not raise an error. Warnings are not passed to Visual Basic's Err object.

Using the Connection Object's Errors Collection

All provider errors and provider warnings that occur in the context of a certain Connection object can be accessed through the Connection object's Errors collection. Each Error object of the Errors collection represents an error or warning that has its origin in OLE DB, ODBC, the data provider, or the database itself. Some methods and properties provide warnings that appear as an Error in the Errors collection. These do not stop the application, however, nor do they appear in the Visual Basic intrinsic Err object.

Whenever you perform an operation using ADO, one or more provider errors or warnings can be generated and stored in the Errors collection of the Connection object involved.

An ADO Error object has several properties that provide access to the error number, error description, or error source.

- The Description property of the Error object is a string that describes the kind of error.
- The Source property enables you to determine where the error occurred.
- The Number property, which contains a long integer value, enables you to determine the kind of error that occurred.

- The SQLState property returns a five-character string error code that follows the ANSI SQL standard.

- The NativeError property returns a long value that indicates the provider-specific error code.

To remove all errors from the Errors collection, you can call the Clear method of the collection. This is useful to reset the Errors collection so that no old error is retained.

You can read all Error objects of the Errors collection by iterating over the Errors collection as shown in Listing 3.10.

Listing 3.10   Reading All Error Objects from the Errors Collection

```
 1: Dim ConnError As ADODB.Error
 2: ...
 3: For Each ConnError In conn.Errors
 4:     strDescription = ConnError.Description
 5:     strHelpContext = ConnError.HelpContext
 6:     strHelpFile = ConnError.HelpFile
 7:     strNativeError = ConnError.NativeError
 8:     strNumber = ConnError.Number
 9:     strSource = ConnError.Source
10:     strSqlState = ConnError.SqlState
11:     ...
12: Next
13: ...
```

ANALYSIS   The script retrieves all errors from the Errors collection of the Connection object. The script assumes that the Connection object is stored in the variable named conn. The script uses a For Each ... Next loop to iterate over all errors. ConnError is the iteration variable that contains the current Error object during each iteration. The variable ConnError is defined as ADODB.Error in line 1. In the lines 4–10, all properties of the current Error object are retrieved and stored in some variables for further use in the loop.

Error handling and error management, especially when dealing with ADO, are a very complex topics. An error that occurs during an ADO operation can originate from many different sources—the OLE DB provider, the database, or ODBC.

Every database and database provider can raise different errors. Also, every database has its own rules and behavior. Please refer to the documentation of the database and to the Windows 2000 platform SDK, MSDN (Microsoft Developer Network), or some comparable source for information about error numbers, reasons for specific errors, handling of errors, and steps that can be taken when an error occurs.

Summary

The topics covered in this lesson were inserting data using ADO and handling of errors that occur during an ADO operation.

You have seen the usage of the SQL INSERT statement and how to add a new record to a database by opening a Recordset, adding the record with the AddNew method, and saving the new record to the database.

Other topics covered included error handling and obtaining information about errors that occur while using ADO. To retrieve information about errors, the Visual Basic Err object and the Connection object's Errors collection can be used.

Q&A

Q Is it possible to use a SQL statement, such as the INSERT statement, together with every data source?

A It depends on the capability of the provider whether a SQL statement can be executed. However, most databases and many other data sources allow executing SQL statements.

Q Do any data sources exist that do not allow inserting data using the Recordset object's AddNew method?

A There are some data sources that only allow you to read data from them but not to write into them. Of course, you cannot use the AddNew method for a read-only data source.

Workshop

Quiz

1. Is it possible to execute a SQL statement to insert new data into a database?
2. How do you retrieve an Autonumber value from a database?
3. Which methods do you use to insert BLOB data into a database chunk by chunk?
4. When using Visual Basic, what possibilities does your application have to retrieve information about an error that occurred?
5. How do you delimit date values in an INSERT statement when dealing with Microsoft Access or SQL Server?

Exercise

Write a script that inserts a new customer into the Customers table of the SQL Server Northwind database using an `INSERT` statement. The definition of the table is shown in Figure 3.13. Add some error handling code to prevent the script from terminating when your `INSERT` statement contains an error or violates any database rule—for example, the Primary Key constraint of the CustomerID column. When an error occurs, read all errors from the `Errors` collection and present all properties of each `Error` object to the user.

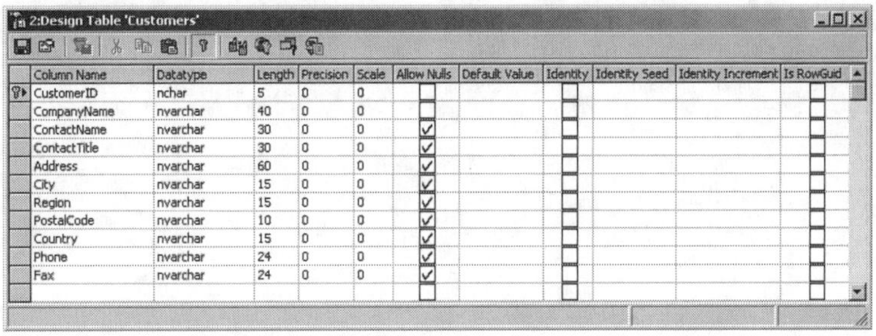

Column Name	Datatype	Length	Precision	Scale	Allow Nulls	Default Value	Identity	Identity Seed	Identity Increment	Is RowGuid
CustomerID	nchar	5	0	0						
CompanyName	nvarchar	40	0	0						
ContactName	nvarchar	30	0	0	✓					
ContactTitle	nvarchar	30	0	0	✓					
Address	nvarchar	60	0	0	✓					
City	nvarchar	15	0	0	✓					
Region	nvarchar	15	0	0	✓					
PostalCode	nvarchar	10	0	0	✓					
Country	nvarchar	15	0	0	✓					
Phone	nvarchar	24	0	0	✓					
Fax	nvarchar	24	0	0	✓					

FIGURE 3.13
Table definition of the Customers table.

3

WEEK 1

DAY 4

Updating and Deleting Database Data

Objectives

You have learned about retrieving data from and inserting data into a database. In this day, you will see how to update and delete data from a database table.

As usual, there are several different ways to update or delete data. You can use SQL statements, such as UPDATE and DELETE, or you can manipulate a Recordset and write it back to the database.

In this lesson, you will learn the following:

- How to update table data
- How to delete database data

Updating Table Data

Beside the basic database tasks to retrieve and insert data, ADO provides multiple ways to update data. Updating data in a database is necessary, for example, when a customer changes his address or when product prices or product stocks change. To reflect these facts in a database, you have to update certain database values.

There are several ways to update database data. The most common methods to change data are the following:

- Execute a SQL UPDATE statement: This is the preferred method when you want to make similar changes to data in more than one record. The SQL UPDATE statement is executed using the Execute method of the Connection object.

- Change data in a Recordset: You can retrieve a Recordset, change some of its data, and write the Recordset back to the database. This is only possible if you prepare the Recordset to be updateable. When you use a Recordset to update database data, you do this in immediate update mode, which means every changed record is updated immediately. You can also update in batch update mode, meaning all changes are cached until the Recordset is written back to the database.

- Use stored procedures: When dealing with a SQL Server database, you can use SQL Server's stored procedures to change data in a database.

The use of these methods to update data, as well as advantages and disadvantages of each, are explained in the following paragraphs.

Using the SQL UPDATE Command

The SQL UPDATE command is simple to use and avoids overhead because you do not have to open a Recordset (as you would to change a Recordset using the Recordset object's Update method). This is explained later in the day.

An outstanding feature of the SQL UPDATE statement is that you can change all the records in a database table that meet certain criteria at once. Also, you can change field values by using the old field values as the basis for the new. This is useful, for instance, to change the prices of products by a certain amount or by a certain percentage.

The general syntax of the SQL UPDATE command is as sfollows:

```
UPDATE TableName SET ColumnName = Expression WHERE Condition
```

The preceding UPDATE statement updates the values in the column ColumnName of the table TableName for all records that meet the criteria specified in Condition. Expression can be, for instance, a valid value for the column or the keyword NULL.

> **Tip**
>
> More complex expressions can also be used. These are described in the Windows 2000 Platform SDK under Data Access Services, Microsoft SQL Server Programmer's Toolkit, Building SQL Server Applications, and Transact-SQL Reference, UPDATE.

The Condition part describes which criteria the records must meet to be updated. Of course, you can use more complex UPDATE statements than the statements previously described.

To update two or more columns at once, you can provide an UPDATE statement as follows:

```
UPDATE TableName SET ColumnName1=Expression1, ColumnName2=Expression2,
➡ ColumnName3 = Expression3, ... WHERE Condition
```

A simple SQL UPDATE statement follows:

```
UPDATE Products SET UnitPrice=12.95 WHERE ProductID=48
```

The UPDATE statement updates the price (UnitPrice) of the product with the ProductID 48 to the value of 12.95.

A typical example of changing more than one column at the same time is when you change the address, city, and postal code of an employee in a database table.

The following statement changes the address data of the employee record with the EmployeeID 8, which is the record of Laura Callahan. The address is updated to 14 People Rd., the postal code to WG2 14PR, and the city to Birmingham.

```
UPDATE Employees SET Address='14 People Rd.', PostalCode='WG2 14PR',
➡ City='Birmingham' WHERE EmployeeID=8
```

> **Caution**
>
> Never forget to specify the correct WHERE clause in your UPDATE statement. When you omit the WHERE clause, all records of the table are affected by the update!

When you build a SQL statement containing string values, you have to make sure that each apostrophe is replaced by two apostrophes and the changed data fits the field definition in the database table. This is the same restriction as for the INSERT statement.

An example of a SQL UPDATE statement is shown in Listing 4.1.

The example updates some data of the employee in the Employees table of the Northwind database who is identified by the EmployeeID 8.

The definition of the Employees table is shown in Figure 4.1

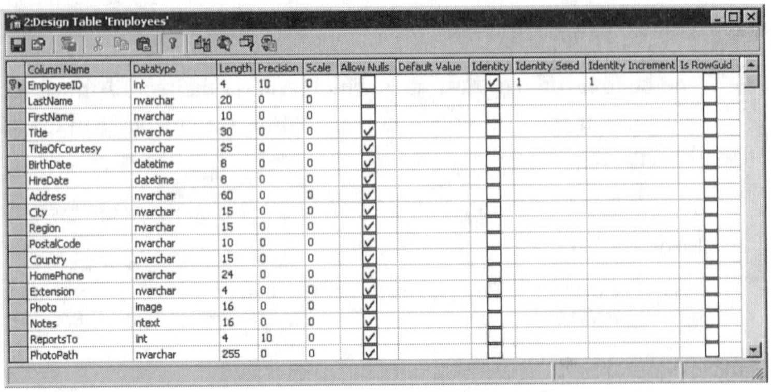

FIGURE 4.1

The definition of the Employees table.

LISTING 4.1   Changing Some Data for EmployeeID 8 in the Employees Table Using the SQL Update Statement

```
 1: Dim conn As ADODB.Connection
 2:
 3: Dim strAddress As String
 4: Dim strPostalCode As String
 5: Dim strCity As String
 6: Dim lngEmployeeID As Long
 7: Dim strSQL As String
 8:
 9: strAddress = "14 People Rd."
10: strPostalCode = "WG2 14PR"
11: strCity = "Birmingham"
12: lngEmployeeID = 8
13:
14: strSQL = "UPDATE Employees SET " & _
15:    "Address='" & Replace(Left(strAddress, 60), "'", "''") & "', " & _
16:    "PostalCode='" & Replace(Left(strPostalCode, 10), "'", "''") & "', " & _
17:    "City='" & Replace(Left(strCity, 15), "'", "''") & "' " & _
18:    "WHERE EmployeeID=" & CLng(lngEmployeeID)
19:
20: Set conn = CreateObject("ADODB.Connection")
21: conn.Open "Provider=SQLOLEDB;Data Source=BoyScout;" & _
22:    "Initial Catalog=Northwind;User ID=sa;Password=;"
23: conn.Execute strSQL
24: conn.Close
25: Set conn = Nothing
```

ANALYSIS   The new values for the employee are stored in the variables strAddress, strPostalCode and strCity. The EmployeeID of the employee whose data is to be updated is stored in the variable lngEmployeeID. The UPDATE statement is built in lines 14–18 and stored in the variable strSQL.

The script takes care of the maximum length allowed for the updated values by cutting string values to the length allowed for the correlating fields in the database (see Figure 4.1 for the definition of the fields in the Employees table). Apostrophes in strings are replaced by two apostrophes. In the lines 20–23, the connection to the Northwind database is opened and the UPDATE statement is executed using the Execute method of the Connection object. Finally, the connection is closed and the resources referenced by the connection variable, conn, are freed.

As mentioned in the preceding paragraph, the UPDATE statement can also be used to change the values of certain records based on their former values. For instance, it is possible to raise by $5 all product prices (UnitPrice) of the products that belong to SupplierID=11 in the Products table. You can use the statement that follows:

```
UPDATE Products SET UnitPrice=UnitPrice+5 WHERE SupplierID=11
```

When you want to increase certain product prices by a certain percentage, you can multiply the old price values to update them. The following UPDATE statement raises the unit price of all products belonging to a certain supplier (SupplierID=11) by 25% when the unit price is lower than $15.

```
UPDATE Products SET UnitPrice=UnitPrice*1.25
➥ WHERE SupplierID=11 AND UnitPrice<15
```

Of course, UPDATE statements can be more complex. For detailed information about the UPDATE statement, please refer to the Windows 2000 Platform SDK or other documentation about SQL.

Updating Database Data Through a Recordset

When you retrieve a Recordset from a database, you can change values in the Recordset and write the Recordset back to the database. The Recordset must be updateable to perform this task.

The Recordset's lock type has to be set to optimistic locking (adLockOptimistic) or batch optimistic locking (adLockBatchOptimistic) if you want to have an updateable Recordset. Use a dynamic, static, or keyset cursor type for an updateable Recordset.

You can prepare a Recordset by setting its lock type to optimistic locking (adLockOptimistic). Such a Recordset is in immediate update mode, and changes in a

4

record are written immediately to the database when you call the Update method of the Recordset object or move the Recordset cursor.

You can also prepare a Recordset to use batch optimistic locking (adLockBatchOptimistic). This Recordset is used in batch update mode, meaning all changed records are cached until you call the UpdateBatch method.

When you use optimistic locking, every updated record is written back to the database when you navigate to the next record or use the Recordset object's Update method. This means you only can change one record before the changes are written back to the database.

In contrast, you can use batch optimistic locking when you want to change several records before ADO updates the database. In this case, you have to use the Recordset object's UpdateBatch method to update all pending changes.

When you update data, whether you use optimistic locking or batch optimistic locking, you use a Recordset with a server-side cursor.

Note

> When you use a server-side cursor, the cursor "knows" which record you are changing. However, when using a client-side cursor, you must retrieve the Primary Key column in your Recordset when you want to change data of a record. The client-side cursor needs this column to unequivocally identify your record. When you change a record that cannot be identified unequivocally, it is possible that several records in the database might be changed (if they contain the same data as the record you intend to change).

Using the Recordset Object's Update Method

When you use a Recordset with optimistic locking, you have to update each record separately. You prepare the Recordset to use optimistic locking, open the Recordset, change a record, and update the record by using the Update method of the Recordset object or by simply moving the Recordset cursor to another record.

Typically, you use the immediate update mode (optimistic locking and updating using the Update method) when you want to write each record back to the database immediately after you have updated it. Using this mode saves resources because you do not have to cache it pending changes.

The script in Listing 4.2 retrieves a Recordset from the Employees table of the Northwind database, changes a record in the Recordset, and writes the changes back to the database. The definition of the Employees table is shown in Figure 4.1

LISTING 4.2 Updating a Record Using the Update Method

```
1: Dim conn As ADODB.Connection
2: Dim rs As ADODB.Recordset
3:
4: Dim strAddress As String
5: Dim strPostalCode As String
6: Dim strCity As String
7: Dim lngEmployeeID As Long
8: Dim strSQL As String
9:
10: strAddress = "14 People Rd."
11: strPostalCode = "WG2 14PR"
12: strCity = "Birmingham"
13: lngEmployeeID = 8
14:
15: Set conn = CreateObject("ADODB.Connection")
16: Set rs = CreateObject("ADODB.Recordset")
17: conn.Open "Provider=SQLOLEDB;Data Source=BoyScout;" & _
18:     "Initial Catalog=Northwind;User ID=sa;Password=;"
19:
20: strSQL = "SELECT EmployeeID, Address, PostalCode, City FROM " & _
21:     " Employees WHERE EmployeeID=" & lngEmployeeID
22:
23: rs.CursorLocation = adUseServer
24: rs.CursorType = adOpenKeyset
25: rs.LockType = adLockOptimistic
26: rs.Open strSQL, conn
27:
28: If Not rs.EOF Then
29:     rs("Address") = Left(strAddress, 60)
30:     rs("PostalCode") = Left(strPostalCode, 10)
31:     rs("City") = Left(strCity, 15)
32:     rs.Update
33:     Debug.Print "Record updated."
34: Else
35:     Debug.Print "Record not found in database."
36: End If
37:
38: rs.Close
39: conn.Close
40: Set rs = Nothing
41: Set conn = Nothing
```

ANALYSIS The script demonstrates the use of the Update method. New data for the employee with the EmployeeID 8 is stored in the variables strAddress, strPostalCode, and strCity. The connection to the SQL Server Northwind database is opened in lines 17–18. The Recordset source is defined in lines 20–21 and stored in the variable strSQL.

The Recordset is prepared in lines 23–25. It is a Recordset that uses a server-side, keyset cursor and optimistic locking. The Recordset is opened in line 26 using the Open method of the Recordset object with the Recordset source and the connection as parameters. When the Recordset contains a record, the values in the fields Address, PostalCode, and City are changed. The script assigns the new values to the fields of the current record and cuts all string values that are longer than the maximum length allowed in the underlying database fields.

> **Caution**
>
> When you change values of a record, you must be sure that you assign valid values to the record's fields. When you use strings that contain more characters than the field in the underlying database can store, you get an error when you try to assign the field values or update the record.

The record is written back to the database in line 32 using the Update method of the Recordset object.

> **Note**
>
> You also can move the Recordset cursor to the next record using the MoveNext method, causing the changed record to be written automatically to the database.

When the update operation is successful, the user is informed about this success in line 33. However, if the SQL statement does not return any Record, a message is written to the user in line 35, and no record is updated. The Recordset does not contain any record that can be updated. As usual, the script closes the Recordset and the Connection objects and frees their resources.

Of course, you can update as many records of the Recordset as you want.

When you have changed values of a record, but you do not want to write the changes back to the database, you have to use the CancelUpdate method of the Recordset object before you move the Recordset's cursor to another record and before you call the Update method.

A sample code for using the CancelUpdate method is shown in Listing 4.3. The variable rs holds the Recordset object.

LISTING 4.3 Cancel the Update of a Record

```
1: ...
2: blnUpdate = False
3: ...
4: If blnUpdate = True Then
5:     rs.Update
6: Else
7:     rs.CancelUpdate
8: End If
9: rs.MoveNext
10: ....
```

Using the `UpdateBatch` Method

When you prepare a Recordset using the batch optimistic lock type, this Recordset is in batch optimistic update mode. A Recordset in this mode caches all changes until you call the UpdateBatch method, which writes all changed records to the database at once.

To illustrate the usage of the UpdateBatch method to update Records of a database, Listing 4.4 shows the steps to open a Recordset, change some of the Records, and write all records back to the database.

Listing 4.4 uses the Customers table from the Northwind database. The listing changes several customer records based on certain field values of the records. Then it updates the whole Recordset at once using UpdateBatch.

Figure 4.2 shows the definition of the Customers table.

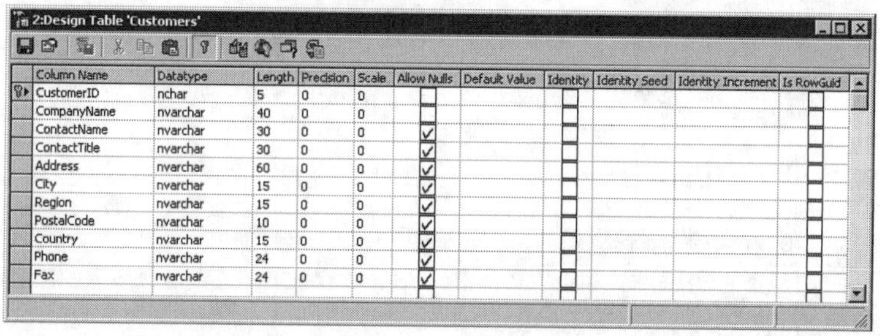

FIGURE 4.2

Definition of the Customers table.

LISTING 4.4 Using the `UpdateBatch` Method to Update a Recordset

```
1: Dim conn As ADODB.Connection
2: Dim rs As ADODB.Recordset
```

continues

LISTING 4.4   continued

```
 3:
 4: Set conn = CreateObject("ADODB.Connection")
 5: Set rs = CreateObject("ADODB.Recordset")
 6: conn.Open "Provider=SQLOLEDB;Data Source=BoyScout;" & _
 7:   "Initial Catalog=Northwind;User ID=sa;Password=;"
 8:
 9: strSQL = "SELECT CustomerID, CompanyName, ContactName, " & _
10:   "ContactTitle, Address, City, Region, PostalCode, " & _
11:   "Country, Phone, Fax FROM Customers"
12:
13: rs.CursorLocation = adUseServer
14: rs.CursorType = adOpenKeyset
15: rs.LockType = adLockBatchOptimistic
16: rs.Open strSQL, conn
17:
18: While Not rs.EOF
19:     If rs("CompanyName") = "Königlich Essen" Then
20:         rs("CompanyName") = "Fürstlich Speisen"
21:     End If
22:
23:     If rs("ContactName") = "Paula Parente" Then
24:         rs("ContactTitle") = "Sales Representative"
25:         rs("Phone") = "(14) 555-78122"
26:         rs("Fax") = "(14) 555-78122-28"
27:     End If
28:
29:     Select Case rs("CustomerID")
30:         Case "LAZYK"
31:             rs("ContactName") = "Remington Steele"
32:         Case "BLAUS"
33:             rs("Phone") = "06721-28460"
34:     End Select
35:     rs.MoveNext
36: Wend
37:
38: rs.UpdateBatch
39:
40: rs.Close
41: conn.Close
42: Set rs = Nothing
43: Set conn = Nothing
```

ANALYSIS The script changes several values of certain records. It renames the company Königlich Essen into Fürstlich Speisen, and it changes the contact title, the phone, and the fax number of all records with the contact name Paula Parente. The script also updates the contact name of the company with the CustomerID LAZYK and changes the telephone number of the company with the CustomerID BLAUS. All these changes are made in the `Recordset`, but are not written to the database until the `UpdateBatch` method of the `Recordset` object is called.

The script performs the following tasks: It opens the connection to the Northwind database in line 6. The SQL statement to retrieve the Recordset is stored in the variable `strSQL` in lines 9–11, and the Recordset is prepared in lines 13–15. The script uses a Recordset with a server-side, keyset cursor and a batch optimistic-locking type. Such a Recordset is updateable in batch optimistic update mode.

Line 16 opens the Recordset using the `Open` method with the SQL `SELECT` statement stored in the variable `strSQL` and the connection as parameters.

Next, the script makes changes in the whole Recordset, but no changes to the Recordset are written to the database until the `UpdateBatch` method is called. The code iterates over all records using a `While ...Wend` loop in lines 18–36. All changes in the Recordset data are performed in this loop.

After that, the `UpdateBatch` method of the `Recordset` object is called in line 38. By using this method all pending changes to the Recordset are written to the database. When you want to cancel the update instead of writing the data to the database, you can use the `CancelBatch` method of the `Recordset` object instead of the `UpdateBatch` method (`rs` stands for a `Recordset` object).

```
rs.CancelBatch
```

Finally the script frees the resources used by the `Connection` and the `Recordset` objects.

Using a Recordset with batch optimistic locking requires more resources than using a Recordset with optimistic locking. All changes in the Recordset have to be stored separately before the pending changes are written to the database using the `UpdateBatch` method.

The advantage of using a Recordset with batch optimistic locking is that you can change several records in a Recordset without any interaction with the database—as long as you do not write the changes to the database. This is important if you want to process a Disconnected Recordset.

NEW TERM   A *Disconnected Recordset* is a Recordset with a client-cursor that no longer has a live connection to the database. If the Recordset needs to access the original database to update or save pending changes, for example, you have to re-establish a connection to the database. A Disconnected Recordset is useful when you need to handle a Recordset for a long time period, but you don't want to waste resources keeping a database connection alive. Disconnected Recordsets are explained in-depth in Day 16, "Working with Disconnected Recordsets."

4

Updating BLOBs

If you want to assign a new value to a BLOB field, you can use the `AppendChunk` method of the `Field` object.

How to use the `AppendChunk` method to manipulate BLOBs is described in Day 3, "Fail-Safe Inserting of Data."

Updating Database Data Using Stored Procedures

When you want to change data in a SQL Server database, you can, of course, use stored procedures. You pass certain parameters to a stored procedure that is defined in a SQL Server database. The stored procedure can perform database tasks, such as updating.

Stored procedures and their usage in ADO are explained in detail in Day 7, "Implementing Application Logic in Stored Procedures."

Retrieving the Original and the Underlying Values

When you change data in a Recordset, especially when using batch optimistic locking, you might want to know what value was stored in a certain field of a Recordset before you made changes to the Recordset. This is where the `OriginalValue` property of the `Field` object is used.

If you want to know the current value of a field in the database, the `UnderlyingValue` property can be used to retrieve this value. This value is retrieved directly from the database.

How to Retrieve the Original Value of a Field

The `OriginalValue` property returns the value of a field prior to any changes. The behavior of the `OriginalValue` property depends on the locking type of the `Recordset` object.

When you are using optimistic locking, the Recordset is in the immediate update mode. In this case, the `OriginalValue` property returns the field value that existed prior to changes. When you call the `Update` method or move the Recordset cursor, the changed value is written to the database and becomes the new `OriginalValue`.

When you are using batch optimistic locking, the Recordset is in the batch update mode. That means that the provider is caching multiple changes until you call the `UpdateBatch` method, which writes the changes into the database. In this case, the `OriginalValue` property returns the field value that existed prior to changes. When you call the `UpdateBatch` method and all changes are written into the database, the changed value becomes the new `OriginalValue`.

The OriginalValue property is only guaranteed to work with a Recordset that can be updated. When you try to access the OriginalValue property of a read-only Recordset, you will receive an error. Certain permutations of LockType, CursorLocation and CursorType might also fail when you access the OriginalValue property—depending on the provider or data source.

The OriginalValue of a field in a Recordset does not need to be the value of the field in the underlying database, it is only the value of the field at the moment you retrieve or update the Recordset.

Reading the Underlying Value of a Field

While you are handling a Recordset, other users can change values in the underlying database. If you want to see whether another application or user has changed values of your Recordset in the underlying database, you can use the UnderlyingValue property of the Field object to retrieve these values.

To retrieve the underlying value of a field you can use a statement as follows (rs is a Recordset object):

```
theValue = rs.("FieldName").UnderlyingValue
```

An Example of Original and Underlying Values

To make it easier to understand the values that are provided by the OriginalValue and UnderlyingValue properties of the Field object, Figure 4.3 shows a process that occurs when two users both retrieve a record, change its values, and write the values back to the database.

In the figure, the left column contains the value in Record 1. The middle column contains the value of the database (that is the UnderlyingValue), and the right column contains the value of Record 2. In the first step, Record 1 and Record 2 are retrieved.

Now let us see what happens in Record 1. In the second step, Record 1 is changed to the value 8. The UnderlyingValue is 7 and the OriginalValue is 7. In the third step, the value in the database is changed. Therefore, the UnderlyingValue returns 5 for Record 1. In the fourth step, the updating of Record 1 is canceled (using the CancelUpdate or CancelBatch method of the Recordset object). Therefore the value of Record 1 is reset to the original value, which is 7.

Similar things happen in Record 2. The value of the Record is changed to 5 in the second step. The OriginalValue is 7 and the UnderlyingValue is 7. The third step writes the data to the database (by the usage of the Update or UpdateBatch method of the Recordset object). Therefore, the OriginalValue of Record 2 is set to the same value that is written to the database. This value is 5.

FIGURE 4.3

UnderlyingValue *and*
OriginalValue.

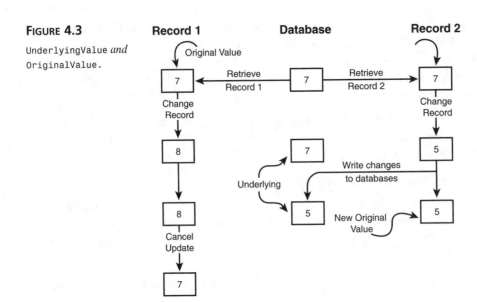

To see how the process shown in Figure 4.3 is done using ADO, Listing 4.5 performs the tasks of the process and retrieves the underlying values and the original values after each step.

LISTING 4.5   Using the OriginalValue and the UnderlyingValue Properties

```
 1: Dim conn As ADODB.Connection
 2: Dim rs1 As ADODB.Recordset
 3: Dim rs2 As ADODB.Recordset
 4: Dim strSQL As String
 5:
 6: Set conn = CreateObject("ADODB.Connection")
 7: Set rs1 = CreateObject("ADODB.Recordset")
 8: Set rs2 = CreateObject("ADODB.Recordset")
 9:
10: conn.Open "Provider=SQLOLEDB;Data Source=BoyScout;" & _
11:     "Initial Catalog=Northwind;User ID=sa;Password=;"
12:
13: strSQL = "SELECT UnitPrice FROM Products WHERE ProductID=52"
14:
15: ' First step: Retrieve Recordsets
16: rs1.CursorType = adOpenKeyset
17: rs1.LockType = adLockOptimistic
18: rs1.Open strSQL, conn
19:
20: rs2.CursorType = adOpenKeyset
```

```
21: rs2.LockType = adLockOptimistic
22: rs2.Open strSQL, conn
23:
24: 'Second step: Change values in Recordsets
25: rs1("UnitPrice") = 8
26: rs2("UnitPrice") = 5
27:
28: Debug.Print "Change Values:"
29: Debug.Print "rs1 = " & rs1("UnitPrice")
30: Debug.Print "rs1 (UnderlyingValue) = " & rs1("UnitPrice").UnderlyingValue
31: Debug.Print "rs1 (OriginalValue) = " & rs1("UnitPrice").OriginalValue
32: Debug.Print
33: Debug.Print "rs2 = " & rs2("UnitPrice")
34: Debug.Print "rs2 (UnderlyingValue) = " & rs2("UnitPrice").UnderlyingValue
35: Debug.Print "rs2 (OriginalValue) = " & rs2("UnitPrice").OriginalValue
36: Debug.Print "---------------------"
37:
38: 'Third step: Write changes in Recordset 2 to database
39: rs2.Update
40:
41: Debug.Print "Update Recordset 2:"
42: Debug.Print "rs1 = " & rs1("UnitPrice")
43: Debug.Print "rs1 (UnderlyingValue) = " & rs1("UnitPrice").UnderlyingValue
44: Debug.Print "rs1 (OriginalValue) = " & rs1("UnitPrice").OriginalValue
45: Debug.Print
46: Debug.Print "rs2 = " & rs2("UnitPrice")
47: Debug.Print "rs2 (UnderlyingValue) = " & rs2("UnitPrice").UnderlyingValue
48: Debug.Print "rs2 (OriginalValue) = " & rs2("UnitPrice").OriginalValue
49: Debug.Print "---------------------"
50:
51: ' Fourth step: Cancel update in Recordset 1
52: rs1.CancelUpdate
53:
54: Debug.Print "Cancel Update of Recordset 1:"
55: Debug.Print "rs1 = " & rs1("UnitPrice")
56: Debug.Print "rs1 (UnderlyingValue) = " & rs1("UnitPrice").UnderlyingValue
57: Debug.Print "rs1 (OriginalValue) = " & rs1("UnitPrice").OriginalValue
58: Debug.Print
59: Debug.Print "rs2 = " & rs2("UnitPrice")
60: Debug.Print "rs2 (UnderlyingValue) = " & rs2("UnitPrice").UnderlyingValue
61: Debug.Print "rs2 (OriginalValue) = " & rs2("UnitPrice").OriginalValue
62: Debug.Print "---------------------"
63:
64: rs1.Close
65: rs2.Close
66: conn.Close
67: Set rs1 = Nothing
68: Set rs2 = Nothing
69: Set conn = Nothing
```

4

The code in Listing 4.5 should produce this output:

```
Change Values:
rs1 = 8
rs1 (UnderlyingValue) = 7
rs1 (OriginalValue) = 7

rs2 = 5
rs2 (UnderlyingValue) = 7
rs2 (OriginalValue) = 7
. . . . . . . . . . . . . . . . . . . . .
Update Recordset 2:
rs1 = 8
rs1 (UnderlyingValue) = 5
rs1 (OriginalValue) = 7

rs2 = 5
rs2 (UnderlyingValue) = 5
rs2 (OriginalValue) = 5
. . . . . . . . . . . . . . . . . . . . .
Cancel Update of Recordset 1:
rs1 = 7
rs1 (UnderlyingValue) = 5
rs1 (OriginalValue) = 7

rs2 = 5
rs2 (UnderlyingValue) = 5
rs2 (OriginalValue) = 5
. . . . . . . . . . . . . . . . . . . . .
```

ANALYSIS   The script creates and opens a connection to the SQL Server Northwind database. Two Recordsets are created and populated using the same data from the database. The data source for both Recordsets is the database record from the Products table that contains the ProductID 52. Strictly speaking only the field with the name UnitPrice is retrieved. The SQL SELECT statement that is used to specify the retrieved Recordsets is stored in the variable strSQL in line 13.

Before the Recordsets are populated, they are prepared to be updateable. Therefore, both use a keyset cursor with optimistic locking as determined in the lines 16–22.

After the Recordsets are retrieved, the value of the UnitPrice field of Recordset 1 is set to 8, although the value in Recordset 2 is set to 5. This value, as well as the underlying and the original value of both Recordsets, is written to the user.

Recordset 2 is updated using the Update method (because the Recordset uses optimistic locking). For both Recordsets, the UnderlyingValue returns the new value in the database, which is 5. The OriginalValue of Recordset 1 remains 7, but the OriginalValue of Recordset 2 changes to 5 because it was written to the database using the Update method.

In the last step, the changes in Recordset 1 are canceled using the CancelUpdate method. This sets the value in Recordset 1 back to the original value, which is 7.

The script is only a sample that provides you an idea of how to use the UnderlyingValue and OriginalValue properties of the Field object. When your application has to serve several users simultaneously, it is likely that a certain record, or a field of a certain record might be used by two users at the same time. To detect if another user has changed any values while your application is handling a Recordset, use the UnderlyingValue property to receive the current value stored in the database and compare it against the OriginalValue of the Recordset.

Deleting Table Data

Deleting records in a database is necessary to keep your database up to date.

There are several ways to delete database records:

- Execute a SQL DELETE statement: This is the preferred method when you want to delete several records (that meet certain criteria) all at once. The SQL DELETE statement is executed using the Execute method of the Connection object.
- Delete data in a Recordset: You can retrieve a Recordset, delete some records and write the changes back to the database. This is only possible if your Recordset is updateable.
- Use stored procedures: Another possibility is deleting data from a SQL Server database by using SQL Server's stored procedures.

Using the SQL DELETE Command

The SQL DELETE command is your first choice when you want to delete records in a database. Just build a SQL DELETE statement that specifies which records in the database should be deleted and execute the SQL statement.

The syntax of a SQL DELETE statement follows:

```
DELETE FROM TableName WHERE Condition
```

This statement deletes all records of the table TableName that meet the conditions specified in the Condition.

Caution

When you do not specify any condition in a DELETE statement, all records are deleted from the database table.

Some examples for DELETE statements are described here:

`DELETE FROM Products WHERE SupplierID=11`

This SQL statement deletes all records from the Products table that contain the value 11 in the column SupplierID.

`DELETE FROM Shippers WHERE CompanyName='United Package'`

This SQL statement deletes all records from the Shippers table that have the value United Package in the CompanyName column.

A SQL DELETE statement can be executed just like any other SQL statement using the Execute method of the Connection object.

Listing 4.6 provides a sample for using the SQL DELETE statement.

LISTING 4.6   Deleting a Record from the Products Table Using the SQL DELETE Statement

```
 1: Dim conn As ADODB.Connection
 2: Dim strSQL As String
 3: Dim lngOrderID As Long
 4:
 5: Set conn = CreateObject("ADODB.Connection")
 6: conn.Open "Provider=SQLOLEDB;Data Source=BoyScout;" & _
 7:    "Initial Catalog=Northwind;User ID=sa;Password=;"
 8:
 9: lngOrderID = 10240
10: strSQL = "DELETE FROM 'Order Details' WHERE OrderID=" & lngOrderID
11:
12: conn.Execute strSQL
13:
14: conn.Close
15: Set conn = Nothing
```

ANALYSIS   Listing 4.6 opens a connection to the SQL Northwind database and deletes all records of the Order Details table that contain the value 10240 in the OrderID column. The SQL DELETE statement is built in line 10 and stored in the variable strSQL. The SQL statement is executed using the Execute method of the Connection object in line 14.

Tip   When you want to make sure that only one record is deleted in the database, use a Primary Key value in the condition part of the DELETE statement to specify that only that particular record should be deleted.

Find the Number of Deleted Records

When using SQL Server as database, you can use the function @@ROWCOUNT to retrieve the number of records deleted by a DELETE statement. The SQL Server function @@ROWCOUNT returns the number of records affected by the last executed SQL statement. Listing 4.7 deletes some records of a SQL Server table and determines the number of records deleted.

LISTING 4.7 Deleting Records from the Order Details Table Using the SQL DELETE Statement

```
 1: Dim conn As ADODB.Connection
 2: Dim rs As ADODB.Recordset
 3: Dim strSQL As String
 4: Dim lngOrderID As Long
 5: Dim lngRecordsDeleted As Long
 6: Set conn = CreateObject("ADODB.Connection")
 7: conn.Open "Provider=SQLOLEDB;Data Source=BoyScout;" & _
 8:    "Initial Catalog=Northwind;User ID=sa;Password=;"
 9:
10: lngOrderID = 10255
11: strSQL = "DELETE FROM [Order Details] WHERE OrderID=" & lngOrderID
12: conn.Execute strSQL
13:
14: strSQL = "SELECT @@ROWCOUNT AS Rows"
15: Set rs = conn.Execute(strSQL)
16: lngRecordsDeleted = rs("Rows")
17:
18: rs.Close
19: conn.Close
20: Set conn = Nothing
21: Set rs = Nothing
22:
23: Debug.Print "Records deleted: " & lngRecordsDeleted
```

ANALYSIS Listing 4.7 deletes all records from the Orders Details table that contain the value 10255 in the OrderID column and retrieves the number of records deleted. The script opens a connection to the SQL Server Northwind database, builds a SQL DELETE statement in line 11, and executes the DELETE statement in line 12. The number of deleted records is retrieved using a SELECT statement that contains the SQL Server @@ROWCOUNT function:

```
SELECT @@ROWCOUNT AS Rows
```

This SELECT statement is executed and the resulting Recordset contains the number of deleted records. The number is read from the Recordset field named Rows and stored in the variable lngRecordsDeleted.

Finally, the script presents the number of deleted records to the user using Debug.Print.

Note

Because the @@ROWCOUNT function contains the number of records affected by the last SQL statement, you have to use it immediately after the SQL DELETE statement to get the number of deleted records. Do not execute another SQL statement between the DELETE statement and the SELECT statement that contains the @@ROWCOUNT function.

When the SQL DELETE Command Fails

When the SQL DELETE command fails, the most frequent reason is that the record cannot be deleted. What circumstances can prevent a record from being deleted? When there is a Foreign Key relationship between two tables, you cannot delete a record that contains a Primary Key value that is referenced as Foreign Key value in another table. In that case, the database rejects the Delete command because deleting the record violates a rule defined in the database. A sample of a Foreign Key relationship is shown in Figure 4.4. The Region table contains the Primary Key in the RegionID column, and the Territories table contains the related Foreign Key column in the RegionID column.

FIGURE 4.4

Relationship between Region and Territories tables.

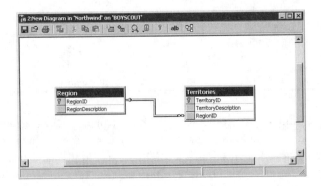

Because a Foreign Key relationship is defined in the database, you cannot delete a record in the Region table if its RegionID value is used as RegionID in any record of the Territories table.

Another thing to watch for is a *cascading delete*, which is a deletion done by the database when a cascading delete relationship (Access) or a Delete Trigger (SQL Server) is defined. When your database uses such a technique to delete a record in a table, the database might also automatically delete records in other tables, depending on the values in the record you originally intended to delete.

You can handle errors that appear using the SQL DELETE command as shown in Day 3, "Fail-Safe Inserting of Data."

Delete Records in a Recordset

You can delete records of an updateable Recordset. This is done using the Recordset object's Delete method.

When you have a Recordset with optimistic locking (immediate update mode), you can delete a record immediately using the Delete method. When your Recordset uses batch optimistic locking (batch update mode), you can mark all records that should be deleted using the Delete method and then delete them using the UpdateBatch method.

Immediate Deletion of Records in a Recordset

If you have an updateable Recordset of optimistic locking type (immediate update mode), you can perform immediate deletion of records in a Recordset. To delete a certain record, use the Delete method of the Recordset object when the recordset cursor is at the position of the record you want to delete.

After you have deleted a record, the Recordset's cursor still points to the deleted record, but the fields of the record are no longer accessible. If you move the Recordset cursor away from the deleted record, the cursor position of the deleted record is also removed, and the deleted record is no longer accessible.

The following script retrieves a Recordset, loops through the Recordset, and deletes the current record if it meets certain criteria.

LISTING 4.8　Deleting Records Using an Updateable Recordset with Optimistic Locking

```
1: Dim conn As ADODB.Connection
2: Dim rs As ADODB.Recordset
3:
4: Set conn = CreateObject("ADODB.Connection")
5: Set rs = CreateObject("ADODB.Recordset")
6: conn.Open "Provider=SQLOLEDB;Data Source=BoyScout;" & _
7:     "Initial Catalog=Northwind;User ID=sa;Password=;"
8:
9: strSQL = "SELECT CustomerID, CompanyName FROM Customers"
10:
11: rs.CursorLocation = adUseServer
```

continues

LISTING 4.8   continued

```
12: rs.CursorType = adOpenKeyset
13: rs.LockType = adLockOptimistic
14: rs.Open strSQL, conn
15:
16: While Not rs.EOF
17:     If rs("CompanyName") = "Kaiserlich Schlemmen" Then
18:         rs.Delete
19:     End If
20:     rs.MoveNext
21: Wend
22:
23: rs.Close
24: conn.Close
25: Set rs = Nothing
26: Set conn = Nothing
```

 ANALYSIS   The script prepares a server-side, keyset Recordset with optimistic locking. This Recordset is populated with the columns CustomerID and CompanyName from the Customers table of the SQL Server Northwind database.

The script loops through all records of the Recordset using the While…Wend loop in the lines 16–21. When the value of the field CompanyName of the current record is Kaiserlich Schlemmen, the record is deleted in line 18 using the Delete method of the Recordset object. The record is deleted immediately because the Recordset is using optimistic locking (immediate update mode).

Note

Listing 4.8 does not delete any customer dataset that has a Foreign Key Relationship. However, if you try to delete a customer other than Kaiserlich Schlemmen, you will get an error message. All original customer datasets have a Foreign Key relationship to datasets in the Orders table, so you can only delete customers, whose CustomerID is not used in any Order dataset.

Batch Deletion of Records in a Recordset

If your application uses a Recordset with batch optimistic locking (batch update mode), you can mark records for deletion in the current Recordset. To delete records from the database, you must execute the UpdateBatch method of the Recordset object. If you do not want to delete the records that are marked for deletion you can execute the CancelBatch method of the Recordset object that rejects all changes made to the Recordset.

The process of deleting records in a Recordset is shown in the example in Listing 4.9.

The sample script retrieves a Recordset that has batch optimistic locking. Some of the records are marked for deletion. Finally, the listing decides whether to delete all marked records or to reject the deletion, depending on the value in a certain variable.

LISTING 4.9   Deleting Records Using an Updateable Recordset With Batch Optimistic Locking

```
 1: Dim conn As ADODB.Connection
 2: Dim rs As ADODB.Recordset
 3: Dim strSQL As String
 4: Dim blnDelete As Boolean
 5:
 6: Set conn = CreateObject("ADODB.Connection")
 7: Set rs = CreateObject("ADODB.Recordset")
 8: conn.Open "Provider=SQLOLEDB;Data Source=BoyScout;" & _
 9:     "Initial Catalog=Northwind;User ID=sa;Password=;"
10:
11: strSQL = "SELECT OrderID FROM [Order Details]"
12:
13: rs.CursorLocation = adUseServer
14: rs.CursorType = adOpenKeyset
15: rs.LockType = adLockBatchOptimistic
16: rs.Open strSQL, conn
17:
18: While Not rs.EOF
19:     If rs("OrderID") = 10250 Then
20:         rs.Delete
21:     End If
22:     rs.MoveNext
23: Wend
24:
25: blnDelete = False
26:
27: If blnDelete = True Then
28:     rs.UpdateBatch
29: Else
30:     rs.CancelBatch
31: End If
32: rs.Close
33: conn.Close
34: Set rs = Nothing
35: Set conn = Nothing
```

ANALYSIS   A connection is opened to the SQL Server Northwind database, and a Recordset is prepared to use a server-side, keyset cursor with batch optimistic locking. The Recordset is opened in line 16 and populated with the column OrderID from the table

Order Details. A `While...Wend` loop iterates over all records and marks every record for deletion if it contains the value `10250` in the field OrderID.

In line 25, the variable `blnDelete`, which indicates if the records should actually be deleted, is set to `False`. The `If` block, in lines 27–31, is responsible for deciding whether the marked `Records` are deleted. When the variable `blnDelete` contains the value `True`, the records marked for deletion are deleted using the `UpdateBatch` method in line 28. But if the variable `blnDelete` contains a value other than `True`, no record is deleted, and all other pending changes are rejected. This is done by the execution of the `CancelBatch` method of the `Recordset` object.

Deleting Records Using Stored Procedures

When you have a SQL Server database, you can, of course, use Stored Procedures to delete records in a database. Using Stored Procedures is explained in detail in Day 7.

Summary

This day's topic was how to update and delete database data. You have examined the usage of the SQL `UPDATE` and `DELETE` methods to update and delete data. You have seen how to use a Recordset to update data or delete records.

Performing updates and deletes of database data are basic database manipulation techniques. Therefore, it is important to be familiar with them if you want to use ADO efficiently in a database application.

Q&A

Q Is it possible to handle errors that are raised while the application updates or deletes database data?

A You can use the same error-handling mechanisms that are described in Day 3, "Fail-Safe Inserting of Data." Use, for instance, the Visual Basic `On Error Resume Next` statement to enable error handling. It retrieves information about the error by reading the properties of the `Err` object. Of course, you can also use the `Errors` collection of the `Connection` object to retrieve errors and warnings that are raised by the data provider.

Q Imagine the following situation. Two applications handle the same database record. Application 1 deletes this record in the database. What happens when Application 2 tries to update the record and write it back to the database?

A Application 2 will raise an error because it tries to update a record that does not exist anymore. The error is raised as the cursor of the Recordset points to a position in the database that does not exist anymore. This is valid for both client-side and server-side cursors. You should include error-handling code in your application in case your application falls into such a trap.

Workshop

The Workshop is designed to help you anticipate possible questions, review what you've learned, and get you thinking about how to put your knowledge into practice. The answers to the quiz are in Appendix A, "Quiz Answers."

Quiz

1. When you want to delete all records from the Products table (see Figure 4.5) that contain the `SupplierID=8`, which SQL statement performs this task?

FIGURE 4.5

Definition of the Products table.

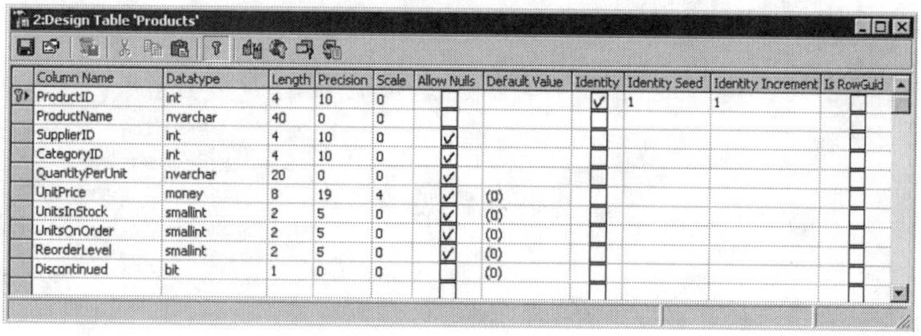

Column Name	Datatype	Length	Precision	Scale	Allow Nulls	Default Value	Identity	Identity Seed	Identity Increment	Is RowGuid
ProductID	int	4	10	0			✓	1	1	
ProductName	nvarchar	40	0	0						
SupplierID	int	4	10	0	✓					
CategoryID	int	4	10	0	✓					
QuantityPerUnit	nvarchar	20	0	0	✓					
UnitPrice	money	8	19	4	✓	(0)				
UnitsInStock	smallint	2	5	0	✓	(0)				
UnitsOnOrder	smallint	2	5	0	✓	(0)				
ReorderLevel	smallint	2	5	0	✓	(0)				
Discontinued	bit	1	0	0		(0)				

2. What are the two locking types that can be used when you want to prepare an updateable Recordset?
3. Design a SQL statement that increases the number of `UnitsInStock` by 5 for the product `ProductID=17`. The products are stored in the Products table.

Exercises

1. Write a script that updates the database record of the Products table with the ProductID 14 so that its UnitsInStock value is set to 25. Use a SQL statement to change the value.

2. Write a script that prepares a Recordset for batch optimistic locking and populates the Recordset with all products from the Products table that have the SupplierID 8. Let the script increase the Unitprice for all products in the Recordset by $2 when the UnitsInStock value is lower than 5 and the value in the column UnitsOnOrder is greater than 10. When more than two product records are changed, the script should write all pending changes to the database.

DAY 5

Filtering and Sorting Resultsets

The former days were about how to retrieve, insert, and update data in a database. Today, you learn how to find specific data in a recordset or sort a recordset.

The Recordset object has many useful properties and functions. Some of them can be used to find certain records in a recordset. Others enable you to sort a recordset or to screen out records you do not need. These techniques can be a good addition to the use of well-defined SQL statements.

The main topics today are

- The use of bookmarks—A bookmark of a recordset is like a dog-eared page corner in a book. It contains information about a certain record and can be used to jump quickly to a specific record.

- Searching in a recordset—The Find method of the Recordset object enables you to find certain records fast without looping through the whole recordset.

- Filtering a recordset—You can apply filters to a recordset to screen out records. Filters can be used similarly to the way you use the WHERE clause in a SELECT statement. You also can find all records of a certain state using a recordset filter. A record can, for instance, have one of the following states: modified, not modified, deleted, new record.

Filtering and Sorting with SQL Statements

When you want to retrieve a recordset, you can specify the content of the recordset using the SQL SELECT statement. In this SELECT statement, the WHERE clause specifies the data you want to retrieve. The sort order of the data is specified by an ORDER BY clause in the SELECT statement. You can use the following statement to determine the kind of data of the recordset and its sort order:

```
SELECT ProductName, UnitPrice FROM Products
WHERE CategoryID = 4
ORDER BY ProductName, UnitPrice
```

The resulting recordset contains all records from the Products table that have the CategoryID 4. The recordset is ordered ascending by the product name (ProductName) and the unit price (UnitPrice). When you want to order a column by its descending values, use the keyword DESC after the column name (ProductName in the following example) in the ORDER BY clause:

```
ORDER BY ProductName DESC, UnitPrice
```

Note   For more information about the possibilities of the SELECT statement, refer to the Microsoft Platform SDK for Windows 2000 or another documentation about SQL.

Of course, you can filter and sort data in a recordset, too. This allows flexibility in using data when you already have retrieved a recordset. The following section introduces details of using a Recordset object in conjunction with finding or sorting data directly in the recordset.

Using Bookmarks in Recordsets

A bookmark of a recordset is like a cursor that points to a certain record in a recordset. You can use bookmarks to return quickly to certain records in a recordset. Bookmarks are sometimes used to identify records for operations such as filtering a recordset.

You can use the `Bookmark` property of the `Recordset` object to retrieve a certain bookmark:

```
varBookmark = rs.Bookmark
```

This statement retrieves the position (bookmark) of the current record in the recordset named `rs` and stores it in the variable `varBookmark`.

The `Bookmark` property can also be used to set the recordset cursor to the position of a stored bookmark:

```
rs.Bookmark = varBookmark
```

No matter where the cursor of the recordset named `rs` has been before, after the operation the cursor is at the position that was stored in the variable `varBookmark`.

Not all recordsets support bookmarks. However, every recordset using a client-side cursor supports the `Bookmark` property. When you use a server-side cursor, whether you can use bookmarks depends on the data provider.

To check whether your recordset supports bookmarks, use the following statement:

```
blnVar = rs.Supports(adBookmark)
```

The `Supports` method with the argument `adBookmark` returns `TRUE` if the recordset supports bookmarks. Therefore, the variable in the example `blnVar` contains the value `TRUE` if the recordset named `rs` supports bookmarks.

Searching for Data in a Recordset

5

The `Recordset` object provides two methods to search for data in a recordset.

You can use the `Find` method of the `Recordset` object to find records with a certain value, and you can use the `Seek` method with the `Index` property to use a table index for your recordset and search for values in this index. Using the `Seek` method has some restrictions; for instance, you cannot use it with a recordset that uses a client-side cursor.

Overview of the `Find` method:

- The `Find` method is a smart way to find records with certain values fast in a recordset without looping through the whole recordset.

- The `Find` method can be used to find values in any column. Just use a search string to find the next record with that has a field value matching the criterium.

- In the search string you can use different comparison operators, such as = (equal), < (less than), > (greater than), <= (less than or equal), >= (greater than or equal), <> (not equal), or like (pattern matching). So you have various possibilities to use the Find method.

Overview of the Seek method:

- The Seek method enables a fast search in a column, especially in a big recordset.

- The Seek method enables you to find only values equal to the search value. There are no other search operations possible.

- The Seek method needs a data provider that enables it to use the Index property and the Seek method. Only a very limited number of data providers can handle the Index property and the Seek method.

- The Seek method requires a server-side recordset cursor that was opened using the Open method and a special parameter to get direct access to the table and its indexes.

- The Seek method can be used only to find values in a column of a recordset that has a so-called index in the underlying database table.

Use the Find Method

You can use the Find method to find a record that contains a certain value in a certain field of the record:

```
rs.Find(SearchString)
```

The SearchString is a string expression that contains the name of a recordset's field, a comparison operator, and the value you want to search for. The comparison operator is allowed to be = (equal), < (less than), > (greater than), <= (less than or equal), >= (greater than or equal), <> (not equal), or like (pattern matching). When the search value is a string, it must be delimited by a single quote ('). When the value is a date, it must be delimited by pound signs (#).

There are some other limitations: You can search for a value in only one field. When you use the like operator, the search value may contain an asterisk (*) to find a certain substring (part of a string), but the asterisk can be used only as the leading and trailing sign of the substring (as in '*ok*') or as the trailing one (as in 'Coo*').

Some examples for search strings are

```
"ProductName = 'Tofu'"
"SupplierID >= 7"
"Freight < 140"
"OrderDate = #9/30/1997#"
```

```
"ProductName like '*hot*'"
"ProductName like 'Out*'"
```

However, the `Find` method provides even more parameters, as shown here:

```
rs.Find(SearchString, SkipRows, SearchDirection, Start)
```

`SkipRows` is an optional `Long` value, whose default value is zero. It specifies the row offset from the current row or `Start` bookmark to begin the search. By default, the search starts in the current row and ends at the last row (when the `SearchDirection` is forward) or the first row of the Recordset (`SearchDirection` backward).

`SearchDirection` indicates the direction the recordset is searched. It is also optional and can be one of the ADO constants `adSearchForward` or `adSearchBackward`. When searching forward and no row is found, the recordset cursor is set beyond the last record and the `EOF` property of the recordset returns `TRUE`. If no match is found while searching backward, the cursor is set before the first record, and the property `BOF` of the recordset returns `TRUE`.

`Start` is an optional parameter that can be set to a start bookmark. You can specify the bookmark that should be used as the starting position for the search.

The use of the `Find` method is as follows:

- You set the recordset cursor to a certain row.

- You invoke the `Find` method.

- When a start bookmark is passed to the `Find` method, the recordset cursor is moved to the start bookmark.

- When a `SkipRows` value is passed to the `Find` method, the recordset cursor moves forward or backward by the number specified in the `SkipRows` parameter. The direction of the movement is indicated by the `SearchDirection` parameter.

- Then the `Find` method searches for the first record that matches the search condition defined by `SearchString`. The search starts at the current cursor position and is performed in the direction indicated by the `SearchDirection` parameter.

- When a matching record is found, the recordset cursor points to the matching row in the recordset. When no row is found, the recordset cursor points to `EOF` (when searching forward) or to `BOF` (when searching backward).

Caution

An error will occur when no current row position is set before calling the `Find` method. Any recordset method that sets the cursor to a certain position, such as `MoveFirst`, should be called before invoking the `Find` method!

5

The Visual Basic example in Listing 5.1 provides an overview of how to use the Find method. It uses the Suppliers table from the SQL Server 7.0 Northwind database as the source for the Recordset.

LISTING 5.1   Example of Using the Find Method

```
 1: Dim conn As ADODB.Connection
 2: Dim rs As ADODB.Recordset
 3: Dim strSQL As String
 4: Dim varBookmark As Variant
 5: Dim strSearch As String
 6:
 7: Set conn = CreateObject("ADODB.Connection")
 8: conn.Open "Provider=SQLOLEDB;Data Source=BoyScout;" & _
 9:     "Initial Catalog=Northwind;User ID=sa;Password=;"
10:
11: Set rs = CreateObject("ADODB.Recordset")
12: strSQL = "SELECT SupplierID, CompanyName, Country FROM Suppliers"
13: rs.CursorLocation = adUseClient
14: rs.Open strSQL, conn
15:
16: rs.MoveFirst
17: strSearch = "Country like 'U*'"
18: rs.Find strSearch, 0, adSearchForward
19:
20: While Not rs.EOF
21:     Debug.Print rs("CompanyName") & "(" & rs("Country") & ")"
22:     varBookmark = rs.Bookmark
23:     rs.Find strSearch, 1, adSearchForward, varBookmark
24: Wend
25:
26: rs.Close
27: conn.Close
28: Set rs = Nothing
29: Set conn = Nothing
```

The code in Listing 5.1 should produce this output:

OUTPUT
```
Exotic Liquids(UK)
New Orleans Cajun Delights(USA)
Grandma Kelly's Homestead(USA)
Specialty Biscuits, Ltd.(UK)
Bigfoot Breweries(USA)
New England Seafood Cannery(USA)
```

ANALYSIS The script opens a connection to the SQL Server 7.0 Northwind database. In lines 11–14, the recordset is created and prepared to use a client-side cursor. Then the recordset is populated with the fields SupplierID, CompanyName, and Country of all records from the Suppliers table (see the SELECT statement in line 12).

After the recordset is opened, its cursor is set to the first record by the MoveFirst method. The search string that is used with the Find method is defined in line 17 and stored in the variable strSearch. In line 18, the script searches for the first occurrence of a record with a value like 'U*' in the Country field.

When no record matches, the recordset cursor is set to EOF. However, when a matching record is found, the While...Wend loop retrieves the company name and country of all suppliers where the country name begins with the letter U. In line 22, the script stores the position (bookmark) of the current record, which is the matching record, in the variable varBookmark and uses it as the start position for the next search. The row offset in the Find method in line 23 is set to 1, so the Find method begins to search 1 row after the position stored in the variable varBookmark (which is the current position of the cursor in the recordset). When no further match is found, the recordset's EOF property returns TRUE and the While...Wend loop terminates. All matching records are written to the user, as shown in the output of Listing 5.1.

Searching with Table Indexes

Searching in a table index is a very specific task. Only a few database providers allow you to use the Index property and the Seek method of the Recordset object to search for values in a table's index. (One of these few database providers is the OLE DB Provider for Microsoft Jet 4.0 that is used to connect to an Access database).

NEW TERM An *index* of a table is like an index in a book. An index in a book enables you to find information quickly without reading the entire book. An index of a table contains information about the position of all values in an indexed column of a database table. Indexing columns consumes some database space and resources. However, the real power of an index shows up in search operations in an indexed column. When you search for a certain value in a nonindex column, the database has to compare all values in the column with the search value. That may take a considerable period of time, especially in tables with thousands of records. In contrast, a search operation in an indexed column is much faster, because the index of the column contains all the information that is necessary to find quickly a database row with a specific value in the indexed column.

You can use an index, which was defined in a database table, for search operations in a recordset. The index must have been declared previously on the underlying database table of the recordset before you can use it in a search operation using the Seek method.

The Index property of the Recordset object can be used to specify the database index to use with the Seek method. The Seek method enables you to perform a fast search for a value in an indexed column.

5

The following are other considerations about using the `Index` property and the `Seek` method:

- The recordset must use a server-side cursor (the recordset's `CursorLocation` property must be `adUseServer`), because the `Seek` method must have direct access to the values in the indexed column at the database (database = server-side).

- The `Seek` method can be used only when the `Recordset` object has been opened using the `CommandTypeEnum` value of `adCmdTableDirect`. This can be done, for example, as follows:
```
objRecordset.Open "Employees", conn, adOpenKeyset,
➥ adLockReadOnly, adCmdTableDirect
```

- The underlying provider must support the `Index` property and the `Seek` method of the `Recordset` object. You can use the `Index` property and the `Seek` method for instance on a recordset retrieved from an Access database when you use the OLE DB Provider for Microsoft Jet 4.0. If a certain provider does not support the `Seek` method, use the `Find` method to search for certain values in a recordset.

> **Tip**
>
> You can check whether the provider supports the `Index` property and the `Seek` method. Open the recordset, use the `Supports` method of the `Recordset` object with the parameters `adIndex` and `adSeek` (The variable `rs` holds the `Recordset` object):
> ```
> If rs.Supports(adIndex) Then
>     Debug.Print "Index property supported!"
> End If
> If rs.Supports(adSeek) Then
>     Debug.Print "Seek method supported!"
> End If
> ```

- To avoid side effects, the `Index` property should be set just after the recordset is opened. It also can be set before you open the recordset. For further information about this topic, refer to the ADO documentation.

Using the `Index` property and the `Seek` method is explained in detail in the following sections.

The `Index` Property

To use the `Index` property, set it to any index name of the table that is the source of the recordset. When you want to use the `Seek` method on a certain indexed column, you set the `Index` property to the name of that index as it is defined in the database table.

Caution The name of the index does not need to be the name of the indexed column, so you cannot expect the name of the index to be the same as the name of the column!

Assuming that you want to use the Seek method to search in the column named EmployeeID, and the index defined for the column is named PrimaryKey, you have to set the Index property to the value PrimaryKey:

```
rs.Index = "PrimaryKey"
```

In some databases (as in Microsoft Access 2000), you do not know the name of a certain index because the name is hidden behind a graphical interface. However, you can retrieve all indexes and the related columns of a table using the script in Listing 5.2.

LISTING 5.2   Retrieve Index Names and Related Columns

```
 1: Dim cat As Object, tbl As Object, idx As Object
 2: Dim idxCol As Object, conn As Object, strTbl As String
 3: ' Define Table Name
 4: strTbl = "Order Details"
 5:
 6: Set cat = CreateObject("ADOX.Catalog")
 7: Set tbl = CreateObject("ADOX.Table")
 8: Set idx = CreateObject("ADOX.Index")
 9: Set idxCol = CreateObject("ADOX.Column")
10: Set conn = CreateObject("ADODB.Connection")
11:
12: ' Open the database (catalog)
13: conn.Open "Provider=Microsoft.Jet.OLEDB.4.0;" & _
14:     "Data Source=J:\ADO25\Northwind\Northwind.mdb;" & _
15:     "user id=admin;password=;"
16:
17: Set cat.ActiveConnection = conn
18: Set tbl = cat.Tables(strTbl)
19:
20: 'Get all Index objects
21: For Each idx In tbl.Indexes
22:     Debug.Print
23:     Debug.Print "Index '" & idx.Name & "' contains the column(s):"
24:     For Each idxCol In idx.Columns
25:         Debug.Print idxCol
26:     Next
27: Next
28: conn.Close
29: Set conn = Nothing
30: Set cat = Nothing
```

5

The code in Listing 5.2 produces the following output for the table named Order Details of the Access 2000 Northwind database:

```
Index 'PrimaryKey' contains the column(s):
OrderID
ProductID

Index 'OrderID' contains the column(s):
OrderID

Index 'OrdersOrder Details' contains the column(s):
OrderID

Index 'ProductID' contains the column(s):
ProductID

Index 'ProductsOrder Details' contains the column(s):
ProductID
```

ANALYSIS The script uses some ADOX (ADO Extensions for DDL and Security; DDL is the shortcut for Data Definition Language) objects to retrieve the index properties of a database table. The use of ADOX is described in detail in Day 14, "Managing Your Database with ADOX."

Briefly, the script in Listing 5.2 does the following: The name of the used database table is defined in line 4 and stored in the variable strTbl. A connection to the database is opened in line 13. The database (or Catalog) is referenced using an ADOX Catalog object. The Table object (variable tbl) is taken from the Tables collection of the Catalog object. The For Each...Next statement in lines 21–27 loops through all Index objects from the Indexes collection of the Table object. Line 23 writes the name of the current Index to the user. The inner For Each...Next loop in lines 24–26 iterates over all Columns that are contained in the current Index and writes their names to the user (see the output of Listing 5.2).

After you know the name of the index related to a certain column, you can use the Index property and the Seek method to search in the index related to the column.

Searching with the Seek Method

After the Index property is set to the name of the table index, you can use the Seek method to search in the column(s) related to the index. When the Seek method finds a matching record, the recordset cursor is set to the matching record. However, when no record is found, the cursor is set to EOF. The syntax of the Seek method is as follows:

```
rs.Seek Array(ColumnValues)
```

The variable rs contains the recordset. Because an index consists of one or more columns, the term ColumnValues stands for the value(s) of the column(s). For instance, when the index with the name PrimaryKey is defined for the column EmployeeID, you can search for the value 7 in the EmployeeID column using the following statements:

```
rs.Index = "PrimaryKey"
rs.Seek Array(7)
```

However, when an index contains more than one column, you have to use the Seek method with an Array that contains the values of all columns that are contained in the index. For example, the Access Northwind table named Order Details has the index named PrimaryKey, which contains the columns OrderID and ProductID. When you want to search for the record with the OrderID 47 and the ProductID 11, use the following Seek statement:

```
rs.Index = "PrimaryKey"
rs.Seek Array(47, 11)
```

To Do: Using the Index Property and Seek Method

A simple recipe for using the Index property and the Seek method is as follows:

1. Create the Recordset and the Connection objects.

2. Open a connection to the database.

3. Do not use a client-side cursor for the recordset. Use a server-side cursor, which is the default cursor.

4. Open the table using the CommandTypeEnum value of adCmdTableDirect, for example:
   ```
   objRecordset.Open "Employees", conn, adOpenKeyset,
   ➥ adLockReadOnly, adCmdTableDirect
   ```

5. Check whether the provider supports the Index property and the Seek method using the Supports method of the recordset together with the arguments adIndex and adSeek.

6. Set the Index property of the recordset to the name of the index in which you want to search.

7. Search for a record using the Seek method.

8. When a record is found, the recordset cursor points to the record. When no matching record is found, the cursor points to EOF.

9. Search for the next matching record using the Seek method again.

▼ To Do

5

The recipe can be understood better when you study an example. Listing 5.3 illustrates the Index property and the Seek method in a Visual Basic script. It shows you the search operation for a certain value in the Employees table of the Access 2000 Northwind database.

LISTING 5.3 Sample for Using Index and Seek

```
 1: Dim conn As ADODB.Connection
 2: Dim rs As ADODB.Recordset
 3: Dim strSQL As String
 4: Dim strIndex As String
 5: Dim lngEmployeeID As Long
 6:
 7: lngEmployeeID = 7
 8:
 9: Set conn = CreateObject("ADODB.Connection")
10: conn.Open "Provider=Microsoft.Jet.OLEDB.4.0;" & _
11:        "Data Source=J:\ADO25\Northwind\Northwind.mdb;" & _
12:        "user id=admin;password=;"
13:
14: Set rs = CreateObject("ADODB.Recordset")
15: rs.CursorLocation = adUseServer
16: rs.Open "Employees", conn, adOpenKeyset,
➥ adLockReadOnly, adCmdTableDirect
17:
18: If rs.Supports(adIndex) = True And rs.Supports(adSeek) = True Then
19:     rs.Index = "Primarykey"
20:     Debug.Print "All records:"
21:     rs.MoveFirst
22:     Do While rs.EOF = False
23:         Debug.Print rs("EmployeeID") & ": " & _
24:             rs("FirstName") & " " & rs("LastName")
25:         rs.MoveNext
26:     Loop
27:     Debug.Print
28:     Debug.Print "Seek for Employee with EmployeeID = " & lngEmployeeID
29:     rs.MoveFirst
30:     rs.Seek Array(lngEmployeeID)
31:     If rs.EOF Then
32:         Debug.Print "No Employee found."
33:     Else
34:         Debug.Print rs("EmployeeID") & ": " & _
35:             rs("FirstName") & " " & rs("LastName")
36:     End If
37: End If
38: rs.Close
39: conn.Close
40: Set rs = Nothing
41: Set conn = Nothing
```

The example in Listing 5.3 provides the following output:

```
All records:
1: Nancy Davolio
2: Andrew Fuller
3: Janet Leverling
4: Margaret Peacock
5: Steven Buchanan
6: Michael Suyama
7: Robert King
8: Laura Callahan
9: Anne Dodsworth

Seek for Employee with EmployeeID = 7
7: Robert King
```

The table Employees of the Access 2000 Northwind database contains the index named PrimaryKey, which indexes the column EmployeeID. The script uses the Seek method on the index PrimaryKey to find a record with the EmployeeID 7. Line 7 defines the EmployeeID to seek for. The EmployeeID is stored in the variable lngEmployeeID. Then the script opens a connection to the Access database. A recordset (with a server-side cursor) is opened using the Open method with the CommandTypeEnum parameter set to adCmdTableDirect. In line 18, the script checks whether the recordset supports the use of the Index property and the Seek method. In line 19, the Index property is set to the name of the index, which is PrimaryKey. This is the index that contains the column EmployeeID. All employees of the Employees table are written to the user in lines 21–26. The Seek method is used in line 30 to search for the record that contains the EmployeeID, which was stored in the variable lngEmployeeID. When the record was not found, the recordset's EOF property returns TRUE and the text No Employee found. is written to the user. However, when the Seek method has found a record with the EmployeeID value 7, the recordset cursor points to this record and the record's values (EmployeeID, FirstName, and LastName) are written to the user.

5

Using the Seek method is possible only with special recordsets (that are opened using the Open method and the CommandTypeEnum parameter set to adCmdTableDirect). I recommend using the Seek method only when your application performs a major number of searches on an opened recordset. Otherwise, you should think about using the SQL SELECT statement to find a certain record in a database table.

Filtering Data in a Recordset

The Filter property of a recordset enables you to selectively screen out records that you do not need at the moment. The filtered recordset becomes the current recordset, and its properties—such as AbsolutePosition, AbsolutePage, RecordCount, or PageCount— are set to values according to the filtered recordset.

You can set the `Filter` property of a recordset to one of the following values:

- `FilterString`—A string of one or more clauses concatenated with `AND` or `OR` operators.
- Array of bookmarks—An array of unique bookmarks that point to certain records in the recordset.
- A so-called `FilterGroupEnum` value—These ADO constants specify certain groups of records. You can use them to view all records that have been changed but not been sent to the server, or you can view all records that could not be updated during the last batch update.

When the `Filter` property has been set, the recordset cursor is set to the first record in the recordset, or to `EOF` if no record is in the filtered recordset.

Apply a `FilterString` to a Recordset

The `Filter` property can be used similarly to the way you use the `WHERE` clause in a `SELECT` statement. Just apply the `FilterString` to the `Filter` property of the recordset to enforce the filter:

```
rs.Filter = "FilterString"
```

An example for a `FilterString` is

```
"(City LIKE 'A*') AND (Country = 'USA')"
```

There are some facts to consider when using a `FilterString`:

- The `FilterString` is made up of clauses in the form `"Fieldname Operator Value"` (for example: `"Country = 'USA'"`).
- The following `Operator`s are allowed: `=`, `<`, `>`, `<=`, `>=`, `LIKE`.
- The `FieldName` must be a valid field name contained in the recordset. When the field name contains spaces, you have to enclose the name with square brackets.
- The `Value` is a value to compare with the field value. Valid values are `'Bianca'`, `#7/24/76#`, `7.18`, `$891.73`. Surround strings with single quotes and surround dates with pound signs. For numbers, you can use decimal points, scientific notification, and dollar signs.
- When the `Operator` is `LIKE`, you can use wildcards, such as the asterisk (`*`) or the percent sign (`%`) in the `Value`. The wildcards must be uses at the last position in the `Value` string, as in `"Company LIKE 'Exotic*'"`. However, you can also use wildcards at the beginning and the end of the `Value`, as in `"Company LIKE '*monde*'"`.

- When a *Value* string contains a single quotation mark, you have to replace it with two single quotation marks. For example, to filter for a value as o'Conner, you should use a filter as "ContactName = 'o''Conner'".

- The *Value* cannot be NULL.

- When using AND or OR, there is no precedence between them. However, clauses can be grouped using parentheses. There is a limitation: You cannot group clauses joined with an OR and then join the grouped clause to another clause using an AND. For example, you cannot use the following:

  "(City = 'London' OR City = 'Madrid') AND (Name = 'Alex')"

  Instead, you have to use a clause such as

  "(City = 'London' AND Name = 'Alex') OR
  ➡ (City = 'Madrid' AND Name = 'Alex')"

- To remove the filter, you can set the FilterString to a zero-length string ("").

Listing 5.4 is an example, written in Visual Basic, that uses the SQL Server 7.0 Northwind sample database to demonstrate the use of a FilterString to filter a Recordset.

LISTING 5.4   Use the Filter Method with a FilterString

```
 1: Dim conn As ADODB.Connection
 2: Dim rs As ADODB.Recordset
 3: Dim strSQL As String
 4:
 5: Set conn = CreateObject("ADODB.Connection")
 6: conn.Open "Provider=SQLOLEDB;Data Source=BoyScout;" & _
 7:    "Initial Catalog=Northwind;User ID=sa;Password=;"
 8:
 9: strSQL = "SELECT * FROM Customers"
10: Set rs = CreateObject("ADODB.Recordset")
11: Set rs.ActiveConnection = conn
12: rs.CursorLocation = adUseServer
13: rs.CursorType = adOpenStatic
14:
15: rs.Open strSQL
16:
17: Debug.Print "records: " & rs.RecordCount
18:
19: rs.Filter = "(City LIKE 'A*') AND (Country = 'USA')"
20: Debug.Print "Filter is set."
21: Debug.Print "records: " & rs.RecordCount
```

5

continues

LISTING **5.4**   continued

```
22: While Not rs.EOF
23:     Debug.Print " " & rs("City")
24:     rs.MoveNext
25: Wend
26:
27: rs.Filter = ""
28: Debug.Print "Filter is removed."
29: Debug.Print "records: " & rs.RecordCount
30:
31: rs.Close
32: conn.Close
33: Set rs = Nothing
34: Set conn = Nothing
```

The code in Listing 5.4 should produce this output:

```
records: 92
Filter is set.
records: 2
 Anchorage
 Albuquerque
Filter is removed.
records: 92
```

ANALYSIS The script opens a connection to the SQL Server 7.0 Northwind database. The recordset to hold all data from the Orders table is prepared in lines 10–13 and opened in line 15. The recordset contains 92 records. However, after the filter is set in line 19, the number of records accessible in the recordset is only 2, as delivered from the RecordCount property of the Recordset object. The script loops through the two records that meet the FilterString in a While...Wend loop. In line 27, the filter is removed by assigning a zero-length string to the Filter property. Therefore, the RecordCount property returns again the value 92.

Using a FilterString is not the only way to use the Filter property. The next section describes how to use an array of bookmarks to filter a recordset.

Use an Array of Bookmarks to Filter a Recordset

Instead of using a FilterString you can use an array of bookmarks to filter a recordset (of course, the recordset must support bookmarks). Listing 5.5 shows two ways to use an array of bookmarks to filter a recordset.

LISTING 5.5 Use the `Filter` Method with an Array of Bookmarks

```
 1: Dim conn As ADODB.Connection, rs As ADODB.Recordset
 2: Dim strSQL As String, intI As Integer
 3: Dim arrBookmark() As Variant
 4:
 5: ReDim arrBookmark(10)
 6:
 7: Set conn = CreateObject("ADODB.Connection")
 8: conn.Open "Provider=SQLOLEDB;Data Source=BoyScout;" & _
 9:     "Initial Catalog=Northwind;User ID=sa;Password=;"
10:
11: strSQL = "SELECT * FROM Customers"
12: Set rs = CreateObject("ADODB.Recordset")
13: rs.Open strSQL, conn, adOpenStatic, adLockReadOnly
14:
15: Debug.Print "records: " & rs.RecordCount
16: ' Get some Bookmarks
17: intI = 0
18: While Not rs.EOF And intI <= 10
19:     arrBookmark(intI) = rs.Bookmark
20:     rs.MoveNext
21:     intI = intI + 1
22: Wend
23: ReDim Preserve arrBookmark(intI - 1)
24:
25: rs.Filter = arrBookmark
26: Debug.Print "Filter with all Bookmarks is set."
27: Debug.Print "records: " & rs.RecordCount
28:
29: If UBound(arrBookmark) >= 4 Then
30:     rs.Filter = Array(arrBookmark(4), arrBookmark(2))
31:     Debug.Print "Filter with 2 Bookmarks is set."
32:     Debug.Print "records: " & rs.RecordCount
33: End If
34:
35: rs.Filter = ""
36: Debug.Print "Filter is removed."
37: Debug.Print "records: " & rs.RecordCount
38:
39: rs.Close
40: conn.Close
41: Set rs = Nothing
42: Set conn = Nothing
```

The code in Listing 5.5 should produce this output:

OUTPUT

```
records: 92
Filter with all Bookmarks is set.
records: 11
Filter with 2 Bookmarks is set.
records: 2
Filter is removed.
records: 92
```

ANALYSIS The script opens a connection to the Northwind database. Then it opens a record-set that contains all 92 records from the Orders table. In lines 17–23, the script retrieves some bookmarks from the recordset and stores them in the dynamic array variable named `arrBookmark`. This array is used in line 25 to filter the recordset by assigning the array to the `Filter` property of the recordset.

> **Caution**
>
> When you assign an array to the `Filter` property, all elements of the array must contain valid bookmarks. When your array has ten elements (indexes 0 to 9 as arrays in Visual Basic are zero-based), all ten elements must contain bookmarks. Otherwise, ADO will return an error when you want to assign the array to the `Filter` property. When you do not know how many bookmarks your program has to store in an array, use a dynamic array and take care that it is resized so that all its elements contain bookmarks before you assign the array to the `Filter` property.

Eleven bookmarks are stored in the array `arrBookmark` (indexes 0 to 10), so the filtered Recordset contains 11 records. When the array `arrBookmark` contains more then 5 elements (indexes 0–4), the program assigns an array with two elements, `arrBookmark(4)` and `arrBookmark(2)`, to the `Filter` property. Therefore, the recordset's `RecordCount` property returns 2, and only the two records stored in the bookmarks of the array are visible in the recordset. Finally, the filter is removed by applying a zero-length string to the `Filter` property.

You have seen how to use a `FilterString` or an array of bookmarks to filter a recordset. The third method of applying a filter to a recordset is by using ADO constants to filter records with a certain state.

Filter Records with a Certain State

During a batch update or another bulk operation, every record is in a certain state. Some examples for record states are

- Record has been modified.
- Record is a new record.

- Record was not modified.

- Record was deleted.

The state of a record can be read from the Status property of the recordset. The following lines check whether the current record of the recordset named rs was modified:

```
If (rs.Status AND adRecModified) <> 0 Then
   Debug.Print "record was modified"
End If
```

You can use the Filter property of the recordset to filter all records with a certain state. You can apply a so-called FilterGroupEnum constant to filter for certain records (see Table 5.1).

TABLE 5.1 FilterGroupEnum Constants

Constant	Description
adFilterPendingRecords	Filters for records that have been changed but not sent to the database. Only applicable in batch update mode.
adFilterAffectedRecords	Filter for records that were affected by the last Delete, Resync, UpdateBatch or CancelBatch call.
adFilterConflictingRecords	Filters for records that failed the last batch update.
adFilterFetchedRecords	Filters for records in the current cache (the results of the last call to retrieve records from the database).
adFilterNone	Removes the current filter and allows to show all records.

Because it is easier to understand in an example how to use the Filter property with a FilterGroupEnum constant, Listing 5.6 provides an example to show the use of the Status property and the Filter property.

LISTING 5.6 Use the Filter Method with an ADO Constant

```
 1: Dim conn As ADODB.Connection, rs As ADODB.Recordset
 2: Dim strSQL As String, lngStatus As Long, strStatus As String
 3:
 4: Set conn = CreateObject("ADODB.Connection")
 5: conn.Open "Provider=SQLOLEDB;Data Source=BoyScout;" & _
 6:    "Initial Catalog=Northwind;User ID=sa;Password=;"
 7:
 8: strSQL = "SELECT * FROM Categories"
 9: Set rs = CreateObject("ADODB.Recordset")
10: rs.CursorLocation = adUseClient
```

continues

5

LISTING 5.6 continued

```
11: rs.Open strSQL, conn, adOpenStatic, adLockBatchOptimistic
12:
13: ' Change some records
14: While Not rs.EOF
15:     If rs("CategoryName") = "Confections" Then
16:         rs("Description").AppendChunk "Desserts, candies"
17:     End If
18:     If rs("CategoryName") = "Meat/Poultry" Then
19:         rs("CategoryName") = "Meat"
20:         rs("Description").AppendChunk "Prepared meats"
21:     End If
22:     rs.MoveNext
23: Wend
24:
25: ' Add new record
26: rs.AddNew
27: rs("CategoryName") = "Poultry"
28: rs("Description").AppendChunk "Chicken, turkey, duck"
29:
30: ' View Status of records
31: rs.MoveFirst
32: While Not rs.EOF
33:     lngStatus = rs.Status
34:     strStatus = ""
35:     If (lngStatus And adRecUnmodified) <> 0 Then
36:         strStatus = strStatus & "Unmodified "
37:     End If
38:     If (lngStatus And adRecModified) <> 0 Then
39:         strStatus = strStatus & "Modified "
40:     End If
41:     If (lngStatus And adRecNew) <> 0 Then
42:         strStatus = strStatus & "New "
43:     End If
44:     Debug.Print rs("CategoryName") & " - " & strStatus
45:     rs.MoveNext
46: Wend
47:
48: Debug.Print
49: ' Filter pending changes:
50: rs.Filter = adFilterPendingRecords
51: Debug.Print "Pending Changes: " & rs.RecordCount
52: While Not rs.EOF
53:     Debug.Print rs("CategoryName")
54:     rs.MoveNext
55: Wend
56:
57: ' Cancel Batch Update
58: rs.CancelBatch
```

```
59:
60: Debug.Print
61: ' Filter affected records:
62: rs.Filter = adFilterAffectedRecords
63: Debug.Print "Records affected by CancelBatch: " & rs.RecordCount
64: While Not rs.EOF
65:     If (rs.Status And adRecDBDeleted) <> 0 Then
66:         Debug.Print " -- - DELETED -- -- "
67:     Else
68:         Debug.Print rs("CategoryName")
69:     End If
70:     rs.MoveNext
71: Wend
72:
73: rs.Close
74: conn.Close
75: Set rs = Nothing
76: Set conn = Nothing
```

The example of Listing 5.6 should produce this output:

```
 1: Beverages - Unmodified
 2: Condiments - Unmodified
 3: Confections - Modified
 4: Dairy Products - Unmodified
 5: Grains/Cereals - Unmodified
 6: Meat - Modified
 7: Produce - Unmodified
 8: Seafood - Unmodified
 9: Poultry - New
10:
11: Pending Changes: 3
12: Confections
13: Meat
14: Poultry
15:
16: Records affected by CancelBatch: 3
17: Confections
18: Meat/Poultry
19:  -- - DELETED -- --
```

ANALYSIS The script in Listing 5.6 performs the following tasks: It prepares a client-side recordset with batch optimistic locking, so that it can be used in batch update mode. Then it retrieves a recordset from the Categories table, changes some of its records, adds a new record, and shows the status (modified, not modified, or new) of all records (lines 1–9 of the output).

5

Further, the script filters for all records that have been changed but not written to the database, by setting the `Filter` property to the ADO constant `adFilterPendingRecords`. The program writes all records from the filtered recordset to the user (lines 11–14 of the output). In line 58, the script performs the `CancelBatch` method to cancel any pending updates.

Setting the `Filter` property to the ADO constant `adFilterAffectedRecords` in line 62 filters all records that are affected by calling the `CancelBatch` method. Note that the resulting recordset contains three records, the two changed records and one record that was added in lines 26–28 and deleted from the recordset by calling the `CancelBatch` method in line 58 (see output lines 16–19).

Using the `Status` property or the `Filter` property together with the `FilterGroupEnum` constants requires more knowledge and experience than today's lesson can impart. However, when you need, for example, to find out which records could not be updated during the call of the `UpdateBatch` method, it is useful to filter all records that failed during the last update and check their status using the `Status` property.

Today, you have seen how to search for certain records and how to apply a filter to a recordset. Sometimes it is necessary to sort a recordset—this is the topic of the next section.

Sorting Data in a Recordset

Similar to using the `ORDER BY` clause in a `SELECT` statement, you can sort a recordset using the `Sort` property of the `Recordset` object. The `Sort` property enables you to sort by one or more fields, ascending or descending.

To sort a recordset, just apply a string to the `Sort` property that contains the name of the field(s) and optionally the keyword `ASC` (for ascending) or `DESC` (for descending). When you want to sort the recordset using two or more fields, separate them with commas. Some examples for using the `Sort` property with a recordset named `rs` are as follows:

```
rs.Sort = "Lastname"
```

```
rs.Sort = "Lastname ASC, HireDate DESC"
```

```
rs.Sort = "Lastname, Firstname, BirthDate, City"
```

However, you must consider the following facts to use the `Sort` property:

- The recordset must use a client-side cursor.
- You cannot use a recordset with a field named ASC or DESC. If you want to retrieve a field with such a name, use aliases:
  ```
  SELECT Desc AS AliasDesc FROM Table
  ```

- Do not apply a filter (using the Filter property) to your recordset when you want to sort it using the Sort property. ADO does not sort a recordset as long as a filter is applied.

Listing 5.7 retrieves all employees from the Employees table (Northwind database) and sorts them ascending by the last name and first name.

LISTING 5.7 Sort a Recordset using the Sort Property

```
 1: Dim conn As ADODB.Connection, rs As ADODB.Recordset
 2: Dim strSQL As String
 3:
 4: Set conn = CreateObject("ADODB.Connection")
 5: conn.Open "Provider=SQLOLEDB;Data Source=BoyScout;" & _
 6:    "Initial Catalog=Northwind;User ID=sa;Password=;"
 7:
 8: strSQL = "SELECT FirstName, LastName, City FROM Employees"
 9: Set rs = CreateObject("ADODB.Recordset")
10: rs.CursorLocation = adUseClient
11: rs.Open strSQL, conn, adOpenStatic, adLockReadOnly
12:
13: ' Sort the Recordset
14: rs.Sort = "LastName, FirstName"
15:
16: While Not rs.EOF
17:    Debug.Print rs("LastName") & " " & rs("FirstName") & _
18:       " (" & rs("City") & ")"
19:    rs.MoveNext
20: Wend
21:
22: rs.Close
23: conn.Close
24: Set rs = Nothing
25: Set conn = Nothing
```

5

Listing 5.7 should produce the following output:

```
Buchanan Steven (London)
Callahan Laura (Seattle)
Davolio Nancy (Seattle)
Dodsworth Anne (London)
Fuller Andrew (Tacoma)
King Robert (London)
Leverling Janet (Kirkland)
Peacock Margaret (Redmond)
Suyama Michael (London)
```

ANALYSIS A recordset with a client-side cursor is prepared and populated with all employees from the Employees table. Then the recordset is sorted in line 14 using the following statement:

```
rs.Sort = "LastName, FirstName"
```

This statement sorts all records of the recordset by the values in the fields LastName and FirstName. The sorted recordset is written to the user in lines 16–20 using a While...Wend loop (see the output of Listing 5.7).

When you want to obtain a sorted recordset, it is often better to use the ORDER BY clause in a SELECT statement than to sort the recordset using the Sort property. When you use the ORDER BY clause, you can use a server-side recordset, which consumes less client resources but more database resources.

Summary

This day was about how to use certain recordset properties and methods to find data, to sort data, or to filter data in a Recordset. The knowledge you gained today is considered advanced because you can write database application without it, but with this knowledge you have the ability to choose between different techniques to write your application more efficiently. It is also important to know these techniques to be able to understand and use someone else's source code.

Today's topics are not used as often as the basic ADO tasks. However, you should know them, because one day you will need to sort or to filter a recordset in your application to avoid round-trips and customize your application straight to your needs.

The following quiz is quite difficult, and it is no shame not to know all the answers. The questions will remind you about the traps you can walk into. So take it with humor.

Q&A

Q Is there a general rule when to use a SELECT statement with a WHERE clause or the Find method of the Recordset object?

A Generally, it is better to use the Find method on tables with fewer records. Using the SELECT statement becomes more efficient the more records are stored in the table, especially when you search for values in indexed columns.

Q My application uses a recordset in UpdateBatch mode. Can I filter the recordset using the Filter property together with a FilterGroupEnum constant and a FilterString at the same time to filter all records that were effected by the last UpdateBatch call and contain a certain value?

A No, it is only possible to apply a `FilterGroupEnum` constant or a `FilterString` to the `Filter` property of a recordset. When you first apply a `FilterGroupEnum` constant and then apply a `FilterString`, the recordset is filtered using only the `FilterString`. A possible solution is to apply the `FilterGroupEnum` constant and then iterate over the resulting recordset to find all records that match the `FilterString`.

Workshop

The quiz questions and exercises are provided for your further understanding. See Appendix A, "Answers," for the answers.

Quiz

1. Which of the following search strings cannot be used as an argument for the `Find` method of the recordset?

   ```
   1: "Product = 'Server"
   2: "UserID >= 7"
   3: "Weight < 140"
   4: "ShippingDate = 9/30/1997"
   5: "FirstName like '*ith'"
   6: "LastName like 'Wil*'"
   7: "Title = 'Good Morning Vietnam'"
   ```

2. When you apply a filter string to the `Filter` property of the `Recordset` object, which one of the following filter strings is invalid?

   ```
   1: "LastName = 'o'Conner'"
   2: "FirstName = '*imson*'"
   3: "Title like 'Teach yourself *'"
   4: "(Age = 7 OR Age = 28) AND (Name = 'Chris')"
   5: "LastName like 'Hom*'"
   6: "City > 'Springf'"
   ```

3. You want to use an Array of bookmarks in conjunction with the `Filter` property of the `Recordset` object. The array named `arrA` is defined as a static Visual Basic array with a statement as follows:

   ```
   Dim arrA(20)
   ```

   Assuming that all elements with the array indexes 1–19 contain valid bookmarks, what can you do to filter your recordset using the array named `arrA`?

4. You are using the following lines of code in an application to populate a recordset named `rs`. Then you want to use the `Sort` property to sort the retrieved recordset. However, using the `Sort` property results in an error. Please correct the code so that it is possible to use the `Sort` method:

```
1: strSQL = "SELECT FirstName, LastName, City FROM Employees"
2: Set rs = CreateObject("ADODB.Recordset")
3: rs.CursorLocation = adUseClient
4: rs.LockType = adLockReadOnly
5: rs.CursorType = adOpenStatic
6: Set rs = conn.Execute(strSQL)
7:
8: ' Sorting the Recordset fails ...
9: rs.Sort = "LastName"
```

Exercise

Write a script that retrieves a recordset with all records from the Employees table of the SQL Server 7.0 Northwind sample database. Let the script filter the recordset using the Filter property with a Filterstring. The filtered recordset should contain all records with a value such as Sales* in the Title column. Then find the first record that contains the value King in the LastName field of the record. Write the values of the following columns of the matching record to the user: Title, LastName, FirstName.

DAY **6**

Working with Large Recordsets

When an application has to work with large recordsets or large database tables, effective navigation is more important than when dealing with small recordsets. It is also important, when dealing with large resultsets, to let users page through a large resultset—especially when used in Web server applications.

NEW TERM *Paging* through a recordset describes the technique in which you present only a certain number of records at once to the user and allow him or her to navigate through the recordset page-by-page.

In an Internet application, this saves Web server and database resources, because only a limited number of records are read at once and sent to the user.

Today, you learn the following:

- To navigate through a recordset using different recordset methods and properties
- Some paging techniques to present a recordset, part by part, to the user

Navigating in a Large Recordset

An application handling a large recordset needs to navigate through the recordset to gain quick access to requested data or to find certain records fast.

The `Recordset` object provides different properties and methods to navigate through it. You can navigate forward and backward, record-by-record, using the `MoveNext` and `MovePrevious` method. You can jump to the beginning and the end of the recordset using the `MoveFirst` and `MoveLast` method. The `Move` method enables you to move the recordset cursor to a record relative to the current record. The current position of the recordset cursor can be retrieved from the `AbsolutePosition` property, which delivers the ordinal number of the current recordset beginning at 1. You also can jump directly to a record by setting the `AbsolutePosition` property to the ordinal number of the record in the recordset.

Caution

When you sort a recordset using the `Sort` property, filter it, or delete and add records to the recordset, the ordinal number of a record changes. After one of these actions has occurred, the record with `AbsolutePosition` 12 might not still be at that position. When you use a cursor type other than static, it is also possible that the records shift when a record is added or deleted in the underlying database table.

Tip

When you want to store the position of a certain record to find it faster in a large recordset, use the `Bookmark` property to retrieve and set the position of the record, as described later in this section.

Another technique, which is very useful when paging through a recordset, enables you to define a recordset page that contains a certain number of records. You can jump to a certain page by specifying the number of the page and then read all records from the recordset page. You can define the number of records on a recordset page by assigning a value for the `PageSize` property (the default value is 10 records per page). Jump to a certain recordset page by specifying the page number using the `AbsolutePage` property.

Caution

You cannot be sure that a certain record remains on a certain page, because records can be added to or deleted from the recordset. Also, actions such as sorting, filtering, or updating a recordset can mix up the order of the records in the recordset and therefore move records from one page to another.

The size of the recordset can be read from two recordset properties: The `RecordCount` property returns the current number of records in the recordset and the `PageCount` property returns the current number of pages in which the recordset is divided.

For example, when you have a recordset with 32 records and a recordset page consists of 10 records, the recordset is divided into 4 pages:

Page 1—Records 1–10

Page 2—Records 11–20

Page 3—Records 21–30

Page 4—Records 31–32

All pages contain 10 records, with the exception of the last page, which can contain between 1 and 10 record(s).

When you navigate through a recordset, the recordset cursor might move beyond the last record or before the first record. The recordset properties `BOF`, `EOF`, `AbsolutePosition`, and `AbsolutePage` return status values that indicate where the recordset cursor points.

It is easier to rate the use of the various navigation techniques when they are presented in a sample code so you can easily understand how to use them in your application code. First, a sample demonstrates navigation that makes use of the various `Move` methods.

Listing 6.1 retrieves a recordset and performs various navigation actions on it. It demonstrates the use of the `RecordCount` and `PageCount` properties of the recordset to get information about the size of the recordset. Then it shows how to use the `AbsolutePosition` property to find the ordinal number of the current record. The script moves the recordset cursor by using the `MovePrevious`, `MoveNext`, `MoveLast`, and `MoveFirst` methods. The script also moves the cursor to a certain ordinal position using the `AbsolutePosition` property. Furthermore, the script provides an idea of how to use the `AbsolutePage` and `PageSize` properties. These properties are useful when you want to present only a part (a page) of the recordset to the user.

6

LISTING 6.1 Navigation in a Recordset

```
1: Dim conn As ADODB.Connection
2: Dim rs As ADODB.Recordset
3: Dim strSQL As String
4: Dim lngPageSize As Long
5: Dim lngCount As Long
```

continues

LISTING 6.1   continued

```
 6:
 7: Set conn = CreateObject("ADODB.Connection")
 8: conn.Open "Provider=SQLOLEDB;Data Source=BoyScout;" & _
 9:     "Initial Catalog=Northwind;User ID=sa;Password=;"
10:
11: Set rs = CreateObject("ADODB.Recordset")
12: strSQL = "SELECT ProductID, ProductName, SupplierID, CategoryID, " & _
13:     "QuantityPerUnit, UnitPrice, UnitsInStock, UnitsOnOrder, " & _
14:     "ReorderLevel, Discontinued FROM Products ORDER BY ProductID"
15:
16: rs.CursorLocation = adUseServer
17: rs.CursorType = adOpenStatic
18: rs.LockType = adLockReadOnly
19: rs.PageSize = 10
20:
21: Set rs.ActiveConnection = conn
22: rs.Open strSQL
23:
24: Debug.Print "Number of records in recordset: " & rs.RecordCount
25: Debug.Print "Number of pages (with " & rs.PageSize & _
26:     " records per page): " & rs.PageCount
27: Debug.Print
28:
29: Debug.Print "Cursor points to first record:"
30: Debug.Print "Cursor position: " & rs.AbsolutePosition
31: Debug.Print "Cursor on page number: " & rs.AbsolutePage
32: Debug.Print
33:
34: Debug.Print "Cursor moves one position backward:"
35: rs.MovePrevious
36:
37: Select Case rs.AbsolutePosition
38:   Case -1
39:     Debug.Print "Cursor Position: (unknown)"
40:     Debug.Print "Cursor on page number: (unknown)"
41:   Case -2
42:     Debug.Print "Cursor Position: (BOF)"
43:     Debug.Print "Cursor on page number: (BOF)"
44:   Case -3
45:     Debug.Print "Cursor Position: (EOF)"
46:     Debug.Print "Cursor on page number: (EOF)"
47:   Case Else
48:     Debug.Print "Cursor position: " & rs.AbsolutePosition
49:     Debug.Print "Cursor on page number: " & rs.AbsolutePage
50: End Select
51: Debug.Print
52:
53: Debug.Print "Cursor moves to last record:"
54: rs.MoveLast
```

```
55: Debug.Print "Cursor position: " & rs.AbsolutePosition
56: Debug.Print "Cursor on page number: " & rs.AbsolutePage
57: Debug.Print
58:
59: Debug.Print "Cursor moves one record forward:"
60: rs.MoveNext
61: Select Case rs.AbsolutePosition
62:   Case -1
63:     Debug.Print "Cursor Position: (unknown)"
64:     Debug.Print "Cursor on page number: (unknown)"
65:   Case -2
66:     Debug.Print "Cursor Position: (BOF)"
67:     Debug.Print "Cursor on page number: (BOF)"
68:   Case -3
69:     Debug.Print "Cursor Position: (EOF)"
70:     Debug.Print "Cursor on page number: (EOF)"
71:   Case Else
72:     Debug.Print "Cursor position: " & rs.AbsolutePosition
73:     Debug.Print "Cursor on page number: " & rs.AbsolutePage
74: End Select
75: Debug.Print
76:
77: Debug.Print "Jump to record position 14:"
78: rs.AbsolutePosition = 14
79: Debug.Print "Cursor position: " & rs.AbsolutePosition
80: Debug.Print "Cursor on page number: " & rs.AbsolutePage
81: Debug.Print
82:
83: Debug.Print "Show all records from page 3:"
84: rs.AbsolutePage = 3
85: lngPageSize = rs.PageSize
86: lngCount = 1
87:
88: Debug.Print "Absolute", "Position", "Page", "Name"
89: Debug.Print "Position", "on Page"
90: While (Not rs.EOF) And (lngCount <= lngPageSize)
91:     Debug.Print rs.AbsolutePosition, lngCount,
➥rs. AbsolutePage, rs("ProductName")
92:     ' Position on Page = AbsolutePosition - (PageSize*(AbsolutePage-1))
93:     rs.MoveNext
94:     lngCount = lngCount + 1
95: Wend
96:
97: rs.Close
98: Set rs = Nothing
99: conn.Close
100: Set conn = Nothing
```

6

OUTPUT The code in Listing 6.1 should produce this output:

```
 1: Number of records in recordset: 75
 2: Number of pages (with 10 records per page): 8
 3:
 4: Cursor points to first record:
 5: Cursor position: 1
 6: Cursor on page number: 1
 7:
 8: Cursor moves one position backward:
 9: Cursor Position: (BOF)
10: Cursor on page number: (BOF)
11:
12: Cursor moves to last record:
13: Cursor position: 75
14: Cursor on page number: 8
15:
16: Cursor moves one record forward:
17: Cursor Position: (EOF)
18: Cursor on page number: (EOF)
19:
20: Jump to record position 14:
21: Cursor position: 14
22: Cursor on page number: 2
23:
24: Show all records from page 3:
25: Absolute       Position      Page        Name
26: Position       on Page
27: 21             1             3           Sir Rodney's Scones
28: 22             2             3           Gustaf's Knäckebröd
29: 23             3             3           Tunnbröd
30: 24             4             3           Guaraná Fantástica
31: 25             5             3           NuNuCa Nuß-Nougat-Creme
32: 26             6             3           Gumbär Gummibärchen
33: 27             7             3           Schoggi Schokolade
34: 28             8             3           Rössle Sauerkraut
35: 29             9             3           Thüringer Rostbratwurst
36: 30             10            3           Nord-Ost Matjeshering
```

ANALYSIS The script prepares a static recordset using a page size of 10 records. All records from the Northwind database table Products are fetched and written into the recordset, which is stored in the variable rs.

The number of records and the number of pages in the recordset are written to the user in lines 24–26 (output lines 1 and 2). The number of records is retrieved from the RecordCount property, whereas the number of pages in the recordset is retrieved from the PageCount property of the recordset. The current position of the recordset cursor is received from the properties AbsolutePosition and AbsolutePage in lines 30 and 31.

`AbsolutePosition` returns the ordinal number of the current records and `AbsolutePage` the ordinal number of the current page. Both values are 1 because the cursor points to the first record of the recordset, which is, of course, on the first page of the recordset (output lines 4–6).

The recordset cursor is moved one record back in line 35 using the `MovePrevious` method. Therefore, the current cursor position is before the first record. This fact can be verified with the `BOF` property.

Next, the script retrieves the value of the `AbsolutePosition`. Normally, the `AbsolutePosition` property returns the ordinal position of the recordset cursor. However, when the cursor points before the first record, the returned value is `-2` (`adPosBOF`). Also, when the cursor's position is beyond the last record, the `AbsolutePosition` property returns `-3` (`adPosEOF`). The `AbsolutePage` property returns the ordinal number of the current page or a position value if the cursor points to `BOF` or `EOF`.

Therefore, the script returns `BOF` as the position of the recordset cursor in lines 37–50 (output lines 8–10) because the script moved from the first record one record backward.

When the cursor moves to the last record, using the `MoveLast` method, the `AbsolutePosition` returns the number of the last record, and `AbsolutePage` provides the number of the last page (output lines 12–14).

As the cursor moves one position forward, it moves beyond the last record. This is indicated by the `AbsolutePosition` property; it returns `-3` (`adPosEOF`). The `EOF` property of the recordset returns `True` in this case, of course. The `AbsolutePosition` and `AbsolutePage` is written to the user (output lines 16–18).

It is possible to move the cursor to a certain record by assigning a value to the `AbsolutePosition` property. In line 78, the script jumps to the record with the current ordinal number 14. The `AbsolutePosition` returns 14, and the `AbsolutePage` property returns 2 (output lines 20–22).

Similarly, you can move the recordset cursor to the beginning of a certain recordset page by assigning a value to the `AbsolutePage` property, as in line 84 of the script.

The script moves the recordset cursor to page 3 and writes all records of the page to the user in lines 88–95. The counter variable `lngCount` indicates the current cursor position on the page. The `While...Wend` loop in lines 90–95 loops through all records of the recordset page until the end of the recordset is reached or the last record of the current page is written to the user. The loop code writes the absolute position, the position on the page, the page number, and the ProductName of each record to the user.

6

The ordinal number of a record on a certain page can be calculated using a counter variable as in the script, or you can calculate the position of the page using the following formula:

```
Position on Page = rs.AbsolutePosition - (rs.PageSize*(rs.AbsolutePage-1))
```

Finally, the script frees the recordset and connection resources.

The script in Listing 6.1 moved the cursor to a certain record using the `AbsolutePosition` or `AbsolutePage` properties. However, when the recordset is filtered or sorted, or records are added and deleted, records change their position in the recordset. How can you store the position of a record in the recordset so that you can jump to this particular record, no matter where it currently resides in the recordset? You can use the `Bookmark` property of the `Recordset` object to store the unique identifier of a certain record in a variable and later jump to that particular record, even if the recordset was sorted or filtered.

> Bookmarks are available only in keyset and static recordsets. You can check whether a recordset supports bookmarks using the `Supports` function:
>
>   blnSupportsBookmarks = *rs*.Supports(adBookmark)
>
> The variable `rs` represents an instance of the `Recordset` object.
>
> When you use a database table with a primary key column for the recordset, in most cases bookmarks are supported when the database provider has the capability of supporting bookmarks.

The script in Listing 6.2 demonstrates the use of the `Bookmark` property for navigation purposes. Use the `Bookmark` property to retrieve and store the position of a record in a variable (of type `Variant`). When assigning the variable value to the `Bookmark` property of the same recordset, the cursor position is set to the record where the bookmark was retrieved.

LISTING 6.2   Using the `Bookmark` Property

```
1: Dim conn As ADODB.Connection
2: Dim rs As ADODB.Recordset
3: Dim strSQL As String
4: Dim lngPageSize As Long
5: Dim lngCount As Long
6: Dim varBookmark50 As Variant
7: Dim blnFound50 As Boolean
8: Dim varBookmarkIkura As Variant
```

```
 9: Dim blnFoundIkura As Boolean
10:
11: Set conn = CreateObject("ADODB.Connection")
12: conn.Open "Provider=SQLOLEDB;Data Source=BoyScout;" & _
13:     "Initial Catalog=Northwind;User ID=sa;Password=;"
14:
15: Set rs = CreateObject("ADODB.Recordset")
16: strSQL = "SELECT ProductID, ProductName, SupplierID, CategoryID, " & _
17:     "QuantityPerUnit, UnitPrice, UnitsInStock, UnitsOnOrder, " & _
18:     "ReorderLevel, Discontinued FROM Products ORDER BY ProductID"
19:
20: rs.CursorLocation = adUseClient
21: rs.CursorType = adOpenStatic
22: rs.LockType = adLockReadOnly
23: rs.PageSize = 10
24:
25: Set rs.ActiveConnection = conn
26: rs.Open strSQL
27:
28: rs.Find "ProductID = 50"
29: If Not rs.EOF Then
30:     varBookmark50 = rs.Bookmark
31:     blnFound50 = True
32:     Debug.Print "Bookmark for ProductID = 50 stored."
33: Else
34:     Debug.Print "Bookmark for ProductID = 50 not found."
35: End If
36:
37: rs.MoveFirst
38: rs.Find "ProductName = 'Ikura'"
39: If Not rs.EOF Then
40:     varBookmarkIkura = rs.Bookmark
41:     blnFoundIkura = True
42:     Debug.Print "Bookmark for ProductName = 'Ikura' stored."
43: Else
44:     Debug.Print "Bookmark for ProductName = 'Ikura' not found."
45: End If
46: Debug.Print
47:
48: If blnFound50 = True Then
49:     Debug.Print "Set cursor to record with ProductID = 50:"
50:     rs.Bookmark = varBookmark50
51:     If Not (rs.AbsolutePosition < 0) Then
52:         Debug.Print "ProductID = " & rs("ProductID")
53:         Debug.Print "ProductName = " & rs("ProductName")
54:     Else
55:         Debug.Print "Record not in current recordset."
56:     End If
57:     Debug.Print
```

6

continues

LISTING 6.2   continued

```
58: End If
59:
60: If blnFoundIkura = True Then
61:     Debug.Print "Set cursor to record with ProductName = 'Ikura':"
62:     rs.Bookmark = varBookmarkIkura
63:     If Not (rs.AbsolutePosition < 0) Then
64:         Debug.Print "ProductID = " & rs("ProductID")
65:         Debug.Print "ProductName = " & rs("ProductName")
66:     Else
67:         Debug.Print "Record not in current recordset."
68:     End If
69:     Debug.Print
70: End If
71:
72: rs.Filter = "ProductID < 14"
73: rs.Sort = "ProductID DESC"
74: Debug.Print "Recordset is filtered for ProductID < 14."
75: Debug.Print "Recordset is sorted ascending by the ProductID."
76: Debug.Print
77:
78: If blnFound50 = True Then
79:     Debug.Print "Set cursor to bookmark varBookmark50:"
80:     rs.Bookmark = varBookmark50
81:     Debug.Print "Current absolute position of record = " & _
82:         rs.AbsolutePosition
83:     Debug.Print "ProductID = " & rs("ProductID")
84:     Debug.Print "ProductName = " & rs("ProductName")
85:     Debug.Print
86: End If
87:
88: If blnFoundIkura = True Then
89:     Debug.Print "Set cursor to bookmark varBookmarkIkura:"
90:     rs.Bookmark = varBookmarkIkura
91:     Debug.Print "Current absolute position of record = " & _
92:         rs.AbsolutePosition
93:     Debug.Print "ProductID = " & rs("ProductID")
94:     Debug.Print "ProductName = " & rs("ProductName")
95:     Debug.Print
96: End If
97:
98: If blnFoundIkura = True And blnFoundIkura = True Then
99:     Debug.Print "Compare Bookmarks: "
100:
101:     Select Case rs.CompareBookmarks(varBookmark50, varBookmarkIkura)
102:         Case adCompareEqual
103:             Debug.Print "Both Bookmarks are equal."
104:         Case adCompareGreaterThan
105:             Debug.Print "Bookmark 50 comes after Bookmark 'Ikura'."
106:         Case adCompareLessThan
```

```
107:              Debug.Print "Bookmark 50 comes before Bookmark 'Ikura'."
108:          Case adCompareNotComparable
109:              Debug.Print "Bookmarks cannot be compared."
110:          Case adCompareNotEqual
111:              Debug.Print "Bookmarks are not equal and not ordered."
112:      End Select
113: End If
114:
115: rs.Close
116: Set rs = Nothing
117: conn.Close
118: Set conn = Nothing
```

OUTPUT   The code in Listing 6.2 should produce this output:

```
 1: Bookmark for ProductID = 50 stored.
 2: Bookmark for ProductName = 'Ikura' stored.
 3:
 4: Set cursor to record with ProductID = 50:
 5: ProductID = 50
 6: ProductName = Valkoinen suklaa
 7:
 8: Set cursor to record with ProductName = 'Ikura':
 9: ProductID = 10
10: ProductName = Ikura
11:
12: Recordset is filtered for ProductID < 14.
13: Recordset is sorted ascending by the ProductID.
14:
15: Set cursor to bookmark varBookmark50:
16: Current absolute position of record = 1
17: ProductID = 13
18: ProductName = Konbu
19:
20: Set cursor to bookmark varBookmarkIkura:
21: Current absolute position of record = 4
22: ProductID = 10
23: PruductName = Ikura
24:
25: Compare Bookmarks:
26: Bookmarks cannot be compared.
```

6

ANALYSIS   The script declares the two variables varBookmark50 and varBookmarkIkura as data type Variant in lines 6 and 8. Every variable that is used to store a recordset bookmark must be declared as Variant. The variables blnFound50 and blnFoundIkura are declared as Boolean and indicate whether the variables varBookmark50 and varBookmarkIkura actually contain valid bookmarks.

In lines 11–26, a static recordset that contains all records of the Products table is opened. Its page size is set to 10 records per page.

The first bookmark, which is stored in the variable varBookmark50, should refer to the record with the ProductID = 50. Therefore, the script uses the Find method in line 28 to search for the record and set the recordset cursor to its position. When the record is not found, the cursor is set to EOF. The bookmark of the record with the ProductID = 50 is retrieved from the current cursor position using the Bookmark property and stored in the variable varBookmark50 in line 30. At the same time, the variable blnFound50 is set to True to indicate that the variable varBookmark50 contains a valid bookmark. The script also indicates this circumstance and writes a message to the user (output line 1).

In lines 37–45, the script searches for the record with the ProductName = Ikura and stores its bookmark in the variable varBookmarkIkura (output line 2).

To jump to a record that belongs to a stored bookmark, you just have to assign the stored bookmark to the Bookmark property of the recordset. The script sets the recordset cursor to the record with the ProductID = 50 by assigning the value of the variable varBookmark50 to the bookmark property of the recordset in line 50. To prove that the cursor points to the correct record, the ProductID and the ProductName of the record are written to the user (output lines 4–6).

The same procedure is done with the record that contains the ProductName Ikura in lines 60–70 using the bookmark stored in varBookmarkIkura.

Caution

When you use a bookmark of a record that has been deleted, the recordset cursor points to the next record after the referred (but deleted) record.

If you assign a variable that does not contain a valid bookmark to the Bookmark property, you get a runtime error (with the error number 3001 in Visual Basic).

Tip

When using bookmarks to find certain records fast in a recordset, it is a good idea to check whether the found record is really the record stored in the bookmark. You can store the primary key value additional to the record's bookmark and compare it with the found record's primary key value to prove this.

Bookmarks are especially useful when you sort or filter your recordset. You still can use them to find certain records, no matter where they are located in the recordset.

Caution

> If you filter a recordset using the `Filter` property, it is possible that the record to which your stored bookmark refers is not visible any more in the recordset. When you assign the bookmark of an invisible record to a filtered recordset, the recordset's cursor is set to another record or to EOF. Strictly speaking, the recordset cursor is set to the next visible record after the record that is referred to in the bookmark value.

To demonstrate the effect of using bookmarks with a filtered and sorted recordset, the script sorts recordset ascending by the ProductID in lines 72 and 73. In the resulting recordset, only records with a `ProductID` less than 14 are visible, and the records are ordered descending by the ProductID. So the record with the `ProductID = 50` is not visible in the current recordset. When the script assigns the bookmark stored in the variable `varBookmark50` to the `Bookmark` property of the recordset, the recordset cursor is set to the next visible record that follows after the record referred to in the bookmark. Consider that all records are ordered descending by the ProductID due to the recordset sorting defined in line 73 (`rs.Sort = "ProductID DESC"`). Therefore, the cursor is set to the record with the `ProductID = 13`, which is the first visible record in the recordset (see the `AbsolutePosition` property) and at the same time the first visible record after the record with the `ProductID = 50` (output lines 15–18).

In contrast to the record with the `ProductID = 50`, the record with the `ProductName = Ikura` is still visible in the filtered recordset because its ProductID is 10 and therefore lower than 14. As the script assigns the bookmark from `varBookmarkIkura` to the `Bookmark` property in line 90, the recordset cursor points to the expected record, which is the record with the `ProductName = Ikura` and `ProductID = 10` (output lines 20–23).

Lines 98–113 of the script demonstrate the use of the Recordset object's method `CompareBookmarks`. This method enables you to determine how two given bookmarks are located relative to each other in the current recordset, which can be filtered and sorted. The bookmark stored in `varBookmark50` is not visible in the current recordset, so `CompareBookmarks` returns the value `adCompareNotComparable` to indicate that the two bookmarks, `varBookmark50` and `varBookmarkIkura`, cannot be compared in the current recordset (output lines 25–26).

When you remove the filter of the recordset, the call of the method

```
CompareBookmarks(varBookmark50, varBookmarkIkura)
```

returns the value `adCompareLessThan` to indicate that in the current recordset the record with the bookmark `varBookmark50` comes before the records with the bookmark `varBookmarkIkura` (because the recordset is sorted descending).

6

The script in Listing 6.2 provides an overview about how to use bookmarks to find certain records again, even if the recordset is sorted or filtered.

For your information, bookmarks are also used in other scenarios:

- You can use bookmarks as starting positions for the Find method to locate certain records.
- The Filter property can be set to an array of bookmarks to specify the filtered recordset.
- In the Move method, you can use a bookmark as starting position.

Paging Through a Large Resultset

When a user requests tabular information that comprises some hundred records, it can be useful to send only a limited number of records (a page) to the user. The user can decide whether he wants to see the following or previous records.

The paging technique enables you to present a large resultset in a clearly arranged way. It also saves database server resources, because only a limited number of records are fetched at once. When using paging in a Web application that serves large database resultsets, you can limit Web server load because you send a large resultset piece-by-piece to the user.

Paging Static Resultsets

When you have database content that rarely changes, you can use a simple paging technique that is based on the built-in paging features of the Recordset object. The Recordset object provides the PageSize and the AbsolutePage properties so that you can define the number of records on a page and jump directly to the first record of a certain page of the recordset.

The script in Listing 6.3 shows a possible paging scenario, wherein the user can choose how many records are shown on each page, and then page forward and backward through the resultset.

LISTING 6.3   Simple Paging Through a Resultset

```
1: Dim conn As ADODB.Connection
2: Dim rs As ADODB.Recordset
3: Dim strSQL As String
4: ' Variables for paging:
5: Dim lngCount As Long
6: Dim lngCurrentPage As Long
```

```
 7: Dim strInput As String
 8: Dim lngInput As Long
 9: Dim strPaging As String
10: Dim blnInputOK As Boolean
11: Dim blnPaging As Boolean
12:
13: Set conn = CreateObject("ADODB.Connection")
14: conn.Open "Provider=SQLOLEDB;Data Source=BoyScout;" & _
15:     "Initial Catalog=Northwind;User ID=sa;Password=;"
16:
17: Set rs = CreateObject("ADODB.Recordset")
18: strSQL = "SELECT ProductID, ProductName, SupplierID, CategoryID, " & _
19:     "QuantityPerUnit, UnitPrice, UnitsInStock, UnitsOnOrder, " & _
20:     "ReorderLevel, Discontinued FROM Products ORDER BY ProductID"
21:
22: rs.CursorLocation = adUseServer
23: rs.CursorType = adOpenStatic
24: rs.LockType = adLockReadOnly
25: rs.PageSize = 10      ' = default value
26: rs.CacheSize = 11     ' = rs.PageSize + 1 for better performance
27:
28: Set rs.ActiveConnection = conn
29: rs.Open strSQL
30:
31: blnInputOK = False
32: While blnInputOK = False
33:     strInput = InputBox("Records per page (1-100)?" & vbCrLf & _
34:          "(0 = Exit)", "Paging in recordset", "10")
35:     strInput = Trim(strInput)
36:     If strInput = "0" Then Exit Function
37:     If IsNumeric(strInput) Then
38:         lngInput = CLng(strInput)
39:         If lngInput >= 1 And lngInput <= 100 Then
40:             blnInputOK = True
41:         End If
42:     End If
43: Wend
44:
45: rs.PageSize = lngInput
46: rs.CacheSize = rs.PageSize + 1
47:
48: ' Begin paging
49:
50: strPaging = "first"
51:
52: blnPaging = True
53: While (blnPaging = True)
54:     Select Case strPaging
55:         Case "first"
56:             lngCurrentPage = 1
```

continues

LISTING 6.3   continued

```
57:             Case "last"
58:                 lngCurrentPage = rs.PageCount
59:             Case "forward"
60:                 lngCurrentPage = lngCurrentPage + 1
61:             Case "backward"
62:                 lngCurrentPage = lngCurrentPage - 1
63:         End Select
64:         ' Check range of page number
65:         If lngCurrentPage < 1 Then
66:             lngCurrentPage = 1
67:         ElseIf lngCurrentPage > rs.PageCount Then
68:             lngCurrentPage = rs.PageCount
69:         End If
70:
71:         ' Set page
72:         rs.AbsolutePage = lngCurrentPage
73:
74:         Debug.Print "Current page: " & rs.AbsolutePage & " / " & rs.PageCount
75:         Debug.Print "Records on page: " & rs.PageSize
76:         Debug.Print
77:
78:         ' Show records of the page
79:         lngCount = 1
80:         Debug.Print "Absolute", "Position", "Pages", "Name"
81:         Debug.Print "Position", "on Page"
82:         While (Not rs.EOF) And (lngCount <= rs.PageSize)
83:             Debug.Print rs.AbsolutePosition, lngCount, rs.PageCount, _
84:                 rs("ProductName")
85:             ' Position on Page = AbsolutePosition-(PageSize*(AbsolutePage-1))
86:             rs.MoveNext
87:             lngCount = lngCount + 1
88:         Wend
89:         Debug.Print "- - - - - - - - - - - - - - - - - - - - - - - - - -"
90:         blnInputOK = False
91:         While blnInputOK = False
92:             strInput = InputBox("Navigate in the recordset." & vbCrLf & _
93:                 "1: Page backward" & vbCrLf & "2: Page forward" & vbCrLf & _
94:                 "0: End paging", "Paging in recordset", "2")
95:             strInput = Trim(strInput)
96:             Select Case strInput
97:                 Case "1"
98:                     strPaging = "backward"
99:                     blnInputOK = True
100:                Case "2"
101:                    strPaging = "forward"
102:                    blnInputOK = True
103:                Case "0"
104:                    blnPaging = False
105:                    blnInputOK = True
```

```
106:          End Select
107:      Wend
108: Wend
109:
```

The code in Listing 6.3 should produce this output:

 First, a window appears where the user can choose the number of records per page, as shown in Figure 6.1.

FIGURE 6.1

Specifying records per page.

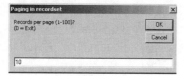

Then, the first page of the resultset is shown in the Immediate pane of the Visual Basic window:

```
 1: Current page: 1 / 8
 2: Records on page: 10
 3:
 4: Absolute      Position      Pages       Name
 5: Position      on Page
 6: 1             1             8           Chai
 7: 2             2             8           Chang
 8: 3             3             8           Aniseed Syrup
 9: 4             4             8           Chef Anton's Cajun Seasoning
10: 5             5             8           Chef Anton's Gumbo Mix
11: 6             6             8           Grandma's Boysenberry Spread
12: 7             7             8           Uncle Bob's Organic Dried Pears
13: 8             8             8           Northwoods Cranberry Sauce
14: 9             9             8           Mishi Kobe Niku
15: 10            10            8           Ikura
16: - - - - - - - - - - - - - - - - - - - - - - - - - - -
```

The paging window appears where you can choose to page forward or backward in the resultset, as shown in Figure 6.2.

FIGURE 6.2

The Paging in record-set window.

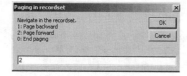

6

When you finally navigate to page 8, the output looks as follows:

```
17: Current page: 8 / 8
18: Records on page: 10
19:
20: Absolute        Position       Pages        Name
21: Position        on Page
22: 71              1              8            Röd Kaviar
23: 72              2              8            Longlife Tofu
24: 73              3              8            Rhönbräu Klosterbier
25: 74              4              8            Lakkalikööri
26: 75              5              8            Original Frankfurter grüne Soße
27: - - - - - - - - - - - - - - - - - - - - - - - - - - - - - -
```

ANALYSIS   The script defines several variables in lines 1–11: Conn holds the connection, rs the recordset, and strSQL the SQL statement to retrieve the recordset. LngCount is used to hold the current record's position on the current page. LngCurrentPage holds the number of the current page during the paging process. The variable strInput is used to receive the user's input from the paging windows. LngInput is used to hold a numeric value retrieved from the user's input string stored in strInput. The variable strPaging can hold values as first, last, forward, or backward and is used to get the navigation action that should be performed in the current paging step. BlnInputOK has the purpose of indicating whether the current user input is valid or not. BlnPaging is True as long as the user wants to page through the recordset; it is set to False to cancel paging.

The static recordset is prepared and its content received from the Products table of the Northwind database. The cache size of the recordset is set to the number of records per page increased by 1. This is done for better performance of the database server and your database application.

Tip

> The database provider caches records in local memory. You can specify how many records are stored at once in the cache using the Recordset object's CacheSize property. Usually, only one record is stored in the cache at once. That means that every record you access is read directly from the database and therefore causes network traffic to the database server and load on the database itself. When you specify a CacheSize of 10, the database provider reads 10 records at once and stores them in local memory. Therefore, accessing these records does not require a round-trip to the database server and therefore is good for the performance of the database application. The only disadvantage is that database changes are not reflected in the cached records. You have to use the Resync method to synchronize the cached content with the database content.

The user can specify the number of records per page in an input box that is created by the script in lines 31–43 (refer also to Figure 6.1). The user's input is checked and written into the variable lngInput when the input is a number between 1 and 100.

In line 45, the value of the variable lngInput is assigned to the PageSize property of the recordset, thus determining the number of records per recordset page. To increase performance, the CacheSize is set to a value that is 1 higher than the PageSize. As the user is beginning paging, the value first is assigned to the variable strPaging in line 50 so that the paging loop in lines 53–108 jumps to the first page of the recordset. In line 52, the variable blnPaging is set to True to indicate that paging is activated. The While...Wend loop runs until blnPaging is set to another value than True.

The paging code in lines 53–108 consists of the following parts:

- Determine the navigation action in lines 54–63—The action is read from the variable strPaging. When paging forward or backward, the number of the current page, which is stored in the variable lngCurrent, is increased or decreased by 1. When strPaging contains first, the page number is set to one; when it contains last, the page number is set to the last page.

- Check the page number (lines 65–69)—The page number must not be less than 1 or greater than the number of pages.

- Navigate to the first recordset of the new page—In line 72, the AbsolutePage property is set to the new page number.

- Output the content of the current page—The number of the current page and the number of all pages is written to the user in line 74. All records of the page—with their absolute position, position on the current page, and then number of the page and the product name stored in the record—are written to the user in lines 79–89 (output lines 1–16 for the first page and lines 17–27 for page 8).

- Determine direction of paging navigation—The script raises an input box in line 92, where the user can specify whether he or she wants to page forward or backward, or exit paging (see Figure 6.2). The user input is evaluated in lines 95–106. If the user wants to page forward, the variable strPaging is set to the value forward. When backward paging is chosen, strPaging is set to backward. When the user wants to exit paging, blnPaging is set to False, which causes the paging loop to terminate.

When you want to use a paging technique, as shown in Listing 6.3, you must have a resultset that does not change too often. When a record in the underlying database is changed during the paging process, records can be moved from one page to another. Consider this especially when your application retrieves the recordset during each paging step. This would be the case in a Web server application written in Active Server Pages (ASP), for instance.

6

Paging with Changing Resultsets in Mind

Listing 6.4 deals with the possibility that a resultset changes while the user pages
through it. This requires a custom paging technique, because it might be possible that a
remarkable number of records is inserted or deleted from the database table while the
user is paging through the resultset.

LISTING 6.4   Custom Paging Through a Resultset

```
 1: Dim conn As ADODB.Connection
 2: Dim rs As ADODB.Recordset
 3: Dim rsID As ADODB.Recordset
 4: Dim strSQL As String
 5: Dim strSQLID As String
 6: Dim strInput As String
 7: Dim lngInput As Long
 8: Dim blnInputOK As Boolean
 9: Dim blnPaging As Boolean
10: Dim IDBegin As Long
11: Dim IDEnd As Long
12: Dim IDTemp As Long
13: Dim strDirection As String
14:
15: blnInputOK = False
16: While blnInputOK = False
17:     strInput = InputBox("Records per page (1-100)?" & vbCrLf & _
18:          "(0 = Exit)", "Paging in recordset", "10")
19:     strInput = Trim(strInput)
20:     If strInput = "0" Then Exit Function
21:     If IsNumeric(strInput) Then
22:         lngInput = CLng(strInput)
23:         If lngInput >= 1 And lngInput <= 100 Then
24:             blnInputOK = True
25:         End If
26:     End If
27: Wend
28:
29: Set conn = CreateObject("ADODB.Connection")
30: conn.Open "Provider=SQLOLEDB;Data Source=BoyScout;" & _
31:     "Initial Catalog=Northwind;User ID=sa;Password=;"
32:
33: Set rs = CreateObject("ADODB.Recordset")
34: rs.CursorLocation = adUseServer
35: rs.CursorType = adOpenStatic
36: rs.LockType = adLockReadOnly
37: rs.CacheSize = lngInput + 1
38:
39: Set rsID = CreateObject("ADODB.Recordset")
40: rsID.CursorLocation = adUseServer
```

```
41: rsID.CursorType = adOpenStatic
42: rsID.LockType = adLockReadOnly
43: rsID.MaxRecords = lngInput
44: rsID.CacheSize = lngInput + 1
45:
46: IDBegin = 0
47: IDEnd = 0
48:
49: If IDBegin > IDEnd Then
50:     IDTemp = IDEnd
51:     IDEnd = IDBegin
52:     IDBegin = IDTemp
53: End If
54:
55: strDirection = "forward"     ' or "backward"
56:
57:
58: blnPaging = True
59: While (blnPaging = True)
60:
61:     Select Case strDirection
62:         Case "forward"
63:             strSQLID = "SELECT ProductID FROM Products " & _
64:                 "WHERE ProductID > " & IDEnd & " ORDER BY ProductID"
65:         Case "backward"
66:             strSQLID = "SELECT ProductID FROM Products " & _
67:                 "WHERE ProductID < " & IDBegin & " ORDER BY ProductID DESC"
68:     End Select
69:
70:     rsID.Open strSQLID, conn
71:     If rsID.EOF And rsID.BOF Then
72:         ' No records found
73:         'IDBegin = 0
74:         'IDEnd = 0
75:     Else
76:         IDBegin = rsID("ProductID")
77:         rsID.MoveLast
78:         IDEnd = rsID("ProductID")
79:     End If
80:     rsID.Close
81:
82:     If IDBegin > IDEnd Then
83:         IDTemp = IDEnd
84:         IDEnd = IDBegin
85:         IDBegin = IDTemp
86:     End If
87:
88:     strSQL = "SELECT ProductID, ProductName, SupplierID, CategoryID, " & _
89:         "QuantityPerUnit, UnitPrice, UnitsInStock, UnitsOnOrder, " & _
90:         "ReorderLevel, Discontinued FROM Products " & _
```

6

continues

LISTING 6.4 continued

```
91:            "WHERE ProductID >= " & IDBegin & " AND ProductID <= " & _
92:            IDEnd & " " & "ORDER BY ProductID"
93:
94:     rs.Open strSQL, conn
95:
96:     ' Show records of the page
97:     Debug.Print "ID", "Product Name"
98:     While (Not rs.EOF)
99:        Debug.Print rs("ProductID"), rs("ProductName")
100:       rs.MoveNext
101:    Wend
102:    Debug.Print "- - - - - - - - - - - - - - - - - - - - - - - -"
103:    rs.Close
104:
105:    blnInputOK = False
106:    While blnInputOK = False
107:       strInput = InputBox("Navigate in the recordset." & vbCrLf & _
108:              "1: Page backward" & vbCrLf & "2: Page forward" & _
109:              vbCrLf & "0: End paging", "Paging in recordset", "2")
110:       strInput = Trim(strInput)
111:       Select Case strInput
112:          Case "1"
113:             strDirection = "backward"
114:             blnInputOK = True
115:          Case "2"
116:             strDirection = "forward"
117:             blnInputOK = True
118:          Case "0"
119:             blnPaging = False
120:             blnInputOK = True
121:       End Select
122:    Wend
123: Wend
124:
125: Set rs = Nothing
126: conn.Close
127: Set conn = Nothing
```

OUTPUT When the user selects 10 records per page, the output of Listing 6.4 looks as follows:

```
1: ID               Product Name
2: 1                Chai
3: 2                Chang
4: 3                Aniseed Syrup
5: 4                Chef Anton's Cajun Seasoning
6: 5                Chef Anton's Gumbo Mix
7: 6                Grandma's Boysenberry Spread
8: 7                Uncle Bob's Organic Dried Pears
```

```
 9:  8              Northwoods Cranberry Sauce
10:  9              Mishi Kobe Niku
11:  10             Ikura
12: - - - - - - - - - - - - - - - - - - - - - - -  -
```

And after some more pages forward:

```
13: ID             Product Name
14:  73            Röd Kaviar
15:  74            Longlife Tofu
16:  75            Rhönbräu Klosterbier
17:  76            Lakkalikööri
18:  77            Original Frankfurter grüne Soße
19: - - - - - - - - - - - - - - - - - - - - - - -  -
```

ANALYSIS All variables are declared in lines 1–13. The variable strSQL is used to store the SQL statement to retrieve the current page from the database.

In the script, a recordset page is a certain set of records whose consecutive ID values are between the two values specified by the variables IDBegin and IDEnd. The recordset page, which has consecutive ID values between IDBegin and IDEnd, and all the record values of the page are stored in the variable rs.

Reading the first and the last value of the recordset rs, the script can determine the ID range of the page.

When the user pages forward, the script uses a SQL statement defined in the variable strSQLID to retrieve a recordset with a certain number (equals the number of records per page increased by 1) of ID values that come right after the value of IDEnd. The script stores the retrieved ID values in the recordset rsID.

The same way, when the user pages backward, the script retrieves a certain number of ID values from the database that comes just before the value of IDBegin. This way, the script can determine the first ID and the last ID of the new page and receive all records whose ID numbers are between IDBegin and IDEnd.

The script can react if certain records are added or deleted between the calls of the pages. It does not matter which ID values the added or deleted records have. The changed records are just displayed on the correct page.

6

The variables strInput and lngInputOK are used to store and process user inputs. Through the variable blnPaging, the script can determine whether the user still wants to page through the resultset. To store the paging direction (backward or forward), the script uses the variable strDirection.

The number of records per page is retrieved from the user in lines 15–27 and stored in the variable lngInput. In lines 29–31, a connection to the Northwind database is opened and stored in `conn`. The two recordsets, `rs` and `rsID`, are prepared in lines 33–44, whereby the `CacheSize` of both recordsets is set to the same value as the number of records per page increased by 1 for better performance of the database queries. The `MaxRecords` property of the recordset `rsID` is set to the number of records per page, so the number of retrieved records is limited exactly to the number of records on one page.

In lines 46–47, the values for the variables `IDBegin` and `IDEnd` are set to 0, and the value for the paging direction is set to `forward`. Using these values in the first paging loop, the first page contains all records whose ID is higher than 0.

The paging itself is performed in the `While...Wend` loop in lines 59–123. First, the script determines the first and the last ID of the new page: According to the current paging direction, the script retrieves the same number of ID values from the database, because there are records in a page. When the paging direction is `forward`, the ID values following the value of `IDEnd` are received. In the paging direction `backward`, the ID values right before the value of `IDBegin` are received and stored in the recordset `rsID`.

If no records are stored in the recordset `rsID`, because you are still on the first or last page, the `IDBegin` and `IDEnd` values remain the same. Otherwise, the `IDBegin` and `IDEnd` values are set to the lowest and highest values of the retrieved recordset `rsID`, respectively.

The recordset with all data is retrieved from the database in lines 88–94, whereby its ID values are between `IDBegin` and `IDEnd`. All records from the recordset are written to the user in lines 96–102 (output lines 1–12 for the first page and lines 13–19 for the last page).

Finally, the user is asked for the new paging direction in lines 105–122. According to the select paging direction, the variable `strDirection` is set to the value `forward` or `backward`.

Listing 6.4 provides only an idea of the possibilities for paging through a recordset. You can use the technique of the script in an ASP application, even when the ASP application retrieves a recordset from the database every time the user navigates a page forward or backward.

Summary

Today, you learned how to navigate in a large resultset. You used the various `Move` methods and the `Bookmark` property of the recordset to specify a new position of the recordset cursor. You also studied two paging examples to introduce you to the techniques of recordset paging.

When you want to save database and application resources, it is often better to use a paging technique to access only a page of data at once. However, it requires some overhead for the paging mechanism when you want to provide comfortable paging techniques.

Q&A

Q I want to provide a paging feature in a database-driven Web server application using ASP and ADO. The content of the database changes very fast. I know that I could retrieve a recordset and store it for a user's session in a `Session` variable on the server. However, I expect a huge number of simultaneous users and this would waste Web server resources and even database resources, because I would have to retrieve the whole database content at once for every new user.

Should I use the mechanism of Listing 6.4 as the base for the paging technique in my Web server application?

A You surely have to adapt the script and even the paging technique to fulfill the needs of a Web server application. However, when you understand how the script in Listing 6.4 works, you will be able to create and develop your own paging technique fast.

Workshop

The quiz questions and exercises are provided for your further understanding. See Appendix A, "Answers," for the answers.

Quiz

1. What properties and methods does the `Recordset` object provide to enable dividing a recordset into several pages?
2. What methods can you use to navigate in a recordset?
3. What property do you have to use when you want to find a specific record fast?
4. What can happen if you have a filtered recordset and you want to jump to a certain record using the `Bookmark` property?
5. What does the `AbsolutePosition` property return, and what else can you use the `AbsolutePosition` property for?
6. How can you determine the number of records in the current recordset?

Exercise

Rewrite Listing 6.3 (simple paging through a recordset) so that the user can also jump to the first and the last page. In addition, include the feature that enables the user to jump 5 pages forward or backward at once.

6

DAY 7

Implementing Application Logic in Stored Procedures

Stored procedures are scripts written in T-SQL (SQL Server's SQL version named Transact SQL) that are executed directly on a SQL Server. With a stored procedure, you can implement application logic directly in the database when you are using a SQL Server database.

A stored procedure is similar to a function in Visual Basic because you can use input and output parameters, but a stored procedure can also return one or more Recordsets.

The benefits of using stored procedures are

- Modular programming: Stored procedures can be used as defined interfaces for database tasks. When you want to change the way the database tasks are executed, you change only the stored procedure. You do not have to change the code of your application.

- Faster execution: Stored procedures are already parsed and stored in the memory of the database server after their first execution. A call to the stored procedure is faster than using the SQL statements of the stored procedure directly because the statements have to be parsed at every call.

- Reduced network traffic: Because the whole SQL code is stored on the SQL Server, you do not need to send large SQL statements from the client (application) to the server (database).

- Database security: You can modify the security of users in a SQL Server database so that certain users cannot access database data directly, but rather must use stored procedures as defined interfaces for database access.

You can execute a stored procedure from your application using ADO, as shown in this day's lesson.

The main topics of this day are

- How to program stored procedures: You will see the basics of stored procedures and how to add new stored procedures to SQL Server 7.0 databases.

- How to call a stored procedure: There are different ways to call stored procedures. You can call a simple stored procedure using the Execute method of the Connection object. More complex stored procedures that use output parameters or return codes can be invoked using the ADO Command object.

- How to use input and output parameters: See how to use ADO to pass values to, or receive values from, a stored procedure.

Programming Stored Procedures

A stored procedure is a SQL script that is stored in a SQL Server database and executed on the SQL Server machine. It can contain variables, loops, and conditional statements. It is written in T-SQL, the SQL version used in SQL Server. The stored procedure can use input parameters, perform various tasks, and return one or more output parameters and Recordsets.

The basic syntax of a stored procedure is

```
CREATE PROCEDURE procedure_name
@parameter_name1 datatype1,
@parameter_name2 datatype2  OUTPUT,
@parameter_name3 datatype3
AS
sql_statements
```

You can use as many parameters as you want, from zero to more than ten. A parameter that returns a value from the stored procedure is called an output parameter and is indicated by the keyword OUTPUT after the data type. All other parameters are input parameters that pass a value to the stored procedure.

The stored procedure can contain one or more SELECT statements, loops such as the T-SQL WHILE construct, or conditional statements, such as the T-SQL IF...ELSE or the CASE expression. Additionally, you can use input and output parameters in the same way as you use variables. It is also possible to declare additional variables in the stored procedure using the T-SQL DECLARE statement:

```
DECLARE @parameter_name datatype
```

A variable has a @ as the first character in the variable name. For the variable data type, you can use any SQL Server system-supplied or user-defined data type—as long as you do not use a data type as text, ntext, or image. However, for input parameters, you can use the data type text, ntext, or image.

Examine a Simple Stored Procedure

A simple stored procedure is the Ten Most Expensive Products stored procedure from the SQL Server 7.0 Northwind database. To view its code you have to perform the following steps.

To Do: View the Ten Most Expensive Products Stored Procedure

1. You must have installed SQL Server 7.0 Enterprise Manager to gain access to the administration of SQL Server 7.0, and you must be able to access the SQL Server 7.0 database server from your computer. (Please refer to the SQL Server documentation for details.)

2. Open the SQL Server 7.0 Enterprise Manager, which can be accessed through the Start button, Programs, Microsoft SQL Server 7.0, Enterprise Manager.

3. Expand the tree in the Enterprise Manager (see Figure 7.1) to view Microsoft SQL Server, SQL Server Group, SQL Server (this should be the SQL Server on which the Northwind database resides; in Figure 7.1 the server is called BOYSCOUT), Databases, Northwind. The content in your Enterprise Manager should now look similar to Figure 7.1.

4. Click Stored Procedures in the tree beyond the Northwind database. You see about 25 stored procedures (see Figure 7.2) in the right pane. The stored procedure named Ten Most Expensive Products is the last one.

▲ To Do

▼

7

FIGURE 7.1

The expanded tree in the SQL Server 7.0 Enterprise Manager.

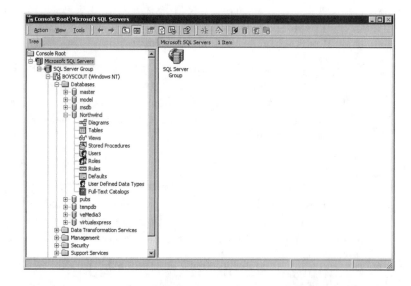

FIGURE 7.2

Stored procedures of the Northwind database.

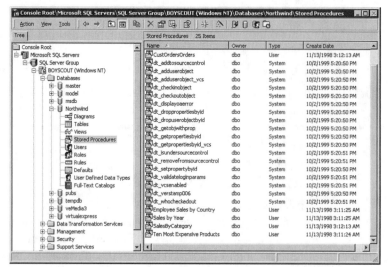

5. Double-click on the stored procedure Ten Most Expensive Products in the right pane. The Stored Procedure Properties window comes up (see Figure 7.3).

6. Now you can see the code of the stored procedure (see Figure 7.3 and Listing 7.1).

FIGURE 7.3

The stored procedure Ten Most Expensive Products.

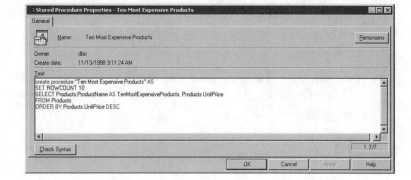

LISTING 7.1 The Stored Procedure Ten Most Expensive Products

```
1: create procedure "Ten Most Expensive Products" AS
2: SET ROWCOUNT 10
3: SELECT Products.ProductName AS TenMostExpensiveProducts,
➥ Products.UnitPrice
4: FROM Products
5: ORDER BY Products.UnitPrice DESC
```

ANALYSIS Take a look at the code in Listing 7.1. The stored procedure returns a Recordset with the ten most expensive products from the Northwind Products table. In line 1, the stored procedure begins with the command CREATE PROCEDURE, followed by the stored procedure's name and the keyword AS, which indicates the beginning of the stored procedure's body.

The body contains the following T-SQL statements. In line 2, the maximum number of rows returned from any SELECT statement in the stored procedure is limited to 10. Lines 3–5 contain a SQL SELECT statement, which returns a Recordset that consists of the product name and the unit price of every item stored in the Products table, ordered descending by the unit price. The returned Recordset can be accessed using ADO, as shown in Listing 7.6 later in this lesson.

As you can see, the stored procedure is simple because it does not receive any input parameters and just returns a simple Recordset. However, the real power of the stored procedure concept is that you can pass parameters to a stored procedure. These parameters can be used as variables in the stored procedures code. Furthermore, you can declare additional variables and use them to store values, control loops, or conditional statements.

7

Define Input Parameters in a Stored Procedure

Input parameters are values that are handed over to a stored procedure. Input parameters can be of any T-SQL data type, even text, ntext, or image.

When you look at the code of Northwind's stored procedure CustOrdersOrders, you can see how an input parameter is declared and used. Listing 7.2 contains the code of the stored procedure.

LISTING 7.2   The Stored Procedure CustOrdersOrders

```
 1: CREATE PROCEDURE CustOrdersOrders
 2:     @CustomerID nchar(5)
 3: AS
 4: SELECT OrderID,
 5:        OrderDate,
 6:        RequiredDate,
 7:        ShippedDate
 8: FROM Orders
 9: WHERE CustomerID = @CustomerID
10: ORDER BY OrderID
```

ANALYSIS   In line 1, the stored procedure begins with the keywords CREATE PROCEDURE, followed by the name of the stored procedure. In line 2, only the input parameter named @CustomerID is declared using the data type nchar(5), which stands for the Unicode fixed-length character data type of length 5. Each parameter declaration consists of *@parameter_name* and *data_type*. If a stored procedure has more than one parameter, the parameters are separated by commas.

Following all parameters, the body of the stored procedure begins after the keyword AS. The SELECT statement in lines 4–10 uses the input parameter @CustomerID to select only the records in which the CustomerID is equal to the value in the input parameter @CustomerID (see line 9). The SELECT statement returns the columns OrderID, OrderDate, RequiredDate, and ShippedDate of all records in the Orders table where the CustomerID is equal to the value in @CustomerID. It also sorts the Recordset by the values in the OrderID column. The Recordset returned from the SELECT statement can be read using ADO, as shown later in this lesson.

As mentioned before, stored procedures can also contain conditional statements. Look at the stored procedure SalesByCategory from the Northwind database in Listing 7.3.

```
 1: CREATE PROCEDURE SalesByCategory
 2:     @CategoryName nvarchar(15),
 3:     @OrdYear nvarchar(4) = '1998'
 4: AS
 5: IF @OrdYear != '1996' AND @OrdYear != '1997' AND @OrdYear != '1998'
 6: BEGIN
 7:     SELECT @OrdYear = '1998'
 8: END
 9:
10: SELECT ProductName,
11:     TotalPurchase=ROUND(SUM(CONVERT(decimal(14,2),
➥ OD.Quantity * (1-OD.Discount) * OD.UnitPrice)), 0)
12: FROM [Order Details] OD, Orders O, Products P, Categories C
13: WHERE OD.OrderID = O.OrderID
14:     AND OD.ProductID = P.ProductID
15:     AND P.CategoryID = C.CategoryID
16:     AND C.CategoryName = @CategoryName
17:     AND SUBSTRING(CONVERT(nvarchar(22), O.OrderDate, 111), 1, 4) =
➥ @OrdYear
18: GROUP BY ProductName
19: ORDER BY ProductName
```

ANALYSIS   The SalesByCategory stored procedure uses two input parameters, @CategoryName and @OrdYear. The first one is declared as nvarchar(15), which is the variable-length, Unicode-character data type of length 15. The second parameter is declared as nvarchar(4) and set to a default value of 1998. As the second parameter has a default value assigned, you can even call the stored procedure passing only one parameter to it. The second parameter is optional because it is assigned to the default value when no value is provided.

The conditional statement in Listing 7.3 is declared in lines 5–8 as follows:

```
IF @OrdYear != '1996' AND @OrdYear != '1997' AND @OrdYear != '1998'
BEGIN
    SELECT @OrdYear = '1998'
END
```

The IF statement assigns the value 1998 to the variable @OrdYear when the value of the variable is not 1996, 1997, or 1998 (the meaning of != is not equal).

The simple IF statement consists of three parts: the keyword IF, the condition, and one SQL statement that should be executed when the condition returns TRUE. Note that instead of using one SQL statement, you can also use several SQL statements when they are surrounded by the keywords BEGIN and END.

7

The Syntax for IF...ELSE in T-SQL

The following code shows the syntax for the T-SQL conditional construct IF...ELSE.

```
IF Boolean_expression
    sql_statement1
ELSE
    sql_statement2
```

When the Boolean_expression returns TRUE, the statement sql_statement1 is executed. When it returns FALSE, then sql_statement2 is executed instead. You can also use code blocks (BEGIN...END) instead of a simple SQL statements for the expression in sql_statement1 or sql_statement2. Note that there is a simple form of the IF statement:

```
IF Boolean_expression
    sql_statement1
```

In the IF statement in Listing 7.3, there is the following SELECT statement:

```
SELECT @OrdYear = '1998'
```

This usage of the SELECT statement assigns the value '1998' to the variable @OrdYear.

The Syntax to Assign a Value to a Variable

```
SELECT @Variable_Name = Variable_Value
```

or

```
SET @Variable_Name = Variable_Value
```

The lines 10–19 in Listing 7.3 use a complex SELECT statement to return a Recordset to the caller of the stored procedure. For information about the T-SQL functions used in Listing 7.3, refer to the SQL Server 7.0 documentation.

Using Output Parameters in a Stored Procedure

A stored procedure can return values through output parameters. Output parameters are often used when you want to return single values instead of (or in addition to) a Recordset. For an output parameter, you can use any T-SQL data type with the exception of the T-SQL data types text, ntext, and image.

The stored procedure in Listing 7.4, named LastShippingAustria, returns an output parameter.

LISTING 7.4 The Stored Procedure `LastShippingAustria`

```
1: CREATE PROCEDURE LastShippingAustria
2:    @ShippedDate datetime OUTPUT
3: AS
4: SELECT @ShippedDate = MAX(ShippedDate) FROM Orders
5:    WHERE ShipCountry = 'Austria'
```

ANALYSIS The output parameter `@ShippedDate` is declared in line 2 using the keyword `OUTPUT`. A value is assigned to the output parameter in line 4 using a `SELECT` statement. This `SELECT` statement assigns the latest shipping date from all orders, that have `Austria` as the shipping country to the variable `@ShippedDate`. The output parameter of the stored procedure can be retrieved using the `Parameters` collection of the `Command` object, as shown later in this lesson.

Using Return Codes

Return codes are similar to output parameters with these important differences:

- Return codes can only return SQL integer values (corresponding with Visual Basic long data type).
- The stored procedure uses the T-SQL `RETURN` statement to return a value to the calling application. When the following T-SQL code is executed, the stored procedure returns the value 5 as the value of the return code:

  `RETURN 5`

  When the following T-SQL statement is executed, the stored procedure returns the value of the variable `@ret`:

  `RETURN @ret`

- When using a stored procedure that returns a return code, the first created and appended parameter of the `Command` object must be the one that holds the return code.
- You can only receive one return code from a stored procedure.

The stored procedure in Listing 7.5 returns an output parameter that contains the value of the last shipping date from the record in the Orders table that has the ShipCountry field set to `Austria`. It also returns a return code, which is set to 1 if there are any orders with the ShipCountry field set to `Austria`, or 0 if there are none.

7

LISTING 7.5   The Stored Procedure with an Output Parameter and Return Code

```
 1: CREATE PROCEDURE LastShippingAustria2
 2:     @ShippedDate datetime OUTPUT
 3: AS
 4: SELECT @ShippedDate = MAX(ShippedDate) FROM Orders
 5:     WHERE ShipCountry = 'Austria'
 6:
 7: IF @ShippedDate IS NULL
 8:     RETURN 0
 9: ELSE
10:     RETURN 1
```

ANALYSIS   A value is assigned to the output parameter `@ShippedDate` in line 4 using a SELECT statement. When no shipment exists with the ShipCountry set to Austria, the SQL aggregate function MAX() returns NULL. The value of the MAX() function is stored in the variable `@ShippedDate`, which is also the output parameter. Depending on whether a shipment exists or not, the return code is either assigned the value 1 or 0. No shipment is indicated by a value of NULL for `@ShippedDate`, which results in a return code value of 0.

Write Your Own Stored Procedure

You can perform the following steps to add your own stored procedure to the Northwind database using the SQL Server 7.0 Enterprise Manager.

To Do: Add Your Own Stored Procedure

1. Open the SQL Server 7.0 Enterprise Manager, which can be accessed through the Start button, Programs, Microsoft SQL Server 7.0, Enterprise Manager.

2. Expand the tree in the Enterprise Manager (refer to Figure 7.1) to view Microsoft SQL Servers, SQL Server Group, *SQL Server* (which should be the SQL Server where the Northwind database resides), Databases, Northwind, Stored Procedures.

3. Right-click on Stored Procedures in the left pane and choose New Stored Procedure from the context menu. Now the Stored Procedure Properties window appears.

4. Write the text of the stored procedure in the window.

5. Check the syntax by clicking the Check Syntax button. Dismiss the information window and correct errors that arise.

6. Click OK to store the stored procedure.

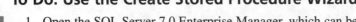

In the special case when you want to use simple T-SQL INSERT, UPDATE, or DELETE statements in your stored procedure, you can use the Create Stored Procedure Wizard. For instance, if you want to create a stored procedure that inserts rows into the Orders table, you can use the Create Stored Procedure Wizard as shown in the following "To Do" section.

To Do: Use the Create Stored Procedure Wizard

1. Open the SQL Server 7.0 Enterprise Manager, which can be accessed via the Start button, Programs, Microsoft SQL Server 7.0, Enterprise Manager.

2. Expand the Tree in the Enterprise Manager, and select the server that contains the database where you want to create the stored procedure, and choose Wizards from the Tools menu in the Enterprise Manager.

3. Expand Database in the Select Wizard and double click on the Create Stored Procedure Wizard (see Figure 7.4). The Create Stored Procedure Wizard dialog box appears.

FIGURE 7.4

The Select Wizard dialog box.

4. Click on Next in the Create Stored Procedure Wizard window.

5. Select the database in which you want to create your stored procedure (for instance, in the Northwind database).

6. Now select the action that your stored procedure should perform. When you want to insert rows into the Orders table of the Northwind database, you have to select the Insert column of the row where the table name Orders appears (see Figure 7.5) and click on the Next button.

7

▼   7. You have completed the steps required to create the new stored procedure. If you want, you can change the stored procedure using the Edit button (see Figure 7.6).

FIGURE 7.5

Select actions in the Create Stored Procedure Wizard.

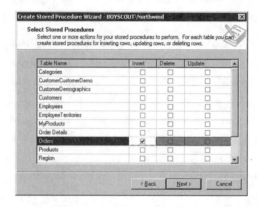

FIGURE 7.6

The Completing the Create Stored Procedure Wizard window.

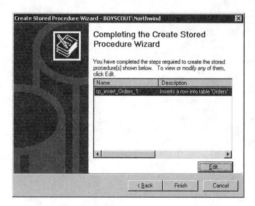

8. When you click on the Edit button, the Edit Stored Procedures Window appears where you can select which columns you want to insert or update. You can even change the SQL code of the stored procedure when you click on the Edit SQL button (see Figure 7.7).

9. The code of the stored procedure is created automatically for you by the Create
▼   Stored Procedure Wizard (see Figure 7.8).

FIGURE 7.7

Select columns that should be manipulated by the stored procedure.

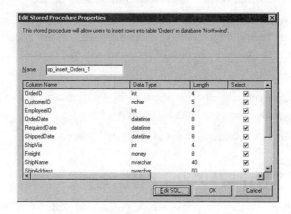

FIGURE 7.8

Code of the created stored procedure.

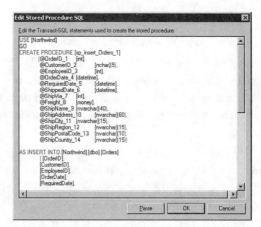

Change a Stored Procedure

Of course, you can change a stored procedure in the Stored Procedure Properties window of the SQL Server 7.0 Enterprise Manager.

To Do: Change a Stored Procedure

1. Open the SQL Server 7.0 Enterprise Manager, which can be accessed through the Start button, Programs, Microsoft SQL Server 7.0, Enterprise Manager.

2. Expand the tree in the Enterprise Manager (refer to Figure 7.1) to view Microsoft SQL Servers, SQL Server Group, *SQL Server* (which should be the SQL Server

7

▼   where the database with the stored procedure resides), Databases, *Database Name*
           (the database that contains the stored procedure), Stored Procedures.

       3. Click on Stored Procedures in the left pane of the SQL Server 7.0 Enterprise
           Manager. Then double-click on the name of the stored procedure that you want to
           change. The Stored Procedures Properties window appears.

       4. Change the text of the stored procedure.

       5. Check the syntax by clicking the Check Syntax button. Dismiss the information
           window and correct errors that you might have introduced.

▲   6. Click OK to store the changes to the stored procedure.

Invoking Stored Procedures

This section presents how to invoke stored procedures from your application using ADO.

You will see how to perform the following tasks:

- Calling a stored procedure: When a stored procedure only returns a Recordset, you
  can call it using the `Execute` method of the `Connection` object.

- Usage of input and output parameters: When you call a stored procedure that
  returns output parameters, you have to use the `Command` object. With the `Command`
  object you can create `Parameter` objects that are used to handle the input and output parameters.

- Usage of return codes: From the view of ADO, a return code is a special case of an
  output parameter of a stored procedure. It can only return long integer numbers and
  is used to indicate a status of the stored procedure—for instance, whether the
  stored procedure can perform a certain action.

Simple Call of a Stored Procedure

As you have seen in Listing 7.1, the declaration of the stored procedure `Ten Most`
`Expensive Products` does not have an input or output parameter and only returns a
Recordset. This Recordset can be retrieved when you execute the stored procedure using
the `Execute` method of the `Connection` object:

```
Set rs = conn.Execute("EXECUTE [Ten Most Expensive Products]")
```

The variable conn stands for a `Connection` object with an open connection to the SQL
Server Northwind database, the variable rs contains the Recordset that was returned by
the stored procedure. The T-SQL statement `EXECUTE`, followed by the name of a stored
procedure, executes the stored procedure at the SQL Server. The name of the stored

procedure is surrounded by square brackets. This is only necessary when its name contains spaces. When you call the stored procedure, the SELECT statement defined in the stored procedure returns a Recordset with the fields TenMostExpensiveProducts and UnitPrice. You can retrieve the values of the fields as shown in Listing 7.6.

LISTING 7.6   Calling the Stored Procedure Ten Most Expensive Products

```
1: Dim conn As ADODB.Connection
2: Dim rs As ADODB.Recordset
3:
4: Set conn = CreateObject("ADODB.Connection")
5: conn.Open "Provider=SQLOLEDB;Data Source=BoyScout;" & _
6:    "Initial Catalog=Northwind;User ID=sa;Password=;"
7: Set rs = conn.Execute("EXECUTE [Ten Most Expensive Products]")
8: While Not rs.EOF
9:     Debug.Print "Productname: " & rs("TenMostExpensiveProducts")
10:    Debug.Print "Price: " & rs("UnitPrice")
11:    Debug.Print
12:    rs.MoveNext
13: Wend
14:
15: rs.Close
16: conn.Close
17: Set rs = Nothing
18: Set conn = Nothing
```

ANALYSIS   The code opens a connection to the Northwind database. In line 7 the stored procedure named Ten Most Expensive Products is executed using the Execute method of the Connection object. The While...Wend loop (in lines 8–13) retrieves the values of all records in the Recordset. The field values are retrieved using the field names TenMostExpensiveProducts and UnitPrice, because these are the fields that are returned by the SELECT statement in the stored procedure.

You have seen how to call a stored procedure that does not have input or output parameters, but what about a stored procedure that only uses input parameters and returns a Recordset? Can it be executed by simply using ADO's Execute method of the Connection object?

You can call a stored procedure that uses input parameters, but no output parameters or return codes, similar to a stored procedure that has no parameters. Just use the following T-SQL statement to execute a stored procedure that uses input parameters but does not return output parameters or return codes:

EXECUTE *StoredProcedure_Name Parameter1, Parameter2*

7

All parameter values are separated by commas.

The procedure CustOrdersOrders of the Northwind database (see Listing 7.2) is a stored procedure that has one input parameter, no output parameters, and no return code.

The example in Listing 7.7 executes the stored procedure CustOrdersOrders.

LISTING 7.7   Execute the Stored Procedure CustOrdersOrders

```
 1: Dim conn As ADODB.Connection
 2: Dim rs As ADODB.Recordset
 3: Dim strSQL As String
 4: Dim strCustomerID As String
 5:
 6: strCustomerID = "DRACD"
 7: strSQL = "EXECUTE CustOrdersOrders '" & _
 8:     Replace(strCustomerID, "'", "''") & "'"
 9:
10: Set conn = CreateObject("ADODB.Connection")
11: conn.Open "Provider=SQLOLEDB;Data Source=BoyScout;" & _
12:     "Initial Catalog=Northwind;User ID=sa;Password=;"
13:
14: Set rs = conn.Execute(strSQL)
15:
16: While Not rs.EOF
17:     Debug.Print "OrderID: " & rs("OrderID")
18:     Debug.Print "Order Date: " & rs("OrderDate")
19:     Debug.Print "Required Date: " & rs("RequiredDate")
20:     Debug.Print "Shipped Date: " & rs("ShippedDate")
21:     Debug.Print
22:     rs.MoveNext
23: Wend
24:
25: rs.Close
26: conn.Close
27: Set rs = Nothing
28: Set conn = Nothing
```

ANALYSIS   Listing 7.7 opens a connection to the Northwind database, where the stored procedure CustOrdersOrders resides. The T-SQL EXECUTE statement is built in the lines 6–8. It is as follows:

```
EXECUTE CustOrdersOrders 'DRACD'
```

This statement executes the stored procedure CustOrdersOrders using one input parameter with the value 'DRACD'. The stored procedure is executed in line 14, and the returned Recordset is stored in the variable rs. The SELECT statement in the stored procedure returns a Recordset with the fields OrderID, OrderDate, RequiredDate, and ShippedDate. All values of these fields are read in the While...Wend loop in the lines 16–23.

Keep in mind that you cannot retrieve output parameters or a return code when you execute a stored procedure using the Execute method of ADO's Connection object.

Execute a Stored Procedure Using the Command Object

A Command object represents a certain command that should be executed against a data source. When you want to execute a stored procedure on a SQL Server, this is done best using the Command object.

A stored procedure is something like a function. It has input and output parameters and is able to return one or more Recordsets.

All input and output parameters for a stored procedure can be defined and accessed using the Command object and its Parameters collection. You can think of the Command object as a command that can be executed against a data source. The usage of the Command object (for instance, to execute a stored procedure) is as follows:

- Specify the text and type of the command you want to execute by assigning values to the CommandText and CommandType properties of the Command object. The CommandText can be the name of a stored procedure, for instance.
- Use the ActiveConnection property to assign a connection to the Command object that is used to connect to the database.
- Add input and output parameters to the Command's Parameters collection.
- Execute a Command and return a Recordset.
- Read the returned output parameters (or a return code) using the Parameters collection.

In Figure 7.9 you can see how the Command object is related to other ADO objects.

To see how to use the Command object in conjunction with a stored procedure that uses input parameters take a look at the following paragraphs.

A Command object can be created and stored in a variable using the following statement:

```
Set objCmd = CreateObject("ADODB.Command")
```

After you have created the Command object you have to specify the name of the stored procedure and the type of command you are using:

```
objCmd.CommandText = "StoredProcedure_Name"
objCmd.CommandType = adCmdStoredProc
```

7

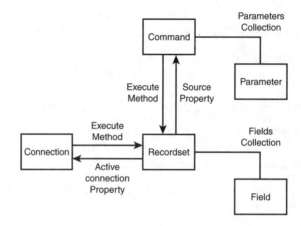

FIGURE 7.9

The relationship between the Command *and other ADO objects.*

The Command object needs to have a connection assigned. The Command object performs database access through this connection. When the connection is opened (after it is created and stored in the variable conn), you can assign it to the Command object using the following statement:

```
Set objCmd.ActiveConnection = conn
```

When you want to pass input or output parameters, you have to assign Parameter objects to the Command object. First create a Parameter object and then append it to the Parameters collection of the Command object. This is done using the following syntax:

```
Set objParam = objCmd.CreateParameter(Name, Type, Direction, Size, Value)
objCmd.Parameters.Append objParam
```

The Name value contains the name of the Parameter object. It is optional and used to reference the Parameter by its name instead of by its position in the Parameters collection of the Command object.

Type provides the ADO data type of the parameter. The Type specified must be compatible with the data type used in the stored procedure for that parameter, and it must conform to the kind of value used in the Value parameter of the CreateParameter method.

The correct correlation for Visual Basic data types, SQL Server 7.0 data types, and ADO constants (for use as Type in the CreateParameter method of the Command object) is shown in Table 7.1. The correct Size value for certain data types is shown in Table 7.2. (The Size value in the CreateParameter method equals the SQL Server data length for all T-SQL data types with the exception of the SQL Server datatypes text, ntext, and image.)

TABLE 7.1   Mapping SQL Server 7.0 Data Types to Visual Basic Data Types, ADO Constants

Visual Basic	SQL Server 7.0	ADO Constant (Type)
Long	int	adInteger
Integer	smallint	adSmallInt
Byte	tinyint	adTinyInt
Boolean	bit	adBoolean
Double	float	adDouble
Single	real	adSingle
Currency	money	adCurrency
Date	datetime	adDate
String (fixed-length)	char	adChar
String (variable-length)	varchar	adVarChar
String (more than 8000 characters)	text	adLongVarChar
Unicode String (fixed-length)	nchar	adWChar
Unicode String (variable-length)	nvarchar	adVarWChar
Unicode String (more than 4000 characters)	ntext	adLongVarWChar
Array of Bytes	image	adVarBinary

TABLE 7.2   SQL Server 7.0 Data Type, ADO Constants, and Size Value for Parameters

SQL Server 7.0	ADO Constant (Type)	Size
int	adInteger	4
smallint	adSmallInt	2
tinyint	adTinyInt	1
bit	adBoolean	1
float	adDouble	8
real	adSingle	4
money	adCurrency	8

7

continues

TABLE 7.2   continued

SQL Server 7.0	ADO Constant (Type)	Size
datetime	adDate	8
char	adChar	1-8000
varchar	adVarChar	1-8000
text	adLongVarChar	2147483647
nchar	adWChar	1-4000
nvarchar	adVarWChar	1-4000
ntext	adLongVarWChar	1073741823
image	adVarBinary	2147483647

Caution   You cannot use output parameters of T-SQL type text, ntext, or image in SQL Server 7.0.

The Direction value of the CreateParameter method determines if the created parameter is an input or output parameter.

An input parameter is used to pass a value to the stored procedure. Its Direction is indicated by the value adParamInput. An output parameter contains a value returned from the stored procedure, and its Direction is indicated by the value adParamOutput. A return code's Direction is indicated by the value adParamReturnValue.

The Size value used in the CreateParameter method indicates the size in bytes or characters according to the used data type. The Size value used for the different SQL Server 7.0 data types is shown in Table 7.2.

Finally, the Value is the value that is passed to the input parameter of the stored procedure. When you define an output parameter or a return code, omit the Value when creating a new Parameter.

The Value for an input parameter should always be compatible with the data type used for the input parameter (refer to Table 7.1). For instance, you should pass a value or variable of the Visual Basic data type Date to the stored procedure when the stored procedure expects a value of the SQL Server data type DateTime. Also, the length of the data passed as Value is important. When the input parameter is defined as SQL Server data type VarChar (variable-length string) with a maximum length of 25 characters, you cannot pass a string that exceeds the length of 25 characters. If you do, you will get an error message when you try to execute the Command object.

In the special case when you are using an input parameter of the type text, ntext, or image, you can also use the AppendChunk method on the Parameter object to assign a value to the input parameter. This is done using the following syntax:

```
Set objParam = objCmd.CreateParameter(Name, Type, adParamInput, Size)
objCmd.Parameters.Append objParam
objCmd.Parameters(Name).AppendChunk Value
```

For instance, to add a long Visual Basic string to an input parameter of the T-SQL type text, you can use statements as follows:

```
Set objParam = objCmd.CreateParameter(Name, adLongVarChar, adParamInput,
2147483647)
objCmd.Parameters.Append objParam
objCmd.Parameters(Name).AppendChunk Value
```

The creation and usage of input and output parameters is illustrated in the following sections.

Using an Input Parameter

When you want to call a stored procedure that uses an input parameter (as the stored procedure CustOrdersOrders in Listing 7.2 does), create a Parameter object of the correct type, assign a value to it, and append it to the Parameters collection of the Command object. This must, of course, be done before you call the stored procedure by executing the Command object.

The input parameter in the SP CustOrdersOrders is defined as nchar(5). To create an input parameter that is defined as the SQL Server data type nchar(5) (fixed-length Unicode string with a length of five characters), use the following code:

```
Set objParam = objCmd.CreateParameter("CustomerID", adWChar, adParamInput, 5,
strParameter)
objCmd.Parameters.Append objParam
```

The name of the created parameter is CustomerID. It is used only to identify the parameter in the Parameters collection later on. The type of the parameter data is set to adWChar because this is the correct ADO data type constant for data of the type fixed-length Unicode String (refer to Table 7.1). The parameter direction is set to adParamInput to create an input parameter. The size (data length) of the value passed to the input parameter is set to 5 (characters). The value, which is passed to the input parameter, is set to the value of the variable strParameter.

After the Parameter object is created, it must be appended to the Parameters collection of the Command object. This is done by the Append method of the Command's Parameters collection.

7

Using an Output Parameter

To retrieve the value of the output parameter of a stored procedure, perform the following steps:

- Prepare the Command object.
- Create the output parameter and append it to the Parameters collection of the Command object.
- Execute the Command object.
- Retrieve the value of the output parameter by reading its value from the Parameters collection.

An output parameter is created and appended to the Parameters collection of the Command object in the following way:

```
Set objParam = objCmd.CreateParameter(Name, Type, adParamOutput , Size)
objCmd.Parameters.Append objParam
```

The variable objCmd contains the Command object, and the variable objParam contains the ADO Parameter object.

After you have executed the Command object, you can read the value of the output parameter from the Parameters collection:

```
OutputValue = objCmd.Parameters(Name)
```

For example, when you want to access the output parameter of the stored procedure named LastShippingAustria (see Listing 7.4), you must know that the parameter is of the SQL Server data type datetime. As you can see in Table 7.1, the corresponding ADO data type constant is adDate with a data length of 8.

Therefore, the statement to create the output parameter might look as follows:

```
Set objParam = objCmd.CreateParameter("ShippedDate",adDate,adParamOutput ,8)
objCmd.Parameters.Append objParam
```

The name of the created parameter is ShippedDate. Its type is set to adDate. The direction indicates an output parameter (adParamOutput), and the data size is 8.

To retrieve the value of the output parameter, execute the command

```
objCmd.Execute
```

Now you can read the value of the output parameter from the Parameters collection:

```
OutputValue = objCmd.Parameters("ShippedDate")
```

As mentioned before you cannot use T-SQL data type as text, ntext, or image for an output parameter. If you want to pass values of those data types from the stored procedure to your application, pass them in a Recordset (using a SELECT statement, for instance).

Using Return Codes

A return code is a special case of an output parameter. You can only retrieve one return code from a stored procedure, and its value is of the SQL Server data type int (corresponding to the data type Long in Visual Basic).

When a stored procedure returns a return code, the first parameter appended to the Parameters collection of the Command object must be the return code.

To create a return code and append it to the Command object, you can use a statement as follows:

```
Set objParam = objCmd.CreateParameter("ReturnCode",
➥ adInteger, adParamReturnValue, 4)
objCmd.Parameters.Append objParam
```

After you have executed the Command, you can use the following statement to read the value of the return code with the name ReturnCode:

```
lngRetCode  = objCmd.Parameters("ReturnCode")
```

That is enough theory about using input parameters, output parameters, and return codes. The next example calls a stored procedure with two input parameters.

Calling a Stored Procedure

An example for a stored procedure (SP) with input parameters is the SP named Sales by Year from SQL Server's Northwind sample database (see Listing 7.8).

LISTING 7.8   The Stored Procedure Sales by Year

```
1: CREATE PROCEDURE "Sales by Year"
2:     @Beginning_Date DateTime,
3:     @Ending_Date DateTime
4: AS
5: SELECT Orders.ShippedDate, Orders.OrderID, "Order Subtotals".Subtotal,
6:     DATENAME(yy,ShippedDate) AS Year
7: FROM Orders INNER JOIN "Order Subtotals" ON
8:     Orders.OrderID = "Order Subtotals".OrderID
9: WHERE Orders.ShippedDate BETWEEN @Beginning_Date AND @Ending_Date
```

The stored procedure Sales by Year has two input parameters. The first is @Beginning_Date and the second @Ending_Date. Both parameters are of the SQL Server

7

data type `DateTime`, which represents a date and time value such as `11/11/2000` `8:21:33 PM` or `7/24/1976`.

The SP `Sales by Year` returns a Recordset, but no output parameters.

How can you invoke this stored procedure using the `Command` object?

The example in Listing 7.9 provides an answer. It invokes the stored procedure `Sales by Year`, provides the two input parameters, and handles the returned Recordset.

In Listing 7.9, it is assumed that the Northwind database is located on the SQL Server 7.0 database that runs on a machine named `BoyScout` and that the database can be accessed using the user ID sa without a password.

LISTING 7.9 Invoking the Stored Procedure `Sales by Year`

```
 1: ' ### Declare Variables
 2: Dim strConn As String
 3: Dim dateBegin As Date
 4: Dim dateEnd As Date
 5: ' ### Declare ADO objects
 6: Dim conn As ADODB.Connection
 7: Dim cmd As ADODB.Command
 8: Dim tmpParam As ADODB.Parameter
 9: Dim rs As ADODB.Recordset
10:
11: ' ### Set some sample dates
12: dateBegin = #1/1/1997#
13: dateEnd = #1/5/1997#
14:
15: ' ### Define ConnectionString
16: strConn = "Provider=SQLOLEDB;Data Source=BoyScout;" & _
17:          "Initial Catalog=Northwind;User ID=sa;Password=;"
18:
19:  ' ### Create Connection object and open Connection
20:  Set conn = CreateObject("ADODB.Connection")
21:  conn.Open strConn
22:
23: ' ### Create Command object
24: Set cmd = CreateObject("ADODB.Command")
25:
26: ' ### Prepare Command
27: cmd.CommandText = "[Sales by Year]"
28: ' Or = """Sales by Year"""
29: cmd.CommandType = adCmdStoredProc
30: Set cmd.ActiveConnection = conn
31:
32: ' ### Create Parameters and apppend them to cmd
33: ' Attention Parameters values that are handed over from
```

```
34: ' the variables must be of correct type and correct length
35: Set tmpParam = cmd.CreateParameter("@Beginning_Date",
➥    adDate, adParamInput, 8, CDate(dateBegin))
36: cmd.Parameters.Append tmpParam
37:
38: Set tmpParam = cmd.CreateParameter("@End_Date",
➥         adDate, adParamInput, 8, CDate(dateEnd))
39: cmd.Parameters.Append tmpParam
40:
41: ' ### Execute cmd and retrieve Recordset
42: ' ### Recordset is then stored in rs
43: Set rs = cmd.Execute
44:
45 ' ### Read returned Recordset
46: Do While (Not (rs.EOF))
47:    strResult = "Shipped Date = " & rs("ShippedDate") & vbCrLf
48:    strResult = strResult & "OrderID = " & rs("OrderID") & vbCrLf
49:    strResult = strResult & "Subtotal = " & rs("Subtotal") & vbCrLf
50:    strResult = strResult & "Year = " & rs("Year") & vbCrLf
51:    Output strResult
52:    rs.MoveNext
53: Loop
54:
55: rs.Close
56: conn.Close
57:
58: Set rs = Nothing
59: Set conn = Nothing
60: Set tmpParam = Nothing
61: Set cmd = Nothing
```

ANALYSIS The script declares some variables in the lines 2–9. The variable strConn contains the ConnectionString; dateBegin and dateEnd contain two dates as input values for the stored procedure. The variable conn contains a Connection object. cmd is the Command object. The variable tmpParam is used to store a temporary Parameter object used to add parameters to the Parameters collection of the Command object. The variable rs contains the Recordset object that is returned after the call of the stored procedure.

Some sample dates are assigned to the variables dateBegin and dateEnd in lines 12–13.

The connection string is stored in the variable strConn in lines 16–17. It contains all the data necessary to connect to the SQL Server database Northwind that is located on the SQL Server machine named BoyScout. The content of the connection string is shown here.

```
Provider=SQLOLEDB;Data Source=BoyScout;Initial Catalog=Northwind;
User ID=sa;Password=;
```

7

The connection string contains the data provider SQLOLEDB, thus specifying the OLE DB Provider for SQL Server. (You can also use the OLE DB Provider for ODBC, together with the ODBC Driver for SQL Server.) The Data Source is the name of the SQL Server machine (or its IP address) to which your application connects across your network to access the database. If the computer where the application is running is the same one that runs SQL Server 7.0, you can use the keyword (local) instead of the machine name. The Initial Catalog specifies the SQL Server database that should be accessed. User ID and Password are used to allow the application to gain access to the SQL Server 7.0 database. They must be a valid user ID/password pair for the database.

Line 20 creates the Connection object, which is used to connect to the database, and stores it in the variable conn. In line 21, the connection is opened using the connection string stored in strConn, which specifies the kind of connection, the database, and the database provider.

The Command object is created in line 24 and stored in the variable cmd. Because you want the Command object to execute the stored procedure, you must prepare the Command object and provide necessary data, such as the name of the stored procedure and the connection to use. To speed up processing, you also can specify the type of command to execute. This all is done in the lines 27–30.

The name of the stored procedure (Sales by Year) is assigned to the CommandText property of the Command object. Square brackets surround the name of the stored procedure because the name contains spaces (quotation marks would also do the trick, as shown in line 28). The CommandType is set to adCmdStoredProc to indicate that a stored procedure is to be executed. This is optional, but it increases speed. When it is used, the ADO provider does not need to determine which kind of statement is to be executed. The ActiveConnection property is set to the Connection stored in the variable conn. This is done to determine which connection to use for accessing the database.

The two input parameters of the stored procedure are created and appended to the Command object in lines 35–39.

Each parameter is represented by a Parameter object. Both parameters are created using the CreateParameter method of the Command object.

```
38: Set tmpParam = cmd.CreateParameter("@End_Date",
➥            adDate, adParamInput, 8, CDate(dateEnd))
```

Compare this to the syntax of the CreateParameter method:

```
Set parameter = command.CreateParameter (Name, Type, Direction, Size, Value)
```

The prepared Command object is executed in line 43, and the returned Recordset is stored in the variable rs. You can use this Recordset as usual, navigate through it, and read fields of its records as shown in lines 46–53. The function named Output is not a Visual Basic function, but it stands for a custom function that shows the data to the user.

After all database actions are finished, the Recordset object and the Connection object are closed in lines 55 and 56. This is done to free the database connection in case there are a restricted number of concurrent connections available from the database or the provider.

To free all ADO resources, the objects used in the script are explicitly released and set to Nothing in the lines 58–61.

Populating the Parameters Collection

Instead of specifying the data type for each input and output parameter, you can also use the Refresh method of the Parameters collection to populate the Parameters collection with Parameter objects of the correct data type, parameter direction, and data size.

Listing 7.10 shows how to use the Refresh method to retrieve the data type, direction, and data size of the Northwind stored procedure named SalesByCategory. The stored procedure SalesByCategory has two input parameters, defined in T-SQL as follows:

```
@CategoryName nvarchar(15),
@OrdYear nvarchar(4)
```

Listing 7.10 uses the Refresh method, assigns some values to the input parameters, and calls the stored procedure SalesByCategory. The code processing the returned Recordset is omitted in Listing 7.10.

LISTING 7.10   Populating a Parameters Collection Using the Refresh Method

```
 1: Dim conn As ADODB.Connection
 2: Dim cmd As ADODB.Command
 3: Dim Param As ADODB.Parameter
 4: Dim rs As ADODB.Recordset
 5:
 6: Set conn = CreateObject("ADODB.Connection")
 7: conn.Open "Provider=SQLOLEDB;Data Source=BoyScout;" & _
 8:    "Initial Catalog=Northwind;User ID=sa;Password=;"
 9:
10: Set cmd = CreateObject("ADODB.Command")
11:
12: cmd.CommandText = "SalesByCategory"
13: cmd.CommandType = adCmdStoredProc
14: Set cmd.ActiveConnection = conn
15:
```

7

continues

LISTING 7.10 continued

```
16: cmd.Parameters.Refresh
17:
18: For Each Param In cmd.Parameters
19:     Debug.Print "Name: " & Param.Name
20:     Debug.Print "Type: " & Param.Type
21:     Debug.Print "Direction: " & Param.Direction
22:     Debug.Print "Size: " & Param.Size
23:     Debug.Print
24: Next
25:
26: cmd.Parameters("@CategoryName") = "Beverages"
27: cmd.Parameters("@OrdYear") = "1998"
28:
29: Set rs = cmd.Execute
30:
31: ' ... Process the Recordset
32:
33: rs.Close
34: conn.Close
35: Set rs = Nothing
36: Set cmd = Nothing
37: Set Param = Nothing
38: Set conn = Nothing
```

OUTPUT

```
Name: RETURN_VALUE
Type: 3
Direction: 4
Size: 0

Name: @CategoryName
Type: 202
Direction: 1
Size: 15

Name: @OrdYear
Type: 202
Direction: 1
Size: 4
```

ANALYSIS In lines 10–14 the script prepares a Command object named cmd to call the stored procedure named SalesByCategory. To populate the Parameters collection of the Command object, the script calls the Refresh method in line 16. Now all Parameter objects in the Parameters collection have the correct type, direction, and size. The name of the Parameter objects is the same as the parameter name specified in the stored procedure (including the trailing @). The name of the return code is RETURN_VALUE.

To show the name, type, direction, and size values of all parameters, the script writes the values to the user in the lines 18–24 (see also output of Listing 7.10). The values of the type and the direction are the integer values of the according ADO constants. A type value of 3 stands for the ADO type constant adInteger, and a type value of 202 stands for adVarWChar. The direction value of 4 is the integer value of the ADO direction constant adParamReturnValue, and the direction value 1 stands for adParamInput. The size value indicates the size value of the parameter in characters or bytes.

Using the Refresh method sometimes makes it easier to write an application that calls a stored procedure. However, calling the Refresh method of the Parameters collection requires a round trip to the SQL database server to retrieve all parameter data. This slows down performance. Besides, errors (such as mixing up values for parameters) cannot be detected as easily as when you explicitly specify each parameter.

Summary

You have seen how to program and to use stored procedures. They are scripts written in T-SQL. Stored procedure are stored in a SQL Server database and executed directly at the SQL Server machine. You can pass parameter values to or retrieve them from the stored procedure. Only input parameters can be the SQL Server data type text, ntext, or image. Output parameters or variables in stored procedures must not be of T-SQL data type text, ntext, or image.

The main advantage of using stored procedures, instead of sending SQL statements to the SQL server, is that stored procedures perform at higher speed. SQL statements that are sent to the SQL Server database have to be parsed every time you execute them. Stored procedures are parsed and stored at the server after they are executed the first time.

Another important advantage is that stored procedures can be used as defined interfaces. An application can use this interface only—instead of dealing with the inner structure of the database.

Q&A

Q **Is SQL Server the only database system that uses stored procedures?**

A Other database systems, such as Oracle for instance, support stored procedures. However, they use different programming languages than SQL Server does. The OLE DB provider or the database driver determine how stored procedures of these database systems must be called.

7

Q Can I use stored procedures to perform administrative tasks on the SQL Server, such as deleting a database or creating a new user?

A If you have enough knowledge about the inner structure of a SQL Server database system, you can write your own stored procedures to perform such tasks. However, a SQL 7.0 Server already has included System Stored Procedures and Extended Stored Procedures. Using these procedures, you can easily perform administrative and informative activities at the SQL Server. When you call such stored procedures from your application, you must log on with a user account that has the permission and administrative privileges to execute the stored procedures.

Workshop

The Workshop is designed to help you anticipate possible questions, review what you've learned, and get you thinking about how to put your knowledge into practice. The answers to the quiz are in Appendix A, "Answers."

Quiz

1. What is characteristic of the name of a variable or parameter in a stored procedure?
2. Can a stored procedure return a Recordset?
3. In which language is a stored procedure for a SQL Server database written?
4. What kind of data cannot be used as values for stored procedure output parameters?

Exercises

1. Write a script in Visual Basic or VBScript that executes the SQL Server 7.0 stored procedure LastShippingAustria (see Listing 7.4) and reads its output parameter.
2. Write a stored procedure that uses one input parameter named @EmployeeID. Return the number of orders from the Northwind Orders table in the output parameter @OrdersTotal that have the same value in the column EmployeeID as the value in the parameter @EmployeeID. Also, return a Recordset that contains all the records that have the value of the variable @EmployeeID in the column EmployeeID. The data type of the parameter @EmployeeID is the same as of the column EmployeeID in the Orders table (SQL Server data type int). Note that you can use the T-SQL function COUNT to get the number of records:

```
SELECT COUNT(*) WHERE Condition
```

WEEK 1
In Review

To review this week, let's explore a case study for the ficti-
tious company "Austrian Aircraft Supply," which sells spare
aircraft parts to all major European airlines.

Austrian Aircraft Supply (AAS Inc.) has its headquarters in
Vienna. It started out as a small one-man shop that delivered
spare parts for hobby pilots' machines. The owner quickly got
in touch with pilots from major Austrian airlines, which
helped him get contracts with their airlines' repair centers.
AAS Inc. then started expanding very fast and now also delivers parts to airlines in France, Belgium, and Sweden.

AAS Inc. has two subsidiaries: one in Frankfurt, Germany,
the other at the Charles de Gaulle airport in Paris. All sales in
the subsidiaries are currently faxed to the headquarters in
Austria, where they are entered into the order entry system
(which is based on an Access 97 solution). For order tracking,
the sales agents in France and Germany have to call their col-
leagues in Vienna. Lists of spare parts and their prices are
sent to the subsidiaries once a week.

The company is about to open two more subsidiaries
(Belgium and Sweden) this year, and another four next year.
The company owner also wants to allow airline customers to
order directly via a secure Web site. Clearly, the current solution isn't adequate for this kind of expansion. You are hired as
a consultant to propose a better solution.

What can you propose to solve the company's pressing business needs? The first mandatory change is to switch to a powerful database back end, such as SQL Server 7. Access isn't
suited for distributed applications, which are needed for the
new order entry system and the Web business-to-business
ordering system. SQL Server offers much better performance,
and you can easily import data from the existing application.

1

2

3

4

5

6

7

This change also mandates that AAS Inc. has to recode its order entry. However, you recommend that it rewrite the DAO code to ADO, because this code also can be reused for the secure Web site for airline orders.

To ensure good performance over the WAN links from the subsidiaries to the headquarters in Vienna—as well as adding an extra level of security for data manipulation—all data access code must be implemented in stored procedures. This allows less changes to the order entry front end while still allowing changes at the database back end.

You also propose to add an order tracking system to the secure Web site, because when the sales agents from the subsidiaries visit their customers, these most likely have Internet access. Now they can answer questions about part availability and shipping immediately.

WEEK 2

At A Glance

This week, you move from basic ADO tasks to more advanced topics. You acquire mandatory knowledge about transaction processing, explore Online Analytical Processing (OLAP) systems, integrate semistructured data in your database application, develop applications that access hierarchical data, and learn how to manage existing databases.

- Day 8—You safeguard your application's data modification tasks with database transactions that allow you to either commit or abort all operations as if they were one single task.
- Day 9—You acquire the necessary skills to create applications that work asynchronously with databases.
- Day 10—You learn how to create hierarchical recordsets using the MSDataShape provider and the SHAPE language.
- Day 11—You explore the basics of what OLAP is, and why it is important for a business. You apply this knowledge to SQL Server 7 OLAP Services.
- Day 12—You build applications on top of the cubes that you created in Day 11. You use ADO MD and the MDX query language to return information from the OLAP Services cubes.
- Day 13—You access semistructured data, such as files on Web servers or the Exchange Web store, using ADO. You learn about new objects that were introduced with ADO 2.5.
- Day 14—You discover the power of ADO X for managing your Access databases—both the definition and the security of database objects.

8

9

10

11

12

13

14

DAY **8**

Enrolling in Transactions

In business applications—especially in database applications—it is often necessary that a unit of work is done in a single and atomic operation (Consider transferring money from a bank account to another). For illustration think about an e-commerce application—when your application processes a customer's order, it has to perform several tasks—initiating to send the goods to the customer, decreasing the number of items in stock stored in the database. Furthermore, the application writes the order details and the order revenue into the database to provide an instant overview in earnings and deliveries.

To make sure that the order process is finally succeeds or fails, you can enclose all tasks of the order process in a transaction. A transaction checks whether every part of the transaction was finished successfully before it commits all the changes and makes them permanent. If any of the tasks in the transaction fails, no matter what the reason, all changes in the whole transaction are rolled back. Furthermore, transactions can be explicitly aborted or committed by your application.

The application must have a means to make sure that the chain of actions—sending the ordered goods and performing all database tasks—is always performed as a whole, and never executed partially.

Multiple database tasks that all either have to succeed or be canceled entirely must be encapsulated in a so-called database transaction.

NEW TERM A *database transaction* is a series of database changes that either have to be saved or canceled as a single unit. A typical transaction occurs when you buy something in a shop. You give the salesman the money and get in exchange the goods you bought. You cannot receive the goods without paying or pay the money and get nothing in exchange. Both actions—handing over the money and receiving the goods—must be performed as a single unit.

A transaction is especially important when you keep in mind that computer hardware or software may fail in the middle of a set of database tasks. To protect your application from such failure and to enforce database integrity, you can use the built-in transaction mechanisms of ADO.

Because you are dealing with database transactions and their use today, you will learn the following:

- Managing database transactions using the ADO `Connection` object and its methods
- Controlling transactions on Active Server Pages using the `TRANSACTION` directive

Enforcing Transactions Using ADO

Whenever you need transaction support when dealing with database changes, you can use mechanisms that are provided by ADO itself. The ADO `Connection` object supports transactions on a single database connection. Use the built-in methods of the `Connection` object to enforce database transactions.

NEW TERM You can start, commit, or reject all database changes encapsulated in a transaction. Furthermore, you can establish transactions that contain other transactions. Such a construct is called a *nested transaction*. An ADO transaction runs in the following typical steps:

1. Open a database connection.
2. Start a new transaction on the connection.
3. Perform the database changes that are encapsulated by the transaction.
4. Commit the transaction so that all database changes are saved or roll back the transaction and cancel all database changes made in the context of the transaction.
5. Close the database connection.

Performing a Simple Transaction

A simple transaction contains several database tasks that are either saved or canceled at the end of the transaction.

The Connection object provides three methods to manage a transaction:

- The BeginTrans method starts a new transaction.
- The CommitTrans method saves all database changes encapsulated in the transaction.
- The RollbackTrans method cancels all pending changes instead of saving them.

Using these methods to manage a transaction in a database application are explained in Listing 8.1, which represents a simple but typical database transaction example using the ADO Connection object to enforce a transaction.

LISTING 8.1   Simple Database Transaction

```
 1: Dim conn As ADODB.Connection
 2: Dim rs As ADODB.Recordset
 3: Dim lngOrderID As Long
 4: Dim lngProductID As Long
 5: Dim lngEmployeeID As Long
 6: Dim lngUnits As Long
 7: Dim lngUnitsInStock As Long
 8: Dim curUnitPrice As Currency
 9: Dim TransDLLProp As Variant
10: Dim blnCommit As Boolean
11:
12: lngEmployeeID = 3
13: lngProductID = 14
14: curUnitPrice = 24.25
15: lngUnits = 5
16: blnCommit = False    ' Set to True to perform updates
17:
18: Set conn = CreateObject("ADODB.Connection")
19: conn.Open "Provider=SQLOLEDB;Data Source=BoyScout;" & _
20:    "Initial Catalog=Northwind;User ID=sa;Password=;"
21:
22: Set rs = CreateObject("ADODB.Recordset")
23: rs.CursorLocation = adUseServer
24: rs.LockType = adLockOptimistic
25: rs.CursorType = adOpenKeyset
26:
27: ' Check if provider supports transactions
28: On Error Resume Next
29: TransDLLProp = conn.Properties("Transaction DDL")
```

continues

LISTING 8.1   continued

```
30: If Err.Number = 3265 Then
31:     Debug.Print "Transactions are not supported by the provider!"
32:     Err.Number = 0
33:     On Error GoTo 0
34:     conn.Close
35:     Exit Function
36: Else
37:     On Error GoTo 0
38:     Debug.Print "Transactions are supported."
39: End If
40:
41: ' Begin Transaction
42: conn.BeginTrans
43:
44: rs.Open "SELECT * FROM Orders WHERE 1=0", conn
45: rs.AddNew
46: rs("EmployeeID") = lngEmployeeID
47: rs("OrderDate") = Now
48: rs.Update
49: lngOrderID = rs("OrderID")
50: rs.Close
51:
52: rs.Open "SELECT * FROM [Order Details] WHERE 1=0", conn
53: rs.AddNew
54: rs("OrderID") = lngOrderID
55: rs("ProductID") = lngProductID
56: rs("UnitPrice") = curUnitPrice
57: rs("Quantity") = lngUnits
58: rs("Discount") = 0
59: rs.Update
60: rs.Close
61:
62: If blnCommit = True Then
63:     conn.CommitTrans
64:     Debug.Print "Order with Order ID = " & lngOrderID &
➥ " inserted into database."
65: Else
66:     conn.RollbackTrans
67:     Debug.Print "Order with Order ID = " & lngOrderID &
➥ " was canceled."
68: End If
69:
70: conn.Close
```

The code in Listing 8.1 should produce this output (Order ID may vary):

OUTPUT
```
Transactions are supported.
Order with Order ID = 11095 was canceled.
```

ANALYSIS The database transaction sample basically performs two database tasks: First it writes a new dataset into the Orders table of the Northwind database. Second, the sample writes another dataset into the Order Details table. Both database changes are encapsulated in a transaction. Either both changes are committed to the database as a single unit, or no database changes are performed. It does not matter whether the application crashes after inserting the first dataset. The transaction mechanism enforces the database to roll back the transaction so that the first insert is canceled.

In lines 12–16, the ProductID, EmployeeID, UnitPrice, and number of units is defined. These values are part of the two datasets inserted into the database tables. The value in the variable blnCommit defines whether the transaction is committed or rolled back when all database changes are performed. In the listing, its value is set to False so that all database changes are canceled at the end of the script.

To perform the database changes, the connection to the database is defined and opened. A Recordset object is created and prepared to use optimistic locking and a keyset cursor. These recordset options enable inserting new records into the database table using the AddNew method.

It is important for the application whether the database provider supports transactions. To get at this critical information, the script accesses the Transaction DLL item of the connection's Properties connection. When the Transaction DDL item is missing, the database provider does not support transactions. Accessing a missing item causes a runtime error in line 29, which is intercepted using the On Error Resume Next statement in line 28. When transactions are not supported, the script writes a message to the user and aborts processing the script in line 35.

Tip | To make sure that the database provider does support transactions, read the Transaction DDL item from the connection's Properties collection.

Usually, the script writes the message to the user that transactions are supported, because almost all database providers now support them.

The transaction begins in line 42 and is started by calling the BeginTrans method of the database connection.

The first dataset is written to the Orders table in lines 44–50 using the AddNew and Update methods. Because the application needs to know the OrderID of the inserted record, the OrderID of the recordset rs is read, after calling the Update method, and stored in the variable lngOrderID.

Then the second dataset is stored in the database table named Order Details. Because this record refers to the record formerly stored in the Orders table, the OrderID value of the record is set to the value stored in the variable lngOrderID in line 54. All other values of the record are predefined by the application. The second record is written to the database calling the Update method in line 59.

Finally, depending on the value stored in blnCommit, the transaction is committed or rolled back. If the transaction is committed calling the CommitTrans method of the connection, both new records are saved permanently in the database in lines 63 and 64 and a message is written to the user.

When the application calls the RollbackTrans method of the connection, the transaction is rolled back and both inserted records are deleted from the database.

Here is a summary of this listing: To enforce a transaction, the script opens a connection to a database provider, which should support transactions. Then the transaction is started for a certain connection, calling the BeginTrans method of the Connection object. All database changes made using the connection are now included in a single transaction until the CommitTrans or RollbackTrans method is called. Calling the CommitTrans method saves the database changes of the transaction. However, when calling the RollbackTrans method, all database changes contained in the transaction are canceled.

Of course, you can use as many transactions you want—one after the other. For instance, you can call transactions as in Listing 8.2.

LISTING 8.2   Multiple Independent Transactions

```
 1: ' conn contains an open database connection
 2: ' Start Transaction 1
 3: conn.BeginTrans
 4:    ...
 5: conn.CommitTrans / conn.RollbackTrans
 6: ...
 7: ' Start Transaction 2
 8: conn.BeginTrans
 9:    ...
10: ' End Transaction 2
11: conn.CommitTrans / conn.RollbackTrans
```

ANALYSIS   The first transaction is enforced in lines 3–5. After the first transaction is finished, the second transaction is started in line 8 and ends in line 11.

When you want your application to start a new transaction automatically after calling CommitTrans or RollbackTrans, set the Attributes property of the Connection object to a certain value that indicates if a new transaction is started automatically after calling

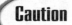

CommitTrans or RollbackTrans. Automatically starting a new transaction has the advantage that you only have to write a statement in your application code to start the first transaction. You can omit all other transaction start statements and therefore have to write less code.

When no transaction should be started automatically, set the Attributes property to 0:

```
conn.Attributes = 0
```

> **Tip**
>
> In ADO 2.5, the default value of the Attributes property is 0 (and no transaction starts automatically after calling CommitTrans or RollbackTrans). However, it is a good idea to set its value to 0 explicitly as a database provider or the connection might return another default value, which overwrites the ADO default value.

To start a new transaction automatically after calling CommitTrans, use the following statement:

```
conn.Attributes = adXactCommitRetaining
```

You can enforce automatically starting transactions after calling RollbackTrans with this statement:

```
conn.Attributes = adXactAbortRetaining
```

When you want your application to start a new transaction automatically when either CommitTrans or RollbackTrans is called, include the following statement in your script:

```
conn.Attributes = adXactAbortRetaining Or adXactCommitRetaining
```

Nested Transactions

As mentioned earlier, ADO also enables a transaction to contain other transactions, called nested transactions. In Figure 8.1, transaction 1 contains the child transactions named transaction 2 and transaction 3.

> **Caution**
>
> Nested transactions are supported by ADO 2.5. However, whether you can use nested transactions in a database application depends on the database provider. For instance, the OLE DB Provider for SQL Server 7.0, as well as the ODBC Provider for OLE DB, does not support nested transactions. The most important database provider supporting nested transactions is the OLE DB Provider for Microsoft Jet (Microsoft.Jet.OLEDB.4.0), which connects to an Access 2000 database (see also the example in Listing 8.4).

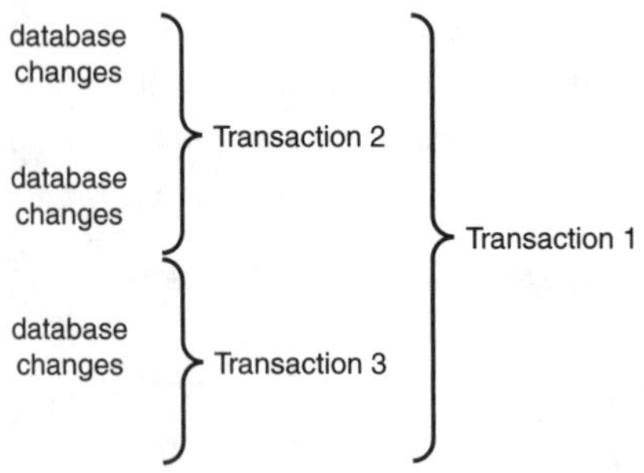

FIGURE 8.1

Schematic diagram of nested transactions.

database
changes
                    } Transaction 2
database
changes   } Transaction 1

database
changes   } Transaction 3

> **Tip**
>
> To check whether your data source provider supports nested transactions, you have to write a little test script that contains a simple nested transaction and execute it against your data source using the provider.

You can begin a new transaction in the context of a parent connection by calling the BeginTrans method. The level of the new transaction can be obtained when calling the BeginTrans method:

```
TransLevel = conn.BeginTrans()
```

The variable conn contains an open connection. When calling the BeginTrans method, the level of the new transaction is returned and stored in the variable TransLevel.

Nested transactions can be enforced, as in Listing 8.3.

LISTING 8.3   Schema of Nested Transactions

```
 1: ' conn contains an open database connection
 2: ' Start Transaction 1
 3: conn.BeginTrans
 4:    ...
 5:    ' Start Transaction 2
 6:    conn.BeginTrans
 7:       ...
 8:    ' End Transaction 2
 9:    conn.CommitTrans / conn.RollbackTrans
10:    ...
11:    ' Start Transaction 3
12:    conn.BeginTrans
13:       ...
14:    ' End Transaction 3
15:    conn.CommitTrans / conn.RollbackTrans
16:    ...
17: ' End Transaction 1
18: conn.CommitTrans / conn.RollbackTrans
```

8

ANALYSIS Transaction 1 is enforced from line 3 to line 18. Transaction 2 (line 6–9) and transaction 3 (lines 11–15) are contained in transaction 1. Transactions 2 and 3 can either be committed or rolled back independently. However, if transaction 1 is rolled back, transaction 2 and transaction 3 are also rolled back automatically—even when transaction 2 or transaction 3 have been committed in their transaction level before (No task included in a transaction is committed permanently until all parent transactions are also committed).

This behavior is easy to understand when you keep in mind that when a transaction is rolled back all contained database changes are canceled. This is even true when a child transaction (such as transaction 2) is committed, because the database changes are also contained in the parent transaction (transaction 1).

Listing 8.4 illustrates the general use of nested transactions.

LISTING 8.4   Nested Transaction

```
 1: Dim conn As ADODB.Connection
 2: Dim rs As ADODB.Recordset
 3: Dim rsProd As ADODB.Recordset
 4: Dim lngOrderID As Long
 5: Dim lngProductID As Long
 6: Dim lngEmployeeID As Long
 7: Dim lngUnits As Long
 8: Dim lngUnitsInStock As Long
 9: Dim curUnitPrice As Currency
10: Dim TransDLLProp As Variant
11: Dim blnCommit As Boolean
12: Dim TransLevel As Long
13:
14: lngEmployeeID = 3
15: lngProductID = 14
16: lngUnits = 5
17: blnCommit = False    ' Set to true to perform updates of transaction
18:
19: Set conn = CreateObject("ADODB.Connection")
20: conn.Open "Provider=Microsoft.Jet.OLEDB.4.0;" & _
21:    "Data Source=J:\ADO25\Northwind\Northwind.mdb;" & _
22:    "user id=admin;password=;"
23:
24: Set rsProd = CreateObject("ADODB.Recordset")
25: rsProd.CursorLocation = adUseServer
26: rsProd.LockType = adLockOptimistic
27: rsProd.CursorType = adOpenKeyset
28:
29: Set rs = CreateObject("ADODB.Recordset")
```

continues

LISTING 8.4   continued

```
30: rs.CursorLocation = adUseServer
31: rs.LockType = adLockOptimistic
32: rs.CursorType = adOpenKeyset
33:
34: ' Check if provider supports transactions
35: On Error Resume Next
36: TransDLLProp = conn.Properties("Transaction DDL")
37: If Err.Number = 3265 Then
38:     Debug.Print "Transactions are not supported by the provider!"
39:     Err.Number = 0
40:     On Error GoTo 0
41:     conn.Close
42:     Exit Function
43: Else
44:     On Error GoTo 0
45: End If
46:
47: ' Do not start a new transaction after
48: ' calling CommitTrans or RollbackTrans
49: conn.Attributes = 0
50:
51: ' Begin Parent Transaction
52: TransLevel = conn.BeginTrans()
53: Debug.Print "Begin Transaction Level " & TransLevel
54:
55: rsProd.Open "SELECT * FROM Products WHERE ProductID = " & _
56:     lngProductID, conn
57: curUnitPrice = rsProd("UnitPrice")
58: lngUnitsInStock = rsProd("UnitsInStock")
59:
60: If lngUnitsInStock < lngUnits Then
61:     ' To less units in stock, abort processing
62:     ' Roll back Parent Transaction
63:     Debug.Print "Rollback Transaction Level " & TransLevel
64:     conn.RollbackTrans
65:     Debug.Print "Not enough items in stocks, processing aborted."
66: Else
67:     ' Begin Child Transaction
68:     TransLevel = conn.BeginTrans()
69:     Debug.Print "   Begin Transaction Level " & TransLevel
70:
71:     rs.Open "SELECT * FROM Orders WHERE 1=0", conn
72:     rs.AddNew
73:     rs("EmployeeID") = lngEmployeeID
74:     rs("OrderDate") = Now
75:     rs.Update
76:     lngOrderID = rs("OrderID")
77:     Debug.Print "    Order ID = " & lngOrderID
78:     rs.Close
79:
```

8

```
80:      rs.Open "SELECT * FROM [Order Details] WHERE 1=0", conn
81:      rs.AddNew
82:      rs("OrderID") = lngOrderID
83:      rs("ProductID") = lngProductID
84:      rs("UnitPrice") = curUnitPrice
85:      rs("Quantity") = lngUnits
86:      rs("Discount") = 0
87:      rs.Update
88:      rs.Close
89:
90:      ' Commit Child Transaction
91:      Debug.Print "   Commit Transaction Level " & TransLevel
92:      conn.CommitTrans
93:      TransLevel = TransLevel - 1
94:
95:      If blnCommit = True Then
96:          ' Commit Parent Transaction
97:          Debug.Print "Commit Transaction Level " & TransLevel
98:          conn.CommitTrans
99:      Else
100:          ' Rollback Parent Transaction
101:          Debug.Print "Rollback Transaction Level " & TransLevel
102:          conn.RollbackTrans
103:      End If
104: End If
105:
106: rsProd.Close
107: conn.Close
```

OUTPUT The output of Listing 8.4 could be as follows:

```
Begin Transaction Level 1
   Begin Transaction Level 2
      Order ID = 11083
   Commit Transaction Level 2
Rollback Transaction Level 1
```

ANALYSIS The script contains a parent transaction and a child transaction. The child transaction contains two database changes that consist of adding a new record to the Orders and the Order Details table. The parent transaction contains the child transaction and also a database change where one value of a record in the Products table is changed.

In line 20, a connection to the Access 2000 Northwind sample database is opened. The OLE DB Provider for Microsoft Jet is used in the sample because it supports nested transactions. The recordsets rsProd and rs are created and prepared in lines 24–32. Both are using optimistic locking and a keyset cursor. In lines 35–45, the script checks whether the database provider supports transactions.

Note   The value returned from the Transaction DDL property of the connection is of type long. Its value is provider-specific and not generally defined for ADO.

When using nested transactions, you can specify whether a new transaction is started automatically after calling CommitTrans or RollbackTrans. Setting the Attributes property of the connection to 0 means that no new transaction is automatically started after calling CommitTrans or RollbackTrans.

Caution   When using nested transactions, the value of the Attributes property must be set to zero before calling the last CommitTrans or RollbackTrans of a child transaction. Otherwise, a new transaction is started automatically, and the application could never finish the parent transaction by a call of CommitTrans or RollbackTrans.

The parent transaction is started in line 51 calling the BeginTrans method. The returned value is the level of the started transaction; it is stored in the variable TransLevel for further use in the script.

In line 55, the record with the ProductID specified in lngProductID is retrieved from the Products table. The UnitPrice of the retrieved record is stored in the variable curUnitPrice, and the number of units in stock is stored in lngUnitsInStock. When there are not as many units in stock as specified in the variable lngUnits, the transaction is rolled back in line 64 and the execution of the script is aborted. Otherwise, the child transaction is established in line 68, and its transaction level stored in TransLevel.

Lines 71–78 add a new record to the Orders table and retrieve the OrderID value from the Orders table after the record is written to the table in line 75 by the Update method. The value of the retrieved OrderID is written to the user in line 77. Another new record is written to the Order Details table in lines 80–88.

The child transaction is committed in line 92 using the CommitTrans method. To reflect that this causes the transaction to go to the next level, the value of TransLevel is decreased by 1 in line 93.

When the value in blnCommit is True, the parent transaction is committed and all database changes are saved. When blnCommit does not contain True, the parent transaction is rolled back and all database changes are canceled—even the changes performed in the child transaction.

Running Transactions on SQL Server 7.0

8

When your application is using SQL Server 7.0, you can make use of stored procedures. T-SQL, the SQL version of SQL Server, enables you to enforce transactions in stored procedures using statements such as BEGIN TRANSACTION, COMMIT TRANSACTION, and ROLLBACK TRANSACTION.

Listing 8.5 is a simple stored procedure containing a transaction.

LISTING 8.5 Stored Procedure Containing a Transaction

```
1: CREATE PROCEDURE MyProcedure
2:    @MyValue VARCHAR(25) AS
3: BEGIN TRANSACTION TransactionName
4:    INSERT INTO MyTable1 VALUES (@MyValue)
5:    INSERT INTO MyTable2 VALUES (@MyValue)
6: COMMIT TRANSACTION TransactionName
```

ANALYSIS The transaction named TransactionName begins in line 3 of the stored procedure and ends in line 6. All statements between the beginning and the end of the transaction are either all executed or all canceled.

Use ADO to call the stored procedure named MyProcedure with the following statement, for instance:

```
conn.Execute " MyProcedure 'MyValue' "
```

Of course, you can call a stored procedure containing one or more transactions the same way as calling any other stored procedure (see also Day 7, "Implementing Application Logic in Stored Procedures").

It is also possible to use T-SQL transaction statements for a certain connection by executing them against a SQL Server database.

Listing 8.6 adds two records to a SQL Server 7.0 database. The insertion of both records is encapsulated in a transaction that is provided directly by the SQL Server database.

LISTING 8.6 Enforcing Transaction Using T-SQL Statements

```
1: Dim conn As ADODB.Connection
2: Dim rs As ADODB.Recordset
3: Dim lngOrderID As Long
4: Dim lngProductID As Long
5: Dim lngEmployeeID As Long
6: Dim lngUnits As Long
7: Dim curUnitPrice As Currency
```

continues

LISTING 8.6 continued

```
 8: Dim blnCommit As Boolean
 9:
10: lngEmployeeID = 3
11: lngProductID = 14
12: curUnitPrice = 24.25
13: lngUnits = 5
14: blnCommit = False     ' Set to True to perform updates
15:
16: Set conn = CreateObject("ADODB.Connection")
17: conn.Open "Provider=SQLOLEDB;Data Source=BoyScout;" & _
18:     "Initial Catalog=Northwind;User ID=sa;Password=;"
19:
20: ' Begin transaction
21: conn.Execute "BEGIN TRANSACTION MyTransaction"
22:
23: ' Insert record
24: conn.Execute "INSERT INTO Orders (EmployeeID, OrderDate) " & _
25:     "VALUES(" & lngEmployeeID & ",'" & CStr(Now) & "')"
26:
27: ' Get Identity column value of last insert
28: Set rs = conn.Execute("SELECT @@IDENTITY AS OrderID")
29: lngOrderID = rs("OrderID")
30: rs.Close
31:
32: ' Insert record
33: conn.Execute "INSERT INTO [Order Details] " & _
34:     "(OrderID, ProductID, UnitPrice, Quantity) " & _
35:     "VALUES(" & lngOrderID & "," & lngProductID & "," & curUnitPrice & _
36:     "," & lngUnits & ")"
37:
38: ' Commit or cancel all database changes
39: If blnCommit = True Then
40:     conn.Execute "COMMIT TRANSACTION MyTransaction"
41:     Debug.Print "Order with Order ID = " & lngOrderID & _
42:     " inserted into database."
43: Else
44:     conn.Execute "ROLLBACK TRANSACTION MyTransaction"
45:     Debug.Print "Order with Order ID = " & lngOrderID & " was canceled."
46: End If
47:
48: conn.Close
```

ANALYSIS The script opens a connection named conn to the SQL Server 7.0 Northwind database in line 17. The transaction of the connection named conn is started in line 21 by executing the following T-SQL statement against the database:

```
BEGIN TRANSACTION MyTransaction
```

This T-SQL Statement starts the transaction named MyTransaction on the SQL Server connection.

In lines 24–36, two records are inserted into the Northwind database using INSERT statements. When the variable blnCommit is set to True, the transaction is committed in line 40 by executing the following T-SQL statement:

```
COMMIT TRANSACTION MyTransaction
```

When blnCommit contains a value other than True, the transaction is aborted, and all database changes are rolled back in line 44 using the T-SQL statement:

```
ROLLBACK TRANSACTION MyTransaction
```

Tip

> Using T-SQL statements to enforce transactions against a SQL Server database instead of using the Connection object's BeginTrans, CommitTrans, or RollbackTrans method is very useful when you want to use nested transactions in your application. The OLE DB Provider for SQL Server is not capable of nested transactions; however, when invoking transactions by executing transaction SQL statements directly against the SQL Server database, you can enforce nested transactions.

For further details about transactions on SQL Server, refer to SQL Server Books Online, the Microsoft Platform SDK, or another in-depth documentation about SQL Server 7.0.

Use of Transactions in Active Server Pages

When you use Active Server Pages (as in a Web or intranet application), you can use the built-in transaction support of ASP to enclose all ADO tasks in one transaction.

A transaction in ASP is a set of instructions that succeed or fail as a whole. Using ASP on IIS 5.0 (and IIS 4.0), the @TRANSACTION directive can be set in the very first line of an ASP script:

```
<%@TRANSACTION = value %>
```

For the value parameter in IIS 5.0, you can use either Required or Requires_New to initiate a transaction automatically; or you use the values Supported or Not_Supported, which will not initiate a transaction.

Day 15, "Creating Scalable Solutions in COM+," explains in detail how transactions are handled by the operating system.

The transaction ends automatically when the script finishes processing. However, you can cancel the effect of all ASP statements within the transaction by calling the following method of the ASP-intrinsic ObjectContext object:

```
ObjectContext.SetAbort
```

When you explicitly want to complete the transaction immediately, use the following statement:

```
ObjectContext.SetComplete
```

Calling the `SetComplete` method forces the ASP script to complete the transaction. However, ASP is waiting for all components participating in the transaction to return `SetComplete`. Then the transaction is completed.

When using a transaction in ASP, the whole ASP page is considered as a transaction. All objects that support transactions cancel their operations when an object aborts the transaction. Of course, the ADO object supports transactions when the used database provider does so. All changes in files on hard disk and changes in ASP Session and `Application` variables are not rolled back. The transaction is committed if all objects on the ASP page indicate that their transactional tasks were successful.

A typical transactional ASP script is shown in Listing 8.7.

LISTING 8.7   ASP Transaction Page

```
 1: <% @TRANSACTION = Required %>
 2: <%
 3:     'Buffer output
 4:     Response.Buffer = True
 5:     ...
 6:     ' Perform some actions
 7:     ...
 8:     If blnOK = True Then
 9:         ' Commit transaction
10:         ObjectContext.SetComplete
11:         Response.Write "Transaction completed."
12:     Else
13:         ' Rollback transaction
14:         ObjectContext.SetAbort
15:         Response.Write "Transaction aborted."
16:     End If
17: %>
```

ANALYSIS   In line 1, the ASP page is declared to use a transaction. All objects of the ASP page that support transactions are part of the ASP page transaction. When `blnOK` contains `True`, the transaction is committed explicitly in line 10 calling the `ObjectContext.SetComplete` method. Otherwise, the transaction is rolled back in line 14 calling the `ObjectContext.SetAbort` method.

Instead of explicitly committing or aborting the transaction, you could make use of events that are triggered when the transaction commits or fails in the ASP script.

8

An ASP transaction triggers two events. When the transaction is successful, the OnTransactionCommit event is triggered and the OnTransactionCommit sub of the ASP page is executed. When the transaction fails, the OnTransactionAbort event is triggered and the OnTransactionAbort sub is executed.

Note

The events OnTransactionCommit and OnTransactionAbort are ASP-specific. However, in Day 9, "Working Asynchronously with ADO Events," you will learn about ADO events and their use.

The ASP page in Listing 8.8 provides an idea of how to use the events OnTransactionCommit and OnTransactionAbort.

LISTING 8.8   ASP Transaction Page Using Events

```
 1: <% @TRANSACTION = Required %>
 2: <%
 3:    'Buffer output
 4:    Response.Buffer = True
 5:    ...
 6:    ' Perform some actions
 7:    ...
 8:    ' End of ASP page
 9:
10: ' Transaction event handlers
11: Sub OnTransactionCommit
12:    ' Executed after transaction was committed
13:    Response.Write "Transaction completed."
14: End Sub
15:
16: Sub OnTransactionAbort
17:    ' Executed after transaction was aborted
18:    Response.Write "Transaction aborted."
19: End Sub
20: %>
```

ANALYSIS   The transaction is initiated in line 1 using the ASP TRANSACTION directive. When the transaction fails, the OnTransactionAbort event is triggered by the transaction and the OnTransactionAbort sub in lines 16–19 is called and executed.

When the transaction finishes successfully, the OnTransactionCommit event is triggered and the OnTransactionCommit sub in lines 11–14 is executed.

Summary

Today, you explored database transactions, their use and their enforcement. A database transaction is used to make sure that dependent database tasks are executed or canceled as a whole. Transactions are necessary for database applications that must remain in a defined state even when the application crashes after it has executed only a part of dependent database tasks. The transaction mechanisms ensure that when an application crashes, the transaction is rolled back and the database is restored to its state before the beginning of the transaction. Even when a part of the application fails (such as an object used by the application), the transaction mechanisms enables you to restore the application to the state before the transaction began.

The most important techniques for enforcing transactions in database applications are

- Using the methods `BeginTrans`, `CommitTrans`, and `RollbackTrans` of the ADO `Connection` object to define a transaction for a certain database connection

- Establishing transactions in SQL Server stored procedures using statements provided by T-SQL

- Enforcing transactions in Active Server Pages using the `TRANSACTION` directive in the first line of the ASP page

Q&A

Q I have heard about so-called implicit transactions. What does that term mean?

A When you change more than one record in a table at once, the database or database provider automatically enforces an implicit transaction. The idea behind this procedure is to make sure that all records affected by a database statement are changed at once. For instance, when two users execute `UPDATE` statements that affect many records of a table at once, some records might be changed according to the first user's `UPDATE` statement and some might be changed as specified in the second `UPDATE` statement. To avoid such an unexpected and mysterious behavior, the execution of an `UPDATE` statement is encapsulated automatically in an implicit transaction.

All transactions discussed today are *explicit* transactions, because they are enforced by executing explicit statements or methods.

Q Is it possible to use the `Connection` object's methods to enforce transactions when using an ODBC database provider?

A The OLE DB Provider for ODBC supports transactions. However, whether transactions can be enforced against a data source depends on the ODBC database driver. SQL Server 7.0 and Access 2000, for instance, enable you to enforce simple transactions over ODBC when using the latest ODBC drivers. Note that nested transactions are not supported by the ODBC drivers contained in MDAC 2.5.

8

Workshop

The quiz questions and exercises are provided for your further understanding. See Appendix A, "Answers," for the answers.

Quiz

1. You are using two database connections in a script at the same time. When using methods of only the ADO Connection object, can you enforce a transaction that covers the database tasks executed against both connections?

2. When using Active Server Pages, how can you easily wrap two different database connections in one transaction?

3. Is it possible to enforce a transaction on every data source connection when using the methods of the ADO Connection object?

Exercises

1. Change Listing 8.6 ("Enforcing Transaction Using T-SQL Statements") so that the first INSERT statement is encapsulated in a SQL Server transaction named InnerTransaction.

2. Write a script that connects to the SQL Server 7.0 Northwind database. In the Products table, lower the value in the UnitsInStock field by 105 in the record with the ProductID = 6. Retrieve the new value of the field UnitsInStock. When it is lower than 20, abort the transaction, cancel all changes, and write a message to the user. When the values is 20 at minimum, commit the transaction and save the changes.

DAY 9

Working Asynchronously with ADO Events

An ADO event is fired when a certain ADO action is executed. For instance, when you disconnect an ADO connection, this action triggers the Disconnect event.

NEW TERM To *trigger* means that a piece of code (the event code) is executed automatically when a certain action takes place. The execution of the event code is triggered by the action.

Various ADO actions have triggers assigned. A triggered event can be used to check the circumstances and parameters of the object and its action. You can check whether the action finished successfully or whether an error occurred during performing the action.

Usually, you use synchronous operations in an ADO script, which means that an operation initiated by the code is completed before the next operation is started. However, it is often useful to use asynchronous operations—for instance, when an operation needs a long time to be executed and you want your application to perform other tasks in the meantime. When you open a very large recordset, it may be useful to perform other operations until the whole recordset is populated. When the recordset is populated, it then triggers the FetchComplete event. You can assign a certain subroutine to this FetchComplete event. Then you have a way to notify your application that from now on, it can use the populated recordset for certain recordset operations—to read or change field values and to save the recordset back to the data source.

Capturing ADO Events in Visual Basic

Events can be used in Visual Basic (VB); in Visual Basic for Applications (VBA); and in Visual Basic, Scripting Edition (VBScript). ADO itself has supported events since ADO 2.0. To use events in a Visual Basic application, you have to consider several facts that are explained in this section.

When using ADO in VBScript, you cannot use ADO events directly in the VBScript code. Generally, VBScript cannot handle events. However, there are some exceptions to that rule. You can, for instance, use transaction events in an ASP script when using the TRANSACTION directive; you also can use various events in a DHTML document, because the DHTML object model supports events.

Note

> To use ADO events from a VBScript application, you have to encapsulate the ADO operations and the events in an object and instantiate the object in the VBScript code to use it.

To enable event handling for a certain ADO operation, both the ADO operation, which triggers the event, and the ADO event handling code must be contained in the same class module. The ADO event object must be defined using the WithEvents keyword in the Dim statement, and it must be of such scope that it is visible to all code in the module.

 A *class module* in Visual Basic is a module in a Visual Basic project that contains the definition of a class, including its properties and methods. The methods are defined in subroutines that can be accessed from outside the class module (public methods).

A class module is handled similarly to an object. You assign the class module reference to a variable creating a new instance of the class module. The instance is referenced using the variable name.

The following steps explain how to create a simple class module in VBA. The programming environment for this sample is Excel 2000. However, Visual Basic 6.0, VBA for Word 2000, and Access 2000 are nearly identical.

To Do: Creating a Simple Class Module in VBA

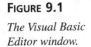

Follow these steps to create a simple class module in VBA using Excel 2000:

1. Start Excel 2000 and save the workbook as MyClassModule.xls.

2. Open the Visual Basic Editor window by pressing Alt+F11 (or choose Tools, Macro, Visual Basic Editor from the menu).

   The Visual Basic Editor window appears (see Figure 9.1).

9

FIGURE 9.1

The Visual Basic Editor window.

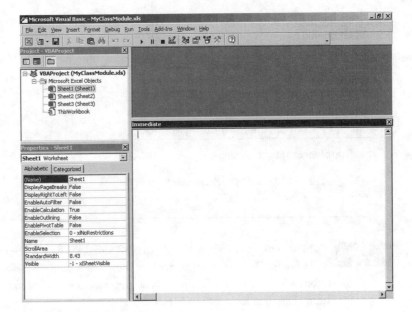

3. In the Editor window, choose Insert, Class Module from the menu. A new class module named Class1 appears in the upper-left pane.

4. In the lower-left pane, change the name from Class1 to MyClass. Click in the field that contains Class1 and overwrite it with MyClass. The window looks similar to Figure 9.2.

5. To add a method to the class, you add the code of the method as sub or function into the class modules code pane, which is the upper-right pane.

▼ 6. Add the method named MyMethod as a sub into the code pane (see Listing 9.1):

FIGURE 9.2

Class named MyClass *added to VBA project.*

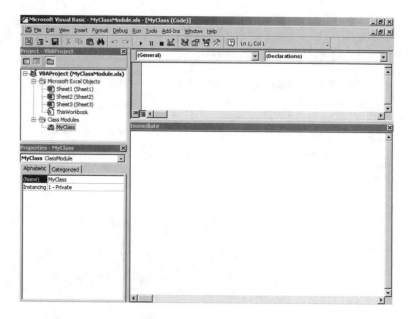

LISTING 9.1 Code of the Method MyMethod

```
1: Option Explicit
2:
3: Public Sub MyMethod(MyText As String)
4:     Debug.Print MyText
5: End Sub
```

ANALYSIS Option Explicit indicates only that all variables have to be defined using Dim statements. The method MyMethod of the class module is defined in lines 3–5 as public sub. The method retrieves a string value and writes this value to the Immediate window of the VB Editor.

7. Before you can use a class module and its methods, you have to create an instance of the class and assign it to a variable. However, you must do so in a module.

8. To add a module to your VBA project, choose Insert, Module from the menu of the Editor window. Change the name of the new module from Module1 to MyModule in the lower-left pane of the Editor (see Figure 9.3).

9. Add a subroutine named Start to the code of MyModule that creates an instance of the class module MyClass and calls the method MyMethod (see Listing 9.2).

FIGURE 9.3

Module named
`MyModule` *added to*
VBA project.

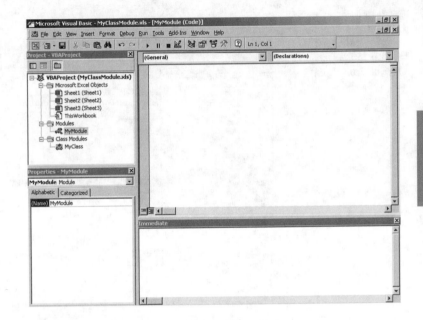

9

LISTING 9.2   Code of the sub `Start`

```
1: Option Explicit
2:
3: Sub Start()
4:     Dim objClass As New MyClass
5:     objClass.MyMethod "Running Class module code."
6:     Set objClass = Nothing
7: End Sub
```

OUTPUT

When you run the sub `Start` (for instance, by typing `start` into the Immediate window and pressing the Return key), the following output appears:

`Running Class module code.`

ANALYSIS

The sub `Start` creates a new instance of the class module `MyClass` and assigns it to the variable `objClass` in line 4. The method `MyMethod` of the class `MyClass` is called in line 5 using the `MyMethod` method of the object named `objClass`. The sub `MyMethod` is called with a string as parameter and writes the string to the Immediate window (see Figure 9.4).

10. Save the VBA project and all its modules for further use by choosing File, Save `MyClassModule.xls` from the menu.

▼

FIGURE 9.4

After calling the sub Start *of the module* MyModule.

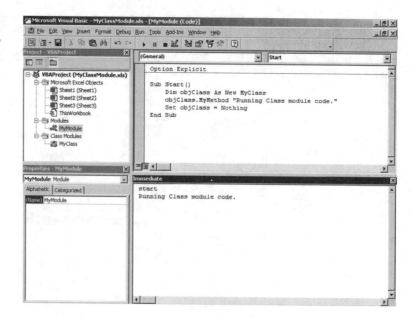

Basic Use of ADO Events in Class Modules

When you want to use ADO events in Visual Basic or VBA, the ADO object and the accordant event handling code must be in the same class module. Listing 9.3 shows how to use an ADO object and its corresponding event in a class module.

LISTING 9.3 Use of an ADO Object and Its Events

```
 1: Dim WithEvents objVarEvent As ADODB.Object
 2: Dim objVar As New ADODB.Object
 3:
 4: Sub MySub()
 5:     Set objVarEvent = objVar      ' Enable event support.
 6:     ' Do something with ADO object objVar
 7:     ...
 8:     Set objVarEvent = Nothing     ' Disable event support.
 9:     ...
10: End Sub
11:
12: Sub objVarEvent_EventName(Eventparameters)
13:     ' The event code goes here
14:     ...
15: End Sub
```

ANALYSIS The code of Listing 9.3 shows how to create the ADO object named *objVar* and its accordant event named *objVarEvent*. The ADO object named *objVar* is created in line 2 using the Dim statement with the New keyword.

In the sub MySub, event handling is enabled in line 5 by setting the reference of the event *objVarEvent* to the reference of the ADO object *objVar*. In lines 6 and 7, any action can be performed with the ADO object *objVar*. When an action is performed that triggers the event with the name *EventName*, the sub named *objVarEvent_EventName* is triggered and executed.

Instead of using a separate definition for the ADO object (using early binding) and a definition for the events object, you can unite both in one object, as shown in Listing 9.4.

LISTING 9.4   ADO Object and Event Object United

```
 1: Dim WithEvents objVar As ADODB.Object
 2:
 3: Sub MySub()
 4:     Set objVar = New ADODB.Object    ' Create object, enable events.
 5:     ' Do something with ADO object objVar
 6:     ...
 7:     Set objVar = Nothing             ' Disable event support.
 8:     ...
 9: End Sub
10:
11: Sub objVar_EventName(Eventparameters)
12:     ' The event code goes here
13:     ...
14: End Sub
```

ANALYSIS The code of Listing 9.4 shows how to define the ADO object named *objVar*. In the definition of *objVar*, the keyword WithEvents is used to indicate that the object supports events. The object itself is created in line 4 using the Set statement. Creating the object automatically enables event support. To disable the event support and its resources, set the object to Nothing, as done in line 7.

The event for the object *objVar* is defined in lines 11–14; the name of the event subroutine consists of the name of the object, an underscore, and the name of the triggered event. (For event names, see Table 9.1, "ADO Connection Event Summary," and Table 9.2, "ADO Recordset Event Summary," later today.)

The ADO object model provides various events for the Connection and Recordset objects:

- Connection events are triggered when a connection starts or ends; when a transaction on a connection begins, is committed, or is rolled back; when a Command object is executed; and when a warning or error is raised during any connection event.

- Recordset events are fired when you open a Recordset with a client-side cursor, navigate through the recordset, change a record or a field of a record, or make any other change in the recordset.

ADO Connection Events Summary

Connection events are triggered when a connection starts or ends; when a transaction on a connection begins, is committed, or is rolled back; when a Command object is executed; and when a warning or error is raised during any connection event (see Table 9.1).

TABLE 9.1   ADO Connection Event Summary

Connection Event	Description
BeginTransComplete, CommitTransComplete, RollbackTransComplete	Events of transaction management, triggered when the current transaction on the connection is started, committed, or rolled back
WillConnect, ConnectComplete, Disconnect	Events for connection management, triggered when the connection is starting, has started, or has ended
WillExecute, ExecuteComplete	Events triggered by command execution management, issued when the execution of the current command on the connection will start or has ended
InfoMessage	Informational event that indicates additional information about the current connection operation

The next section provides a sample with connection events in a Visual Basic class module.

Exploring the Use of ADO Connection Events

With a sample code of a Visual Basic class module, you can explore the use of a Connection object and its events.

Listing 9.5 contains all the code of a sample for a class module named MyClass using the ADO Connection object and some of its events.

LISTING 9.5   ADO Connection Object and Events (Code of Class Module Named MyClass)

```
1: Option Explicit
2:
```

```
 3: Dim conn As New ADODB.Connection
 4: Dim WithEvents connEvent As ADODB.Connection
 5:
 6: Sub MyMethodSync()
 7:     ' Enable Error handling
 8:     On Error GoTo MyMethodSyncError
 9:
10:     Debug.Print "Begin MyClass.MyMethodSync()"
11:     Set connEvent = conn          ' Enable event support.
12:
13:     Debug.Print "Opening connection synchronously..."
14:     ' Open connection synchronously
15:     conn.Open "MyNorthwind", "admin", ""
16:     'conn.Open "Provider=SQLOLEDB;Data Source=BoyScout;" & _
17:       "Initial Catalog=Northwind", "sa", ""
18:     Debug.Print "Connection was opened synchronously..."
19:
20:     ' ...
21:
22:     Debug.Print "Closing Connection..."
23:     conn.Close                    ' Close Connection
24:     Debug.Print "Connection was closed..."
25:
26:     Set connEvent = Nothing       ' Disable event support.
27:
28:     Debug.Print "End MyClass.MyMethodSync()"
29:     Exit Sub
30: MyMethodSyncError:
31:     Debug.Print "Run-time Error in MyMethodSync!"
32:     Debug.Print err.Description
33:     Debug.Print err.Source
34: End Sub
35:
36: Private Sub connEvent_InfoMessage(ByVal pError As ADODB.Error,
 ➥ adStatus As ADODB.EventStatusEnum,
 ➥ ByVal pConnection As ADODB.Connection)
37:     Debug.Print
38:     Debug.Print "Connection InfoMessage was triggered."
39:     Debug.Print "Error Description: " & pError.Description
40:     Debug.Print "Error Source: " & pError.Source
41:
42:     Debug.Print "Connection Status Number: " & adStatus
43:     Debug.Print
44: End Sub
45:
46: Private Sub connEvent_WillConnect(ConnectionString As String,
 ➥ UserID As String, Password As String, Options As Long,
 ➥ adStatus As ADODB.EventStatusEnum,
 ➥ ByVal pConnection As ADODB.Connection)
```

continues

LISTING 9.5   Continued

```
47:
48:     Debug.Print "Connection WillConnect event was triggered."
49: End Sub
50:
51: Private Sub connEvent_ConnectComplete(ByVal pError As ADODB.Error,
➥ adStatus As ADODB.EventStatusEnum,
➥ ByVal pConnection As ADODB.Connection)
52:     Debug.Print "Connection ConnectComplete event was triggered."
53: End Sub
54:
55: Private Sub connEvent_Disconnect(adStatus As ADODB.EventStatusEnum,
➥ ByVal pConnection As ADODB.Connection)
56:     Debug.Print "Connection Disconnect event was triggered."
57: End Sub
```

When working with a Visual Basic Editor, you can obtain a skeleton code for the event with all the event's parameters as follows: Choose the ADO object from the left drop-down box of the code window in the VB Editor as a connection object named connEvent for instance. Then select the type of event in the right drop-down box, for instance the connection event ConnectComplete. Then the skeleton code is created automatically (see Figure 9.5).

FIGURE 9.5

Creating a skeleton code for the event ConnectComplete.

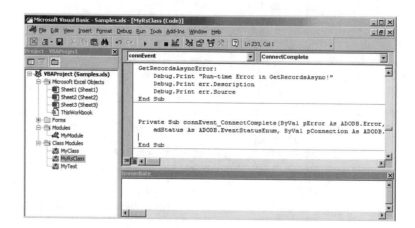

The method MyMethodSync can be called from another sub in a module of the Visual Basic project, as in Listing 9.6.

LISTING 9.6   Call MyMethodSync from MyClass (Code of Module Named MyModule)

```
1: Option Explicit
2:
```

```
3: Sub StartSync()
4:     Dim clsTest As New MyClass
5:     'or: Dim clsTest As New VBAProject.MyClass
6:     clsTest.MyMethodSync
7: End Sub
```

When you call the sub named StartSync, an instance of the class MyClass is created and the method MyMethodSync is called. The output of calling MyClass.MyMethodSync, which is the output of Listing 9.5, might be as follows (depending on the system you are using, the info message in lines 6–9 may appear or not):

9

OUTPUT

```
 1: Begin MyClass.MyMethodSync()
 2: Opening connection synchronously...
 3: Connection WillConnect event was triggered.
 4: Connection ConnectComplete event was triggered.
 5:
 6: Connection InfoMessage was triggered.
 7: Error Description: [Microsoft][ODBC Driver Manager]
➥ Driver's SQLSetConnectAttr failed
 8: Error Source: Microsoft OLE DB Provider for ODBC Drivers
 9: Connection Status Number: 1
10:
11: Connection was opened synchronously...
12: Closing Connection...
13: Connection Disconnect event was triggered.
14: Connection was closed...
15: End MyClass.MyMethodSync()
```

ANALYSIS Listing 9.6 is only used to call the class module code of Listing 9.5. In Listing 9.5, the Connection object named conn is defined and created in line 3. Another Connection object, named connEvent, is defined in line 4 using the keyword WithEvents in the Dim statement. connEvent becomes an event object, which is used to enable and disable event support of the object conn.

The method MyMethodSync is defined as sub in the class module named MyClass. Error handling is enabled in the method using the On Error GoTo statement in line 8. The accordant error handling code for runtime errors appearing in sub MyMethodSync is defined in lines 30–33. Event handling is enabled in line 11 by assigning the reference of the conn object to the connEvent object, thus making both variables reference the same Connection object. Every time you perform certain actions on the connection named conn, the action is also notified by the connection named connEvent, because both connection variables reference the same Connection object.

Therefore, when you open the connection named conn in line 15, a WillConnect event is triggered by the variable connEvent, and the event code defined in the sub connEvent_WillConnect (see lines 46–49) is executed.

The sub connEvent_WillConnect handles the event and automatically hands over parameters, such as ConnectionString, UserID, and adStatus (which indicates the status of the execution of the event). Because the adStatus parameter is handed over by reference, you can, for instance, check all parameters and cancel the execution of the event by assigning the EventStatusEnum value adStatusCancel to the variable adStatus. In Listing 9.5, the event connEvent_WillConnect only notifies the user that the WillConnect event was triggered (output line 3).

When the connection is finally opened, the ConnectComplete event is triggered and the code of the sub named connEvent_ConnectComplete is executed. The event only writes a message to the user (output line 4).

In line 15, when you open the connection, the connection string indicates to open the database defined in the System ODBC DSN named MyNorthwind. Instead of using an ODBC data source, you can also open a connection using the OLE DB Provider for SQL Server, for instance, as shown in lines 15 and 16.

 Note

The ODBC warning message in lines 6–9 of the output is ODBC-specific, so it would not appear when you use the OLE DB Provider from lines 15 and 16. The OLE DB provider opens the SQL Server 7.0 database named Northwind on the database server named BoyScout.

The connection is opened synchronously because no additional parameter was provided for the Open method in line 15. *Synchronously* means that the connection waits until the connecting process is finished. Then the application is allowed to continue with execution in line 18.

After the connection process is finished, it triggers an InfoMessage event to hand over a warning that appeared during the connection process. The InfoMessage event executes the sub connEvent_InfoMessage that writes a message with the error description, the error source, and the connection status number to the user (output lines 6–9). A connection status number of 1 (adStatusOK) indicates that the connection was opened successfully.

Lines 19–21 of Listing 9.5 act as placeholders for statements using the Connection object named conn to perform various database tasks, such as retrieving recordsets or executing commands. Of course, using the Connection object may trigger further connection events.

The connection conn is closed in line 23, which triggers the connection's Disconnect event. This event executes the sub named connEvent_Disconnect, as defined in lines 55–57, and writes a simple message to the user (output line 13).

Finally, in line 26, the event connection variable connEvent is set to Nothing to disable event support and free its resources used.

9

> **Tip**
>
> You can disable and enable event handling of the ADO object by setting the event object to Nothing and to the ADO object again. For instance, in Listing 9.5 you can disable event support using the following line:
>
>   Set connEvent = Nothing
>
> and you can enable event support using
>
>   Set connEvent = conn
>
> When event support for an object is disabled, no event is triggered and no accordant event subroutine is executed.

> **Tip**
>
> Instead of defining two variables, conn for the ADO Connection object and connEvent for the event object, you can unite both into one object, as shown before in Listing 9.4.

The class module code in Listing 9.5 contains the definition for a VB class (named MyClass) with the method MyMethodSync. Listing 9.6 contains the code of a VB module named MyModule. This code contains the sub StartSync. When you call StartSync, the variable clsTest is defined as a new instance of the class named MyClass (which is the class defined in the class module named MyClass in Listing 9.5).

In line 4 of Listing 9.6, the variable clsTest is defined and contains a new instance of the class named MyClass. Instead of using only the class name MyClass, you can use the full application and class name, as shown in line 5. The method MyMethodSync of the instance of the class MyClass is called in line 6 using a statement such as *ClassVariable.Method*. When you execute clsTest.MyMethodSync in line 6, the MyMethodSync method of the class MyClass, which is referenced in the variable clsTest, is executed.

ADO Recordset Events Summary

Recordset events are triggered for various reasons, such as fetching a Recordset object asynchronously, navigation through a recordset, or changing a field of a Record object or a record of the Recordset object. Events are also triggered for any other changes performed on a recordset.

A summary of recordset events provided by ADO is shown in Table 9.2.

TABLE 9.2   ADO Recordset Event Summary

Recordset Event	Description
FetchProgress, FetchComplete	Indicates the retrieval status of a recordset. FetchProgress is triggered periodically during a lasting asynchronous record-set fetch. FetchComplete notifies that the retrieval operation has completed.
WillChangeField, FieldChangeComplete	Events triggered by the field change management when a field value is about to change or has changed.
WillMove, MoveComplete, EndOfRecordset	Notification from navigation management that the row position in a recordset will change or has changed, or that the recordset cursor has reached the end of the recordset.
WillChangeRecord, RecordChangeComplete	Used for row change management. Events are triggered when something in a row of the recordset will change or has changed.
WillChangeRecordset, RecordsetChangeComplete	Enforced to notify that something in the current recordset will change or has changed.

The next section provides a sample with recordset events in a Visual Basic class module.

Experiencing the Possibilities of ADO Recordset Events

Recordset events are used to check whether an asynchronous opening of a recordset is finished, whether a record or field has been changed, and whether the recordset cursor has been moved.

Most events can be used as pairs. When you move the recordset cursor, the WillMove and MoveComplete events are triggered. The WillMove event is triggered before the recordset cursor is actually moved; the MoveComplete event is triggered afterward.

Recordset events are used similarly to connection events—for instance, you can use them in Visual Basic classes.

Listing 9.7 defines a recordset to use events and event handlers. Several actions performed on the recordset trigger the events and therefore execute the accordant event handler subroutines.

LISTING 9.7   ADO Recordset Object and Events (Code of Class MyRsClass)

```
1: Option Explicit
2:
```

```
 3: ' Define Recordset object and the accordant Event object
 4: Dim rs As New ADODB.Recordset
 5: Dim WithEvents rsEvent As ADODB.Recordset
 6:
 7:
 8: ' METHOD:
 9: Sub GetRecords()
10:     Dim conn As New ADODB.Connection
11:     Dim strSQL As String
12:     conn.Open "Provider=SQLOLEDB;Data Source=BoyScout;" & _
13:       "Initial Catalog=Northwind", "sa", ""
14:
15:     Set rsEvent = rs    ' Enable event support.
16:
17:     strSQL = "SELECT EmployeeID, LastName, FirstName FROM Employees"
18:
19:     rs.CursorLocation = adUseServer    ' or adUseClient
20:     Debug.Print "Open recordset..."
21:     rs.Open strSQL, conn, adOpenStatic, adLockBatchOptimistic
22:
23:     Debug.Print "Move recordset cursor..."
24:     rs.MoveNext
25:
26:     Debug.Print "Move recordset cursor to last record..."
27:     rs.MoveLast
28:
29:     Debug.Print "Move recordset cursor beyond last record..."
30:     rs.MoveNext
31:
32:     Debug.Print "Move recordset cursor to first record..."
33:     rs.MoveFirst
34:
35:
36:     Debug.Print "Search for record with EmployeeID = 5..."
37:     rs.Find "EmployeeID = 5"
38:
39:     If Not (rs.EOF Or rs.BOF) Then
40:         If rs("EmployeeID") = 5 Then
41:             Debug.Print "Record with EmployeeID = 5 found..."
42:
43:             Debug.Print "Change record with EmployeeID = 5..."
44:             Debug.Print "Change FirstName..."
45:             rs("FirstName") = "Richard"
46:             Debug.Print "Change LastName..."
47:             rs("LastName") = "Strauss"
48:             Debug.Print "Record changed..."
49:
50:         End If
51:     End If
52:
```

continues

LISTING **9.7**   Continued

```
53:     Debug.Print "Cancel Batch Update..."
54:     rs.CancelBatch
55:
56:     Debug.Print "Close recordset..."
57:     rs.Close
58:
59:     Set rsEvent = Nothing     ' Disable event support.
60:     conn.Close
61:     Set conn = Nothing
62: End Sub
63:
64: ' EVENTS:
65: Private Sub rsEvent_EndOfRecordset(fMoreData As Boolean, adStatus As
➡ ADODB.EventStatusEnum, ByVal pRecordset As ADODB.Recordset)
66:     Debug.Print "> Recordset EndOfRecordset event was triggered."
67: End Sub
68:
69: Private Sub rsEvent_FetchComplete(ByVal pError As ADODB.Error, adStatus
➡ As ADODB.EventStatusEnum, ByVal pRecordset As ADODB.Recordset)
70:     Debug.Print "> Recordset FetchComplete event was triggered."
71: End Sub
72:
73: Private Sub rsEvent_FieldChangeComplete(ByVal cFields As Long,
➡ ByVal Fields As Variant, ByVal pError As ADODB.Error, adStatus
➡ As ADODB.EventStatusEnum, ByVal pRecordset As ADODB.Recordset)
74:     Debug.Print "> Recordset FieldChangeComplete event was triggered."
75: End Sub
76:
77: Private Sub rsEvent_MoveComplete(ByVal adReason As ADODB.EventReasonEnum,
➡ ByVal pError As ADODB.Error, adStatus As ADODB.EventStatusEnum,
➡ ByVal pRecordset As ADODB.Recordset)
78:     Debug.Print "> Recordset MoveComplete event was triggered."
79: End Sub
80:
81: Private Sub rsEvent_RecordChangeComplete(ByVal adReason As
➡ ADODB.EventReasonEnum, ByVal cRecords As Long, ByVal pError As
➡ ADODB.Error, adStatus As ADODB.EventStatusEnum,
➡ ByVal pRecordset As ADODB.Recordset)
82:     Debug.Print "> Recordset RecordChangeComplete event was triggered."
83: End Sub
84:
85: Private Sub rsEvent_RecordsetChangeComplete(ByVal adReason As
➡ ADODB.EventReasonEnum, ByVal pError As ADODB.Error, adStatus As
➡ ADODB.EventStatusEnum, ByVal pRecordset As ADODB.Recordset)
86:     Debug.Print "> Recordset RecordsetChangeComplete event was triggered."
87: End Sub
88:
89: Private Sub rsEvent_WillChangeField(ByVal cFields As Long,
➡ ByVal Fields As Variant, adStatus As ADODB.EventStatusEnum,
➡ ByVal pRecordset As ADODB.Recordset)
```

```
90:     Debug.Print "> Recordset WillChangeField event was triggered."
91: End Sub
92:
93: Private Sub rsEvent_WillChangeRecord(ByVal adReason As
➥ ADODB.EventReasonEnum, ByVal cRecords As Long, adStatus As
➥ ADODB.EventStatusEnum, ByVal pRecordset As ADODB.Recordset)
94:     Debug.Print "> Recordset WillChangeRecord event was triggered."
95: End Sub
96:
97: Private Sub rsEvent_WillChangeRecordset(ByVal adReason As
➥ ADODB.EventReasonEnum, adStatus As ADODB.EventStatusEnum,
➥ ByVal pRecordset As ADODB.Recordset)
98:     Debug.Print "> Recordset WillChangeRecordset event was triggered."
99: End Sub
100:
101: Private Sub rsEvent_WillMove(ByVal adReason As ADODB.EventReasonEnum,
➥ adStatus As ADODB.EventStatusEnum,
➥ ByVal pRecordset As ADODB.Recordset)
102:     Debug.Print "> Recordset WillMove event was triggered."
103: End Sub
```

The method `GetRecords` of the class module named `MyRsClass` can be called, for instance, from a sub in a module of the Visual Basic project (see Listing 9.8).

LISTING 9.8 Call `GetRecords` from Class `MyRsClass` (Code of module `MyModule`)

```
1: Option Explicit
2:
3: Sub StartGetRecords()
4:     Dim clsRs As New MyRsClass
5:     'Dim clsRs As New VBAProject.MyRsClass
6:     clsRs.GetRecords
7: End Sub
```

When sub `StartGetRecords` is called, an instance of the class `MyRsClass` is created and the method `GetRecords` of Listing 9.7 is called. The resulting output in the Intermediate window of the VB Editor might be as follows:

OUTPUT

```
1: Open recordset...
2: > Recordset WillMove event was triggered.
3: > Recordset MoveComplete event was triggered.
4: Move recordset cursor...
5: > Recordset WillMove event was triggered.
6: > Recordset MoveComplete event was triggered.
7: Move recordset cursor to last record...
```

```
 8: > Recordset WillMove event was triggered.
 9: > Recordset MoveComplete event was triggered.
10: Move recordset cursor beyond last record...
11: > Recordset WillMove event was triggered.
12: > Recordset EndOfRecordset event was triggered.
13: > Recordset MoveComplete event was triggered.
14: Move recordset cursor to first record...
15: > Recordset WillMove event was triggered.
16: > Recordset MoveComplete event was triggered.
17: Search for record with EmployeeID = 5...
18: > Recordset WillMove event was triggered.
19: > Recordset MoveComplete event was triggered.
20: Record with EmployeeID = 5 found...
21: Change record with EmployeeID = 5...
22: Change FirstName...
23: > Recordset WillChangeRecord event was triggered.
24: > Recordset WillChangeField event was triggered.
25: > Recordset FieldChangeComplete event was triggered.
26: > Recordset RecordChangeComplete event was triggered.
27: Change LastName...
28: > Recordset WillChangeField event was triggered.
29: > Recordset FieldChangeComplete event was triggered.
30: Record changed...
31: Cancel Batch Update...
32: > Recordset WillChangeRecord event was triggered.
33: > Recordset RecordChangeComplete event was triggered.
34: Close recordset...
35: > Recordset RecordsetChangeComplete event was triggered.
```

ANALYSIS   The Recordset object rs is defined and created in line 4. The accordant event object rsEvent is defined in line 5 using the keyword WithEvents. The object rsEvent supports trigger events. The method GetRecords of the class module MyRsClass is defined in lines 9–62. When you call the method GetRecords, a connection to the SQL Server 7.0 Northwind database is opened in line 12. The event support for the Recordset object rs is enabled in line 15 by setting rsEvent to rs.

The recordset rs is prepared and opened in line 21. When the recordset rs is opened, the WillMove (lines 101–103) and MoveComplete (lines 77–79) events of the rsEvent object are triggered (output lines 1–3).

Moving the recordset cursor using the MoveNext method in line 24 also triggers the WillMove and MoveComplete events. Both events are also triggered when executing the MoveLast method of rs. When you move the recordset cursor beyond the last record, as done in line 30, the EndOfRecordset event (lines 65–67) is triggered, in addition to the WillMove and MoveComplete events (output lines 10–13). When you move the recordset cursor to the first record, only the WillMove and MoveComplete events are triggered.

The script executes the `Find` method on the recordset `rs` in line 37 to set the recordset cursor to the record that contains an `EmployeeID` of 5. When a matching record is found, the recordset cursor is not set to `EOF` or `BOF`. When the recordset `rs` may be filtered and therefore the recordset cursor is set to the first record after the matching record, the value of the `EmployeeID` is checked in line 40. After the record is found, its `FirstName` field value is changed in line 45, triggering the following events: `WillChangeRecord` (lines 93–95), `WillChangeField` (lines 89–91), `FieldChangeComplete` (lines 73–75), and `RecordChangeComplete` (lines 81–83). See also output lines 22–26.

The `LastName` field value of the current record is changed in line 47, which triggers only the events `WillChangeField` and `FieldChangeComplete`. The `WillChangeRecord` and `RecordChangeComplete` are not called again, because the record has already been changed (output lines 27–29).

In line 54, the batch update is canceled so that no values in the database are changed. This action triggers the `WillChangeRecord` and `RecordChangeComplete` events. If you call the `UpdateBatch` method instead of the `CancelBatch` method in line 54, the same events are called.

The recordset `rs` is closed in line 57, triggering the `RecordsetChangeComplete` event (lines 85–87).

Events are often used to validate that a certain action is allowed to be executed with the values and parameters involved. For instance, when you change a field value, the event handler code can check whether the field value meets certain criteria defined by the demands of the application. Events can be used for validation purposes, to make sure that a certain action is executed only when valid data or parameters are provided for the ADO action.

Another purpose of an event can be to notify the application—by changing a global variable (property of the class module)—that a certain event has taken place.

Validating ADO Actions Using Events

When a recordset event is triggered, the accordant event handler subroutine of the code is executed. You have the possibility of checking whether you want to perform an action in that particular case; you can abort the action or change some parameters involved in it.

When you change the field of a recordset named `rsEvent`, for example, the following event handlers could be triggered: Before field changes are performed, the `WillChangeField` event is triggered. Using this event enables you to check all pending field changes of the ADO action that triggered the current `WillChangeField` event and cancel the pending changes when necessary (see Listing 9.9).

LISTING 9.9   `WillChangeField` Event Handler

```
 1: Private Sub rsEvent_WillChangeField(ByVal cFields As Long,
➥ ByVal Fields As Variant, adStatus As ADODB.EventStatusEnum,
➥ ByVal pRecordset As ADODB.Recordset)
 2:     Dim intI as Long
 3:     For intI = 0 To UBound(Fields)
 4:         Debug.Print Fields(intI).Name, Fields(intI).Value
 5:         If LCase(Fields(intI).Name) = "lastname" Then
 6:             If Len(Fields(intI).Value) < 4 Then
 7:                 If adStatus <> adStatusCantDeny Then
 8:                     adStatus = adStatusCancel
 9:                 End If
10:             End If
11:         End If
12:     Next
13:
14:     Debug.Print "> Recordset WillChangeField event was triggered."
15: End Sub
```

ANALYSIS   The `WillChangeField` event handler of the `Recordset` object `rsEvent` has the name `rsEvent_WillChangeField`. Four parameters are handed over to the sub (line 1).

The parameter `cFields` provides the number of `Field` objects in the array `Fields`. The array in the parameter `Fields` contains all `Fields` with pending changes. The parameter `adStatus` indicates whether the pending field changes caused an error (`adStatus` contains `adStatusErrorsOccurred`). An `adStatus` value different from `adStatusCantDeny` indicates that the pending changes can be canceled by setting the value of `adStatus` to `adStatusCancel` in the event handler code.

Caution

> When you cancel an event by setting the adStatus parameter to adStatusCancel, the event raises a runtime error that is handed over to the application that invoked the class module. Make sure to enable error-handling in each method of the class module to avoid the cancellation of an ADO operation. When an ADO operation is canceled in an event, it might cause the entire application to stop.

The parameter `pRecordset` contains the `Recordset` object for which the event occurred.

You can read all field names and field values from the `Fields` array, which contains all `Field` objects with pending changes, as demonstrated in the `For..Next` loop in lines 3–12. The field names and values are written to the user in line 4. You can check the field values and cancel the ADO operation by setting adStatus to adStatusCancel. This is demonstrated in lines 5–11. Line 5 checks whether the field name is lastname. Line 6 provides the condition for a field value in a lastname field. When the lastname field contains a string that is shorter than four characters, the script tries to cancel the pending field change by setting adStatus to adStatusCancel in line 8.

Because the WillChangeField event is triggered before field values are changed, the FieldChangeComplete event is triggered after the field values are changed (see Listing 9.10).

LISTING 9.10 FieldChangeComplete Event Handler

```
1: Private Sub rsEvent_FieldChangeComplete(ByVal cFields As Long,
[ ByVal Fields As Variant, ByVal pError As ADODB.Error, adStatus
[ As ADODB.EventStatusEnum, ByVal pRecordset As ADODB.Recordset)
2:
3:      Debug.Print "> Recordset FieldChangeComplete event was triggered."
4: End Sub
```

ANALYSIS The FieldChangeComplete event is executed after one or more fields of a recordset are changed. The parameters cFields, Fields, adStatus, and pRecordset are used analogous to the parameters of the WillChangeField event. When the parameter adStatus contains the value adStatusErrorsOccurred, the pError parameter contains the ADO Error object that describes the error that occurred during the ADO operation.

All samples presented before today used synchronous connection and recordset operations. The effects of asynchronous ADO operations and the use of their triggers are explained in the next section.

Performing Asynchronous ADO Operations with Events

ADO allows you to perform asynchronous operations when opening a connection to a database, or when fetching a recordset. Asynchronous operations are useful to let the calling application continue executing while the ADO operation is still in progress. The advantage of using asynchronous operations is that your application speeds up. The disadvantage is that the application has to know when the asynchronous operation is finished. Otherwise, it would be possible for the application to try to access a connection that is not opened or a recordset that is not fully retrieved.

The characteristic of an asynchronous ADO operation is that it hands over control to the calling application before the ADO operation has actually finished execution. For instance, when you retrieve a recordset in asynchronous mode from a data source, the calling application continues execution while the recordset is fetched. As long as the recordset is fetched asynchronously, the `FetchProgress` event is triggered periodically. You can use this event to provide information to the user about the progress of opening a large recordset.

When the recordset is fully retrieved, the `FetchComplete` event is triggered. This event is useful, for instance, to notify the application that the recordset is fully available.

An ADO connection provides a similar behavior when opened in asynchronous mode. The connection's `WillConnect` event is triggered before the connection starts to connect to the data source.

 Caution When an asynchronous connection process is finished, the `ConnectComplete` event is not triggered in ADO 2.5. The `ConnectComplete` event is triggered only when you establish a connection synchronously.

Connecting Asynchronously to a Data Source

You can open a connection in asynchronous mode when supplying the `adAsyncConnect` option parameter:

`conn.Open ConnectionString, UserID, Password, adAsyncConnect`

The variable conn contains the `Connection` object, and `ConnectionString` specifies the data source to connect to. The `UserID` and `Password` parameters are used for user identification. Finally, the `adAsyncConnect` parameter indicates that the connection is opened asynchronously.

The sample in Listing 9.11 provides an idea of what it means to open a connection in asynchronous mode, and how the accordant event `WillConnect` is triggered. You also see that the event `ConnectComplete` is not triggered when you open a connection asynchronously.

LISTING 9.11 Opening a Connection Asynchronously (Code of Class MyClass)

```
1: Option Explicit
2:
3: Dim WithEvents connEvent As ADODB.Connection
```

```
 4: Dim conn As New ADODB.Connection
 5:
 6: Sub MySubAsync()
 7:     Dim lngNotOpen As Long
 8:     Dim lngClosed As Long
 9:     Dim lngConnecting As Long
10:     ' Enable Error handling
11:     On Error GoTo MySubAsyncError
12:
13:     Debug.Print "Begin MyClass.MySubAsync()"
14:     Set connEvent = conn          ' Enable event support.
15:
16:     Debug.Print "Opening connection..."
17:      ' Open connection asynchronously
18:     conn.Open "MyNorthwind", "admin", "", adAsyncConnect
19:     'conn.Open "Provider=SQLOLEDB;Data Source=BoyScout;" & _
20:       "Initial Catalog=Northwind", "sa", "", adAsyncConnect
21:
22:     Debug.Print "Connection was opened asynchronously..."
23:
24:     lngNotOpen = 0
25:     lngClosed = 0
26:     lngConnecting = 0
27:     While (conn.State And adStateOpen) = 0
28:         ' Wait until opened
29:         lngNotOpen = lngNotOpen + 1
30:         If (conn.State And adStateClosed) > 0 Then
31:             lngClosed = lngClosed + 1
32:         End If
33:         If (conn.State And adStateConnecting) > 0 Then
34:             lngConnecting = lngConnecting + 1
35:         End If
36:     Wend
37:     Debug.Print CStr(lngClosed) & " cycles with closed connection..."
38:     Debug.Print CStr(lngConnecting) & " cycles while connecting..."
39:     Debug.Print CStr(lngNotOpen) & " cycles until connected..."
40:
41:     ' Performing operations on the ADO connection:
42:     ' ...
43:
44:     Debug.Print "Closing Connection..."
45:     conn.Close                ' Close Connection
46:     Debug.Print "Connection was closed..."
47:
48:     Set connEvent = Nothing    ' Disable event support.
49:     Set conn = Nothing         ' Free resources
50:     Debug.Print "End MyClass.MySubAsync()"
51:     Exit Sub
52: MySubAsyncError:
53:     Debug.Print "Run-time Error in MySubAsync!"
```

9

continues

LISTING 9.11 Continued

```
54:       Debug.Print err.Description
55:       Debug.Print err.Source
56: End Sub
57:
58: ' EVENTS:
59: Private Sub connEvent_WillConnect(ConnectionString As String,
➥ UserID As String, Password As String, Options As Long,
➥ adStatus As ADODB.EventStatusEnum,
➥ ByVal pConnection As ADODB.Connection)
60:       Debug.Print "Connection WillConnect event was triggered."
61: End Sub
62:
63: Private Sub connEvent_ConnectComplete(ByVal pError As ADODB.Error,
➥ adStatus As ADODB.EventStatusEnum,
➥ ByVal pConnection As ADODB.Connection)
64:       Debug.Print "Connection ConnectComplete event was triggered."
65: End Sub
66:
67: Private Sub connEvent_Disconnect(adStatus As ADODB.EventStatusEnum,
➥ ByVal pConnection As ADODB.Connection)
68:       Debug.Print "Connection Disconnect event was triggered."
69: End Sub
```

The output of running the method MySubAsync of the class module MyClass should be as
follows (the number of cycles may vary due to performance of the database, server, or
database connection):

OUTPUT

```
 1: Begin MyClass.MySubAsync()
 2: Opening connection...
 3: Connection WillConnect event was triggered.
 4: Connection was opened asynchronously...
 5: 0 cycles with closed connection...
 6: 13398 cycles while connecting...
 7: 13399 cycles until connected...
 8: Closing Connection...
 9: Connection Disconnect event was triggered.
10: Connection was closed...
11: End MyClass.MySubAsync()
```

ANALYSIS The Connection objects connEvent and conn are defined in lines 3 and 4. The
variable connEvent is used to pass on the connection events of the connection held
in the variable conn. When you define connEvent, the WithEvents keyword is used in
the Dim statement. The connection conn is created in line 4 using the New keyword in the
Dim statement.

The sub `MySubAsync` performs the ADO action. The code enables error handling in line 11 using the `OnError GoTo` statement. When a runtime error occurs in the sub, the code in lines 52–55 is executed. Event support for the connection `conn` is enabled in line 14 by setting the variable `connEvent` to `conn`. This statement allows the ADO connection, defined and created using the variable `conn`, to use the ADO connection events that are assigned to the connection variable `connEvent`.

To open the connection stored in the variable `conn`, the `Open` method is performed in line 18 using the `adAsyncConnect` as the fourth parameter. This forces the connection to open asynchronously, which means that the script in Listing 9.11 continuous executing before the ADO connection is established. Calling the `Open` method also triggers the connection's `WillConnect` event. The event handler code of `WillConnect` (lines 59–61) writes a message to the user (output line 3).

Caution

You might think that opening a connection always triggers the `ConnectComplete` event. This is true when you open a connection synchronously. However, when you open a connection in asynchronous mode, only the `WillConnect` event is triggered and the `ConnectComplete` event does not come up, as you see in the output of Listing 9.11.

When you cancel the `WillConnect` event by setting its adStatus parameter to adStatusCancel in the `WillConnect` event handler code, the `ConnectComplete` event is triggered and executes the corresponding event handler code before a runtime error is raised.

When the connection is established, its `State` property returns `adStateOpen` to indicate that you can use the connection for database operations.

Until the connection is opened, the script performs a `While...Wend` loop in lines 27–36. In this loop, the script checks whether the connection is still closed (`State = adStateClosed`) or whether the connection is still to be established (`State = adStateConnecting`). In every loop, the `State` property of the connection `conn` returns `adStateClosed` and the counter `lngClosed` is increased by 1. While ADO is establishing the connection, the counter variable `lngConnecting` is increased by 1. Finally, the `While...Wend` loop is terminated when the connection `conn` is established and its `State` property returns `adStateOpen`.

The number of loop cycles is written to the user: the total amount, the number of cycles while connecting, and the number of cycles while the connection was closed (output 5–7).

When you close the connection in line 45, the connection's Disconnect event is triggered. Its event handler in lines 67–69 also writes a message to the user (output line 9). Event support for the connection conn is disabled in line 48 by setting the variable connEvent to Nothing.

The event handlers in lines 59–69 could be used for much more than writing a message to the user.

 Tip   Please refer to the Microsoft Platform SDK or another documentation about ADO 2.5 to discover the meaning and use of the event parameters in every event handler code.

Fetching Data Asynchronously from a Data Source

To populate a Recordset object with data, you can use various ADO methods, such as the Open method of the Recordset object, or the Execute method of the Connection or Command object.

To execute a SQL statement asynchronously using the Execute method of the Connection object, use the following syntax:

```
Set rs = conn.Execute(strSQL, lngRecordsAffected, AsyncOption)
```

The variable conn is the database connection, strSQL contains the SQL statement, and lngRecordsAffected returns the number of records affected by the execution of the statement specified in strSQL. The Recordset object rs is used to access the retrieved records.

The AsyncOption parameter specifies whether the command should be executed asynchronously or not. The following values for the AsyncOption parameter are possible in regard to asynchronous operations:

- adAsyncExecute—The command should be executed asynchronously. The initial number of records (as specified in the CacheSize property) is fetched asynchronously.

- adAsyncFetch—Remaining records after the initial quantity (CacheSize) of records should be retrieved asynchronously.

- adAsyncFetchNonBlocking—While retrieving records, the main thread never blocks. This means that the script initiates the fetching of records but does not stop executing further commands even when the recordset is not fetched completely. If a requested record has not been retrieved, the recordset's EOF property returns True to indicate that the recordset cursor points beyond the last fetched record.

> **Note**
>
> To use two or three AsyncOption parameters together, you have to combine their values using the OR operator. For instance, to use the adAsyncExecute and adAsyncFetch parameters, you can use a statement such as the following:
>
> ```
> Set rs = conn.Execute(strSQL, lngRecordsAffected,
> ➥ (adAsyncExecute OR adAsyncFetch))
> ```

When you populate a recordset using the Open method of the Recordset object, you can specify an AsyncOption parameter (adAsyncExecute, adAsyncFetch, or adAsyncFetchNonBlocking) using the following syntax:

```
rs.Open strSQL, conn, CursorType, LockType, AsyncOption
```

The variable strSQL contains the statement that is executed against the data source using the connection conn and returns the records that can be accessed through the recordset variable rs. For the value of AsyncOption, you can use the values adAsyncExecute, adAsyncFetch, adAsyncFetchNonBlocking, or a combination of them.

You also can use the Command object and its Execute method to fill a recordset with data:

```
Set rs = command.Execute(lngRecordsAffected, Parameters, AsyncOption)
```

The variable rs contains the fetched recordset, command contains a prepared Command object, lngRecordsAffected returns the number of records affected, and the optional Parameters parameter enables you to pass an array with parameter values to the command. The AsyncOption parameter specifies which asynchronous operations the Execute method performs when receiving records from the database source. Its use is the same as in the Execution method of the Connection object.

You can open recordsets asynchronously, but you can also open a Record or Stream object asynchronously. Refer to the Microsoft Platform SDK or another documentation about the ADO Record or Stream object to get the syntax of the Open method.

When you open a connection or recordset asynchronously, recordset and connection events can be triggered.

The following sample populates a recordset using the Open method of the Recordset object with various combinations of asynchronous option parameters (see Listing 9.12).

LISTING 9.12 Populate a Recordset in Asynchronous Mode (Code of Class MyAsyncRsClass)

```
1: Option Explicit
2:
3: ' Define Recordset object and the accordant Event object
```

continues

LISTING 9.12   Continued

```
 4: Dim rs As New ADODB.Recordset
 5: Dim WithEvents rsEvent As ADODB.Recordset
 6: ' Define Connection object and the accordant Event object
 7: Dim conn As New ADODB.Connection
 8: Dim WithEvents connEvent As ADODB.Connection
 9:
10:
11: Sub GetRecordsAsync()
12:     Dim intI As Long
13:     Dim intK As Long
14:     Dim intL As Long
15:
16:     Dim strConnectionString As String
17:     Dim strSQL As String
18:     Dim lngTotal As Long
19:     Dim lngClosed As Long
20:     Dim lngOpened As Long
21:     Dim lngConnecting As Long
22:     Dim lngExecuting As Long
23:     Dim lngFetching As Long
24:     Dim strClosed As String
25:     Dim strOpened As String
26:     Dim strConnecting As String
27:     Dim strExecuting As String
28:     Dim strFetching As String
29:     Dim lngClG As Long
30:     Dim lngOpG As Long
31:     Dim lngCoG As Long
32:     Dim lngExG As Long
33:     Dim lngFeG As Long
34:     Dim arrGraph As Variant
35:     Dim arrValue(7) As Long
36:     Dim arrDesc(7) As String
37:     Dim lngArr As Long
38:     Dim lngPart As Long
39:     Dim lngState As Long
40:     Dim blnRun As Boolean
41:
42:     On Error GoTo GetRecordsAsyncError
43:
44:     arrGraph = Array(" ", ".", ".", ".", ".", "o", "o", "o", _
45:         "O", "O", "O")
46:
47:     lngArr = -1
48:     For intI = 0 To 1
49:         For intK = 0 To 1
50:             For intL = 0 To 1
51:                 lngArr = lngArr + 1
52:                 arrValue(lngArr) = ((intI * adAsyncExecute) Or _
```

```
53:                               (intK * adAsyncFetchNonBlocking) Or _
54:                               (intL * adAsyncFetch))
55:              Next
56:          Next
57:      Next
58:
59:      Debug.Print "Event Support enabled..."
60:      Set connEvent = conn ' Enable event support for Connection.
61:      Set rsEvent = rs      ' Enable event support for Connection.
62:
63:      strConnectionString = "Provider=SQLOLEDB;Data Source=BoyScout;" & _
64:          "Initial Catalog=Northwind;uid=sa;pwd="
65:      strSQL = "SELECT OrderID, CustomerID, OrderDate, EmployeeID " & _
66:          "FROM Orders ORDER BY EmployeeID"
67:
68:      For intI = 0 To 7
69:          Debug.Print
70:          Debug.Print "### Loop " & intI + 1 & " ###"
71:          If (arrValue(intI) And adAsyncExecute) <> 0 Then
72:              Debug.Print "(AsyncExecute)"
73:          End If
74:          If (arrValue(intI) And adAsyncFetchNonBlocking) <> 0 Then
75:              Debug.Print "(AsyncFetchNonBlocking)"
76:          End If
77:          If (arrValue(intI) And adAsyncFetch) <> 0 Then
78:              Debug.Print "(AsyncFetch)"
79:          End If
80:
81:          rs.CursorLocation = adUseClient
82:          rs.CacheSize = 250
83:
84:          conn.Open strConnectionString
85:          rs.Open strSQL, conn, adOpenDynamic, adLockBatchOptimistic, _
86:              arrValue(intI) Or adCmdText
87:          lngTotal = 0
88:          lngClosed = 0: lngClG = 0
89:          lngOpened = 0: lngOpG = 0
90:          lngConnecting = 0: lngCoG = 0
91:          lngExecuting = 0: lngExG = 0
92:          lngFetching = 0: lngFeG = 0
93:          strClosed = "": strOpened = ""
94:          strConnecting = "": strExecuting = ""
95:          strFetching = ""
96:
97:          lngPart = 350
98:          blnRun = True
99:          While (blnRun = True)
100:             lngState = rs.State
101:             If lngState = adStateOpen Then
102:                 blnRun = False
```

continues

LISTING 9.12 Continued

```
103:              End If
104:
105:              lngTotal = lngTotal + 1
106:              If ((lngState And adStateClosed) <> 0) Then
107:                  lngClosed = lngClosed + 1: lngClG = lngClG + 1
108:              End If
109:              If ((lngState And adStateOpen) <> 0) Then
110:                  lngOpened = lngOpened + 1: lngOpG = lngOpG + 1
111:              End If
112:              If ((lngState And adStateConnecting) <> 0) Then
113:                  lngConnecting = lngConnecting + 1: lngCoG = lngCoG + 1
114:              End If
115:              If ((lngState And adStateExecuting) <> 0) Then
116:                  lngExecuting = lngExecuting + 1: lngExG = lngExG + 1
117:              End If
118:              If ((lngState And adStateFetching) <> 0) Then
119:                  lngFetching = lngFetching + 1: lngFeG = lngFeG + 1
120:              End If
121:
122:              If ((lngTotal Mod lngPart) = 0) Or (blnRun = False) Then
123:                  strClosed = strClosed & _
124:                      arrGraph(Int(lngClG * 10 / lngPart))
125:                  strOpened = strOpened & _
126:                      arrGraph(Int(lngOpG * 10 / lngPart))
127:                  strConnecting = strConnecting & _
128:                      arrGraph(Int(lngCoG * 10 / lngPart))
129:                  strExecuting = strExecuting & _
130:                      arrGraph(Int(lngExG * 10 / lngPart))
131:                  strFetching = strFetching & _
132:                      arrGraph(Int(lngFeG * 10 / lngPart))
133:                  lngClG = 0: lngOpG = 0: lngCoG = 0
134:                  lngExG = 0: lngFeG = 0
135:              End If
136:          Wend
137:
138:          Debug.Print lngClosed & " cycles with closed recordset..."
139:          Debug.Print lngOpened & " cycles with open recordset..."
140:          Debug.Print lngConnecting & " cycles while connecting..."
141:          Debug.Print lngExecuting & " cycles while executing..."
142:          Debug.Print lngFetching & " cycles while fetching..."
143:
144:          Debug.Print "Closed:     " & strClosed
145:          Debug.Print "Opened:     " & strOpened
146:          Debug.Print "Connecting: " & strConnecting
147:          Debug.Print "Executing:  " & strExecuting
148:          Debug.Print "Fetching:   " & strFetching
149:          Debug.Print rs("OrderID"), rs("CustomerID"), rs("OrderDate")
150:
151:          rs.Close
```

```
152:          rs.CacheSize = 1
153:          rs.CursorLocation = adUseServer
154:          conn.Close
155:          If intI = 0 Then
156:              Debug.Print "Event Support disabled..."
157:              ' Disable event support for Recordset and Connection
158:              Set rsEvent = Nothing
159:              Set connEvent = Nothing
160:          End If
161:      Next
162:
163:      Exit Sub
164: GetRecordsAsyncError:
165:      Debug.Print "Run-time Error in GetRecordsAsync!"
166:      Debug.Print err.Description
167:      Debug.Print err.Source
168: End Sub
169:
170:
171: ' EVENTS:
172: ' Recordset:
173: Private Sub rsEvent_EndOfRecordset(fMoreData As Boolean, adStatus As _
174:     ADODB.EventStatusEnum, ByVal pRecordset As ADODB.Recordset)
175:      Debug.Print "> Recordset EndOfRecordset event was triggered."
176: End Sub
177:
178: Private Sub rsEvent_FetchComplete(ByVal pError As ADODB.Error, _
179:   adStatus As ADODB.EventStatusEnum, _
180:   ByVal pRecordset As ADODB.Recordset)
181:      Debug.Print "> Recordset FetchComplete event was triggered."
182: End Sub
183:
184: Private Sub rsEvent_FieldChangeComplete(ByVal cFields As Long, _
185:   ByVal Fields As Variant, ByVal pError As ADODB.Error, adStatus _
186:   As ADODB.EventStatusEnum, ByVal pRecordset As ADODB.Recordset)
187:      Debug.Print "> Recordset FieldChangeComplete event was triggered."
188: End Sub
189:
190: Private Sub rsEvent_MoveComplete(ByVal adReason As _
191:     ADODB.EventReasonEnum, ByVal pError As ADODB.Error, adStatus As _
192:     ADODB.EventStatusEnum, ByVal pRecordset As ADODB.Recordset)
193:      Debug.Print "> Recordset MoveComplete event was triggered."
194: End Sub
195:
196: Private Sub rsEvent_RecordChangeComplete(ByVal adReason As _
197:     ADODB.EventReasonEnum, ByVal cRecords As Long, ByVal pError As _
198:     ADODB.Error, adStatus As ADODB.EventStatusEnum, _
199:   ByVal pRecordset As ADODB.Recordset)
200:      Debug.Print "> Recordset RecordChangeComplete event was triggered."
201: End Sub
```

9

continues

LISTING 9.12   Continued

```
202:
203: Private Sub rsEvent_RecordsetChangeComplete(ByVal adReason As _
204:   ADODB.EventReasonEnum, ByVal pError As ADODB.Error, adStatus _
205:   As ADODB.EventStatusEnum, ByVal pRecordset As ADODB.Recordset)
206:     Debug.Print "> Recordset RecordsetChangeComplete event was triggered."
207: End Sub
208:
209: Private Sub rsEvent_WillChangeField(ByVal cFields As Long, ByVal Fields _
210:   As Variant, adStatus As ADODB.EventStatusEnum, _
211:   ByVal pRecordset As ADODB.Recordset)
212:     Debug.Print "> Recordset WillChangeField event was triggered."
213: End Sub
214:
215: Private Sub rsEvent_WillChangeRecord(ByVal adReason As _
216:   ADODB.EventReasonEnum, ByVal cRecords As Long, _
217:   adStatus As ADODB.EventStatusEnum, ByVal pRecordset _
218:   As ADODB.Recordset)
219:     Debug.Print "> Recordset WillChangeRecord event was triggered."
220: End Sub
221:
222: Private Sub rsEvent_WillChangeRecordset(ByVal adReason As _
223:   ADODB.EventReasonEnum, adStatus As ADODB.EventStatusEnum, _
224:   ByVal pRecordset As ADODB.Recordset)
225:     Debug.Print "> Recordset WillChangeRecordset event was triggered."
226: End Sub
227:
228: Private Sub rsEvent_WillMove(ByVal adReason As ADODB.EventReasonEnum, _
229:   adStatus As ADODB.EventStatusEnum, ByVal pRecordset As ADODB.Recordset)
230:     Debug.Print "> Recordset WillMove event was triggered."
231: End Sub
232:
233:
234: ' Connection:
235: Private Sub connEvent_InfoMessage(ByVal pError As ADODB.Error, _
236:   adStatus As ADODB.EventStatusEnum, ByVal pConnection As ADODB.Connection)
237:     Debug.Print
238:     Debug.Print "> Connection InfoMessage was triggered."
239:     Debug.Print "Error Description: " & pError.Description
240:     Debug.Print "Error Source: " & pError.Source
241:
242:     Debug.Print "Connection Status Number: " & adStatus
243:     Debug.Print
244: End Sub
245:
246: Private Sub connEvent_WillConnect(ConnectionString As String, _
247:   UserID As String, Password As String, Options As Long, adStatus _
248:   As ADODB.EventStatusEnum, ByVal pConnection As ADODB.Connection)
249:     Debug.Print "> Connection WillConnect event was triggered."
250: End Sub
```

```
251:
252: Private Sub connEvent_ConnectComplete(ByVal pError As ADODB.Error, _
253:    adStatus As ADODB.EventStatusEnum, _
254:    ByVal pConnection As ADODB.Connection)
255:      Debug.Print "> Connection ConnectComplete event was triggered."
256: End Sub
257:
258: Private Sub connEvent_Disconnect(adStatus As ADODB.EventStatusEnum, _
259:    ByVal pConnection As ADODB.Connection)
260:      Debug.Print "> Connection Disconnect event was triggered."
261: End Sub
```

When you run the method GetRecordsAsync of the class module MyAsyncRsClass, the output might be as follows (the number of cycles may vary due to performance of the database, server, or database connection).

OUTPUT

```
1: Event Support enabled...
2:
3: ### Loop 1 ###
4: > Connection WillConnect event was triggered.
5: > Connection ConnectComplete event was triggered.
6: > Recordset WillMove event was triggered.
7: > Recordset MoveComplete event was triggered.
8: 0 cycles with closed recordset...
9: 1 cycles with open recordset...
10: 0 cycles while connecting...
11: 0 cycles while executing...
12: 0 cycles while fetching...
13: Closed:
14: Opened:
15: Connecting:
16: Executing:
17: Fetching:
18: > Recordset WillMove event was triggered.
19: > Recordset MoveComplete event was triggered.
20:   10258        ERNSH        7/17/1996
21: > Recordset RecordsetChangeComplete event was triggered.
22: > Connection Disconnect event was triggered.
23: Event Support disabled...
24:
25: ### Loop 2 ###
26: (AsyncFetch)
27: 0 cycles with closed recordset...
28: 10036 cycles with open recordset...
29: 0 cycles while connecting...
30: 0 cycles while executing...
31: 10035 cycles while fetching...
```

9

```
32: Closed:
33: Opened:       OOOOOOOOOOOOOOOOOOOOOOOOOOOOOOo
34: Connecting:
35: Executing:
36: Fetching:     OOOOOOOOOOOOOOOOOOOOOOOOOOOOOOo
37:  10258          ERNSH          7/17/1996
38:
39: ### Loop 3 ###
40: (AsyncFetchNonBlocking)
41: 0 cycles with closed recordset...
42: 5978 cycles with open recordset...
43: 0 cycles while connecting...
44: 0 cycles while executing...
45: 5977 cycles while fetching...
46: Closed:
47: Opened:       OOOOOOOOOOOOOOOO
48: Connecting:
49: Executing:
50: Fetching:     OOOOOOOOOOOOOOOO
51:  10258          ERNSH          7/17/1996
52:
53: ### Loop 4 ###
54: (AsyncFetchNonBlocking)
55: (AsyncFetch)
56: 0 cycles with closed recordset...
57: 10602 cycles with open recordset...
58: 0 cycles while connecting...
59: 0 cycles while executing...
60: 10601 cycles while fetching...
61: Closed:
62: Opened:       OOOOOOOOOOOOOOOOOOOOOOOOOOOOOO.
63: Connecting:
64: Executing:
65: Fetching:     OOOOOOOOOOOOOOOOOOOOOOOOOOOOOO.
66:  10258          ERNSH          7/17/1996
67:
68: ### Loop 5 ###
69: (AsyncExecute)
70: 0 cycles with closed recordset...
71: 1 cycles with open recordset...
72: 0 cycles while connecting...
73: 19336 cycles while executing...
74: 0 cycles while fetching...
75: Closed:
76: Opened:
77: Connecting:
78: Executing:  OOOOOOOOOOOOOOOOOOOOOOOOOOOOOOOOOOOOOOOOOOOOOOOOOOOOOOOOOOOO.
79: Fetching:
80:  10258          ERNSH          7/17/1996
81:
82: ### Loop 6 ###
```

```
83: (AsyncExecute)
84: (AsyncFetch)
85: 0 cycles with closed recordset...
86: 7272 cycles with open recordset...
87: 0 cycles while connecting...
88: 9397 cycles while executing...
89: 7271 cycles while fetching...
90: Closed:
91: Opened:                                    .OOOOOOOOOOOOOOOOOOOOOo
92: Connecting:
93: Executing:   OOOOOOOOOOOOOOOOOOOOOOOOOOOOO
94: Fetching:                                  .OOOOOOOOOOOOOOOOOOOOOo
95:  10258        ERNSH        7/17/1996
96:
97: ### Loop 7 ###
98: (AsyncExecute)
99: (AsyncFetchNonBlocking)
100: 0 cycles with closed recordset...
101: 7038 cycles with open recordset...
102: 0 cycles while connecting...
103: 12800 cycles while executing...
104: 7037 cycles while fetching...
105: Closed:
106: Opened:                                   .OOOOOOOOOOOOOOOOOOOOOo
107: Connecting:
108: Executing:   OOOOOOOOOOOOOOOOOOOOOOOOOOOOOOOOOOOOOOOOOo
109: Fetching:                                 .OOOOOOOOOOOOOOOOOOOOOo
110:  10258        ERNSH        7/17/1996
111:
112: ### Loop 8 ###
113: (AsyncExecute)
114: (AsyncFetchNonBlocking)
115: (AsyncFetch)
116: 0 cycles with closed recordset...
117: 6106 cycles with open recordset...
118: 0 cycles while connecting...
119: 12829 cycles while executing...
120: 6105 cycles while fetching...
121: Closed:
122: Opened:                                   .OOOOOOOOOOOOOOOOOO.
123: Connecting:
124: Executing:   OOOOOOOOOOOOOOOOOOOOOOOOOOOOOOOOOOOOOOOOOo
125: Fetching:                                 .OOOOOOOOOOOOOOOOOO
126:  10258        ERNSH        7/17/1996
```

ANALYSIS   The script in Listing 9.12 creates the array arrGraph in line 44. It is used to indicate how often a certain recordset state appeared during executing the recordset command and fetching the records asynchronously.

The event messages are not explained in detail in this analysis. See output lines 4–22 for the events that are triggered by the Connection and Recordset objects.

To demonstrate all possible asynchronous modes when you open a recordset, all permutations of the asynchronous options adAsyncExecute, adAsyncFetchNonBlocking, and adAsyncFetch are written into the array arrValue. To achieve the option that indicates adAsyncExecute and adAsyncFetchNonBlocking, you have to use the following value:

```
adAsyncExecute OR adAsyncFetchNonBlocking
```

Event support is enabled for both the recordset rs and the connection conn in lines 60–61.

The connection string, which specifies a connection to the SQL Server 7.0 Northwind database, is stored in the strConnectionString in line 63. The SQL statement to retrieve the recordset is stored in the variable strSQL in line 65. It fetches all records from the Orders table, ordered by EmployeeIDs.

The first loop, which uses the asynchronous option parameter stored in the first element of the array arrValue, is executed in lines 69–160. During a loop, all used asynchronous option parameters for the current loop are written to the user in lines 71–79 of the listing (output lines 26, 40, 113–115, and others).

In lines 81–84 the recordset rs is prepared and the connection conn is opened. Line 85 opens the recordset using the recordset's Open method with the connection conn, executes the SQL statement stored in strSQL, and fetches the records returned from the data source. The asynchronous option parameter for the Open method is specified by the element with the index number of the loop pass (=intI) in the array arrValue. This asynchronous option parameter is superimposed with an execution option parameter using the Or operator.

The execution of the While...Wend loop (lines 99–136) is prepared by initializing various variables to their initial values. Counter variables, such as lngClosed or lngExecuting, are used to count the number of loops with a certain recordset state (closed or executing). Variables such as lngClG or lngExG are used for the graphical illustration. For instance, the variable lngExG (Execution Graphical) sums up the number of loops where the recordset's State property returns adStateExecuting. After a certain number of loops, as specified in lngPart, the percentage of loops with State set to adStateExecuting is evaluated and an accordant character (space, dot, lowercase o, or uppercase O) is added to the graphical string variable strExecuting. The variable lngExG is set to 0 to evaluate the percentage of the following loops.

To see the content of strExecuting or strFetching, look at output lines 93 and 94.

The While...Wend loop is executed as long as the State property of the Recordset object rs contains another value than adStateOpen. The value of rs.State is stored in lngState during each pass of the While loop.

When the property rs.State returns adStateOpen, the variable blnRun is set to False to indicate that the current pass of the While loop is the last one.

The total number of passes of the While loop is tracked in the variable lngTotal in line 105. The number of passes, where the State property of the recordset indicates a closed recordset, is tracked in lngClosed. The variable lngOpened tracks the number of cycles of the While loop where the recordset is already opened. The number of passes where the recordset statement is executed is stored in lngExecuting, and the number of passes where the recordset fetches records is tracked in lngFetching.

The code in lines 122–135 is used to compose the graphical strings strFetching and strExecuting. These strings serve as indicators of how often and when a certain record-set state was engaged during processing of the While loop.

After the While loop, the number of loop cycles with a certain recordset state is written to the user in lines 138–142 (output lines 85–89, for instance). The graphical illustration of the frequency of a certain recordset mode is written to the user in lines 144–148 using variables such as strConnecting, strExecuting, or strFetching.

Lines 151–154 close the recordset rs and reset its properties. The connection conn is closed in line 154. At the end of the first pass of the While loop, the script disables event support for both the Connection and the Recordset objects.

All event handler codes for the Recordset object rs are defined in lines 172–231. The event handler subs for the events triggered by the Connection object conn are defined in lines 235–261.

Summary

Today, you learned how to use events that are triggered by ADO objects. Both the Recordset and the Connection objects fire events, which indicate whether actions—such as closing a connection, fetching records into a recordset, beginning a transaction, moving the recordset record, or changing a field's content—are engaged.

Generally, events can be used only in Visual Basic or VBA class or form modules. In VBScript, you can use events only in special environments. For instance, Active Server Pages support transactional events. VBScript in a DHTML page can also use the events defined by the DHTML object model.

You also explored the execution of asynchronous ADO actions, such as connecting to a data source, executing a statement against a data source, or populating a recordset with records. Using asynchronous events enables you to continue execution of your application while ADO is connecting to a data source or fetching records into a recordset.

Remember that not every event is triggered as expected at first sight. When you open a recordset, for example, the `WillMove` and `MoveComplete` events are triggered. When you open a connection asynchronously, the `ConnectComplete` event is not triggered as long as you do not set `adStatus` parameter in the `WillConnect` event handler code to `adStatusCancel`.

Q&A

Q **I found out that certain events are not triggered as expected. For instance, the `ConnectComplete` event is not triggered when I open an ADO connection in asynchronous mode. How can I find out which events are triggered in which situation?**

A The ADO documentation in the field of ADO events does not tell you much about whether an event is triggered. The only safe possibility is to use a test sample code that uses the same connection and recordset option parameters as the application and then force an event to be triggered. In the event handler code, for example, you write a message in the Immediate window of Visual Basic to see whether an event was triggered.

Workshop

The quiz questions and exercises are provided for your further understanding. See Appendix A, "Answers," for the answers.

Quiz

1. What do you have to check before you use a connection that was opened asynchronously?

2. What name do you have to use for the `WillConnect` event handler subroutine when using the following definitions for the Connection object:Dim conn As New ADODB.

   ```
   Connection Dim WithEvents connEvent As ADODB.Connection
   ```

   Assume that the script uses the `Connection` object named conn to perform the ADO actions.

3. Provide the name of the `WillChangeField` event handler subroutine for the record-set `objRs`, which is defined as follows:

```
Dim WithEvents objRs as ADODB.Recordset
```

4. Listing 9.13 does not execute the event handler subroutine named `rs_EndOfRecordset`. Change the script so that the event handler sub is executed.

LISTING 9.13   No Events Are Triggered

```
 1: Dim rs As New ADODB.Recordset
 2: Dim WithEvents rsEvent As ADODB.Recordset
 3:
 4: Sub NoEvents()
 5:     Dim conn As New ADODB.Connection
 6:
 7:     On Error GoTo NoEventsError
 8:
 9:     conn.Open "Provider=SQLOLEDB;Data Source=BoyScout;" & _
10:     "Initial Catalog=Northwind", "sa", ""
11:
12:     Set rsEvent = rs    ' Enable event handler
13:     Set rs = conn.Execute("SELECT * FROM Customers")
14:
15:     While Not rs.EOF
16:         Debug.Print rs("CustomerID"), rs("CompanyName")
17:         rs.MoveNext
18:     Wend
19:
20:     rs.Close
21:     conn.Close
22:     Set conn = Nothing
23:     Set rs = Nothing
24:     Exit Sub
25:
26: NoEventsError:
27:     Debug.Print err.Description
28:     Debug.Print err.Source
29: End Sub
30:
31: ' Recordset Events:
32: Private Sub rs_EndOfRecordset(fMoreData As Boolean, adStatus As _
33:     ADODB.EventStatusEnum, ByVal pRecordset As ADODB.Recordset)
34:     Debug.Print "> Recordset EndOfRecordset event was triggered."
35: End Sub
```

9

Exercises

1. Rewrite Listing 9.5 so that only one object named objConn is used instead of the objects named conn and connEvent. Of course, the object objConn should support events so that the function of the code remains the same.

2. Write a class module with the method named ADOAction. In the sub named ADOAction, the class module has to retrieve all records from the Employees table from the SQL Server 7.0 Northwind database. Open the connection asynchronously and fetch all records from the Employees table into a recordset named rsEmployees; use the Execute method of the Connection object with an SQL statement and the asynchronous option parameters adAsyncExecute and adAsyncFetch. Also, provide the option parameter adCmdText to indicate that the first parameter of the Execute method is a SQL statement, because this accelerates retrieving the recordset. Then write all values from the FirstName and the LastName field to the user.

DAY 10

Shaping Your Data into Hierarchical Recordsets

Objectives

Relationships in a database form a hierarchy that is, most often, a one-to-many relationship, such as Customer to Orders. However, when you retrieve the data, you usually retrieve it separately (or in some combined form), not in the hierarchy. Today, you'll learn about a technique that enables you to create hierarchies with Recordsets—Data Shaping. With it, you can navigate the relational data in a tree.

Today, you will learn the how to do following:

- Define the contents of a shaped recordset.
- Decide the type of hierarchy to build.
- Create parameterized hierarchies for minimum memory usage.
- Aggregate child recordset information, as well as calculate row results.
- Control the freshness of child resultsets.
- Reshape hierarchies to prototype and experiment with data.

Understanding Data Shaping

As a database developer, you are used to working with relational data in a relational database. When you look at database diagrams of the Northwind database, for example, you have various foreign key relationships defined among the tables (see Figure 10.1).

FIGURE 10.1

The relationships among the Customers, Orders, and Order Details tables.

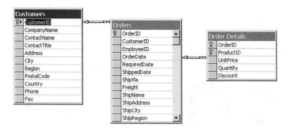

The diagram of Figure 10.1 is a really simple one. It only contains a subset of the tables that are in this database. It shows the relationship between the tables used for customer and order tracking.

How would you display information about a customer, including the orders? There are several ways to do this:

- JOINing the tables: A very common solution is to create an INNER JOIN between the Customers and Orders tables (see Figure 10.2).

FIGURE 10.2

Creating an INNER JOIN between the Customers and Orders tables.

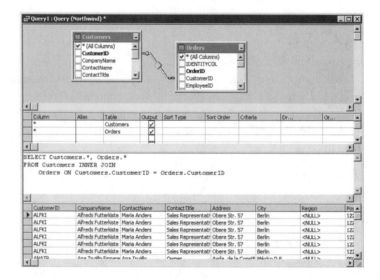

There are a few disadvantages to this approach. The most important is that, because you have joined two tables, you cannot make updates to the underlying data. The second severe disadvantage is that, because there can be multiple orders for a single customer, you might be duplicating data—the customer data is duplicated in each order row.

- Two table-level rowsets: Another solution is to open two Recordsets, one for the Customers table, and a second one for the Orders table. To see a customer's orders, you apply a FILTER statement to the Orders Recordset.

  The disadvantage of this approach is that you open potentially large resultsets, which can severely impact performance in multiuser environments. On the plus side, you can update both customer and order data.

- Prepared statements: Similar to the previous approach, you open the Customers table. However, for the Orders table, you create a prepared statement (or even stored procedure with an ADO Command object), which has a parameter for CustomerID.

  The advantage of this approach is that both tables can be updated directly, and that the Orders resultset is small. It is limited to the current customer's data only. If you are paging through many customers, you incur a high number of round-trips to the database server because the prepared statement has to be executed for every customer.

- Shaped Recordsets: This solution allows for the best of the last two approaches, and they are my topic today. Shaped Recordsets allow you to build hierarchies of Recordsets that can be updated, contain aggregates, and have additional fabricated columns and hierarchy reshaping.

Before going into any depth with Shaped Recordsets—how can you visualize them? If you have Access 2000 installed on your machine, simply open the Northwind database's Customers table and expand the nodes (see Figure 10.3).

If you page back to Figure 10.1, you can see that Access converted the three tables (Customers, Orders and Order Details) into a hierarchy. Each child table is related to its parent table via the foreign key relationship. If you give it a try, you'll learn that you can update data at any level in the hierarchy.

This is a practical example of how Shaped Recordsets can be used to create hierarchies. Now I want you to take a closer look at what Data Shaping is and how it actually works behind the scenes.

10

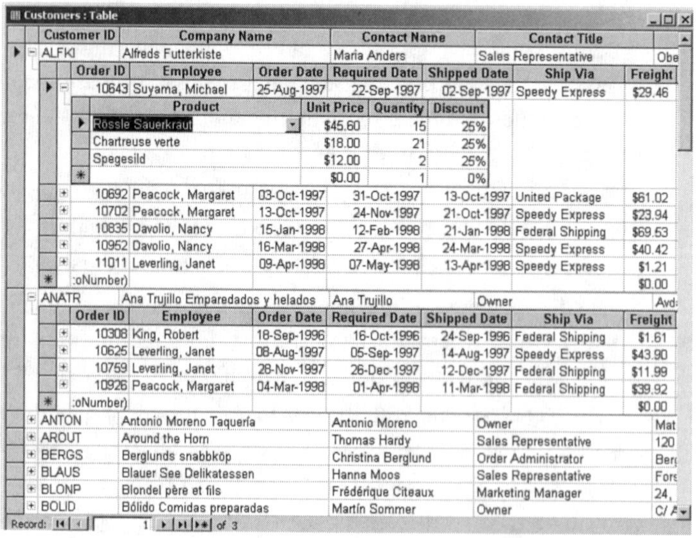

FIGURE 10.3

Access 2000 uses Shaped Recordsets to display one-to-many relationships between tables.

How Does Data Shaping Work?

Up to this point, I've only let you in on the fact that you can use Data Shaping to create hierarchies with Shaped Recordsets. A complete definition of Data Shaping is presented below:

Data Shaping encompasses the definition of columns in a Shaped Recordset, the creation of relationships that had not previously existed between keys, fields, or rowsets, as well as the way the Recordsets are actually filled with data.

As you can see from this definition, you are not limited to creating hierarchies based on foreign key relationships only—you can create hierarchies based on any field or any grouping you can imagine.

Data Shaping is implemented by the Data Shaping Service for OLE DB, which is actually an OLE DB Provider. You tell this provider how to create the hierarchies using the SHAPE language (which is described later in the section "Using SHAPE Commands"). The entire process is shown in the model of Figure 10.4.

The following steps are performed to retrieve a hierarchical Recordset:

1. Your application connects to the Data Shaping provider (service provider) and supplies the name of the data provider (such as SQLOLE) in the connection properties. The SHAPE construct is supplied in Recordset.Open.

2. ADO passes the SHAPE construct on to the Data Shaping provider, which parses it. The Data Shaping provider then issues the SQL statements against the data provider (SQLOLE in this example) to query SQL Server for the necessary data. The returned data is shaped into hierarchical Recordsets according to the SHAPE instructions.

FIGURE 10.4

The process of creating hierarchical Recordsets.

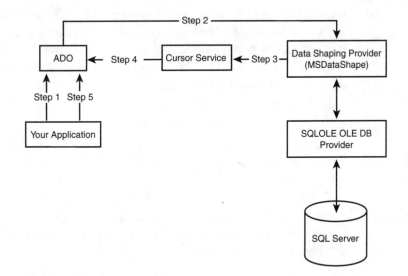

3. The Shaped Data is loaded in the Cursor Engine Service.
4. The Shaped Data is now available in ADO (steps 2 and 3 happened at the OLE DB level).
5. Your application can access the hierarchical Recordsets.

From this process model, you can see that the Data Shaping provider is independent of the database because it employs a data provider to actually connect to the data it is told to shape.

The next interesting thing to know is what you can store in such a Shaped Recordset.

Contents of a Shaped Recordset

Although you haven't seen a single SHAPE command, let's start examining what you can put into a Shaped Recordset using the SHAPE language.

The following column types can be part of a Shaped Recordset:

- *Data field*: This is one of the most common types of columns in Shaped Recordsets. It is a field that is returned by a SQL command issued to a data provider or a previously Shaped Recordset (this is part of the reshaping feature discussed later in section "Reshaping Hierarchies").

- *Chapter*: A child Recordset stored by reference in the parent Recordset is called a *Chapter*. You use the Chapter to access the child Recordset and thus the underlying records in the child recordset. For example, the Orders table's Recordset is stored as a Chapter in the Customers table's recordset when you build this hierarchy.

- *Aggregate*: The value of this column is created by executing an aggregate function on all the rows (or specific columns) of a child Recordset. You learn more on this in the section titled "Aggregating Information."

- *Calculated Expression*: Using the JET Expression Service, you can calculate columns using familiar Visual Basic for Applications expressions. However, you are limited to the current row's columns for your calculations. In-depth coverage is provided in "Calculating Expressions."

- *Fabricated Field*: If the existing fields don't fit your bill, you can create your own. These can be populated at a later time (or never). A discussion is provided in "Fabricating Fields."

Aggregates, Chapters, and calculated expressions give you a lot of power—but how do you use it? The next section gives you some hints and guidelines.

Usage Scenarios

The SHAPE language enables you to construct a wide variety of hierarchies. You can create hierarchical relations between rowsets, as long as they have at least one column value in common (and be the data type only!). You can create one-to-one, one-to-many, many-to-many, or many-to-one relationships by simply appending a child rowset to a parent rowset. As you can see in Figure 10.5, even childless rowsets are allowed.

Given the column types that you can add to a Shaped Recordset, there are basically two types of hierarchies you can build:

- Relation-based hierarchies
- Group-based hierarchies

FIGURE 10.5

The SHAPE language enables you to build quite different hierarchies.

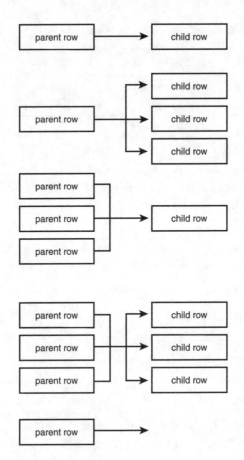

10

Relation-Based Hierarchies

This hierarchy is easy to imagine because you build a parent-child relationship between the rowsets. You can create the relationship either explicitly or via a parameterized data provider command.

What kinds of relationships can you build? That depends mainly on the parent columns in the parent rowset. If these form a key, you can build one-to-one or one-to-many relationships. If they do not form a key, you get many-to-many or many-to-one relationships. Table 10.1 will help you decide which kind of relationship is formed.

TABLE 10.1 Relationships Formed Dependent on Keys

	Key in Parent Rowset	No Key in Parent Rowset
Key in child rowset	One-to-one	Many-to-one
No key in child rowset	One-to-many	Many-to-many

Group-Based Hierarchies

The group-based, or computed, hierarchical rowsets are constructed when you use aggregate functions in your SHAPE constructs. In fact, the parent rowset is fabricated based on the data found in the child rowsets: The parent rowset contains one row for each child.

Although the parent rowset will contain computed columns as well as the Chapter column, you can also add other columns (just as you can in relation-based hierarchies).

You can build the following hierarchy definitions:

- Aggregated group hierarchy
- Hierarchy with multiple groupings
- Hierarchy showing grand totals
- One parent with two child rowsets, a group detail, and a parameterized hierarchy
- Nested hierarchies
- Grandchild grouping to skip one level when summing
- Computed rowsets that have a one-to-one or a one-to-many relationship and are members of multiple groups

Using SHAPE Commands

You now have a good understanding of what Data Shaping is, what you can put into a Shaped Recordset, and where to use it. The only piece missing is how to actually build a Shaped Recordset using the SHAPE language.

This section presents the following topics for your understanding of the SHAPE language:

- The general syntax
- Parameterized hierarchies
- Aggregating information
- Calculating expressions
- Fabricating fields

The General Syntax

If you recall what you've already learned today, you know that there are two possible types of hierarchies: relation-based and group-based hierarchies. (The latter ones are described in section "Aggregating Information.") These two hierarchies are reflected in the syntax of the SHAPE language.

The SHAPE Syntax for Relation-Based Hierarchies

▼ SYNTAX

The following code shows the syntax for the SHAPE command used to build relation-based hierarchies.

```
SHAPE {parent-command} [[AS] parent-alias]
APPEND ({child-command} [[AS] child-alias]
RELATE parent-column TO child-column) [[AS] chapter-alias]
```

Although it might look confusing at first, it isn't. Every SHAPE command starts with SHAPE. Because you are building a relation-based hierarchy, the parent-command goes first. For example

```
SELECT * FROM Customers
```

Although it is strictly optional to do so, you can alias this command using the AS clause. The next step is to APPEND columns to the parent recordset. In this case, you are appending a child recordset. A good example is

```
SELECT * FROM Orders
```

Now the only thing missing for the Data Shaping provider is how the two (parent and child) RELATE to each other, that is, which parent-column matches which child-column. As both are linked via the CustomerID field, a complete SHAPE command looks like this:

```
SHAPE { SELECT * FROM Customers }
APPEND ({ SELECT * FROM Orders }
RELATE CustomerID TO CustomerID)
```

I have deliberately omitted the Chapter alias—why would you want to name it? There is a good reason to name it—this alias identifies the Chapter that references the child recordset. The default Chapter name is ChapterX, where X is a number starting at 1.

To name your chapter rsOrders, the final SHAPE command look like this:

```
SHAPE { SELECT * FROM Customers }
APPEND ({ SELECT * FROM Orders }
▲ RELATE CustomerID TO CustomerID) AS rsOrders
```

How do you know that your SHAPE command is valid? You can write a simple test program that enables you to verify your commands.

10

To Do: Creating a SHAPE Command Tool in Excel

Follow these steps to create a tool for verifying SHAPE commands in Excel:

1. Start Excel. Right-click on any visible toolbar and make sure that the Control Toolbox toolbar is selected.

2. From the Control Toolbox, activate the Text Box tool (the cursor changes to a thin crosshair cursor).

3. Click in the center of the A2 cell and drag the text box to the center of G17.

4. Right-click on the newly created text box and choose Properties from the context menu. The Properties dialog box for "TextBox1" pops up.

5. Change the name to txtShapeCommand and set the EnterKeyBehavior, MultiLine, and TabKeyBehavior properties to True. This will enable you to use the Enter and Tab keys to format your SHAPE commands.

6. The only additional adjustment to make is to set the Scrollbars property to fmScrollbarsBoth. You are now done preparing the text box.

7. Select Command Button from the Control Toolbox. Create a command button from the center of cell A18 to D20. Rename the button to cmdShapeIt, and change the caption to Shape It!.

8. Double-click the button to open the Visual Basic Editor with the event procedure selected. Insert the code from Listing 10.1.

LISTING 10.1   The Event Procedure for the Shape It! Button

```
 1: Private Sub cmdShapeIt_Click()
 2:     Dim strShapeCmd As String, cn As ADODB.Connection, rs As ADODB.Recordset
 3:
 4:     ' get the shape command
 5:     strShapeCmd = Me.txtShapeCommand.Text
 6:
 7:     ' create the objects, and then open the connection
 8:     Set cn = New ADODB.Connection
 9:     Set rs = New ADODB.Recordset
10:     cn.Provider = "MSDataShape"
11:     cn.Open "data provider=sqloledb.1;user id=sa;password=;
➥initial catalog=northwind;data source=strangelove"
12:
13:     rs.Open strShapeCmd, cn
14:     MsgBox "Successfully created command!"
15: End Sub
```

▼ You will need to adjust the connection string in line 11 according to your setup.

9. Make a reference to the ADO 2.5 library.

10. Switch back to the worksheet and exit design mode (you can do that in the Control Toolbox). Save the workbook so you do not lose your work in case of a later crash.

11. Try the following SHAPE command by pasting it into the textbox:

```
SHAPE { SELECT * FROM Customers }
APPEND ({ SELECT * FROM Orders }
RELATE CustomerID TO CustomerID) AS rsOrders
```

▲ 12. If all went well, you should get a success message for this SHAPE command.

Instead of analyzing the previous example, it is better to expand it so it is more useful—and includes decent error handling that doesn't exist in this example.

A useful extension is to create a tree that includes all column names from each rowset, be it parent or child. Listing 10.2 shows the complete code for the Visual Basic module.

10

LISTING 10.2 Listing All Columns in a Shaped Recordset

```
 1: Option Explicit
 2:
 3: Private Sub cmdShapeIt_Click()
 4: On Error GoTo Err_cmdShapeIt
 5:     ' declare the variables
 6:     Dim strShapeCmd As String, cn As ADODB.Connection, rs As ADODB.Recordset
 7:     Dim strResult As String
 8:
 9:     ' get the shape command
10:     strShapeCmd = Me.txtShapeCommand.Text
11:
12:     ' create the objects, and then open the connection
13:     Set cn = New ADODB.Connection
14:     Set rs = New ADODB.Recordset
15:     cn.Provider = "MSDataShape"
16:     cn.Open "data provider=sqloledb.1;user id=sa;password=;
➥initial catalog=northwind;data source=strangelove"
17:
18:     rs.Open strShapeCmd, cn
19:     CreateHierarchy rs.Fields, strResult, 0
20:     MsgBox strResult
21:
22:     Exit Sub
23: Err_cmdShapeIt:
24:     MsgBox Err.Description
25:     Exit Sub
26: End Sub
27:
```

continues

LISTING 10.2   continued

```
28: Sub CreateHierarchy(ByRef flds As ADODB.Fields, ByRef strFields As String,
➥ByVal nNestDepth As Integer)
29:     Dim fld As ADODB.Field
30:     For Each fld In flds
31:         strFields = strFields & Space(nNestDepth * 2) & fld.Name & vbCrLf
32:         If adChapter = fld.Type Then
33:             CreateHierarchy fld.Value.Fields, strFields, nNestDepth + 1
34:         End If
35:     Next
36: End Sub
```

ANALYSIS   The differences start at the top—I added the OPTION EXPLICIT statement to make variable declaration mandatory, which rules out most errors you usually make in VB (typos). Besides the declaration of strResult, everything else including line 18 remains the same. Line 19 calls a custom procedure:

```
CreateHierarchy rs.Fields, strResult, 0
```

In the definition for this procedure, I am passing the Fields collection by reference, as well as passing the resulting string that I generate. The third parameter is the nesting level, which indicates the level where I am currently. Because I am at the parent level, this is 0.

The CreateHierarchy procedure consists of a For Each loop to iterate over all columns in a Recordset. There's only one special check, the one to detect Chapters:

```
If adChapter = fld.Type Then
```

When a Chapter (a child) is detected, as indicated by the field type of adChapter (value is 136), the CreateHierarchy procedure is called recursively to iterate over the child Recordset. This is the only special case handled. All other columns are simply appended to the result string.

On return from the CreateHierarchy procedure, the result string is displayed in a message box. This is not very sophisticated, but it does its job to illustrate the point (see Figure 10.6).

Parameterized Hierarchies

The previously presented SHAPE command has one major downside—all the data is retrieved from the database to create the hierarchy. If there are a large number of orders in the database, this can drain performance quite a bit, and it is entirely undesirable for multiuser environments.

FIGURE 10.6

*The output for the
sample* SHAPE
command.

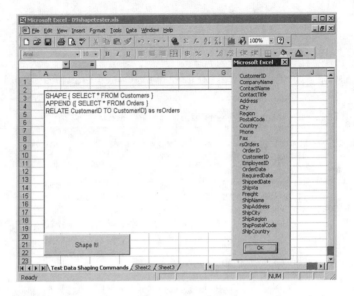

10

To circumvent the problem of retrieving large amounts of child data, you can use
parameterized commands. The hierarchical result of a parameter-based hierarchy has
exactly the same structure as when you use the standard RELATE clause. However, child
data is fetched from the database when you move from one parent record to the next.

> **Note**
>
> Because Chapters are fetched when you move to a new parent record, there
> must be an active database connection. If you make a number of round-trips
> to the database server, it is recommended to use parameterized hierarchies
> with only a few Chapters.

How would the Customers-Orders SHAPE command look if you use parameterized hierarchies? Not much different:

```
SHAPE {select * from Customers}
APPEND ({select * from Orders where CustomerID = ?}
RELATE CustomerID TO PARAMETER 0) AS rsOrders
```

If you are used to prepared statements, the general syntax for defining a parameter isn't
new for you. All you have to do is provide a question mark as placeholder. Parameters
are referenced by ordinal position starting at 0, as you can see in the RELATE clause.
Instead of relating to a column name, you relate to a parameter. Now the Chapter members are fetched when you move to a new parent record that references the parameter.

Please note that the PARAMETER clause has absolutely nothing to do with the ADO Parameters collection or Parameter object. The PARAMETER clause only pertains to the SHAPE language.

Listing 10.3 shows how to iterate over the entire hierarchical recordset.

LISTING 10.3   Iterating over a Hierarchical Recordset

```
1:      Dim strShapeCmd As String, cn As ADODB.Connection, rs As ADODB.Recordset
2:      Dim chapter As ADODB.Recordset
3:
4:      strShapeCmd = "SHAPE {select * from Customers}   "
5:      strShapeCmd = strShapeCmd & "APPEND ({select * from Orders where
➥ CustomerID = ?} "
6:      strShapeCmd = strShapeCmd & "RELATE CustomerID TO PARAMETER 0) AS
➥ rsOrders"
7:
8:      Set cn = New ADODB.Connection
9:      Set rs = New ADODB.Recordset
10:     cn.Provider = "MSDataShape"
11:     cn.Open "data provider=sqloledb.1;user id=sa;password=;
➥initial catalog=northwind;data source=strangelove"
12:
13:     rs.Open strShapeCmd, cn
14:     While Not rs.EOF
15:         Set chapter = rs("rsOrders").Value
16:         ' do something actually really useful with the chapter
17:         rs.MoveNext
18:     Wend
```

ANALYSIS   The SHAPE command is created in lines 4–6 and executed against the Northwind database in line 13. Although the While Wend loop actually does nothing, you can measure a time difference between this SHAPE command and the original one:

```
SHAPE {select * from Customers}
APPEND ({select * from Orders}
RELATE CustomerID TO CustomerID) AS rsOrders
```

This one is faster for smaller amounts of data because data is fetched in one batch (because the resultset isn't too large). Therefore, use the parameterized hierarchical Recordsets only when you intend to use a small number of Chapters.

Aggregating Information

You definitely remember the aggregate columns that can be added to shaped Recordsets. These lead to the group-based or computed hierarchies, because parent columns are computed based on child resultsets.

The SHAPE Syntax for Group-Based Hierarchies

The SHAPE syntax for computed hierarchies differs from that of relation-based hierarchies because a child recordset is partitioned using the aggregate functions (see Table 10.1). One row for each partition is created in the parent recordset.

```
SHAPE {child-command} [AS] child-alias
COMPUTE child-alias [, aggregate-command-field-list]
[BY grp-field-list]
```

The child-command is not new, but here it appears at the top of the SHAPE command. To illustrate my point, you are going to calculate the total for each order placed. The child-command is the following:

```
SELECT OrderID,UnitPrice*Quantity*(1.0-Discount) AS SubTotal

➥FROM [Order Details]
```

You have to name the child-command before you can use it in the COMPUTE clause:

```
AS chOrderDetails
```

What do you need to compute? You want a SUM of all SubTotals, and you want to include the child Recordset as a Chapter (in this case, the COMPUTE clause works just like APPEND). Therefore, the COMPUTE clause is

```
COMPUTE chOrderDetails, SUM(chOrderDetails.SubTotal)
```

All you finally need is to specify BY which column(s) you want to group. Obviously, this is the OrderID column. The complete SHAPE command is

```
SHAPE { SELECT OrderID,UnitPrice*Quantity*(1.0-Discount) AS SubTotal
        FROM [Order Details]}
AS chOrderDetails
COMPUTE chOrderDetails, SUM(chOrderDetails.SubTotal) AS OrderTotal
BY OrderID
```

The only addition I made was to rename to SUMmation of the SubTotal fields.

Which columns are in the parent recordset? These are the Chapter chOrderDetails, the OrderTotal, and the OrderID columns. Give this SHAPE command a try in the Excel SHAPE command tester.

Which aggregate functions are available for use? Take a look at Table 10.2. Most of these will already be familiar from standard SQL.

▼ SYNTAX

10

TABLE 10.2 Aggregate Functions in the SHAPE Language

Aggregate Function	Description
SUM(chapter-alias.column-name)	Calculates the sum for all values of a column in the Chapter
AVG(chapter-alias.column-name)	Determines the average of all values of a column
MAX(chapter-alias.column-name)	Finds the maximum value of all values
MIN(chapter-alias.column-name)	Finds the minimum value of all values in a given column
COUNT(chapter-alias[.column-name])	Counts the number of rows in a given chapter
STDEV(chapter-alias.column-name)	Calculates the standard deviation for the column given
ANY(chapter-alias.column-name)	Returns the value of a column where the value of the column is the same for all rows

In the example presented for the group-based hierarchies SHAPE syntax, I have used only one grouping. However, you are definitely not limited to using only one grouping. The Data Shaping provider can be used to group any number of times, and you can produce totals at any level you want.

To illustrate this, rewrite the SHAPE command

```
SHAPE { SELECT OrderID,UnitPrice*Quantity*(1.0-Discount) AS SubTotal
        FROM [Order Details]}
AS chOrderDetails
COMPUTE chOrderDetails, SUM(chOrderDetails.SubTotal) AS OrderTotal
BY OrderID
```

to include the CustomerID from the Customers table. You are now able to group by Order, then by Customer. Figure 10.7 illustrates the structure of the recordset.

The SHAPE command to produce the result as desired in Figure 10.7 is presented in Listing 10.4.

FIGURE 10.7

Two groupings create this hierarchy—one by OrderID, the other by CustomerID.

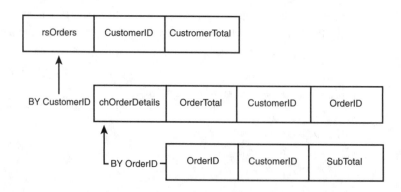

LISTING 10.4 Multiple Groupings in the SHAPE Language

```
 1: SHAPE
 2: (
 3:  SHAPE { SELECT Customers.CustomerID,[Order Details].OrderID,UnitPrice*
➥Quantity*(1.0-Discount) AS SubTotal
 4:         FROM [Order Details],Orders,Customers WHERE Customers.CustomerID =
➥Orders.CustomerID AND Orders.OrderID=[Order Details].OrderID}
 5:    AS chOrderDetails
 6:    COMPUTE chOrderDetails,
 7:            SUM(chOrderDetails.SubTotal) AS OrderTotal,
 8:            ANY(chOrderDetails.CustomerID) AS CustomerID
 9:    BY OrderID
10: )
11: AS rsOrders
12: COMPUTE rsOrders, SUM(rsOrders.OrderTotal) AS CustomerTotal
13: BY CustomerID
```

ANALYSIS What is new to this SHAPE command? First of all, I had to add the Orders and Customers table in line 4, together with the WHERE statements to join the tables (INNER JOINs would be better, but they also add more clutter). The next addition is ANY(...) in line 8. This is necessary to add the CustomerID connected to each order.

The outer SHAPE command creates the parent rowset, which includes the CustomerID (the BY statement in line 13), the rsOrders Chapter for each customer (line 12) and, finally, the total of all orders placed by the customer (also line 12).

Although this construct looks intimidating at first, ask yourself, How long would it take to create all these calculations without Shaped Recordsets?

Calculating Expressions

Another part of a COMPUTE or APPEND statement can be a calculated expression. Calculated expressions can only be applied to the columns of a single row in which the expression is contained. The statement is as simple as

CALC(expression)

What kind of expression can this be? You have a really large number of choices because you have functions from the MS Jet Expression Service at your disposal. To give you an idea of the functionality, I have provided the following paragraph listing the functions only.

10

Abs	Day	LeftB$	Second
Asc	DDB	Len	Sgn
Atn	Error	Log	Sin
CBool	Error$	LTrim	SLN
CByte	Exp	LTrim$	Space
CCur	Fix	Mid	Space$
CDate	Format	Mid$	Sqr
CDbl	Format$	Minute	Str
Chr	FV	MIRR	Str$
ChrB	Hex	Month	StrComp
ChrW	Hex$	Now	StrConv
Chr$	Hour	NPer	String
ChrB$	IIF	NPV	String$
CInt	InStr	Oct	SYD
CLng	Int	Oct$	Tan
Cos	IPmt	Pmt	Time
CSng	IRR	PPmt	Time$
CStr	IsDate	PV	Timer
Cvar	IsEmpty	QBColor	TimeSerial
CVDate	IsError	Rate	TimeValue
CVErr	IsNull	RGB	Trim
Date	IsNumeric	Right	Trim$
Date$	IsObject	RightB	TypeName
DateAdd	LCase	Right$	UCase
DateDiff	LCase$	RightB$	UCase$
DatePart	Left	Rnd	Val
DateSerial	LeftB	RTrim	VarType
DateValue	Left$	RTrim$	Weekday
			Year

That's quite a lot. Because this is not a reference book, I can't explain every function in detail—please look them up in the Platform SDK documentation.

What does a SHAPE command that employs a function from the Jet Expression Service look like? I have provided a short example below that adds a computed column with the first three letters of the company to the parent Recordset:

```
SHAPE { select * from Customers }
APPEND ({ select * from ORDERS }
RELATE CustomerId to CustomerId) as rsOrders,
CALC(Left(CompanyName,3)) AS TLA
```

The same syntax holds true for the COMPUTE clause; however, be aware that you must not reference the Chapter's columns in the CALC expression. The CALC expression can work on a single row only.

Fabricating Fields

In case a Shaped Recordset doesn't come with all the fields you'd like to see, you can add new ones with the NEW keyword. You are not limited to fabricating columns only—you can create entire hierarchies on your own.

Before trying too much, start by adding a single column. The general syntax for NEW is

```
NEW field-type [(width | scale | precision | error [, scale | error])]
```

If you have ever created a new table in SQL Server, the fields named width, scale, precision, and so forth will look familiar to you. But what do you supply for field-type? The ADO data type constants are a good bet (see Table 10.3). To show you that the actual underpinnings of ADO are OLE DB, I have compared OLE DB and ADO data type constants in this table.

TABLE 10.3 Mapping of OLE DB Data Types to ADO Data Types

OLE DB Data Types	ADO Data Type Equivalent(s)
DBTYPE_BSTR	adBSTR
DBTYPE_BOOL	adBoolean
DBTYPE_DECIMAL	adDecimal
DBTYPE_UI1	adUnsignedTinyInt
DBTYPE_I1	adTinyInt
DBTYPE_UI2	adUnsignedSmallInt
DBTYPE_UI4	adUnsignedInt
DBTYPE_I8	adBigInt

continues

TABLE **10.3** continued

OLE DB Data Types	ADO Data Type Equivalent(s)
DBTYPE_UI8	adUnsignedBigInt
DBTYPE_GUID	adGuid
DBTYPE_BYTES	adBinary, adVarBinary, adLongVarBinary
DBTYPE_STR	adChar, adVarChar, adLongVarChar
DBTYPE_WSTR	adWChar, adVarWChar, adLongVarWChar
DBTYPE_NUMERIC	adNumeric
DBTYPE_DBDATE	adDBDate
DBTYPE_DBTIME	adDBTime
DBTYPE_DBTIMESTAMP	adDBTimeStamp
DBTYPE_VARNUMERIC	adVarNumeric
DBTYPE_FILETIME	adFileTime
DBTYPE_ERROR	adError

To put it into practice, you can add a new VarChar field of length 20 to the parent Recordset using the following SHAPE command:

```
SHAPE { select * from Customers }
APPEND ({ select * from ORDERS }
RELATE CustomerId to CustomerId) as rsOrders,
NEW adVarChar(20) AS myNewField
```

The length of the field is supplied in parentheses. Remembering Table 10.3, you can rewrite the last line to

```
NEW DBTYPE_STR(20) AS myNewField
```

and it would still work.

What about creating an entirely new Recordset using the NEW keyword? No problem. As an example, you can create a table to store ISO country codes. The SHAPE language would be

```
SHAPE APPEND
   NEW adChar(2) AS CountryCode,
   NEW adVarChar(128) AS CountryName
```

When you are creating entirely new hierarchies, you can change the data provider to NONE (even if I didn't provide children), because you do not necessarily need to retrieve data. Therefore, my VB code for creating the fabricated Recordset looks like Listing 10.5.

10

LISTING 10.5 Creating an Entirely Fabricated Recordset

```
 1: Sub Fabricate()
 2:     Dim strShapeCmd As String, cn As ADODB.Connection, rs As ADODB.Recordset
 3:     Dim fld As ADODB.Field
 4:
 5:     strShapeCmd = "SHAPE APPEND   "
 6:     strShapeCmd = strShapeCmd & "NEW adChar(2) AS CountryCode, "
 7:     strShapeCmd = strShapeCmd & "NEW adVarChar(128) AS CountryName"
 8:
 9:     Set cn = New ADODB.Connection
10:     Set rs = New ADODB.Recordset
11:     cn.Provider = "MSDataShape"
12:     cn.Open "data provider=none;provider=MSDataShape"
13:
14:     rs.Open strShapeCmd, cn
15:     For Each fld In rs.Fields
16:         Debug.Print fld.Name & " " & fld.Type
17:     Next
18: End Sub
```

ANALYSIS Note that in line 12 I have both the service provider (MSDataShape) and the data provider (NONE) in the same connection string. This is entirely legal and saves one line for the assignment of the Provider property. Besides this change, there is nothing new to this listing.

Working with Shaped Recordsets

You have a solid foundation for using the SHAPE language and forming SHAPE commands. The only thing left to do is to take a closer look at how to work effectively and quickly with Shaped Recordsets.

In this section you learn about the following topics:

- Iterating through a hierarchical Recordset
- Controlling the freshness of child results
- Reshaping hierarchies

Iterating Through a Hierarchical Recordset

The samples presented so far have never output the actual data—only the column names that are in the respective rowsets. To put it together, I take the parameterized SHAPE command and display the results in an Excel worksheet (see Listing 10.6).

LISTING 10.6   Iterating Through a Hierarchical Recordset

```
 1: Dim strShapeCmd As String, cn As ADODB.Connection, rs As ADODB.Recordset
 2: Dim chapter As ADODB.Recordset, fld As ADODB.Field, nCounter As Integer,
➥strResult As String
 3:
 4: strShapeCmd = "SHAPE {select * from Customers}   "
 5: strShapeCmd = strShapeCmd & "APPEND ({select * from Orders where
➥CustomerID = ?} "
 6: strShapeCmd = strShapeCmd & "RELATE CustomerID TO PARAMETER 0)
➥AS rsOrders"
 7:
 8: Set cn = New ADODB.Connection
 9: Set rs = New ADODB.Recordset
10: cn.Provider = "MSDataShape"
11: cn.Open "data provider=sqloledb.1;user id=sa;password=;
➥initial catalog=northwind;data source=strangelove"
12:
13: rs.Open strShapeCmd, cn
14: nCounter = 1
15: While Not rs.EOF
16:     For Each fld In rs.Fields
17:         If fld.Type <> adChapter Then strResult = strResult & " " &
➥fld.Value
18:     Next
19:     ActiveWorkbook.Worksheets(2).Cells(nCounter, 1) = strResult
20:     nCounter = nCounter + 1
21:     strResult = ""
22:
23:     Set chapter = rs("rsOrders").Value
24:     While Not chapter.EOF
25:         For Each fld In chapter.Fields
26:             strResult = strResult & " " & fld.Value
27:         Next
28:         ActiveWorkbook.Worksheets(2).Cells(nCounter, 2) = strResult
29:         nCounter = nCounter + 1
30:         strResult = ""
31:         chapter.MoveNext
32:     Wend
33:     rs.MoveNext
34: Wend
```

ANALYSIS   The Shaped Recordset is opened as usual; however, starting with line 15, I output the data in the Recordset to the Excel worksheet. The first For Each loop iterates over all fields ignoring the Chapter (lines 16–18). This is the data of the parent Recordset. Next, I access the child via the rsOrders Chapter:

```
Set chapter = rs("rsOrders").Value
```

Notice that I assign the value of the field to a Recordset variable. This is done for faster access later on. The `While Wend` loop in lines 24–32 iterates over all child records because it is a one-to-many relationship. The data is written to a cell that is one to the right from the parent data (line 28).

I have intentionally duplicated code that you usually put in procedures to make it more appealing and structured. However, my main point is that, except for the additional field type of chapter, Shaped Recordsets just behave like normal Recordsets.

Controlling the Freshness of Child Results

When working with Recordsets, don't use stale data. You must have some way either to guarantee the freshness of data or to have the option to explicitly update the data in your hierarchy.

For relation-based and group-based hierarchies, there are some common ways to requery and resync the hierarchy. For parameterized hierarchies, there is one additional way to do so.

10

Requerying the Hierarchy

You can refresh the data in your hierarchy using the `Requery` method of the `Recordset` object. When you execute it on any Recordset in the hierarchy, it will close and reopen all Recordsets that are affected.

Issuing a call to Requery is especially useful when you expect changes to all tables included in the query. Note that the call can consume considerable amounts of memory and network bandwidth.

Resyncing the Hierarchy

If you don't want to use that much bandwidth, you can issue `Resync` against the parent row. This causes only the child Recordset's chapter to be cleared (the data is not deleted, only the association). As soon as you access the parent again, the child rows are re-associated appropriately.

You should employ `Resync` when a parent column is changed that links to the children (a field used in the `RELATE` clause such as `OrderID`).

Caching Behavior of Parameterized Hierarchies

Parameterized hierarchies are different because the Chapters are populated only when you move to a new parent row. However, the already accessed child Recordset's Chapters are cached, so that when you issue `MovePrevious` on the parent rowset, the child Recordset isn't refetched from the database.

Although this default caching behavior is conserving network bandwidth, it can sometimes get in your way. To turn off caching for parameterized hierarchies, set the Cache
Child Rows for the parent rowset:

```
rsParent.Properties("Cache Child Rows") = False
```

Reshaping Hierarchies

The term *reshaping* might be a bit misleading at first, but it is actually best described as
prune and *graft*. Before I get too technical, take a look at a sample that employs
reshaping (see Listing 10.7).

LISTING 10.7 Simple Reshaping in Action

```
 1: Dim rs As ADODB.Recordset, cn As ADODB.Connection,
➥reshape As ADODB.Recordset
 2: Dim strShapeCmd As String, strReshapeCmd As String
 3:
 4: Set cn = New ADODB.Connection
 5: Set rs = New ADODB.Recordset
 6: Set reshape = New ADODB.Recordset
 7:
 8: cn.Provider = "MSDataShape"
 9: cn.Open "data provider=sqloledb.1;user id=sa;password=;
➥initial catalog=northwind;data source=strangelove"
10:
11: strShapeCmd = "SHAPE {select * from Customers} AS rsCustomers "
12: strShapeCmd = strShapeCmd & "APPEND ({select * from Orders} AS rsOrders "
13: strShapeCmd = strShapeCmd & "RELATE CustomerID TO CustomerID)"
14:
15: rs.Open strShapeCmd, cn
16:
17: strReshapeCmd = "SHAPE rsOrders"
18:
19: reshape.Open strReshapeCmd, cn
```

ANALYSIS In line 15, the Shaped Recordset, rs, is opened. You have done that many times.
What is new is the bare-bones SHAPE command in line 17. It references the
Shaped Recordset that was created in the SHAPE command—lines 11–13—the rsOrders
recordset.

What happens when I reuse the rsOrders Shaped Recordset in the second ADO
Recordset? The existing rowset rsOrders is completely unaffected, except that it
acquires a new parent. Why would you want to use reshaping? The reshape operations
are performed outside the data store. This allows easy experimentation and prototyping
with the data.

There are some limitations to reshaping of which you need to be aware. The most important limitation is that you can refer only to Recordsets that are created in the same session (this is the MSDataShape service session, not to be confused with the connection).

Also, you cannot append new columns to an already existing shaped recordset. A last important limitation is that you cannot reshape parameterized rowsets.

Summary

Today, you learned how to build hierarchies from your relational data. The types of hierarchies you can construct are relation-based or group-based hierarchies, and both are defined using the SHAPE language. This language is used by the Data Shaping OLE DB provider to construct the hierarchies.

The SHAPE language enables you to build Shaped Recordsets that contain data, Chapter, aggregate, calculated expression, or even new columns. In case you are not happy with the hierarchies you build, you can fabricate entirely new hierarchies or reshape your existing hierarchies.

10

Q&A

Q During the day, I have looked up information in the ADO section of the Platform SDK, however, I couldn't find much information on reshaping there. Where is this information hidden?

A You can find a lot of really good information about Data Shaping in general and Reshaping in particular in the "Using the Data Shaping Service for OLE DB" in the Microsoft OLE DB documentation (in the section on OLE DB providers).

Q You have talked about the updating of Shaped Recordsets, but you haven't shown an example. Why?

A The reason is simple—it is too simple! If you really want to know more, see Day 3, "Fail-Safe Inserting of Data."

Workshop

The quiz questions and exercises are provided for your further understanding. See Appendix A, "Answers," for the solutions.

Quiz

1. Write down the SHAPE command for relating the Shippers table to the Orders table.

2. When you issue a MovePrevious in the parent rowset of a parameterized hierarchy, will the child Recordset be fetched from the database server or taken from the cache?

3. What is the difference between a service provider and a data provider?

4. Are the following two NEW statements equal?

    ```
    NEW adChar(20) AS myNewField
    NEW DBTYPE_BSTR(20) AS myNewField
    ```

5. Name at least two limitations of reshaping.

6. Why are parameterized hierarchies dependent on an active connection?

7. Which refreshing takes more network bandwidth: Requerying or Resyncing?

Exercise

Take the SHAPE command from Quiz Question 1 and output all field names and data types in the Excel worksheet. It should be generalized to work with any level of nesting.

DAY 11

Analyzing Businesses with OLAP

A new tool that ships with SQL Server 7 is the Online Analytical Processing (OLAP) Service, which enables you to efficiently analyze data warehouses by transforming data optimized for transactional processing into multidimensional structures (cubes) optimized to enable rapid access for analysis. OLAP Services are firmly rooted in OLE DB, on the server and client sides.

You are learning about the concepts of OLAP, the advantages of using OLAP, and how to interactively query OLAP cubes today—programming cubes with ADO is tomorrow's topic.

This is an overview of what you will learn today:

- How to move from OLTP data to OLAP analysis
- What roles OLAP Services and the PivotTable Service play
- The steps necessary to prepare an OLAP cube for analysis
- Analyzing data in Excel 2000 using the PivotTable Service

- Enhancing cubes with calculated members, member properties, virtual dimensions, and multiple hierarchies
- Publishing PivotTable charts to the intranet

Understanding Data Warehousing and OLAP

When using a database today, you are working with a relational database. Tables are related to each other by foreign key relationships in such a way that you are not duplicating data across tables. For example, each order line item stores only a product ID, and not the product data, such as name or supplier (see Figure 11.1).

FIGURE 11.1

Relationship of the Order Details and Products tables.

NEW TERM This kind of table design is typical for *Online Transaction Processing* (*OLTP*) systems. An *OLTP* system's design is usually complex, optimized to support a large number of concurrent users that add or modify data, and, of course, tuned for transactional activity. It is the company's database for day-to-day operations.

Such a system is great for the purpose it was built for, but what about other business needs, such as analyzing business activity? In this case, OLTP systems' advantages immediately turn out to be drawbacks. The complexity of the structures are, at best, hard to grasp for analysts (which are most often executive-level users), and creating ad hoc queries turns out to be a major headache. Also, because the performance was optimized for transactional processing, the performance for analysis typically isn't good.

NEW TERM To overcome the limitations of OLTP systems, data needed for analytical processing is transformed into *data warehouses*. These are usually filled with all data from an organization, extracted from the OLTP systems.

Tip

> The extraction, cleansing, and data transformation necessary can be performed with the Data Transformation Services (DTS) found in SQL Server 7. Because DTS is important for this usage scenario, I recommend that you take the time to learn this powerful tool.

The goals of a data warehouse are to have the right information in the right form at the right time. The information can come from multiple sources and be summarized from details. *Right form* means that flexible analysis must be allowed, and that the delivery should be flexible, too. Because executive-level users are the target audience, data warehouses must offer a fast turnaround and rapid query response.

Why are you going to build up a data warehousing solution? Typically, not because you have the technical opportunity, and also rarely because someone decided that a global plan to analyze might be nice. Pressing business needs lead you implement a data warehouse.

The number one reason for a data warehouse is that you want to understand your customers—this is especially important now with e-commerce shops. Another reason that is closely linked to the first is that you want to manage your company by profitability—for example, profitability of products, channels, or geography. If this information is accessible fast and in understandable format, you gain an edge over competition.

The goals you have to meet for a data warehouse are not always easy to achieve because of the following requirements:

- Different database servers for different departments or tasks might be used and must be integrated in the solution (Oracle, Informix, SQL Server, and so forth).
- Decentralized, incremental development must be allowed.
- You have to deploy it rapidly and it will keep changing continuously.
- Daily refreshed data is required in most data marts.
- It must be fast and easy to understand by end users.

 A data warehouse can consist of multiple *data marts* that aggregate data at a lower level. The data is then used in the data warehouse.

If you take these requirements into account, the only thing to do is to cleanly separate your architecture. Take a look at the diagram in Figure 11.2.

FIGURE 11.2

An overview of the data warehousing process.

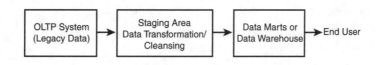

The first step is to transform the legacy data from the OLTP system in the data staging area. In the staging area, the data is cleaned and prepared, but no query service is provided. From the data staging area, the data is transferred to the data mart. This is the presentation server that serves the end user's queries.

NEW TERM
The *Online Analytical Processing* (*OLAP*) component enables an end user to efficiently query data warehouses. Although the terms *data warehouse* and *OLAP* are often used interchangeably, both refer to different components of a decision support system. A data warehouse contains data that supports analysis, and OLAP performs this analysis.

Data Warehousing and Dimensional Data

Data warehouses are built using dimensional databases. A dimensional database stores facts about business activity—such as sales—in the context of dimensions—such as time, customer, or geography.

The relevant facts, such as sales in dollars, are stored in a facts table. This table is dependent on dimension tables, and the facts table's primary key consists of foreign keys from the dimension tables. Figure 11.3 shows a star schema in which the sales_fact_1998 table is the facts table, and time_by_day, customer, and store are the dimension tables.

FIGURE 11.3

A star schema for dimensional data.

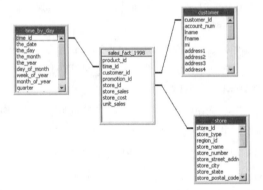

NEW TERM
The facts (such as store_sales, store_cost, and unit_sales) of the facts table are referred to as *measures*. A *measure* is a column in the facts table that represents the values that are analyzed, and it must be a numerical data type.

NEW TERM
The members of the dimension tables are used to *slice* (also referred to as filter) the data. With the dimension tables in this example, you can create slices, such as store sales by time, product sales per store, and so on. The members of the dimension tables can be used to browse the facts table.

A second schema that can be built is the snowflake schema (see Figure 11.4). In this case, the dimension tables are normalized—split into multiple, related tables.

FIGURE 11.4

A snowflake schema for dimensional data.

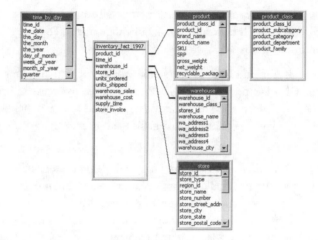

You now have a good understanding of why and how to use data warehousing and OLAP. After this general introduction, we now go to specifics on the OLAP Services that ship with SQL Server 7.

The Data Warehousing Framework

You learned how data is transformed into a data warehouse in a previous section, "Understanding Data Warehousing and OLAP." The Data Warehousing Framework put in place by OLAP Services is shown in Figure 11.5, and it describes the relationships between the various components used in the process of building, using, and managing a data warehouse.

FIGURE 11.5

The components of the Data Warehousing Framework.

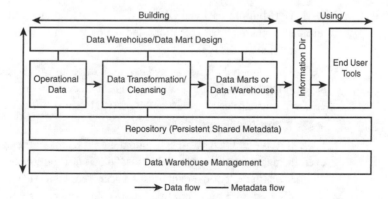

The parts you already know about are operational sources (the legacy data from the OLTP systems), data transformation, and the data marts. These are part of the Building section in Figure 11.5.

End-user tools, ranging from desktop productivity tools to custom programs written against the OLE DB provider for OLAP, can be used to access information in the data warehouse. The information directory that is located between the data marts and the end user provides a layer of security and enables end-user searches for appropriate and relevant data.

NEW TERM The Repository provides an integrated *metadata* repository that is shared by the various components used in the data warehousing process. *Metadata* is comprised of information about properties of the data, such as data type of a column, design of dimensions and so on. You can transparently integrate multiple products from different vendors using shared metadata without the need to create specialized interfaces between all the products.

Introducing the Microsoft OLAP Services

SQL Server 7's OLAP Services is implemented as a middle-tier service to intelligently build, query, and manage data cubes that are built from data stored in data warehouses.

NEW TERM *Cubes* are the multidimensional structures that are built from data warehouses to allow for fast analysis. The analysis is performed via dimensions and measures, which define the cube's structure.

Cube data itself is stored in one of three types of dimensional data storage, and all are supported with SQL Server OLAP Services:

- MOLAP (Multidimensional OLAP)—Data is stored in a multidimensional structure that contains the aggregations and the base data. Because MOLAP stores aggregations, access is fast.

- ROLAP (Relational OLAP)—ROLAP uses the data warehouse's relational database to store a cube's aggregations. This can become costly in terms of disk storage, and it usually isn't as fast as MOLAP. However, it scales better and leverages existing investments.

- HOLAP (Hybrid OLAP)—The original data remains in the data warehouse; however, the aggregations are stored in a MOLAP fashion. If you drill down to the detail level, the relational data must be accessed, which can be slow. HOLAP is generally best used for cubes that require rapid query response for summaries based on a large amount of data.

Before diving deeper into the details of OLAP cubes, you need to install OLAP Services to follow the examples. The requirements for the OLAP Services installation are presented in Table 11.1.

TABLE 11.1 Hardware/Software Requirements for OLAP Services

Hardware/Software	Requirements
Computer	Pentium 133MHz or higher
Memory (RAM)	32MB minimum (64MB recommended)
Disk drive	CD-ROM drive
Hard disk space	85MB including common files and samples
Operating system	Microsoft Windows NT Server 4.0 with Service Pack 4 or later, or Windows NT Workstation 4.0 with Service Pack 4
Network protocol	TCP/IP
Online Product Documentation Viewer	Microsoft Internet Explorer version 4.01 or later with Service Pack 1

Of course, you must be logged in as Administrator in order to perform the installation. However, you do not need to have SQL Server 7 installed on the same machine.

To Do: Installing OLAP Services

To Do

1. Depending on whether you install from a SQL 7 CD-ROM or the Microsoft BackOffice CD-ROMs, the installation program location will differ slightly. For the BackOffice Developers Edition, the install folder is shown in Figure 11.6.

   Start `setup.exe` to initiate the installation.

FIGURE 11.6

Installing OLAP Services from CD2 of the BackOffice Developers Edition.

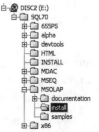

2. Accept the license agreement and enter your CD key.

3. You are asked for the destination folder. By default, OLAP Services are installed in the Program Files folder. Change it if necessary.

4. The next question pertains to the data folder and where it should be located. The data folder is where OLAP cube data is stored. Place it on a disk that has enough capacity and meets your speed requirements (such as RAID disks).

11

▼   5. Select the components you want to install. By default, all components are selected (see Figure 11.7). Make sure that you leave Sample applications selected, because the demonstrations in today's lesson use the sample FoodMart cubes.

FIGURE 11.7

Choose the appropriate installation options.

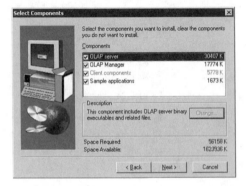

6. The final question is about the name of the program group in which to create the icons. Stick with the default.

7. Installation is completed and you are asked to restart your computer. Do it now to finish.

When the server comes back online, OLAP Services are already running, and the sample database you have installed alongside can be accessed. How is this access handled and which system components are responsible? These questions are addressed in the next section.

The PivotTable Service

You wouldn't find a lesson on any topic in this book if it weren't connected to ADO in some way. For OLAP, the connection to OLE DB and hence ADO is the PivotTable Service.

NEW TERM   *PivotTable Service* is the client-side of the Microsoft SQL Server OLAP Services. The *PivotTable Service* is an in-process desktop OLAP server that provides client applications access to OLAP Services, including online and offline data analysis capabilities.

The PivotTable Service provides the layer necessary for client applications to access OLAP cubes. Sitting on top of the PivotTable Service are OLE DB for OLAP or ADO MD, ADO Multidimensional (see Figure 11.8).

FIGURE 11.8

The architecture of the PivotTable Service.

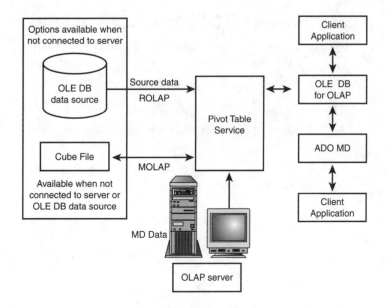

An important feature of the PivotTable Service is that it can cache user queries, meta data, and data itself. Therefore, new queries can be satisfied by data that was fetched earlier rather than needing a round-trip to the OLAP server.

Another important message is that the PivotTable Service and OLAP Services share a great deal of code. This means that the PivotTable Service comes with the capability of multidimensional calculation and query management features right on the client machine. The PivotTable Service also supports disconnected operations by enabling parts of a cube to be stored on the client machine for later analysis.

Client applications access OLAP cubes using the PivotTable Service, and as mentioned earlier, these can range from desktop productivity applications to custom applications. For example, Excel 2000 has OLAP support out of the box and can be used to analyze data.

The SQL 7 OLAP Services

When you have cleansed and transformed your data into the data mart, you can put OLAP Services to work. Before you can get your first analytical result, you must perform the following steps to get up and running on the server side:

- Creating a new database for analysis
- Creating a cube
- Designing the cube storage

Creating a New Database for Analysis

The first step in getting started with multidimensional analysis is to create a database and connect it to the data mart. The example database created in this section uses the FoodMart data mart that is installed as a sample application with OLAP Services.

To Do: Creating a New Database

1. Open OLAP Manager from the Microsoft SQL Server 7/OLAP Services program group.
2. Select the server you want to add a new database to, right-click, and select New Database from the context menu (see Figure 11.9).

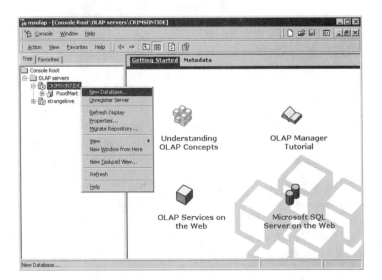

3. To create a new database, you provide a name; in this case, use TYS ADO 21 Days (see Figure 11.10). Click OK to create the database.

FIGURE **11.10**

Provide the name and a description to create a new OLAP database.

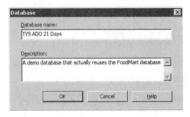

As you can see, there isn't much needed to create a new database; however, it has no data mart connections, which are necessary to perform analysis.

To Do: Adding a Data Source to the Database

1. In OLAP Manager, expand the newly created database and open the Library folder. There is an item named Data Sources (see Figure 11.11). Right-click and select New Data Source from the context menu.

FIGURE 11.11

The Library contains the Data Sources folder.

2. The Data Link Properties dialog box opens (see Figure 11.12). By default, the Microsoft OLE DB Provider for ODBC Drivers is selected. Stick with this selection, because an ODBC connection exists for the FoodMart database. Click Next to proceed.

FIGURE 11.12

Select the OLE DB provider in the first tab of the Data Link Properties dialog box.

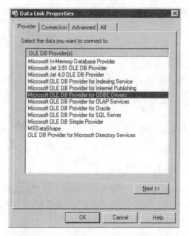

11

3. On the Connection tab, select the FoodMart data source from the Use data source name drop-down list. Because it is an Access database, you don't need to specify a username or password (see Figure 11.13).

▼

FIGURE 11.13

Choosing the FoodMart data source.

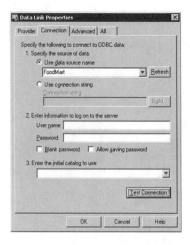

▲   4. Click OK to create the data source.

Now your OLAP database is connected to a data mart. However, this data still doesn't meet the requirements for fast analysis—you have to define cubes.

Creating a Cube

The data mart is connected; now you have to create the new cube. Though you usually should carefully plan a cube, this time you create it ad hoc based on the sales facts for 1998. The number of dimensions is limited to two: Time and Products.

To Do: Creating a New Cube with the Cube Wizard

1. Right-click on the Cubes folder in the TYS ADO 21 Days database and select New Cube/Wizard from the context menu.

2. The Cube Wizard starts (skip the Welcome screen if necessary). The first thing you have to select is the facts table. Choose sales_fact_1998 for the new cube, and then click Next.

3. Now you have to define the measures for the facts table (you can choose numeric columns only!). Select the only three non-ID columns, which are store_sales, store_cost, and unit_sales. Click Next to proceed.

4. This step is about defining dimensions for the cube. Because you created an entirely new database, there are no shared dimensions that you could select from. Therefore, click New Dimension to create a new one.

5. The Dimension Wizard starts with the star schema selection. Accept the default
▼   schema and click Next to proceed.

6. Select the time_by_day table and then click Next. Choose Time dimension as dimension type and move on to the next step.

7. You are asked to create time dimension levels. The defaults are just fine, so stick with these.

8. In the last step, enter Time as the dimension name and click Finish to create this new dimension.

9. To make the cube more interesting, add another dimension—for products. Start the Dimension Wizard by clicking New Dimension, and this time select snowflake schema.

10. As dimension tables, select product and product_class. Upon clicking Next, you can now edit the relationships (see Figure 11.14). As the defaults are just fine, leave them in place.

FIGURE 11.14

Defining the joins for the snowflake schema.

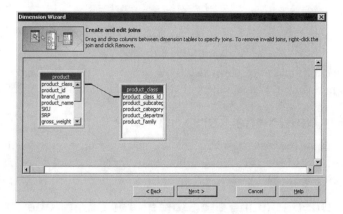

11. In contrast to the Time dimension, you now need to define the dimension levels. A good choice is product_category, product_subcategory, and brand_name.

12. On the final step, name the new dimension Product and click Finish.

13. Instead of building more dimensions (see the Help file of OLAP Services), you now proceed to the final step—naming the cube. Enter DemoCube and click Finish. The Cube Editor is opened with the definition of the new cube (see Figure 11.15).

14. Click the Save button in the toolbar to save your new cube.

▼

FIGURE **11.15**

*The cube is finished
and can be fine-tuned
in the Cube Editor.*

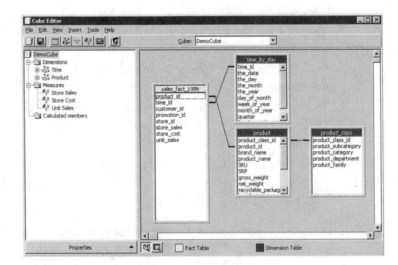

▲

The cube's definition now exists; however, it isn't processed and therefore is not ready
for querying. This final preparation step is shown in the next section.

Designing the Cube Storage

Recall the dimensional storage options that are available for OLAP Services: MOLAP,
ROLAP, and HOLAP. You can choose one for a cube you have defined in an OLAP database. You can even change the storage option later.

To Do: Designing the Storage for DemoCube

1. You should still have the Cube Editor open. To get started with designing the stor-
    age options, it is easiest to close the Cube Editor for a new cube—you are automat-
    ically asked to set the storage options.

2. The first step in the Storage Design Wizard is to choose the storage type for the
    data. In the case of our sample data, MOLAP is the best option, because the data
    mart is an Access database—the MOLAP cube definitely offers better performance
    than the Access database in an ROLAP scenario.

3. Now you can choose the aggregation options.

    Aggregations are precalculated summaries of data that help performance when
    querying data. The downsides are that aggregations increase the storage needs for a
    cube, and take time to calculate when creating the cube.

    Therefore, you can limit the amount of aggregations either by a storage limit or a cer-
    tain percentage of performance gain (manually selecting the gain is also possible).

▼

▼   Because your cube is small, limit the storage to 2MB and click the Start button. As you can see from the performance-versus-size diagram, 100% performance gain is already reached at 800KB—2MB wouldn't be necessary for cube storage.

4. Click Next to reach the final step of the Storage Design Wizard. You can schedule the cube creation, or you can process it now. Stick with Process now and click Finish to start the process. You get a status window that shows what action is currently performed by OLAP Services. Because it is a small cube, it should finish in
▲   less than two minutes.

Congratulations! You have just created your first cube, which can be analyzed in Excel using the PivotTable Service.

Analyzing OLAP Data in Excel

Excel can analyze data from OLAP cubes using the PivotTable Service that ships with it. It is exactly the tool you want executive-level users to use.

> **Note**   You need to have Microsoft Query, which comes with Microsoft Office 2000 installed on the machine; otherwise, you can't use the PivotTable feature of Excel.

11

To get immediate results with the PivotTable feature, use the following steps:

- Creating a PivotTable
- Drilling the data

Creating a PivotTable

The first step involves connecting to the data source and attaching to the relevant cube. Additionally, you have to choose which measure to examine and how to slice the cube—which dimensions you want to use.

To Do: Adding a PivotTable to an Excel Worksheet

1. Start Excel 2000 and select PivotTable and PivotChart Report from the Data menu. The PivotTable and PivotChart Wizard starts (see Figure 11.16).

2. Select External data source. Click Next to proceed.

3. You are asked where your external data is stored (see Figure 11.17). Click the Get Data button to establish a connection to the FoodMart database.

FIGURE 11.16

*In the first step, choose
the data source to use.*

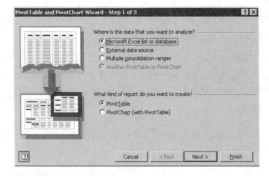

FIGURE 11.17

*Choosing the external
data source.*

4. The Choose Data Source dialog box opens (see Figure 11.18). By default, you are
on the Database tab. Switch to the OLAP Cubes tab.

FIGURE 11.18

*The Choose Data
Source dialog box.*

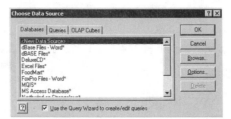

5. The <New Data Source> item is already selected. Click OK to create a new data
source.

6. In the Create New Data Source dialog box, enter the name first. Choose Demo of
FoodMart.

7. Next, you have to select an OLAP provider from the drop-down list. Choose
Microsoft OLE DB Provider for OLAP Services. Click the Connect button to proceed.

8. You are now presented the first step in the Multi-Dimensional Connection Wizard.
Here, you have to provide either a server name or a cube file. Stick with server
name, and in case you have installed OLAP Services on your local computer, the
name is localhost (see Figure 11.19). Click Next to proceed.

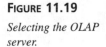

FIGURE 11.19

Selecting the OLAP server.

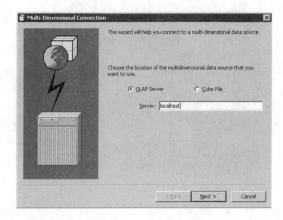

9. The next step presents a choice of databases installed on your OLAP server. Choose the FoodMart database and click Finish to return to the Create New Data Source dialog box.

10. The final choice is which cube this data source refers to. Select the Sales cube. The choices are shown in Figure 11.20.

FIGURE 11.20

Reviewing all choices for the new OLAP data source.

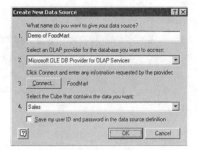

11. Click OK to create the new data source.

12. You are back in the Choose Data Source dialog box with the newly created data source selected. Click OK to dismiss this dialog box.

13. Click Next to proceed to the final step of the PivotTable Wizard. Put the PivotTable on the current worksheet at the position A1.

14. To define the layout, click the Layout button.

15. In this example, you create a rather simple PivotTable. Drag the Profit measure to the DATA section, the Store dimension to the ROW section and the Time dimension to the COLUMN section (see Figure 11.21). Click OK to accept the Layout.

FIGURE 11.21

Deciding the layout of your PivotTable.

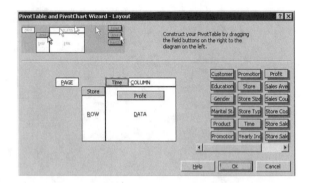

16. Click Finish to create the PivotTable. It should look like Figure 11.22.

FIGURE 11.22

The PivotTable is now finished and ready to be analyzed.

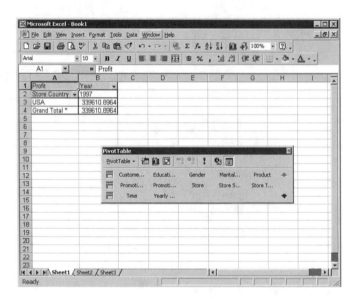

The PivotTable is placed on the worksheet and already contains data from the OLAP cube—at the highest level for each dimension. When you are interested in more detailed results, you have to drill the data. You can either drill up to the most summarized level, or drill down to the most detailed level.

Drilling the Data

Each dimension can have multiple levels; the Time dimension, for example, has levels of Year, Quarter, and Month. The Store dimension has even more: Store Country, Store State, Store City, and Store Name. Drilling to the level of detail you need enables you to get a clearer picture of what is going on in your business.

To Do: Exploring the Cube Data

1. Because the measure is given in dollars, you have to format the corresponding cells using the Currency format. To do this, right-click the Grand Total cell, select Format Cells from the context menu, and choose Currency from the Category list. Apply the same formatting to the USA Total cell.

2. To drill down on the Store dimension, double-click USA. Now you can see the sales totals broken down by state. If you double-click on state (California, for example), profits are shown for each city. Double-clicking on the city takes you down to the store level, which is the last one (see Figure 11.23).

FIGURE 11.23

Drilling down to the shop level.

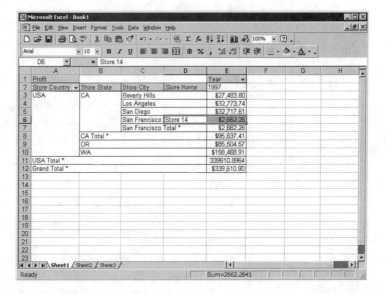

3. Now you do the same for the Time dimension. The first level is quarters, followed by months.

4. Click on the drop-down list next to Year. In the tree of the dimension, you can select which quarter or which month to show in the PivotTable (see Figure 11.24).

5. Save the workbook.

FIGURE 11.24

Selecting individual dimension levels.

This is a very simple example of how to analyze OLAP data in Excel 2000. You could do more right now, and you can do even more when you enhance your OLAP cubes.

Enhancing OLAP Cubes

This section can hardly scratch the surface of advanced topics relating to OLAP Services. However, I'm going to present the following common enhancements for OLAP cubes you need for your day-to-day work with OLAP Services:

- Adding calculated members
- Defining member properties
- Multiple hierarchies per dimension

Adding Calculated Members

A calculated member can either be a dimension member or it can be defined as a measure. Both are calculated at runtime using the expression you specify, and only the definition is stored for a calculated member. Values are calculated in memory.

The obvious advantage of a calculated member is that the size of the cube does not increase. Although a calculated member must be based on data that already exists in the cube, you can create complex expressions by combining the data with operators and functions. OLAP Services comes with more than 100 built-in functions, and you can extend the reach by installing your own.

Nice talking, but how does it work in the real world? The following example shows how to add a new calculated member to the already existing Sales cube. The member's name is ProfitMargin, and it is a measure with the following formula: [Store Profit]/[Store Sales].

To Do: Adding `ProfitMargin` as a New Calculated Member

▼ To Do

1. In OLAP Manager, select the Sales cube in the FoodMart database. Right click on the cube and select Edit from the context menu.

2. You are now in the Cube Editor and see the Dimensions, Measures, and Calculated members. There are already two defined: Profit and Sales Average. To view the definition of Profit, right click Profit and then select Edit from the context menu. The Calculated Member Builder opens and shows how this calculated member is created (see Figure 11.25). Close it when you are finished exploring its properties.

FIGURE 11.25

Viewing the definition of the Profit calculated member.

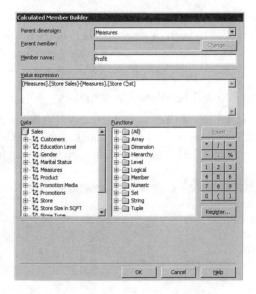

3. To create the new calculated member, right-click on Calculated members and choose New Calculated Member from the context menu.

4. You are once again in the Calculated Member Builder. Name the new member Profit Margin.

5. The profit margin is calculated by dividing the profit by store sales. Therefore, expand the Measures folder in the Data list box. Drag the Profit to the Value expression text box, add a divide symbol, and then drag the Store Sales to Value expression.

6. Click OK to create the new calculated member.

7. Save your changes and then exit the Cube Editor. Because it is a calculated member, you don't have to rebuild the cube.

▲

11

In the last step, I mention that you don't have to rebuild the cube. Don't trust me—give it a try in Excel by inserting a new PivotTable and using Profit Margin as measure.

Defining Member Properties

If you want to tag attributes to a dimension member, member properties are your choice, although at the moment only very few OLAP tools support this feature. A member property's name and type is the same for all dimension members at the same hierarchy level; however, the values can differ for each member (for example, a member property Store Manager has the same name and type for each Store; however, the value differs).

Why could member properties be useful? Client applications can provide information about member properties in flyovers or store member aliases in member properties (so you can switch between the member name and its alias—product ID versus product name, for example).

To Do: Creating New Member Properties

1. In OLAP Manager, open the Library folder of the FoodMart database. Drill down to the Shared Dimensions folder and right-click the Store dimension. Select Edit from the context menu. The Dimension Editor opens (see Figure 11.26).

FIGURE 11.26

Working in the Dimension Editor.

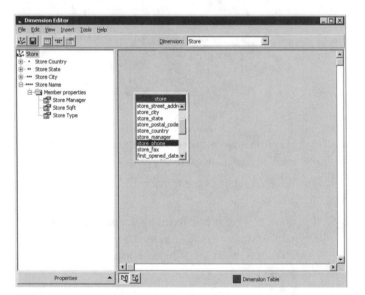

2. From Figure 11.26 you can see that I have already expanded the Store Name level to view the existing member properties: Store Manager, Store Sqft, and Store Type.

▼   To add a new property, select the store_phone column in the store dimension table
           and drag it to the member properties of the store. A name is assigned, which can be
           changed by choosing Rename from the context menu.

       3. Close the Dimension Editor and save the changes you made when prompted.

       4. To make your changes visible in the cube, you have to update it. Select Process
           from the Sales cube's context menu and make an Incremental Update with all
▲   defaults in place.

Up to this point, the member property doesn't serve a really cool purpose. You can easily
change that by transforming the member property into a virtual dimension. Why would
you want to do so? Virtual dimensions enable you to filter OLAP queries based on member properties, even if the client applications wouldn't enable you to do so.

To Do: Making Virtual Dimensions out of Member Properties

       1. Expand FoodMart, Library, Virtual Dimensions. There you can see that two virtual
           dimensions are already defined (Store Size in SQFT and Store Type).

       2. To add a new virtual dimension for the Store Manager, select New Virtual
           Dimension from the context menu. The Virtual Dimension Wizard starts up.

       3. First, you have to select which member property you want to use for your new vir-
           tual dimension. Make sure to select the Store Manager (see Figure 11.27).

FIGURE 11.27

*Select the Store
Manager member
property of the Store
dimension.*

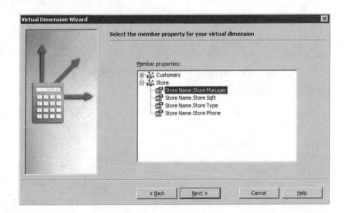

       4. Name the virtual dimension Store Manager and click Finish to create it.

       5. Open the Cube Editor for the Sales cube.

       6. Right-click on Dimensions and select Dimension Manager from the context menu.

       7. Choose the Store Manager from the shared dimensions list box and add it to the
▼   Cube dimensions list box.

▼ 8. Click OK to make your changes stick.

9. When you close the Cube Editor and choose to save your cube changes, you are asked to design the storage options because you added a new dimension. Click Yes to open the Storage Design Wizard.

10. As type of storage, stick with the default choice of MOLAP.

11. The Storage Design Wizard now presents you with aggregation options. You can limit aggregations by storage size or performance gain, or you can manually balance control between storage size or performance gain (see Figure 11.28).

FIGURE 11.28

Choosing aggregation options for the Sales cube.

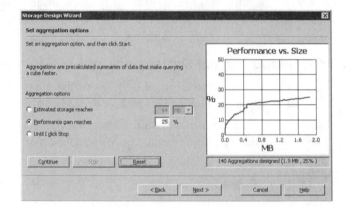

12. Select the Performance gain reaches option and set the threshold to 25%. Click Start, and as you can see from the estimates shown, you get the most gain up to roughly 20%, and afterward the performance gain curve flattens dramatically (this means that more aggregations won't return any performance gains).

13. Click Next, select Process Now, and click the Finish button to update the cube. You see the processing window (see Figure 11.29) until the cube is finished. You can now use the new dimension.

▼

FIGURE **11.29**

During cube processing, you can see what is going on in the Process window.

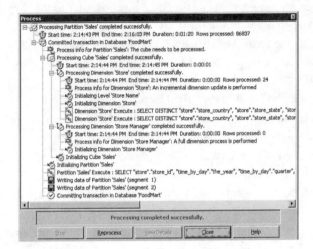

In the next task, you take a different look at the OLAP data with the virtual dimension—in Internet Explorer, as a chart—and can change the PivotTable's settings. It sounds like
▲ a lot of work, but with Excel 2000 it's only a few mouse clicks away.

To Do: Creating a Web Chart Using the Virtual Dimension

1. Create a new workbook in Excel. Insert a PivotTable connected to the Sales cube; however, do not set the layout options. The worksheet should look like Figure 11.30.

FIGURE **11.30**

A blank PivotTable connected to the Sales cube.

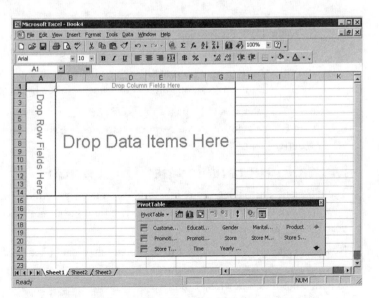

▼

▼ 2. From the PivotTable toolbar, select the Store Manager dimension and drag it to the Column Items area. Drag the Store Size in SQFT to the Row Items area. Both dimensions are now defined.

3. Select the Profit Margin calculated measure from the toolbar (you have to scroll down to see it) and drag it to the Data Items area. The PivotTable is populated with data, though sparsely.

4. Format the Profit Margin field as percentage.

5. To create a more meaningful diagram, click the Chart Wizard toolbar icon. The chart shows the profitability of each store by square feet.

6. The final step is to create a Web page out of this chart. Therefore, select Save as Web Page from the File menu.

7. Save the Chart and make it interactive (see Figure 11.31). Store it to the Desktop to more easily locate it.

FIGURE 11.31

Storing the chart as HTML with the interactivity option selected.

8. Go to the Desktop and double-click the newly created HTML document. IE starts and the chart connects to the PivotTable service to retrieve the data.

9. To prove that it is really interactive, swap the column and row dimensions by simply dragging them from one area to the other. Notice how the chart changes.

You can create canned HTML pages or Excel sheets for your executive-level users. Publishing OLAP analysis to the corporate intranet is easy now and might make some of
▲ your executives really happy.

Multiple Hierarchies per Dimension

Though many times a hierarchy in a dimension is easy to find, sometimes you can come up with more than one. The best example from the business world is definitely calendar year versus fiscal year.

How can you deal with a request to be able to slice data once for fiscal year, another time for calendar year? You can implement multiple hierarchies per dimension, which are easy to define but little-known and rarely used.

To Do: Adding a New Time Hierarchy

1. In the FoodMart database, go to Library/Shared Dimensions. Right-click and select New Dimension/Wizard from the context menu.

2. Leave the default choice in place, which is to create the new dimension from a single dimension table.

3. Next, you have to choose the dimension table. Select the time_by_day table. Proceed by clicking Next.

4. The dimension type for this new dimension is Time dimension. Make sure to select it, because it isn't the default choice.

5. Now you have to decide when the year starts. Because you are creating the fiscal year dimension first, choose July 1 as the year's start date.

6. You have now reached the final step—naming the new dimension. To make dimension hierarchies work, it must be a two-part name separated by a period. Type `SharedTime.Fiscal` as the name and click Finish to create the dimension.

7. The Dimension Editor opens automatically. Close it; you don't need to make any other changes.

8. Start again at step 1 and create the second hierarchy for the SharedTime dimension. The only differences are that this time the year starts on January 1, and you name the dimension `SharedTime.Calendar`.

9. Create a new cube that uses the new dimensions. In the Cube Wizard, select inventory_fact_1997 as the fact table (see Figure 11.32).

FIGURE 11.32

Selecting the fact table for the new cube.

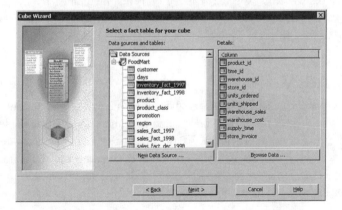

10. Next, you have to define the measures. Choose warehouse_sales and warehouse_cost.

▼   11. Still missing for the cube are the dimensions. For this cube, select Store, Product,
         Warehouse, and both SharedTime dimensions (see Figure 11.33).

FIGURE **11.33**

*Adding the appropriate
dimensions to the
cube.*

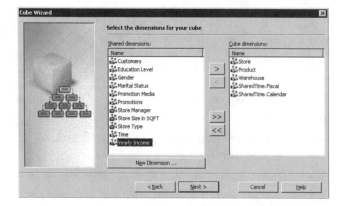

     12. You have reached the final step. Name the cube Warehouse Time Cube and click
         Finish. The Cube Editor is opened with the definition of the new cube.

     13. Save the cube definition and design the storage as asked for by the OLAP
         Manager. This time, choose a performance gain of 80%. Process the cube. Now
▲   you have a cube with the SharedTime dimension containing multiple hierarchies.

If you try to build a PivotTable based on the SharedTime dimension, you will see that it
shows up in Excel as SharedTime.Calendar and as SharedTime.Fiscal—maybe not
quite the way you expected. The reason is that hierarchies are treated as dimensions;
however, you can overcome these limitations with MDX queries—which are an integral
part of tomorrow's close look at ADO MD and OLAP.

Summary

Data warehousing and OLAP are becoming increasingly important in the field of business because of the need to understand customers and analyze the business for profitability. SQL Server ships with OLAP Services—that is, implemented as middle-tier service
for analytical processing of data stored in data marts. The client side of OLAP Services
is the PivotTable service, which shares code with its server-side counterpart to enable
data caching and query optimization.

Today, you haven't coded a single line of ADO; however, you have worked with OLE DB all day. Because OLAP is such an important and complicated field, today's lesson served the purpose of introducing you to cubes and analysis with high-level tools—tomorrow, you write code for the drag-and-drop operations you performed today.

Q&A

Q I have a large data mart, and when I select a 30% optimization, the storage space needed is more than I have on a single disk in that server. However, I need this amount of optimization because otherwise queries are so slow. Is there a possibility of achieving the 30% optimization?

A If you run the Enterprise Edition of OLAP Services, there is an option for you: partitions. These enable you to store a single cube across multiple partitions.

Q You have shown Excel 2000 as a tool for analyzing OLAP data—are there others I should know about?

A Definitely! One is Seagate Worksheet with write-back functionality (yes, OLAP Services allows write-enabled cubes), which is free; another is OLAP@Work for Excel, which also supports the write-back capabilities of OLAP Services.

11

Workshop

The quiz questions are provided for your further understanding. See Appendix A, "Answers," for the answers.

Quiz

1. What does the acronym *OLTP* stand for?
2. Which SQL Server 7 service lends itself to filling a data warehouse?
3. How are dimension tables and the fact table linked?
4. Where is base data stored for the ROLAP dimensional storage option?
5. Which schemas can you choose to relate facts and dimension tables?
6. When you design storage options, what are your options for deciding the level of aggregation?

DAY 12

Building Applications with ADO MD

ADO Multidimensional is an extension to ADO's capability to enable access to multidimensional data stores. Yesterday, you learned about the basics of OLAP, how SQL Server OLAP Services work, and how to access cubes via Excel using the PivotTable Service, which is the OLE DB provider for OLAP.

Accessing multidimensional data via Excel or any other OLAP tool might be sufficient for executive-level users; however, the need for multidimensional data in your company's custom application will probably arise at some point. Then you need to programmatically access OLAP cubes, retrieve data, and maybe even create your own cubes.

Today, you learn the following tasks:

- Creating a simple MDX statement and executing it using the MDX Sample Application
- Working with level members and children and defining slicer specifications in MDX statements

- Adding calculated members to MDX statements and filtering and sorting them
- Accessing axes and cellset items using ADO MD
- Working with metadata to access cube definitions of OLAP Services' cubes
- Creating cubes on the local machine for use in analytical software

Multidimensional Expressions

In Excel, all you have to do is select the cube and create a layout with dimensions and measures, and the PivotTable is populated automatically with cube data. The interesting question is how Excel accesses the cube data—the answer lies in the query language for accessing multidimensional data: Multidimensional Expressions (MDX).

The MDX query language not only supports querying cube data, but also creating it. As you will see today, MDX is a really powerful and sophisticated language that enables you to perform the trickiest analysis—much better than Excel can.

The sample MDX statements presented today run against the Sales cube in the FoodMart database. Therefore, it is good to know which dimensions and measures exist in this database. The easiest way to view this information is to open OLAP Manager, select the cube in question, and choose to view Metadata in the right pane (see Figure 12.1).

FIGURE **12.1**

The Metadata option enables you to get a quick overview of a cube's definition.

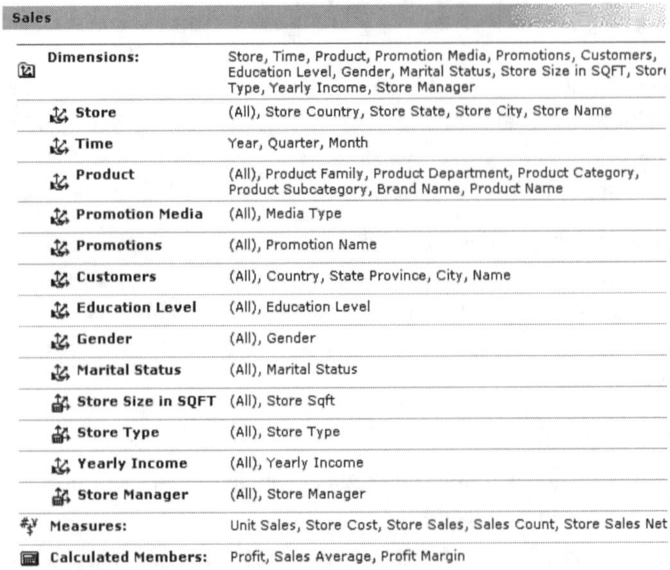

Sales	
Dimensions:	Store, Time, Product, Promotion Media, Promotions, Customers, Education Level, Gender, Marital Status, Store Size in SQFT, Store Type, Yearly Income, Store Manager
Store	(All), Store Country, Store State, Store City, Store Name
Time	Year, Quarter, Month
Product	(All), Product Family, Product Department, Product Category, Product Subcategory, Brand Name, Product Name
Promotion Media	(All), Media Type
Promotions	(All), Promotion Name
Customers	(All), Country, State Province, City, Name
Education Level	(All), Education Level
Gender	(All), Gender
Marital Status	(All), Marital Status
Store Size in SQFT	(All), Store Sqft
Store Type	(All), Store Type
Yearly Income	(All), Yearly Income
Store Manager	(All), Store Manager
Measures:	Unit Sales, Store Cost, Store Sales, Sales Count, Store Sales Net
Calculated Members:	Profit, Sales Average, Profit Margin

Although this overview can get you started, it doesn't always cut the mustard. Most of the time you create MDX statements that are directed toward a specific level of a dimension. In order to review all dimension levels, you can open the Cube Editor for the cube in question (see Figure 12.2).

FIGURE 12.2

In the Cube Editor, you can drill down on any dimension, measure, or calculated member.

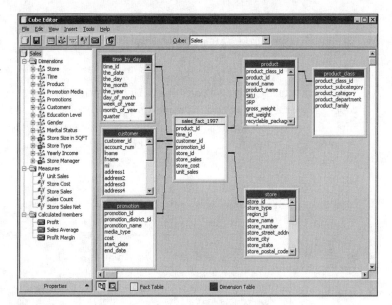

With this information, you can create MDX statements that become more sophisticated with each step:

- The basics of MDX
- Working with members and children
- Defining slicer specifications
- Adding calculated members and named sets
- Hierarchical navigation
- Applying filters and sorting
- Cross-joining dimensions
- Adding numeric functions
- User-defined functions and conditional expressions

12

The Basics of MDX

There are two ways to learn something new: look at a piece of code someone else wrote, or look at a definition. The first is great when the syntax of the sample is easy; however, MDX can quickly become complicated.

Therefore, let's take a look at the most common form of an MDX statement:

```
SELECT <axis_specification> [, <axis_specification>...]
FROM <cube_specification>
WHERE <slicer_specification>
```

There are actually only two parts that must be specified: *axis_specification* and *cube_specification*. From the names of the placeholders, you can already guess that the first one defines the axis, and the latter one defines which cube is to be queried. The *slicer_specification* is described in the "Defining Slicer Specifications" section later in this lesson.

The axis specification selects the members that are displayed on the axis. These members can come from any dimension, including the Measures dimension.

 Note

Time, Store, and others form a dimension. All measures are contained in a dimension, the Measures dimension. Although the word *cube* implies three dimensions, there can be up to 64 dimensions. Because the Measures dimension counts as one, there are 63 "real" dimensions possible per cube.

A simple MDX statement could look like the following:

```
SELECT Measures.MEMBERS ON COLUMNS FROM Sales
```

Before analyzing this statement, I want you to try it out in the MDX Sample Application that ships with OLAP Services.

To Do: Executing MDX Queries in the MDX Sample Application

1. Start the MDX Sample Application from the Microsoft SQL Server 7.0/OLAP Services program group.

2. You are asked to provide the name of the OLAP server and the OLE DB provider. If you are running OLAP Services on the local machine, the defaults should be okay.

3. The main screen is now active; however, no cube has been selected so far. From the Cube drop-down list, select Sales. Notice that all dimensions are retrieved from the Sales cube, which enables you to easily select them when creating statements (see Figure 12.3).

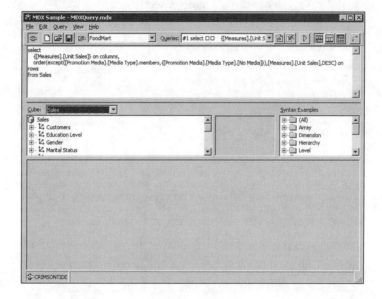

FIGURE 12.3

The MDX Sample Application enables you to browse the dimensions found in the cubes.

4. Remove the default MDX statement by clicking the New Query button on the toolbar.

5. Enter the MDX statement

   ```
   SELECT Measures.MEMBERS ON COLUMNS FROM Sales
   ```

6. Click the Run Query button in the toolbar, or alternatively press the F5 key. The results pane is populated with the members of the Measures dimension displayed in the column with their respective aggregation values.

Tip

The source code for the MDX Sample Application is installed in the `Samples\MDXSample` folder off the OLAP Services installation root. The application is written in Visual Basic and shows how to use ADO MD—which is discussed later today—in a custom OLAP application. It is highly recommended that you review this code.

Now that you know that

```
SELECT Measures.MEMBERS ON COLUMNS FROM Sales
```

is actually a working MDX statement, what does the ON COLUMNS stand for? It describes where—on which axis—the dimension is to be displayed. As you might guess, the next axis specification is ROWS, followed by PAGES, CHAPTERS, and finally SECTIONS.

12

A good question is what you do when there are more than five axes you want to select. In this case, you can use the more general syntax ON AXIS(index), where index starts at zero. Therefore, COLUMNS, ROWS, PAGES, CHAPTERS, and SECTIONS are equal to AXIS(0) to AXIS(4).

 Caution
> The axis names CHAPTERS and SECTIONS are optional. If you want to rely on them in your application, you should check the provider property MDPROP_AXES to see whether these names are supported.

For example, to select two dimensions, an MDX statement looks like this:

```
SELECT Measures.MEMBERS on AXIS(0), [Store].MEMBERS ON AXIS(1) FROM Sales
```

Using the syntax with named columns, it looks like this:

```
SELECT Measures.MEMBERS on COLUMNS, [Store].MEMBERS ON ROWS FROM Sales
```

The only thing I didn't take on so far is what measure is actually returned from the Sales cube, because the WHERE statement was omitted. The answer is that the default measure is returned.

One final note before going on: the square brackets serve the same purpose as in standard SQL—as delimiters for identifiers with embedded spaces. In this statement, therefore, I could have left them out.

Working with Members and Children

The preceding MDX statement returned the MEMBERS for a specified dimension. When you recall the results you got for the MEMBERS of Measures and Store, you can see that MEMBERS included all members for the specified dimension. This included the All Stores member as well as each individual store.

If you go to a dimension level, only the members for the specific dimension level are returned:

```
SELECT Measures.MEMBERS on COLUMNS,
           [Store].[Store State].MEMBERS ON ROWS
FROM Sales
```

Taking a closer look at the result, you'll notice that all measures are there, but all calculated members (such as Profit or Sales Average) are missing. To add the calculated members to the output, rewrite the statement:

```
SELECT ADDCALCULATEDMEMBERS(Measures.MEMBERS) on COLUMNS,
            [Store].[Store State].MEMBERS ON ROWS
FROM Sales
```

Calculated members must be explicitly requested using the ADDCALCULATEDMEMBERS function.

If you don't want to see all members for a dimension, but just a few, you can also enumerate them:

```
SELECT Measures.MEMBERS on COLUMNS,
            {[Store].[Store State].[WA], [Store].[Store State].[Yucatan],
             [Store].[Store State].[Veracruz]} ON ROWS
FROM Sales
```

Enumerations are enclosed in curly braces. However, you still might not be satisfied with what you get. Maybe you are just interested in stores that are located in Oregon. How can you view those only? A possible solution is

```
SELECT Measures.MEMBERS on COLUMNS,
            Store.[Store State].[OR].CHILDREN
            ON ROWS
FROM Sales
```

When you take a closer look at this expression, you can see that I enclosed both Store State and OR in square brackets. Following the rule I gave earlier, I shouldn't be required to enclose OR, so why did I have to? If the brackets are not used, an invalid token error results because OR is used in MDX itself. When you query for WA, you don't see this error. Therefore, it is always advisable to use the square brackets.

The CHILDREN clause returns only the immediate children of the specified member of a dimension. Sometimes, this isn't flexible enough. Then you can use DESCENDANTS of a member at a specified level:

```
DESCENDANTS(<member>, <level> [, <desc_flags>])
```

For example, if you want to rewrite the previous statement using DESCENDANTS, it would look like this:

```
SELECT Measures.MEMBERS on COLUMNS,
            DESCENDANTS([Store].[Store State].[OR],[Store City])
            ON ROWS
FROM Sales
```

This statement returns exactly the same result, so why would you bother using it? The reason is *desc_flags*, which is a flag describing what to include in the result. The default is SELF, which refers to the *level* itself. In addition to the SELF value, you can also specify BEFORE, AFTER, or the all-encompassing BEFORE_AND_AFTER.

12

Defining Slicer Specifications

Until now, not all MDX statements included a WHERE statement, which is also referred to as *slicer specification*. Because of this omission, the default measure was returned. To specify which slice of the cube you want to retrieve, use the Measures dimension:

```
SELECT [Product].[Product Family].MEMBERS ON COLUMNS,
       [Store].[Store State].MEMBERS ON ROWS
FROM Sales
WHERE [Measures].[Profit]
```

This statement queries the profit summary for each product family, cross-referenced to store state. Because you are hunting for slices, you could add additional dimensions to limit the range. For example, you could look at profit summaries for Q1 1997 only:

```
SELECT [Product].[Product Family].MEMBERS ON COLUMNS,
           [Store].[Store State].MEMBERS ON ROWS
FROM Sales
WHERE ([Measures].[Profit], [Time].[Year].[1997].[Q1])
```

Notice that a slice statement does not reduce the number of axis members; it only affects the values that go into the axis members. This is in contrast to filtering, which is described in a later section.

Adding Calculated Members and Named Sets

Of course, you not only want to retrieve data, you also want to perform some calculations on data. With a little SQL knowledge, you might come up with a profit calculation such as the following one:

```
SELECT [Store].[Store State].MEMBERS ON COLUMNS,
       ([Measures].[Profit]/[Measures].[Store Sales]) ON ROWS
FROM Sales
```

The only problem is that you get a formula error for this statement. You cannot put calculations inside the SELECT statement; you put them before it, using the WITH MEMBER statement to define a new member:

```
WITH MEMBER [Measures].[Local Profit Margin]
   AS '([Measures].[Profit]/[Measures].[Store Sales])'
SELECT  [Time].[1997].CHILDREN ON COLUMNS,
        [Store].[Store State].MEMBERS ON ROWS
FROM Sales
WHERE [Measures].[Local Profit Margin]
```

Each new member must be part of a dimension, and because the Measures dimension counts as one, you can add it there. The remainder is the definition of the formula—hence the general syntax

```
WITH MEMBER parent.name AS 'formula'
```

Caution Support for the WITH clause is optional for providers (OLAP Services supports it). You should check the provider property MDPROP_MDX_FORMULAS to see whether a provider supports the WITH clause.

If you look back at the result your MDX statement generated, it doesn't look like a percentage. Although you could do that later programmatically, wouldn't it be easier if the MDX query already returned properly formatted values? In case you want this, you can set the cell property FORMAT_STRING:

```
WITH MEMBER [Measures].[Local Profit Margin]
    AS '([Measures].[Profit]/[Measures].[Store Sales])',
    FORMAT_STRING='#.00%'
```

Now the output is in percent and properly formatted. If you want to learn more about the options of FORMAT_STRING, look up the section "Contents of FORMAT_STRING" in the OLE DB Programmer's Reference of the Platform SDK.

When you are using more than one calculated member, it becomes necessary to define the solve order of the expressions when there are dependencies between formulas. You can resolve such issues with the solve order specification, which is simply appended to a calculated MEMBER:

```
WITH MEMBER [Measures].[Local Profit Margin]
    AS '([Measures].[Profit]/[Measures].[Store Sales])',
    FORMAT_STRING='#.00%',
    SOLVE_ORDER=1
```

By default, SOLVE_ORDER is 0. If you assign higher values, these expressions are evaluated first. When there are expressions with the same solve order, it is up to the OLE DB provider to choose which to evaluate first.

Hierarchical Navigation

Several calculation scenarios necessitate that you can access other member values in the hierarchy. The following list contains member value expressions you can use; the first three are the ones used most often:

- PREVMEMBER returns the previous member on the same level. For example, you could calculate quarterly sales changes using this approach:

```
WITH MEMBER [Measures].[QSalesChange] AS
    '(Measures.[Store Sales]/Measures.[Store Sales].PREVMEMBER)',
    FORMAT_STRING = '#.00%'
```

12

- NEXTMEMBER gets the value of the next member on the same level. Its use is similar to the last example.
- FIRSTCHILD returns the first child of a member.
- LASTCHILD returns the last child of a member.
- PARENT enables access to the parent of a member. You could append multiple PARENT statements to walk up the hierarchy. For example, to access the Store State for the current store, you could write

  ```
  [Store Name].CURRENTMEMBER.PARENT.PARENT
  ```

- CURRENTMEMBER gives the current member. Although it wouldn't be necessary in the last statement, the concept of a current member becomes important with functions such as GENERATE. CURRENTMEMBER is useful whenever iterations are required.
- LEAD(*<index>*) accesses the member that is *<index>* positions away on the same dimension. The index is zero-based.
- FIRSTSIBLING and LASTSIBLING return the first or the last sibling of a member at the parent level. For example, if you use it for Q3, the results are Q1 and Q4.
- ANCESTOR(*<member>*, *<level>*) returns the ancestor of *<member>* at the specified *<level>*. This removes the need for repetitive calls to PARENT, as in the following example:

  ```
  ANCESTOR([Store Name].CURRENTMEMBER, [Store State])
  ```

- COUSIN(*<member>*, *<ancestor_member>*) enables you to find cousins; for example, find Q1 1994 based on Q1 1997—both Q1s are cousins.

With these member value expressions, you can build time-based analysis; however, there are some functions you can use immediately: the time series functions. When you use such a function, comparing quarterly results or the like becomes a snap.

Some time series functions are YTD, QTD, MTD, and WTD (year-, quarter-, month-, and week-to-date). These are applicable to Time dimensions only. For example, to calculate the average profit to date, you can create the following calculated member:

```
WITH MEMBER [Measures].[Avg Profit 2 Date] AS
 'AVG(YTD(), [Profit])'
```

Of course, these are not the only time series functions. Others include PARALLELPERIOD, CLOSINGPERIOD, OPENINGPERIOD, and PERIODSDATE. These work equally well with dimensions other than Time dimensions.

Applying Filters and Sorting

The slicer specification does not restrict the number of the members on the axis, as I mentioned earlier. However, sometimes it is necessary to actually reduce the number of members on an axis. You can do this using filters.

For example, the following is an MDX statement:

```
SELECT Measures.MEMBERS on COLUMNS,
          [Store].[Store State].MEMBERS ON ROWS
FROM Sales
```

When you look at the result pane in the MDX Sample Application, you can see that many states do not return any values. To eliminate these empty rows, add the NON EMPTY clause:

```
SELECT Measures.MEMBERS on COLUMNS,
          NON EMPTY [Store].[Store State].MEMBERS ON ROWS
FROM Sales
```

The grid contains only nonempty cells after executing the previous query. You will agree that though this is useful filtering, it isn't powerful filtering. If you opt for powerful filter conditions, use the FILTER function:

```
FILTER(<set>, <search_condition>)
```

This function filters a set based on a specified search condition. Here is an example of a FILTER condition:

```
SELECT [Product].[Product Family].MEMBERS ON COLUMNS,
       FILTER( [Store].[Store Name].MEMBERS,
       (Measures.[Unit Sales],[Time].[1997]) > 10000) ON ROWS
FROM Sales
WHERE (Measures.[Unit Sales],[Time].[1997].[Q1])
```

The FILTER condition is set to exclude all members whose yearly unit sales for 1997 are lower or equal to 10,000. However, notice that the slicer specification is limited to the first quarter of 1997. This is perfectly legal.

Now that you have limited the results to the ones you wanted, you also want to present them nicely ordered. In this case, use the ORDER function:

```
ORDER(<set>, {<string_value_expression> | <numeric_value_expression>}
  [, ASC | DESC | BASC | BDESC])
```

The latter two options—BASC and BDESC—enable you to break the hierarchical order, arranging members in the set without regard to their hierarchical position. ASC and DESC, in contrast, create a hierarchical order by first arranging members according to their position in the hierarchy and then ordering each level.

12

The ORDER function orders a set based on a value expression that can be either numerical or string-based. To order Store States ascending by Unit Sales for 1997, you add the following ORDER statement:

```
ORDER([Store].[Store State], ([Measures].[Unit Sales],[Time].[1997]), ASC)
```

The important thing to learn is that the set does not need to be connected to the value expression.

Cross-Joining Dimensions

As long as you are working with COLUMNS and ROWS, you can display all data in a simple 2D chart. However, when you need to add a PAGES dimension (for example relating store sales to store type, city, and product family), unless you would like to create a 3D chart, you are out of display methods.

The original MDX statement looks like this:

```
SELECT [Store Type].MEMBERS on COLUMNS,
           [Store].[Store City].MEMBERS ON ROWS,
           [Product].[Product Family].MEMBERS ON PAGES
FROM Sales
WHERE ([Measures].[Store Sales],[Time].[1997])
```

Trying to run this in the MDX Sample Application results in an error (cellsets with more than two axes are not supported). To circumvent this problem and display the results on a 2D grid, you have to add the CROSSJOIN function. This function creates all combinations of two sets:

```
SELECT [Store Type].MEMBERS on COLUMNS,
        CROSSJOIN([Store].[Store City].MEMBERS,
           [Product].[Product Family].MEMBERS) ON ROWS
FROM Sales
WHERE ([Measures].[Store Sales],[Time].[1997])
```

However, this results in a sparse matrix with lots of combinations that simply don't return values. You can apply NON EMPTY to the CROSSJOIN to simplify the matrix:

```
SELECT [Store Type].MEMBERS on COLUMNS,
        NON EMPTY(CROSSJOIN([Store].[Store City].MEMBERS,
           [Product].[Product Family].MEMBERS)) ON ROWS
FROM Sales
WHERE ([Measures].[Store Sales],[Time].[1997])
```

When you execute this query in the MDX Sample Application, the result should look like Figure 12.4.

FIGURE 12.4

*Cross-joined sets
enable three axes to fit
into two.*

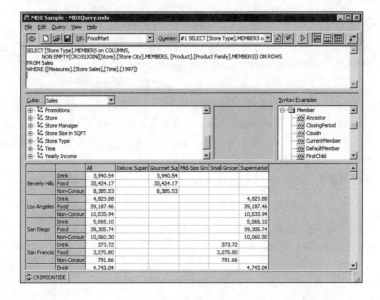

Numeric Functions and Conditional Expressions

MDX supports a wide range of numeric functions, which include SUM, COUNT, AVG, MIN, MAX, and many others. These are built-in functions, which can be supplemented by user-defined functions (UDFs).

Note

> A UDF can be created in any language that supports COM, such as Visual C++ or Visual Basic. The Visual Basic Expressions library is already registered and can be used immediately in addition to the built-in functions. Please see Day 10, "Shaping Your Data into Hierarchical Recordsets," for a list of functions supported by this library.

12

One example of a user-defined function is the conditional clause IIF (immediate-if) that comes with the VBA expression library. It enables you to choose between two values based on a test condition. For example, when you make calculations based on PREVMEMBER, it could be zero when you are calculating the very first member and that can cause division by zero errors. In this case, you can include an immediate check for zero, where you do nothing, and the other case, where you calculate your member.

Retrieving Multidimensional Data

All the MDX statements you have created were run inside the MDX Sample Application. So far, you have dealt with query language issues only. Now let's switch gears and return to ADO and its sibling, ADO Multidimensional (ADO MD).

A question that might have come up when using the MDX Sample Application is how you could retrieve all databases and cubes that are stored on an OLAP server. This is fairly easy and doesn't involve ADO MD at all, as can be seen in Listing 12.1.

LISTING 12.1 Listing All Databases and Cubes on an OLAP Server

```
 1: Option Explicit
 2:
 3: Sub ShowDBsAndCubes()
 4:     Dim cn As ADODB.Connection, i As Integer, strCatalog As String
 5:     Dim rsCatalogs As ADODB.Recordset, rsCubes As ADODB.Recordset
 6:
 7:     Worksheets(1).Activate
 8:     Cells.Clear
 9:
10:     Set cn = CreateObject("ADODB.Connection")
11:     cn.Open "Provider=MSOLAP;Data Source=localhost"
12:     Set rsCatalogs = cn.OpenSchema(adSchemaCatalogs)
13:
14:     While Not rsCatalogs.EOF
15:         i = i + 1
16:         strCatalog = rsCatalogs.Fields("CATALOG_NAME")
17:         Cells(i, 1) = strCatalog
18:
19:         ' enumerate the cubes that are in this database
20:         cn.DefaultDatabase = strCatalog
21:         Set rsCubes = cn.OpenSchema(adSchemaCubes)
22:         While Not rsCubes.EOF
23:             i = i + 1
24:             Cells(i, 2) = rsCubes("CUBE_NAME")
25:             rsCubes.MoveNext
26:         Wend
27:
28:         ' clear the cubes recordset and proceed to next catalog
29:         Set rsCubes = Nothing
30:         rsCatalogs.MoveNext
31:     Wend
32:     Set rsCatalogs = Nothing
33:     cn.Close
34:     Set cn = Nothing
35: End Sub
```

ANALYSIS   The code presented in Listing 12.1 uses the ADODB Type Library as you can see in the variable declarations in lines 4 and 5. This function was designed for use in Excel; therefore, an active worksheet has to be selected and old output cleared (lines 7–8).

Line 10 creates a Connection object, and it is connected to the local OLAP Services in the next line via the MSOLAP OLE DB provider and the localhost data source. In line 12, the schema definition Recordset for catalogs (databases) is opened. This schema information Recordset contains two columns, CATALOG_NAME and DESCRIPTION.

Because you are interested in catalogs, the name of the catalog is retrieved in line 16 and assigned to a local variable named strCatalog. The code needs to access the catalog more than once, so a local variable is faster than a further access to the Recordset.

To be able to enumerate the cubes in a database, you have to set a default database for the connection. This is done in line 20:

```
cn.DefaultDatabase = strCatalog
```

After the assignment of the default database, the script opens a new schema information Recordset, this time for the cubes in the database. In contrast to the catalogs, this Recordset contains some more information: CATALOG_NAME, SCHEMA_NAME, CUBE_NAME, CUBE_TYPE, CUBE_GUID, CREATED_ON, LAST_SCHEMA_UPDATE, SCHEMA_UPDATED_BY, LAST_DATA_UPDATE, DATA_UPDATED_BY, and DESCRIPTION. However, for clarity purposes, only the cube name is printed in the output cell (line 24).

The remainder of the code is needed for looping through two Recordsets and outputting the results to the Excel worksheet.

With the information you gain from the previous script, you can populate drop-down boxes with available databases and cubes for an OLAP server. The next step is then to connect to the catalog (database) and access data from a cube. You need ADO MD for this task, which exposes additional objects for cube access.

The ADO MD object model is split in two; one is the CellSet object model for cube data access presented in this section, and the other one is the CubeDef object model presented later when you manipulate cubes that reside on an OLAP server. The CellSet object model is shown in Figure 12.5.

12

FIGURE 12.5

The CellSet *object
model represents the
data access in a cube.*

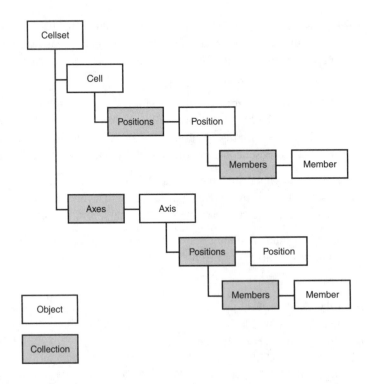

Though not shown in Figure 12.5, the Axis, Cell, Cellset, and Member objects each
have a standard ADO Properties collection. If you already took a look at ADO MD, you
might notice that I left out the Catalog object—it is optional just like the Connection
object is in standard ADO; therefore, I removed it from the top of the hierarchy to make
the tree easier to read.

The Axes branch of the object model is responsible for—you guessed it—the axes you
have defined in your MDX statement. The Cell object holds the data slice that is to be
displayed for each group of axes items.

To finally get started with coding ADO MD, here are the topics you're going to explore
in detail for your application and OLAP connectivity:

- Retrieving axes definitions
- Working with cell data

Retrieving Axes Definitions

When you compare how tabular OLE DB providers and the OLE DB provider for OLAP
retrieve data, there isn't too much difference (see Figure 12.6). As you can see, the OLE

DB provider for OLAP performs one step for you—it executes the query against the database, and it also caches the dataset on the client side (this is the PivotTable Service).

FIGURE 12.6

How the OLE DB provider for OLAP retrieves data.

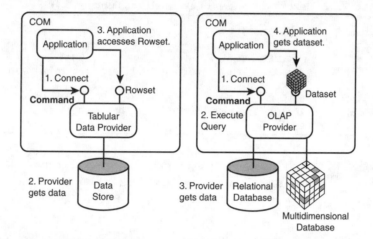

Judging from the similarities between the two retrieval methods, it is a safe assumption that the data access methods via ADO MD don't differ vastly from those with ADO. Therefore, let's start with the first ADO MD application. To make it more useful, I have created a front end for simple MDX queries in Excel (see Figure 12.7).

FIGURE 12.7

How the front end for retrieving axes defini-tions should look.

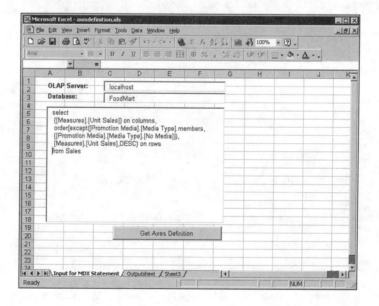

12

The only code that is located on this worksheet is presented in Listing 12.2.

LISTING 12.2 Invoking the `GetAxesDefinitions` Function

```
1: Private Sub cmdGetAxes_Click()
2:     If "" = Me.txtDatabase Or "" = Me.txtServer Or
➡"" = Me.txtMDXStatement Then
3:         MsgBox "You did not enter all required information!"
4:         Exit Sub
5:     End If
6:     GetAxesDefinitions Me.txtServer, Me.txtDatabase, Me.txtMDXStatement
7: End Sub
```

ANALYSIS The code performs simple string sanity checks and then calls the method `GetAxesDefinitions` that is presented in Listing 12.3. Therefore, if you don't like my front end, you can easily go with this function only and test it in the Immediate Window.

Before you type the following code, I have to advise you of some changes to the usual practices—you now need to set a different reference. You need the ADO (Multi-dimensional) Library (see Figure 12.8).

FIGURE 12.8

Adding the ADO MD Type Library to your project.

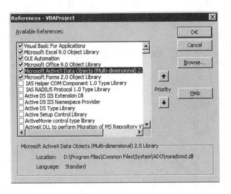

After this addition, you can start coding Listing 12.3.

LISTING 12.3 Implementing the `GetAxesDefinitions` Function

```
1: Option Explicit
2:
3: Global Const strSampleQuery = "select {[Measures].[Unit Sales]} on columns,
➡order(except([Promotion Media].[Media Type].members,
➡{[Promotion Media].[Media Type].[No Media]}),[Measures].[Unit Sales],DESC)
➡on rows from Sales"
```

```
 4:
 5: Function CreateMDDataSource(strServer As String, strDatabase As String)
➥As String
 6:     Dim strDSN As String
 7:     strDSN = "Provider=MSOLAP;Data Source=" & strServer & ";"
 8:     strDSN = strDSN & "Location=" & strDatabase
 9:     CreateMDDataSource = strDSN
10: End Function
11:
12: Sub GetAxesDefinitions(strServer As String, strDatabase As String,
➥strMDX As String)
13: On Error GoTo Err_GAD
14:     Dim cs As ADOMD.Cellset, strDSN As String
15:     Set cs = New ADOMD.Cellset
16:
17:     Worksheets(2).Activate
18:     Cells.Clear
19:
20:     strDSN = CreateMDDataSource(strServer, strDatabase)
21:     cs.Open strMDX, strDSN
22:
23:     Dim i As Integer, pos As ADOMD.Position
24:
25:     i = 1
26:     For Each pos In cs.Axes(0).Positions
27:         i = i + 1
28:         Cells(1, i) = pos.Members(0).Name
29:     Next
30:     i = 1
31:     For Each pos In cs.Axes(1).Positions
32:         i = i + 1
33:         Cells(i, 1) = pos.Members(0).Name
34:     Next
35:
36:     Exit Sub
37: Err_GAD:
38:     MsgBox Err.Description
39:     Exit Sub
40: End Sub
```

12

ANALYSIS Option Explicit is very useful—it automatically catches typos and speeds up your code at execution time. Line 3 contains a sample MDX statement I took from the MDX Sample Application, so in case you interactively test the function GetAxesDefinitions, you don't have to type an MDX statement in the Immediate Window.

The first function in the module is CreateMDDataSource. I invented this neat little helper so I could avoid duplicating DSN creation code throughout the main function. It takes the server and database names as input and returns a completed DSN to the caller. You are free to either add more options or come up with sophisticated validity checking.

The main function you are interested in starts on line 12. Input parameters are server and database names, as well as the MDX statement. In line 14, I declare the variable cs as type ADOMD.Cellset. This variable is going to hold the resultset from my MDX query. However, before I can open the resultset, I have to create the connection string using the helper function CreateMDDataSource (line 20).

It is fairly simple to connect to an MD data source and execute an MDX statement, as shown in line 21:

```
cs.Open strMDX, strDSN
```

This is really all it takes to go to the OLAP server, execute the query, get at the data, and start working with it. Because "working" for this application means getting at the axes definitions, I have included two loops for each axis:

```
For Each pos In cs.Axes(0).Positions
    i = i + 1
    Cells(1, i) = pos.Members(0).Name
Next
```

This iterates over all Positions on the first axis (COLUMNS). Each Position has a Members collection (see the Cellset object model in Figure 12.5); however, as I assumed that there can be only one member displayed in a cell, I take only the first member's name.

 Note

> This example is overly simple in terms of error handling. A good example of how to implement error handling is the MDX Sample Application, which also has decent documentation about what's going on in the code.

Executing the code results in column and row headers, but the data is still missing. This is added in the next section.

Working with Cell Data

You have retrieved all data and displayed the axes on the worksheet. An important thing is missing: the cell items (the data). To illustrate different ways to get at data, I have implemented a new function ExecuteMDX (see Listing 12.4) that uses a different way to connect to the OLAP server as well as a slightly different way to display axes and cell items.

LISTING 12.4 Displaying a Two-Dimensional Cellset

```
 1: Sub ExecuteMDX(strServer As String, strDatabase As String, strMDX As String)
 2: On Error GoTo Err_GAD
 3:     Dim cs As ADOMD.Cellset, strDSN As String, cat As ADOMD.Catalog
 4:     Set cat = New ADOMD.Catalog
 5:     Set cs = New ADOMD.Cellset
 6:
 7:     Worksheets(2).Activate
 8:     Cells.Clear
 9:
10:     strDSN = CreateMDDataSource(strServer, strDatabase)
11:     cat.ActiveConnection = strDSN
12:     cs.Source = strMDX
13:     Set cs.ActiveConnection = cat.ActiveConnection
14:     cs.Open
15:
16:     Dim nColPositions As Integer, nRowPositions As Integer, i As Integer
17:     Dim pos As ADOMD.Position, j As Integer
18:
19:     nColPositions = cs.Axes(0).Positions.Count
20:     nRowPositions = cs.Axes(1).Positions.Count
21:
22:     For i = 0 To nColPositions - 1
23:         Cells(1, i + 2) = cs.Axes(0).Positions(i).Members(0).Name
24:     Next
25:
26:     For i = 0 To nRowPositions - 1
27:         Cells(i + 2, 1) = cs.Axes(1).Positions(i).Members(0).Name
28:
29:         For j = 0 To nColPositions - 1
30:             Cells(i + 2, j + 2) = cs(j, i).FormattedValue
31:         Next
32:     Next
33:
34:     Exit Sub
35: Err_GAD:
36:     MsgBox Err.Description
37:     Exit Sub
38: End Sub
```

ANALYSIS In this script, I connect to the OLAP database using a variable of type `ADOMD.Catalog` (created on line 4). The connection string is assigned to the `ActiveConnection` property of the `Catalog` object in 11, and the MDX statement to the Cellset's `Source` property in line 12. All that remains to be done is to associate the Cellset's `ActiveConnection` property with the Catalog's `ActiveConnection` property and call `Cellset.Open` to execute the MDX statement against the database and get the resulting dataset from the server.

12

Also changed from the previous script is how I iterate over the axis' members. First, I get the number of axis members (lines 19–20). Then I display the axis descriptions for the columns (lines 22–24).

To finish the output, I still have to iterate over the rows and the cell items. I decided to display one row at a time, including both the row headers (line 27) and the row data (lines 29–31). Each Cell object I access is retrieved via the Item default property of the Cellset object. Then I call FormattedValue to display the value according to FORMAT_STRING assignment in the MDX query.

With the code presented in the preceding two examples, you can display data successfully, and with the help of the DrilledDown property of the Member object, you can create drill-down code, such as in Excel.

The MDX Sample Application shows how to use ADO MD in conjunction with grid controls, which I can't do here. However, I want to take a look at another area that is implemented in the MDX Sample Application: how to retrieve cube metadata to get at measures, dimensions, and more.

Working with Metadata

You definitely remember that when you selected a cube in the MDX Sample Application, all dimensions with their hierarchies were returned and made available in a tree view. What is going on behind the scenes when you select a cube? The sample application goes to the OLAP server and requests metadata information about the cube (the definition). This metadata is available through the CubeDef object model of ADO MD (see Figure 12.9).

This is quite a deep object model, and it is also powerful. You already know the top-level object from the last example; however, this time it is mandatory to connect to the catalog first, because otherwise you have no way of accessing the CubeDefs.

Each CubeDef holds a collection of Dimensions, which contain hierarchies, levels, and members. With the OLAP Cube Editor in mind, it is easy to map this object model to the dimensions and their properties in the cube. For example, Time has only one hierarchy; however, SharedTime, which we created yesterday, has two hierarchies. The levels are also easy—for example, Year, Quarter, and Month for the Time dimension. The members for the level Year are 1997, and so on. You see, it is easy.

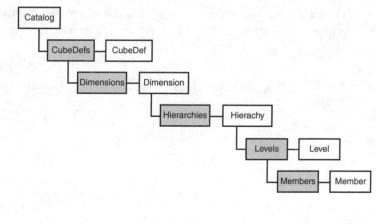

FIGURE 12.9

The CubeDef *object model for working with metadata.*

Object	(white box)
Collection	(shaded box)

Note Remember, the measures of a cube are contained in a dimension of their own, the Measures dimension.

12

With the explanations in place, I want to start exploring the following topics regarding cubes and their definitions:

- Dumping a cube's definition
- Creating a cube programmatically

Dumping a Cube's Definition

A cube's definition contains a lot of information that can be used in an analysis application to guide the user through the process of interactively creating an analysis—just remember the layout feature found in Excel's PivotTable.

As I mentioned earlier, the only way to get at a CubeDef (the name already tells all) is to first open a catalog, which is ADO MD's equivalent of a Connection object. When you are connected to a catalog, you can iterate over all CubeDefs and drill down the object to retrieve information about dimensions, levels, and members.

All this is done in Listing 12.5. It might look overwhelming at first because it contains everything you might want to look up. However, a thorough analysis follows the code monster.

LISTING 12.5 Getting at a Cube's Most Important Information and Displaying It in an Excel Worksheet

```
 1: Option Explicit
 2:
 3: Const bShowProperties = False
 4:
 5: Sub DumpCubeDef()
 6:     Dim cat As ADOMD.Catalog, cdf As ADOMD.CubeDef
 7:     Dim i As Integer, j As Integer, nCellRow As Integer
 8:     Dim di As Integer, hi As Integer, le As Integer
 9:
10:     Set cat = CreateObject("ADOMD.Catalog")
11:
12:     cat.ActiveConnection = "Data Source=localhost;" & _
13:         "Initial Catalog=FoodMart;Provider=msolap;"
14:
15:     Set cdf = cat.CubeDefs("Sales")
16:
17:     ' show properties for the cubedef on sheet 1
18:     Worksheets(1).Activate
19:     Cells.Clear
20:     For i = 0 To cdf.Properties.Count - 1
21:         Cells(i + 1, 1) = cdf.Properties(i).Name
22:         Cells(i + 1, 2) = cdf.Properties(i).Value
23:     Next
24:
25:     ' show dimension names and properties for the cubedef on sheet 2
26:     Worksheets(2).Activate
27:     Cells.Clear
28:
29:     For di = 0 To cdf.Dimensions.Count - 1
30:         nCellRow = nCellRow + 1
31:         Cells(nCellRow, 1) = cdf.Dimensions(di).Name
32:
33:         If bShowProperties Then
34:             nCellRow = nCellRow + 1
35:             Cells(nCellRow, 2) = ">Dimension Properties"
36:
37:             For j = 0 To cdf.Dimensions(di).Properties.Count - 1
38:                 nCellRow = nCellRow + 1
39:                 Cells(nCellRow, 3) = cdf.Dimensions(di).Properties(j).Name
40:                 Cells(nCellRow, 4) = cdf.Dimensions(di).Properties(j).Value
41:             Next
42:         End If
```

```
43:
44:            nCellRow = nCellRow + 1
45:            Cells(nCellRow, 2) = ">Hierarchy"
46:
47:            ' loop hierarchy names and properties
48:            For hi = 0 To cdf.Dimensions(di).Hierarchies.Count - 1
49:               nCellRow = nCellRow + 1
50:               Cells(nCellRow, 3) = cdf.Dimensions(di) & _
51:                   .Hierarchies(hi).UniqueName
52:
53:               If bShowProperties Then
54:                  For j = 0 To cdf.Dimensions(di).Hierarchies(hi)
➥.Properties.Count - 1
55:                     nCellRow = nCellRow + 1
56:                     Cells(nCellRow, 4) = cdf.Dimensions(di) & _
57:                        .Hierarchies(hi).Properties(j).Name
58:                  Next
59:               End If
60:
61:               ' display level name and properties
62:               For le=0 To cdf.Dimensions(di).Hierarchies(hi).Levels.Count-1
63:                  nCellRow = nCellRow + 1
64:                  Cells(nCellRow, 4) = "Level: " & _
65:                     cdf.Dimensions(di).Hierarchies(hi).Levels(le).Name & _
66:                     " has " & _
67:                     cdf.Dimensions(di).Hierarchies(hi).Levels(le) & _
68:                        .Properties("LEVEL_CARDINALITY") & _
69:                     " members"
70:
71:                  If bShowProperties Then
72:                     For j = 0 To cdf.Dimensions(di).Hierarchies(hi) & _
73:                           .Levels(le).Properties.Count - 1
74:                        nCellRow = nCellRow + 1
75:                        Cells(nCellRow, 5) = cdf.Dimensions(di) & _
76:                           .Hierarchies(hi).Levels(le).Properties(j).Name
77:                        Cells(nCellRow, 6) = cdf.Dimensions(di) & _
78:                           .Hierarchies(hi).Levels(le).Properties(j).Value
79:                     Next
80:                  End If
81:               Next
82:            Next
83:         Next
84: End Sub
```

ANALYSIS Start with the well-known facts: a connection to the catalog FoodMart on the local server is established on lines 12–13. The next step in analyzing a cube is to connect to it, to retrieve its CubeDefs—this is done in line 15:

```
Set cdf = cat.CubeDefs("Sales")
```

The script then clears the first worksheet and proceeds to display the properties for the cube itself (lines 20–23). To keep the cube's properties separate from the cube's hierarchy, the code then switches to sheet 2.

Line 29 dives into the `Dimensions` collection and returns near the end, in line 83. In this entire block, multiple things happen. The first is to print the dimension's name (line 31). Enclosed by the `If...End If` statement in lines 33–42 is the code for dumping the properties of the current dimension. I added a constant to the beginning of the file to be able to turn off properties dumping because it makes reading the Dimension structure harder.

Line 48 then steps into the hierarchies that are available for this Dimension (remember for SharedTime, you created two Dimensions). This block encloses the iteration over the properties for the hierarchies (lines 53–59), as well as iterating over the levels and their properties. When all is completed, the code exits on line 82.

Looking at this code, you can learn a lot about the properties that are available at each level of the object model. Though the example dumped the information on a worksheet, you can easily take portions to write it to a TreeView control or various drop-down boxes where users can select cube dimensions.

Creating a Cube Programmatically

I won't finish today until I at least give a brief rundown on a feature that can be extremely important for custom analysis software—rolling out your own cubes on a client machine using the `CREATE CUBE` statement.

 Note

> The `CREATE CUBE` statement can be used only to create local cubes using the PivotTable Service. `CREATE CUBE` statements cannot be issued against an OLAP Services catalog.

The cube creation script presented in Listing 12.6 is a modification to a sample found in the Platform SDK. I have stripped some lines (indicated by ...) to make it shorter and clearer to understand what's behind creating a local cube.

LISTING 12.6 Creating a Cube and Populating It with Data

```
1: Sub CreateCubeProgrammatically()
2: On Error GoTo Err_CCP
3:     Dim cn As ADODB.Connection
4:     Dim strExec As String, strProvider As String, strInsertInto As String
5:     Dim strDataSource As String, strSourceDSN As String,
```

```
➡strCreateCube As String
 6:
 7:      strProvider = "PROVIDER=MSOLAP"
 8:      strDataSource = "DATA SOURCE=C:\NewCube.cube"
 9:      strSourceDSN = "SOURCE_DSN=FoodMart"
10:
11:      ' create cube statements; doesn't fill it with data
12:      strCreateCube = "CREATECUBE=CREATE CUBE Sample( "
13:      strCreateCube = strCreateCube & "DIMENSION [Product],"
14:          strCreateCube = strCreateCube & "LEVEL [All Products] TYPE ALL,"
15:          strCreateCube = strCreateCube & "LEVEL [Product Family] ,"
16:          strCreateCube = strCreateCube & "LEVEL [Product Department] ,"
17:          strCreateCube = strCreateCube & "LEVEL [Product Category] ,"
18:          strCreateCube = strCreateCube & "LEVEL [Product Subcategory] ,"
19:          strCreateCube = strCreateCube & "LEVEL [Brand Name] ,"
20:          strCreateCube = strCreateCube & "LEVEL [Product Name] ,"
21: ...
22:      strCreateCube = strCreateCube & "DIMENSION [Time] TYPE TIME,"
23:          strCreateCube = strCreateCube & "HIERARCHY [Column],"
24:          strCreateCube = strCreateCube & "LEVEL [All Time]  TYPE ALL,"
25:          strCreateCube = strCreateCube & "LEVEL [Year]  TYPE YEAR,"
26:          strCreateCube = strCreateCube & "LEVEL [Quarter]  TYPE QUARTER,"
27:          strCreateCube = strCreateCube & "LEVEL [Month]  TYPE MONTH,"
28:          strCreateCube = strCreateCube & "LEVEL [Week]  TYPE WEEK,"
29:          strCreateCube = strCreateCube & "LEVEL [Day]  TYPE DAY,"
30:          strCreateCube = strCreateCube & "HIERARCHY [Formula],"
31:          strCreateCube = strCreateCube & _
32:              "LEVEL [All Formula Time]  TYPE ALL,"
33:          strCreateCube = strCreateCube & "LEVEL [Year]  TYPE YEAR,"
34:          strCreateCube = strCreateCube & "LEVEL [Quarter]  TYPE QUARTER,"
35:          strCreateCube = strCreateCube & _
36:              "LEVEL [Month]  TYPE MONTH OPTIONS (SORTBYKEY) ,"
37:      strCreateCube = strCreateCube & "DIMENSION [Warehouse],"
38:          strCreateCube = strCreateCube & _
39:              "LEVEL [All Warehouses]  TYPE ALL,"
40:          strCreateCube = strCreateCube & "LEVEL [Country] ,"
41:          strCreateCube = strCreateCube & "LEVEL [State Province] ,"
42:          strCreateCube = strCreateCube & "LEVEL [City] ,"
43:          strCreateCube = strCreateCube & "LEVEL [Warehouse Name] ,"
44:      strCreateCube = strCreateCube & "MEASURE [Store Invoice] "
45:          strCreateCube = strCreateCube & "Function Sum "
46:          strCreateCube = strCreateCube & "Format '#.#',"
47: ...
48:      strCreateCube = strCreateCube & "MEASURE [Units Ordered] "
49:          strCreateCube = strCreateCube & "Function Sum "
50:          strCreateCube = strCreateCube & "Format '#.#')"
51:
52:      ' the insert into statement for filling the cube with data
53:      strInsertInto = strInsertInto & _
```

12

continues

LISTING 12.6 continued

```
54:          "INSERTINTO=INSERT INTO Sample( " & _
55:            "Product.[Product Family], Product.[Product Department],"
56: ...
57:      strInsertInto = strInsertInto & _
58:        "Measures.[Units Shipped], Measures.[Units Ordered] )"
59:
60:      ' select statements that define where the data comes from
61:      strInsertInto = strInsertInto & _
62:        "SELECT product_class.product_family AS Col1,"
63: ...
64:      strInsertInto = strInsertInto & _
65:        "inventory_fact_1997.units_ordered AS Col26 "
66:      strInsertInto = strInsertInto & _
67:        "From [inventory_fact_1997], [product], [product_class], " & _
68:          "[time_by_day], [store], [warehouse] "
69:      strInsertInto = strInsertInto & _
70:        "Where [inventory_fact_1997].[product_id] = [product]." & _
71:          "[product_id] And "
72: ...
73:      strInsertInto = strInsertInto & _
74:        "[inventory_fact_1997].[warehouse_id] = [warehouse].[warehouse_id]"
75:
76:
77:      ' create the cube with CREATE statement and INSERT statement
78:      Set cn = New ADODB.Connection
79:      strExec = strProvider & ";" & strDataSource & ";" & strSourceDSN & _
80:        ";" & strCreateCube & ";" & strInsertInto & ";"
81:      cn.Open strExec
82:
83:      ' this cube is now accessible immediately
84:      Dim cat As New ADOMD.Catalog
85:      Dim cdf As ADOMD.CubeDef
86:
87:      cat.ActiveConnection = strProvider & ";" & strDataSource
88:      Set cdf = cat.CubeDefs("Sample")
89:
90:      Exit Sub
91: Err_CCP:
92:      MsgBox Err.Description
93:      Exit Sub
94: End Sub
```

ANALYSIS Though I removed many lines, it still takes nearly 100 lines just to show how it works. In the first 10 lines, variables are defined and initialized. The only one I specifically want to mention is strDataSource:

```
strDataSource = "DATA SOURCE=C:\NewCube.cub"
```

It contains the file location for the cube this script is creating. Then, in lines 12–50, the CREATE CUBE statement is built. I have left in the different LEVEL declarations to look at—for syntax specifics, please take a look at the Platform SDK for SQL Server.

When the CREATE CUBE statement is built, you still have no data for the cube—you have to insert it into the cube somehow. Provide an INSERT INTO statement, which is created in lines 53–58.

Though part of the INSERT INTO statement, the SELECT statement (lines 61 and following) needs further attention: the OLAP provider passes this on to the underlying database—it usually doesn't parse and execute it itself. The statement is completed on line 74.

You have finally reached the ADO code for creating the connection (line 78) and building the connection string. Notice that both the CREATE CUBE statement and the INSERT INTO statement are concatenated and executed against the connection (the cube file) in line 81:

```
cn.Open strExec
```

If everything went well, no error was raised and the code on the remaining lines connects to the newly created cube and retrieves the CubeDef and the metadata. You could also issue MDX statements against this newly created cube.

This example shows a very advanced use of the PivotTable Service for creating your own cubes on the client. Actually, the PivotTable Service uses similar code to cache a cube from OLAP Services on the local computer.

12

Summary

Today, you learned how to create a multidimensional expression that you can use to retrieve datasets from an OLAP cube. You added slicer specifications, filtered and ordered the results, created calculated members, cross-joined dimensions, and did hierarchical navigation. Take some time to practice your MDX skills.

The remainder of today was dedicated to using ADO MD to retrieve data using the MDX statements you wrote, or getting at cube metadata and displaying it for various purposes. Because the object model is large, it might take you some time to get really acquainted with it.

Q&A

Q **How can I extend the functionality of OLAP Services?**

A Look up the section "Decision Support Objects" in the Platform SDK. The DSO are intended for enhancing, augmenting, and automating OLAP installations.

Q **I have looked up the ADO MD documentation, but there isn't good information on MDX—where is it located?**

A Go to the OLE DB Programmers Reference, Part 3. Chapters 4, 5, and 6 are dedicated to MDX.

Workshop

The quiz questions and exercises are provided for your further understanding. See Appendix A, "Answers," for the answers.

Quiz

1. In case you omit the slicer specification, what is returned by OLAP Services?

2. Are the following two lines of code equal?

```
Measures.MEMBERS ON AXIS(3)
Measures.MEMBERS ON CHAPTERS
```

3. When you display the members of the Measures dimension on the COLUMNS axis, are there any obstacles you have to observe?

4. Is the following MDX statement valid?

```
SELECT [Product].[Product Family].MEMBERS ON COLUMNS,
       [Store].Store State.MEMBERS ON ROWS
FROM Sales
WHERE [Measures].[Profit]
```

5. What are the differences between BDESC and DESC?

6. Why would you want to cross-join sets?

7. Do you need to open a Cellset object to get at cell data?

8. Which service creates the cube when you issue a CREATE CUBE statement?

Exercises

1. Create the MDX that enables you to display sales profit and change from month to month for the year of 1997. *Hint:* Use PREVMEMBER and DESCENDANTS.

2. Your boss asks you to create an MDX query for him. He needs to query year-to-date sales monthly, for each product category in 1997. *Hint:* Use SUM, YTD, and DESCENDANTS.

DAY 13

Accessing Non-Relational Data

Not all data in your enterprise is stored in a relational database. You have important data in your file systems, in mail systems, and even in Web pages. To access data stored in those locations, you had to use different access methods— until now. Beginning with ADO 2.5, you can access semistructured data with ADO as well.

Today, you learn the following tasks:

- How ADO can be used to access semistructured data using `Record` and `Stream` objects
- Configuring a Web directory for WebDAV so you can access Web pages using ADO
- Uploading and downloading files from a Web server
- Managing Exchange 2000's Web store with ADO
- Working with mailboxes and public folders

ADO Extension for Semistructured Data

Because you weren't able to access semistructured data until now, it is a safe assumption that there must have been some changes and additions to ADO 2.5. The most obvious change is that two new objects were added to the ADO object model: the Record and Stream objects (see Figure 13.1).

FIGURE 13.1

The Record *and* Stream *objects are new for ADO 2.5.*

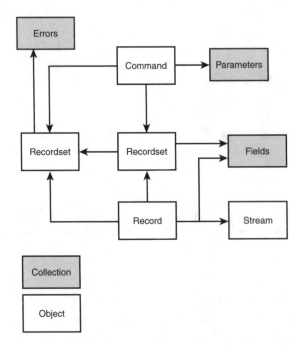

The Record object provides methods and properties to manage either files and directories, or messages and folders. Management tasks can include copying records, deleting records, or creating records. In addition to this use in semistructured data access scenarios, a Record object can also represent a row in a recordset.

The Stream object is used to access the data that comprises a message or file. Using the Stream object, you can read from a file, write to file, and modify the file's contents. A Stream object is usually used in conjunction with a Record object.

To illustrate the power of the additions for semistructured data, you are going to work with two different data stores today: a Web server (Internet Information Server) and a mail server (Exchange 2000). You are going to explore the capabilities of Record and Stream objects in examples that exploit the two systems; however, I want to introduce two topics first:

- URL binding
- Representing recordset rows as record

URL Binding

To access semistructured data, you have to provide a URL to the provider. The URL can specify an HTML page, image, and so on, and in general form looks like this:

```
scheme://server/path/resource
```

The *scheme* specifies how the resource is to be accessed, the *server* specifies on which machine it is located, and the *path* specifies the directory structure where it resides. For the HTTP scheme, a URL looks like the following:

```
http://localhost/myfolder/myfile.txt
```

This is an absolute URL because it contains the entire path to the file, but you can also use relative URLs. These are best compared to databases and tables: a connection to a database is established with the Connection object (absolute URL, provider, server name, and database), and a table is accessed via a Recordset object (relative URL and the name of the table). Translated to the HTTP example, the absolute parent URL would be

```
http://localhost/
```

and the relative URL to the file would be

```
myfolder/myfile.txt
```

As you might guess, there is not only the HTTP scheme. Additional schemes out of the box are LDAP, for accessing Active Directory, and file, installed by Exchange 2000.

You will see how to use schemes and URLs throughout today's examples—enough time to get used to these concepts.

Representing Recordset Rows as Record

Before starting with the in-depth data access tutorials for Web servers and mail servers, let's look a little closer at the Record object. Not only can it represent a resource, such as a message or file, but the Record object can also represent a row of a recordset. With this information at hand, you should be able to write database code such as Listing 13.1.

13

LISTING 13.1 The Record Object and Database Providers

```
 1: Sub ReadRecordAndStream()
 2:     Dim cn As ADODB.Connection, rs As ADODB.Recordset, rec As ADODB.Record
 3:     Dim strSQL As String, n As Integer, i As Integer
 4:
 5:     ' create the objects, and then open the connection
 6:     Set cn = New ADODB.Connection
 7:     Set rs = New ADODB.Recordset
 8:
 9:     cn.Open "provider=sqloledb.1;user id=sa;password=;
➥initial catalog=northwind;data source=strangelove"
10:     ' cn.Open "Provider=Microsoft.Jet.OLEDB.4.0;
➥Data Source=c:\NorthWind.mdb;"
11:
12:     strSQL = "select * from Suppliers"
13:     rs.Open strSQL, cn
14:
15:     Set rec = New ADODB.Record
16:     While Not rs.EOF
17:         rec.Open rs
18:         ' do some operations with the Record object
19:         ' move to the next record
20:         rec.Close
21:         rs.MoveNext
22:     Wend
23: End Sub
```

ANALYSIS Except for the declaration of the Record variable, there is nothing special about the database code until line 17, where the current row is assigned to the Record object. However, in this line, the code will fail for both connection strings—SQL Server and Access—with the error number adErrFeatureNotAvailable.

Didn't I say that a record can represent a row of a recordset? Yes. However, the provider must allow the user to retrieve records or change the position while holding previously retrieved records with pending changes. Neither SQL Server nor Jet providers support this functionality, and you can verify whether a provider supports the Record object by checking

```
If True = rs.Properties("Hold Rows") Then ' yes!
```

Having said that representing rows as Record objects is a provider-specific feature, let's move on to a provider that supports this functionality.

Web Publishing

NEW TERM Internet Information Server (IIS) 5 supports *WebDAV* (Web Distributed Authoring and Versioning), which is an extension to the HTTP 1.1 protocol. WebDAV enables clients to access files on a Web server, including for creation, deletion, and modification of files. A client can be Windows 2000 through Network Neighborhood, Internet Explorer 5, or even Microsoft Office 2000—and let's not forget ADO.

To access anything with ADO you need a data provider, and WebDAV is no exception to this rule. The provider is named MS Distributed Authoring Internet Publishing Provider, or Internet Publishing Provider (IPP). It allows you to modify files on the Web server. The following sections will get you, as a database developer, started with authoring Web content:

- Configuring WebDAV
- Connecting to Web Resources
- Listing a Folder
- Downloading Files
- Uploading Files

Configuring WebDAV

Before you can start your career as Web site manager, you have to prepare your server—though it is no database server, but a Web server. Also, you are not dealing with tables, but with directories.

The configuration tasks are not complicated, but you have to perform them:

- Creating a publishing directory
- Security implications

Creating a Publishing Directory

Before you can start exploring the capabilities of WebDAV and the OLE DB IPP, you need to set up a sandbox in which you can safely test the features that are available (so that you don't ruin your entire machine). To be really on the safe side, you create a virtual directory that has all WebDAV features enabled.

13

To Do: Creating a WebDAV directory

Follow these steps to create a directory that is enabled for upload and download:

1. In Windows Explorer, create a directory named WebDAV (such as `c:\WebDAV`) that will be used to explore the WebDAV functionality. Copy some files into this directory.

2. Start Internet Services Manager and expand the Default Web Site. Right-click and select New, Virtual Directory from the context menu (see Figure 13.2).

FIGURE 13.2

Creating a new virtual directory.

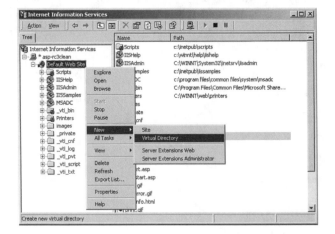

3. The Virtual Directory Creation Wizard starts. Skip the start screen and proceed to step two, assigning an alias for the virtual directory. Enter **WebDAV** as the alias name.

4. Browse for the physical directory you created in step one. This is where the Web site will serve content from when the alias is requested.

5. You are now asked for access permissions to this directory. In addition to Read and Run scripts, select Write and Browse (see Figure 13.3).

6. Finish the Wizard. Note that the new directory is shown in the right-hand pane.

7. Select the directory and choose Properties from the context menu.

8. In the Properties dialog box, select the Script source access permission (see Figure 13.4). This enables you to upload and download scripts such as ASP pages.

FIGURE 13.3

Setting access permissions for the new virtual directory.

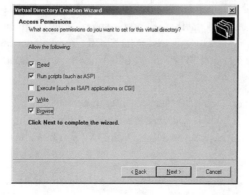

FIGURE 13.4

Adding additional access permissions to the WebDAV virtual directory.

9. Click OK to make your changes stick.

10. Use Internet Explorer to view the contents of the new virtual directory (`http://localhost/WebDAV/`). Because browsing is allowed, you will get a directory listing (if you didn't copy a default document to the directory in the first step).

If you are already a Web professional, you might argue that creating a virtual directory is overkill, because you can set the same permissions for any directory that is part of the Web site. You are right; however, because you are modifying the Default Web Site, it is a good idea to be on the safe side.

Enabling read, write, browse, and even script uploading can be dangerous; therefore before proceeding, let's take a look at security in a WebDAV-enabled environment.

13

Security Implications

When you listed the contents of the new virtual directory in the last step of the preceding task, you weren't asked for a username and password unless you created the WebDAV physical directory on an already-secured NTFS disk. You had access as the anonymous user for browsing the resource. The same holds true for writing data—unless you tighten security.

Though this book is not about Web servers, it is important to know how to protect an environment—especially when you enable such sensitive tasks as modifying data and scripts. To be more secure, let's review the WebDAV settings and how they interact with each other:

- Read enabled—This is the default for all Web directories you create. Users can download files via Internet Explorer, for example, or using WebDAV. All scripts are executed before they are downloaded; the code itself cannot be downloaded.
- Read and Browse enabled—Users can list the contents of a directory and then download files.
- Write enabled, Read and Browse disabled—Users can upload files; however, they can't list the contents of the directory, nor can they download files. This scenario is useful when you want users to upload files; however, they should not be able to view what else was uploaded.
- Read and Write enabled, Browse disabled—Allow users to upload and download files; however, disallow to view all files. This scenario enables you to selectively provide files for download.
- Read, Write and Browse enabled—Users may download, upload, and view what they want to.
- Read and Script enabled—Users can download scripts (ASP pages, for example) without the code being executed, thus being able to see your code.
- Write and Script enabled—Users are allowed to upload script files. If Write only is allowed without Script, uploading scripts fails.

For the last two items, I omitted the combinations with Browse because they can be easily imagined. However, even if you limit the options listed, not only authorized persons have the permissions. Anonymous Web clients also have them.

Because we don't have the time to discuss all the various authentication schemes that are provided with IIS, I can give you only an overview and hand you over to the documentation of IIS to get proficient. The following schemes can be used:

- Anonymous
- Basic
- Windows Integrated
- Digest

Each of these has strengths and weaknesses; however, they have in common that they rely on access control lists that are applied to files in Windows Explorer. By setting access permissions to files on the NTFS level, clients are forced to authenticate using one of the schemes outlined and provide sufficient security credentials to be able to access the resource in the desired way.

Connecting to Web Resources

Your WebDAV-enabled directory is up and running and is waiting to be accessed using ADO and the OLE DB provider for Internet Publishing. To show you how many different ways there are to connect to a Web resource using the Record object, I used three methods in Listing 13.2 to attach to file myfile.txt in the WebDAV folder.

LISTING 13.2   Connecting to a WebDAV Resource

```
 1: Option Explicit
 2:
 3: Const cstrServerName = "localhost"
 4: Const cstrDAVDirectory = "/WebDAV/"
 5:
 6: ' Three different ways to bind to a URL
 7: Sub UrlBinding()
 8:     Dim cn As New Connection
 9:     Dim rec As New Record
10:
11:     rec.Open "myfile.txt", "URL=http://" & cstrServerName & cstrDAVDirectory
12:     rec.Close
13:
14:     rec.Open "http://" & cstrServerName & cstrDAVDirectory & _
15:             "myfile.txt"
16:     rec.Close
17:
18:     cn.Open "URL=http://" & cstrServerName & cstrDAVDirectory
19:     rec.Open "myfile.txt", cn
20: End Sub
```

13

ANALYSIS   I'm not doing anything fancy with the file yet, just connecting to it three times. For this task, I hard-coded the server name and DAV directory in lines 3 and 4, which you can change easily to adapt to your environment. For the Default Web Site, however, it should work out of the box. Because `Connection` and `Record` variables are declared in lines 8 and 9, you need to reference the ADO type library. It is necessary for all examples in this chapter (again).

The first connection is set up by calling `Record.Open` with

```
Record.Open Source, ActiveConnection
```

I do not need to deal with the other options:

```
Record.Open Source, ActiveConnection, Mode, CreateOptions, Options,
➡ UserName, Password
```

Because you are going to revisit `Mode`, `CreateOptions`, and `Options` later in detail, let's look at `Username` and `Password` first. I did not need to specify them in the example because our sample directory does not require any special user accounts. It allows anonymous access; therefore I didn't need these options.

Line 12 closes the `Record` variable:

```
Rec.Close
```

This statement is necessary to be able to reopen the `Record` variable on another resource, though it is the same (line 14):

```
Rec.Open "http://" & cstrServerName & cstrDAVDirectory & "myfile.txt"
```

I do not need to specify the connection because the URL already points to the file itself. To reuse the variable, I close the `Record` variable again.

The final option is presented in lines 18 and 19:

```
cn.Open "URL=http://" & cstrServerName & cstrDAVDirectory
rec.Open "myfile.txt", cn
```

A connection to the WebDAV folder is opened and then passed as parameter for `ActiveConnection`. I did not need to specify the provider because I used the `URL=` syntax, which automatically invokes the IPP. However, if you like to do it manually, you can rewrite it to

```
cn.Provider = "MSDAIPP.DSO"
cn.Open "http://" & cstrServerName & cstrDAVDirectory
rec.Open "myfile.txt", cn
```

When you recall the object model for the `Record` object, you know that it contains a `Fields` collection. This poses quite an interesting question: What is contained in this collection for a WebDAV resource? To test it, I created a folder named `"TestFolder"` in the sample directory and then ran the script in Listing 13.3.

LISTING 13.3   Showing the Properties for a Resource Record

```
1: Sub FolderProperties()
2:     Dim rec As New Record, fld As Field
3:     rec.Open "TestFolder", "URL=http://" & cstrServerName & cstrDAVDirectory
4:
5:     For Each fld In rec.Fields
6:         Debug.Print fld.Name, " = ", fld.Value
7:     Next
8: End Sub
```

When you run this code, it produces output similar to the following:

OUTPUT

```
RESOURCE_PARSENAME              =    TestFolder
RESOURCE_PARENTNAME             =    http://192.168.1.105/WebDAV
RESOURCE_ABSOLUTEPARSENAME      =    http://192.168.1.105/WebDAV/TestFolder
RESOURCE_ISHIDDEN               =    False
RESOURCE_ISREADONLY             =
RESOURCE_CONTENTTYPE            =
RESOURCE_CONTENTCLASS           =    application/octet-stream
RESOURCE_CONTENTLANGUAGE        =
RESOURCE_CREATIONTIME           =    11/18/1999 11:48:42 AM
RESOURCE_LASTACCESSTIME         =
RESOURCE_LASTWRITETIME          =    11/18/1999 11:57:32 AM
RESOURCE_STREAMSIZE             =    0
RESOURCE_ISCOLLECTION           =    True
RESOURCE_ISSTRUCTUREDDOCUMENT   =
DEFAULT_DOCUMENT                =
RESOURCE_DISPLAYNAME            =    TestFolder
RESOURCE_ISROOT                 =
RESOURCE_ISMARKEDFOROFFLINE     =    False
DAV:getcontentlength            =    0
DAV:creationdate                =    11/18/1999 11:48:42 AM
DAV:displayname                 =    TestFolder
DAV:getetag                     =    "6c67ca18bc31bf1:8928"
DAV:getlastmodified             =    11/18/1999 11:57:32 AM
DAV:ishidden                    =    False
DAV:iscollection                =    True
DAV:getcontenttype              =    application/octet-stream
```

ANALYSIS   The code in Listing 13.3 doesn't contain any tricks you need to pay extra attention to. The more interesting part is the output—the properties for the resource you accessed. When you look at the output, you notice that some RESOURCE_ column names are equal to DAV: properties. In general, there'd be an equivalent for each (see Table 13.1); however, not all are meaningful in the current situation.

13

TABLE 13.1   Record Type Information

Column Name	DAV Property	Description
RESOURCE_ PARSENAME	`DAV: lastpathsegment`	Defines the URL of a resource. Usually, this is a relative URL. For tree roots, this is defined to be empty.
RESOURCE_ PARENTNAME	`DAV:parentname`	Specifies the parent URL, which is always an absolute URL.
RESOURCE_ ABSOLUTEPARSENAME	`DAV:href`	Returns the absolute path of a resource. For nonroot items, it is the concatenation of parent and parse name.
RESOURCE_ ISHIDDEN	`DAV:ishidden`	Determines whether a resource is hidden or visible.
RESOURCE_ ISREADONLY	`DAV:isreadonly`	Determines whether a resource is read-only.
RESOURCE_ CONTENTTYPE	`DAV: getcontenttype`	Returns the MIME type of a resource.
RESOURCE_ CONTENTCLASS	`DAV:contentclass`	Informs about the most likely use of a document, such as which application was used to create it.
RESOURCE_ CONTENTLANGUAGE	`DAV: getcontent language`	Specifies the language in which the content was created.
RESOURCE_ CREATIONTIME	`DAV: creationdate`	Determines the time the resource was initially created.
RESOURCE_ LASTACCESSTIME	`DAV:lastaccessed`	Determines the time the resource was accessed for the last time.
RESOURCE_ LASTWRITETIME	`DAV: getlastmodified`	Determines the time when the resource was updated the last time.
RESOURCE_ STREAMSIZE	`DAV: getcontentlength`	Specifies the size of the default stream if one exists.
RESOURCE_ ISCOLLECTION	`DAV:iscollection`	Returns True if the Record is a collection or False when the Record is atomic.
RESOURCE_ ISSTRUCTURED DOCUMENT	`DAV: isstructured document`	Determines whether the current resource is a structured document.

Column Name	DAV Property	Description
DEFAULT_DOCUMENT	DAV: defaultdocument	Returns the current default document for a folder or the structured document it represents.
CHAPTERED_ CHILDREN		Specifies the chapter that contains the children for the current resource.
RESOURCE_ DISPLAYNAME	DAV:displayname	The display name of the resource.
RESOURCE_ISROOT	DAV:isroot	If True, the current item is the root of a collection.

Notice that CHAPTERED_CHILDREN doesn't have a DAV: equivalent—it is directly implemented in the GetChildren method shown in the next section.

Listing a Folder

After connecting to a folder, it is interesting to know what is actually contained in this folder (given that Browse access is enabled). You can achieve the goal by using the code presented in Listing 13.4.

LISTING 13.4 Displaying a Folder's Contents

```
 1: Sub IterateFolder()
 2:     Dim rec As New Record
 3:     Dim rs As New Recordset
 4:
 5:     rec.Open "TestFolder", "URL=http://" & cstrServerName & cstrDAVDirectory
 6:
 7:     If adCollectionRecord = rec.RecordType Then
 8:         Set rs = rec.GetChildren
 9:         ' now print all the contents that were found
10:         While Not rs.EOF
11:             Debug.Print rs(0)
12:             rs.MoveNext
13:         Wend
14:     End If
15: End Sub
```

13

ANALYSIS In line 5, I open a Record object for the folder named "TestFolder". Then I check whether this is a collection (folder) in the If statement in line 7. You could also rewrite the statement to

```
If True = rec.Fields("RESOURCE_ISCOLLECTION") Then
```

However, accessing the `RecordType` property of the `Record` object is much more friendly, and it provides named constants for each record type: `adSimpleRecord`, `adCollectionRecord`, and `adStructDoc` (this is extracted from the RESOURCE_ISSTRUCTUREDDOCUMENT field). You see once again that ADO is a nice wrapper around hard-core functionality.

In line 8, I retrieve the chaptered children, which is a recordset that represents the files and subfolders in the `TestFolder` directory. I then simply iterate over the recordset and dump all information to the Immediate Window. The information at index zero is RESOURCE_PARSENAME.

Because the IPP is very versatile, there is another way to get at a directory listing. You can find the code for listing a directory's content using a Recordset in Listing 13.5.

LISTING 13.5   Another Method for Retrieving Folder Listings

```
 1: Sub ViewFilesForURL(strURL As String)
 2:      Dim rs As ADODB.Recordset
 3:      Dim cn As ADODB.Connection
 4:      Dim nRow As Integer
 5:
 6:      Set rs = New ADODB.Recordset
 7:      Set cn = New ADODB.Connection
 8:
 9:      ' set up the connection object
10:      cn.Mode = adModeRead
11:      cn.Provider = "MSDAIPP.DSO"
12:      cn.ConnectionString = "Data Source=" & strURL
13:
14:      cn.Open
15:
16:      ' open the recordset to the url
17:      rs.Open strURL, cn, adOpenForwardOnly, adLockPessimistic,adCmdTableDirect
18:
19:      Worksheets(2).Activate
20:      Cells.Clear
21:
22:      While Not rs.EOF
23:          nRow = nRow + 1
24:          If (True = rs("RESOURCE_ISCOLLECTION")) Then
25:              Cells(nRow, 1) = "(+)" & rs("RESOURCE_DISPLAYNAME")
26:          Else
27:              Cells(nRow, 1) = rs("RESOURCE_DISPLAYNAME")
28:          End If
29:          rs.MoveNext
30:      Wend
31:
32:      rs.Close
33:      cn.Close
34: End Sub
```

ANALYSIS In this example, an explicit connection is opened using the IPP (line 11). The URL is specified using the `Data Source` property, which is equivalent to the URL for this provider. After the connection is opened, a recordset is assigned to the directory listing. The cursor is set to forward-only, pessimistic locking is enforced, and you access the directory as a table using the `adCmdTableDirect` parameter.

After this initial setup, the recordset now contains a directory listing with rows that are comprised of all properties presented in Table 13.1. To distinguish files from folders, a check is implemented in line 24 using the RESOURCE_ISCOLLECTION property. And in contrast to earlier examples, RESOURCE_DISPLAYNAME is used to present the resource.

Downloading Files

Now that you know which files are available, you might want to download one of them. This is no hard task, as shown in Listing 13.6. File handling using the `FileSystemObject` is even harder!

LISTING 13.6 Downloading a File from a Web Site

```
 1: Sub Download(strURL As String, strFilePath As String)
 2:     Dim rec As ADODB.Record
 3:     Dim stm As ADODB.Stream
 4:
 5:     Set rec = New ADODB.Record
 6:     rec.Open strURL, , adModeRead
 7:     Set stm = rec.Fields(adDefaultStream).Value
 8:
 9:     stm.Type = adTypeBinary
10:     stm.SaveToFile strFilePath, adSaveCreateOverWrite
11: End Sub
```

ANALYSIS The `Download` method takes two parameters: a URL to the file you want to download (for example `http://192.168.1.105/WebDav/myfile.txt`) and a path to where you want to locally store the downloaded file (ie `c:\myfile.txt`). The URL you pass is used on line 6 to establish a connection to the file on the server:

```
rec.Open strURL, , adModeRead
```

This time, only `Source` is specified, and `ActiveConnection` is omitted (the URL already fully qualifies the resource you want to access).

To be on the safe side with permissions, I tell the provider which connection mode I need for the file: read mode (`adModeRead`). There are some more connection modes available, which are documented for the `Mode` property of the `Record` object.

13

After the file has been opened, you need to access the stream that represents the contents of the file. Because you accessed a file with the `Record` object, its `DEFAULT_DOCUMENT` already points to the default stream. You access the stream as shown in line 7:

```
Set stm = rec.Fields(adDefaultStream).Value
```

You have full access to the stream in read mode—merely transfer it to the local machine's hard disk. To achieve this, you first set the type of the stream to binary and then call `SaveToFile`, which takes the following parameters:

```
Stream.SaveToFile FileName, SaveOptions
```

The `Filename` parameter is pretty obvious, and `SaveOptions` can be either `adSaveCreateNotExist` to download the file only when the destination does not exist, or `adSaveCreateOverwrite` when you want to overwrite any existing local file.

Downloading a file with ADO `Record` and `Stream` objects is easy; however, keep in mind that you need proper access permissions and that to be able to download script files in source code, you need Script access permissions.

Uploading Files

To complete the feature set of DAV, you can also upload files to a Web server. Again, it can be achieved with `Record` and `Stream` objects using the IPP, as shown in Listing 13.7.

LISTING 13.7 Uploading a File to a Web Server

```
 1: Sub Upload(strURL As String, strFilePath As String)
 2:     Dim rec As ADODB.Record, stm As ADODB.Stream
 3:
 4:     Set rec = New ADODB.Record
 5:     Set stm = New ADODB.Stream
 6:
 7:     ' create the file if it doesn't exist
 8:     rec.Mode = adModeReadWrite
 9:     rec.Open strURL, , , adCreateNonCollection Or adCreateOverwrite
10:     ' it must be open, otherwise an error occurs
11:     If (adStateOpen = rec.State) Then
12:         rec.Close
13:     End If
14:
15:     stm.Type = adTypeBinary
16:     stm.Open "URL=" & strURL, adModeWrite Or adModeShareDenyWrite
17:
18:     ' upload from the local file to the stream
19:     stm.LoadFromFile strFilePath
20:     stm.Flush
21: End Sub
```

The Upload function takes a URL for the destination location and a path to a local file. Both the Stream and Record objects are initialized (lines 4 and 5). The Record object's Mode is set to adModeReadWrite to allow for uploading. Then the destination URL is opened with the record creation options of adCreateNonCollection and adCreateOverwrite, which tell the Web server to create a simple file that can overwrite already existing ones.

After the Record object creates the file, it is closed again (lines 11–13), because the Stream object takes over in line 16. It opens the file for read mode and denies all other processes write mode. You upload the file to the server using LoadFromFile, passing it the local filename as parameter. Flush is used only to clear the buffers immediately.

To show you that there's always at least a second way to solve a problem, Listing 13.8 shows how to implement uploading using a slightly different approach.

LISTING 13.8   Uploading via the Default Stream

```
 1: Sub Upload2(strURL As String, strFilePath As String)
 2:     Dim rec As ADODB.Record, stm As ADODB.Stream
 3:
 4:     Set rec = New ADODB.Record
 5:
 6:     ' create the file if it doesn't exist
 7:     rec.Mode = adModeReadWrite
 8:     rec.Open strURL, , , adCreateNonCollection Or adCreateOverwrite
 9:
10:     Set stm = rec.Fields(adDefaultStream).Value
11:     stm.Type = adTypeBinary
12:
13:     ' upload from the local file to the stream
14:     stm.LoadFromFile strFilePath
15:     stm.Flush
16:     rec.Close
17: End Sub
```

ANALYSIS   This code doesn't differ too much; however, the Record object isn't closed but its default stream is attached to the Stream object (line 10). With this link, the file can be uploaded immediately. No need to close the Record object first.

With the examples presented for the IPP, you can build your own scripts to maintain an entire Web site. Applications range from listing directories to even a content replication program. Knowledge about these technologies definitely comes in handy when maintaining your Web site.

13

Managing Exchange's Web store

To prove the versatility of Record and Stream objects, you can also access Exchange 2000's databases, the Web stores. A Web store is an object-oriented database that makes its items available through the WebDAV protocol, the one you have already used to access files on Web servers. A further similarity is that the items are organized in a hierarchy of folders, and each item can have properties.

 Note

> You need a functioning Exchange 2000 server and some knowledge of how to administer it to follow the examples presented here. Preparation could take a few hours if you are building a server from scratch.

To show the real-world use, I picked two folders that you might be interested in: mailboxes and public folders (public folders are similar to Internet newsgroups). Therefore, the organization of this section is as follows:

- The Web Store
- Accessing Mailboxes
- Working with Public Folders

The Web Store

The introduction mentioned that the Web store is an object-oriented database. It is managed with folders and items, and acts as a single repository for email, documents, and other items. In contrast to a database server, it is semistructured and allows you to add new schemas. Another difference is that you don't have relationships between items, such as one-to-many.

Before diving into actually accessing items in the Web store, let's look at two more topics:

- Accessing the Web Store
- Searching the Web Store

Accessing the Web Store

One secret is already out—you can use WebDAV to access a Web store. However, this is not the only protocol you can use to get to items in the Web store. The following protocols are also available:

- Microsoft Exchange OLE DB Provider
- Exchange Installable File System (ExIFS)

- Internet Explorer 5.0 XML Components
- IMAP4
- POP3
- MAPI

As you might guess, the one that you are going to use throughout the rest of this chapter is the Exchange OLE DB provider.

Note

The OLE DB provider can be used on the local host only, which means on the Exchange server machine on which the Web store resides.

Items in a Web store are accessed exactly the same way as items in a WebDAV store—using a URL. Instead of prefixing the URL with http://, you use file://, which automatically invokes the Exchange OLE DB provider, ExOleDb. The root URL to a Web store is

```
file://./backofficestorage/domain.tld/
```

where `domain.tld` is replaced with the domain name you are using. For example, a local domain named dev run under alfasierrapapa.com would be addressed with

```
file://./backofficestorage/dev.alfasierrapapa.com/
```

From that point, you can navigate the hierarchy, because there are mailboxes and public folders. To see how the hierarchy looks, you can use Windows Explorer to access the Web store with ExIFS (see Figure 13.5). The Web store is automatically mounted as drive M: on the Exchange 2000 server machine.

Take a look at the mailbox I opened in Figure 13.5. What would be the URL for it? No problem:

```
file://./backofficestorage/dev.alfasierrapapa.com/MBX/christophw
```

Navigating the Web store isn't difficult, because you are already familiar with URLs. However, because Web stores also act as databases, you need to learn one more thing: how to query the Web store.

Searching the Web Store

Hierarchical navigation does not solve all problems. For example, you might want to search for all messages received on a certain date in all folders of a mailbox. Manually traversing all possible folders isn't the ideal solution to this problem—searching the Web store is.

13

FIGURE 13.5

Accessing the Web store with Windows Explorer.

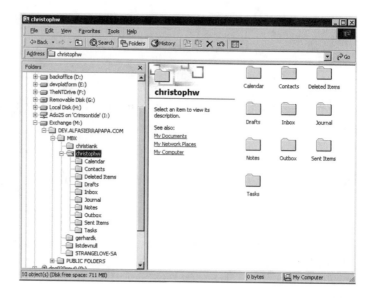

The good news is that searching the Web store uses the familiar SELECT * syntax, and there are only a few modifications you need to be aware of. Basically, a DAV:sql statement looks like this:

```
SELECT * | select-list
FROM SCOPE( resource-list)
[WHERE search-condition]
[order-by-clause]
```

For example, to search the Inbox for all messages, you use a statement like this one:

```
SELECT "dav:href", "dav:displayname" FROM
"file://./backofficestorage/dev.alfasierrapapa.com/MBX/christophw/Inbox"
WHERE "DAV:isfolder" = False
```

This statement returns the URL and display name for all messages in my Inbox that are not folders. Notice that I left out the SCOPE statement. Leaving out the SCOPE statement defaults the search to shallow traversal, limiting it to the current folder and ignoring subfolders. If you want a deep traversal, you could write

```
SELECT "dav:href", "dav:displayname" FROM
SCOPE('deep traversal of
"file://./backofficestorage/dev.alfasierrapapa.com/MBX/christophw/Inbox"')
WHERE "DAV:isfolder" = False
```

This returns all messages in the Inbox and all subfolders of the Inbox.

Where can you learn more about the column names you can use? Because today we are dealing with messages, you need only basic knowledge about the DAV:, `urn:schemas:mailheader:`, and `urn:schemas:httpmail:` namespaces. You can find all field definitions for these namespaces in the Exchange 2000 SDK section Reference, Web store, Web store schema, or Properties by namespace.

However, though we can't discuss each field contained in every namespace, you can use the query feature immediately: I will provide the field names for you.

Accessing Mailboxes

Now that you are familiar with the principles of the Web store and how you can access it, let's put the theory to work by working with mailboxes.

You are going to perform the following tasks with a user's mailbox:

- Listing subfolders
- Viewing the Inbox
- Deleting a message

Listing Subfolders

When you refer to Figure 13.5, you can see that a user's mailbox consists of multiple subfolders—these are also the folders you have in the Outlook client. Therefore, the first task to complete is to list all the folders for a given mailbox, which is shown in Listing 13.9. In order to be able to run the code, you must be logged on to the Exchange 2000 server as the owner of the mailbox (the value of `strMailbox`).

 Note | All examples presented for the Exchange Web store can be run only on the Exchange server.

LISTING 13.9 Listing a Mailbox's Subfolders

```
 1: Option Explicit
 2:
 3: Sub ListFolders4Mailbox(strDomain As String, strMailbox As String)
 4:     Dim Rec As ADODB.Record, Rs As ADODB.Recordset
 5:     Dim strURL As String, strQuery As String, nRow As Integer
 6:
 7:     Worksheets(1).Activate
 8:     Cells.Clear
 9:
10:     Set Rec = New ADODB.Record
11:     Set Rs = New ADODB.Recordset
12:
```

13

continues

LISTING 13.9 Continued

```
13:         'this URL is to a user's mailbox
14:         strURL = "file://./backofficestorage/" & strDomain & "/MBX/" & _
15:           strMailbox
16:         Rec.Open strURL
17:
18:         strQuery = "select "
19:         strQuery = strQuery & " ""urn:schemas:mailheader:content-class"" "
20:         strQuery = strQuery & ", ""DAV:href"" "
21:         strQuery = strQuery & ", ""DAV:displayname"" "
22:         strQuery = strQuery & ", ""DAV:isfolder"" "
23:         strQuery = strQuery & " from scope ('shallow traversal of "
24:         strQuery = strQuery & Chr(34) & strURL & Chr(34) & "')"
25:         strQuery = strQuery & " WHERE ""DAV:isfolder"" = TRUE"
26:         strQuery = strQuery & " ORDER BY ""DAV:displayname"" "
27:
28:         Rs.Open strQuery, Rec.ActiveConnection
29:
30:         While Not Rs.EOF
31:             nRow = nRow + 1
32:             Cells(nRow, 1) = Rs.Fields("DAV:displayname").Value
33:             Rs.MoveNext
34:         Wend
35:
36:         Rs.Close
37:         Rec.Close
38: End Sub
```

ANALYSIS The input parameters for this method are the Exchange domain and the user-name. Both parameters are used to build the Webstore URL in lines 14 and 15. Then the mailbox is opened, given that you are currently logged in as the user whose mailbox you are accessing. Notice that I don't need to specify the provider, because the file schema is reserved for the Exchange OLE DB provider.

The next step is to build a query that returns all subfolders at the current level. To achieve this, you create a SELECT statement for shallow traversal of the user's mailbox and add a WHERE statement for DAV:isfolder. The fields you return are either urn: or DAV:.

In line 28, I open the recordset using the query string and the connection of the Record object (which point to the mailbox). Upon successful retrieval, the contents of the record-set are written to the cells of the Excel sheet. A sample output is shown in Figure 13.6.

There are quite a lot of folders, such as Calendar, Contacts, and so forth. The most important one, however, will always be the user's Inbox, because it contains all the incoming messages.

FIGURE 13.6

Listing the folders in a user's mailbox.

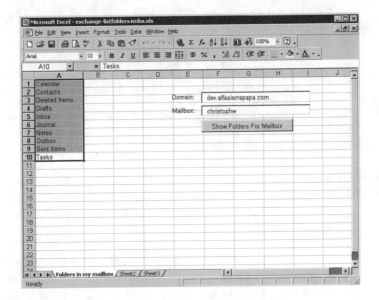

Viewing the Inbox

The first question you need to answer is how the URL must look to access a user's Inbox—you are right, simply append the string Inbox to the URL of the user's mailbox. To start, you retrieve the properties of the Inbox in the first step (Listing 13.10).

LISTING 13.10 Viewing Properties for a User's Inbox

```
1: Option Explicit
2:
3: Sub GetInboxProperties()
4:     Dim cn As ADODB.Connection
5:     Dim rs As ADODB.Recordset
6:     Dim rec As ADODB.Record
7:     Dim fld As ADODB.Field, strDebugString As String
8:
9:     Set cn = New ADODB.Connection
10:    cn.Provider = "ExOleDb.DataSource"
11:    cn.Open "file://./backofficestorage/dev.alfasierrapapa.com/MBX/
➥christophw"
12:
13:    Set rec = New ADODB.Record
14:    rec.Open "Inbox", cn
15:
16:    For Each fld In rec.Fields
17:        strDebugString = fld.Name & "="
```

continues

13

LISTING 13.10   Continued

```
18:          If IsNull(fld.Value) Then
19:              strDebugString = strDebugString & "Null"
20:          Else
21:              strDebugString = strDebugString & fld.Value
22:          End If
23:          Debug.Print strDebugString
24:      Next
25: End Sub
```

ANALYSIS   In this listing, I explicitly name the provider to be used for the connection in line 10: `ExOleDb.DataSource`. The next line then simply opens the connection to the mailbox, which is hard-coded to mine—you need to change this line to make it work for your account.

The `Record` object is created in line 13 and opened and attached to the Inbox in line 14. From this point, it is again a simple enumeration of the `Fields` collection; however, it includes handling for `Null` values that otherwise would cause problems in string concatenation.

The promise of this section was to view the messages in a user's Inbox. This is what Listing 13.11 does—it opens the Inbox for a user that is specified via a parameter, and it runs a `SELECT` statement to retrieve only messages that meet certain criteria.

LISTING 13.11   Viewing Messages in the Inbox

```
 1: Sub ShowMyInbox(strDomain As String, strUsername As String)
 2:     Dim rec As ADODB.Record, Rs As ADODB.Recordset, fld As ADODB.Field
 3:     Dim strURL As String, nRow As Integer, nCol As Integer
 4:
 5:     Set rec = New ADODB.Record
 6:     Set Rs = New ADODB.Recordset
 7:
 8:     'this URL is to a user's mailbox
 9:     strURL = "file://./backofficestorage/" & strDomain & "/MBX/" & _
10:         strUsername & "/inbox"
11:     rec.Open strURL
12:
13:     Dim strView As String
14:     strView = "select " _
15:         & "   ""DAV:href""" _
16:         & ", ""urn:schemas:mailheader:content-class""" _
17:         & ", ""urn:schemas:httpmail:datereceived""" _
18:         & ", ""DAV:isfolder""" _
19:         & ", ""DAV:getcontentlength""" _
20:         & ", ""urn:schemas:httpmail:from""" _
```

```
21:         & ", ""urn:schemas:httpmail:subject""" _
22:         & ", ""urn:schemas:mailheader:importance""" _
23:         & ", ""urn:schemas:httpmail:hasattachment""" _
24:         & ", ""urn:schemas:httpmail:read""" _
25:         & " from scope ('shallow traversal of """ _
26:         & strURL & """') " _
27:         & " WHERE ""DAV:isfolder"" = false AND ""DAV:ishidden"" = false" _
28:         & " ORDER BY ""urn:schemas:httpmail:datereceived"" DESC"
29:
30:     Rs.Open strView, rec.ActiveConnection
31:
32:     If Rs.RecordCount = 0 Then
33:         MsgBox "There are no items in your inbox"
34:     Else
35:       Rs.MoveFirst
36:       Worksheets(2).Activate
37:       Cells.Clear
38:       nRow = nRow + 1
39:       For Each fld In Rs.Fields
40:         nCol = nCol + 1
41:         Cells(nRow, nCol) = fld.Name
42:       Next
43:
44:       While Not Rs.EOF
45:         nCol = 0
46:         nRow = nRow + 1
47:         For Each fld In Rs.Fields
48:             nCol = nCol + 1
49:             Cells(nRow, nCol) = fld.Value
50:         Next
51:         Rs.MoveNext
52:       Wend
53:     End If
54: End Sub
```

ANALYSIS In contrast to the previous listing, I pass the domain name and username to the method so it isn't locked to my mailbox. However, now I have to build the URL—see lines 9 and 10. Take a closer look at the SELECT statement in lines 14–28, because it contains a lot of urn:s and DAV:s. Messages are sorted descending by date received, and folders and hidden messages are not retrieved. The columns that are retrieved are common for email messages: subject, sender, importance, and so forth.

The query statement is executed against the Web store when you open the recordset in line 30. Because it could be possible that you have no mail, the first check is for RecordCount. If no mail exists, a message box is displayed. Otherwise, the column names are written to the sheet (lines 38–42) followed by all mail (lines 44–52).

13

Though the presentation is not neat, it shows some of the power of queries that can be executed against the Web store. When retrieving results from the Web store, make sure that you include DAV:href, because you need it if you want to deal with an item later, such as when you want to delete it.

Deleting a Message

A common fate of mail messages is that you delete them. Instead of pressing the Delete key, you can do it programmatically using the Record object. All you need is the URL to the message, for example:

```
file://./backofficestorage/dev.alfasierrapapa.com/MBX/christophw/
➥Inbox/Check this out.EML
```

All messages have an .EML extension, and their names are derived from the message's subject. In order to delete it, you pass this URL to the DeleteMessage method presented in Listing 13.12.

LISTING 13.12   Deleting a Message Using DAV:href

```
1: Sub DeleteMessage(strURL As String)
2:     Dim rec As ADODB.Record
3:     Set rec = CreateObject("ADODB.Record")
4:
5:     rec.Open strURL
6:     rec.DeleteRecord
7:     Set rec = Nothing
8: End Sub
```

 It is really simple—just create a Record object, attach it to the message's URL, and then call DeleteRecord. It was never easier to recycle electrons.

Working with Public Folders

Mailboxes are the private storage area of a single user; however, sometimes multiple users need to share the same data. This is where Exchange's public folders come into the picture, which enable you to do that—share data such as messages and files between users.

Because listing messages in a public folder is no different from viewing mail in the Inbox, I'm going to show you different approaches this time:

- Creating public folders
- Copying from folder to folder

Creating Public Folders

Before someone can use a public folder, you have to create it. You can perform this task manually, or you can achieve it programmatically. Both scenarios are shown, starting with the manual creation of a public folder.

To Do: Manually creating a public folder

Follow these steps to create a new public folder named ADO Forums:

1. Open Exchange Management and go to Folders, Public Folders. Select New, Public Folder from the context menu (see Figure 13.7).

FIGURE 13.7

Creating a new public folder in Exchange Management.

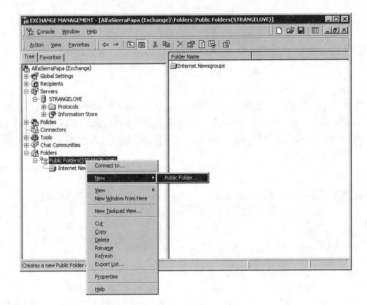

2. The Properties dialog box for the new public folder opens. Enter the name ADO Forums and a description (see Figure 13.8).

▼ 3. Click OK to apply your changes and create the public folder.

13

FIGURE 13.8

Naming the new public folder in the Properties dialog box.

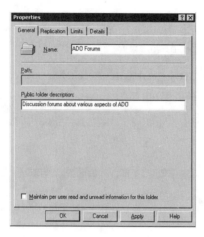

The public folder is now available to all users through Outlook. Though the process of manually creating public folders isn't exactly painful, it can come in handy to create new folders automatically via script. Listing 13.13 shows how to create an entire public folder hierarchy.

LISTING 13.13 Creating a Public Folder Hierarchy for ADO Lists

```
 1: Option Explicit
 2:
 3: Const cstrDomain = "dev.alfasierrapapa.com"
 4:
 5: Sub CreatePublicFolders()
 6:     Dim recFolder As New ADODB.Record, i As Integer
 7:     Dim strURL As String, strFolderURL As String, varFolders As Variant
 8:
 9:     varFolders = Array("OLAP", "ADO-X", "ADO Multidimensional", "RDS", _
10:         "Internet Publishing")
11:
12:     ' create a URL for the basic public folder and open it
13:     strURL = "file://./backofficestorage/" & cstrDomain & _
14:         "/Public Folders/ADO Lists/"
15:     recFolder.Open strURL, , adModeReadWrite, adCreateCollection
16:     recFolder.Fields("urn:mailheader:content-class").Value = _
17:         "urn:content-classes:folder"
18:     recFolder.Fields.Update
19:     recFolder.Close
20:
21:     For i = 0 To UBound(varFolders)
22:         strFolderURL = strURL & varFolders(i)
```

```
23:        recFolder.Open strFolderURL, , adModeReadWrite, adCreateCollection
24:        recFolder.Fields("urn:mailheader:content-class").Value = _
25:            "urn:content-classes:folder"
26:        recFolder.Fields.Update
27:        recFolder.Close
28:    Next
29: End Sub
```

ANALYSIS The Exchange domain is stored in a constant (line 3), which is used in the
CreatePublicFolders method to build the URLs. This method has a variable
varFolders (line 9) to hold an array of public folders to be created below the root folder
ADO Lists.

The first public folder created is the top-level ADO Lists public folder. The URL is com-
posed in line 13, and the folder is created in line 15:

```
recFolder.Open strURL, , adModeReadWrite, adCreateCollection
```

The Record object is opened for read and write operations, and it is a collection record,
because it holds messages and other folders. To define what content is stored in this public folder, the field urn:mailheader:content-class is set to the content class folder,
which identifies a message folder. Line 18 updates the field's value within Exchange, and
then the newly created folder is closed.

The child folders for ADO Lists are created in the For loop in lines 21–28. It is the same
code as for the creation of the top-level folder—the only difference is the path, of course.

The folders are created, and are ready to be used immediately. You can check this by
connecting to the folder hierarchy in Outlook 2000 (see Figure 13.9).

FIGURE 13.9

*Verifying the new pub-
lic folder hierarchy in
Outlook 2000.*

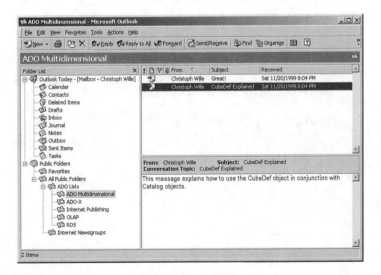

13

In addition to that, you can go back to Exchange Management and view the folder hierarchy there—with the additional benefit of being able to administer folder security and replication settings (see Figure 13.10).

FIGURE 13.10

Public folder management in Exchange 2000's management console.

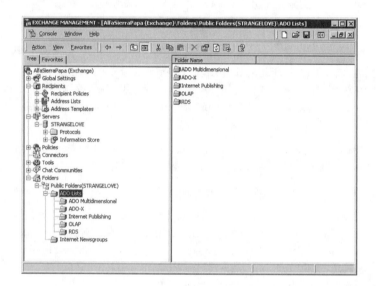

The example presented in the preceding listing is simple because the code creates folders that are predetermined. However, you can also create scripts that take folder names as input parameters, and you also can modify more properties when you access folders using Collaboration Data Objects (CDO).

CDO's capabilities are vast, and it fills many books by itself, some of which are even thicker than this one; therefore, I can't elaborate here. Anyway, you can't do Exchange development without CDO.

When you refer to Figure 13.9, you can see that I entered messages into the ADO Multidimensional folder. What if you want to mirror these messages in the OLAP folder? Then you need to copy the contents from one folder to the other.

Copying from Folder to Folder

It happens more than once that you want to copy records from one location to another, and this also holds true for messages or entire folders. The entire folder approach is demonstrated in Listing 13.14.

LISTING 13.14 Copying Between Folders

```
 1: Option Explicit
 2:
 3: Const cstrDomain = "dev.alfasierrapapa.com"
 4:
 5: Sub CopyFolderItems()
 6:     Dim rec As ADODB.Record, strURL As String
 7:     Dim strSourcePath As String, strDestinationPath As String
 8:
 9:     strSourcePath = "public folders/ADO Lists/ADO Multidimensional"
10:     strDestinationPath = "public folders/ADO Lists/OLAP"
11:
12:     Set rec = New ADODB.Record
13:     strURL = "file://./backofficestorage/" & cstrDomain & "/" & _
14:         strSourcePath
15:     rec.Open strURL
16:     rec.CopyRecord , "file://./backofficestorage/" & cstrDomain & "/" & _
17:         strDestinationPath, , , adCopyOverWrite
18:     rec.Close
19: End Sub
```

ANALYSIS To copy a record, you need a source and a destination (lines 9 and 10). With the source URL, you open the `Record` object, as done in line 15. The command to copy a record is `CopyRecord`, and it takes the following command-line parameters:

```
Record.CopyRecord Source, Destination, UserName, Password, Options, Async
```

Because you have already opened the Record, you can omit the `Source` parameter. The `Destination` parameter can be a connection or URL, which is used in this example. The next two parameters are `Username` and `Password`, which are not used here. To overwrite any existing data, I have set the `Options` parameter to `adCopyOverWrite`. Other `Options` values can be found in the Platform SDK under the topic CopyRecordOptionsEnum. Finally, the `Record` object is closed.

The `CopyRecord` command is, of course, not limited to Exchange's Webstore—you also can copy files on a Web server.

13

Summary

Today, you did not work with relational databases, but you still accessed data stores: WebDAV-enabled directories and Exchange's Web stores.

After a short introduction to semistructured data access, you learned how to enumerate files on a Web server, download files, and upload files. In addition to these ADO tasks, you created WebDAV folders and read about security implications—and I recommend that you learn more about these security implications before deploying WebDAV on a large scale.

The second semistructured data store you examined was the Exchange Web store. You learned how to enumerate folders, access a user's inbox and retrieve messages using the `dav:sql` statements. After deleting messages, you switched gears from private message storage to public folders, where I showed you how to perform administrative tasks, such as creating public folders with ADO or copying folder contents.

Q&A

Q **When I perform a large download, my application locks up until the file is entirely retrieved. Is there a way to circumvent this lockup?**

A You can open a record in asynchronous mode. When you initiate downloads, control returns immediately to your application. You can check the status of the download with the `State` property. To learn more, search the Platform SDK for the term RecordOpenOptionsEnum.

Q **Can I use the `Stream` object to display the data that is retrieved?**

A Yes. There is an example in the Platform SDK that shows how to read and display files: the Internet Publishing Scenario.

Workshop

The quiz questions and exercise are provided for your further understanding. See Appendix A, "Answers," for the answers.

Quiz

1. Which provider property do you need to query to obtain information about whether `Record` objects are supported?

2. What permissions do you need to set so users cannot upload script files?

3. Is the following a valid way to bind a resource to a `Record` object?
   ```
   cn.Open "URL=http://localhost/WebDAV/
   rec.Open "yourfile.txt", cn
   ```

4. What is the `DAV:` namespace equivalent for CHAPTERED_CHILDREN?

5. What is the most severe limitation of the Exchange OLE DB provider?

6. When searching the Web store, why would you limit the `dav:sql` statement to deep traversal?

7. What `CreateOption` do you need to supply to `Record.Open` when creating a new public folder?

Exercise

Create a program that recursively dumps all files and folders of a Web site branch. Write it in a way so it could be easily used to traverse a public folder structure of an Exchange Web store.

DAY 14

Managing Your Database with ADOX

You want to do more than just store and retrieve data from a database. You also want to manage your database, including its tables, views, procedures, and access permissions for users and groups. These management tasks are made easier by the ADO Extension for Data Definition Language and Security, which because of its object-oriented nature, also offers the advantage of being database-system neutral.

Today, you will learn how to perform the following tasks:

- Browsing a database's schema using ADO's OpenSchema method
- Opening and creating catalogs
- Creating tables, adding columns, creating indexes and relationships
- Working with views and procedures
- Managing database security

Browsing a Database's Structure with ADO

Sometimes data isn't the only thing you need from the database. To work efficiently, you also need more information about the schema (definition) of tables, procedures, and other objects that comprise a database. This information can help you with situations ranging from creating simple optimizations for a Seek statement to working with sophisticated applications that need to adapt to different databases.

With ADO, you have two options to retrieve schema information from databases and their objects:

- Using OpenSchema
- Using ADOX

Using OpenSchema

A method to browse the schema of a database is to use the OpenSchema method that has been part of ADO for a long time now. It allows you to browse schema definitions ranging from databases to table privileges. However, OpenSchema has one severe limitation: It only allows you to browse a schema; it does not allow you to change it.

I won't go into every detail of OpenSchema; however, I will give you an example. See Listing 14.1 on how to list all tables in a database.

LISTING 14.1   Retrieving Tables from a Database

```
 1: Public Sub OpenTableSchema()
 2:     Dim cn As New ADODB.Connection
 3:     Dim rsSchema As ADODB.Recordset
 4:
 5:     cn.Open "Provider=sqloledb;Data Source=strangelove;
➥Initial Catalog=Northwind;User Id=sa;Password=; "
 6:     Set rsSchema = cn.OpenSchema(adSchemaTables)
 7:
 8:     While Not rsSchema.EOF
 9:         Debug.Print "Table name: " & rsSchema("TABLE_NAME") & " of type "
➥& rsSchema("TABLE_TYPE")
10:         rsSchema.MoveNext
11:     Wend
12:
13:     rsSchema.Close
14:     cn.Close
15: End Sub
```

ANALYSIS A connection to the tried-and-true Northwind database on SQL Server is established in line 5. Right after opening the connection, the script calls OpenSchema with the constant adSchemaTables, which returns a Recordset that contains information about all tables in the Northwind database. The fields of the returned schema Recordset are described in Table 14.1.

TABLE 14.1   The TABLES Rowset's Columns

Column name	Description
TABLE_CATALOG	The catalog the table resides in. This is Null if the provider does not support catalogs.
TABLE_SCHEMA	The unqualified schema name. This is Null if the provider does not support schemas.
TABLE_NAME	The name of the table, which cannot be Null.
TABLE_TYPE	The type of table. The following provider-specific values are possible: ALIAS, TABLE, SYNONYM, SYSTEM TABLE, VIEW, GLOBAL TEMPORARY, LOCAL TEMPORARY, SYSTEM VIEW.
TABLE_GUID	The GUID (globally unique identifier) that identifies the table.
DESCRIPTION	A description about the table.
TABLE_PROPID	The property ID of the table. This is Null, if not supported by the provider.
DATE_CREATED	Date when the table was created.
DATE_MODIFIED	Date when the table was last modified.

From the table information that is returned, the script only writes the table's name and its type to the Immediate Window. After all tables are listed, the connection and the Recordset are closed.

Although OpenSchema is a powerful and straightforward means of retrieving schema information from within standard ADO, the fact that it does not permit modification of the schema definition weighs in heavily. This is where ADOX (ADO Extensions for DDL and Security) comes in the picture. Besides retrieving schema information, ADOX also allows you to modify existing objects or create entirely new ones.

Using ADOX

The Microsoft ADO Extensions for Data Definition Language (DDL) and Security are—as the name implies—extensions of the standard ADO object model. ADOX comes with objects for manipulating schemas and security. It gives you access to various data sources because of its object-oriented approach.

14

Because it is an extension, ADOX is not an integral part of ADO, but a companion library that needs a separate type library to work correctly—the Microsoft ADO Extension 2.5 for DDL and Security type library. This library exposes the object model shown in Figure 14.1.

FIGURE **14.1**

The ADOX object model allows you to manage tables, views, procedures, and security.

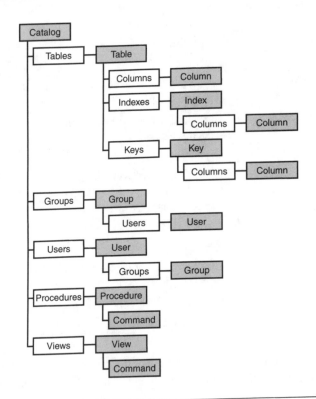

> **Note**
>
> If you are programming ASP pages, then you can import the definitions for the ADOX constants in each page (or global.asa) using the following statement:
>
> ```
> <!--METADATA NAME="Microsoft ADO Ext. 2.5 for DDL and Security"
> ➥TYPE="TypeLib" UUID="{00000600-0000-0010-8000-00AA006D2EA4}"-->
> ```

Although not shown in this diagram, each table, index, and column object has an additional Properties collection. With the objects provided by ADOX, you can manage tables, views, and procedures, and administer the security of all these objects using groups and users.

Before starting with the top-level object, the `Catalog`, I want to point out some possible limitations of ADOX. First, only OLE DB providers are supported as data sources, not ODBC drivers. This won't be a severe limitation, however. The second limitation can be more troublesome: Only the Jet OLE DB provider supports the entire ADOX functionality. Other providers might implement only parts of ADOX. Therefore, to harness the full power of ADOX, this lesson works with Jet databases. If you want to use other providers, please check their documentation to learn which level of support for ADOX is included in the provider you want to use.

Catalog Basics

When working with ADOX, the root object is the `Catalog` object. It allows you to access and maintain tables, views, procedures, and security objects. There are two ways to obtain a `Catalog` object:

- Opening a catalog
- Creating a new catalog

Opening a Catalog

The most-often-used approach is to open an already existing catalog—this can be an Access database, a SQL Server database, or a database whose provider supports the necessary interfaces. While I am on the subject of interfaces, remember that whenever you use ADOX objects, you need to reference the Microsoft ADO Extension 2.5 for DDL and Security type library (see Figure 14.2).

FIGURE 14.2

Before typing in the code, make sure that you have made a reference to the ADO Extension 2.5 for DDL and Security type library.

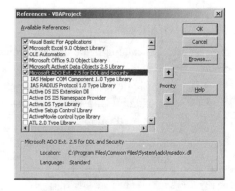

14

To open a catalog, you can either use a `Connection` object or a simple connection string. Both methods are shown in Listing 14.2.

LISTING 14.2   Connecting to a Catalog Using Various Methods

```
 1: Sub ConnectToCatalog()
 2:     Dim cn As ADODB.Connection
 3:     Dim cat As ADOX.Catalog
 4:
 5:     Set cn = New ADODB.Connection
 6:     Set cat = New ADOX.Catalog
 7:
 8:     ' this assumes that you copied the Northwind db to c:\
 9:     cn.Open "Provider=Microsoft.Jet.OLEDB.4.0;Data Source=c:\Northwind.mdb"
10:     Set cat.ActiveConnection = cn
11:
12:     ' this time, we don't need the connection object
13:     cat.ActiveConnection = "provider=sqloledb.1;user id=sa;password=;
➥initial catalog=northwind;data source=strangelove"
14:     Set cat = Nothing
15: End Sub
```

ANALYSIS   The variable cat of type ADOX.Catalog is declared in line 3 and initialized on line 6. For the connection to the Access Northwind database, you first open a Connection object (line 9), which you assign to the ActiveConnection property in the following line. Notice that you have to use Set because you are assigning an object variable.

The second connection attempt is for the SQL Server Northwind database. This time, you pass a connection string to the ActiveConnection property of the Catalog object. As you can see, it takes only one line, and you don't have to close the connection to the Access Northwind database first.

Creating a New Catalog

Although I said that opening an existing catalog is the most common scenario, it is sometimes necessary to create a new catalog—when you want to backup data from other databases, for example. All it takes is a single-line Create statement to create an Access database as shown in Listing 14.3. An example of a valid parameter you can pass to the CreateJetCatalog method would be "c:\mydb.mdb".

LISTING 14.3   Creating a New Access Database

```
1: Sub CreateJetCatalog(ByVal strFilename As String)
2:     Dim cat As New ADOX.Catalog
3:     cat.Create "Provider=Microsoft.Jet.OLEDB.4.0;Data Source=" & strFilename
4: End Sub
```

ANALYSIS After declaring and initializing the Catalog variable, the only action necessary to create a new Access database is to call the `Catalog.Create` function with a connection string that specifies the filename of the new database in the `Data Source` property. This single line creates an entirely new database.

Wouldn't it be great if you could create SQL Server databases the same way? It would be. However, it doesn't work because the SQLOLEDB provider does not have full ADOX support, and creating catalogs is one of the features that is not available.

Managing Tables

You are connected to your catalog, and now you want to manage your tables. In contrast to `OpenSchema`, you cannot only enumerate information with ADOX, you can also make modifications to tables or create entirely new ones. The most common tasks are described in the following sections:

- Querying table definitions
- Creating tables
- Modifying existing tables

Querying Table Definitions

When you want to perform `Filter` or `Seek` operations on Recordsets, you need to know what key columns are available. To get this information, ADOX sports the `Table` object with its children—columns, indexes, and keys. Of course, the use of this information is not limited to search scenarios only. You can create a nifty online tool to examine table structures, and it is also a good starting point for making modifications.

Listing 14.4 shows you how to view table information such as table properties, column definition, and index and key setup. Please note that you need to add a fourth worksheet to your Excel workbook in order to run the following code.

LISTING 14.4 Viewing a Table's Definition

```
1: Option Explicit
2:
3: Const cstrJetsource = "Provider=Microsoft.Jet.OLEDB.4.0;
➥Data Source=c:\Northwind.mdb"
4:
5: Sub DumpTableProperties()
6:     Dim cn As ADODB.Connection
```

continues

14

LISTING 14.4   continued

```
 7:      Dim cat As ADOX.Catalog, tbl As ADOX.Table
 8:
 9:      Set cn = New ADODB.Connection
10:      Set cat = New ADOX.Catalog
11:      cn.ConnectionString = cstrJetsource
12:      cn.Open
13:      Set cat.ActiveConnection = cn
14:
15:      Dim col As ADOX.Column, objKey As ADOX.key
16:      Dim objProp As ADOX.Property, objIndex As ADOX.index
17:      Dim strIndex As String, nRow As Integer
18:
19:      Set tbl = cat.Tables("Suppliers")
20:
21:      Worksheets(1).Activate
22:      Cells.Clear
23:      nRow = 0
24:      For Each objProp In tbl.Properties
25:          nRow = nRow + 1
26:          Cells(nRow, 1) = objProp.Name
27:          Cells(nRow, 2) = objProp.Value
28:      Next
29:
30:      Worksheets(2).Activate
31:      Cells.Clear
32:      nRow = 0
33:      For Each col In tbl.Columns
34:          nRow = nRow + 1
35:          Cells(nRow, 1) = col.Name
36:          Cells(nRow, 2) = col.Type
37:          Cells(nRow, 3) = col.DefinedSize
38:          Cells(nRow, 4) = col.NumericScale
39:          Cells(nRow, 5) = col.Precision
40:      Next
41:
42:      Worksheets(3).Activate
43:      Cells.Clear
44:      nRow = 0
45:      For Each objIndex In tbl.Indexes
46:          nRow = nRow + 1
47:          Cells(nRow, 1) = objIndex.Name
48:          strIndex = ""
49:          For Each col In objIndex.Columns
50:              strIndex = strIndex & col.Name & " "
51:          Next
52:          Cells(nRow, 2) = strIndex
53:      Next
54:
```

```
55:        Worksheets(4).Activate
56:        Cells.Clear
57:        nRow = 0
58:        For Each objKey In tbl.Keys
59:            nRow = nRow + 1
60:            Cells(nRow, 1) = objKey.Name
61:            Cells(nRow, 2) = objKey.RelatedTable
62:            strIndex = ""
63:            For Each col In objKey.Columns
64:                strIndex = strIndex & col.Name & " "
65:            Next
66:            Cells(nRow, 3) = strIndex
67:        Next
68: End Sub
```

ANALYSIS   The Catalog is opened using a `Connection` object (line 13), and the table to be shown is selected in line 19, which is the Suppliers table. It is retrieved from the `Tables` collection and assigned to a local `Table` variable.

The table's properties (shown in lines 21–28), are available in the `Properties` collection. Then, the script takes on the columns (lines 30–40). The script iterates over all columns in the `Columns` collection of the table and displays the following column properties: `Name`, `Type`, `DefinedSize`, `NumericScale`, and `Precision`. The latter two are significant for numeric data only; however, the first three are defined for all columns in a table.

Now you move on to the indexes of the table. The index information is dumped in lines 42–53. Because an index can span more than one column, you create a string representing the column names (lines 48–51), which is then written to the currently active worksheet.

The final information that is available for a `Table` object is the `Keys` collection. Here you can gather information about primary, foreign, and unique keys. The code segment, in lines 55–67, collects information for a key's name, its related table (which is available only if it is a foreign key), and the columns that make up the key.

Accessing a table's information with ADOX is much easier than using `OpenSchema`, and ADOX lets you create additional tables if you want to.

Creating Tables

The database you created earlier in Listing 14.3 is totally empty. It does not contain any tables you can query. To change this, you will add two tables to the database in the course of the following sections: tUserData and tUserTracking (see Figure 14.3).

14

FIGURE **14.3**

The two tables that are added to the new catalog.

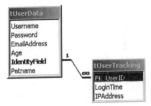

The tUserData table holds user information, and tUserTracking tracks logins, as well as the IP address from which they originated. To make full use of ADOX's capabilities, you have added some primary indexes and keys.

However, let's start from the very beginning by adding the tUserData table to the catalog (see Listing 14.5).

LISTING **14.5**   Creating a Bare-Bones Table with ADOX

```
 1: Sub CreateTable()
 2:     Dim cat As ADOX.Catalog
 3:     Dim tbl As ADOX.Table
 4:
 5:     Set cat = New ADOX.Catalog
 6:     cat.ActiveConnection = "Provider=Microsoft.Jet.OLEDB.4.0;
➥Data Source=c:\new.mdb"
 7:
 8:     Set tbl = New ADOX.Table
 9:     tbl.Name = "tUserData"
10:     cat.Tables.Append tbl
11: End Sub
```

ANALYSIS   Notice that the `ActiveConnection` points to the Data Source c:\new.mdb—this is the filename you chose when creating the new catalog. You have declared one instance of ADOX.Table, which is initialized in line 8 and assigned a name in the next line. The newly created table is then appended to the `Tables` collection of the catalog:

`cat.Tables.Append tbl`

Notice that the table doesn't contain a single column, not to mention indexes or the like. These are added to the new table in these sections:

- Adding columns
- Creating indexes
- Setting up foreign-key relationships

Adding Columns

Although it is perfectly okay to create a table that has no columns, it doesn't make sense to leave it that way. After all, you want to store values in columns of a table. To make this possible, you have to add columns. This process is shown in Listing 14.6.

LISTING **14.6**   Adding Columns to a Table

```
1: Sub AppendColumns()
2:     Dim cat As ADOX.Catalog
3:     Dim tbl As ADOX.Table
4:
5:     Set cat = New ADOX.Catalog
6:     cat.ActiveConnection = "Provider=Microsoft.Jet.OLEDB.4.0;
➥Data Source=c:\new.mdb"
7:     Set tbl = cat.Tables("tUserData")
8:
9:     Dim col As ADOX.Column
10:
11:     Set col = New ADOX.Column
12:     With col
13:         .Name = "Username"
14:         .Type = adVarWChar
15:         .DefinedSize = 64
16:     End With
17:     tbl.Columns.Append col
18:
19:     tbl.Columns.Append "Password", adVarWChar, 12
20:     tbl.Columns.Append "EmailAddress", , 96
21:     tbl.Columns.Append "Age", adInteger, 4
22:
23:     Set col = New ADOX.Column
24:     With col
25:         .Name = "IdentityField"
26:         .Type = adInteger
27:     End With
28:     Set col.ParentCatalog = cat
29:     col.Properties("Autoincrement") = True
30:     tbl.Columns.Append col
31: End Sub
```

ANALYSIS   After various variable declarations, the catalog is connected to the database. In line 7, you retrieve the table that was created in the previous example.

The first column, Username, is added in the script block in lines 11–17. First, you create a new instance of the ADOX.Column object, which is then used in the With block to assign the column name, data type, and its defined size. Because Username is textual data,

14

choose the variable `widechar` data and set the maximum length to 64 characters. After all assignments are complete, the column is appended to the table's `Columns` collection.

Because creating an object every time you create a column can become tedious, there's a shorthand for creating columns and immediately appending them to the `Columns` collection:

```
tbl.Columns.Append Column [, Type] [, DefinedSize]
```

Only the column name is mandatory. You can leave out `Type` (defaults to `adVarWChar`) and `DefinedSize` (determined by the database). The columns Password, EmailAddress, and Age are added in this way.

Now for the final column, which is special. It is an Autonumber field, which SQL Server aficionados also know as an Identity field. To keep ADOX more general, (because these fields are provider-specific), there is no Autonumber property in the `Column` object. Instead, it is a dynamic property that can be accessed and changed via the `Properties` collection (line 29). However, because it is provider specific, the column must first be connected to the catalog—this is what line 28 achieves.

```
Set col.ParentCatalog = cat
```

Now the table is complete.

Where did I learn about the provider-specific dynamic properties that are available for the `Column` object? I created a script that dumps all properties for an existing column as shown in Listing 14.7.

LISTING 14.7 Viewing Provider-Specific Properties for a Column

```
 1: Sub DumpDynamicProperties()
 2:     Dim cat As ADOX.Catalog
 3:     Dim col As ADOX.Column, prop As ADOX.Property
 4:
 5:     Set cat = New ADOX.Catalog
 6:     cat.ActiveConnection = "Provider=Microsoft.Jet.OLEDB.4.0;
➥Data Source=c:\new.mdb"
 7:     Set col = cat.Tables("tUserData").Columns("IdentityField")
 8:
 9:     For Each prop In col.Properties
10:         Debug.Print prop.Name & "=" & prop.Value
11:     Next
12: End Sub
```

Creating Indexes

The columns are there—but searching and sorting won't be fast because there are no indexes and keys on the table's columns. Also, the most important index is missing: the primary key index.

To create a primary key, you need to choose a column that only stores unique values. A good choice for the tUserData table is the IdentityField column, because AutoNumber guarantees unique values for each row. You learn how to create a primary key index on this column in Listing 14.8.

LISTING 14.8   Creating a Primary Key Index on the IdentityField Column

```
 1: Sub CreateIndex()
 2:     Dim tbl As Table, cat As ADOX.Catalog
 3:     Dim idx As ADOX.Index
 4:
 5:     Set cat = New ADOX.Catalog
 6:     cat.ActiveConnection = "Provider=Microsoft.Jet.OLEDB.4.0;
➡Data Source=c:\new.mdb"
 7:
 8:     Set idx = New ADOX.Index
 9:     With idx
10:         .Name = "PrimaryKey"
11:         .IndexNulls = adIndexNullsDisallow
12:         .PrimaryKey = True
13:         .Unique = True
14:         .Columns.Append "IdentityField"
15:     End With
16:
17:     Set tbl = cat.Tables("tUserData")
18:     tbl.Indexes.Append idx
19: End Sub
```

ANALYSIS   The idx object is initialized in line 8, and a With block to set multiple properties for it starts the following line. First, the name of the index is determined. Because Access names primary key indexes PrimaryKey, I chose to use the same name here. Because it is a primary key, it must not contain Null values, as defined by setting the IndexNulls property to adIndexNullsDisallow. A very obvious choice is to set the PrimaryKey and Unique properties to True. All that's left to do is to add columns to this index—as shown in line 14. The only column in this primary key is the IdentityField column.

14

The `Index` object is still not connected to any table. This is finally done in line 18 using the `Indexes.Append` method. Now the tUserData table has a primary key that allows for faster searching and for creating foreign-key relationships to other tables.

Setting Up Foreign-Key Relationships

A foreign key defines the relationship between two tables; however, you still have only one table in your database, the tUserData table. To remedy the situation, you can run the script in Listing 14.9 to create the tUserTracking table that will participate in the foreign-key relationship.

LISTING **14.9**   Creating the tUserTracking Table Using ADOX

```
 1: Sub CreateDependentTable()
 2:     Dim cat As ADOX.Catalog
 3:     Dim tbl As ADOX.Table
 4:     Dim idx As ADOX.Index
 5:
 6:     Set cat = New ADOX.Catalog
 7:     cat.ActiveConnection = "Provider=Microsoft.Jet.OLEDB.4.0;
➥Data Source=c:\new.mdb"
 8:
 9:     Set tbl = New ADOX.Table
10:     tbl.Name = "tUserTracking"
11:     cat.Tables.Append tbl
12:
13:     tbl.Columns.Append "FK_UserID", adInteger
14:     tbl.Columns.Append "LoginTime", adDate
15:     tbl.Columns.Append "IPAddress", adWChar, 15
16:
17:     Set idx = New ADOX.Index
18:     With idx
19:         .Name = "FK_Index"
20:         .IndexNulls = adIndexNullsDisallow
21:         .PrimaryKey = False
22:         .Unique = False
23:         .Columns.Append "FK_UserID"
24:     End With
25:
26:     tbl.Indexes.Append idx
27: End Sub
```

ANALYSIS   There are three columns in this table: FK_UserID, LoginTime, and IPAddress. Because a primary key is not mandatory, you omit a column to serve as the key column. Although you create no primary key, there's key creation code in this listing. Why? When you create a foreign-key relationship, the tables are joined on the linked fields, and hence having a non-unique key on the linked column in the child table improves performance considerably.

It is clear why you create an index that disallows Nulls (otherwise, no connection can be established to the parent table) and why you set the Unique and PrimaryKey columns to False. The index is created on the column FK_UserID (see line 23). The index is appended to the table's Indexes collection in line 26, which completes the creation of the tUserTracking table.

Now both tUserData and tUserTracking are ready to be joined in a foreign-key relationship. The code to create this relationship is contained in Listing 14.10.

LISTING 14.10   Creating the Foreign-Key Relationship Between tUserData and tUserTracking

```
 1: Sub CreateFKRelationship()
 2:     Dim cat As ADOX.Catalog, objKey As ADOX.Key
 3:
 4:     Set cat = New ADOX.Catalog
 5:     cat.ActiveConnection = "Provider=Microsoft.Jet.OLEDB.4.0;
➥Data Source=c:\new.mdb"
 6:
 7:     Set objKey = New ADOX.Key
 8:     With objKey
 9:         .Name = "FKR_tUserData"
10:         .Type = adKeyForeign
11:         .RelatedTable = "tUserData"
12:         .Columns.Append "FK_UserID", adInteger
13:         .Columns("FK_UserID").RelatedColumn = "IdentityField"
14:         .UpdateRule = adRICascade
15:     End With
16:
17:     ' Append the foreign key
18:     cat.Tables("tUserTracking").Keys.Append objKey
19: End Sub
```

ANALYSIS   The setup of the foreign key is handled in lines 7–15. First of all, you have to name the new key (see line 9). Next, you define the Type of the key: adKeyForeign. Because foreign keys are always created on the child table, the RelatedTable property has to contain the parent table, which is tUserData. The next step is to append the columns that form the foreign key in the child table:

```
.Columns.Append "FK_UserID", adInteger
```

You could have omitted the data type because it is already defined for that column, however, it doesn't prevent the code from working properly. With the child column decided,

14

you now have to relate it to a parent column, which in this case is named
IdentityField:

```
.Columns("FK_UserID").RelatedColumn = "IdentityField"
```

The final decision is about how parent updates are propagated to the child table. You can
pass the following constants to UpdateRule:

- adRICascade: All parent changes are propagated to the child, and hence the connection between parent row and child rows is never broken.
- adRINone: When the parent column changes, no action is taken (the old value is
  preserved). However, the child columns are no longer connected to a parent row.
  They are now orphaned.
- adRISetDefault: Changes to the parent column result in setting the child column
  to its database default value. This also causes the child rows to be orphaned; however, they can be easily searched for.
- adRISetNull: A change in the parent column causes the child column's value to
  change to Null. In this case, the child column must allow Null values (as must all
  indexes that are created on this column).

With the foreign key now professionally prepared, the final task at hand is to attach it to
the child table. This is done in line 18 using the following statement:

```
cat.Tables("tUserTracking").Keys.Append objKey
```

Now you have created a simple but complete relational database that contains a working
relationship between two tables.

Modifying Existing Tables

An application often needs to store more information than it was originally designed to
store. When this happens, you have to modify the table design (schema) to fulfill the
needs. Basically, adding a column is not very different from creating columns up front,
as shown in Listing 14.11.

LISTING 14.11   Adding a New Column to the tUserData Table

```
1: Sub AddColumn()
2:     Dim cat As ADOX.Catalog
3:     Dim col As ADOX.Column, tbl As ADOX.Table
4:
5:     Set cat = New ADOX.Catalog
6:     cat.ActiveConnection = "Provider=Microsoft.Jet.OLEDB.4.0;Data
➥Source=c:\new.mdb"
```

```
 7:
 8:        Set tbl = cat.Tables("tUserData")
 9:        Set col = New ADOX.Column
10:        With col
11:            Set .ParentCatalog = cat
12:            .Name = "Petname"
13:            .Type = adVarWChar
14:            .DefinedSize = 64
15:            .Attributes = adColNullable
16:        End With
17:        tbl.Columns.Append col
18:
19:        Debug.Print cat.Tables("tUserData").DateCreated
20:        Debug.Print cat.Tables("tUserData").DateModified
21: End Sub
```

ANALYSIS   The script in the preceding listing adds a new column Petname to the tUserData table. The code in lines 8–17 for creating and appending the column is very similar to creating columns up front; however, there is one important difference, shown in line 15:

```
.Attributes = adColNullable
```

This attribute must be set for columns that are added after data has been inserted in a table. You can't enforce non-nullability for records that already exist—because these records don't have a value for this column.

To illustrate two more properties of the Table object, the script prints the creation and last modification date for the table tUserData. This allows you to review the modification history of each table in a database.

Managing Views and Procedures

Although data is stored in tables, a database can offer more: views to create virtual tables and procedures to execute code on the database server. You have already used both, and even created some yourself. However, you always had to interact with the database system directly.

When you manage views and procedures with ADOX, you do so without having to deal with database specifics. This is why ADOX comes in handy for the following tasks:

- Working with views
- Creating a procedure

14

Working with Views

Views are SQL statements that are stored on the database server and create virtual tables that are either subsets of a single table or a joined result of multiple tables. These statements enable you to create views of data that normal tables wouldn't allow.

To demonstrate how easy it is, Listing 14.12 creates a new view that returns all users from the tUserData table ordered by Username.

LISTING 14.12 Creating a New View to Select All Users from the tUserData Table

```
1: Sub CreateView()
2:     Dim cmd As New ADODB.Command
3:     Dim cat As New ADOX.Catalog
4:
5:     cat.ActiveConnection = "Provider=Microsoft.Jet.OLEDB.4.0;
➥Data Source=c:\new.mdb"
6:     cmd.CommandText = "SELECT * FROM tUserData ORDER BY Username"
7:     cat.Views.Append "AllUsers", cmd
8: End Sub
```

ANALYSIS To create a view, you must have a Command object that stores the CommandText. Therefore, you must reference both the ADODB and ADOX type libraries to access the objects you need.

In line 5, the script establishes a connection to the database. Next, the Command object's CommandText property is set to the SQL statement you will use to create a view (you can compare it to a prepared statement). After the Command object is prepared, all you need to do is to pass the Command object to the Views.Append method, which takes the new view's name as its first parameter and the Command object as its second parameter. Now you have a new view in your database.

After the view is added, how can you display all views that are available in a database? Listing 14.13 shows a possible solution.

LISTING 14.13 Showing All Views Available in a Database

```
1: Sub ViewViews()
2:     Dim cat As New ADOX.Catalog, objView As ADOX.View
3:
4:     cat.ActiveConnection = "Provider=Microsoft.Jet.OLEDB.4.0;
➥Data Source=c:\new.mdb"
5:
6:     For Each objView In cat.Views
7:         Debug.Print objView.Name
8:     Next
9: End Sub
```

ANALYSIS There isn't much to analyze—after connecting to the database, a For...Next loop is used to iterate over views that are contained in the Views collection. Each view's name is written to the Immediate Window.

At some point in time, you might no longer need the view you have created. To delete it, you can use ADOX, as demonstrated in Listing 14.14.

LISTING 14.14 Deleting a View That Is No Longer Needed

```
1: Sub DeleteView()
2:     Dim cat As New ADOX.Catalog
3:     cat.ActiveConnection = "Provider=Microsoft.Jet.OLEDB.4.0;
➥Data Source=c:\new.mdb"
4:     cat.Views.Delete "AllUsers"
5: End Sub
```

ANALYSIS You only need a single line to delete a view—all you need to know is the name of the view. The method to use is Delete, which is part of the Views collection.

Creating a Procedure

Managing procedures is similar to managing views. Therefore, I only present how to create a procedure. Deleting and enumerating procedures are nearly identical processes to those used for deleting and enumerating views.

Listing 14.15 creates a procedure for an Access database that takes one input parameter. It allows you to filter the tUserData table for a certain Username.

LISTING 14.15 Creating a New Procedure

```
1: Sub CreateProcedure()
2:     Dim cmd As New ADODB.Command
3:     Dim cat As New ADOX.Catalog
4:
5:     cat.ActiveConnection = "Provider=Microsoft.Jet.OLEDB.4.0;
➥Data Source=c:\new.mdb"
6:
7:     ' parameters are Jet-specific
8:     cmd.CommandText = "PARAMETERS [UsernameParam] Text;" & _
9:         "SELECT * FROM tUserData WHERE Username = [UsernameParam]"
10:
11:     cat.Procedures.Append "GetSingleUser", cmd
12: End Sub
```

14

The `CommandText` is prepared in lines 8–9. It contains one `PARAMETERS` statement, and a `SELECT` clause that is restricted to `Username = [parametervalue]`. Now that the `CommandText` is created, all that is left to do is to append the procedure to the catalog:

```
cat.Procedures.Append "GetSingleUser", cmd
```

The procedure can be invoked using the `Command` object and specifying one parameter for the Username.

Managing Security

Security is a topic that is emphasized over and over again in this book. It is important to be security-conscious: The data in your databases is one of your most valuable assets. Therefore, you have to guard it against unauthorized access.

Just like Windows NT, most database systems implement security with users and groups (of users). Each user that may access the database gets a user account. This user account is part of one or more groups. Ideally, access permissions to objects in the database are granted to the groups. This makes adding users a pleasant experience.

Because security is an important thing to manage, ADOX also supports the following tasks:

- Working with groups
- Working with users
- Assigning object owners
- Setting access permissions

Working with Groups

The role of a group is to be a container for users who share common access privileges. For example, the Accounting group can access the Payroll table, whereas the Engineering group is explicitly not permitted to do that.

Groups and users are managed in a way that is very dependent on the database system being used. For example, Microsoft Access uses workgroup files to maintain security information for databases. Therefore, when working with the Jet OLEDB provider, you must specify which workgroup you are currently administering. This is shown in Listing 14.16.

Note

You can manage workgroup files in the MS Access Workgroup Administrator, which, by default, is located in the \Program Files\Microsoft Office\Office folder. This program also allows you to create new workgroup files. Because you can't create new workgroup files from ADOX, this provides the only way to get at blank workgroup security databases.

When working with a blank security database (the shipping default of Microsoft Access 2000), you are automatically logged in as user Admin with no password. With this privlege, you can add users and groups and assign permissions to database objects.

LISTING 14.16   Creating New Groups

```
 1: Sub CreateGroup()
 2:     Dim cat As New ADOX.Catalog
 3:     Dim objGroup As ADOX.Group
 4:
 5:     cat.ActiveConnection = "Provider=Microsoft.Jet.OLEDB.4.0;" & _
 6:         "Data Source=c:\new.mdb;" & _
 7:         "jet oledb:system database=c:\system.mdw"
 8:
 9:     cat.Groups.Append "DB Administrators"
10:
11:     Set objGroup = New ADOX.Group
12:     objGroup.Name = "DB Users"
13:     cat.Groups.Append objGroup
14: End Sub
```

ANALYSIS   The workgroup database is specified as part of the connection string:

```
jet oledb:system database=c:\system.mdw
```

Notice that you use a copy of the system.mdw that is, by default, installed in the Office folder hierarchy. I copied it to the root of c: so that you don't have to specify overly long pathnames.

Adding groups can be achieved using two different approaches: You can pass the group's name directly to Groups.Append (line 9), or you can create a Group object first (line 11). You have to assign the Name property, and pass the constructed object to Groups.Append.

Now you have two new groups in your workgroup database. Groups are containers for User objects. Adding users to groups is shown in the next section.

14

Working with Users

Let's get started with the most important task of user management: adding new users. Once again, there is more than one solution to the problem, as demonstrated by the code in Listing 14.17.

LISTING **14.17** Adding Users and Assigning These to Certain Groups

```
 1: Sub AddUsersToGroup()
 2:     Dim cat As New ADOX.Catalog
 3:     Dim objGroup As ADOX.Group, objUser As ADOX.User
 4:
 5:     cat.ActiveConnection = "Provider=Microsoft.Jet.OLEDB.4.0;" & _
 6:         "Data Source=c:\new.mdb;" & _
 7:         "jet oledb:system database=c:\system.mdw"
 8:
 9:     Set objGroup = cat.Groups("DB Administrators")
10:
11:     Set objUser = New ADOX.User
12:     objUser.Name = "christophw"
13:     objUser.ChangePassword "", "topsecret"
14:
15:     cat.Users.Append objUser
16:     objUser.Groups.Append "DB Administrators"
17:
18:     cat.Users.Append "christiank", "poem"
19:
20:     Set objGroup = cat.Groups("DB Users")
21:     objGroup.Users.Append (cat.Users("christiank"))
22: End Sub
```

ANALYSIS   Lines 5–7 build the already familiar connection string that includes the reference to the system database. Line 9 opens the DB Administrators group and assigns the group to a local variable, although it is not necessary to do so at this point. Then you start creating the first user by creating an object of type ADOX.User (line 11).

The Name property for the User object is then assigned (this is the login name), and by calling the ChangePassword method, you assign an initial password of topsecret. The first parameter passes the old password; however, because there is none in this case, you pass an empty string.

The user is created, but not yet known to the catalog. Therefore, you have to append it to the Users collection of the catalog:

```
cat.Users.Append objUser
```

Because the user is now known in the catalog, it can also be appended to Groups, which is done in line 16:

```
objUser.Groups.Append "DB Administrators"
```

Finally, the new user christophw is a DB Administrator.

The second way to add users to the database is illustrated by the code in lines 19 and following. First, the user is appended immediately to the catalog's Users collection by calling Append with Username and Password as parameters. However, because when assigning group membership you can only deal with objects, line 21 does not look very elegant:

```
objGroup.Users.Append (cat.Users("christiank"))
```

To prove that the users were really added, you can execute the code in Listing 14.18, which dumps all users in the DB Administrators group.

LISTING 14.18 Dumping All Users in the DB Administrators Group

```
 1: Sub EnumerateUsers()
 2:     Dim cat As New ADOX.Catalog, strGroups As String, n As Integer
 3:     Dim objGroup As ADOX.Group, objUser As ADOX.User
 4:
 5:     cat.ActiveConnection = "Provider=Microsoft.Jet.OLEDB.4.0;" & _
 6:         "Data Source=c:\new.mdb;" & _
 7:         "jet oledb:system database=c:\system.mdw"
 8:
 9:     Set objGroup = cat.Groups("DB Administrators")
10:
11:     For Each objUser In objGroup.Users
12:         ' a user can be in multiple groups
13:         strGroups = ""
14:         For n = 0 To objUser.Groups.Count - 1
15:             strGroups = strGroups & " " & objUser.Groups(n).Name
16:         Next
17:         Debug.Print objUser.Name; " is member of: " & strGroups
18:     Next
19: End Sub
```

ANALYSIS After you open the DB Administrators group in line 9, a For Each loop follows that iterates over all group members (users). Because a user can belong to multiple groups, the script iterates over the User's Groups collection and creates a string that represents all group memberships (lines 13–16). Then the user's Name and group membership is dumped to the Immediate Window (line 17).

14

The groups and users are set up and just waiting to be used to assign permissions to objects.

Assigning Object Owners

Every database object has an owner, usually the person who created the object in the first place. To be able to transfer object ownership, ADOX supports two methods for the Catalog that are demonstrated in Listing 14.19.

LISTING **14.19** Changing the Owner of an Object

```
 1: Sub SetOwner()
 2:     Dim tbl As New ADOX.Table, cat As New ADOX.Catalog
 3:     Dim strOwner As String
 4:
 5:     cat.ActiveConnection = "Provider=Microsoft.Jet.OLEDB.4.0;" & _
 6:         "Data Source=c:\new.mdb;" & _
 7:         "jet oledb:system database=c:\system.mdw"
 8:
 9:     ' get the current owner
10:     strOwner = cat.GetObjectOwner("tUserData", adPermObjTable)
11:     Debug.Print "Owner of tUserData: " & strOwner
12:
13:     ' change owner to DB Administrators
14:     cat.SetObjectOwner "tUserData", adPermObjTable, "DB Administrators"
15: End Sub
```

ANALYSIS The first method retrieves the current owner of an object:

```
cat.GetObjectOwner(Object, ObjectType)
```

The Object parameter is the name of the object whose owner you want to find. Because multiple objects of different types can have the same name, you must also specify which object type you are accessing. Object types can be adPermObjectDatabase, adPermObjectView, or adPermObjectProcedure to name a few.

In line 11, the current owner of the object is written to the Immediate Windows, followed by the statement in line 14, which changes the owner to the DB Administrators group. The general syntax for SetObjectOwner is:

```
Catalog.SetObjectOwner ObjectName, ObjectType , OwnerName [, ObjectTypeId]
```

The first three parameters are mandatory. Only the ObjectTypeId parameter can be omitted (and usually you do so, because it is a GUID for a provider object type).

You have successfully transferred the ownership of a database object to one of the new groups. However, ownership doesn't necessarily result in great access permissions. No one except the owner can access the object. Therefore, you have to set more granular access permissions.

Setting Access Permissions

Before blindly changing permissions, you should know how the permissions were defined. Therefore, you need to check permissions as shown in Listing 14.20.

LISTING 14.20 Checking for a Specific Permission

```
 1: Sub ViewPermissions()
 2:     Dim cat As New ADOX.Catalog
 3:     Dim nRights As Long
 4:
 5:     cat.ActiveConnection = "Provider=Microsoft.Jet.OLEDB.4.0;" & _
 6:         "Data Source=c:\new.mdb;" & _
 7:         "jet oledb:system database=c:\system.mdw"
 8:
 9:     nRights = cat.Users("christiank").GetPermissions("tUserData",
↳adPermObjTable)
10:
11:     Debug.Print "Read permissions: " & (adRightRead And nRights)
12: End Sub
```

ANALYSIS Line 9 answers the question about what access permissions a user holds on an object. Permissions returned from the GetPermissions method are represented as a bitmask of RightEnums constants (because there are more than 15 constants, see the Platform SDK for details). Therefore, to determine whether a specific permission was granted, you have to And the bitmask with the constant, and if the result is equal to the constant, the permission was granted (line 11).

When you run and debug the script, you can see that Christian doesn't have any rights on the table—because he isn't the owner, and he hasn't been granted any rights on the table yet. Listing 14.21 changes this situation by granting Christian the right to drop the table (delete it from the database).

14

LISTING 14.21 Setting New Permissions for an Object

```
 1: Sub SetPermissions()
 2:     Dim cat As New ADOX.Catalog
 3:     Dim nRights As Long
 4:
 5:     cat.ActiveConnection = "Provider=Microsoft.Jet.OLEDB.4.0;" & _
 6:         "Data Source=c:\new.mdb;" & _
 7:         "jet oledb:system database=c:\system.mdw"
 8:
 9:     nRights = cat.Users("christiank").GetPermissions("tUserData",
➥adPermObjTable)
10:
11:     cat.Users("christiank").SetPermissions "tUserData", adPermObjTable, _
12:         adAccessSet, nRights Or adRightDrop
13: End Sub
```

ANALYSIS When you change permissions for an object, keep in mind that you have two choices: replace any existing rights, or selectively add rights. In case you want to do the latter, you first have to retrieve the current rights (line 9), and then add the new right by OR'ing the right's constant to the current bitmask. The new bitmask is then applied using the SetPermissions method:

```
GroupOrUser.SetPermissions Name, ObjectType, Action, Rights
```

The Action you perform for changing rights is adAccessSet, however, when you want to selectively change rights, you can also use adAccessGrant.

Assume that you added more rights in the meantime. Now, you decide that Christian is no longer trustworthy. You want to remove all access rights immediately. Listing 14.22 contains code for this scenario.

LISTING 14.22 Revoking a User's Permissions on an Object

```
 1: Sub RevokeAllPermissions()
 2:     Dim cat As New ADOX.Catalog
 3:     Dim nRights As Long
 4:
 5:     cat.ActiveConnection = "Provider=Microsoft.Jet.OLEDB.4.0;" & _
 6:         "Data Source=c:\new.mdb;" & _
 7:         "jet oledb:system database=c:\system.mdw"
 8:
 9:     ' Revoke all permissions
10:     cat.Users("christiank").SetPermissions "tUserData", adPermObjTable, _
11:         adAccessRevoke, adRightFull
12: End Sub
```

ANALYSIS A user's permissions can be revoked when you call `SetPermissions` with an Action constant of `adAccessRevoke`, and access permission `adRightFull`, which removes any rights you've ever granted to a user. Christian no longer can access the table.

Summary

In today's lesson, you learned how to harness the power of ADOX in various areas. You started by opening existing catalogs and creating new ones using single-line statements. Into this new catalog, you put tables with primary key indexes, and you established a foreign-key relationship between two tables. This is part of the Data Definition Language feature set of ADOX.

The second part of ADOX is security management. You exploited the functionality by creating groups and users and assigning access permissions and owners for database objects. Security is a recurring topic as data is one of your most valuable assets (if not the most valuable one).

Q&A

Q **You were creating a procedure for an Access database—but Access databases only support queries, so the term *view* is also wrong, or did I miss something?**

A Query is just how views are named in an Access database. Though Access does not support procedures that match stored procedures, such as the ones in SQL Server, parameterized queries are managed as procedures. Just remember that SQL Server views cannot take parameters.

Workshop

The Workshop is designed to help you anticipate possible questions, review what you've learned, and get you thinking about how to put your knowledge into practice. The answers to the quiz are in Appendix A, "Quiz Answers."

Quiz

1. What is the limitation of using `OpenSchema`?
2. Does the Jet OLE DB provider support the creation of new catalogs?
3. What are dynamic properties? Why are they used in ADOX, and can you name one?

14

4. When creating a primary key index, which important properties do you need to set?

5. What is the advantage of cascaded relational integrity?

6. Why do you need to reference the ADODB type library when creating views and procedures?

7. What does a connection string look like when you are administering security?

Exercise

1. Create a new catalog named mydb.mdb using the Jet OLE DB provider. Add a new table named tExercise to this catalog. This table contains the following columns: ExerciseID (Autonumber), Chapter (Integer), Description (VarChar, 255) and DifficultyLevel (Integer). ExerciseID is a primary key that does not allow Nulls.

   To test the database, insert a row with following values: Chapter=14, Description=Create a new catalog, DifficultyLevel=0. Use INSERT INTO for the insert operation.

WEEK 2
In Review

For our second week in review, we will look at a Web Brokerage Company. This company, Demaine Brokerage Services, allows customers to buy and sell shares over the Internet. Business has been booming and the number of customers and share trades carried out each day has been steadily rising.

As part of its service, Demaine Brokerage Services provides detailed information to each customer on the share trades they have carried out. As well, each customer has a trading account for which the balance can be displayed. When a customer purchases shares, money is withdrawn from their trading account to cover the cost of the transaction. When a customer sells shares, the money from the transaction is deposited into their trading account.

Unfortunately, on an irregular basis, a number of customers have contacted the company complaining that their trading account balance does not tally with their detailed shared trade information. One customer in particular has complained that $10,000 has been withdrawn from his account but he can find no corresponding share trade!

You have been called in to investigate and hopefully provide a solution. You first look at the code that deposits and withdraws from the trading account, and everything looks fine. You then look at the code that inserts the details of the transaction to a transaction table. Again, everything looks fine. You then realize that both these pieces of code are running in two separate (implicit) transactions! This accounts for the earlier discrepancies. You determine that on occasion the following sequence of events is occurring:

The account balance is updated and the implicit transaction committed.

This is followed, in a separate implicit transaction, by the insert of the transaction details into the transaction table, which is encountering an error and being rolled back.

Your solution is to combine both of the above actions into the same explicit transaction, so that there will never be a discrepancy between the account balance and the transaction details. Either both will be committed, or both will be rolled back.

Demaine Brokerage Services then ask if you can help in another area. As a small but rapidly growing company, they want to analyze how their customers are using their services. In particular, they are interested in categories of shares being traded (i.e. Industrial, Transport, Technology and so on) by volume and dollar amounts at various intervals (i.e. hourly, daily, weekly, monthly and yearly).

They also make it clear that they are not quite sure what sort of analysis they want to undertake, but would like you to provide a way that they can undertake their analysis with some flexibility. They clearly state that a simple report won't do.

Immediately you recognize a perfect use for the OLAP features of SQL Server 7. You realize that volume and dollar amounts are facts, and categories, customers, and intervals will be your dimensions used to slice the facts.

You suggest to Demaine Brokerage Services that you design and implement a data warehouse, explaining the benefits of such an approach.

WEEK 3
At A Glance

This week, you concentrate on using advanced features of ADO and services offered by the operating system, such as COM+ applications for enhancing scalability. You acquire knowledge about disconnected recordsets, explore standard RDS functionality, extend RDS with custom data factories, develop XML-enabled code, secure your applications, and finally tune them.

- Day 15—You learn how to leverage the COM+ infrastructure of Windows 2000 to create scalable database applications. You build COM components that work well in transactional usage scenarios.

- Day 16—You create disconnected recordsets that can be used when having an open connection to a database is too costly in terms of network bandwidth and processing power. You store recordsets to disk and later open them again to update the data store.

- Day 17—You extend your ADO knowledge to the largest network of the world—the Internet. You discover how to use RDS to access SQL data sources via the IIS Web services.

- Day 18—You take the concept of RDS one step further by creating your own data source objects, the so-called custom data factories. These allow you to harden security and enforce business rules.

- Day 19—You explore the advantages of using XML in conjunction with ADO to present data efficiently on the Internet, as well as use XML to transfer database data to other platforms.

- Day 20—You plug security holes and learn how to not open ones yourself. You lock down your SQL Server installation and revisit several security concepts that are necessary to run a server machine.

15

16

17

18

19

20

21

- Day 21—You tune the applications that use ADO to squeeze out that last bit of performance that is crucial when building large-scale database applications. You also learn how to debug multitier applications effectively.

Day 15

Creating Scalable Solutions with COM+

Objectives

Today's applications need to scale to large numbers of concurrent users; however, they must still be easy to program. If you write all scalability code yourself, you won't be able to achieve this goal. However, if you stick with COM+, you get all the necessary plumbing for free.

Although you are not building an entire COM+ application today, you will learn the following:

- Implementing a three-tiered application design
- Browsing data using a data-tier object
- Encapsulating stored procedures in the data tier
- Adding COM+ transaction support
- Improving scalability by exploiting JIT and other COM+ mechanisms

Three-Tiered Application Design

Up to this point, you have accessed the database directly from what is called the presentation layer (a.k.a. front end). You worked in a client-server environment, where the client is directly connected to the data store.

In larger deployments, the client-server model quickly turns out to be a pain in the neck. The number one problem is that a client application usually acquires a database connection at startup and keeps it for the entire lifetime. This is costly in terms of database connections and also poses a performance problem.

Second, the database manipulation is implemented in the client application, which causes problems in various areas. For example, when you need to update the database manipulation code, you have to roll out your changes to every desktop, effectively reinstalling the application. Additionally, you're bitten when you need to implement different front ends, such as a Windows client and Web clients. Spreading database code in various front ends turns maintenance into a severe headache.

For all these problems there is a solution: the three-tiered application design (see Figure 15.1).

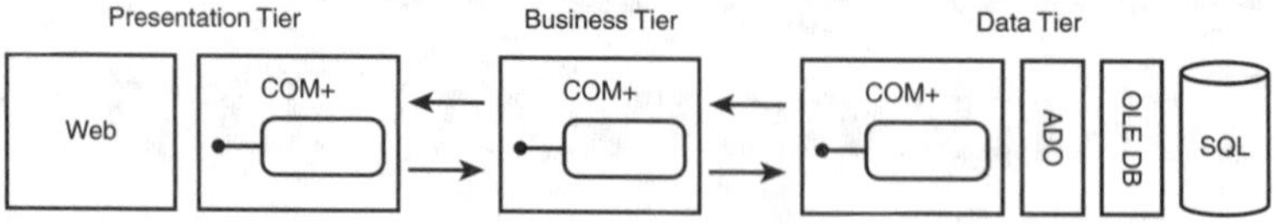

FIGURE 15.1

The three tiers are the presentation, business, and data tiers.

With this approach, the client is no longer directly connected to the database, nor does it contain business logic. The advantages are clear: Should you ever need to change the business logic, you can do so in the business components that reside in the business tier. Also, because business tier and data tier shield you from database access logic, you can reuse the components in many different clients, such as standard Windows applications or Active Server Pages applications on IIS.

I already mentioned that, in the business tier, the code is implemented in components. You have worked with components already. For example, the ActiveX Data Objects are components. These are provided *as is* for you. However, when you need to implement your business logic or data access methods, you have to create components on your own.

The easiest and fastest way to roll out components on your own is to use Visual Basic. You don't have to learn too much to get up to speed—you can even copy unmodified code from the Excel examples.

15

Because the most important tier for you, as the database developer, is the data tier, I'm going to focus on this layer. The business tier is already a consumer of services provided by the data tier.

> **Tip**
>
> A three-tiered application should be thoroughly designed (and that topic can fill another book). If you are using Visual Basic, you get Visual Modeler for free. It is a scaled-down version of the excellent Rose tool from Rational.

Creating a Data-Tier Component

What are the tasks that business tier and presentation tier must be able to perform? In general, you can break them down into four data-related tasks:

- Browsing
- Adding
- Changing
- Removing

Browsing can be achieved by simply executing a SQL SELECT statement. For the latter three tasks, you can use SQL statements or Recordset operations. For speed and security reasons, the most powerful way to implement these tasks is using stored procedures, which are compiled SQL statements.

Now that you have determined what you need, you can go about putting the pieces together:

- Adding necessary stored procedures
- Browsing with disconnected Recordsets
- Encapsulating the stored procedures
- Testing the component

Adding Necessary Stored Procedures

One more time, the victim of your ADO explorations is the Northwind database in SQL Server 7. All examples use the Suppliers table. Its structure is shown in Figure 15.2.

FIGURE 15.2

The structure of the Suppliers table.

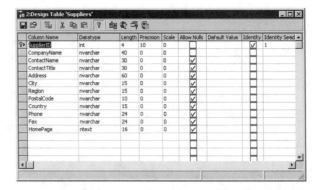

To add the necessary stored procedures for inserting, updating, and deleting data, you use the Stored Procedure Wizard (already introduced in Chapter 7, "Implementing Application Logic in Stored Procedures").

To Do: Creating the Stored Procedures on the Suppliers Table

1. Open SQL Server Enterprise Manager and connect to the SQL Server that contains the Northwind database.

2. Open the Create Stored Procedure Wizard (from the Tools menu, select Wizards, expand Database, and then launch the Create Stored Procedure Wizard).

3. Select the Northwind database, if it is not already selected.

4. Scroll to the Suppliers table and check all three types of stored procedures (see Figure 15.3).

FIGURE 15.3

Select all three types of stored procedures for the Suppliers table.

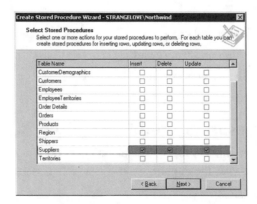

▼

▼ 5. You are now presented with the last step of the Stored Procedure Wizard (see Figure 15.4). Select the UPDATE stored procedure and click Edit to begin the change process.

FIGURE 15.4

The stored procedures are created with default names and default SQL statements.

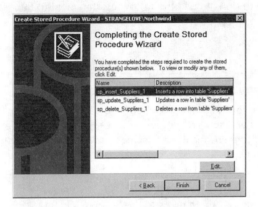

6. First, change the name to sp_update_Suppliers. Next, remove the check mark in the Include in Set Clause for the SupplierID column because it is the Identity column (see Figure 15.5). Click OK to make your changes permanent.

FIGURE 15.5

Changing the column selection for the UPDATE stored procedure.

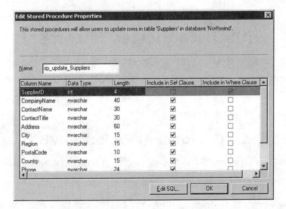

7. Now edit the DELETE stored procedure. All you have to do is to change the name to sp_delete_Suppliers.

8. The final stored procedure that needs to be changed is the INSERT stored procedure. First, change the name to sp_insert_Suppliers. Next, deselect the SupplierID
▼ column because it will be automatically generated.

▼ 9. Click the Edit SQL button to open the Edit Stored Procedure SQL dialog box.
      Although it is a perfectly legal SQL statement, you need one change: Return the
      Identity value generated for the SupplierID column.

      All you have to do is to add the following statement to the very end of the stored
      procedure:

      ```
      RETURN @@IDENTITY
      ```

> **Caution** The @@IDENTITY variable is connection global and returns the last identity
> value for the connection, not for the table. This means if the INSERT state-
> ment on Suppliers triggers an INSERT on a second table, the @@IDENTITY vari-
> able contains the identity value from that table. In this case, however, it can
> be safely used.

    10. Click OK to save your changes to the SQL statement.

    11. Back in the Create Stored Procedure Wizard, click Finish to create the three stored
▲   procedures.

You can give the stored procedures a try by running them in SQL Server Enterprise
Manager.

Browsing with Disconnected Recordsets

Instead of immediately encapsulating the stored procedures in the data tier object,
start with an easier task: adding the code necessary to browse the existing records.
However, there are some up-front duties, such as creating the project in Visual Basic,
before you can start coding.

To Do: Creating a Component Project in VB

    1. Start Visual Basic from the Visual Studio program group.

    2. Select ActiveX DLL from the New tab in Visual Basic.

    3. The new Project1 is opened with one class module Class1 already created (see
       Figure 15.6).

    4. Rename the project to ADO25Northwind, and change the class to Suppliers. When
       you later create an instance of the Suppliers class, you will be using the following
       syntax:

▼   ```
    Set xObj = CreateObject("ADO25Northwind.Suppliers")
    ```
    ```

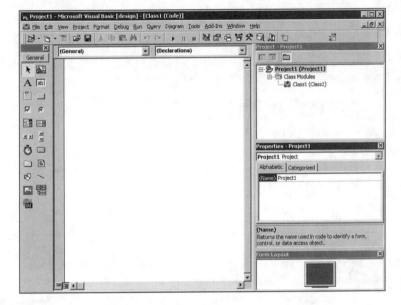

FIGURE 15.6

The newly created project is opened.

5. Save the project to a location of your choosing (File/Save Project). When you are asked for names of both the class and the project, stick with the default suggestions.

With the project saved and ProgId determined, you can start adding the functionality that is to be provided by the object. The first function is being able to browse the Suppliers, as shown in Listing 15.1.

LISTING 15.1 First Implementation of the `BrowseTable` Function

```
1: Option Explicit
2:
3: Const cstrConnection = "provider=sqloledb.1;user id=sa;password=;
▶initial catalog=northwind;data source=strangelove"
4:
5: Public Function BrowseTable() As ADODB.Recordset
6: On Error GoTo Err_Browse
7:     Dim cn As ADODB.Connection
8:     Dim rs As ADODB.Recordset
9:
10:     Set cn = New ADODB.Connection
```

continues

LISTING 15.1 continued

```
11:     cn.Open cstrConnection
12:
13:     Set rs = New ADODB.Recordset
14:     rs.CursorLocation = adUseClient
15:     rs.LockType = adLockBatchOptimistic
16:     rs.CursorType = adOpenForwardOnly
17:
18:     rs.Open "select * from Suppliers", cn
19:     Set rs.ActiveConnection = Nothing
20:     Set BrowseTable = rs
21:
22:     Exit Function
23: Err_Browse:
24:     Set rs = Nothing
25:     Set cn = Nothing
26:     Err.Raise Err.Number, Err.Source, Err.Description
27: End Function
```

ANALYSIS To start work with components slowly and simply, I kept the tricks to a minimum. The connection string is declared as a constant in line 3, and the function that encapsulates the browsing functionality starts in line 5. Notice that the function has a `Public` attribute, which means that it can be accessed from outside the object:

```
Set rs = xObj.BrowseTable
```

The function itself doesn't perform magic. The cursor location is set to the client (line 14) and the ActiveConnection is set to `Nothing` after obtaining the Recordset (line 19). This is all it takes to create a Recordset that is disconnected from the database. You'll learn more about disconnected Recordsets tomorrow in "Disconnecting Data From the Database."

The approach presented in Listing 15.1 isn't flexible, nor is it fast. Flexibility is hampered because I have hard coded the connection string, including username and password. Furthermore, I always select the entire contents of the table and don't allow sorting or filtering. To overcome these limitations, I have modified the code as shown in Listing 15.2.

LISTING 15.2 Browsing the Table

```
1: Public Function BrowseTable(Optional ByVal strSelect As Variant, _
2:          Optional ByVal strDSN As Variant) As ADODB.Recordset
3: On Error GoTo Err_Browse
4:     Dim cn As ADODB.Connection
```

```
 5:    Dim rs As ADODB.Recordset
 6:
 7:    If IsMissing(strDSN) Then
 8:        strDSN = cstrConnection
 9:    End If
10:
11:    Set cn = New ADODB.Connection
12:    cn.Open strDSN
13:
14:    Set rs = New ADODB.Recordset
15:    rs.CursorLocation = adUseClient
16:    rs.LockType = adLockBatchOptimistic
17:    rs.CursorType = adOpenForwardOnly
18:
19:    If IsMissing(strSelect) Then
20:        rs.Open "select * from Suppliers", cn
21:    Else
22:        rs.Open strSelect, cn
23:    End If
24:
25:    Set rs.ActiveConnection = Nothing
26:    Set BrowseTable = rs
27:
28:    Exit Function
29: Err_Browse:
30:    Set rs = Nothing
31:    Set cn = Nothing
32:    Err.Raise Err.Number, Err.Source, Err.Description
33: End Function
```

ANALYSIS The major difference is that there are now two optional parameters for a SELECT statement and DSN. Notice that both are declared as ByVal—passing parameters by value greatly reduces the overhead necessary to transfer values from the caller to the callee (your object). This improvement in speed is especially important when deploying your objects later in distributed environments.

Take a look at the statement in lines 7–9:

```
If IsMissing(strDSN) Then
   strDSN = cstrConnection
End If
```

If the DSN parameter is not passed, the component falls back to the DSN that is defined in the constant cstrConnection. This provides the capability to deliver the component with a defined connection string; however, you can change it at any time by passing it as an optional parameter.

The same approach is taken for the SELECT statement—if it is not passed, the default is used. There is one caveat to this approach: In its current implementation, you can pass any SQL statement for any table. You can add checks for the correct table. You can view this, however, as an advantage. You only have to implement the browse functionality once!

 Note

> In a correct implementation, you implement an object on its own for the browse functionality. However, because I picked only one table, it is perfectly okay to mix common functionality (browsing) with specific functionality (modifying data in a specific table).

Encapsulating the Stored Procedures

Browsing records is only part of the functionality you need for the data tier. You also need to be able to insert, update, and delete records in a table. The following sections introduce these concepts:

- Deleting records
- Updating existing records
- Inserting new data

Deleting Records

You'll start with the easiest of the three. Take a look at how you implement the record deletion code in Listing 15.3.

LISTING 15.3 Deleting a Record

```
 1: Public Function DeleteRecord(ByVal nSupplierId As Long, _
 2:                              Optional ByVal strDSN As Variant) As Boolean
 3: On Error GoTo Err_Delete
 4:     Dim cmd As ADODB.Command
 5:     Dim tmpParam As ADODB.Parameter
 6:
 7:     DeleteRecord = False
 8:     If IsMissing(strDSN) Then
 9:         strDSN = cstrConnection
10:     End If
11:
12:     Set cmd = New ADODB.Command
```

```
13:    cmd.ActiveConnection = strDSN
14:    cmd.CommandType = adCmdStoredProc
15:    cmd.CommandText = "sp_delete_Suppliers"
16:
17:    Set tmpParam = cmd.CreateParameter("@SupplierId", adInteger,
➥adParamInput, 4, nSupplierId)
18:    cmd.Parameters.Append tmpParam
19:
20:    cmd.Execute
21:    DeleteRecord = True
22:
23:    Exit Function
24: Err_Delete:
25:    Set cmd = Nothing
26:    Err.Raise Err.Number, Err.Source, Err.Description
27: End Function
```

ANALYSIS   Remember that, in the stored procedure's SQL, there is only one parameter that needs to be passed—the SupplierID, which is the primary key. Therefore, the only mandatory parameter for the DeleteRecord function is nSupplierId, and strDSN is once again the optional parameter.

For record deletion, I use only a Command object, which is created in line 12. The active connection is set to the connection string, and the Command's type is set to adCmdStoredProc to indicate a stored procedure. Line 15 supplies the CommandText, which is the name of the stored procedure.

The final input missing is the stored procedure's input parameter for SupplierID. This is created in line 17 and added to the Parameters collection of the Command object in line 18. The parameter is an input parameter of type integer, and the value is nSupplierId, which is passed to the function.

The command is executed in line 20 (cmd.Execute), and if it is successful, the return value is set to True (line 21). The error-handling code simply passes the error to the caller.

 Note

> When you recall the relationships in the Northwind database, you might argue that I won't be able to delete any Supplier because foreign key relationships exist. This is why error-handling code must be in components.

Updating Existing Records

Records often require updating. There are at least two ways to update records: via a recordset or via an UPDATE statement. In a three-tiered architecture, the latter method is usually faster because there is no object remoting involved, as there is with the Recordset object.

The UPDATE stored procedure is encapsulated in the code in Listing 15.4.

LISTING **15.4**   Updating a Row in a Database

```
 1: Public Function UpdateRecord(ByVal nSupplierId As Long, _
 2:                             ByVal strCompanyName As String, _
 3:                             ByVal strContactName As String, _
 4:                             ByVal strContactTitle As String, _
 5:                             ByVal strAddress As String, _
 6:                             ByVal strCity As String, _
 7:                             ByVal strRegion As String, _
 8:                             ByVal strPostalCode As String, _
 9:                             ByVal strCountry As String, _
10:                             ByVal strPhone As String, _
11:                             ByVal strFax As String, _
12:                             ByVal strHomepage As String, _
13:                             Optional ByVal strDSN As Variant) As Boolean
14: On Error GoTo Err_Update
15:     Dim cn As ADODB.Connection
16:     Dim cmd As ADODB.Command
17:
18:     UpdateRecord = False
19:     If IsMissing(strDSN) Then
20:         strDSN = cstrConnection
21:     End If
22:
23:     Set cn = New ADODB.Connection
24:     cn.ConnectionString = strDSN
25:     cn.Open
26:
27:     Set cmd = New ADODB.Command
28:     Set cmd.ActiveConnection = cn
29:     cmd.CommandType = adCmdStoredProc
30:     cmd.CommandText = "sp_update_Suppliers"
31:
32:     cmd.Parameters.Append cmd.CreateParameter("RETURN_VALUE",
➥adInteger, adParamReturnValue)
33:     cmd.Parameters.Append cmd.CreateParameter("@SupplierID_1", adInteger,
➥adParamInput, , nSupplierId)
34:     cmd.Parameters.Append cmd.CreateParameter("@CompanyName_2",
➥adVarWChar, adParamInput, 40, strCompanyName)
35:     cmd.Parameters.Append cmd.CreateParameter("@ContactName_3",
```

```
↪adVarWChar, adParamInput, 30, strContactName)
36:     cmd.Parameters.Append cmd.CreateParameter("@ContactTitle_4",
↪adVarWChar, adParamInput, 30, strContactTitle)
37:     cmd.Parameters.Append cmd.CreateParameter("@Address_5",
↪adVarWChar, adParamInput, 60, strAddress)
38:     cmd.Parameters.Append cmd.CreateParameter("@City_6",
↪adVarWChar, adParamInput, 15, strCity)
39:     cmd.Parameters.Append cmd.CreateParameter("@Region_7",
↪adVarWChar, adParamInput, 15, strRegion)
40:     cmd.Parameters.Append cmd.CreateParameter("@PostalCode_8",
↪adVarWChar, adParamInput, 10, strPostalCode)
41:     cmd.Parameters.Append cmd.CreateParameter("@Country_9",
↪adVarWChar, adParamInput, 15, strCountry)
42:     cmd.Parameters.Append cmd.CreateParameter("@Phone_10",
↪adVarWChar, adParamInput, 24, strPhone)
43:     cmd.Parameters.Append cmd.CreateParameter("@Fax_11",
↪adVarWChar, adParamInput, 24, strFax)
44:     cmd.Parameters.Append cmd.CreateParameter("@HomePage_12",
↪adVarWChar, adParamInput, 1073741823, strHomepage)
45:
46:     cmd.Execute
47:     UpdateRecord = True
48:
49:     Exit Function
50: Err_Update:
51:     Set cmd = Nothing
52:     Err.Raise Err.Number, Err.Source, Err.Description
53: End Function
```

ANALYSIS   The size of this listing results from the number of parameters that need to be passed around. First, you have to get all table columns into the function (lines 1–13). In the function, a connection to the database is established using the Connection object. Line 30 determines the stored procedure that is called, and starting in line 32, you add the parameters—you've already learned that in Chapter 7.

The command is executed against the database in line 46, and success or failure is then reported back to the user (constraint violations, duplicates, and so forth).

Inserting New Data

Before you can add a product, you must insert a supplier for that product into the Suppliers table. For that purpose, you can create a stored procedure with the Stored Procedure Wizard. It also returns the identity value for the SupplierID. Listing 15.5 shows how to wrap the functionality of inserting suppliers.

LISTING 15.5   Inserting a New Supplier in the Suppliers Table

```
 1: Public Function InsertRecord(ByVal strCompanyName As String, _
 2:                              ByVal strContactName As String, _
 3:                              ByVal strContactTitle As String, _
 4:                              ByVal strAddress As String, _
 5:                              ByVal strCity As String, _
 6:                              ByVal strRegion As String, _
 7:                              ByVal strPostalCode As String, _
 8:                              ByVal strCountry As String, _
 9:                              ByVal strPhone As String, _
10:                              ByVal strFax As String, _
11:                              ByVal strHomepage As String, _
12:                              Optional ByVal strDSN As Variant) As Integer
13: On Error GoTo Err_Insert
14:     Dim cn As ADODB.Connection
15:     Dim cmd As ADODB.Command
16:
17:     InsertRecord = -1
18:     If IsMissing(strDSN) Then
19:         strDSN = cstrConnection
20:     End If
21:
22:     Set cn = New ADODB.Connection
23:     cn.ConnectionString = strDSN
24:     cn.Open
25:
26:     Set cmd = New ADODB.Command
27:     Set cmd.ActiveConnection = cn
28:     cmd.CommandType = adCmdStoredProc
29:     cmd.CommandText = "sp_insert_Suppliers"
30:     cmd.Parameters.Refresh
31:
32:     With cmd.Parameters
33:         ' item zero is the return value
34:         .Item(1).Value = strCompanyName
35:         .Item(2).Value = strContactName
36:         .Item(3).Value = strContactTitle
37:         .Item(4).Value = strAddress
38:         .Item(5).Value = strCity
39:         .Item(6).Value = strRegion
40:         .Item(7).Value = strPostalCode
41:         .Item(8).Value = strCountry
42:         .Item(9).Value = strPhone
43:         .Item(10).Value = strFax
44:         .Item(11).Value = strHomepage
45:     End With
```

```
46:
47:      cmd.Execute
48:      InsertRecord = cmd.Parameters(0).Value
49:
50:      Exit Function
51: Err_Insert:
52:      Set cmd = Nothing
53:      Err.Raise Err.Number, Err.Source, Err.Description
54: End Function
```

ANALYSIS The function's parameters are declared in lines 1–12, and the connection to the database is established in line 24 via an instance of the Connection object. The parameters for the Command object are not created manually, but they are retrieved using the Refresh method (line 30):

```
cmd.Parameters.Refresh
```

The values for the parameters are set in the With block in lines 32–45. Notice that the index for the collection starts at zero, but the first element is the return value. After all values are set, the stored procedure is executed. On a successful return, the function's return value is set to the return value of the stored procedure, which is the @@IDENTITY variable.

Although I used the Refresh method for this example, I strongly discourage you from using it in component code. If you use it, every time you want to execute the stored procedure, a round-trip is made to the database server first to get the parameter information. This is extremely costly for a three-tiered application. Therefore, always declare parameters explicitly.

Testing the Component

Up to this point, you had to trust that the code I presented actually works. Now you are going to test it for yourself.

The most efficient way to test ActiveX components is from within VB using a second project, making it a project group with the ActiveX project. This allows you to debug from the client (standalone application) into the component, without having to deal with extra tricks.

To start, you first have to compile the ActiveX DLL project. Choose Make ADO25Northwind.dll from the File menu to create it. The process will halt only if there are errors in your code.

To Do: Testing the Component in Visual Basic

1. With the ADO25Northwind project selected, open the File menu and select Add Project.

2. Select Standard Exe and create the project. Rename it to ObjTester, and change the form name to frmTest. Save the project—you are also asked to provide a name for the project group (the EXE and DLL projects form a group). Choose ADO25Group as the group name.

3. Right click on the ObjTester project and select Set as start up. This allows you to click the Run button and automatically start the test application.

4. Just as with all component projects, you need to set a reference to the objects you want to use. Pick ADO25Northwind in the References dialog box (see Figure 15.7). It can be reached via Project, References.

FIGURE 15.7

Adding a reference to the ADO25Northwind project.

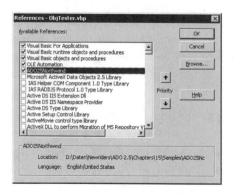

5. Place a button on frmTest and name it cmdTest. Double click on the button to create the Click event.

6. Enter the following code for the click event:

```
Private Sub cmdTest_Click()
    Dim objTest As New Suppliers, bResult As Boolean
    bResult = objTest.DeleteRecord(5)
End Sub
```

7. Place a breakpoint on the last line and start debugging. Notice that you can step into the component's code.

If you run the code, you will inevitably enter the error label because the foreign-key relationships disallow the deletion of the record. However, you know that your component handles error conditions correctly. You can give UpdateRecord and InsertRecord a try, too.

Adding COM+ Support

15

The component you have created is already a good citizen in the data tier; however, it could do more. This is where COM+ comes into the picture. Although you are definitely not interested in everything that COM+ encompasses, I'm going to pick the most important parts for the data-tier developer.

> **Note**
>
> COM+ is only available on Windows 2000 or later. Although you can achieve most of what is explained here on Windows NT 4 with service pack 3 or higher, this section focuses on Windows 2000 technologies.

 COM+ is the next evolutionary step of COM, the Component Object Model. It includes formerly separate technologies, such as Transaction Server or Message Queue Server. The most important task that COM+ performs for you is handling resource allocation tasks that developers previously had to do on their own.

The most important part for you as a database developer is transaction support: a component that can participate in a transaction, such as the classical example of money transfer—a crediting and a debiting component run in one transaction.

These are the features of COM+ that I will emphasize because I feel they are important for you, as a developer:

- Transaction support
- Object construction

Transaction Support

In the business world, a transaction is defined as an atomic task that either succeeds or fails as a whole. The famous example is the ATM: Your account is debited only if you also get the money (and no other way).

Transactions shield your applications from problems, be they system failures or fail conditions. Transactions are characterized by the ACID properties:

- Atomicity: Ensures that all actions governed by a transaction are either committed to the store or entirely rolled back.
- Consistency: Guarantees that a transaction changes data from one consistent state to another consistent state.

- Isolation: Allows parts of a transaction to run as if they were the only transaction running—shielding concurrent transactions from seeing each other's uncommitted changes.

- Durability: Ensures that after a transaction has been completed, all data is permanently stored in the database, even in case of system failures.

In each part of a transaction, there can be only success or failure. The outcome of the entire transaction is determined by whether all parts report success. If even one part reports an error, the entire transaction rolls back.

Now, put on the hat of a programmer again. I said that each part of a transaction can either fail or succeed. How do you tell COM+ about the outcome of your operations? You need to obtain the object context and call either SetComplete or SetAbort—if you think this is too easy, see for yourself in Listing 15.6.

LISTING 15.6   SetComplete and SetAbort

```
 1: Public Function DeleteRecord(ByVal nSupplierId As Long, _
 2:                              Optional ByVal strDSN As Variant) As Boolean
 3: On Error GoTo Err_Delete
 4:     Dim cmd As ADODB.Command
 5:     Dim tmpParam As ADODB.Parameter
 6:
 7:     DeleteRecord = False
 8:     If IsMissing(strDSN) Then
 9:         strDSN = cstrConnection
10:     End If
11:
12:     Set cmd = New ADODB.Command
13:     cmd.ActiveConnection = strDSN
14:     cmd.CommandType = adCmdStoredProc
15:     cmd.CommandText = "sp_delete_Suppliers"
16:
17:     Set tmpParam = cmd.CreateParameter("@SupplierId", adInteger,
➥adParamInput, 4, nSupplierId)
18:     cmd.Parameters.Append tmpParam
19:
20:     cmd.Execute
21:     DeleteRecord = True
22:     GetObjectContext().SetComplete
23:
24:     Exit Function
25: Err_Delete:
26:     Set cmd = Nothing
27:     GetObjectContext().SetAbort
28:     Err.Raise Err.Number, Err.Source, Err.Description
29: End Function
```

15

ANALYSIS The only differences from the previously discussed `DeleteRecord` code are lines 22 and 27, which contain calls to `SetComplete` and `SetAbort` through the `ObjectContext` object. Normally, you'd write

```
Set objContext = GetObjectContext()
objContext.SetComplete
```

but I decided to use the shorter version. There is one thing I must mention: The `ObjectContext` and all other COM+ functionality are provided by the COM+ Services Type Library, which you must reference in your project.

If you call your object now, it won't behave as expected—you first have to configure it in a COM+ application.

To Do: Creating a COM+ Application

1. From the Administrative Tools folder, start the Component Services management console.
2. Expand the Component Services node until you reach COM+ Applications (see Figure 15.8).

FIGURE 15.8

Managing COM+ applications for the local machine.

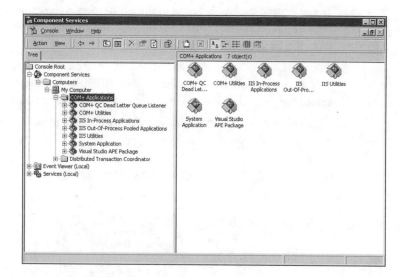

3. Right-click on COM+ Applications and select New, Application from the context menu. The COM Application Install Wizard starts.
4. In the wizard's second step, choose to create an empty application. Later, you can use the Install Prebuilt Applications feature to deploy your solution to multiple machines.

▼   5. You are asked for a name; enter ADO++ Test. Also, choose Library Application—
          this will run the components of the application in the process of the caller. They
          will run fast and behave as do "normal" DLL components (see Figure 15.9).

FIGURE 15.9

*Naming the new appli-
cation and setting acti-
vation properties.*

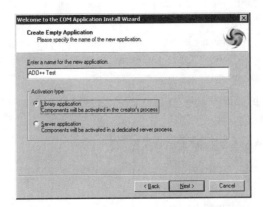

      6. You've reached the final step. Click Finish to create the application

      7. If you expand the nodes found in the application, you see that there are no compo-
          nents in this application. To add our Suppliers component, select New, Component
          from the context menu.

      8. Your first choice is whether to install new components, install already registered
          components, or install new event classes. Because the Suppliers component is
          already registered, choose to import components that are already registered.

      9. Choose the ADO25Northwind.Suppliers from the component list (see Figure
          15.10) and click Next to proceed.

FIGURE 15.10

*Selecting the compo-
nent you want to add
to the package.*

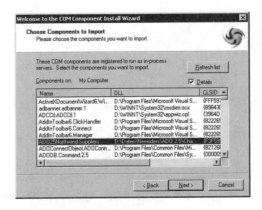

▲   10. The component is added to the application.

15

I hate to tell you, but you are still not entirely done configuring your component in the COM+ application. I intentionally left out a small configuration detail when adding the object context to the component. I did not change the MTSTransactionMode property for the Suppliers class, which, by default, is set to Not Supported. Because Component Services honor this property, our component was registered with no transaction support, as you can see in the Properties dialog box of the component (see Figure 15.11).

FIGURE 15.11

Verifying the transaction level that is set for the current component.

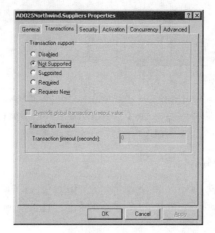

There are five transaction attributes:

- Disabled: With this option set, COM+ ignores transactional requirements of the component. The main use of this attribute is for COM components that must run as if they were not part of a COM+ application.

- Not Supported: Determines that the object will not participate in any transaction. Therefore, the object also cannot vote on the outcome of the transaction.

- Supported: The object will participate in a transaction if there is one. Transactions are shared with a caller.

- Required: Indicates that the object requires a transaction. This transaction can be one from the caller or a new one created for the component. Transaction context is passed to all objects that are created within this component. This setting should be the default for all your components that access or modify resources.

- Requires New: The component requires a new transaction, regardless of the transactional status of the caller. The component is the root of a new transaction.

Therefore, for the Suppliers component to be a better citizen in the COM+ world, set the transaction attribute to Required. And for all your new components, make sure that you set the MTSTransactionMode property for your classes to RequiresTransaction (see Figure 15.12).

FIGURE 15.12

Making the
RequiresTransaction
setting the default for
the Suppliers compo-
nent.

Now your component always participates in a transaction, and it votes in the transaction with SetComplete and SetAbort—for the DeleteRecord function only. Make the necessary changes so all functions work correctly within transactions.

Object Construction

You might wonder why today's chapter has *scalable* in its title. Did you add code to the component that made it more scalable than before? Yes, you did—by adding SetComplete and SetAbort.

The reason is JIT (just in time) activation. It enables you to manage resources more efficiently, because COM+ can at times deactivate a component while a client still holds a reference to an instance. When the client accesses the instance again, the same or a different instance is activated. COM+ manages a pool of components that can serve a large client base because of the JIT mechanism.

The critical essence of the previous paragraph is that JIT activation does not necessarily return the original instance of the component to the caller. This happens because you told COM+ about the deactivation of your component by setting the deactivation bit to True via calls to SetComplete and SetAbort. Deactivation also encompasses the deletion of instance data (state) that was stored in the component.

Though it is generally not a good idea to store state (because it severely hampers scalability), you can force COM+ to keep the instance of the component around between method calls. Even if the component stays activated after a method invocation, it can vote on a transaction outcome, as shown in Listing 15.7.

LISTING 15.7 Setting the Done Bit Using the `IContextState` Interface

```
 1: Public Sub StayAround()
 2:     Dim objContext As ObjectContext
 3:     Dim ctxState As IContextState
 4:
 5:     Set objContext = GetObjectContext()
 6:
 7:     ' Get the IContextState interface
 8:     Set ctxState = objContext
 9:
10:     ctxState.SetMyTransactionVote TxCommit
11:     ctxState.SetDeactivateOnReturn False
12: End Sub
```

ANALYSIS   The object context is obtained in line 5 and cast to the `IContextState` interface in line 8. This interface supports more granular and, sometimes, even more intuitive control than does the default interface of the object context for the Done bit (line 11) and transaction vote (line 10). With COM+ under Windows 2000, I'd recommend these methods instead of `SetComplete` and `SetAbort`—unless you really only need to report on the outcome and vote on the transaction.

If you visit the Activation tab of the component's Properties dialog box in Component Services, you can see that JIT activation is enabled by default (see Figure 15.13).

FIGURE 15.13

Activation options for the component.

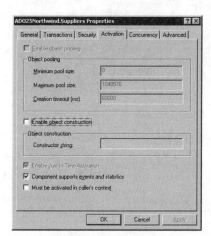

When employing Visual Basic 6 components, this tab has only one really useful setting that makes life much easier: Enable Object Construction. This allows you to pass a constructor string to the object when it is first created. And what is the most important string for a data tier component? Yes, the connection string! Now you have an elegant way of changing connection strings without hard coding it into the component or proliferating it through the calling code.

To Do: Setting the Constructor String

1. In Component Services, right-click on the component you want to manage and select Properties from the context menu.

2. Switch to the Activation tab and check the Enable Object Construction check box.

3. Enter the connection string in the Constructor String text box (see Figure 15.14).

FIGURE 15.14

Setting the constructor string to the connection string.

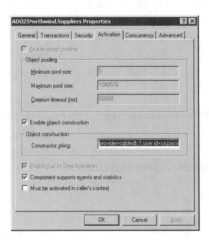

4. Click OK to make your changes stick.

The constructor string is set, but it is still not available to your component. In order to get at the constructor string, you have to implement the IObjectConstruct interface in your object. The code necessary to do so is presented in Listing 15.8.

LISTING 15.8 Code Necessary to Evaluate the Constructor String

```
1: Implements IObjectConstruct
2:
3: Private m_strConnString As String
4:
5: Private Sub IObjectConstruct_Construct(ByVal pCtorObj As Object)
6:     m_strConnString = pCtorObj.ConstructString
7: End Sub
```

15

ANALYSIS It takes only five lines of code to get at the constructor string and store it as a variable in the object. The `Implements` keyword is used to tell VB that this class implements the `IObjectConstruct` interface, and lines 5–7 implement the `Construct` method of this interface. All that needs to be done is to get the constructor string and assign it to the connection string variable (line 6).

Because of JIT, the use of `IObjectConstruct` allows for better performance because instances are reused for multiple clients, but the connection string is passed only once. Also, the connection string can be managed from a convenient location, without its being hard coded, either in the component or in any other script file.

Summary

Today, you learned about the differences between the client-server model and the three-tiered application design. I gave an overview of the responsibilities of each tier. These include the presentation tier for front ends, the business tier for implementing business logic, and the data tier for providing access to the database in a fast and organized way.

The remainder of the chapter dealt with programming components on the data tier. First, you created a plain-vanilla component that did not take advantage of any of the COM+ features, transaction support and object construction. You learned how to use different levels of transaction support and how to leverage the JIT feature of COM+. Finally you saw how to use object construction to pass initial parameters such as connection strings.

Q&A

Q There are several levels of transaction support, but how can I find out if an instance of my component actually takes part in a transaction?

A Check the `IsInTransaction` property of the `ObjectContext`. It returns `True` if your object takes part in a transaction.

Q When exploring the COM+ application I saw a folder named Roles. What is this folder about?

A COM+ applications support a security model that is built on a roles model—just like SQL Server 7. You can query in your component if a caller is in a role and deny access to specific features if she isn't. (For example, you can impose credit limit for bank clerks. Only managers can give unlimited credits.)

Workshop

The Workshop is designed to help you anticipate possible questions, review what you've learned, and get you thinking about how to put your knowledge into practice. The answers to the quiz are in Appendix A,"Answers."

Quiz

1. Why would you set the transaction level to Disabled?
2. How do you set the Done bit in your component?
3. Which interface implements the `Construct` method that is used to pass the constructor string?
4. Why should you never use the `Refresh` method on the `Parameters` collection of the `Command` object?
5. What is the primary advantage of stateless components?
6. Which type library do you need to reference in order to be able to use COM+ services?

Exercise

1. Create an entirely new component project named ADO25Exercise. Add a class named `Browser`, which supports transactions (but does not influence them) and has the following function:

    `GetRecordset(strSQL) As String`

    The String that is returned is the Recordset persisted using the `Save` function as XML (hint: use the `Stream` object and its `ReadText` function).

    The connection string is passed via the component's constructor string.

DAY 16

Working with Disconnected Recordsets

A disconnected recordset is a client-side recordset that has no active connection to a data source or database. Such a recordset seems to be rather useless at first sight. Where should someone use a disconnected recordset?

Think about a database server that can handle only a limited number of connections at the same time. When an application waits for user input or other actions, it would be a waste in connection resources to keep the connection open all the time.

Disconnected recordsets provide a solution for this problem. You can retrieve data from a data source, store the data in a recordset, and then disconnect the recordset from the data source to release the connection resources. The application that holds the recordset can change data in it or add new records to the recordset. After the application has performed all changes in the disconnected recordset, you can reconnect the recordset to the data source and write all pending changes to the data source.

Using this technique, a database server can serve many more clients, because only a limited number of open connections are required at the same time.

There are other scenarios where disconnected recordsets can be used. Because a disconnected recordset can be created without any data source, you can view the recordset as some kind of complex array that can store and organize data. Furthermore, the data in the recordset can be sorted or filtered very easily using the built-in functions and methods of the `Recordset` object. You might use disconnected recordsets instead of arrays in future applications and use the built-in sorting feature instead of writing sorting routines on your own.

Today, you will learn the following:

- Creating disconnected recordsets with or without a data source
- Performing tasks, such as sorting, searching for values, and filtering for certain data on disconnected recordsets
- Writing back changes in a disconnected recordset to the data store
- Dealing with concurrency problems that arise when multiple users change the same data while the recordsets are still handled by the users
- Using the mechanisms of ADO to detect concurrency errors and possibilities to use ADO for solving these errors
- Managing disconnected recordsets, storing them as persistent recordsets on a disk

Creating a Disconnected Recordset

This section shows the different methods of creating a disconnected recordset. A disconnected recordset is a recordset that has no active connection assigned. In order to create such a recordset, you must have a client-side, static cursor, and locking must be set to batch optimistic locking so that you can change its data without changing the data in an underlying data store immediately. A disconnected recordset uses records with fields to store data, as any other recordset does.

There are two techniques to define the structure of a disconnected recordset:

- Prepare and open a client-side recordset and populate it with data from a database, using a SQL statement, for instance. Then disconnect the recordset by setting the recordset's `ActiveConnection` property to `Nothing`. All fields, the field type, and data length of the disconnected recordset are now defined, and you have already populated the recordset with data.

- Prepare a client-side recordset and define the properties of its fields. Use the Open method to allow the disconnected recordset to be filled with records. No connection is assigned to the recordset. Use the recordset as some kind of data store. You can add new records to it or perform other recordset actions.

No matter how you create a disconnected recordset and fill it with data, you can change the data in the recordset, add records, and delete records as usual. Furthermore, you can sort the recordset using the Sort property, or search in it for records with certain values using the Find method or the Filter property. First, you will see how to create a disconnected recordset without using any data source. Such a recordset needs no connection even at creation time. However, you can use the disconnected recordset as any other client-side recordset, add records to it, delete records, and perform tasks such as sorting or filtering to manage the recordset data.

Creating a Recordset Without Using a Data Source

You can create a recordset without an underlying query or table definition—you are fabricating a recordset. The structure of the recordset is not implicitly defined by retrieving a recordset from the database, but you create the structure of the recordset explicitly by defining its fields, field types, and field names.

Such a fabricated recordset can be used in any application that needs to store data temporary in a tabular form. Using the features of the Recordset object you can sort or filter the stored data very easily.

The Recordset object enables you to define and add new fields to it. Strictly speaking, you can add new fields to the Fields collection of the Recordset object using the Append method, which has the following syntax:

```
objRecordset.Fields.Append FieldName, FieldType, DefinedSize, Attributes
```

objRecordset is the Recordset object where you want to append the new field. FieldName specifies the name of the recordset field. FieldType defines the type of the field (see Table 16.1).

TABLE 16.1   Mapping Visual Basic Data Types to ADO Field Type Constants

Visual Basic	ADO Field Type
Long	adInteger
Integer	adSmallInt
Byte	adTinyInt

continues

TABLE 16.1   continued

Visual Basic	ADO Field Type
Boolean	adBoolean
Double	adDouble
Single	adSingle
Currency	adCurrency
Date	adDate
String (fixed-length)	adChar
String (variable-length)	adVarChar
String (more than 8,000 characters)	adLongVarChar
Unicode String (fixed-length)	adWChar
Unicode String (variable-length)	adVarWChar
Unicode String (more than 4,000 characters)	adLongVarWChar
Array of Bytes	adVarBinary

The optional *DefinedSize* parameter defines the size (in characters or bytes) of the new field. Its default value is derived from the *FieldType* parameter.

Finally, the optional *Attributes* parameter specifies attributes for the new fields. It can contain NULL values, for instance. For more information, search for the term FieldAttributeEnum in the Microsoft Platform SDK.

A typical example for creating a recordset and defining its structure using the Fields collection's Append method is provided in Listing 16.1.

LISTING 16.1   Creating a Disconnected Recordset Without a Data Source

```
 1: Dim rs As ADODB.Recordset
 2:
 3: ' Create Client-Side Recordset
 4: Set rs = CreateObject("ADODB.Recordset")
 5: rs.CursorLocation = adUseClient         ' Optional
 6: rs.CursorType = adOpenStatic            ' Optional
 7: rs.LockType = adLockBatchOptimistic     ' Optional
 8: ' No Connection assigned to the Recordset
 9:
10: ' Define Recordset
11: rs.Fields.Append "FirstName", adVarChar, 30, adFldMayBeNull
12: rs.Fields.Append "LastName", adVarChar, 35, adFldMayBeNull
13:
14: ' Open Recordset
15: rs.Open
16: ...
```

ANALYSIS In line 4, the `Recordset` object is created and stored in the variable `rs`. The recordset is prepared in lines 5–7 to use a client-side, static cursor with batch optimistic locking. You can omit lines 5–7 because the recordset is automatically prepared this way when using the `Open` method without any parameters on a `Recordset` object that has no active connection assigned.

The fields for the recordset are defined in lines 11 and 12. The two fields defined are `FirstName`, which can hold strings up to 30 characters, and `LastName`, which stores strings with a maximum length of 35 characters.

After the recordset is opened in line 15, you can add new records to the recordset using the `AddNew` method and perform various actions on the recordset and its data, such as sorting or filtering the recordset.

It is often useful to construct a recordset on your own, but the real power of the recordset object is that you can retrieve data from a data source, disconnect the recordset, and use the data immediately. How to disconnect a recordset that was retrieved from a data source is explained in the next section.

Creating a Recordset Using a Data Source

Disconnected recordsets are often used to enable an application to process database data without consuming connection resources during all the time the recordset is held by the application.

For instance, when your application serves many users at the same time, you might use disconnected recordsets to save database server resources. Every user can retrieve a recordset, disconnect the recordset, and close the database connection. Then the user can process the recordset even over a period of hours without a connection to the database. Finally, when the user wants to synchronize his changes with the database data, the database connection is attached to the recordset, all changes are written to the database, and the connection is closed.

Disconnected recordsets that are retrieved from a database can also be very useful when you need only a snapshot of a database and certain recordset features to represent the data in a comfortable way.

Instead of programmatically defining the fields for a recordset, you retrieve a recordset (with or without any data) and use the delivered fields definition from the underlying data source to determine the recordset structure implicitly.

You just have to retrieve a recordset from a data source and then disconnect its connection to obtain a disconnected recordset. An example is given in Listing 16.2.

16

```
 1: Dim rs As ADODB.Recordset
 2: Dim conn As ADODB.Connection
 3: Dim strSQL As String
 4:
 5: Set conn = CreateObject("ADODB.Connection")
 6: conn.Open "Provider=SQLOLEDB;Data Source=BoyScout;" & _
 7:    "Initial Catalog=Northwind;User ID=sa;Password=;"
 8:
 9: Set rs = CreateObject("ADODB.Recordset")
10: rs.CursorLocation = adUseClient
11: rs.CursorType = adOpenStatic
12: rs.LockType = adLockBatchOptimistic
13:
14: ' Connect to Data Source and Retrieve Recordset
15: Set rs.ActiveConnection = conn
16: strSQL = "SELECT CustomerID, CompanyName FROM Customers"
17: rs.Open strSQL
18:
19: ' Disconnect Recordset from Data Source
20: Set rs.ActiveConnection = Nothing
21: ...
```

ANALYSIS   The script opens a connection to the SQL Server Northwind database in line 6.
Then it creates a Recordset object and prepares it to use a client-side and static
cursor. The locking type of the recordset is set to batch optimistic locking. In line 15, the
connection to the data source is attached to the Recordset object. Line 17 opens the
recordset and populates it with the values of the columns CustomerID and CompanyName
from all records of the Customers table. The script disconnects the recordset from the
data source in line 20 by setting the ActiveConnection property to Nothing. From then,
the script can use the disconnected recordset even when the connection in the variable
conn is closed.

You can use the disconnected recordset as any other recordset—manipulate its data, sort
the recordset, or search for certain records.

In the next sections, you will see some examples of the use of disconnected recordsets.

Storing and Organizing Data in a Disconnected Recordset

When your application needs to store data temporarily in a tabular form, a disconnected
recordset is the first choice for this task. You can organize the data using the various
built-in functions of the Recordset object.

After you have created a disconnected recordset, you can add new records to it or manipulate its data. The most important advantage when using a disconnected recordset for storing and organizing data is that you can use the Recordset object's built-in features:

- The Sort property enables you to organize the recordset data by ascending or descending values of a certain field.
- The Filter property enables you to view only the recordset's data that meet certain criteria.
- The Find method can search for a record that satisfies complex criteria.
- The Count property of the Records collection delivers the number of records in the recordset.
- Using the Bookmark property of the Recordset object enables you to save the position of a certain record, so you can return to that record very quickly.
- Retrieve data directly from a data source.
- Save the whole recordset (structure and data) to disk using the Recordset's Save method.

It is easy to sort the data in a recordset, and it is no expense to find records with certain data or properties.

Even better, you can fill a recordset directly with data from a database using a SQL statement, for instance. When you want to save the recordset back to the database, you can use all the features provided by ADO.

Another important advantage of a disconnected recordset is that you can easily persist the recordset to a file on disk so that it becomes transferable and can even be sent by email to another user. The Recordset object provides all the functions to manage such recordset files, to retrieve data from such a file, and to write data into it.

The procedure to create a disconnected recordset, populate it with data, and perform several actions on it is explained best by using an example.

Listing 16.3 shows how to use the built-in recordset methods and properties to organize data that are stored temporarily in a tabular form as recordset data.

The following script creates a recordset without a data source, adds some records, and performs typical recordset tasks.

LISTING 16.3   Using a Disconnected Recordset as a Data Store

```
1: ' Create Record without Data Source
2: Dim rs As ADODB.Recordset
3: Dim varBookmark As Variant
```

continues

LISTING **16.3**   continued

```
 4:
 5: ' Create Client-Side Recordset
 6: Set rs = CreateObject("ADODB.Recordset")
 7: rs.CursorLocation = adUseClient      ' Optional
 8: rs.CursorType = adOpenStatic         ' Optional
 9: rs.LockType = adLockBatchOptimistic ' Optional
10: ' No Connection assigned to the Recordset
11:
12: ' Define Recordset
13: rs.Fields.Append "FirstName", adVarChar, 30, adFldMayBeNull
14: rs.Fields.Append "LastName", adVarChar, 35, adFldMayBeNull
15:
16: ' Open Recordset
17: rs.Open
18:
19: ' Add Records
20: rs.AddNew
21: rs("FirstName") = "Desmond"
22: rs("LastName") = "Tutu"
23:
24: rs.AddNew
25: rs("FirstName") = "Dalai"
26: rs("LastName") = "Lama"
27:
28: rs.AddNew
29: rs("FirstName") = "Mother"
30: rs("LastName") = "Teresa"
31:
32:
33: ' Show Original Recordset
34: rs.MoveFirst
35: Debug.Print "Original Recordset:"
36: While Not rs.EOF
37:     Debug.Print rs("FirstName") & " " & rs("LastName")
38:     rs.MoveNext
39: Wend
40: Debug.Print
41:
42: ' Sort Recordset
43: rs.Sort = "LastName DESC, FirstName DESC"
44: rs.MoveFirst
45: Debug.Print "Sorted Recordset:"
46: While Not rs.EOF
47:     Debug.Print rs("FirstName") & " " & rs("LastName")
48:     rs.MoveNext
49: Wend
50: Debug.Print
51:
52: ' Search in Recordset
53: rs.MoveFirst
54: strSearch = "FirstName LIKE 'D*'"
```

16

```
55: Debug.Print "Searching for: " & strSearch
56: rs.Find strSearch
57: While Not (rs.EOF)
58:     Debug.Print rs("FirstName") & " " & rs("LastName")
59:     varBookmark = rs.Bookmark
60:     rs.Find strSearch, 1, adSearchForward, varBookmark
61: Wend
62: Debug.Print
63:
64: ' Change a Record
65: rs.MoveFirst
66: rs.Find "LastName LIKE 'Tutu*'"
67: If Not rs.EOF Then
68:     rs("LastName") = "Tutu (Bishop)"
69:     Debug.Print "Record changed ..."
70: End If
71:
72:
73: ' Delete a Record
74: rs.MoveFirst
75: rs.Find "FirstName = 'Dalai'"
76: If Not rs.EOF Then
77:     rs.Delete
78:     Debug.Print "Record deleted ..."
79: End If
80: Debug.Print
81:
82: ' Show Final Recordset
83: rs.MoveFirst
84: Debug.Print "Final Recordset:"
85: While Not rs.EOF
86:     Debug.Print rs("FirstName") & " " & rs("LastName")
87:     rs.MoveNext
88: Wend
89:
90: rs.Close
91: Set rs = Nothing
```

The code in Listing 16.3 should produce this output:

OUTPUT

```
 1: Original Recordset:
 2: Desmond Tutu
 3: Dalai Lama
 4: Mother Teresa
 5:
 6: Sorted Recordset:
 7: Desmond Tutu
 8: Mother Teresa
 9: Dalai Lama
10:
11: Searching for: FirstName LIKE 'D*'
12: Desmond Tutu
```

```
13: Dalai Lama
14:
15: Record changed ...
16: Record deleted ...
17:
18: Final Recordset:
19: Desmond Tutu (Bishop)
20: Mother Teresa
```

 The script creates and prepares a recordset in lines 6–9. The cursor location is set to client-side, the cursor type is static, and the lock type is set to batch optimistic locking. The fields of the recordset are defined in lines 13 and 14. The first field is named FirstName and can store strings with a maximum length of 30 characters. The second field's name is LastName; it can hold strings up to a length of 35 characters. Both fields are allowed to contain NULL.

After the recordset is defined, it is opened in line 17 using the Open method. Note that the recordset does not make use of any database connection. As the recordset is a client-side recordset, it is stored on the user's computer similar to a variable. Three records are added to the recordset in lines 20–30. You can navigate in the disconnected recordset using the MoveFirst or MoveNext method.

In lines 34–39, the content of the recordset is written to the user (output lines 1–4).

> **Caution**
>
> Performing the MoveFirst method on an empty recordset will result in a runtime error! Therefore, you should check whether the recordset is empty before using the MoveFirst method. When no record is stored in the recordset, the EOF and BOF properties both return True. You should always check for an empty recordset before using the MoveFirst method.

You can perform several tasks on the recordset and its data. In line 43, the recordset is sorted descending by the values in the fields LastName and FirstName. The sorted recordset is written to the user in lines 45–49. The result is shown in the output in lines 6–9.

There is also a way to search for records with certain values. In line 53, the cursor's start position for the search is set to the first record in the recordset. The search string is defined in line 54 and stored in the variable strSearch:

```
FirstName LIKE 'D*'
```

In line 56, the search string is used as argument for the Find method of the Recordset object. This forces the recordset's cursor to point to the first record whose FirstName value starts with the character D. If no record is found, the cursor points beyond the last record and the recordset's EOF property returns TRUE. The content of the found record is written to the user in line 58.

The bookmark of the current record is stored in the variable varBookmark to define the start position for the next search pass. In line 60, the Find method is invoked using the search string stored in the variable strSearch. The offset of 1 and the search direction Forward is used, and the current cursor position (varBookmark) is used as the starting position for the search. The Find method begins one position (offset of 1) after the current position (varBookmark) to search for another record that meets the search string stored in strSearch. The content of all records that meet the search condition is written to the user (output lines 11–13). When no further matching record is found, the While...Wend loop (lines 57–61) terminates.

To demonstrate that the content of a disconnected recordset can be changed easily, the script searches for the record with a LastName LIKE Tutu and changes its LastName value to Tutu (Bishop) in lines 65–68.

Of course, you can also delete records from the recordset. In lines 74–79, the script searches for the first record that contains the value Dalai in the FirstName field. When a record is found, it is deleted in line 77.

Finally, the resulting recordset is shown to the user in lines 84–88; see also output lines 18–20. The record Desmond Tutu has been changed into Desmond Tutu (Bishop), the record Dalai Lama has been deleted, and the record Mother Teresa remained untouched.

 Note   Another possible task that you can do with a disconnected recordset is to filter it to view only the records that meet certain conditions.

In the previous script, the recordset structure was defined in the script. Instead of building a disconnected recordset's structure on your own, you can open a connection to a database, retrieve a recordset from there, and then disconnect the recordset. This disconnected recordset can be used to read its data, change the data, and sort or filter the recordset, depending on your demands.

The script in Listing 16.4 retrieves such a recordset from a database, disconnects it, and performs various recordset tasks on the disconnected recordset.

LISTING 16.4 Disconnecting a Recordset

```
 1: Dim conn As ADODB.Connection
 2: Dim rs As ADODB.Recordset
 3: Dim strSQL As String
 4:
 5: Set conn = CreateObject("ADODB.Connection")
 6: conn.Open "Provider=SQLOLEDB;Data Source=BoyScout;" & _
 7:     "Initial Catalog=Northwind;User ID=sa;Password=;"
 8:
 9: Set rs = CreateObject("ADODB.Recordset")
10: strSQL = "SELECT SupplierID, CompanyName, Country FROM Suppliers " & _
11:     "WHERE Country LIKE 'U%'"
12: rs.CursorLocation = adUseClient
13: rs.CursorType = adOpenStatic
14: rs.LockType = adLockBatchOptimistic
15: Set rs.ActiveConnection = conn
16: rs.Open strSQL
17:
18: ' Disconnect Client-Side Recordset
19: Set rs.ActiveConnection = Nothing
20:
21: conn.Close
22: Set conn = Nothing
23:
24: ' Perform some Tasks on the Recordset
25: Debug.Print "Unsorted, Disconnected Recordset:"
26: While Not rs.EOF
27:     Debug.Print rs("CompanyName") & "(" & rs("Country") & ")"
28:     rs.MoveNext
29: Wend
30: Debug.Print
31:
32: Debug.Print "Sorted, Disconnected Recordset:"
33: rs.Sort = "CompanyName ASC, Country ASC"
34: While Not rs.EOF
35:     Debug.Print rs("CompanyName") & "(" & rs("Country") & ")"
36:     rs.MoveNext
37: Wend
38: Debug.Print
39:
40: strFilter = "(CompanyName LIKE 'New*') AND (Country='USA')"
41: Debug.Print "Filtered Recordset: "
42: rs.Filter = strFilter
43: While Not rs.EOF
44:     Debug.Print rs("CompanyName") & "(" & rs("Country") & ")"
45:     rs.MoveNext
46: Wend
47:
48: rs.Close
49: Set rs = Nothing
```

The code in Listing 16.4 should produce this output:

```
 1: Unsorted, Disconnected Recordset:
 2: Exotic Liquids(UK)
 3: New Orleans Cajun Delights(USA)
 4: Grandma Kelly's Homestead(USA)
 5: Specialty Biscuits, Ltd.(UK)
 6: Bigfoot Breweries(USA)
 7: New England Seafood Cannery(USA)
 8:
 9: Sorted, Disconnected Recordset:
10: Bigfoot Breweries(USA)
11: Exotic Liquids(UK)
12: Grandma Kelly's Homestead(USA)
13: New England Seafood Cannery(USA)
14: New Orleans Cajun Delights(USA)
15: Specialty Biscuits, Ltd.(UK)
16:
17: Filtered Recordset:
18: New England Seafood Cannery(USA)
19: New Orleans Cajun Delights(USA)
```

ANALYSIS

Listing 16.4 retrieves all Suppliers from the Northwind database whose country starts with the character U. The records are stored in a client-side recordset. In line 19, the connection is removed from the recordset, making it a disconnected recordset. Because the script does not need the database connection any more, the connection is closed in line 21. The disconnected recordset is written to the user in lines 25–29; see also output lines 1–7.

In line 33, the recordset is sorted ascending by the values in the CompanyName and the Country field of the records. The loop in lines 34–37 writes the sorted recordset to the user (output lines 9–15).

In line 40, a filter string is prepared and stored in the variable strFilter. In line 42, the filter string is assigned to the Filter property of the recordset so that the resulting recordset contains only records where the CompanyName starts with New and the Country field contains the value USA. The filtered recordset is shown to the user in lines 43–46 (output lines 17–19). Finally, the recordset is closed and its resources released.

In the last two listings, you examined how to create a disconnected recordset, populate it with data, and perform several tasks on it. It does not matter how you created and populated the disconnected recordset; you can use it to store, manage, and organize data in a tabular form.

Additionally, when you retrieve a recordset from a database, it is very common to write the changed recordset back to the database. In the next sections, the most common scenarios when writing back (updating) data to a database are explained. The most important problems and pitfalls are described using some sample listings.

Synchronizing Changes in a Disconnected Recordset with the Database Data

The last sections explained how to retrieve a recordset, disconnect it from the database, and change some of its data. The next advanced step, how to synchronize the data of the disconnected recordset with the database data, is explained in this section.

When using disconnected recordsets, you can retrieve the recordset from a database without using a database connection any longer then necessary. The client can hold the recordset as long as he or she wants—even several days—change some data of the recordset, and finally write the changed recordset back to the database.

Before you can write the changed data to the database, you have to reconnect the record-set to the database. Do so by assigning an open connection to the `ActiveConnection` property of the recordset:

```
Set rs.ActiveConnection = conn
```

The variable rs contains the `Recordset` object, and the variable conn contains the open connection.

After you have reestablished the connection, you can write the recordset to the database using the `UpdateBatch` method:

```
rs.UpdateBatch
```

This sounds simple; however, you have to consider many things to avoid problems, unintended results, and other pitfalls.

Here is a brief checklist with the actions and checks you should perform when you want to write a disconnected recordset back to a database:

- The recordset should contain all primary key columns of the table. Otherwise, it is possible that some records cannot be written back to the database.
- Because many runtime errors can appear when writing a recordset to a database, you should always use error handling in your application when calling the `UpdateBatch`, `Resync`, or `Refresh` method.
- If an update failed due to concurrency problems, you can use the `Filter` property to find the records that caused the error. Sometimes you can use the `Resync` method of the `Recordset` object to solve concurrency errors when the record in the underlying database was not deleted.
- Use the `Filter` property and the `Status` property of the `Recordset` object to determine which records could not be written to the database and to find out the reasons for the problem.

However, before diving into these issues at length, I want to start with a simple update operation.

Performing a Simple Update of a Recordset

Listing 16.5 performs the simple task to retrieve a disconnected recordset from a database, change a value, and write the changed recordset back to the database.

LISTING 16.5   Simple Update of a Disconnected Recordset

```
 1: Dim conn As ADODB.Connection
 2: Dim rs As ADODB.Recordset
 3: Dim strSQL As String
 4: Dim blnUpdate As Boolean
 5:
 6: Set conn = CreateObject("ADODB.Connection")
 7: conn.Open "Provider=SQLOLEDB;Data Source=BoyScout;" & _
 8:     "Initial Catalog=Northwind;User ID=sa;Password=;"
 9:
10: Set rs = CreateObject("ADODB.Recordset")
11: rs.CursorLocation = adUseClient
12: rs.CursorType = adOpenStatic
13: rs.LockType = adLockBatchOptimistic
14: Set rs.ActiveConnection = conn
15: strSQL = "SELECT SupplierID, CompanyName, Country FROM Suppliers"
16: rs.Open strSQL
17:
18: ' Disconnect Recordset
19: Set rs.ActiveConnection = Nothing
20:
21: rs.Find "CompanyName = 'Bigfoot Breweries'"
22: If Not (rs.EOF Or rs.BOF) Then
23:     rs("CompanyName") = "Greyhound Breweries"
24:     Debug.Print
25:     Debug.Print "Original Value: " & rs("CompanyName").OriginalValue
26:     Debug.Print "New Value: " & rs("CompanyName")
27: End If
28: Debug.Print
29:
30: ' Reconnect Recordset
31: Set rs.ActiveConnection = conn
32:
33: blnUpdate = True
34: If blnUpdate = True Then
35:     rs.UpdateBatch
36:     Debug.Print "Recordset written to Database."
37: Else
38:     rs.CancelBatch
39:     Debug.Print "Recordset not written to Database."
```

continues

LISTING **16.5**   continued

```
40: End If
41:
42: ' Restore Record in Database
43: conn.Execute "UPDATE Suppliers SET CompanyName = 'Bigfoot Breweries'" & _
44:      " WHERE (CompanyName = 'Greyhound Breweries')"
45:
46: rs.Close
47: Set rs = Nothing
48: conn.Close
49: Set conn = Nothing
```

The output of Listing 16.5 is as follows:

OUTPUT
```
1: Original Value: Bigfoot Breweries
2: New Value: Greyhound Breweries
3:
4: Recordset written to Database.
```

ANALYSIS The script opens a connection to the SQL Server 7.0 Northwind database. You could also use a connection to the Access 2000 Northwind database. In lines 10–14, the Recordset object is created and prepared with a client-side, static cursor and batch optimistic locking. The SQL statement, which is used to populate the recordset, is stored in the variable strSQL in line 15. This SQL statement is executed in line 16 to retrieve all values of the columns SupplierID, CompanyName, and Country from the Suppliers table and store them in the recordset in the variable rs.

Caution | When you want to create a recordset that can be updated (even when the underlying table contains similar records), you must include all primary key columns of the table in the recordset. When you open the recordset using a SQL SELECT statement, make sure that all primary key columns of the table are included in the SELECT column list. When you retrieve the recordset from a stored procedure, also make sure that the stored procedure returns all primary key columns of the database table!

Note that the primary key column (SupplierID) is retrieved from the Suppliers table and stored in the recordset to make sure that the recordset can later be updated. When updating a changed record, the record can be identified by ADO using the unequivocal value(s) of the primary key column(s).

The retrieved recordset is disconnected in line 19 from the database by setting the Recordset's ActiveConnection property to Nothing.

In line 21, the first record with the CompanyName value of Bigfoot Breweries is searched for using the Find method. When a matching record is found, the CompanyName value is changed to Greyhound Breweries in line 23. The originally retrieved value of the CompanyName field (Bigfoot Breweries) is written to the user in line 25 using the OriginalValue property (output line 1). The new value of CompanyName field (Greyhound Breweries) is written to the user in line 26 (output line 2).

In lines 31–35, the changed recordset is written back to the database. First, the recordset is reconnected to the database. Then the changes of the recordset are written to the database in line 35 using the UpdateBatch method.

When you want to reject the changes in the recordset, call the CancelBatch method as in line 38 (before calling the UpdateBatch method).

16

> **Note**
>
> You can call the CancelBatch method even when no connection is attached to the recordset. This is useful to cancel all changes performed to the recordset since it was retrieved, or to call the UpdateBatch method the last time.

The UPDATE statement in line 43 is executed only to restore the Suppliers table to its original state.

As long as only one user changes database data, synchronizing the disconnected recordset and the underlying database data is no problem at all.

However, when multiple users access the database at the same time, various problems can arise out of concurrency of changes in the user's recordsets. The next section shows how to deal with a multiuser application, the problems and pitfalls.

Fail-Safe Updates with Multiple Users in Mind

In a multiuser environment it is very likely that while a user works with a disconnected recordset, some data in the underlying table are changed or deleted. This fact raises a so-called concurrency problem, because multiple users want to change the same set of data. In contrast to classical concurrency, where changes occur nearly at the same time, concurrency issues with disconnected recordsets might occur much delayed.

This results in problems when you want to write a disconnected recordset back to the database. Some of the data in the disconnected recordset can be lost, or changes from other users can be overwritten.

Furthermore, you get a runtime error when you want to write a changed record from a disconnected recordset into a database when the underlying record of the database has been changed.

You have to consider such concurrency problems when designing a database application using disconnected recordsets. Depending on the demands of the application, you have to decide how to deal with concurrency problems in specific scenarios and situations.

Other problems can arise out of the database design. For instance, if you add a new record to a disconnected recordset, including the value for the primary key, it is possible that the primary key value already exists in the database and therefore the insertion of the record will fail.

The most common pitfalls and scenarios are shown in the next sections, with certain approaches for solving the problems that are raised.

Dealing with Updates by Other Users

When using disconnected recordsets in multiuser environments, it is likely that one user changes some database data while another user works with a disconnected recordset that contains the original and unchanged data.

How does ADO deal with concurrency problems? ADO uses a special mechanism to find out whether a record has been changed or deleted by another user. This mechanism is used to detect concurrency problems, as you will see in this section.

A recordset contains not only the actual values of the record fields, but also the original values and the underlying values of the database.

The original values contain the values that were received from the database during populating the recordset. After a successful UpdateBatch call, the original value is overwritten with the actual value.

The underlying values reflect the values of the corresponding record in the database. However, the underlying values do not actually return the values of the database as long as you are using a client-side cursor.

If you are using a client-side cursor, the underlying value of the recordset field is updated with the current value from the database when you are calling the UpdateBatch method (with batch optimistic locking).

Take a look at the following scenario. You have retrieved a client-side recordset with two records from the database (see Table 16.2).

TABLE 16.2 Recordset Retrieved from Database

Record	Value	Original Value	Underlying Value	Database
Record 1	8	8	8	8
Record 2	3	3	3	3

Then you change the recordset's value in record 1 from 8 to 4 (see Table 16.3).

16

TABLE 16.3 Recordset After Change

Record	Value	Original Value	Underlying Value	Database
Record 1	4	8	8	8
Record 2	3	3	3	3

During the time you are working with the client-side recordset, somebody changes the value of record 1 in the database from 8 to 7 and the value of record 2 from 3 to 9 (see Table 16.4).

TABLE 16.4 Database Values Changed by Other Users

Record	Value	Original Value	Underlying Value	Database
Record 1	4	8	8	7
Record 2	3	3	3	9

Now ADO can detect whether another user has changed a certain record by comparing the UnderlyingValue in the recordset and the value in the database.

When you write the recordset back to the database, calling the UpdateBatch method, ADO compares the Value and OriginalValue to check whether a record has been changed in the recordset. ADO compares the UnderlyingValue and the value in the database to detect concurrency collision in all changed records—whether another user has changed a value in the underlying database.

All changed records without a concurrency conflict are written to the database when calling the UpdateBatch method.

Therefore, after calling the UpdateBatch method, the recordset and the database values are as shown in Table 16.5.

TABLE 16.5   Recordset Value After `UpdateBatch`

Record	Value	Original Value	Underlying Value	Database
Record 1	4	8	8	7
Record 2	3	3	3	9

The value of record 1 was not written to the database because it has a conflict between database value and `UnderlyingValue`.

The value of record 2 was not written to the database, because its value has not been changed (`OriginalValue` and `Value` are the same). Also, its `UnderlyingValue` was not changed.

 Note

> When a record field is written to the database using the `Update` or `UpdateBatch` method, the `UnderlyingValue` is changed to the value of the record field.

When you want to allow ADO to write the value of record 1 to the database, you have to refresh the `UnderlyingValue` in record 1 so that it becomes synchronous to the database value. Otherwise, ADO will always detect a concurrency collision and not write the record to the database to prevent the value in the database, which was changed by another user, from being overwritten.

To refresh all `UnderlyingValues` of the recordset, you have to apply a special filter to the recordset and call the `Recordset` object's `Resync` method with special parameters, as in Listing 16.6.

LISTING 16.6   Detecting Concurrency Problems Because of Update or Delete in an Underlying Table

```
 1: On Error Resume Next
 2: rs.UpdateBatch
 3: On Error GoTo 0
 4: rs.Filter = adFilterConflictingRecords
 5: If rs.BOF And rs.EOF Then
 6:     ' No conflicting Records in Recordset
 7: Else
 8:     ' Resynchronise conflicting Records
 9:    rs.Resync adAffectGroup, adResyncUnderlyingValues
10: End If
```

ANALYSIS The last `UpdateBatch` call can result in some records with concurrency conflicts. When you apply a special filter to the recordset, as in line 4, you get a recordset that contains only records with conflicts. When no records with conflicts exist, the filtered recordset is empty, and both the `BOF` and `EOF` property return `TRUE`.

However, when any conflicting records exist, you can resynchronize the `UnderlyingValues` using the `Resync` method of the recordset with two special parameters, as shown in line 9. The parameter `adAffectGroup` forces the `Resync` method to affect only records that satisfy the current `Filter` property setting (records with conflicts). The parameter `adResyncUnderlyingValues` tells the `Resync` method to affect only the `UnderlyingValues` of the recordset (no other values are overwritten and pending updates are not canceled).

After calling the `Resync` method as described in Listing 16.6, the `UnderlyingValue` of the first record is synchronous to the database value, and the recordset has the values in Table 16.6.

TABLE 16.6 Values After `Resync` of `UnderlyingValues` in Records with Conflicts

Record	Value	Original Value	Underlying Value	Database
Record 1	4	8	7	7
Record 2	3	3	3	9

Now you can call the `UpdateBatch` method again to update also the records that failed to update (due to concurrency problems) during the last call of the `UpdateBatch` method:

```
rs.UpdateBatch
```

 Caution Synchronizing the recordset's underlying values and updating the conflicted record values without further checks is only admissible when the application goal allows that all conflicting data in the database is lost.

Then the values in the recordset and the database are as shown in Table 16.7.

TABLE 16.7 Values After Second `UpdateBatch`

Record	Value	Original Value	Underlying Value	Database
Record 1	4	4	4	4
Record 2	3	3	3	9

Note It is possible that calling the UpdateBatch method this time also fails due to other changes in the database between calling Resync and UpdateBatch. Therefore, you should always check for concurrency problems after calling UpdateBatch.

The schematic description of this procedure is shown in Figure 16.1.

FIGURE 16.1

Schematic description of using UpdateBatch *and* Resync *for solving concurrency collisions.*

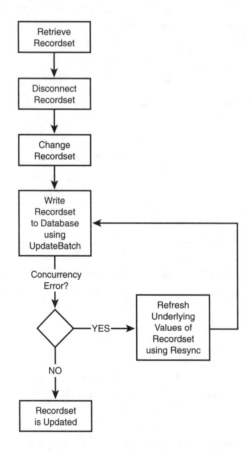

After you have retrieved the disconnected recordset, you can make changes to the recordset. When you attempt to write the changed recordset data back to the database using UpdateBatch, there can be some concurrency collisions. Check for collisions and try to solve them by refreshing the UnderlyingValues of the recordset. After refreshing the UnderlyingValues, call the UpdateBatch method again to write the changes to the database.

When calling the `UpdateBatch` method, there can appear other runtime errors than concurrency errors. Use efficient error-handling code to distinguish between errors raised due to concurrency problems and other errors. Errors can also appear when calling the `Resync` method. For a well-designed database application that deals with all possible scenarios, you have to use plenty of error-handling code.

Detecting and Handling Deletions Performed by Other Users

As outlined in the previous section, you might not be the only one modifying the database. You also have concurrency problems when you are processing a disconnected recordset and another user deletes some of the recordset's data in the database before you write the recordset back to the database.

The following scenario shows how to deal with a concurrency problem caused by the fact that another user deleted data from the underlying database:

You have retrieved a client-side recordset with two records from the database. As shown before, you have the value, the original value, and the underlying value stored in the recordset (see Table 16.8).

TABLE 16.8   Recordset Retrieved from Database

Record	Value	Original Value	Underlying Value	Database
Record 1	4	4	4	4
Record 2	6	6	6	6

Then you change the value in record 1 from 4 to 5 (see Table 16.9).

TABLE 16.9   Changed Recordset

Record	Value	Original Value	Underlying Value	Database
Record 1	5	4	4	4
Record 2	6	6	6	6

While you are working with the client-side recordset, somebody deletes record 1 in the database (see Table 16.10).

TABLE 16.10 Database Value Deleted by Other User

Record	Value	Original Value	Underlying Value	Database
Record 1	5	4	4	(DELETED)
Record 2	6	6	6	6

What happens when you update the recordset using the UpdateBatch method? First, you cannot update record 1 in the database with the values of record 1 from the recordset, because there is no longer a record 1 in the database.

Now we must take a closer look at some ADO details. How does ADO know to which database record a recordset record refers? ADO identifies a recordset row, for instance, by its primary key value(s). But what happens if your recordset or the underlying database table does not have a primary key? ADO tries to update a record in the database that has the same values as the OriginalValues of the record in the recordset.

> **Caution**
>
> It is strongly recommended that you use only database tables that have a primary key defined for disconnected recordsets when you want to write the changed recordset back to the database.
>
> Make sure to retrieve a recordset that contains the primary key column(s) of the underlying database table. Only this step ensures that the recordset can be written back to the data source.

> **Note**
>
> When using a SQL Server 7.0 database table with a primary key defined as a data source for a disconnected recordset, you can update the recordset even when the recordset does not contain the primary key column(s). The reason is that ADO also retrieves the primary key values from the database when populating the recordset and uses them to uniquely identify the records when writing them back to the database.
>
> For the more interested reader: The undocumented SQL Server 7.0 switch NO_BROWSETABLE is used by the SQL database provider to force the SQL Server to deliver primary key and time stamp columns in addition to the requested columns when executing a SELECT statement.

When you write the recordset of Table 16.10 back to the database, you get a runtime error. This error tells you that a row cannot be located for updating. Record 1 cannot be located in the database because it was deleted!

You must use some error-handling code to intercept the runtime error, examine the reason for the error, and perform an appropriate action, as in Listing 16.7.

LISTING 16.7   Update and Error Handling

```
 1: On Error Resume Next
 2: rs.UpdateBatch
 3:
 4: If (Err.Number - vbObjectError) = 3640 Then
 5:    ' Changes in underlying table since last reading
 6:    ' Perform some appropriate action
 7:    On Error GoTo 0
 8:    ...
 9: ElseIf Err.Number <> 0 Then
10:    ' Other error occurred
11:    On Error GoTo 0
12:    ...
13: End If
```

ANALYSIS   Imagine that the script in Listing 16.7 is part of a larger script that produced a disconnected recordset. The disconnected recordset is written back to the database in line 2 of Listing 16.7. Error handling is enabled in line 1 using the `On Error Resume Next` statement. In line 2, the update of the recordset is performed using the `UpdateBatch` method. When a record of the underlying database table is changed or deleted, an error is raised in line 2. The error could also be raised by another reason (maybe the database connection is broken and timed out or the database is full).

When the error is caused by the fact that a value of the recordset in the underlying table was changed or deleted by another user (concurrency error), the `Err` object returns the custom error number 3640. The script checks in line 4 for the custom error number and performs appropriate actions when a concurrency error is raised. When another error occurs, the script executes line 11–13.

Now that you know how to use error handling when calling the `UpdateBatch` method, what happens to the recordset of Table 16.10 when calling `UpdateBatch` with enabled error handling?

When calling the `UpdateBatch` method with enabled error handling on a recordset, as shown in Table 16.10, the recordset and the database look like Table 16.11 after calling `UpdateBatch`.

TABLE 16.11 Value After `UpdateBatch`

Record	Value	Original Value	Underlying Value	Database
Record 1	5	4	4	(DELETED)
Record 2	6	6	6	6

When the `UpdateBatch` statement tries to locate the position of record 1 in the database, an error is raised by ADO because no record 1 is found. When you enable error handling, the update of record 1 is canceled and the `UpdateBatch` statement tries to update all other records of the recordset.

Because record 1 only raises an error, no value in record 1 is changed in the recordset. It depends on you to deal with the situation. Based on the business rules of your application, you have to decide whether you add record 1 as a new record to the database or delete it from the recordset.

How can you detect whether a record could not be updated in the database—because the record was deleted from the database, for instance?

When you loop through all records of the recordset and read their `Status` properties, every `Status` property of an updated record returns the value `adRecOK` or `adRecUnmodified`. Any record that does not return the `Status` value `adRecOK` or `adRecUnmodified` immediately after calling `UpdateBatch` was not written to the database. Listing 16.8 provides an overview of how to check for records that could not be updated during the `UpdateBatch` call.

LISTING 16.8 Check for Records That Were Not Updated

```
 1: On Error Resume Next
 2: rs.UpdateBatch
 3: On Error GoTo 0
 4: If Not (rs.EOF And rs.BOF) Then
 5:     rs.MoveFirst
 6:     ' Records that could not be updated:
 7:     While Not rs.EOF
 8:         If rs.Status <> adRecOK And rs.Status <> adRecUnmodified Then
 9:             ' Current Record was not updated
10:             ' Perform some action on current Record
```

```
11:              ...
12:          End If
13:          rs.MoveNext
14:      Wend
15: End If
```

ANALYSIS In line 1, the error handling is enabled to allow the script to continue even when a runtime error occurs. Line 2 executes the `UpdateBatch` method of the recordset stored in the variable `rs`. The error handling is disabled in line 3. The script loops through all records of the recordset in lines 5–14. Because the `MoveFirst` method (in line 5) would raise an error when the recordset is empty, the script checks in line 4 to determine whether any record is in the recordset. The `While...Wend` loop in lines 7–14 iterates over all records of the recordset.

The `Status` property of every record is checked. If a record failed to update in line 2, its `Status` property is different from `adRecOK` and `adRecUnmodified`. According to the business rules of your application, the script can perform certain actions on records that could not be updated due to concurrency problems in lines 9–11.

As shown in Listing 16.6, you can check for conflicting records using the `Filter` property with the `adFilterConflictingRecords` parameter. Applying this filter results in a recordset that contains only records with conflicts during the last call of `UpdateBatch`.

As mentioned before, many concurrency problems are raised by the fact that the `UnderlyingValue` of a record differs from the database value. You can refresh the `UnderlyingValues` of all records using the `Resync` method with some special parameters to synchronize the `UnderlyingValues` and the database values:

```
rs.Resync adAffectGroup, adResyncUnderlyingValues
```

After refreshing the `UnderlyingValues` of records with conflicts, you can write all records from the recordset whose underlying database values have changed (but were not deleted), to the database. To write them to the database, you use another `UpdateBatch` call (see also the earlier section "Dealing with Updates by Other Users).

What happens to the recordset's records whose database records have been deleted when you call the `Resync` method? When an underlying record of the recordset is deleted in the database, calling the `Resync` method returns a runtime error. The error description looks as follows:

```
Key value for this row was changed or deleted at the data store.
➡ The local row is now deleted.
```

This error message is a little confusing. In fact, the error was caused by the recordset's record whose underlying record in the database was deleted. However, contrary to the error description, the local record is not deleted. It is still in the local recordset.

You can intercept the runtime error using error handling. You also can find out which records are affected by the call of the Resync method, as shown in Listing 16.9.

LISTING 16.9   Check for Status of Records After Resync of UnderlyingValues

```
 1: ' Update Recordset
 2: On Error Resume Next
 3: rs.UpdateBatch
 4: On Error GoTo 0
 5:
 6: rs.Filter = adFilterConflictingRecords
 7: If rs.EOF And rs.BOF Then
 8:     ' No conflicting Records
 9: Else
10:     ' Conflicting Records
11:     ' Resyncronize UnderlyingValues of Records with Conflicts
12:     On Error Resume Next
13:     rs.Resync adAffectGroup, adResyncUnderlyingValues
14:     On Error GoTo 0
15:     rs.Filter = adFilterAffectedRecords
16:     ' Records Affected by Resync:
17:     While Not rs.EOF
18:         ' Check Status of Recordset
19:         Debug.Print "Status: 0x" & Hex(rs.Status)
20:         If (rs.Status And adRecModified) = adRecModified Then
21:             ' Record was modified
22:             ...
23:         End If
24:         If (rs.Status And adRecDBDeleted) = adRecDBDeleted Then
25:             ' Record was deleted from Data source
26:             ...
27:         End If
28:         ...
29:         rs.MoveNext
30:     Wend
31: End If
```

ANALYSIS   When the UpdateBatch method returns records with concurrency conflicts, the script tries to refresh the UnderlyingValues of all records that have conflicts. The refresh is performed in line 13 using the Resync method of the Recordset object. When the recordset in the variable rs contains records whose underlying records in the database are deleted, the Resync method raises a runtime error. Therefore, you need some error-handling code in lines 12 and 14.

After calling the `Resync` method, the script applies a filter to the recordset using the `adFilterAffectedRecords` parameter in line 15. This filter enables you to loop through all records that were affected by the `Resync` method. All affected records are examined in the `While...Wend` loop in lines 17–30. In line 19, the hexadecimal value of the recordset status is written to the user. The recordset status can be compared with certain ADO constants, as shown in lines 20–27. For the description of the ADO status constants, see Table 16.12.

16

> **Caution**
>
> If you read the `Status` property of a record, the values you receive depend on the `Filter` you applied to the recordset. Suppose you have a recordset with a special record whose underlying record has been deleted. After calling `Resync` and applying an `adFilterAffectedRecords` filter to the recordset, the `Status` property of the special record returns only a status of `adRecModified`, which indicates that the record was modified. However, when applying an `adFilterAffectedRecords` or `adFilterConflictingRecords` filter to the recordset, the `Status` property of the special record returns a status of `adRecModified` and `adRecDBDeleted`. The status `adRecDBDeleted` indicates that the record in the underlying database has been deleted.

> **Note**
>
> Of course, the action of the script must depend on the business rules of your application. You have to decide whether you want to write records to the database when other users still have changed values of the records in the underlying database. When you want to write them to the database anyway, you have to refresh the `UnderlyingValues` of all records with concurrency conflicts. Otherwise, you can send a message to the user or decide for each record whether to write it to the database or not.

TABLE 16.12   Status of a Record

ADO Constant (Value)	Description
`adRecOK` (0)	Record was updated successfully.
`adRecNew` (0x1)	Record is new.
`adRecModified` (0x2)	Record was modified.

continues

TABLE 16.12 continued

ADO Constant (Value)	Description
adRecDeleted (0x4)	Record was deleted.
adRecUnmodified (0x8)	Record was not modified.
adRecInvalid (0x10)	Record was not saved; its bookmark is invalid.
adRecMultipleChanges (0x40)	Record was not saved; it would have affected multiple records.
adRecPendingChanges (0x80)	Record was not saved; it refers to a pending insert.
adRecCanceled (0x100)	Record was not saved because operation was canceled.
adRecCantRelease (0x400)	New record was not saved because the existing record was locked.
adRecConcurrencyViolation (0x800)	Record was not saved because optimistic concurrency is in use.
adRecIntegrityViolation (0x1000)	Record was not saved because of violation of integrity constraints.
adRecMaxChangesExceeded (0x2000)	Record was not saved because there were too many pending changes.
adRecObjectOpen (0x4000)	Record was not saved because of conflict with an open storage.
adRecOutOfMemory (0x8000)	Record was not saved because computer has run out of memory.
adRecPermissionDenied (0x10000)	Record was not saved; user has insufficient permissions.
adRecSchemaViolation (0x20000)	Record was not saved; it violates the structure of the underlying database.
adRecDBDeleted (0x40000)	Record has already been deleted from the data source.

What happens to the recordset from Table 16.11 after refreshing its UnderlyingValues? The UnderlyingValue of record 1 is marked as deleted (see Table 16.13).

TABLE 16.13 Value After Refresh of `UnderlyingValues`

Record	Value	Original Value	Underlying Value	Database
Record 1	5	4	(DELETED)	(DELETED)
Record 2	6	6	6	6

When accessing the `UnderlyingValue` property of record 1, you get a runtime error as follows:

```
Row handle referred to a deleted row or a row marked for deletion.
```

This error message indicates that record 1 has no underlying value any more because its underlying record in the database is deleted.

You could delete record 1 in the local recordset, or you could write the record as a new record in the database by copying all its values to a new record in the recordset.

After you have refreshed the `UnderlyingValues` of the database, you have to call `UpdateBatch` once more to write the records with a former concurrency conflict to the database (see Table 16.14).

TABLE 16.14 Values After second `UpdateBatch`

Record	Value	Original Value	Underlying Value	Database
Record 1	5	4	(DELETED)	(DELETED)
Record 2	6	6	6	6

The values remain the same. Because record 1 was deleted from the database, calling the `UpdateBatch` method raises a runtime error. However, when applying a `Filter` using the `adFilterConflictingRecords` parameter, record 1 is not among the records with concurrency conflicts. This is clear when you remember that only records where the `UnderlyingValue` differs from the database value can be recognized by ADO as records with concurrency conflicts.

However, when you check the `Status` property of all records, you will see that the `Status` property of record 1 returns the value `adRecModified`. This value indicates that the record has been changed in the local recordset, but the changes have not been written to the database. The `Status` property of a record, which has been written successfully to the database, returns the value `adRecOK` or `adRecUnmodified`.

16

A Sample Solution for Handling Concurrency Issues

You have seen how to deal with concurrency errors that were raised by changed or deleted records of the database. The next step is to use this knowledge and build a sample application that deals with both changed and deleted records in the database. This sample application must create a disconnected recordset and change some of its data and the underlying database data to simulate a concurrency problem. Lots of error-handling code and code to solve the concurrency problem is needed in the application.

Such an application can be built similar to the sample application in Listing 16.10.

LISTING 16.10   Concurrency Problems Because of Update or Delete in an Underlying Table

```
 1: Dim conn As ADODB.Connection
 2: Dim rs As ADODB.Recordset
 3: Dim strSQL As String, strUV As String
 4: Dim blnUpdated As Boolean
 5: Dim lngLoop As Long
 6: Dim strUpdateDelete As String
 7: strUpdateDelete = "Update"  ' or Delete
 8: 'strUpdateDelete = "Delete"
 9:
10: Set conn = CreateObject("ADODB.Connection")
11: conn.Open "Provider=SQLOLEDB;Data Source=BoyScout;" & _
12:     "Initial Catalog=Northwind;User ID=sa;Password=;"
13:
14: ' Add New Record to Database
15: conn.Execute "INSERT INTO Suppliers(CompanyName, Country) " & _
16:     "VALUES('Taurus Beer','Austria')"
17:
18: Set rs = CreateObject("ADODB.Recordset")
19: strSQL = "SELECT SupplierID, CompanyName, Country " & _
20    "FROM Suppliers WHERE SupplierID > 26"
21: rs.CursorLocation = adUseClient
22: rs.CursorType = adOpenStatic
23: rs.LockType = adLockBatchOptimistic
24: Set rs.ActiveConnection = conn
25: rs.Open strSQL
26:
27: Set rs.ActiveConnection = Nothing
28:
29: rs.MoveFirst
30: rs.Find "CompanyName = 'Taurus Beer'"
31: If Not (rs.EOF Or rs.BOF) Then
32:     ' Record found: Change CompanyName
33:     rs("CompanyName") = "Greyhound Beer"
34:     Debug.Print "Record in Disconnected Recordset changed ..."
```

```
35:     Debug.Print
36: End If
37:
38: ' Change Taurus Beer Record in Database
39: If LCase(strUpdateDelete) = "update" Then
40:     conn.Execute "UPDATE Suppliers SET CompanyName = 'Bull Beer' " & _
41:         "WHERE CompanyName = 'Taurus Beer' And Country = 'Austria'"
42:     Debug.Print "Data in Underlying Table changed ..."
43: ElseIf LCase(strUpdateDelete) = "delete" Then
44:     conn.Execute "DELETE FROM Suppliers WHERE " & _
45:         "CompanyName = 'Taurus Beer' And Country = 'Austria'"
46:     Debug.Print "Data in Underlying Table deleted ..."
47: End If
48:
49: lngLoop = 0
50: blnUpdated = False
51: Set rs.ActiveConnection = conn
52:
53: Do While (lngLoop < 5 And blnUpdated = False)
54:     lngLoop = lngLoop + 1
55:     Debug.Print lngLoop & ". Attempt to Write Recordset into Database:"
56:     rs.Filter = adFilterNone
57:     On Error Resume Next
58:     rs.UpdateBatch
59:
60:     If (Err.Number - vbObjectError) = 3640 Then
61:         ' Changes in underlying table since last reading
62:         Debug.Print "Error During Update was caused by " & _
63:             "Conflicting Records ..."
64:     ElseIf Err.Number <> 0 Then
65:         Debug.Print "An Error Occurred During Update:"
66:         Debug.Print "Error Description: " & Err.Description
67:         Debug.Print "Error Source: " & Err.Source
68:         Debug.Print "Application Error: " & Err.Number - vbObjectError
69:         Debug.Print
70:     End If
71:     On Error GoTo 0
72:
73:     If Not (rs.EOF And rs.BOF) Then
74:         rs.MoveFirst
75:         Debug.Print "*** Records that could not be updated: ***"
76:         While Not rs.EOF
77:             If rs.Status <> adRecOK And rs.Status <> adRecUnmodified Then
78:                 ' Record was not updated
79:                 Debug.Print rs("SupplierID"), rs("CompanyName"),
➥ "Status: 0x" & Hex(rs.Status)
80:                 On Error Resume Next
81:                 ' Access the Underlying Value
82:                 strUV = rs("CompanyName").UnderlyingValue
83:                 If (Err.Number - vbObjectError) = 3619 Then
84:                     ' Row Handle referred to a Deleted Row
```

continues

LISTING **16.10**   continued

```
85:                         Debug.Print "UnderlyingValue: (Deleted Row Handle)"
86:                 ElseIf Err.Number <> 0 Then
87:                         Debug.Print "UnderlyingValue: (Error occurred)"
88:                 Else
89:                         Debug.Print "UnderlyingValue: " &
➥ rs("CompanyName").UnderlyingValue
90:                 End If
91:                 On Error GoTo 0
92:                 Debug.Print "OriginalValue: " &
➥ rs("CompanyName").OriginalValue
93:             End If
94:             rs.MoveNext
95:         Wend
96:     End If
97:     ' Filter for Records with Conflicts During Update
98:     rs.Filter = adFilterConflictingRecords
99:     If (rs.EOF And rs.BOF) Then
100:         ' No Conflicting Records
101:         ' Update is OK
102:         Debug.Print "> No conflicting Records any more."
103:         blnUpdated = True
104:     Else
105:         ' Examine Problems During UpdateBatch
106:         Debug.Print "*** Records with Problems During UpdateBatch: ***"
107:         While Not rs.EOF
108:             Debug.Print rs("SupplierID"), rs("CompanyName"),
➥ "Status: 0x" & Hex(rs.Status)
109:             Debug.Print "UnderlyingValue: " &
➥ rs("CompanyName").UnderlyingValue
110:             Debug.Print "OriginalValue: " &
➥ rs("CompanyName").OriginalValue
111:             rs.MoveNext
112:         Wend
113:
114:         ' Resyncronize Underlying Values of Recordset
115:         On Error Resume Next
116:         rs.Resync adAffectGroup, adResyncUnderlyingValues
117:
118:         If Err.Number <> 0 Then
119:             Debug.Print "An error occurred during refreshing
➥ the UnderlyingValues:"
120:             Debug.Print "Error Description: " & Err.Description
121:             Debug.Print "Error Source: " & Err.Source
122:             Debug.Print "Error Number: " & Err.Number
123:             Debug.Print "Application Error: " &
```

```
➥ (Err.Number - vbObjectError)
124:            Debug.Print
125:        End If
126:        On Error GoTo 0
127:
128:        rs.Filter = adFilterAffectedRecords
129:        Debug.Print "*** Records Affected by Resync: ***"
130:        While Not rs.EOF
131:            Debug.Print rs("SupplierID"), rs("CompanyName"),
➥ "Status: 0x" & Hex(rs.Status)
132:            On Error Resume Next
133:            ' Access the Underlying Value
134:            strUV = rs("CompanyName").UnderlyingValue
135:            If (Err.Number - vbObjectError) = 3619 Then
136:                ' Row Handle referred to a Deleted Row
137:                Debug.Print "UnderlyingValue: (Deleted Row Handle)"
138:            ElseIf Err.Number <> 0 Then
139:                Debug.Print "UnderlyingValue: (Error occurred)"
140:            Else
141:                Debug.Print "UnderlyingValue: " &
➥ rs("CompanyName").UnderlyingValue
142:            End If
143:            On Error GoTo 0
144:            Debug.Print "OriginalValue: " &
➥ rs("CompanyName").OriginalValue
145:            rs.MoveNext
146:        Wend
147:        Debug.Print "> Recordset's UnderlyingValues were refreshed."
148:    End If
149:    Debug.Print
150: Loop
151:
152: If blnUpdated = True Then
153:     Debug.Print "> Update Successful."
154: Else
155:     Debug.Print "> Update Failed."
156: End If
157:
158: ' Delete Record from Database
159: conn.Execute "DELETE FROM Suppliers WHERE (CompanyName = " & _
160:     "'Taurus Beer') OR (CompanyName = 'Greyhound Beer') " & _
161:     "AND Country = 'Austria'"
162:
163: rs.Close
164: Set rs = Nothing
165: conn.Close
166: Set conn = Nothing
```

The output of Listing 16.10 is as follows:

```
 1: Record in Disconnected Recordset changed ...
 2:
 3: Data in Underlying Table changed ...
 4: 1. Attempt to Write Recordset into Database:
 5: Error During Update was caused by Conflicting Records ...
 6: *** Records that could not be updated: ***
 7:  30              Greyhound Beer              Status: 0x802
 8: UnderlyingValue: Taurus Beer
 9: OriginalValue: Taurus Beer
10: *** Records with Problems During UpdateBatch: ***
11:  30              Greyhound Beer              Status: 0x802
12: UnderlyingValue: Taurus Beer
13: OriginalValue: Taurus Beer
14: *** Records Affected by Resync: ***
15:  30              Greyhound Beer              Status: 0x2
16: UnderlyingValue: Bull Beer
17: OriginalValue: Taurus Beer
18: > Recordset's UnderlyingValues were refreshed.
19:
20: 2. Attempt to Write Recordset into Database:
21: *** Records that could not be updated: ***
22: > No conflicting Records any more.
23:
24: > Update Successful.
```

In short terms, the code in Listing 16.10 performs the following actions: It adds a record to the database and retrieves a disconnected recordset that contains the added record. Then it changes (updates) or deletes the added record in the database to produce a concurrency problem between the disconnected recordset and the underlying database data.

When the script has changed the local recordset and writes it back to the database, the script has to handle the runtime errors that occur and retrieve information about the kind of error. It searches for the record that caused the error and tries to resolve the error when possible. When the error is caused because the UnderlyingValue of a record differs from the value in the database, the script tries to refresh the UnderlyingValues to enable the UpdateBatch method to write the records from the recordset back to the database—even when the data in both the local recordset and the database have been changed.

In line 7, the variable strUpdateDelete is assigned to the value Update. This value indicates whether the listing should change (update) or delete an underlying record of the disconnected recordset. A new record is inserted in the Suppliers table of the SQL Server 7.0 Northwind database in line 15. The disconnected recordset is retrieved from the Suppliers table in lines 18–27. The next step is to change the record with the

CompanyName `Taurus Beer` of the disconnected recordset and assign the new CompanyName `Greyhound Beer` to it (see listing lines 29–36 and output line 1). In lines 38–47, the record `Taurus Beer` in the database is changed (`strUpdateDelete` contains `Update`) or deleted (`strUpdateDelete` contains `Delete`).

The variable `lngLoop` is set to `0` in line 49. It is a counter variable with the purpose of limiting the number of passes of the `While... Wend` loop in lines 53–150. The variable `blnUpdated` is set to `False` in line 50. Its purpose is to determine whether the changed records of the disconnected recordset could be written to the database successfully.

In line 51, the disconnected recordset is reconnected to the database to enable writing the recordset's data to the database. The `While...Wend` loop in lines 53–150 tries to write the recordset to the database and checks for concurrency problems. The code tries to write the recordset to the database five times at maximum. In line 56, any filter of the recordset is removed to write all changed records to the database. Line 58 tries to call the `UpdateBatch` method, which writes records to the database. All errors that occur during the `UpdateBatch` are examined in lines 60–70; see also output line 5.

The `If` statement in line 73 is used only to avoid a runtime error that would appear in line 74 when calling `MoveFirst` on an empty recordset.

All records that could not be updated are written to the user in lines 76–95. Any record that was updated has a `Status` of `adRecOK` or `adRecUnmodified`. The script writes all records with a differing `Status` property value to the user (output lines 6–9). A `Status` value of `0x802` indicates that the record was modified (`0x2`, `adRecModified`), and the record was not saved (written to the database) because of concurrency problems (`0x800`, `adRecConcurrencyViolation`). See also Table 16.12 (`Status` value of a record).

In line 98, all conflicted records are filtered. When there are records with concurrency conflicts, they are written to the user in lines 106–112 (output lines 10–13). When no conflicting records are found, the variable `blnUpdate` is set to `True` in line 103 to indicate that no more records with concurrency conflicts are in the recordset.

The script refreshes all `UnderlyingValues` of the records with concurrency problems. This is done in line 116 using the `Resync` method with the parameters `adAffectGroup` and `adResyncUnderlyingValues`. The parameter `adAffectGroup` forces the `Resync` method only to refresh the records affected by the current filter settings (`Filter` was set in line 98 to show the conflicted records). The other parameter ensures that only the `UnderlyingValues` of the filtered recordset are refreshed.

The error-handling code in lines 115 and 126 is necessary, because the `Resync` method raises a runtime error when you try to refresh a record whose underlying record in the database has already been deleted. When an error occurs, the error description, the source, and the error number are written to the user in lines 118–125.

In line 128, a filter is applied to the recordset so that the resulting recordset shows only the records that were affected by the call of the `Resync` method in line 116.

The resulting recordset is written to the user in lines 129–146 (output lines 14–17). In line 131, the SupplierID, the CompanyName, and the record's `Status` are written to the user. A `Status` value of `0x2` (`adRecModified`), as in line 15 of the output, means that the record was modified and not written to the database yet (after a record is written to the database, its `Status` is either `0x0` for `adRecModified` or `0x8` for `adRecUnmodified`).

In lines 132–143, the `UnderlyingValue` is written to the user. When the `UnderlyingValue` is deleted, accessing the `UnderlyingValue` of a record, as done in line 134, raises a runtime error. Therefore, the error-handling code in lines 132 and 143 is needed. When the `UnderlyingValue` is deleted, a runtime error with the user-defined error number 3619 is raised in line 134, and the script writes a message to the user in line 137. When another error occurs in line 134, the script writes the message `Error occurred` to the user. When the `UnderlyingValue` can be accessed, it is written to the user in line 141 (output line 16). The `OriginalValue` is written to the user in line 144.

The message that the recordset's `UnderlyingValues` were refreshed is written to the user in line 147; see also output line 18.

Then the script jumps back to the beginning of the `While` ... `Wend` loop from line 150 to line 53. There, the script checks whether the variable `blnUpdated` is set to `True` or whether 5 loops have already been passed. In both cases, the loop terminates and the script continues at line 152. In every pass of the loop, the script tries to write the records of the recordset to the database using the `UpdateBatch` method. When a concurrency problem is detected during the call of the `UpdateBatch` method, the script refreshes the `UnderlyingValues` of the recordset and calls `UpdateBatch` again.

The script reports to the user whether the `Update` was successful (`blnUpdate` is `TRUE`) or failed (`blnUpdate` is `FALSE`) in lines 152–156.

Finally, the record, which was written to the database in line 15, is deleted in line 159.

Until here you have seen what the script in Listing 16.10 does when the variable `strUpdateDelete` is set to `Update` in line 7, which raises a concurrency problem because a record is changed in the database while the script changes the record in the disconnected recordset.

When you change the value in the variable `strUpdateDelete` into the value `Delete`, in line 44 the script deletes a record in the database while the script changes the record in the client-side recordset. The output of Listing 16.10 in this scenario looks as follows:

OUTPUT

```
 1: Record in Disconnected Recordset changed ...
 2:
 3: Data in Underlying Table deleted ...
 4: 1. Attempt to Write Recordset into Database:
 5: Error During Update was caused by Conflicting Records ...
 6: *** Records that could not be updated: ***
 7: 31             Greyhound Beer              Status: 0x802
 8: UnderlyingValue: Taurus Beer
 9: OriginalValue: Taurus Beer
10: *** Records with Problems During UpdateBatch: ***
11: 31             Greyhound Beer              Status: 0x802
12: UnderlyingValue: Taurus Beer
13: OriginalValue: Taurus Beer
14: An error occurred during refreshing the UnderlyingValues:
15: Error Description: Key value for this row was changed or deleted
➡ at the data store. The local row is now deleted.
16: Error Source: Microsoft Cursor Engine
17: Error Number: -2147217885
18: Application Error: 3619
19:
20: *** Records Affected by Resync: ***
21: 31             Greyhound Beer              Status: 0x40002
22: UnderlyingValue: (Deleted Row Handle)
23: OriginalValue: Taurus Beer
24: > Recordset's UnderlyingValues were refreshed.
25:
26: 2. Attempt to Write Recordset into Database:
27: An Error Occurred During Update:
28: Error Description: Row handle referred to a deleted row or a row
marked for deletion.
29: Error Source: Microsoft Cursor Engine
30: Application Error: 3619
31:
32: *** Records that could not be updated: ***
33: 31             Greyhound Beer              Status: 0x2
34: UnderlyingValue: (Deleted Row Handle)
35: OriginalValue: Taurus Beer
36: > No conflicting Records any more.
37:
38: > Update Successful.
```

ANALYSIS   There are some differences in the behavior of Listing 16.10 when deleting the
record from the database instead of changing it. When calling the UpdateBatch
method, a concurrency error also occurs. However, when you refresh the
UnderlyingValues of the recordset using the Resync method, you get a runtime error in
line 116 of the script. The error message itself is written to the user in lines 119–123
(output lines 14–18). The error description tells you that a record's key value, which is
used to identify a record unequivocally, was changed or deleted. However, the message
that the local row (record) is deleted is misleading. In fact, the record that caused the
error is not deleted from the recordset.

16

The records that were affected by calling the Resync method are shown in the output in lines 20–23. The record with the CompanyName Greyhound Beer was affected by the Resync method because the local record was changed and the underlying record in the database was deleted.

When the Resync method tries to refresh the UnderlyingValues of this record, it finds out that the underlying record in the database does not exist any more. This fact is reflected in the Status property of the record; see also output line 21. Its record status of 0x40002 indicates that the record was modified (adRecModified or 0x2) and not saved in the database.

Note When a record is saved in the database during the call of the UpdateBatch method, its Status property returns 0x0 (adRecOK) or 0x8 (adRecUnmodified).

The other information you get from the status is that the record has been deleted from the data source (adRecDBDeleted or 0x40000). Calling the Resync method also changes the UnderlyingValue of the record with the deleted row handle. Accessing its UnderlyingValue results in a runtime error with the application-defined error number 3619 (listing lines 83–85 and output line 22).

Caution The Status value of adRecDBDeleted (0x40000) is shown only when you apply the filter adFilterAffectedRecords to make only the affected records visible in the recordset. Without applying this filter to the recordset, the Status value adRecDBDeleted (0x40000) is not provided by the Status property even when the underlying record in the database has been deleted and the records UnderlyingValues have been refreshed using the Resync method.

When calling the UpdateBatch method in line 58—the second attempt to write the changed recordset to the database—another runtime error appears. This error is also caused by the fact that the UpdateBatch method tries to update a record with a deleted row handle. The record still could not be updated and therefore is shown in lines 32–35 of the output.

Tip

> If you want to write the record with the deleted row handle to the database
> anyway, you have to use the AddNew method to create a new record in the
> disconnected recordset. Copy all values (but not the UnderlyingValues or
> OriginalValues) from the record with the deleted row handle to the new
> record, and call the UpdateBatch method to save the new record to the
> database.

16

ANALYSIS Although the record is not written to the database, ADO does not recognize the
record as a record with a concurrency conflict. Its UnderlyingValue indicates
that the record was deleted in the database since refreshing its UnderlyingValue. In fact,
the same status has the value of the record in the database because it was also deleted.
This fact is shown in line 36 of the output.

Because the variable blnUpdated has the value True in line 152, the message Update
Successful is written to the user (output line 38).

It can be rather complicated to create a fail-safe application that uses disconnected
recordsets in a multiuser environment because concurrency problems can appear and
much error-handling code is necessary to protect your application from crashing when a
concurrency problem appears.

Storing a Disconnected Recordset to Disk

ADO enables you to store a Recordset object in a file on your disk. Of course, you can
retrieve a recordset from that file later and use it as disconnected recordset again.

NEW TERM Such a recordset stored in a file is called a *persistent recordset*.

It is also possible to retrieve a recordset from a database, perform some changes, store it
in a file, retrieve the recordset from the file, and write it back to the database.

The Recordset object provides two methods that enable you to save a recordset to a file
and to retrieve the saved recordset from a file.

The Save method enables you to save a recordset in a file:

```
rs.Save DestinationFile, PersistFormat
```

The variable *rs* holds the Recordset object, which is saved in the file *DestinationFile*
using the file format specified in *PersistFormat* enumeration. You can save a recordset
in the ADTG (Advanced Data TableGram) or in the XML (eXtensible Markup
Language) format by setting the *PersistFormat* parameter to adPersistADTG or
adPersistXML.

Caution You can use the Save method only when the file specified in the
DestinationFile parameter does not exist. However, there is one exception. When you open a recordset from a file, you can save it back to the
same file calling the Save method.

The `Open` method of the `Recordset` object, on the other hand, enables you to retrieve a
recordset from a file:

```
rs.Open SourceFile, "Provider=MSPersist"
```

or

```
rs.Open SourceFile
```

The variable *rs* holds the recordset object, which is retrieved from the file with the complete pathname specified in *SourceFile*.

The `Provider=MSPersist` specifies the Microsoft OLE DB Persistence Provider, which
enables you to save a recordset into a file and later restore it from the file.

Listing 16.11 provides an idea about the possibilities of saving a disconnected recordset
into a file.

LISTING 16.11 Turn a Disconnected Recordset into a Persistent Recordset

```
 1: Dim rs As ADODB.Recordset
 2: Dim swapRs As ADODB.Recordset
 3: Dim conn As ADODB.Connection
 4: Dim strFile As String
 5: Dim lngI As Long
 6:
 7: ' Create Client-Side, Disconnected Recordset
 8: Set rs = CreateObject("ADODB.Recordset")
 9: rs.CursorLocation = adUseClient
10: rs.CursorType = adOpenStatic
11: rs.LockType = adLockBatchOptimistic
12: ' No Connection assigned to the Recordset
13:
14: ' Define Recordset
15: rs.Fields.Append "FirstName", adVarChar, 30, adFldMayBeNull
16: rs.Fields.Append "LastName", adVarChar, 35, adFldMayBeNull
17:
18: ' Open Recordset
19: rs.Open
20:
21: ' Add 3 Records
22: rs.AddNew
```

16

```
23: rs("FirstName") = "Desmond"
24: rs("LastName") = "Tutu"
25: rs.AddNew
26: rs("FirstName") = "Dalai"
27: rs("LastName") = "Lama"
28: rs.AddNew
29: rs("FirstName") = "Mother"
30: rs("LastName") = "Teresa"
31:
32: ' Write Recordset as Persistent Recordset to a File
33: strFile = "C:\PersRec.xml"
34: On Error Resume Next
35: rs.Save strFile, adPersistXML
36:
37: If Err.Number = 58 Then
38:     ' File already exists
39:     On Error GoTo 0
40:     Err.Number = 0
41:
42:     ' Open swap Recordset that connects to existing file
43:     Set swapRs = CreateObject("ADODB.Recordset")
44:     swapRs.Open strFile, "Provider=MSPersist"
45:
46:     ' Delete all records from swap Recordset
47:     While Not swapRs.EOF
48:         swapRs.Delete
49:         swapRs.MoveNext
50:     Wend
51:
52:     ' Write all values from Recordset (rs) into swap Recordset (swapRs)
53:     If Not (rs.BOF And rs.EOF) Then
54:         rs.MoveFirst
55:         While Not rs.EOF
56:             swapRs.AddNew
57:             For lngI = 0 To rs.Fields.Count - 1
58:                 swapRs(lngI) = rs(lngI)
59:             Next
60:             rs.MoveNext
61:         Wend
62:     End If
63:     ' Save swap Recordset to file
64:     swapRs.Save strFile, adPersistXML
65:
66:     Debug.Print "Recordset in file " & strFile & " was updated."
67: ElseIf Err.Number <> 0 Then
68:     On Error GoTo 0
69:     Debug.Print "An error occurred."
70: Else
71:     On Error GoTo 0
72:     Debug.Print "Recordset was written to file " & strFile & "."
```

continues

LISTING 16.11 continued

```
73: End If
74:
75: ' Close Disconnected Recordset
76: rs.Close
77: Set rs = Nothing
```

When the file `C:\PersRec.xml` does not exist, the output of Listing 16.11 looks as follows:

OUTPUT `Recordset was written to file C:\PersRec.xml.`

When the file `C:\PersRec.xml` is already created, the output looks as follows:

`Recordset in file C:\PersRec.xml was updated.`

The content of the file `C:\PersRec.xml` looks as follows:

OUTPUT
```
<xml xmlns:s='uuid:BDC6E3F0-6DA3-11d1-A2A3-00AA00C14882'
  xmlns:dt='uuid:C2F41010-65B3-11d1-A29F-00AA00C14882'
  xmlns:rs='urn:schemas-microsoft-com:rowset'
  xmlns:z='#RowsetSchema'>
<s:Schema id='RowsetSchema'>
  <s:ElementType name='row' content='eltOnly' rs:updatable='true'>
    <s:AttributeType name='FirstName' rs:number='1' rs:write='true'>
      <s:datatype dt:type='string' rs:dbtype='str' dt:maxLength='30'
➡ rs:precision='0'/>
    </s:AttributeType>
    <s:AttributeType name='LastName' rs:number='2' rs:write='true'>
      <s:datatype dt:type='string' rs:dbtype='str' dt:maxLength='35'
➡ rs:precision='0'/>
    </s:AttributeType>
    <s:extends type='rs:rowbase'/>
  </s:ElementType>
</s:Schema>
<rs:data>
  <rs:insert>
    <z:row FirstName='Desmond' LastName='Tutu'/>
    <z:row FirstName='Dalai' LastName='Lama'/>
    <z:row FirstName='Mother' LastName='Teresa'/>
  </rs:insert>
</rs:data>
</xml>
```

ANALYSIS The script of Listing 16.11 creates a disconnected recordset and defines the columns of the recordset in lines 8–16. After the recordset is opened in line 19, three records are added in lines 22–30.

In line 33, the filename of the persistent recordset is defined and stored in the variable `strFile`. In line 35, the recordset is stored in the file using the XML format. The `Save` method creates a new file and writes the recordset into it.

The `Save` method fails when a file with the filename stored in `strFile` already exists, and a runtime error is raised with the error number 58.

When the file already exists, the script uses a trick to update the values of the recordset stored in the file. The `Save` method cannot overwrite an existing file. However, you can store a recordset back to a file when you open the recordset from the file.

Therefore, the script opens the persistent recordset (named `swapRs`) from the file using the `Open` method of the `Recordset` object. The script deletes all records from the `swapRs` recordset. Then it copies all values from the disconnected recordset (`rs`) to the `swapRs` recordset in lines 47–62.

Note   The copy section in lines 53–60 works only when the disconnected recordset and the recordset retrieved from the file contain the same fields in the same order.

The `swapRs` recordset is written back to the file using the `Save` method in line 64.

Of course, you can retrieve the content of the file as recordset and perform various actions on it. Listing 16.12 retrieves the content of the file `C:\PersRec.xml` and shows the content of the retrieved recordset to the user.

LISTING 16.12   Retrieve a Recordset from a Persistent Recordset File

```
 1: ' Retrieve Persistent Recordset from File
 2: Dim lngField As Long
 3: Dim newrs As ADODB.Recordset
 4: Dim newconn As ADODB.Connection
 5: Dim strNewFile
 6: strNewFile = "C:\PersRec.xml"
 7:
 8: Set newrs = CreateObject("ADODB.Recordset")
 9: newrs.CursorLocation = adUseClient
10: newrs.CursorType = adOpenStatic
11: newrs.LockType = adLockBatchOptimistic
12:
13: On Error Resume Next
14: ' Open implicitly creates a Connection to the File
15: newrs.Open strNewFile
16: If Err.Number = 3709 Then
```

continues

LISTING **16.12**   continued

```
17:        ' File not found
18:        On Error GoTo 0
19:        Debug.Print "File " & strNewFile & " not found!"
20: ElseIf Err.Number <> 0 Then
21:        On Error GoTo 0
22:        Debug.Print "An error occurred."
23: Else
24:        ' File Found and Recordset retrieved
25:        On Error GoTo 0
26:        ' No more error handling
27:
28:        ' Show Content of Disconnected Recordset
29:        Debug.Print "Recordset retrieved from file " & strNewFile & ":"
30:        Debug.Print
31:        While Not newrs.EOF
32:            Debug.Print "Record #" & newrs.AbsolutePosition
33:            For lngField = 0 To newrs.Fields.Count - 1
34:                Debug.Print newrs(lngField).Name & "=" &
➥ newrs(lngField).Value
35:            Next
36:            Debug.Print
37:            newrs.MoveNext
38:        Wend
39:        newrs.Close
40: End If
41:
42: Set newrs = Nothing
```

The output of Listing 16.12 looks as follows:

```
Recordset retrieved from file C:\PersRec.xml:

Record #1
FirstName=Desmond
LastName=Tutu

Record #2
FirstName=Dalai
LastName=Lama

Record #3
FirstName=Mother
LastName=Teresa
```

ANALYSIS   In line 6, the name of the file, which contains the persisted recordset, is stored in the variable strNewFile.

A disconnected recordset is prepared in lines 8–11. You could omit the preparation, because a recordset retrieved from a file is always a disconnected recordset.

In line 15, the recordset is opened from the file using the Open method of the Recordset object. Because the argument of the Open method is a filename, the Open method automatically uses the OLE DB Persistence Provider. When a file with the filename stored in the variable strNewFile does not exist, a runtime error appears. The error-handling code in lines 13 and 18 enables you to intercept any errors. When the file specified in strNewFile cannot be opened, the code of the error is 3709.

When no error occurs, the recordset newrs is retrieved from the file in line 15. The recordset is automatically retrieved from a file as a disconnected recordset. The whole content of the recordset is shown in lines 29–38 (see output).

Persisted recordsets can be used to store a recordset on a floppy disk or sent by email. You do not need a database to store a persisted recordset, and you maintain the full recordset structure and all data of a recordset when you store it as persisted recordset.

Summary

Today's topic is the use and update of disconnected recordsets. You learned about the basic mechanisms that you can use to write a disconnected recordset back to a database. You saw some of the problems in multiuser applications that arise out of concurrency collisions.

Generally spoken, disconnected recordsets can be used in two main scenarios:

- Use a disconnected recordset to store data in a tabular form and use the features of the Recordset object to organize the data.
- Manipulate database data without consuming connection resources longer than necessary through the use of disconnected recordsets.

ADO itself uses and provides several internal techniques to detect and solve concurrency problems. The most important advantage of disconnected recordsets is that they do not consume any database connection resources while the application handles them. However, the disadvantage is that you must consider several facts when you want to write a disconnected recordset back to a database.

Another important advantage of a disconnected recordset is that you can store it on a normal floppy disk or laptop, and even send it over the Internet for further use in a form that can be read by ADO applications very easily.

Q&A

Q **I have a database table in which one column is defined as primary key. This primary key is not an Autonumber or Identity field. I retrieve a recordset from the database table and change some of its values. What happens when I want to write the disconnected recordset into the database table and a record in the recordset has the same value in the primary key column as a record in the database? Is the record in the database just overwritten, or does a runtime error appear?**

A When you add a new record to the disconnected recordset, which has the same primary key value as a record in the database, the record is not written into the database. The `Status` property of the new recordset declares it as a new record. Because it is a new record, it is clear to ADO that it was not retrieved from the database table, and therefore ADO returns a concurrency error.

However, if you retrieve a record with a primary key value from the database table and change it in the disconnected recordset, you can, of course, write the changes back to the database.

In the unlikely case that you retrieved a record and its underlying record in the table is deleted while you process the disconnected Recordset, the record cannot be written to the table and a concurrency error is raised. ADO detects this scenario because the `Status` property of the record indicates that the record was only modified but not added as a new record to the recordset. Therefore, ADO knows that the record must have been retrieved from the database table. Because ADO cannot find the record in the underlying table, a concurrency error is raised.

Even when you change the value of the primary key field of the record, the record is not written as a new record in the database. When you change the primary key of a record and the record in the underlying table is not changed or deleted, the record is added as a new record to the database table.

Workshop

The quiz questions and exercises are provided for your further understanding. See Appendix A, "Answers," for the answers.

Quiz

1. Which statement refreshes the `UnderlyingValues` of the recordset that is stored in the variable `rs`?

2. How can ADO detect concurrency problems when you update disconnected recordsets and write them back in the database?

3. What cursor type, cursor location, and lock type must a disconnected recordset have?

4. What kind of columns should a recordset retrieve from a table when you want to change values in the recordset and write it back to the database?

5. Which possibilities do you have to obtain a disconnected recordset with or without using a data source?

Exercise

Write a script that adds two new records to the Customers table of the SQL 7.0 Northwind database. The two new records should have the values AAAAA and AABBB in the CustomerID column. Note that you also must provide a value in the CompanyName column.

Prepare a disconnected recordset and populate it with all records from the Customers table, where the CustomerID is less than the value ALF. Then disconnect the recordset and write the content and the `Status` property of each record to the user.

Use SQL statements to delete the record with the CustomerID AAAAA and change the record with the CustomerID AABBB in the database.

Add a new customer record with the CustomerID ALLLL to the disconnected recordset.

Reattach a connection to the disconnected recordset, enable error handling, and write the recordset's content to the database using the `UpdateBatch` method. When an error occurs during calling of the `UpdateBatch` method, write the error description to the user.

Set a filter to make only the records with conflicts during the call of the `UpdateBatch` method visible (the `Filter` property is set to the `adFilterConflictingRecords` argument). Write the `Status` property, the CustomerID, and the CompanyName of each conflicting record to the user. Set a filter to view only affected records (`adFilterAffectedRecords`) and write all records that were affected by the call of the `UpdateBatch` to the user. Then remove the filter (set it to `adFilterNone`) and show the `Status` property, the CustomerID, and the CompanyName of all records from the recordset to the user.

Refresh the data of the recordset using the `Resync` method. Intercept any error that might appear and write all records (and their `Status` property) that had conflicts during the refresh to the user (use the `Filter` property with `adFilterConflictingRecords`). Then show the `Status` property values and some values of all records affected by the refresh using the `Filter` property with the argument `adFilterAffectedRecords`. Show the `Status` property of all records in the recordset.

Finally, delete the records from the Customers table, where the CustomerID is either AABBB or ALLLL.

DAY 17

Remoting Data Using RDS

Yesterday, you learned about disconnecting recordsets from a database and how to use these disconnected recordsets for various tasks. A disconnected recordset can be used on the same machine or on a remote computer via DCOM. You can take this remoting one step further by employing Remote Data Services (RDS), which enables you to access data via the HTTP protocol.

Today, you will learn the following tasks:

- Configuring your RDS environment
- Listing records that are returned via RDS
- Filtering and sorting cached RDS recordsets
- Editing recordsets and submitting the changes to the server
- Securing the RDS environment with handlers

Overview of RDS

RDS takes the concept of disconnected recordsets one step further. RDS is built for an environment where a client application requests that an object that resides on a server will return the desired data. This object resides on the middle tier and can be accessed either on the local machine, via DCOM on a remote server, or via HTTP, thus being able to get remote data across the Internet.

There are two possible usage scenarios with RDS—you can use RDS to access data via a Web server using a component that ships with RDS, or you can build your own components that work with RDS. The first scenario is very common and the topic of today. The advanced topic of custom business objects for RDS is discussed tomorrow in Day 18, "Creating RDS Business Objects."

The following sections get you started with RDS:

- The RDS Data Path
- Strengths and Limitations

The RDS Data Path

An important question to ask about a technology is how it actually works. The diagram in Figure 17.1 shows the flow of data in an RDS environment you are going to explore today: Internet Explorer on the presentation tier, Internet Information Server (IIS) on the business tier, and SQL Server on the data tier.

The following steps are performed:

1. There are two components of RDS that reside on the client: the RDS `DataControl` and the RDS `DataSpace`. The `DataControl` fulfills one purpose: providing easy access to data on a Web server. To fulfill the data needs, it uses the `DataSpace` component to cross the Internet to access the server-side `DataFactory` component.

2. On the server, the RDS `DataFactory` takes over. It issues the query that was passed from the client against the database.

3. The data tier is OLE DB territory. The query is executed and the results are retrieved.

4. When the execution has finished, the resultset is passed back to the `DataFactory`.

5. The `DataFactory` packages the resultset for Internet transfer and starts sending it to the client—to the `DataSpace` component.

6. When the data is received, it is cached on the client side (for sorting and filtering, for example). The `DataSpace` component then passes control back to the `DataControl`.

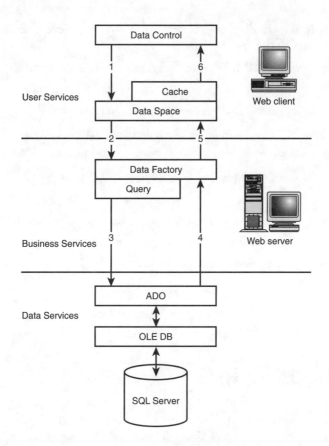

As you can see from the diagram, the `DataControl` is a front end to more complicated RDS technology, such as `DataSpace` and `DataFactory`. You can customize quite a lot of this functionality, which is shown in Day 18.

Strengths and Limitations

Every technology has its strengths and weaknesses, including RDS; therefore, you should be aware of them when deciding when to employ it.

Let's start with the strengths:

- RDS is automatically installed with IE 4 or higher and therefore can be used immediately.
- The RDS components (`DataFactory`) communicate directly with ADO—there's no interim layer.

- In asynchronous environments, you can rely on events fired by the RDS DataControl.

- Dynamic HTML is a great container for the RDS DataControl.

- You need not use ASP for RDS to work; it is independent of ASP.

- Client-side caching is transparent to the programmer.

For an intranet application, these strengths are definitely worth a look. However, no technology has strengths only. The following are downsides of RDS:

- The data is returned as-is from the query.

- You cannot use hierarchical recordsets.

- In case you fancy multiselect list boxes, you cannot use RDS.

- Complex JOIN statements are not supported by RDS.

- Calculated fields cannot be updated via RDS.

- RDS is not supported by Netscape Navigator.

This gives you an idea of where and when to employ RDS. The examples presented today also should get you started with the most common tasks.

Configuring RDS

Before you can start using RDS, you need to perform some setup work on your Web server, because with the default installation in place, you won't be able to follow the examples presented today. You will learn the following common tasks necessary to get up and running with RDS and IIS:

- Reconfiguring the default Web site

- Configuring Web sites

- Disabling the default handler

Reconfiguring the Default Web Site

When you are using IIS on Windows 2000 Professional, you have only one Web site for your work: the default Web site. You cannot create additional sites and must deploy your RDS solution to this site.

The default Web site comes with the necessary preconfigured virtual directory named MSADC; however, access to it is restricted to the local machine only. This is okay as long as you are testing on the same computer, but as soon as you want to access your RDS pages from another machine, you get access errors. Therefore, you have to remove the access restrictions, which are based on IP addresses.

To Do: Enabling Remote Access to the MSADC Directory

Follow these steps in ISM to allow remote access to the MSADC virtual directory:

1. Open Internet Services Manager and open Default Web Site (see Figure 17.2). Select the MSADC directory.

FIGURE 17.2

The MSADC virtual directory contains the files necessary for RDS.

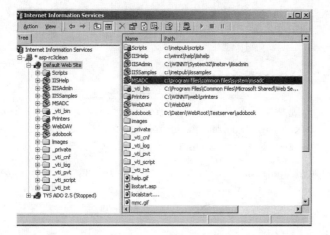

17

2. Right-click and select Properties from the context menu.
3. Switch to the Directory Security tab. In the IP address and domain restrictions frame, click the Edit button (see Figure 17.3).

FIGURE 17.3

Configuring access permissions to the MSADC directory.

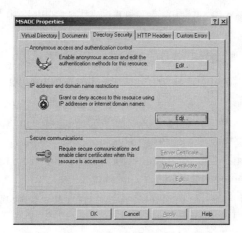

▼ 4. By default, all computers are denied access except localhost (127.1.1.1), as shown in Figure 17.4. Select the restriction and click Remove. Change the access setting to Granted Access.

FIGURE 17.4

On the default Web site, all computers except the localhost are denied access.

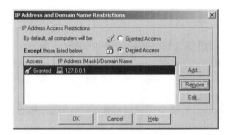

5. Click OK to save your changes. Close the Properties dialog box with OK and the
▲   new loose restrictions will be in place.

If you are using your RDS pages in an intranet scenario while serving Internet-accessible pages from the same Web site, I recommend that you restrict access to MSADC to all internal IP addresses. Each additional security layer makes your valuable data safer.

Configuring Web Sites

In the previous section you configured a site that you usually won't use for publishing on Windows 2000 Server or upward—the default Web site. You will be creating additional Web sites.

When you create new Web sites, these do not have the required MSADC virtual directory preconfigured for you. You have to add it. If you forget to, RDS won't work at all.

To Do: Creating the MSADC Virtual Directory

Follow these steps to create the MSADC virtual directory for any Web site different from the default Web site:

1. In Internet Services Manager, select the Web site you want to enable RDS for. Right-click and select New, Virtual Directory from the context menu.

2. Enter MSADC as the alias for this directory. This is the name used by RDS to retrieve data from the RDS ISAPI application.

3. You are asked for the physical directory where the files for the virtual directory shall be served. If you installed on drive C:, the directory is C:\Program
▼   Files\Common Files\System\msadc.

▼ 4. The final step is about access permissions. By default, Read and Script permissions
      are enabled. However, this is not sufficient for ISAPI applications—these also need
      Execute permissions (see Figure 17.5).

FIGURE 17.5

*Adding Execute per-
missions for the
MSADC directory.*

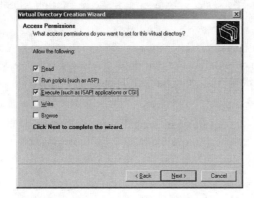

5. Click Next to create the virtual directory MSADC. It is now added to the Web site
   (see Figure 17.6).

FIGURE 17.6

*The MSADC directory
is added to the Web
site.*

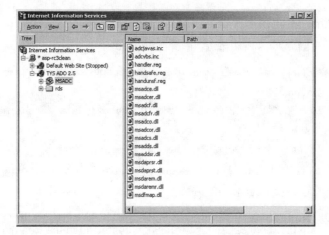

The steps in this task are mandatory for each Web site that employs RDS pages; howev-
▲ er, there's nothing complicated about it.

17

Disabling the Default Handler

As you will see later in the examples, you can do a lot with RDS, including things that pose a real security threat to your data. The good news is that by default this possible security hole is perfectly sealed; however, it makes exploring RDS harder.

The "plugs" in the security hole are handlers (more information is presented in the section "Working With Handlers," later today). Though these can be custom-built objects, RDS ships with one default handler that prevents users from accessing arbitrary databases or executing harmful SQL statements. It is enabled by default (the good news), but it makes it more difficult to learn (the bad news).

Therefore, to follow the examples presented today, complete the instructions to remove the default handler. After exploring the basics, you will close the security hole again in the section "Working With Handlers."

> **Caution** When dealing with the registry, be careful. Making a wrong modification can lead to a Windows system that no longer boots.

To Do: Disabling the default handler

Follow these steps to disable the default handler:

1. Open the Registry Editor. In the Run dialog box, enter `regedit.exe` and click OK.
2. Navigate to the `HKEY_LOCAL_MACHINE\SOFTWARE\Microsoft\DataFactory\HandlerInfo` key (see Figure 17.7).
3. Right-click on DefaultHandler and select Delete.
4. Double-click the HandlerRequired item and change the value to 0.
5. Close the Registry Editor.
6. For the changes to take effect, you have to stop and restart the Web service. To stop the service, issue the following command in the Run dialog box:

   `net stop w3svc`
7. When it has completed, restart the Web service with

   `net start w3svc`

   Now RDS can be used without using the default handler.

Your Web site is now set up with loose security to learn RDS. Later, you will lock down your site and change the scripts presented now to work in a more tightly secured environment.

FIGURE 17.7

Navigating to the `HandlerInfo` *key.*

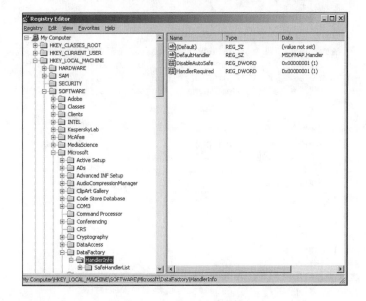

Creating RDS-Enabled Web Pages

You have heard enough about configuration tasks; let's switch back to what is really interesting—exploiting RDS to create great data-enabled Web pages. I have partitioned RDS along the following most common tasks:

- Tabular listing of records
- Sorting records
- Filtering records
- Editing records
- Submitting changes to the server

Tabular Listing of Records

The first example with database technology is retrieving records and displaying them. Listing 17.1 retrieves data from the Suppliers table in the Northwind database and displays the returned results in an HTML table.

LISTING 17.1 Creating a Tabular Listing of Records

```
 1: <html>
 2: <head>
 3:   <title>Listing Suppliers using a handler</title>
 4: </head>
 5: <body bgcolor="#ffffff">
 6: <%
 7: strServer = Request.ServerVariables("SERVER_NAME")
 8: strConnect = "provider=sqloledb.1;user id=sa;password=;
➥initial catalog=northwind;data source=strangelove"
 9: strSQL = "SELECT CompanyName,Address,City,Country FROM Suppliers"
10: %>
11:
12: <OBJECT classid="clsid:BD96C556-65A3-11D0-983A-00C04FC29E33"
➥ID="rdsDC" height=0 width=0>
13:     <PARAM NAME="SQL" VALUE="<%=strSQL %>">
14:     <PARAM NAME="SERVER" VALUE="http://<%=strServer%>">
15:     <PARAM NAME="CONNECT" VALUE="<%=strConnect %>">
16: </OBJECT>
17:
18: <h2>Suppliers in the database</h2>
19: <TABLE DATASRC="#rdsDC">
20: <TBODY>
21:     <TR>
22:       <TD><SPAN DATAFLD="CompanyName"></SPAN></TD>
23:       <TD><SPAN DATAFLD="Address"></SPAN></TD>
24:       <TD><SPAN DATAFLD="City"></SPAN></TD>
25:       <TD><SPAN DATAFLD="Country"></SPAN></TD>
26:     </TR>
27: </TBODY>
28: </TABLE>
29:
30: </body>
31: </html>
```

ANALYSIS The listing contains server-side code (ASP); therefore you have to store it with the extension .asp and not .htm. The ASP code is used to define the variables strServer, strConnect, and strSQL (lines 7–9), which are later used to create the <OBJECT> tag that is evaluated by the client. In general, the <OBJECT> tag looks like this:

```
<OBJECT classid="clsid:BD96C556-65A3-11D0-983A-00C04FC29E33" ID="rdsDC">
</OBJECT>
```

Though the ClassId is not very intuitive, it represents the MSADC.DataControl object, which is used to establish a connection to an MSADC.DataFactory object on the server. To get started with a DataControl, you need the URL of the Web server (the one with the MSADC directory), the database connection string, and the SQL statement that should be executed (lines 13–15).

To be able to reference the `DataControl` as a data source for elements on the page, you have to name it using the ID attribute. In this example, the `DataControl` is named `rdsDC`.

After the control is initialized, it automatically executes the SQL statement on the server and returns with query results, if there are any. These results are displayed in the `<TABLE>` tag in lines 19–28. The part that creates the rows for each record is the `<TBODY>` tag in lines 20–27. To display a column's value, simply use

```
<SPAN DATAFLD="City"></SPAN>
```

The `DATAFLD` attribute references the column that is displayed, but where is the data source I kept talking about? The data source (the `DataControl`) is already specified in the `<TABLE>` tag (line 19):

```
<TABLE DATASRC="#rdsDC">
```

Because it is a page-relative context, you have to prefix the control's name with a pound sign.

I didn't need to use server-side ASP to create this page; simple HTML with hard-coded strings would have been sufficient. However, when later maintaining this script, it will be easier (SQL statements in include files, and so forth).

Sorting Records

Sometimes you want to sort results in a way that suits their needs. In a server-side–only environment, you would incur round-trips for each request to change the sort order, because ASP returns static HTML. This is where RDS becomes handy.

In the previous example, I didn't add any sort order (with `ORDER BY`) to the resultset. But now I want to, and using RDS and a few lines of VBScript, you can do so without going back to the Web server to ask for sorted data (see Listing 17.2).

LISTING 17.2 Sorting an Existing RDS Recordset on the Client

```
1: <html>
2: <head>
3:   <title>Listing Suppliers with sorting</title>
4: </head>
5: <body bgcolor="#ffffff">
6: <%
7: strSQL = "SELECT * FROM Suppliers"
8: strServer = Request.ServerVariables("SERVER_NAME")
```

continues

17

LISTING 17.2   continued

```
 9: strConnStr = "provider=sqloledb.1;user id=sa;password=;
➥initial catalog=northwind;data source=strangelove"
10: %>
11:
12: <OBJECT classid="clsid:BD96C556-65A3-11D0-983A-00C04FC29E33"
➥ID="rdsDC" height=0 width=0>
13:     <PARAM NAME="SQL" VALUE="<%=strSQL %>">
14:     <PARAM NAME="SERVER" VALUE="http://<%=strServer%>">
15:     <PARAM NAME="CONNECT" VALUE="<%=strConnStr %>">
16: </OBJECT>
17:
18: <h2>Suppliers</h2>
19: <p style="width:750px;height:450px;overflow:scroll">
20: <TABLE DATASRC="#rdsDC" ID="SuppliersTable">
21: <thead>
22: <tr>
23:    <th id="CompanyName">Company</th>
24:    <th id="Address">Address</th>
25:    <th id="City">City</th>
26:    <th id="Country">Country</th>
27: </tr>
28: </thead>
29: <TBODY>
30:     <TR>
31:      <TD><SPAN DATAFLD="CompanyName"></SPAN></TD>
32:      <TD><SPAN DATAFLD="Address"></SPAN></TD>
33:      <TD><SPAN DATAFLD="City"></SPAN></TD>
34:      <TD><SPAN DATAFLD="Country"></SPAN></TD>
35:     </TR>
36: </TBODY>
37: </TABLE>
38: </p>
39:
40: <SCRIPT LANGUAGE="VBSCRIPT">
41: Sub SuppliersTable_onClick()
42:    if ("TH" = window.event.srcElement.tagName) then
43:      strSortColumn = window.event.srcElement.id
44:      rdsDC.SortColumn = strSortColumn
45:      bSortDirection = rdsDC.SortDirection
46:      rdsDC.SortDirection = Not bSortDirection
47:      rdsDC.Reset
48:    end if
49: End Sub
50: </SCRIPT>
51:
52: </body>
53: </html>
```

ANALYSIS The first sixteen lines are the same as in Listing 17.1. The interesting part for resorting starts once again in the `<TABLE>` tag:

```
<TABLE DATASRC="#rdsDC" ID="SuppliersTable">
```

In contrast to the previous example, now `<TABLE>` has an `ID` attribute too, which is used to fire the `OnClick` event procedure for this table (lines 41–49). This event procedure checks which element in the table (`TH` or `TD`) fired the event. If it was a `TH` (table header) element, it performs the sort operation.

You know which `TH` element fired the event, so you also know its `ID`, which I used to store the table column names (lines 23–26). With the column name, you can sort the RDS recordset:

```
rdsDC.SortColumn = strSortColumn
bSortDirection = rdsDC.SortDirection
rdsDC.SortDirection = Not bSortDirection
rdsDC.Reset
```

To enable switching between ascending (`True`) and descending (`False`) sort order, the script first reads the previous sort order and then inverts it and assigns it to the `SortDirection` property again.

If you forget the `Reset` method call, nothing will happen to the display. To view your sort order changes, you have to call `Reset`. `Reset` takes one Boolean parameter that defaults to `True`, which means that changing the sort order does not remove filters. To remove a filter, you have to call `Reset` with a value of `False`.

Filtering Records

Before removing a filter, there should be one in the first place. Adding a filter can be condensed to four lines of code, but then you have no user interface that allows users to choose the filtering they want.

Because my users usually want sophisticated filtering, I created a page that allows users to filter for all columns in the Suppliers recordset, and as an additional bonus, highlights selected rows. The resulting page is shown in Figure 17.8.

Listing 17.3 contains the code necessary to create the filtering outlined.

17

FIGURE 17.8

Filtering a recordset and highlighting rows.

LISTING 17.3 Filtering for Records

```
 1: <html>
 2: <head>
 3:   <title>Filtering Suppliers</title>
 4:   <STYLE TYPE="text/css">
 5:     .active {font-weight:bold; background-color : silver;}
 6:     .normal {font-weight:normal; background-color : white;}
 7:   </STYLE>
 8: </head>
 9: <body bgcolor="#ffffff">
10: <%
11: strSQL = "SELECT CompanyName,Address,City,Country FROM Suppliers"
12: strServer = Request.ServerVariables("SERVER_NAME")
13: strConnStr = "provider=sqloledb.1;user id=sa;password=;
➥initial catalog=northwind;data source=strangelove"
14: %>
15:
16: <table>
17: <tr><td>Filter Value:</td><td>
18: <INPUT TYPE="TEXT" NAME="txtFilterValue"></td></tr>
19: <tr><td>Filter Column:</td><td>
20: <SELECT NAME="cbFilterColumn">
21:   <OPTION VALUE="CompanyName">Company
22:   <OPTION VALUE="Address">Address
23:   <OPTION VALUE="City">City
24:   <OPTION VALUE="Country">Country
25: </SELECT></td></tr>
26: <tr><td>Filter Criterion:</td><td>
```

```
27: <SELECT NAME="cbFilterCriterion">
28:   <OPTION VALUE=""></OPTION>
29:   <OPTION VALUE="=">=</OPTION>
30:   <OPTION VALUE="&gt;">&gt;</OPTION>
31:   <OPTION VALUE="&lt;">&lt;</OPTION>
32:   <OPTION VALUE="&gt;=">&gt;=</OPTION>
33:   <OPTION VALUE="&lt;=">&lt;=</OPTION>
34:   <OPTION VALUE="&lt;&gt;">&lt;&gt;</OPTION>
35: </SELECT></td></tr>
36: </table>
37: <INPUT TYPE="BUTTON" NAME="btnApplyFilter" VALUE="Apply Filter">
38: <INPUT TYPE="BUTTON" NAME="btnClearFilter" VALUE="Clear Filter">
39:
40: <OBJECT classid="clsid:BD96C556-65A3-11D0-983A-00C04FC29E33"
➥ID="rdsDC" height=0 width=0>
41:    <PARAM NAME="SQL" VALUE="<%=strSQL %>">
42:    <PARAM NAME="SERVER" VALUE="http://<%=strServer%>">
43:    <PARAM NAME="CONNECT" VALUE="<%=strConnStr %>">
44: </OBJECT>
45:
46: <p style="width:750px;height:450px;overflow:scroll">
47: <TABLE DATASRC="#rdsDC" ID="SuppliersTable">
48: <thead>
49: <tr>
50:   <th>Company</th>
51:   <th>Address</th>
52:   <th>City</th>
53:   <th>Country</th>
54: </tr>
55: </thead>
56: <TBODY>
57:   <TR>
58:     <TD><SPAN DATAFLD="CompanyName"></SPAN></TD>
59:    <TD><SPAN DATAFLD="Address"></SPAN></TD>
60:    <TD><SPAN DATAFLD="City"></SPAN></TD>
61:     <TD><SPAN DATAFLD="Country"></SPAN></TD>
62:   </TR>
63: </TBODY>
64: </TABLE>
65: </p>
66:
67: <SCRIPT LANGUAGE="VBSCRIPT">
68: Dim activeRow
69: activeRow = -1
70:
71: Sub btnApplyFilter_onClick()
72:   strFilterColumn = cbFilterColumn.Options(cbFilterColumn.selectedIndex).
➥Value
73:   if ("" <> strFilterColumn) then
74:     rdsDC.FilterColumn = strFilterColumn
75:   end if
```

17

continues

LISTING **17.3** continued

```
76:
77:    strFilterCriterion = cbFilterCriterion.Options(cbFilterCriterion.
➥selectedIndex).Value
78:    if ("" <> strFilterCriterion) then
79:      rdsDC.FilterCriterion = strFilterCriterion
80:    End If
81:
82:    If ("" <> txtFilterValue.Value) Then
83:      rdsDC.FilterValue = txtFilterValue.Value
84:    End If
85:
86:    rdsDC.Reset
87:    activeRow = -1
88: End Sub
89:
90: Sub btnClearFilter_OnClick()
91:    cbFilterColumn.selectedIndex = 0
92:    cbFilterCriterion.selectedIndex = 0
93:    txtFilterValue.Value = ""
94:
95:    rdsDC.FilterCriterion = ""
96:    rdsDC.Reset False
97:    activeRow = -1
98: End Sub
99:
100: Sub SuppliersTable_OnClick()
101:    strTagName = window.event.srcElement.tagName
102:    strTagParent = window.event.srcElement.parentElement.tagName
103:
104:    nRow = -1
105:    if ("SPAN" = strTagName And "TD" = strTagParent) then
106:      nRow = window.event.srcElement.parentElement.parentElement.sourceIndex
107:    end if
108:    if ("TD" = strTagName) then
109:      nRow = window.event.srcElement.parentElement.sourceIndex
110:    end if
111:
112:    if -1 <> nRow then
113:      if (activeRow <> -1) then
114:        document.all.item(activeRow).className = "normal"
115:      end if
116:
117:      document.all.item(nRow).className = "active"
118:      activeRow = nRow
119:    end if
120: End Sub
121: </SCRIPT>
122:
123: </body>
124: </html>
```

ANALYSIS The listing starts with a STYLE definition (lines 4–7) that is used later to highlight rows. This definition is followed by the usual definitions for server, SQL statement, and connection string.

The code block in lines 16–38 creates an input box where users can enter the filter value, a combo box where users can choose the column they want to apply the filter to, and another combo box where users can choose the filter criterion (=, <, >, >= , <=, or <>). The block closes with two buttons: one for applying the filter, and another one for removing the filter.

Next is the well-known <OBJECT> tag for the DataControl, as well as the <TABLE> tag to display the resultset, which closes in line 64.

Now let's take a look at the client-side code for applying a filter. The OnClick event procedure for the Apply button starts in line 71. It consists mostly of sanity checks for the values and can be distilled to

```
rdsDC.FilterColumn = strFilterColumn
rdsDC.FilterCriterion = strFilterCriterion
rdsDC.FilterValue = txtFilterValue.Value
rdsDC.Reset
```

These are the four lines of code I was talking about at the beginning of this section.

The code for the Clear button (lines 90–98) clears all input fields, removes the filter value and the filter criterion, and then resets the recordset to its original state.

The activeRow variable is used for the OnClick event procedure of the <TABLE> tag (lines 100 and following) to remove highlighting from the previously active row—and when you change a filter or remove it, the active row is set to -1.

The code in SupplierTable_OnClick is intended to demonstrate that you can create a cool front end using Web pages. It has nothing to do with RDS itself, so I won't discuss it at length here. To sum up what it does: if a user clicks in a row (either in the SPAN or TD tag), the previously active row is deactivated and the newly selected row activated.

If you put in more work for client-side presentation, you can come close to the comfort a VB-based or Access-based solution provides for the end user.

Editing Records

A nice presentation of data is only a part of what users need from a Web-based solution. The users also want to be able to edit records, as shown in Figure 17.9.

FIGURE **17.9**

Editing records in an
online form.

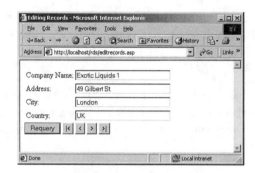

With your knowledge in displaying data, it is not complicated to create this online form.
The code for this form is shown in Listing 17.4.

LISTING 17.4   Editing Records with RDS

```
 1: <html>
 2: <head>
 3:   <title>Editing Records</title>
 4: </head>
 5: <body bgcolor="#ffffff">
 6:
 7: <OBJECT classid="clsid:BD96C556-65A3-11D0-983A-00C04FC29E33"
 8:   ID="rdsDC" HEIGHT=0 WIDTH=0>
 9: </OBJECT>
10:
11: <table>
12: <tr><td>Company Name:</td>
13: <td>
14:   <INPUT TYPE=TEXT NAME=COL0 SIZE=30 DATASRC="#rdsDC" DATAFLD="CompanyName">
15: </td></tr>
16: <tr><td>Address:</td>
17: <td>
18:   <INPUT TYPE=TEXT NAME=COL1 SIZE=30 DATASRC="#rdsDC" DATAFLD="Address">
19: </td></tr>
20: <tr><td>City:</td>
21: <td>
22:   <INPUT TYPE=TEXT NAME=COL2 SIZE=30 DATASRC="#rdsDC" DATAFLD="City">
23: </td></tr>
24: <tr><td>Country:</td>
25: <td>
26:   <INPUT TYPE=TEXT NAME=COL3 SIZE=30 DATASRC="#rdsDC" DATAFLD="Country">
27: </td></tr>
28: </table>
29:
30: <INPUT TYPE=BUTTON NAME="btnRequery" VALUE="Requery">
31: <INPUT TYPE=BUTTON NAME="btnFirst" VALUE=" |&lt; ">
```

```
32: <INPUT TYPE=BUTTON NAME="btnPrevious" VALUE=" &lt; ">
33: <INPUT TYPE=BUTTON NAME="btnNext" VALUE=" &gt; ">
34: <INPUT TYPE=BUTTON NAME="btnLast" VALUE=" &gt;| ">
35:
36: <SCRIPT LANGUAGE="VBSCRIPT">
37: <!-- #include file="adcvbs.inc" -->
38: Sub btnRequery_OnClick
39:   strSQL = "SELECT * FROM Suppliers"
40:   strServer = "http://<%=Request.ServerVariables("SERVER_NAME")%>"
41:   strConnStr = "provider=sqloledb.1;user id=sa;password=;
➥initial catalog=northwind;data source=strangelove"
42:
43:   rdsDC.Server = strServer
44:   rdsDC.Connect = strConnStr
45:   rdsDC.SQL = strSQL
46:   rdsDC.ExecuteOptions = adcExecSync
47:   rdsDC.FetchOptions = adcFetchBackground
48:   rdsDC.Refresh
49: End Sub
50:
51: Sub btnFirst_OnClick
52:   MoveRSPointer "First"
53: End Sub
54:
55: Sub btnPrevious_OnClick
56:   MoveRSPointer "Prev"
57: End Sub
58:
59: Sub btnNext_OnClick
60:   MoveRSPointer "Next"
61: End Sub
62:
63: Sub btnLast_OnClick
64:   MoveRSPointer "Last"
65: End Sub
66:
67: Sub MoveRSPointer(strDirection)
68:   If rdsDC.Recordset.State = adcStateClosed Then
69:     If rdsDC.ReadyState = adcReadyStateComplete Then
70:       Msgbox "No query results arrived. Check the error state."
71:     End If
72:     If rdsDC.ReadyState = adcReadyStateLoaded Then
73:       Msgbox "Query results have not yet arrived."
74:     End If
75:   Else
76:     If rdsDC.Recordset.State = adcStateOpen Then
77:       Select Case strDirection
78:         Case "First"
79:           rdsDC.Recordset.MoveFirst
```

17

continues

LISTING **17.4** continued

```
80:          Case "Next"
81:            If Not rdsDC.Recordset.EOF Then
82:              rdsDC.Recordset.MoveNext
83:            End If
84:          Case "Last"
85:            rdsDC.Recordset.MoveLast
86:          Case "Prev"
87:            If Not rdsDC.Recordset.BOF Then
88:              rdsDC.Recordset.MovePrevious
89:            End If
90:        End Select
91:      Else
92:          Msgbox "An unexpected error has occurred."
93:        End If
94:    End If
95: End Sub
96: </SCRIPT>
97:
98: </body>
99: </html>
```

ANALYSIS If you look at the DataControl <OBJECT> tag (lines 7–9), you will notice that this time there are no settings for the server, SQL statement, or connection string. These are set programmatically later on, when the user clicks the Requery button.

The input part of the form begins in line 11 and continues until line 34. It contains four input fields, one for each column that needs to be displayed:

```
<INPUT TYPE=TEXT NAME=COL0 SIZE=30 DATASRC="#rdsDC" DATAFLD="CompanyName">
```

Because I want only one record per page (not a listing in a table), I assign the DATASRC and DATAFLD attributes. Now this field binds to the current row of the recordset provided by the DataControl.

Lines 30–34 contain button definitions for Requery and move operations (first, previous, next, and last). Each of these buttons has an event procedure.

The Requery button is responsible for connecting the DataControl to the Web server and retrieving the data. Instead of passing the parameters to the control through PARAM statements, the parameters are set at runtime using the corresponding properties (lines 43–45). Before retrieving the recordset, two more properties are set:

```
rdsDC.ExecuteOptions = adcExecSync
rdsDC.FetchOptions = adcFetchBackground
```

ExecuteOptions can be either adcExecSync or adcExecAsync (default). This setting tells RDS whether to execute the Refresh method synchronously—returning when the statement was executed—or asynchronously—returning immediately without waiting for success or failure. The second property is FetchOptions, which can be one of the following values:

- adFetchUpFront—All records are fetched before Refresh returns.

- adFetchBackground—Control is returned to the caller of Refresh when the first batch of records is returned from the caller.

- adFetchAsync—Control is returned immediately to the caller. Records are fetched in the background. If you access a record that hasn't been fetched yet, the closest fetched record is returned. This is the default behavior.

These constants bring me back to the issue of named constants and where they are defined. The constants I mentioned are defined in the adcvbs.inc file, which is included for client-side use through the ASP server-side include statement in line 37:

```
<!-- #include file="adcvbs.inc" -->
```

The adcvbs.inc file is presented in Listing 17.5.

LISTING 17.5   The Constants Defined in adcvbs.inc

```
'---- enum Values ----
Const adcExecSync = 1
Const adcExecAsync = 2

'---- enum Values ----
Const adcFetchUpFront = 1
Const adcFetchBackground = 2
Const adcFetchAsync = 3

'---- enum Values ----
Const adcStateClosed = &H00000000
Const adcStateOpen = &H00000001
Const adcStateConnecting = &H00000002
Const adcStateExecuting = &H00000004
Const adcStateFetching = &H00000008

'---- enum Values ----
Const adcReadyStateUninitialized = 0
Const adcReadyStateLoading = 1
Const adcReadyStateLoaded = 2
Const adcReadyStateInteractive = 3
Const adcReadyStateComplete = 4
```

17

With the constants defined and `ExecuteOptions` and `FetchOptions` set, `Refresh` starts populating the recordset for us (line 48).

Now that we have data to display, you have to enable a user to switch between records. This is handled by the `OnClick` events for the First, Previous, Next, and Last buttons (lines 51–65). All these event procedures delegate to the `MoveRSPointer` function in line 67.

Because of the possible asynchronous nature of RDS, you have to take care of recordsets that are not fully loaded (but already executed) or security problems if someone is not allowed to get results. This is all handled in the `If` statements of lines 68–75.

When no error occurred, the `Move` operations of the underlying recordset are executed (see the `Select` statement in lines 77–90).

Now your users are much happier because they can view a record per page and change values—but wait, they can't update the database with the values they changed. This functionality is added in the next section.

Submitting Changes to the Server

You are now adding the last piece to your database front end—updating data at the back end. The example presented in Listing 17.6 builds on the previous listing and adds support for the `DataControl`'s events you can use for asynchronous processing.

LISTING 17.6 Submitting the Changes to the Database

```
 1: <html>
 2: <head>
 3:   <title>Editing Records</title>
 4: </head>
 5: <body bgcolor="#ffffff">
 6:
 7: <OBJECT classid="clsid:BD96C556-65A3-11D0-983A-00C04FC29E33"
 8:   ID="rdsDC" HEIGHT=0 WIDTH=0>
 9: </OBJECT>
10:
11: <table>
12: <tr><td>Company Name:</td>
13: <td>
14:   <INPUT TYPE=TEXT NAME=COL0 SIZE=30 DATASRC="#rdsDC" DATAFLD="CompanyName">
15: </td></tr>
16: <tr><td>Address:</td>
17: <td>
18:   <INPUT TYPE=TEXT NAME=COL1 SIZE=30 DATASRC="#rdsDC" DATAFLD="Address">
19: </td></tr>
20: <tr><td>City:</td>
```

```
21: <td>
22:  <INPUT TYPE=TEXT NAME=COL2 SIZE=30 DATASRC="#rdsDC" DATAFLD="City">
23: </td></tr>
24: <tr><td>Country:</td>
25: <td>
26:  <INPUT TYPE=TEXT NAME=COL3 SIZE=30 DATASRC="#rdsDC" DATAFLD="Country">
27: </td></tr>
28: </table>
29:
30: <INPUT TYPE=BUTTON NAME="btnRequery" VALUE="Requery">
31: <INPUT TYPE=BUTTON NAME="btnFirst" VALUE=" |&lt; ">
32: <INPUT TYPE=BUTTON NAME="btnPrevious" VALUE=" &lt; ">
33: <INPUT TYPE=BUTTON NAME="btnNext" VALUE=" &gt; ">
34: <INPUT TYPE=BUTTON NAME="btnLast" VALUE=" &gt;| ">
35: <INPUT TYPE=BUTTON NAME="btnSaveChanges" VALUE="Save changes">
36:
37: <SCRIPT LANGUAGE="VBSCRIPT">
38: <!-- #include file="adcvbs.inc" -->
39: Sub btnRequery_OnClick
40:    strSQL = "SELECT * FROM Suppliers"
41:    strServer = "http://<%=Request.ServerVariables("SERVER_NAME")%>"
42:    strConnStr = "provider=sqloledb.1;user id=sa;password=;
➡initial catalog=northwind;data source=strangelove"
43:
44:    rdsDC.Server = strServer
45:    rdsDC.Connect = strConnStr
46:    rdsDC.SQL = strSQL
47:    rdsDC.ExecuteOptions = adcExecSync
48:    rdsDC.FetchOptions = adcFetchBackground
49:    rdsDC.Refresh
50: End Sub
51:
52: Sub btnFirst_OnClick
53:    MoveRSPointer "First"
54: End Sub
55:
56: Sub btnPrevious_OnClick
57:    MoveRSPointer "Prev"
58: End Sub
59:
60: Sub btnNext_OnClick
61:    MoveRSPointer "Next"
62: End Sub
63:
64: Sub btnLast_OnClick
65:    MoveRSPointer "Last"
66: End Sub
67:
68: Sub MoveRSPointer(strDirection)
```

17

continues

LISTING 17.6   continued

```
69:    If rdsDC.Recordset.State = adcStateClosed Then
70:     If rdsDC.ReadyState = adcReadyStateComplete Then
71:       Msgbox "No query results arrived. Check the error state."
72:     End If
73:     If rdsDC.ReadyState = adcReadyStateLoaded Then
74:       Msgbox "Query results have not yet arrived."
75:     End If
76:   Else
77:     If rdsDC.Recordset.State = adcStateOpen Then
78:       Select Case strDirection
79:         Case "First"
80:           rdsDC.Recordset.MoveFirst
81:         Case "Next"
82:           If Not rdsDC.Recordset.EOF Then
83:             rdsDC.Recordset.MoveNext
84:           End If
85:         Case "Last"
86:           rdsDC.Recordset.MoveLast
87:         Case "Prev"
88:           If Not rdsDC.Recordset.BOF Then
89:             rdsDC.Recordset.MovePrevious
90:           End If
91:       End Select
92:     Else
93:         Msgbox "An unexpected error has occurred."
94:       End If
95:   End If
96: End Sub
97:
98: Sub rdsDC_OnDataSetChanged
99:    MsgBox "Execution is completed!"
100: End Sub
101:
102: Sub rdsDC_OnDataSetComplete
103:    MsgBox "Fetching of rows is complete!"
104: End Sub
105:
106: Sub rdsDC_onReadyStateChange
107:    ' adcReadyStateUninitialized
108:    ' adcReadyStateLoading
109:    ' adcReadyStateLoaded
110:    ' adcReadyStateInteractive
111:    ' adcReadyStateComplete
112: End Sub
113:
114: Sub rdsDC_onError(SCode, Description, Source, CancelDisplay)
115:    MsgBox "onError: " & Description
116: End Sub
```

```
117:
118: Sub btnSaveChanges_OnClick()
119:    rdsDC.SubmitChanges
120:    rdsDC.Refresh
121: End Sub
122: </SCRIPT>
123:
124: </body>
125: </html>
```

ANALYSIS Line 35 adds a Save changes button, but otherwise the script is identical until line 96 (take the time to read the `MoveRSPointer` method again).

The first event of the `DataControl` is line 98's `OnDataSetChanged`. This event is fired when the execution of a SQL statement is complete, but it does not mean that any rows are here. The event that indicates all rows are here is `OnDataSetComplete`—it fires when all rows are received (lines 102–104).

Though it is good to know about these milestones, a more granular information control is provided by the `onReadyStateChange` event (line 106). It is called whenever the `ReadyState` property changes. `adcReadyStateLoaded` and `adcReadyStateComplete` match the events presented in the previous paragraph. The other `ReadyStates` return information on the status of the record retrieval. Complete documentation can be found in the Platform SDK.

Before finally submitting data changes, let's take a quick look at a very important event: `onError`. It returns error information for asynchronous operations and can give invaluable debugging information. With the `CancelDisplay` variable set to `False`, you can even suppress the error message in the synchronous case (silent fail).

Okay, enough distracters have been shown—let's get to the two-line meat of the script, saving changes a user made (119 and 120):

```
rdsDC.SubmitChanges
rdsDC.Refresh
```

You merely call `SubmitChanges` and then call `Refresh` to get any updates that were made by other users.

Now the script is complete, and it took us only 120 lines to create it. If combined with the list, filter, and sort feature—as well as some more DHTML—a complete client-side front end would consume about 250 lines of code.

17

Working with Handlers

You will have noticed that when you select View Source for your RDS pages, there is a lot of information you don't want to show users: the database server's name, database server login information, and SQL statements. The worst is that a user could build his or her own RDS page and try to wreak havoc on your database by creating malicious SQL statements.

NEW TERM   Because this is a severe security problem, IIS ships with a default handler. A *handler* is a piece of software that fits into the RDS data path, as shown in Figure 17.10.

FIGURE 17.10

The RDS data path with a handler.

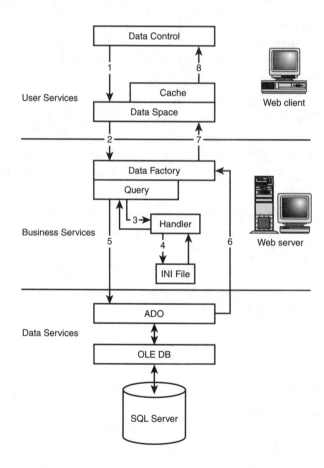

The difference to the normal RDS data path is that before a query is executed, the handler has to approve it. The default handler MSDFMAP goes even one step further—it maps incoming queries to real SQL statements. This enables you to issue single-word statements that map to the full SQL statement on the server. MSDFMAP also hides the Connect to the SQL Server in its INI file. Now your users are out of luck: no login information and only approved SQL statements.

As you remember, you disabled the default handler, enabling you to try all the features live from the Web page. You are now experienced, so in the next sections, you tighten the security again and change your scripts accordingly.

Installing a Default Handler

To lock down your server against unauthorized use, you must install a default handler. If you have a default handler in place, no one can issue SQL statements or access databases other than the ones allowed by the default handler.

A default handler is installed for security reasons by default. Recall that you uninstalled the default handler for learning purposes. To reinstall the MSDFMAP handler, use the following task.

To Do: Installing a default handler

Follow these steps to install a mandatory default handler:

1. Open the Registry Editor and open the registry key HKEY_LOCAL_MACHINE\SOFT-WARE\Microsoft\DataFactory\HandlerInfo.
2. In the right-hand pane, right-click and select New, String Value from the context menu (see Figure 17.11).
3. A string value named New Value #1 is created. Enter DefaultHandler instead.
4. Double-click DefaultHandler and enter MSDFMAP.Handler as the string value.
5. Double-click HandlerRequired and change the value to 1.
6. Stop and restart the Web service to make your changes stick. First, issue net stop w3svc, and then net start w3svc to restart the Web service.

When you try to run one of the scripts you created earlier today, you'll notice that you don't get any data—errors are the only results you get back from the server. The reason is that all requests are now handled by the MSDFMAP handler, which looks up all allowed operations in the INI file MSDFMAP.INI, and your operations are not allowed—at least until now.

FIGURE **17.11**

*Adding a new string
value to the Registry.*

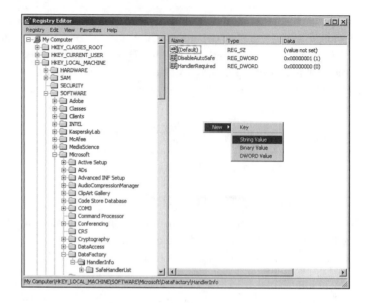

Note

The MSDFMAP handler is not limited to using only one INI file—you can have
multiple files. However, they share one commonality: They all must reside in
the WINNT folder.

To get your first script up and running, you need to create an INI file such as the one presented in Listing 17.7.

LISTING 17.7 A Simple MSDFMAP INI file named tysado25.ini

```
 1: [connect default]
 2: Access=NoAccess
 3:
 4: [sql default]
 5: Sql=" "
 6:
 7: [connect NorthwindDatabase]
 8: Access=ReadWrite
 9: Connect="provider=sqloledb.1;user id=sa;password=;
➡initial catalog=northwind;data source=strangelove"
10:
11: [sql SuppliersRDS]
12: Sql="SELECT CompanyName,Address,City,Country FROM Suppliers"
```

ANALYSIS You can do a lot for security in the MSDFMAP handler files. For example, I created a default Connect, for which I set the access permission to NoAccess. Any RDS client that does not specify a Connect is rejected automatically.

Next, I do the same for the default SQL statement—if someone tries to hack you with these settings in place, you have no defaults that make your server exploitable. However, you need to be able to access certain databases and execute specific SQL statements.

Any database and SQL access is specified in a parent [connect] section and one or more child [sql] sections. The example of the MSDFMAP INI file contains only one [connect] section, the NorthwindDatabase Connect. Access is granted for ReadWrite, and the actual Connect string is provided, hence hiding your user accounts and server settings.

After you have declared the [connect], you need to specify all the [sql] sections, again hiding your database secrets.

Before showing you how to change your RDS pages, I want to mention that these are not all settings you can make in the INI file. One important one is

```
[Logs]
err='c:\MSDFMapErr.log'
```

to enable error logging. Further information about other sections can be found in the Platform SDK.

Changing Your Scripts

The tysado25.ini file for the MSDFMAP handler is placed in the WINNT folder, and all that is left to do is to modify the listings to use the handler, the INI file, and the settings contained in it. Listing 17.8 shows the minimal modifications necessary to use a handler for the supplier listing page.

LISTING 17.8 Using a Handler to List Suppliers

```
 1: <html>
 2: <head>
 3:   <title>Listing Suppliers using a handler</title>
 4: </head>
 5: <body bgcolor="#ffffff">
 6: <%
 7: strHandler = "MSDFMAP.Handler,TysAdo25.ini"
 8: strServer = Request.ServerVariables("SERVER_NAME")
 9: strConnect = "Data Source=NorthwindDatabase"
10: strSQL = "SuppliersRDS"
11: %>
```

continues

LISTING 17.8 continued

```
12:
13: <OBJECT classid="clsid:BD96C556-65A3-11D0-983A-00C04FC29E33"
➥ID="rdsDC" height=0 width=0>
14:     <PARAM NAME="SQL" VALUE="<%=strSQL %>">
15:     <PARAM NAME="SERVER" VALUE="http://<%=strServer%>">
16:     <PARAM NAME="CONNECT" VALUE="<%=strConnect %>">
17:     <PARAM NAME="HANDLER" VALUE="<%=strHandler %>">
18: </OBJECT>
19:
20: <h2>Suppliers in the database</h2>
21: <TABLE DATASRC="#rdsDC">
22: <TBODY>
23:     <TR>
24:        <TD><SPAN DATAFLD="CompanyName"></SPAN></TD>
25:      <TD><SPAN DATAFLD="Address"></SPAN></TD>
26:      <TD><SPAN DATAFLD="City"></SPAN></TD>
27:        <TD><SPAN DATAFLD="Country"></SPAN></TD>
28:     </TR>
29: </TBODY>
30: </TABLE>
31:
32: </body>
33: </html>
```

ANALYSIS The first major change is line 7's strHandler variable:

```
strHandler = "MSDFMAP.Handler,TysAdo25.ini"
```

It specifies the handler and the INI file used to map the requests. The connect string is set to the name of the [connect] section (line 9), and the SQL statement to the name of the [sql] section.

The final addition is the HANDLER parameter in line 17 to open the DataControl. Now the sample works fine with the MSDFMAP handler and all your sensitive database information (server name, SQL statement, and user accounts) are hidden on the server. And best of all, no one can execute statements other than the ones authorized in the INI files.

Summary

With RDS, you can easily access data across the Internet. All you need is some setup work on your Web server to make the RDS ISAPI application functional, which is responsible for sending the data to the client.

The client uses the RDS `DataControl` to request data from the server, which in turn uses the underlying `DataSpace` and `DataControl` components that are described in Day 18. RDS uses ADO as the data access method, and it can operate in asynchronous mode to be more responsive to user input.

If you want to deploy RDS, it is recommended that you tighten security to not only use the `MSDFMAP` handler (or a custom one), but to require its use. With this security in place, users can access only precanned data connections and SQL statements.

Q&A

Q The `MSDFMAP` handler is a great tool, but what if I need to pass parameters to my SQL query—for example, to select a specific supplier?

A The `MSDFMAP` handler supports the use of parameters. In the INI file, you need to create the following SQL statement:

```
[sql SupplierById]
SELECT * FROM Suppliers WHERE SupplierId=?
```

In your RDS page, set the following SQL statement:

```
rdsDC.SQL = "SupplierById(8)"
```

Q How do I add new records via RDS?

A Take a look at the example of editing the records—you were using the `MoveFirst` and other methods of the `Recordset` object. Just move beyond the last record and start editing.

Workshop

The quiz questions and exercises are provided for your further understanding. See Appendix A, "Answers," for the answers.

Quiz

1. What permission do you need to set on the MSADC virtual directory?
2. Which registry keys must be changed so the `MSDFMAP.Handler` is the required default handler?
3. Give some reasons why you would use the `MSDFMAP` handler.
4. What is the name of the client-side RDS component that is used by the `DataControl` to contact the server's `DataFactory`?

Exercise

Create an RDS page that uses the MSDFMAP handler. It will return all records of the Suppliers table, but display only ten records per page. (In a table, see the DATAPA-GESIZE property.) The user must be able to page with the Next and Previous buttons. In addition, display page-of-pages and the RecordCount.

DAY **18**

Creating RDS Business Objects

Yesterday, you learned the basics of RDS, especially how to get along with the `DataFactory` and the MSDFMAP handler. Though you can customize quite a bit with these two, RDS is capable of going above and beyond this functionality. There are two technologies that enable you to add business logic to the RDS scenario on IIS: custom handlers and dedicated business objects.

Today, you will learn the following tasks:

- Choosing the right approach for your needs
- Creating a custom handler
- Installing and testing the custom handler
- Implementing a business object for your three-tiered application
- Invoking the business object across the Internet

Deciding Your Approach

Today's introduction mentioned that you have two choices to implement your business logic using RDS: a custom handler or a business object. Before examining either, take a look at the basic RDS object model again (see Figure 18.1).

FIGURE 18.1

The RDS object model with the default DataFactory *business object on the server side.*

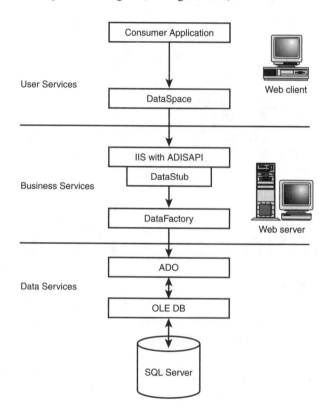

This figure depicts the scenario where the DataFactory is invoked by the client-side DataSpace object. The DataSpace object creates the DataFactory on the server, and all method calls are marshaled across the Internet using HTTP.

NEW TERM   To be able to call a server-side object, the DataSpace object creates a *proxy* of the DataFactory on the client side. An object's proxy acts much like a Web proxy: An object proxy operates on behalf of the real component, whereas a Web proxy acts on behalf of a user.

NEW TERM When data is marshaled across process boundaries—with the Internet being an extreme case of a boundary—this data must be unpackaged on the server and passed to the component that was created for the `DataSpace` component. This task is handled by the *stub*, which is the server-side counterpart of the proxy.

This entire process of packaging and unpackaging is going on behind the scenes for you when you invoke RDS using the `DataControl`. However, you add more or different layers to this process when you introduce one of the following:

- Custom handlers
- Business objects

Custom Handlers

Yesterday, you examined a case that used a custom handler. The one that ships with RDS is the `MSDFMAP` handler allowing you to hide connection strings, SQL statements, and access information in custom INI files. However, you are not limited to using only this one—you can create your own and place it in the object model (see Figure 18.2).

FIGURE 18.2

A custom handler is invoked by the `DataFactory` *object.*

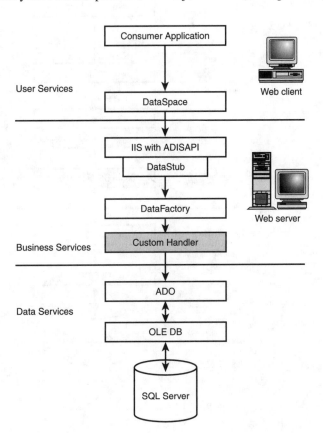

18

The custom handler is automatically invoked by the DataFactory object, and hence its operation is transparent to the client. This is the big boon of using a custom handler, because the client needs only to specify the handler and the rest is taken care of by the server-side DataFactory.

For the DataFactory to be able to invoke a custom handler, the handler object must implement a specific interface—the IDataFactoryHandler interface. This process is shown in the section "Implementing a Custom Handler" later today.

Business Objects

Because you implement a specific interface in the handler object, its use is more-or-less limited to RDS only. That means you'd be creating an object for RDS only, possibly duplicating development efforts that were put into business objects. Therefore, a more general approach is to extend your business objects to the Internet (see Figure 18.3) and RDS.

FIGURE 18.3

A custom business object takes the place of the DataFactory *object.*

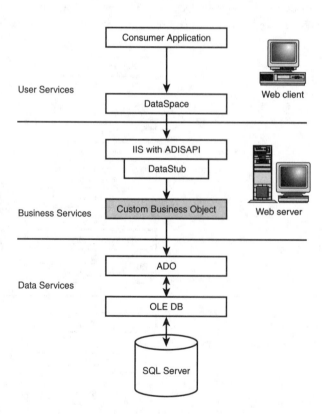

In this scenario, your business object takes the role of the DataFactory. As you will see in the section "Implementing a Business Object," all you have to do in addition to creating a business object is set a registry key. Creating a business object is therefore my personal favorite; however, let's start with a thorough look at handlers and how you can use them to enforce business rules via RDS applications.

Implementing a Custom Handler

As described earlier, implementing a custom handler enables you to integrate seamlessly with the RDS DataFactory on the server side. A custom handler is implemented as a COM component, so you don't have to learn too many new tricks.

The recipe to get up and running with RDS custom handlers is as follows:

- Creating the handler
- Registering the handler
- Working with the handler

Creating the Handler

You can implement the custom handler in any programming language that supports COM. However, in order for the RDS DataFactory to be able to talk to your handler, your handler must implement one specific interface—the IDataFactoryHandler interface. Its definition is shown in Figure 18.4.

18

FIGURE 18.4

The
IDataFactoryHandler
interface's three methods must be implemented by your handler.

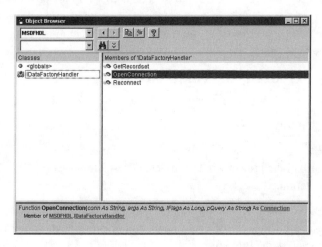

The interface has three methods, which must be implemented by your handler:

- GetRecordset—Returns a recordset for a given connection string, SQL statement, and argument string.
- Reconnect—Connects a disconnected recordset to the database. A connection string and argument string are passed.
- OpenConnection—Primarily serves the purpose of enabling the MS Remote Provider to talk to a handler; however, it can act as a replacement of the other two methods. OpenConnection was introduced with MDAC 2.1.

If you recall Day 15, "Creating Scalable Solutions with COM+," you know that in Visual Basic when implementing an interface, you have to reference the type library and use the Implements keyword in your class. The problem is that you won't easily find the type library for IDataFactoryHandler—that's why we have provided it on the accompanying website in the Samples directory.

Now that you know what is mandatory to succeed in building the handler, let's examine the process of creating, deploying, and testing it. The following sections introduce you to the building part:

- Setting up the project
- Coding the handler

Setting Up the Project

The first step before writing a line of code is to set up the project for the handler. As the handler is referenced via its ProgId, the project and class name decide it. The handler's ProgId will be Custom.Handler; therefore, the project must be named Custom and the handler class named Handler.

To Do: Creating the Handler Project

To Do ►

Follow these steps to create and customize the handler project:

1. Start Visual Basic and select ActiveX DLL as project type.
2. In the project window, select Project1 and rename it Custom.
3. Still in the project window, rename Class1 to Handler. Now the ProgId is correctly determined.
4. Save the project.
5. Right-click on the project's name and select Custom Properties from the context menu. In the Properties dialog box see Figure 18.5, select Unattended Execution and Retained in Memory).

▼

▼ Unattended Execution suppresses any dialog boxes (important for server process-es), and Retained in Memory tells the VB runtime to cache class structures in memory to allow fast creation of instances of your objects.

FIGURE 18.5

Setting project options to speed up the handler.

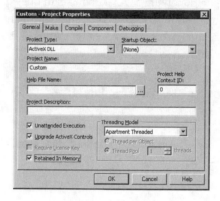

6. You have to add the necessary type library references. Select References from the Project menu and click Browse to locate the `msdfhdl.tlb` file that holds the type library for the `IDataFactoryHandler` interface. Add it to the references.

7. Next, add the ADO type library. The References dialog box should now look like Figure 18.6.

FIGURE 18.6

You have added two type libraries: the ADO type library and the MSDFHDL library.

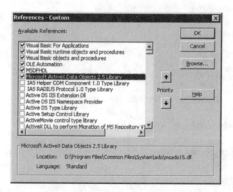

▲ 8. Save the changes to your project.

The project is configured properly, and you can start coding the actual handler function-ality. This is shown in the next section.

18

Coding the Handler

You know that you must implement the `IDataFactoryHandler` interface; however, it is completely up to you what you do in these three methods. For example, the MSDFMAP handler is capable of mapping incoming SQL statements to ones that are stored in an INI file, doing the same with connection strings. The example in Listing 18.1 is not that sophisticated—it simply ignores incoming connection strings and SQL statements and returns data only for those hard-coded in the handler.

LISTING 18.1 The Code for the `Handler` Class Module

```
1: Option Explicit
2:
3: Const cstrConnStr = "provider=sqloledb.1;user id=sa;password=;
➥initial catalog=northwind;data source=strangelove"
4: Const cWriteAccessFlag = 1
5: Const cModifyQueryFlag = 2
6:
7: Implements MSDFHDL.IDataFactoryHandler
8:
9: ' get a recordset from the database
10: Private Function IDataFactoryHandler_GetRecordset(ByVal conn As String,
➥ByVal args As String, ByVal query As String) As ADODB.Recordset
11: On Error GoTo Err_GetRecordset
12:     Dim cn As ADODB.Connection
13:     Dim rs As ADODB.Recordset
14:
15:     Set cn = IDataFactoryHandler_OpenConnection(conn, args,
➥cModifyQueryFlag, query)
16:
17:     Set rs = New ADODB.Recordset
18:     rs.CursorLocation = adUseClient
19:     rs.CursorType = adOpenStatic
20:     rs.LockType = adLockBatchOptimistic
21:     rs.Open query, cn
22:     Set rs.ActiveConnection = Nothing
23:
24:     Set IDataFactoryHandler_GetRecordset = rs
25:
26:     Exit Function
27: Err_GetRecordset:
28:     Err.Raise Err.Number, Err.Source, Err.Description, _
29:         Err.HelpFile, Err.HelpContext
30:     Exit Function
31: End Function
32:
33: ' reconnect a disconnected recordset to the database
```

```
34: Private Sub IDataFactoryHandler_Reconnect(ByVal conn As String,
➥ByVal args As String, ByVal pRS As ADODB.Recordset)
35: On Error GoTo Err_Reconnect
36:     Dim cn As ADODB.Connection, strQuery As String
37:
38:     Set cn = IDataFactoryHandler_OpenConnection(conn, args,
➥cWriteAccessFlag, strQuery)
39:     pRS.ActiveConnection = cn
40:
41:     Exit Sub
42: Err_Reconnect:
43:     Err.Raise Err.Number, Err.Source, Err.Description, _
44:         Err.HelpFile, Err.HelpContext
45:     Exit Sub
46: End Sub
47:
48: ' MDAC 2.1 and greater supports this function for the MS Remote provider
49: Private Function IDataFactoryHandler_OpenConnection(ByVal conn As String,
➥ByVal args As String, ByVal lFlags As Long, ByRef query As String)
➥As ADODB.Connection
50: On Error GoTo Err_OpenConnection
51:     Dim cn As ADODB.Connection
52:
53:     If (lFlags = cWriteAccessFlag) Then
54:         ' connection is opened for Read/Write
55:         ' fail if you don't want write access (Reconnect)
56:     ElseIf (lFlags = cModifyQueryFlag) Then
57:         ' connection is opened for SQL modification (GetRecordset)
58:         query = "SELECT CompanyName,Address,City,Country FROM Suppliers"
59:     End If
60:
61:     Set cn = New ADODB.Connection
62:     cn.Open cstrConnStr
63:
64:     Set IDataFactoryHandler_OpenConnection = cn
65:
66:     Exit Function
67: Err_OpenConnection:
68:     Err.Raise Err.Number, Err.Source, Err.Description, _
69:         Err.HelpFile, Err.HelpContext
70:     Exit Function
71: End Function
```

18

ANALYSIS Ignoring the first few lines (we'll return to these later on), the first interesting statement is line 7:

```
Implements MSDFHDL.IDataFactoryHandler
```

This tells Visual Basic that our class is implementing the `IDataFactoryHandler` interface. The first method of this interface is implemented from lines 10–31 and has the following definition:

```
Private Function IDataFactoryHandler_GetRecordset(ByVal conn As String,
➥ByVal args As String, ByVal query As String) As ADODB.Recordset
```

It takes three input strings—the connection string, an argument string, and a SQL statement—all of which can be ignored or changed (as the `MSDFMAP` handler does). The return value of the function is a disconnected recordset. When you take a look at the body of the function, you can see that I delegate the chore of creating the connection to the `OpenConnection` function that is also part of this interface. The advantage is that the connection opening code is contained in a single place, one that I had to implement anyway. The remainder of this function is plain code to create a disconnected recordset and return it to the caller.

The next function in the course of our listing is `Reconnect`. Its purpose is to reconnect the previously disconnected recordset to the database again, which would enable the `DataFactory` to execute the `SubmitChanges` function. Once again, the connection opening is delegated to `OpenConnection`, and the `ActiveConnection` property is then set to the new connection.

The workhorse of our code is clearly `OpenConnection`, which starts on line 49. I delegate that much work to it because, starting with MDAC 2.1, it is called most often, especially when you are working with the MS Remote provider. The signature of this function is quite interesting:

```
Private Function IDataFactoryHandler_OpenConnection(ByVal conn As String,
➥ByVal args As String, ByVal lFlags As Long, ByRef query As String)
➥As ADODB.Connection
```

Once more, it takes the connection string and arguments parameters; however, there are two different ones: `lFlags` and `query`. The first one tells `OpenConnection` whether the `DataFactory` wants to create a read/write recordset with your connection or just a disconnected recordset. This enables you to implement security measures, such as generally disallowing write operations (`SubmitChanges`). The interesting news about `query` is that it is passed by reference, which means that if you modify it, the `DataFactory` will honor your changes and create the recordset with the SQL statement you passed back to it (again, this is what MSDFMAP does with the help of its INI files).

The core of the function consists of an `If` statement (lines 53–59), which checks the permissions but changes only the SQL statement when a query modification is requested for creating a disconnected recordset. Note that in line 62 the connection is opened using the string constant defined in line 3.

In this example, the `GetRecordset` and `Reconnect` use `OpenConnection` with the appropriate `lFlags` parameter. `GetRecordset` needs a disconnected recordset; therefore, it calls the function with the query modification flag:

```
IDataFactoryHandler_OpenConnection(conn, args, cModifyQueryFlag, query)
```

`Reconnect`, in contrast, needs a connection that enables you to attach a disconnected recordset and possibly update the database:

```
IDataFactoryHandler_OpenConnection(conn, args, cWriteAccessFlag, strQuery)
```

So, the handler code is already doing what the `DataFactory` would do for clients accessing the handler via `OpenConnection` directly. Before any client can access your handler, however, it must be correctly installed on your Web server. Before installing and registering, you have to compile the Visual Basic DLL.

Registering the Handler

The first step you have to perform, as with any COM component, is register it so someone can create an instance using its `ProgId`. This is performed using the tried and true `regsvr32.exe` program:

```
regsvr32.exe custom.dll
```

With that registration, you could create an instance of `Custom.Handler`, but RDS is not allowed to use it because you must register it as a safe handler. These modifications must be made manually in the registry—as always, perform them cautiously.

To Do: Enabling Your Handler

Follow these steps to register your handler as a safe handler with RDS:

1. Open the Registry Editor by starting `regedit.exe` from the Run dialog box.

2. Navigate to the `HKEY_LOCAL_MACHINE\SOFTWARE\Microsoft\DataFactory\HandlerInfo\SafeHandlerList` key. If you installed the Platform SDK, you'll see two additional handlers installed besides the `MSDFMAP.Handler` key.

3. Right-click on SafeHandlerList and select New, Key from the context menu. Change the key name to `Custom.Handler`.

4. Close the Registry Editor.

5. Restart the Web service by issuing the following commands:

   ```
   net stop w3svc
   net start w3svc
   ```

18

The handler is now available via COM and registered as a safe handler with RDS. This is all you need to do to make your custom handler available to RDS consumers.

Working with the Handler

The best server-side technology, such as handlers, is useless if users don't profit from it. With the handler configured and waiting for requests, you can now code the RDS client for our new handler.

To prove that RDS is not tied to HTML or Internet Explorer, the first of the following two implementations shows how to use Excel to talk to RDS data served via your Web server:

- The RDSServer DataFactory
- The MS Remote Provider

The RDSServer DataFactory

In all the examples you've seen, I used the DataControl to establish a connection to a server-side DataFactory. The DataControl itself didn't directly communicate with the DataFactory; instead, it used the client-side DataSpace component to establish the communication and data transfer with the server.

Therefore, you can code RDS without the DataFactory, relying only on the DataSpace and DataFactory. Listing 18.2 performs all the functionality hidden in the DataControl to get data from the server (it doesn't use our handler yet).

LISTING 18.2   Coding Directly to RDS in Excel

```
 1: Sub Talk2DataFactory()
 2: On Error GoTo Err_Talk2DataFactory
 3:     Dim objRDS As Object
 4:     Dim objBusObj As Object, rs As Object
 5:
 6:     Set objRDS = CreateObject("RDS.DataSpace")
 7:     Set objBusObj = objRDS.CreateObject("RDSServer.DataFactory", _
 8:         "http://192.168.1.105")
 9:     Set rs = objBusObj.Query("provider=sqloledb.1;user id=sa;password=;
➡initial catalog=northwind;data source=strangelove", _
10:         "SELECT * FROM Suppliers")
11:
12:     Exit Sub
13: Err_Talk2DataFactory:
14:     MsgBox Err.Number & " " & Err.Description
15:     Exit Sub
16: End Sub
```

ANALYSIS The project does not reference the RDS type library; therefore, all objects are generically defined (lines 3 and 4). I am on the client-side, so line 6 creates an instance of the `DataSpace` component. Using the `DataSpace`'s `CreateObject` function, I create a `DataFactory` object on a Web server. The general syntax of `CreateObject` is

```
objRDS.CreateObject(ProgId, Location)
```

The `Location` parameter can be either an empty string (local computer), a computer name (invocation via DCOM), or a Web server address (our case).

With the `DataFactory` up and running, I call its `Query` method which takes a connection string and SQL statement (line 9). If nothing goes wrong, I have a disconnected recordset ready to use in my application—a recordset that was served via HTTP.

The example showed how the `DataControl` takes some burden off you by calling the `CreateObject` and `Query` functions. The latter function is the one where `DataFactory` is going to use your handler's `GetRecordset` or `OpenConnection` function. As you can see in Listing 18.3, there aren't too many modifications necessary to talk to your handler.

LISTING 18.3 Telling the `DataFactory` to Use Your Handler

```
 1: Sub Talk2CustomHandler()
 2: On Error GoTo Err_Talk2CustomHandler
 3:     Dim objRDS As Object
 4:     Dim objBusObj As Object, rs As Object
 5:
 6:     Set objRDS = CreateObject("RDS.DataSpace")
 7:     Set objBusObj = objRDS.CreateObject("RDSServer.DataFactory", _
 8:         "http://192.168.1.105")
 9:     Set rs = objBusObj.Query("Handler=Custom.Handler", _
10:        "SELECT * FROM Customers")
11:
12:     Exit Sub
13: Err_Talk2CustomHandler:
14:     MsgBox Err.Number & " " & Err.Description
15:     Exit Sub
16: End Sub
```

18

ANALYSIS Actually the only change is line 9, which specifies a different connection string, and a SQL statement (line 10). The connection string tells the `DataFactory` to invoke your handler and passes the connection string (minus the handler part) as well as the SQL statement to your handler.

What does your handler return? Well, definitely not the data for the SQL statement that is specified in line 10. Instead, it returns specific columns for the Suppliers table. This happens because the handler modifies the query parameter that is passed when a connection is requested.

As you can see, a handler is a convenient way to force a client to do what you want, but still be able to use as little code as possible, which is demonstrated in the next section.

The MS Remote Provider

Let's switch back to the favorite playground of RDS—the Web server and Web client arena. Did you ever wonder how the recordset data was transferred from the server to the client and vice versa? The necessary packaging and unpackaging for the transfer is done by the MS Remote Provider, however, on behalf of the DataFactory object.

Starting with MDAC 2.1, you could forego the DataFactory object and let the MS Remote provider talk directly to your handler. To prove that this is simple, see Listing 18.4, which implements the provider and handler using the already familiar DataControl.

LISTING 18.4 Using the RDS DataControl with Your Handler

```
 1: <html>
 2: <head>
 3:   <title>Listing Suppliers using a handler</title>
 4: </head>
 5: <body bgcolor="#ffffff">
 6: <%
 7: strServer = Request.ServerVariables("SERVER_NAME")
 8: strConnect = "Provider=MS Remote;Handler=Custom.Handler;"
 9: strSQL = "Even this is going to work"
10: %>
11:
12: <OBJECT classid="clsid:BD96C556-65A3-11D0-983A-00C04FC29E33"
➥ID="rdsDC" height=0 width=0>
13:     <PARAM NAME="SQL" VALUE="<%=strSQL %>">
14:     <PARAM NAME="SERVER" VALUE="http://<%=strServer%>">
15:     <PARAM NAME="CONNECT" VALUE="<%=strConnect %>">
16: </OBJECT>
17:
18: <h2>Suppliers in the database</h2>
19: <TABLE DATASRC="#rdsDC">
20: <TBODY>
21:     <TR>
22:        <TD><SPAN DATAFLD="CompanyName"></SPAN></TD>
23:       <TD><SPAN DATAFLD="Address"></SPAN></TD>
24:       <TD><SPAN DATAFLD="City"></SPAN></TD>
25:        <TD><SPAN DATAFLD="Country"></SPAN></TD>
26:     </TR>
27: </TBODY>
```

```
28: </TABLE>
29:
30: </body>
31: </html>
```

ANALYSIS Once again, the RDS page uses some ASP, therefore it must be stored to a file with an .asp extension. The connection string is created in line 8, specifying the MS Remote provider as well as the custom handler. To illustrate more vividly that our handler ignores any SQL statement, I'm passing garbage in line 9. The remainder of the script is no different from the script you saw yesterday.

The examples accessing the custom handler showed clearly that it integrates perfectly in the DataControl code of your RDS pages. Also, it acts as a business object because it enforces rules on how data is accessed and manipulated. However, handlers aren't nearly as flexible as a real business object, nor can handlers be used in any client application.

Implementing a Business Object

If you implement a custom handler, it is closely tied to RDS, which makes it hard and sometimes even impractical to reuse it in other environments, such as a Visual Basic client or a Web front end that is processed on the server side. Though a handler acts like a business object (by being able to decide which action to allow), it is also rooted in the data tier because it directly accesses the data store. If you look at Figure 18.7, however, these two tiers should be separate.

18

FIGURE 18.7

The three-tier programming model.

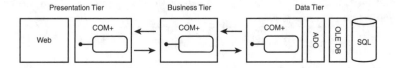

Therefore, if you want a clean design, you should consider building business objects that take advantage of data tier objects to talk to the database. With this approach your business object can be used everywhere, including RDS.

Because there is a different approach between the side of the business object and the client side, this section discusses the following topics:

- Creating the business object
- Registering with COM+ and IIS
- Working with the business object

Creating the Business Object

In a correct three-tier design, the business object talks to the database only via components that reside in the data tier. But do you have a data tier component readily available? Yes, the AD25Northwind.Suppliers component that you created in Day 15.

The business object you create now—BusObj.Test—is using this data tier component and adding some business logic to justify its name. It implements its logic in two methods: GetSuppliers and DeleteSupplier.

The first task at hand before coding, however, is to create a project for the business component. Because it talks to ADO25Northwind.Suppliers and passes a disconnected recordset, you must reference both the ADO25Northwind and ADO type libraries.

To Do: Setting up the Project

Follow these steps to create the project with the necessary references:

1. Create a new ActiveX DLL project in Visual Basic. Name the project BusObj and the class Test.

2. In the References dialog box, make sure to select the ADO type library as well as the ADO25Northwind type library, which defines your Suppliers data tier component.

3. Save the project.

Now that the project is set up, copy the code in Listing 18.5 into the class module.

LISTING **18.5**   The Code of the Business Component for GetSuppliers and DeleteSupplier

```
 1: Option Explicit
 2:
 3: Private Const cstrDSN = "provider=sqloledb.1;user id=sa;password=;
➥initial catalog=northwind;data source=strangelove"
 4: Private Const cstrQuery = "SELECT CompanyName,Address,City,Country
➥FROM Suppliers"
 5:
 6: Public Function GetSuppliers() As ADODB.Recordset
 7: On Error GoTo Err_GetSuppliers
 8:     Dim suppDataObj As ADO25Northwind.Suppliers
 9:
10:     Set suppDataObj = New ADO25Northwind.Suppliers
11:     Set GetSuppliers = suppDataObj.BrowseTable(cstrQuery)
12:
13:     Exit Function
```

```
14: Err_GetSuppliers:
15:     Err.Raise Err.Number, Err.Source, Err.Description, _
16:         Err.HelpFile, Err.HelpContext
17:     Exit Function
18: End Function
19:
20: Public Function DeleteSupplier(ByVal nSupplierId As Variant) As Boolean
21: On Error GoTo Err_DeleteSupplier
22:     Dim bResult As Boolean
23:
24:     If (nSupplierId < 30) Then
25:         Err.Raise vbObjectError + 1, "BusObj.Test", _
26:             "Cannot delete a supplier that ships with the
➥default installation!"
27:         Exit Function
28:     End If
29:
30:     Dim suppDataObj As ADO25Northwind.Suppliers
31:
32:     Set suppDataObj = New ADO25Northwind.Suppliers
33:     bResult = suppDataObj.DeleteRecord(nSupplierId)
34:     DeleteSupplier = bResult
35:
36:     Exit Function
37: Err_DeleteSupplier:
38:     Err.Raise Err.Number, Err.Source, Err.Description, _
39:         Err.HelpFile, Err.HelpContext
40:     Exit Function
41: End Function
```

ANALYSIS I have declared some constants up front, including the data source name. This is only for purposes of testing, because as you can see in the GetSuppliers method in line 11, I call the data tier object without it. The general syntax of BrowseTable is

```
xObj.BrowseTable([sql],[data source])
```

Both parameters are optional, but I pass along only the SQL statement to retrieve the Suppliers. In this way, the business object is shielded from actual database access, but is able to return a disconnected recordset to the presentation tier.

A function that really contains business logic, albeit a simplistic one, is DeleteSupplier, starting in line 20. Please notice that I am passing the parameter nSupplierId as Variant; scripting languages support only Variant as data type. The only downside of Variant is that it is large in terms of size compared to the actual data types, but you can stuff nearly anything into Variant.

18

The business logic contained in this function checks only whether the SupplierId passed to the function is smaller than 30, which would mean that someone wanted to delete one of the sample suppliers that ship with Northwind. As a business rule, I disagree with this delete operation and return an error (line 25). Please note that all custom object errors must be higher than vbObjectError, so I add it to my error constant of 1.

After my business logic has approved the intentions of the client, the code calls the data tier component to do the hard work. Should an error occur, it is returned to the calling client.

You haven't compiled the DLL, so there can't be any clients yet—therefore make and register the DLL now.

Registering with COM+ and IIS

Though the DLL exists and is registered properly, it is no good citizen in the three-tier world. You have to install it in a COM+ application. To make things fast, install it in the ADO++ Test application where the data tier component already resides.

To Do: Registering the Object in ADO++ Test

Follow these steps to add the BusObj.Test component to the ADO++ Test application in Component Services:

1. Start the Component Services MMC application (Start Menu, Programs, Administrative Tools).

2. Expand Component Services, Computers, My Computer, COM+ Applications, ADO++ Test, Components. Your Component Services application should now look like Figure 18.8.

3. Right-click on Components and select Component from the New menu.

4. In the COM Component Install Wizard, choose to Install Components that are already registered.

5. Select the BusObj.Test component from the list of installed components.

6. Finish the installation.

FIGURE 18.8

*Adding a new compo-
nent to the ADO++
Test application.*

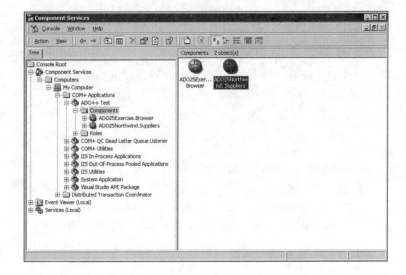

The business object works fine now in environments such as Excel or Visual Basic, for example. However, because of security restrictions, it is not possible to access it via RDS. To make
this happen, you have to grant additional launch permissions.

To Do: Marking the Component Safe for RDS

Follow these steps to mark the component safe for use with RDS:

1. Open the Registry Editor (type `regedit.exe` in the Run dialog box).

2. Go to the
   `HKEY_LOCAL_MACHINE\SYSTEM\CurrentControlSet\Services\W3SVC\Parameters`
   `\ADCLaunch` key.

3. Right-click and select New, Key from the context menu. Change the key name to
   `BusObj.Test`.

4. Close the Registry Editor.

5. Stop and restart the Web server:

   ```
   net stop w3svc
   net start w3svc
   ```

Now your business object is accessible remotely via the Web.

18

Working with the Business Object

If you use the business object directly in Excel or Visual Basic, your code is straightforward, as it would be with every component. If you work across HTTP with RDS, however, you have to code to the `DataSpace` object, and you can do this in many environments, including the following two:

- Using Excel as front end
- Using IE as front end

Using Excel as Front End

I use Excel here as an example of any standalone application development environment. RDS can be accessed from anywhere, because the only thing implied is that the data transfer and object invocation is performed over the HTTP protocol.

The example presented in Listing 18.6 creates an instance of your business object and tests both methods that are supported.

 Note   You must reference the RDS Client type library (Microsoft Remote Data Services 2.5 Library) to be able to use typified access to the `DataSpace` object.

LISTING 18.6   Acquiring an Instance and Testing the Functionality

```
 1: Sub TestCustBusObj()
 2:     Dim objDS As RDS.DataSpace
 3:     Set objDS = New RDS.DataSpace
 4:
 5:     Dim myBusObj As Object
 6:     Set myBusObj = objDS.CreateObject("BusObj.Test", _
 7:         "http://192.168.1.105")
 8:
 9:     Dim rs As ADODB.Recordset
10:     Set rs = myBusObj.GetSuppliers()
11:     Debug.Print rs.RecordCount
12:
13:     ' this generates an error, therefore catch it
14:     On Error Resume Next
15:     Dim bRetVal As Boolean
16:     bRetVal = myBusObj.DeleteSupplier(5)
17:     If Err.Number <> 0 Then
18:         MsgBox "Error #" & (Err.Number - vbObjectError) & _
19:             ", " & Err.Description
20:     Else
21:         MsgBox "Delete Succeeded!"
22:     End If
23: End Sub
```

ANALYSIS An instance of the `DataSpace` object is created in line 3 and used to instantiate your `BusObj.Test` in line 6 using its `CreateObject` method, which takes the `ProgId` and the server (change as necessary).

Because the `DataSpace` object created a proxy of `BusObj.Test` for you, you can now call all methods just as if the business object resided on the local machine. In our case, however, all calls work over HTTP. The first call is for `GetSuppliers` (line 10), which retrieves all our suppliers in the database. The recordset is verified in line 11.

Because the `DeleteSupplier` method can return errors, I decided to use the `On Error Resume Next` statement to catch any errors and create an appropriate output—subtracting the `vbObjectError` constant to get my original error code.

Using IE as Front End

Using RDS with custom business objects on the browser client—that is, Internet Explorer—isn't much different. You can add a twist to it, however. Previously, the `DataControl` did all the work for you, including displaying the data in an HTML table.

With a custom business object, your first guess might be that you have to create the HTML on-the-fly, but there's a nice trick to be able to use the `DataControl` with a `Recordset` returned from a custom business object. See Listing 18.7 for details.

LISTING 18.7 Loading a Recordset and Assigning It to the `DataControl`

```
 1: <html>
 2: <head>
 3:   <title>Attaching Recordsets from a Business Object</title>
 4: </head>
 5: <body bgcolor="#ffffff">
 6: <%
 7: strServer = Request.ServerVariables("SERVER_NAME")
 8: %>
 9:
10: <OBJECT classid="clsid:BD96C556-65A3-11D0-983A-00C04FC29E33"
11:    ID="rdsDC" height=0 width=0>
12:    <PARAM NAME="SERVER" VALUE="http://<%=strServer%>">
13: </OBJECT>
14:
15: <h2>Suppliers in the database</h2>
16: <TABLE DATASRC="#rdsDC">
17: <TBODY>
18:    <TR>
19:       <TD><SPAN DATAFLD="CompanyName"></SPAN></TD>
20:      <TD><SPAN DATAFLD="Address"></SPAN></TD>
21:      <TD><SPAN DATAFLD="City"></SPAN></TD>
22:       <TD><SPAN DATAFLD="Country"></SPAN></TD>
```

continues

18

LISTING 18.7   continued

```
23:     </TR>
24: </TBODY>
25: </TABLE>
26:
27: <input type="button" name="btnLoadBusObj" value="Load Data">
28:
29: <SCRIPT LANGUAGE="VBSCRIPT">
30: Sub btnLoadBusObj_onClick
31:    Set objDS = CreateObject("RDS.DataSpace")
32:    objDS.InternetTimeout = 6000
33:    Set myBusObj = objDS.CreateObject("BusObj.Test","http://<%=strServer%>")
34:    Set rdsDC.SourceRecordset = myBusObj.GetSuppliers()
35: End Sub
36: </SCRIPT>
37:
38: </body>
39: </html>
```

ANALYSIS   Lines 1 through 25 are pretty much the same as for any other RDS page I have presented so far (therefore, you have to store it as an ASP page). The real difference is the script in lines 29–36. In this block of code, I first create a `DataSpace` object, which is then used to retrieve an instance of `BusObj.Test`. I'm using one interesting property here:

```
objDS.InternetTimeout = 6000
```

This tells the `DataSpace` how long to wait before it considers the connection with the HTTP server as terminated. The value is given in milliseconds, and the default is `30,000`, which should be long enough for even the slowest Web server. `InternetTimeout` and `CreateObject` are the only properties and methods of the `DataSpace` object.

The trick I mentioned is line 34:

```
Set rdsDC.SourceRecordset = myBusObj.GetSuppliers()
```

The recordset that is returned by your business object is assigned the `SourceRecordset` property of the `DataControl`, which then performs the task of displaying the recordset in the table. This way you can reuse most RDS code without having to deal with too much DHTML.

Summary

Today, you examined how to make RDS even more powerful by creating your own handler and by implementing a business object that could be instantiated across the Internet. The main advantage of creating a custom handler is that it integrates seamlessly with the `DataFactory`, but isn't well-suited for reuse with other clients. Custom business objects, in contrast, take the place of the `DataFactory` as the server-side object and enable rich access to more methods. However, the biggest advantage is that business objects can be used for any presentation tier application, and not be tied to the RDS environment only.

Q&A

Q You have briefly mentioned the use of proxies and stubs and what marshaling is. Where can I learn more, and why should I?

A These terms are parts of the underpinnings of COM, and usually transparent to the Visual Basic component developer. The advantage of knowing what is happening on behalf of your code is that you can write components that are faster and more reliable. You can learn more either in the Platform SDK, or in books such as *Essential COM*, Don Box, Addison Wesley Press, or *Inside COM*, Dale Rogerson, Microsoft Press.

Q The business component you presented didn't use the `ObjectContext` as the data tier component did. Why?

A To create a correct COM+ component, I should have incorporated the `ObjectContext` to allow for JIT activation and deactivation. However, because RDS allows only one call to the component (stateless), you get a new instance for each method invocation anyway.

Workshop

The quiz questions and exercises are provided for your further understanding. See Appendix A, "Answers," for the answers.

Quiz

1. Which three methods must be implemented for the `IDataFactoryHandler` interface?

2. Where do you need to mark a custom handler as a safe handler?

3. Which security restrictions are in place for custom business objects over RDS?

4. Name the property you have to assign a disconnected recordset to for the `DataControl` to use it for display.

Exercises

1. Write a custom handler `MyHandler.Exercise` that allows read operations only (`Reconnect` and `OpenConnection` with `lFlags` of `cWriteAccessFlag` should fail). The connection string is a constant; however, the SQL statements are to be honored.

2. Create a business object named `MyBusObj.Exercise` that implements one method named `Fetch`. This method takes as input parameter a string (SQL statement) and returns a recordset. The database connection is the Northwind database.

DAY **19**

ADO and XML Integration

On Day 16, "Working with Disconnected Recordsets," you learned how to store recordsets to disk in either ADTG or XML format. Today, you take a closer look at how XML can be used with ADO and how it can help you fulfill needs for data in your applications.

The advantage of using XML in your applications is that XML acts as an open standard data exchange format, which can be used to transfer data from the Web to a standalone application, and from a PC to a UNIX server, for example. You are going to see a lot of solutions built around XML in the future.

Today, you learn the following tasks:

- Identifying sections of the XML persistence format
- Using XML in conjunction with RDS
- Applying style sheets to XML data
- Working with data islands
- Using hierarchical recordsets with XML

The ADO XML Persistence Format

To take full advantage of ADO's XML persistence features, it is important to know how the XML format created by ADO looks. To be able to take a look at the format, however, you have to create XML from a recordset.

Because most of today's XML applications run on the Web, I decided to stick with that scenario in today's lesson. To follow the examples, you must have a Web server with ASP up and running and use Internet Explorer 5 or higher to display the pages. All samples must be stored with an ASP extension.

Now that you know what is necessary to successfully run Listing 19.1, take a look at it.

LISTING 19.1   Creating XML from a Recordset

```
1: <%
2: Set conn = CreateObject("ADODB.Connection")
3: Set rs = CreateObject("ADODB.Recordset")
4: Set stm = CreateObject("ADODB.Stream")
5:
6: conn.Open "provider=sqloledb.1;user id=sa;password=;
►initial catalog=northwind;data source=strangelove"
7:
8: strSQL = "SELECT * FROM Customers"
9: rs.Open strSQL, conn
10:
11: Const adPersistXML = 1
12: rs.Save stm, adPersistXML
13: Response.Write stm.ReadText
14:
15: stm.Close
16: Set stm = Nothing
17:
18: rs.Close
19: Set rs = Nothing
20:
21: conn.Close
22: Set conn = Nothing
23: %>
```

ANALYSIS   Lines 2 through 4 create ADO objects. The first is the connection opened in line 6; the second is the recordset opened in line 9. The third object is a `Stream` object. I declare this object because the `Save` method enables you to save a recordset to a file or any object that supports the IStream interface—and the `Stream` object obviously supports it.

Now that I have a `Stream` object that contains XML, all I have to do is to send this XML to the client. This is done in line 13 using `Response.Write` and the `ReadText` method of the `Stream` object. The remainder of the script deals with correct cleanup of all open objects.

So how is the XML being displayed when you open the page in Internet Explorer? Take a look at Figure 19.1.

FIGURE 19.1

Displaying the XML in Internet Explorer.

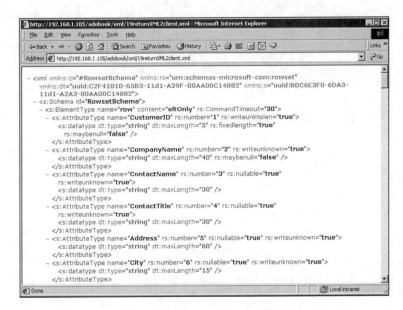

As you can see, it is marked up nicely through a standard formatting template that is provided by Internet Explorer. However, you are more interested in the hard facts of the XML format, and not so much in how Internet Explorer displays it by default.

Listing 19.2 provides a quick overview of the raw format. It is generally broken into two sections: a schema section followed by a data section.

LISTING 19.2 A Quick Look at the XML Format

```
 1: <xml xmlns:s='uuid:BDC6E3F0-6DA3-11d1-A2A3-00AA00C14882'
 2:   xmlns:dt='uuid:C2F41010-65B3-11d1-A29F:00AA00C14882'
 3:   xmlns:rs='urn:schemas-microsoft-com:rowset'
 4:   xmlns:z='#RowsetSchema'>
 5: <s:Schema id='RowsetSchema'>
...
52: </s:Schema>
53: <rs:data>
...
433: </rs:data>
434: </xml>
```

19

ANALYSIS I have skipped the declaration of namespaces on top of the document—if you are going to work with XML a lot, you have to learn how to create them. For our discussion of the format, however, it is sufficient to know what each namespace refers to:

- s refers to the XML-Data namespace, which contains the elements and attributes that define the schema of the current Recordset.
- dt refers to the data type definitions specification.
- rs refers to the namespace that contains the elements and attributes specific to ADO Recordset properties and attributes.
- z refers to the schema of the current rowset.

The Schema Section

The schema section contains definitions for each column that is contained in the record-set. To get a feel for what is contained in this section, take a look at Listing 19.3, which shows the definition for the Customers table recordset.

LISTING **19.3**   The Schema Section of the Recordset

```
 5: <s:Schema id='RowsetSchema'>
 6:   <s:ElementType name='row' content='eltOnly' rs:CommandTimeout='30'>
 7:     <s:AttributeType name='CustomerID' rs:number='1' rs:writeunknown='true'>
 8:       <s:datatype dt:type='string' dt:maxLength='5' rs:fixedlength='true'
 9:         rs:maybenull='false'/>
10:     </s:AttributeType>
11:     <s:AttributeType name='CompanyName' rs:number='2'
➥rs:writeunknown='true'>
12:         <s:datatype dt:type='string' dt:maxLength='40' rs:maybenull='false'/>
13:     </s:AttributeType>
14:     <s:AttributeType name='ContactName' rs:number='3' rs:nullable='true'
15:         rs:writeunknown='true'>
16:       <s:datatype dt:type='string' dt:maxLength='30'/>
17:     </s:AttributeType>
18:     <s:AttributeType name='ContactTitle' rs:number='4' rs:nullable='true'
19:         rs:writeunknown='true'>
20:       <s:datatype dt:type='string' dt:maxLength='30'/>
21:     </s:AttributeType>
22:     <s:AttributeType name='Address' rs:number='5' rs:nullable='true'
23:         rs:writeunknown='true'>
24:       <s:datatype dt:type='string' dt:maxLength='60'/>
25:     </s:AttributeType>
26:     <s:AttributeType name='City' rs:number='6' rs:nullable='true'
27:         rs:writeunknown='true'>
28:       <s:datatype dt:type='string' dt:maxLength='15'/>
29:     </s:AttributeType>
30:     <s:AttributeType name='Region' rs:number='7' rs:nullable='true'
```

```
31:          rs:writeunknown='true'>
32:          <s:datatype dt:type='string' dt:maxLength='15'/>
33:       </s:AttributeType>
34:       <s:AttributeType name='PostalCode' rs:number='8' rs:nullable='true'
35:          rs:writeunknown='true'>
36:          <s:datatype dt:type='string' dt:maxLength='10'/>
37:       </s:AttributeType>
38:       <s:AttributeType name='Country' rs:number='9' rs:nullable='true'
39:          rs:writeunknown='true'>
40:          <s:datatype dt:type='string' dt:maxLength='15'/>
41:       </s:AttributeType>
42:       <s:AttributeType name='Phone' rs:number='10' rs:nullable='true'
43:          rs:writeunknown='true'>
44:          <s:datatype dt:type='string' dt:maxLength='24'/>
45:       </s:AttributeType>
46:       <s:AttributeType name='Fax' rs:number='11' rs:nullable='true'
47:          rs:writeunknown='true'>
48:          <s:datatype dt:type='string' dt:maxLength='24'/>
49:       </s:AttributeType>
50:       <s:extends type='rs:rowbase'/>
51:    </s:ElementType>
52: </s:Schema>
```

ANALYSIS   As you can see, ADO writes out detailed metadata about each column to enable preservation of semantics for the data values. Each column is represented by an s:AttributeType element, which contains the name, the ordinal position in the recordset, and whether the column is nullable or not.

Data Type Representation

Each column must have a data type assigned. For example, the column CompanyName has the following definition:

```
<s:datatype dt:type='string' dt:maxLength='40' rs:maybenull='false'/>
```

Because of the inherent descriptiveness of the ADO XML schema, it is not hard to guess that the column takes a string with a maximum of 40 characters, and that it must not be Null.

The most important dt:type values you are going to encounter are boolean, string, i4, ui1, and char. If you want to learn more, visit http://www.w3.org/TR/1998/ NOTE-XML-data-0105/, section Specific Datatypes.

The Data Section

The data section defines the data of the recordset. It also contains information about any pending updates, insertions, or row deletions. There can be zero or more rows in the data section; however, the `rs:data` element is always there. Listing 19.4 shows the data section for our sample recordset.

LISTING 19.4   The Data Section of the XML Format

```
53: <rs:data>
54:   <z:row CustomerID='ALFKI' CompanyName='Alfreds Futterkiste'
55:       ContactName='Maria Anders' ContactTitle='Sales Representative'
56:       Address='Obere Str. 57' City='Berlin' PostalCode='12209'
57:       Country='Germany' Phone='030-0074321' Fax='030-0076545'/>
...
429:   <z:row CustomerID='WOLZA' CompanyName='Wolski  Zajazd'
430:       ContactName='Zbyszek Piestrzeniewicz' ContactTitle='Owner'
431:       Address='ul. Filtrowa 68' City='Warszawa' PostalCode='01-012'
432:       Country='Poland' Phone='(26) 642-7012' Fax='(26) 642-7012'/>
433: </rs:data>
```

Using XML with RDS

You are now familiar with how ADO stores a recordset in XML format. This knowledge is important when dealing with the various usage scenarios of XML data in client applications. The first scenario you are going to explore is how to use XML recordsets in RDS client applications.

When you recall Day 17, "Remoting Data Using RDS," you'll remember that you had to specify the SERVER, SQL, and CONNECT parameters for the RDS DataControl. These parameters were passed to the server and executed by the RDS ISAPI application, and the results were then returned to the user.

With XML, this changes a bit. First, forget about those three parameters; you need only one: URL. This parameter specifies which XML file to use as the data source for the DataControl. It can be either a static XML file or one that you generate on-the-fly using ASP, as shown in Listing 19.5.

LISTING 19.5   The File `xmlrds.asp` Persists a Recordset via Response's IStream Interface

```
1: <!--METADATA NAME="Microsoft ActiveX Data Objects 2.5 Library"
2:    TYPE="TypeLib"
3:    UUID="{00000205-0000-0010-8000-00AA006D2EA4}"
4: -->
5: <%
6: Set conn = CreateObject("ADODB.Connection")
7: Set rs = CreateObject("ADODB.Recordset")
8:
```

```
 9: conn.Open "provider=sqloledb.1;user id=sa;password=;
➡initial catalog=northwind;data source=strangelove"
10:
11: strSQL = "SELECT * FROM Customers"
12: rs.Open strSQL, conn
13: rs.Save Response, adPersistXML
14: %>
```

ANALYSIS This ASP file is very similar to Listing 19.1; however, it takes advantage of one of the new features in IIS 5.0—that the `Response` object implements the IStream interface and can be passed to the `Save` method of the `Recordset` object (line 13). The only other difference is that the type library definitions for ADO are incorporated using the `METADATA` tag instead of by defining the necessary constants manually.

When you open this ASP in the browser, you again get a color-highlighted version of the XML. Let's see how you can incorporate this output into an RDS client application.

Using XML-Persisted Recordsets in Excel

The easiest—but not strictly RDS—use of the generated XML is to call the `Open` method of the `Recordset` object. The news about this approach is that you are passing the URL of the ASP page, and not a filename on the local computer. See Listing 19.6 to implement it.

LISTING 19.6 Setting the Content Type

```
1: Option Explicit
2:
3: Const cstrWebServer = "http://192.168.1.105/"
4:
5: Sub GetRSFromWebServer()
6:     Dim rs As New ADODB.Recordset
7:     rs.Open cstrWebServer & "/adobook/xml/xmlrds.asp"
8:     Debug.Print rs.RecordCount
9: End Sub
```

19

ANALYSIS The recordset is opened in line 7 using the `Open` method and passing the URL to the dynamic XML file (you might have to adjust the path for your setup). This is actually all you have to do to reactivate the persisted recordset and be able to access it as if it were created from the live data source.

Feeding XML to the RDS DataControl

After completing the little Excel exercise, switch gears back to Web development. I already broke the news that to use XML as the data source in RDS, all you have to do is provide an URL tag to the DataControl. This is what I did in Listing 19.7.

LISTING 19.7　Populating the RDS DataControl with XML Data

```
 1: <html>
 2: <head>
 3:   <title>Listing Customers</title>
 4: </head>
 5: <body bgcolor="#ffffff">
 6:
 7: <%
 8: strURL = "http://"
 9: strURL = strURL & Request.ServerVariables("SERVER_NAME")
10: strURL = strURL & "/adobook/xml/xmlrds.asp"
11: %>
12:
13: <OBJECT classid="clsid:BD96C556-65A3-11D0-983A-00C04FC29E33"
14:    ID="rdsDC" height=0 width=0>
15:     <PARAM NAME="URL" VALUE="<%=strURL%>">
16: </OBJECT>
17:
18: <h2>Customers</h2>
19: <p style="width:750px;height:450px;overflow:scroll">
20: <TABLE DATASRC="#rdsDC" ID="SuppliersTable">
21: <thead>
22: <tr>
23:    <th id="CompanyName">Company</th>
24:    <th id="Address">Address</th>
25:    <th id="City">City</th>
26:    <th id="Country">Country</th>
27: </tr>
28: </thead>
29: <TBODY>
30:    <TR>
31:       <TD><SPAN DATAFLD="CompanyName"></SPAN></TD>
32:     <TD><SPAN DATAFLD="Address"></SPAN></TD>
33:     <TD><SPAN DATAFLD="City"></SPAN></TD>
34:       <TD><SPAN DATAFLD="Country"></SPAN></TD>
35:    </TR>
36: </TBODY>
37: </TABLE>
38: </p>
39:
40: <SCRIPT LANGUAGE="VBSCRIPT">
41: Sub SuppliersTable_onClick()
```

```
42:    if ("TH" = window.event.srcElement.tagName) then
43:       strSortColumn = window.event.srcElement.id
44:       rdsDC.SortColumn = strSortColumn
45:       bSortDirection = rdsDC.SortDirection
46:       rdsDC.SortDirection = Not bSortDirection
47:       rdsDC.Reset
48:    end if
49: End Sub
50: </SCRIPT>
51:
52: </body>
53: </html>
```

ANALYSIS The URL is created in server-side ASP logic in lines 8–10 and assigned to the URL parameter in line 15. The remainder of this listing is the same as found in Day 17.

As you can see, it is simple to designate an XML file as the data source in an RDS application. On the plus side, it enables you to effectively hide connection and implementation details on the server; however, you also lose the ability to update information on the server—at least, it is not as easy as with standard RDS, which you learned in Day 17.

Applying Style Sheets to Persisted Recordsets

NEW TERM If you have worked with XML before, you definitely have run across *XSL*, which is short for *eXtensible Stylesheet Language*. XSL enables you to transform XML to any other format, even a different XML document.

The advantage of using XSL templates is that you can apply various XSL templates to a single XML file; this enables you to target specific needs of varying user groups. Also, XSL either is applied on the client (Internet Explorer 5), or the XML is merged with the XSL on the server to support clients that do not understand XML (Netscape Navigator 4.*x*).

19

> **Note**
>
> We don't have time for an in-depth exploration of all XSL features. I strongly recommend that you go to http://msdn.microsoft.com/xml/, where you can learn more about every facet of XML and its derivatives.

Creating a Style Sheet

In Figure 19.1, the XML was already marked up and had gimmicks, such as collapsible branches. Raw XML can't do that—the trick is that Internet Explorer applies a standard XSL template to every XML document it receives.

What if you want to use a different XSL template? You have to write one on your own. To make the task easier, I have provided a generic template for Recordset XML in Listing 19.8.

LISTING 19.8 The XSL File stylesheet.xsl That Can Be Applied to any Recordset XML

```
 1: <?xml version="1.0"?>
 2: <xsl:stylesheet xmlns:xsl="http://www.w3.org/TR/WD-xsl">
 3: <xsl:template match="/">
 4: <HTML><HEAD><TITLE>Formatting Output with XSL</TITLE></HEAD>
 5:     <BODY>
 6:        <TABLE BORDER="1">
 7:          <TR>
 8:            <xsl:for-each select="*/s:Schema/s:ElementType/s:AttributeType">
 9:               <TD><STRONG><FONT COLOR="#ff0000" size="2">
10:               <xsl:value-of select="@name"/></FONT></STRONG></TD>
11:            </xsl:for-each>
12:          </TR>
13:          <xsl:for-each select="*/rs:data/z:row">
14:             <TR>
15:              <xsl:for-each select="@*">
16:                <TD><FONT size="2"><xsl:value-of/></FONT></TD>
17:              </xsl:for-each>
18:             </TR>
19:          </xsl:for-each>
20:        </TABLE>
21:     </BODY></HTML>
22:    </xsl:template>
23: </xsl:stylesheet>
```

ANALYSIS Because of time and space constraints I cannot go into every detail, but it should be easy for you to understand what is going on. First, I tell Internet Explorer to process all elements within the whole XML document:

```
<xsl:template match="/">
```

The next few lines are plain HTML. It gets interesting again in lines 8–11:

```
<xsl:for-each select="*/s:Schema/s:ElementType/s:AttributeType">
   <TD><STRONG><FONT COLOR="#ff0000" size="2">
   <xsl:value-of select="@name"/></FONT></STRONG></TD>
</xsl:for-each>
```

The first section in a Recordset XML is the s:Schema. It contains one s:ElementType, which has multiple s:AttributeType elements, representing the definition of each column.

I am interested only in the name attribute of s:AttributeType, so I access it via @name. The xsl:for-each loop iterates over all column definitions and then proceeds to the iteration for the data section (lines 13–19):

```
<xsl:for-each select="*/rs:data/z:row">
  <TR>
  <xsl:for-each select="@*">
    <TD><FONT size="2"><xsl:value-of/></FONT></TD>
  </xsl:for-each>
  </TR>
</xsl:for-each>
```

The xsl:for-each loop is similar to the one for the column definitions, but it sports a nested loop that outputs all fields, which are attributes of each z:row.

The XSL template closes the xsl:stylesheet tag as a final action. You need to be careful about each single character in XML and XSL, because validity checking is extremely strict—this is a very unpleasant surprise for HTML developers who don't care about capitalization.

Applying the Style Sheet to XML

To see the XSL template in action, you have to assign it to XML data. The easiest way is to prepend XSL style sheet information to the actual XML content, as shown in Listing 19.9.

LISTING 19.9   Returning XML with an Attached Style Sheet

```
 1: <%
 2: Set conn = CreateObject("ADODB.Connection")
 3: Set rs = CreateObject("ADODB.Recordset")
 4:
 5: conn.Open "provider=sqloledb.1;user id=sa;password=;
➥initial catalog=northwind;data source=strangelove"
 6:
 7: strSQL = "SELECT CustomerID, ContactName, ContactTitle, Address, City
➥FROM Customers"
 8: rs.Open strSQL, conn
 9:
10: Response.Write "<?xml:stylesheet type=""text/xsl"""
11: Response.Write " href=""stylesheet.xsl""?>" & vbCrlf
12: rs.Save Response, 1
13: %>
```

19

ANALYSIS With the exception of lines 10 and 11, you are already familiar with this code. However, even these two lines are not complicated: they only add a reference to the style sheet, which is applied to the XML that follows. The output you receive is shown in Figure 19.2.

FIGURE 19.2

The XSL is automatically applied to the XML data.

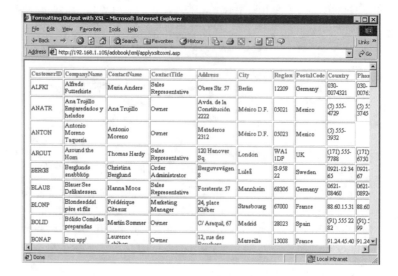

XSL is a very powerful means of transforming XML data to new presentations. I can merely showcase the possibilities, so I strongly recommend that you take a closer look at the capabilities built into these templates to make your Web applications more enticing.

Working with XML Data Islands

NEW TERM It is increasingly important today to have small portions of data in every HTML page—whether a single product record, line items in a shopping bag, or information for an invoice. This data needs to be embedded in *islands* inside the HTML page, and Internet Explorer 5 supports data islands that are written in XML.

Basically, all you need is the following tag in your HTML page:

```
<XML ID="dsoXML"></XML>
```

The XML tag specifies that all that is contained inside is data for the island dsoXML. The ID attribute defines the name of the data island, and it is this ID you use later to access the data island.

I did not include any data in the syntax example, so you can add any valid XML you like. Listing 19.10 shows how to use the data island with some static company information and how to display it to the client.

LISTING 19.10 A Static XML Data Island

```
 1: <html>
 2: <head>
 3:   <title>XML Data Islands</title>
 4: </head>
 5: <body bgcolor="#ffffff">
 6:
 7: <XML ID="dsoCustomers">
 8:   <customer>
 9:     <CompanyName>My Company</CompanyName>
10:   <Address>My Road</Address>
11:   <City>My City</City>
12:   <Country>My Country</Country>
13:   </customer>
14: </XML>
15:
16: <TABLE ID="tblCustomers" DATASRC="#dsoCustomers" BORDER="1">
17:   <TR>
18:     <TD><DIV DATAFLD="CompanyName"></DIV></TD>
19:     <TD><DIV DATAFLD="Address"></DIV></TD>
20:     <TD><DIV DATAFLD="City"></DIV></TD>
21:   <TD><DIV DATAFLD="Country"></DIV></TD>
22:   </TR>
23: </TABLE>
24:
25: </body>
26: </html>4
```

ANALYSIS The data island spans lines 7–14, and it defines a `customer` record with CustomerName, Address, City, and Country. It is a block of XML with tags that I made up—which is, of course, perfectly legal in XML.

The `ID` of the data island is `dsoCustomers`, which is used in line 16 as the `DATASRC` attribute for the HTML table. The table itself contains four `DIV` tags for displaying all fields that are also part of the XML data island.

With the example in Listing 19.10, you already have a good idea of why data islands can be useful; however, you usually won't implement data islands statically. You are going to provide the data via a database or some other means of data store to the island.

19

Implementing a Simple Data Island

There are two ways you can fill a data island with data dynamically. One way is to add ASP code to the XML tag directly in Listing 19.10 and create the necessary XML. The second way is to tell the XML tag where it can fetch the XML data:

```
<XML ID="dsoXML" SRC="myDynData.asp"></XML>
```

The new attribute here is SRC. It enables you to specify where the data island is going to fetch its XML data—in this syntax example, it makes a round trip to the Web server and requests myDynData.asp from the same directory as the calling page. The myDynData.asp file has to take responsibility for generating the appropriate XML data.

The first step in creating a data island that is filled with dynamic data is to prepare an ASP page that returns an XML document generated on a database query. When you are done, you can use this ASP page as input to the SRC property of the XML data island.

Creating the XML Data

The big difference from all previous approaches of displaying ADO recordset data is that you can't simply store the recordset using the Save method—the data island can't cope with that XML. Therefore, you have to generate plain XML on your own.

Listing 19.11 introduces you to a generic approach of dumping a recordset to XML, which can be used in a data island.

LISTING 19.11 Creating XML On-the-Fly for the Data Island (dataforisland.asp)

```
1: <%
2: Set conn = CreateObject("ADODB.Connection")
3: Set rs = CreateObject("ADODB.Recordset")
4:
5: conn.Open "provider=sqloledb.1;user id=sa;password=;
➥initial catalog=northwind;data source=strangelove"
6:
7: strSQL = "select CategoryName, Description from Categories"
8: rs.Open strSQL, conn
9:
10: Response.ContentType="text/xml"
11: Response.Write "<?xml version=""1.0"" encoding=""Windows-1252""?>" & vbCrlf
12: Response.Write "<Categories>" & vbCrlf
13: While Not rs.EOF
14:    Response.Write "<Category>" & vbCrlf
15:    For Each fld in rs.Fields
16:      strFldName = fld.Name
17:      Response.Write "<" & strFldName & ">" & fld.Value & _
18:        "</" & strFldName & ">" & vbCrlf
19:    Next
20:    Response.Write "</Category>" & vbCrlf
```

```
21:    rs.MoveNext
22: Wend
23: Response.Write "</Categories>"
24: %>
```

ANALYSIS The code for opening the connection and recordset are the same as for the last few examples. The interesting part of this listing starts in line 10. First, I explicitly set the ContentType of this ASP page to text/xml, which tells the client that what is transferred to it is actually XML, and not HTML. Line 11 also serves this informational purpose, because it informs the user of the XML that it conforms to XML 1.0 and that the content is encoded in the Windows 1252 codepage.

All code following line 12 deals with creating the appropriate XML structure. The top element of the document is Categories, which contains multiple Category elements. Each Category element represents one row of the recordset, and it is constructed in lines 14–20. Note that the children of the Category element are created entirely with the Fields collection of the record row (lines 15–19).

When you execute this listing, you get an XML document that is very straightforward and definitely easier to read than the ADO recordset persistence format. With the data now available in the appropriate format, you can create the consumer—the data island in your Web page.

Binding the XML Data Source Object to Data

Now that you have your dynamic XML, all that is left to do is link it to the data island so you get a listing of all categories (see Figure 19.3).

19

FIGURE 19.3

The page rendered with the data island.

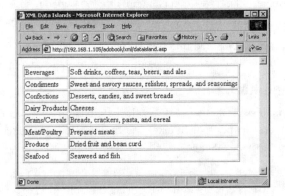

This figure shows the desired result, and Listing 19.12 provides the code that was used to create it.

```
 1: <html>
 2: <head>
 3:    <title>XML Data Islands</title>
 4: </head>
 5: <body bgcolor="#ffffff">
 6:
 7: <XML ID="dsoCategories" SRC="dataforisland.asp"></XML>
 8:
 9: <TABLE ID="tblCategories" DATASRC="#dsoCategories" BORDER="1">
10:    <TR>
11:       <TD><DIV DATAFLD="CategoryName"></DIV></TD>
12:       <TD><DIV DATAFLD="Description"></DIV></TD>
13:    </TR>
14: </TABLE>
15:
16: </body>
17: </html>
```

ANALYSIS   It is actually very simple to bind a data island to dynamic XML: Correctly specify the SRC attribute (see line 7). The remainder of the listing is responsible only for displaying the information the data island contains.

As you can see, it is no big deal to work with data islands; however, you can make them even more useful when you stuff hierarchical recordsets into them.

Displaying Chaptered XML

You learned how to deal with hierarchical recordsets in Day 10, "Shaping Your Data into Hierarchical Recordsets." Now you can apply that knowledge to another area of database applications: a Web page that uses XML data islands to view chaptered recordsets.

Again, the process is separated into two tasks: one creates the ASP page that generates the XML, and the other creates the page that consumes the data in a data island.

Creating the XML Data

The first step is to generate the XML for the data island. I have extended the previous example; the hierarchy consists of categories and the related products. The hierarchy is retrieved using the MSDataShape provider and the appropriate SHAPE command.

To represent the hierarchy, each Category element can contain zero or more Product elements. The XML is created on-the-fly using the definition of each field. See Listing 19.13 for more details.

LISTING 19.13 Creating XML with Child Records (`chapteredxml.asp`)

```
 1: <%
 2: Set conn = CreateObject("ADODB.Connection")
 3: Set rs = CreateObject("ADODB.Recordset")
 4:
 5: conn.Provider = "MSDataShape"
 6: conn.Open "data provider=sqloledb.1;user id=sa;password=;
➥initial catalog=northwind;data source=strangelove"
 7:
 8: strSQL = "SHAPE {select CategoryID,CategoryName,Description from
➥Categories}"
 9: strSQL = strSQL & " APPEND ("
10: strSQL = strSQL & "{select CategoryID,ProductID,ProductName,
➥UnitPrice from Products}"
11: strSQL = strSQL & " RELATE CategoryID to CategoryID) as rsProducts"
12:
13: rs.Open strSQL, conn
14:
15: Response.ContentType="text/xml"
16: Response.Write "<?xml version=""1.0"" encoding=""Windows-1252""?>" & vbCrlf
17: Response.Write "<Categories>" & vbCrlf
18: While Not rs.EOF
19:   Response.Write "<Category>" & vbCrlf
20:   For Each fld in rs.Fields
21:     strFldName = fld.Name
22:     If ("rsProducts" = strFldName) Then
23:       Set rsProducts = fld.Value
24:       If Not rsProducts.EOF Then
25:         While Not rsProducts.EOF
26:           Response.Write "<Product>" & vbCrlf
27:           Response.Write "<ProductID>" & rsProducts(1) & _
28:             "</ProductID>" & vbCrlf
29:           Response.Write "<ProductName>" & rsProducts(2) & _
30:             "</ProductName>" & vbCrlf
31:           Response.Write "<UnitPrice>" & rsProducts(3) & _
32:             "</UnitPrice>" & vbCrlf
33:           Response.Write "</Product>" & vbCrlf
34:           rsProducts.MoveNext
35:         Wend
36:       End If
37:     Else
38:       Response.Write "<" & strFldName & ">" & fld.Value & _
39:         "</" & strFldName & ">" & vbCrlf
40:     End If
41:   Next
42:   Response.Write "</Category>" & vbCrlf
43:   rs.MoveNext
44: Wend
45: Response.Write "</Categories>"
46: %>
```

19

The first part of the listing deals with retrieving the data from the database using the MSDataShape provider. To get you up to speed again on data shaping, I'll cover each task. First, you have to specify the MSDataShape provider for the current connection (line 5). The next step is to designate the data provider and the remainder of the connection string, which enables you to then open the connection to the database (line 6).

Lines 8 to 11 define the SHAPE command that is issued against the connection in line 13. It creates a hierarchy of the Categories and Products tables based on the CategoryID key. The chapter (child recordset) is named rsProducts. This name is later used to distinguish between "normal" fields and the chapter in the recordset.

Now that the recordset is open, you create the appropriate XML. This looks much like the simple version of this script; however, this time you have to deal with a child recordset (lines 22–36). Note that I check for the chapter by the field name—this is not the programmatically perfect way, but another one that you can use.

Implementing the Consumer Page

The XML is waiting to be consumed by your yet-to-be-created data island. To get a preview of what you are going to create, take a look at Figure 19.4.

FIGURE **19.4**

Displaying the hierarchical recordset in a table.

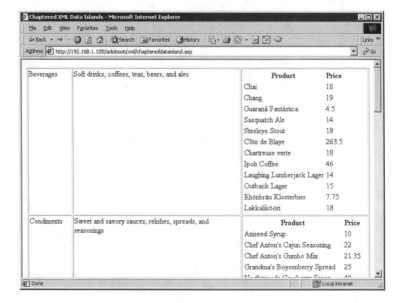

The idea is to display in some way a parent-child relationship using a table in a table. You can add DHTML to it so children disappear and reappear, but user interface design is not your primary concern. Getting at data is your primary concern, as demonstrated in Listing 19.14.

LISTING 19.14 Displaying a Chaptered Recordset

```
 1: <html>
 2: <head>
 3:   <title>Chaptered XML Data Islands</title>
 4: </head>
 5: <body bgcolor="#ffffff">
 6:
 7: <XML ID="dsoXML" SRC="chapteredxml.asp"></XML>
 8:
 9: <TABLE DATASRC="#dsoXML" BORDER="1">
10:   <TR>
11:     <TD VALIGN="TOP"><SPAN DATAFLD="CategoryName"></SPAN></TD>
12:     <TD VALIGN="TOP"><SPAN DATAFLD="Description"></SPAN></TD>
13:   <TD VALIGN="TOP">
14:   <TABLE DATASRC="#dsoXML" DATAFLD="Product" BORDER="0">
15:     <THEAD><TR><TH>Product</TH><TH>Price</TH></TR></THEAD>
16:     <TR>
17:       <TD><SPAN DATAFLD="ProductName"></SPAN></TD>
18:       <TD><SPAN DATAFLD="UnitPrice"></SPAN></TD>
19:     </TR>
20:   </TABLE>
21:   </TD>
22:   </TR>
23: </TABLE>
24:
25: </body>
26: </html>
```

ANALYSIS Take a close look at line 14, because it contains all the magic necessary to make the products appear. I set the DATAFLD attribute to the value Product. Together with the outer table, this tells Internet Explorer that if it finds a Product element inside a Category element (the top level elements of the XML data), it should enumerate all of them and print the ProductName and UnitPrice for them.

As you can see, implementing the data island isn't complicated. Data islands enable you to hide database connection details in server-side ASP files, and if you add some client-side scripting, you can create great Web pages that act much like a standard Windows application.

19

Summary

In today's lesson, you learned how ADO integrates with various XML data access and management techniques. After completing a quick review of the XML format that is used to persist ADO recordsets to XML, you used persisted recordsets to serve as the data source for RDS applications. In this scenario, you can hide data access details in ASP pages.

You also learned to apply XSL style sheets to XML data to generate output that is automatically rendered. In the final section, you acquired the knowledge necessary to effectively employ data islands for flat and for hierarchical recordsets.

Q&A

Q You mentioned that XML is like a universal data interchange format. Where can I learn more about this use scenario?

A There is one good starting point to see what kind of interoperability you can achieve: `http://www.biztalk.org`. At that site, you can find a lot of predefined data interchange formats that are based on XML.

Q Is there a way I can programmatically access the various elements in the XML?

A Yes, the Document Object Model (DOM) provides a rich set of functions to modify, create, and delete nodes in an XML document. Microsoft ships an XML parser with Internet Explorer that exposes the DOM.

Workshop

The quiz questions and exercises are provided for your further understanding. See Appendix A, "Answers," for the answers.

Quiz

1. Which interface must be supported by objects that are passed as first parameter to the Save method of the Recordset object?

2. Can you open persisted recordsets from the local hard disk only, or are other locations also supported?

3. You have a data island defined. How do you refer to it from within a TABLE tag?

4. How does the data island tag look when your data source is a file named data.xml?

5. Is it possible to use a raw persisted ADO recordset as source for a data island?

6. Which attribute do you use in a TABLE tag for child elements in a hierarchical data island to be able to enumerate the children?

Exercises

1. Create a shaped recordset (relate CustomerID to CustomerID for the Customers and Orders tables) and return it as an XML-persisted recordset to the Web client.

2. Use the XML returned from Exercise 1's ASP page to drive an RDS-enabled Web page.

19

DAY **20**

Securing Your ADO/RDS Environment

Because ADO enables you to access databases, today you explore the security in database access and the security for data that is sent across networks.

Remember which scenarios can be used with ADO—You might use ADO in Active Server Pages to access an intranet database server on the request of an Internet ASP page. Or you allow to access an ADO data source via RDS directly from Internet Explorer. When people have access to a data source, potential security problems arise, and the more people that have potential access to your ADO application, the more security becomes important to cover sensitive data and prevent hackers from reading or deleting data.

An application can access a database server in the company network. When the database contains sensitive data, make sure that only authorized people can show and manipulate the data. Because the data is exchanged over the company's network, you also should take necessary steps to encrypt the data. Otherwise, unauthorized people with suitable tools can listen in on the network transmission and read the data, and maybe even learn the user ID and password you sent to the database.

Another scenario is that you use Microsoft Internet Explorer as a client for reading data from a database server in a three-tier environment. The middle tier is the Internet Information Server (IIS), which provides a connection to the client using RDS, and the third tier is the database server, which is accessed by IIS using an ADO connection.

Today, you look at different ways to log into a database embedded in an NT network. This chapter shows how to secure a database for granular access by various users—from the manager with access to all data, to the database administrator with the ability to change and maintain the database, to the desktop user reading product prices from the database.

Today is just an introduction to database security. Nobody can expect to become an expert in one day. However, the scenarios, instructions, tasks, and tips show you the direction you have to go to enforce security on different areas of ADO applications.

Today, you explore the following:

- Authentication modes for identifying users and logging them into the database
- Basic planning considerations for securing a company's database
- Securing an Access database on an IIS Web server
- Closing security holes in ODBC
- Using ADOX to manage users and roles of an Access database from any application

Database Authentication

To make sure that only authorized personnel has access to confidential data, you have to authorize each database access to make sure that the user actually is who he or she claims to be. This process is called authentication.

After a user is authenticated and granted access to a certain database, the database itself enforces the privileges and rights the user has. For instance, certain users may read only publicly available data, and reading any other data by the user is refused by the database. A user with a wide range of privileges is the database administrator, because he or she is responsible for backup and tuning the database or changing the database structure.

Database and application developers might have the right to add new tables and procedures to the database, but reading data may be denied.

There are different ways to authenticate users, as you learn in the next few sections.

Basic Password Authentication

A simple form of authentication is the user ID/password authentication. A user (or group of users) is assigned a unique user ID. Using this ID, the database knows who is trying to log in. The password actually makes sure that the user is authorized to log in.

In the examples in this book, a connection is often established using a user ID and the accordant password. Both user ID and password are provided in the connection string or separately when you invoke the Open method of the Connection object, for instance:

```
objConn.Open "Provider=SQLOLEDB;Data Source=ServerName;
➥ Initial Catalog=DatabaseName; User ID=UserName;
➥ Password=UserPassword;"
```

or

```
objConn.Open "Provider=SQLOLEDB;Data Source=ServerName;
➥ Initial Catalog=DatabaseName;", UserName, UserPassword
```

Using basic password authentication against a database means that you directly send a user ID/password combination to the database, which decides whether to allow or deny the user access.

The kind of privileges and rights a logged-in user has is determined by the respective authorization control, which supervises the connections to a certain security area.

Some users might be able to perform all actions against a database, for instance; others may access only a certain database table with public available data.

Windows NT/2000 Authentication

Another form of authentication when you deal with Windows NT/2000 networks is to use the Windows NT/2000 authentication that is part of the operating system. This form of authentication is provided by the operating system's Security Support Provider Interface (in Win NT/Win 2000) or the Kerberos security protocol (in Windows 2000).

When a client is connecting to a Windows NT/2000 network, a complicated exchange of encrypted security inquiries and responses is enforced to authenticate the user in the network structure.

In most cases, the user that is logged in on the client computer is passed through to the Windows NT/2000 network with all the privileges and rights that are granted on the individual security areas or applications. Security areas are, for instance, the IIS, a SQL Server database, the SQL Server administration, and so on.

Even when users have permission to access a security area, they can be restricted so that certain actions, such as reading product prices from a database, can be performed, and other actions, such as changing their own salaries in the database, are denied.

Using Windows NT/2000 authentication, an application can log into a database using the user context in which the application is running, or by passing through the user context of another Windows NT/2000 application that is connecting to the database application.

Planning Database Security

The purpose of planning security is to identify which users can see which data and perform which actions in a database.

To develop a security plan, the following basic steps are useful:

- List all items and activities in the database that must be controlled through security to prevent data misuse or malicious destruction of database parts.
- Identify the individual users that need access to database data or database functions. Unite users with identical privileges and rights into groups.
- Cross-reference the two lists to identify which users or groups can see which data and perform which activities in the database.

 A *group* of database users is the combination of various users with the same database privileges and access rights. Another word for database group is *role*.

When using groups, you define a certain group and assign all necessary data access and activities privileges to it only once. This can be lot of work in a complex and thought-out database system. The advantage for adding new users is that they can be assigned to an existing group and automatically get all privileges and rights of the group. So you only have to add a user to a group instead of assigning all rights of accessing data, performing database tasks, or executing procedures to the user. Of course, you can always assign special rights to certain users.

The following example shows how to make a security plan for a SQL Server 7.0 database, how to create new groups, and how to assign privileges and rights to them. The example also shows how to create new user accounts, which can be added to groups, or get their database privileges.

Studying a Small Company Case

A small company is building a database application based on SQL Server 7.0 to manage customer, product, and sales data. The database design, tables, procedures, and views are ready, but the security is not planned yet. The company has two managers, a database administrator, two developers, and about 10 employees in the administration.

The managers have full access to all database data. The database administrator must have full access to all data and tasks of the database. The developers are allowed to add new procedures and have full access to data, and the administrative employees have full access to customer and sales data, but read-only permission for all other data.

First, draw up the users-to-activity map for all users or groups (see Table 20.1).

TABLE 20.1 Users-to-Activity Map for Case Study

Role or User Account	Database Activity
Managers	Full access to all data
dbAdmin	Full access to database
Developers	Full access to data, create procedures
Employees	Full access to customer data and sales, read-only for all other data

Then set up the users-to-role map to indicate which users are contained in which role (see Table 20.2). To each role a certain set of allowed activities would be assigned later on.

TABLE 20.2 Users-to-Role Map for Case Study

Database User	Database Role
Jane (manager)	Managers
Alexander (manager)	Managers
Mike (database admin)	dbAdmin
Jack (developer)	Developers
Sue (developer)	Developers
Administrative employees	Employees

In a SQL Server database, every user needs a user ID for the login assigned. This login user ID and an accordant password are defined in a login account, and are used to establish the connection to the database server. Each SQL Server database on the SQL Server has its own set of usernames defined. Usually a username defined in a certain database is equal to the login user ID used to log into the SQL Server database.

20

To Do: Creating a New Login Account on SQL Server 7.0

So you have to create the logins for the users in the SQL Server 7.0 database system. This can be done performing the following steps:

1. Open the Microsoft SQL Server 7.0 Database Administrator by selecting Start button, Programs, Microsoft SQL Server 7.0, Enterprise Manager.

2. In the Tree pane of the Enterprise Manager, expand the database server and the Security folder (see Figure 20.1).

FIGURE 20.1

Logins in SQL Server 7.0 Enterprise Manager.

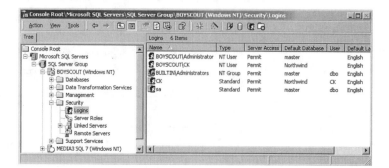

3. Right-click on the Logins icon, choose New Login, and the New Login window appears (see Figure 20.2).

FIGURE 20.2

The SQL Server Login Properties—New Login window.

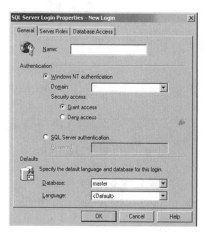

4. Enter the new login user ID in the Name field, choose SQL Server authentication, and supply a password for the login name.

Note

When you choose Windows NT authentication instead of SQL Server authentication, an existing Windows NT/2000 user account is taken for authentication purpose. You have to provide the Windows NT domain and the user defined in that domain to log in to the database. Then the login username consists of domain name and username, separated by a backslash.

5. Specify default values, such as the database you want to access using this login and the default language.

6. Click on OK, confirm the password, and the new login is created. After the New Login window is closed, you see the new login in the left pane of the Enterprise Administrator window.

After you have created all necessary SQL Server database system logins for the users, you can create the roles and users for the company database that is contained in the SQL Server database system.

To Do: Creating a New Role in a SQL Server 7.0 Database

To Do

To create the Managers role (group) in the SQL Server Northwind database example, you perform the following steps:

1. Open the Microsoft SQL Server 7.0 Database Administrator by selecting Start button, Programs, Microsoft SQL Server 7.0, Enterprise Manager.

2. In the Tree pane of the Enterprise Manager window, expand the database server, the folder Databases, and the database to which you want to add a new role (see Figure 20.3).

FIGURE 20.3

Roles in a SQL Server 7.0 database.

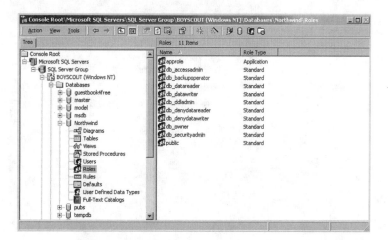

20

▼   3. Right-click on the Roles icon in the Tree pane and select New Database Role.

4. The New Role window opens. Enter the role's name in the Name field (for instance Managers) and click on the OK button. The new role is created but no privileges or rights—permission granted or denied for certain database actions—are set.

5. To assign certain permissions to a role, click on Roles in the left pane of the Enterprise Manager. Then double-click on the role in the right pane and the Database Role Properties window for the role appears (see Figure 20.4).

FIGURE 20.4

The Database Role Properties window.

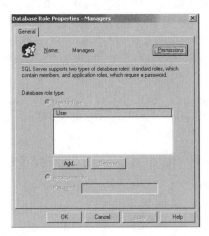

6. Click on the Permissions button and the role permissions window pops up (see Figure 20.5).

FIGURE 20.5

The role permissions window.

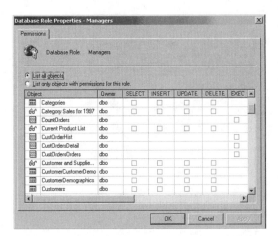

▼

▼   7. In the role permissions window, you can specify the permissions (granted or denied) for actions on database objects. Choose whether the role is allowed to perform a SELECT, INSERT, UPDATE, or DELETE action against a table or view. Select which stored procedures the role may execute (EXEC). A granted permission is indicated by a check, and a denied permission by a red cross. No check or cross indicates a so-called revoked permission, which forces the role to use the permission of the group or role containing the role.

8. Close the role permission window and apply all adjustments by clicking on OK.

9. To add an existing database user to the database role, double-click on the role icon to open the role. Then click on Add, select the users you want to add, and click OK to close the window. You see the role's new users in the User field of the Database Role Properties window.

10. Using a similar procedure, you can remove users from a role. Select the user in the Database Role Properties window and click on the Remove button.

▲   11. Close the Role Properties window by clicking OK.

Of course, you also want to add new users to the SQL Server database and either assign permissions to the users or add some users to roles so that the role's permissions automatically pass over to the user every time the user logs in to the database.

To Do: Creating a New User in a SQL Server 7.0 Database

Use the following steps to add a new user to a SQL Server 7.0 database:

▼   1. Open the Microsoft SQL Server 7.0 Database Administrator by selecting Start button, Programs, Microsoft SQL Server 7.0, Enterprise Manager.

2. Expand the database server in the Tree pane of the Enterprise Manager window. Expand the Databases folder and the database where you want to add the new user.

3. Right-click on the Users icon and select New Database User from the context menu. The Database User Properties window for the new user appears (see Figure 20.6).

4. Choose a login name in the appropriate drop-down box.

5. If necessary, change the username for the database.

6. To assign the user to one or more database roles, select the Database role membership from the lower select box.

7. Click on the OK button to close the window and to create the database user.

8. Open the user again to set additional permissions especially for the user. Double-click on the user icon, click on the Permissions button in the User Properties window and update permissions to your needs. Finally close both windows by a click
▼   on OK.

To Do

20

FIGURE 20.6

*The Database User
Properties window.*

Because you can use stored procedures as defined interfaces for data manipulation in a
SQL Server database, it is possible to deny direct database tables access for certain users.
You can set permissions for those users and allow them to execute only certain stored
procedures. This way, you make sure that only actions defined by the stored procedures
can be performed.

Besides common database actions, such as inserting or deleting data, in SQL Server 7.0
users can have the permission to create tables or stored procedures, or to back up database data and log files.

To Do: Setting up Special Database Permissions for Users of a SQL Server 7.0 Database

Use the following steps to give users permission to create tables or stored procedures, or
to back up database data and log files:

1. Right-click on a database icon in the Tree pane of the SQL Server Enterprise
   Manager and select Properties.

2. Click the Permissions tab in the database Properties window (see Figure 20.7).

3. Grant or withdraw user permissions on creating tables, views, stored procedures
   (SP), and so on according to your security demands.

4. Close the database Properties window with a click on OK.

FIGURE 20.7

The database Properties window, Permissions tab.

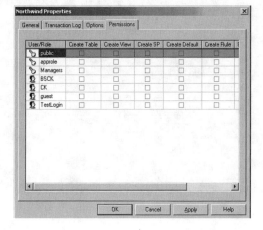

For simple database queries, you also can define so-called views, some kind of virtual table representing data from one or more tables in an alternative way. Then assign the permission to access only particular views and stored procedures to certain users. This allows controlling access and enhances security of your database data.

Additionally, you can set permission for selected users on every database object of a SQL Server 7.0 database.

To Do: Setting User Permissions for Single SQL Server 7.0 Database Objects

Use the following steps to set permission for selected users on every database object of an SQL Server 7.0 database:

1. In the Tree pane of the SQL Server Enterprise Manager expand the database tree so that the desired database object (table, view, or stored procedure) is visible. Double-click on the database object and the Properties window appears (see Figure 20.8).

2. Click on Permissions in the Properties window and select additional permissions for actions on the selected database object, as shown in Figure 20.9.

To Do

20

FIGURE 20.8

The database Table Properties window.

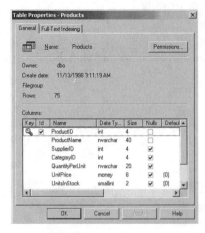

FIGURE 20.9

The Object Properties window.

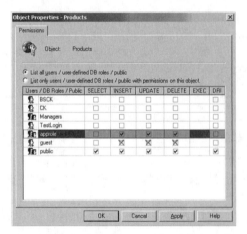

Other Database Security Considerations

The best database software and security technology is not very helpful when your database server machine is directly connected to the Internet or the intranet. You have to shield the whole database server system as well as possible from potential hacker attacks from outside and inside your company. Therefore, security for the database server machine is a very important issue even when you're planning and building a company network.

Firewalls and separate premises for database servers and other important network components with admission control (maybe automatic doors with personal identification) should be considered.

Securing RDS and IIS

For enhanced security of your IIS Web site, you can use encrypted ASP files, so that plaintext user ID and password combinations cannot be read by hackers or Web space provider personnel even if they gain access to the ASP source code.

Encryption of ASP files is a new feature of VBScript 5.0. However, there is third-party technology based on ISAPI filters available that allows using encrypted ASP files to run even on IIS 4.0.

When you're dealing with RDS, the database client is Microsoft Internet Explorer (or an application using the Internet Explorer library). IIS represents the middle tier and exposes an RDS Data Factory, which allows data exchange from the client to IIS.

The database connection between IIS and database is established using ADO and therefore can be secured as any other ADO connection.

However, the RDS connection between client and IIS opens some potential security problems.

As you learned on Day 17, "Remoting Data Using RDS," users can see the user ID and password used to connect from the Internet Explorer to the RDS DataFactory on IIS. Therefore, do not specify a user with more access rights and privileges than necessary. Restrict the access of the user to a narrow window of database actions that cannot change other data.

When connecting from Internet Explorer to the data factory on IIS over potential unsafe networks such as the Internet, consider the possibility of someone intercepting the data exchange between the client and IIS and therefore also reading the user ID, password, and all data transferred. Think about using SSL ports (HTTPS protocol) to access the data factory.

Potential problems when using RDS in intranets can arise from security issues in Internet Explorer itself. Users who access Web sites containing RDS or ADO applications should adjust and check their Internet Explorer security settings. The Internet Explorer should be adjusted in a way so that access to the RDS applications is possible. At the same time Internet Explorer security should be adjusted strong enough to protect their computer from potential damaging Web page controls (applets, ActiveX controls) or applications. Otherwise, destroy data on the hard disk can be destroyed by a malicious Web page control, or some confidential client computer data can be spied out by the creator of such an Web control.

To secure a client computer when you run RDS Web pages, certain features of Internet Explorer allow you to set security levels for RDS and ADO access on the client machine.

20

The security features of Internet Explorer are as follows:

- Internet Explorer security zones
- Internet Explorer security levels
- Restrictions in a trusted environment
- Customized Security Settings and Local Computer Access

Using different security zones allows you to determine the potential danger a certain Web site represents so you can prepare Internet Explorer to deal with the danger adequately.

You can specify in which security zone certain Web domains fall. Examples for security zones are Internet, Local Intranet, Trusted Sites, and Restricted Sites.

For each security zone, you can set predefined security levels (from High to Low) and also customize security settings and behavior in downloading, installing, and executing ActiveX controls, for instance, with other adjustable security settings. Changing the security level affects all security-related behavior of ADO and RDS objects running in the browser in that particular zone.

In Internet Explorer 5.0, you can access the security settings through Tools, Internet Options in the menu. Internet Explorer 4.0 makes the security settings available through the View, Internet Options menu.

In the Internet Options window, choose the Security tab to gain access to security settings. There, you have the possibility of adjusting the security level and setting custom security options (Custom Level button) for each security zone. Define which sites are assigned to which security zone by choosing a security zone (Web content zone) and clicking on the Sites button.

For detailed information and more specific instructions about the behavior of Internet Explorer 4.0 and 5.0, refer to the article titled "ADO and RDS Security Issues in Microsoft Internet Explorer" in the Platform SDK documentation.

Securing Access Databases Located on IIS

An Access database (`*.mdb`) is often used to provide an easy-to-use data store for small ASP applications.

When you put the Access database file in the directory of an IIS Web site, anybody with access to the Web site can easily download the whole Access database (even over the Internet).

To close this security hole, make sure that the directory, where the file is installed, has the IIS Execute permission, but no Directory Browsing or Read permission. However, make sure that the directory has NTFS Write permission because accessing the database file automatically creates the database's current connection file `*.ldb`.

Tip Remember that you can use the Jet and Replication Objects (JRO) to encrypt an Access database if necessary.

In IIS 4.0 and IIS 5.0, you can set directory permissions in a Web site by exploring the directory structure in the Internet Service Manager (ISM). Right-click on the directory, choose Properties, and go to the Directory Settings tab. There, all permissions for the directory and the contained files can be set.

Enforcing Security Using ADOX

As shown on Day 14, "Managing Your Database with ADOX," ADOX can be useful when you're developing an application that has to manage users, groups of users, and their access permissions for specific data sources.

Depending on the OLE DB Provider for a data source, certain ADOX features may not be supported. With MDAC 2.5, ADOX is fully supported only with the OLE DB Provider for Microsoft Jet. Managing security over the ADOX User and Group objects is possible only with the OLE DB Provider for Jet.

The OLE DB Providers for SQL Server, for ODBC, and for Oracle do not support managing security through the User and Group objects. All other OLE DB Providers do not support ADOX.

Through ADOX, an application can take over user management and set security issues. Access permissions for database objects can be granted or denied dynamically from your application.

Use of ADOX with Access databases, with Visual Basic Examples for defining Users and Roles, can be found in the Platform SDK in the article named "Security" among the Microsoft Data Access Technical Articles (MDAC 2.5 SDK).

20

Discussing ODBC Security Issues

Often, database applications use ADO with ODBC to connect to a database. An experienced user can enable ODBC tracing and find out data transmitted over an ODBC connection, including user ID and password when sent as clear text!

Knowing and understanding ODBC security is important for both developers and administrators.

To prevent hacker attacks based on ODBC tracing tools and enhance security of your ODBC environment, you have several possibilities:

- Instead of using plaintext authentication, you can use Windows NT/2000 security and authentication services. For instance, when you connect to a SQL Server 7.0 database, the database server can be configured to use Windows NT/2000 security in Windows NT Authentication mode instead of SQL Server Authentication. Usually, applications carrying the BackOffice logo have to use integrated Windows NT/2000 security.

  To force a SQL Server database system to use Windows NT/2000 authentication, open the SQL Server Enterprise Manager (from the Microsoft SQL Server group in the Start menu). Expand a Server Group, right-click on a server, and select Properties. Change to the Security tab and change the Authentication radio control to Windows NT only.

 Note | Windows NT Authentication Mode is not available when SQL Server is running on Windows 95/98.

- ODBC uses the trace DLL, `Odbctrac.dll`, to trace ODBC calls. The trace DLL can be deleted on Windows 95 and Windows NT systems to prevent its use. However, users with sufficient rights and knowledge could reinstall `Odbctrac.dll` again.

Summary

Today, you explored basic security considerations that are important when you use ADO to connect to a database. You also briefly looked at the protection of the database data itself, ensuring the privacy of data connections, and securing the user ID and password of an application.

Q&A

Q Does every data source provide a mechanism for login to ensure that only authorized users have access to data source data and administrative tasks?

A All major database systems provide the possibility of restricting access using various security levels for database users and groups. However, other data sources, especially when related to the core of the Windows 2000 operating system, automatically use the user context and Windows NT security of the calling application to determine whether a data source access is permitted or denied.

Q **I am connecting to an SQL Server database, using no user ID or password in the connection string. However, the application connecting to the database has access to all database data. How can that be?**

A When an empty user ID is provided to connect to an SQL Server, Windows NT authentication is automatically enforced. When an NT user (`MachineName/UserName`) is allowed to log into the SQL Server database, this user is used to identify and enable access to the database.

Workshop

The quiz questions and exercises are provided for your further understanding. See Appendix A, "Answers," for the answers.

Quiz

1. With ADO 2.5, which database systems allow you to manage users and roles via an ADOX connection?

2. When using an SQL Server 7.0 database, is it possible to adjust database permissions on SQL Server so that only selected stored procedures can be called to shield the database data from direct interaction with the user and malicious SQL statements?

3. On which operation system must a database server run to allow Windows NT authentication?

Exercise

Today is about theory, so there is no exercise.

20

DAY 21

Tuning and Debugging ADO Applications

When you undertake performance tuning, it is important to change only one thing at a time. This way, you can gauge the effect the change has made to your application's performance. For example, let's assume you make two changes to an application. Change 1 improves performance by 50%. Change 2 reduces performance by 40%. If you apply both changes at once, you see an overall improvement in performance of 10%. If you make the changes one at a time, you see that change 2 actually reduces the performance of your application. Instead of a 10% improvement, you get a 50% improvement by applying only change 1.

Typically, the first changes that you make give the largest improvements. Subsequent changes may still improve performance, but usually not to the same extent. Eventually, you reach a point where the effort outweighs the benefits.

If you follow sound design and coding practices, the amount of time you spend on performance tuning should be minimal.

Recordset Options (CursorType, CursorLocation, LockType)

The options you use for CursorType, CursorLocation, and LockType can have a major impact on the performance of an application. Let's examine each one to determine how best to use these parameters to maximize performance.

You have four cursor types to choose from: dynamic, keyset, static, and forward-only. The forward-only cursor is the default cursor type of ADO. The only way to use any of the other cursor types is to specify them before or via the ADO Recordset's Open method.

 Caution
> If a database provider does not support the requested CursorType, it may engage another CursorType. Always check the actual CursorType by reading the CursorType property of the recordset and comparing it with the values of the ADO CursorTypeEnum constants (adOpenForwardOnly, adOpenKeyset, adOpenDynamic, and adOpenStatic). When you are examining the effect of CursorTypes that are not engaged you are only wasting time.

The choice of forward-only cursors as the default is not a coincidence. This type of cursor also happens to be the most efficient, because it reads through the rows in a single pass. When you're dealing with databases where you want to maximize performance, the simple rule is this: the faster, the better. The quicker you carry out your work on the database, the quicker that resources that have been used by your query—such as locks, temporary tables, memory, and so forth—can be released for other queries to use.

Keyset and static cursor both make demands on the temporary storage provided by the server. However, generally the dynamic cursor provides the worst performance of all the cursor types.

When choosing the cursor type, you must, of course, consider what functionality you require. If you must have backward and forward scrolling, for example, you need to use a dynamic, keyset, or static cursor type.

There are two choices for CursorLocation: client or server. For client-side cursors, the resultset is sent from the server to the client machine, where it is cached. This is ideal for small recordsets, because the retrieval of rows from the client's cache is highly efficient. You are moving the processing load from your server to the client machines, making your application more scalable. The resources used on the server in servicing the request also are released quickly so that they can be reused. For large recordsets, a server-side cursor should be considered. This prevents the network from being flooded by the returning resultset, and enables the network traffic between the client and server machines to be controlled. However, server-side cursors also reduce your ability to scale your application, because the resource use is focused on the database server, instead of being spread across multiple database clients.

With LockType, you have four choices: read-only, pessimistic, optimistic, and batch-optimistic. The lock type that you choose affects how many concurrent users your application will support. The following lists the lock types, from maximum to minimum concurrency:

1. Read-only

2. Optimistic, batch-optimistic

3. Pessimistic

When considering what lock type to use for high-volume applications, you should start at the top of this list and work your way down until you arrive at a lock type that meets your requirements.

Size of Returned Recordsets

When developing scalable applications, you should always try to minimize the amount of information being passed across the network between your database client and database server.

Any SQL SELECT statement without a WHERE clause should immediately come under suspicion, because this means that all the rows in a table are potentially being returned when the statement is executed. This doesn't necessarily mean that there is a problem. For example, if the SELECT statement is being issued against a table that contains only a small number of rows, performance of the application will not be impacted.

Some data sources, such as SQL Server 7, enable you to specify in your SQL statement exactly how many rows you want to be returned. For example, the following SELECT statement returns the first 10 rows from the resultset:

```
SELECT TOP 10 * FROM customers ORDER BY companyname, customerid
```

Let's examine this SQL statement further. Because the statement includes an ORDER BY, SQL Server will (if necessary) sort the rows to be returned by companyname and customerid, and then return the first 10 sorted rows. By storing the companyname and companyid of the first and last rows returned and adding a WHERE clause for repositioning,

21

you can return 10 rows at a time and display them to the user, giving the appearance of
backward and forward scrolling. Listing 21.1 defines the stored procedure named
sp_GetNextTen that performs the task of paging forward.

LISTING 21.1   Paging Forward

```
 1: create procedure sp_GetNextTen
 2:      @CompanyName    varchar(40),
 3:      @CustomerId     char(5)
 4: as
 5:      select TOP 10
 6:             CustomerId,
 7:             CompanyName,
 8:             ContactName,
 9:             Address
10:      from Customers
11:      where CustomerId  > @CustomerId
12:        and CompanyName > @CompanyName
13:      order by CompanyName, CustomerId
```

ANALYSIS   The stored procedure sp_GetNextTen returns the first 10 sorted rows that have a
company name and customer ID greater than the name and ID you pass it. You
save the company name and customer ID of the last row from the previous search. You
then pass these to the stored procedure, which returns the next 10 rows sorted by
CompanyName and CustomerId.

To allow moving backward, you have to use another stored procedure. The stored procedure

LISTING 21.2   Paging Backward

```
 1: create procedure sp_GetPreviousTen
 2:      @CompanyName    varchar(40),
 3:      @CustomerId     char(5)
 4: as
 5:      select TOP 10
 6:             CustomerId,
 7:             CompanyName,
 8:             ContactName,
 9:             Address
10:      from Customers
11:      where CustomerId  < @CustomerId
12:        and CompanyName < @CompanyName
13:      order by CompanyName DESC, CustomerId DESC
```

ANALYSIS   To move backward, you need to save the company name and customer ID of the
first row from the previous search. Then you pass these parameters to the stored

procedure `sp_GetPreviousTen`, which returns the previous 10 rows sorted by descending `CompanyName` and `CustomerId`—your application has to turn around the order.

The important point is that to reposition correctly, you must be able to uniquely identify an individual row and reposition exactly before or after it. The company name does not guarantee uniqueness. However, being the primary key of the Customers table, the customer ID does. By using both these fields together, you can ensure that you will always get the next or previous 10 rows from the last search.

This enables you to use a forward-only, client-side, read-only cursor and still provide what appears to the user to be backward and forward scrolling. If you were writing a Web application using ASP (Active Server Pages), you could save the company name and customer ID of the first and last rows from the previous search in session variables. If the user clicked the Next button, you connect to the database and call the `sp_GetNextTen` stored procedure passing the `CustomerId` and `CompanyName` of the last row of the previous search. You then loop through the resultset, updating your session variables with the company name and customer ID of the first and last rows, and return the results to the user. If the user clicked the Previous button, you connect to the database and call the `sp_GetPreviousTen` stored procedure passing the `CustomerId` and `CompanyName` of the first row of the previous search, and so forth.

The functionality described is the same as provided by search engines on the Web. Typically, search engines return results of searches in lots of 10, with Next and Previous buttons provided to access the 10 next or previous results in the search. By limiting the number of rows returned, the application places less demands on the database server and the network. The user also receives a response in a timelier manner.

Now turn your attention to the columns being returned in the recordsets.

You should make sure that only columns that are used by your application are selected. If for example, you are issuing a SQL statement that selects customer first name, last name, and address details, you should ensure that all these details are being used. If they are not, they should be removed from the `SELECT` statement

Also check that the type and sizes of the columns being returned are appropriate. For example, if you come across a column for a customer's last name that had a type of `char(100)`, you should redefine this column to a more reasonable size, such as `char(20)`. This leads to reduced network traffic, because every time you pass a customer's last name you transmit less information. The amount of disk space needed to store the table also is reduced.

When selecting a number of rows from the database, you can use the `CacheSize` property of the `Recordset` object to improve performance. By setting `CacheSize`, you tell ADO the number of rows to fetch and copy to a local memory cache at once. As each row is requested, ADO returns the row from the cache. A request for a row outside of those held

21

in the cache causes the cache contents to be refreshed with the next CacheSize rows. Tuning ADO record cache size is typically a matter of trial and error until a suitable value is found.

Tuning SQL Statements

Not all SQL statements are created equal. Two different query statements that return exactly the same results can execute at very different performance levels. When you code your queries, there are a number of operators that should be avoided if possible, including

- IN
- NOT IN
- OR
- != (Not equal)
- Column aggregate functions, such as SUM, AVG, MAX, or MIN

A join between two or more tables can also be a source of performance problems. When joining tables in a query, always use columns that are indexed. If you would have to use non-indexed columns then create a new index on the columns in the database! In the following statement, which joins the Customers table with the Orders table, all the orders for every customer are returned. The join between these two tables uses the CustomerId column of both tables as the matching data (see Listing 21.3). For optimal performance of a join statement, both tables should have indexes on the CustomerId column.

LISTING 21.3   SELECT Statement Joining Two Tables

```
1: SELECT Customers.CompanyName,
2:        Orders.OrderDate
3:  FROM  Customers INNER JOIN
4:        Orders ON
5:        Customers.CustomerId = Orders.CustomerId
6: ORDER BY Customers.CustomerId, Orders.OrderDate
```

Without suitable indexes, the whole table may have to be scanned to determine what rows of a table should be selected. Depending on the size of the table, this could be prohibitively expensive. Another way to reduce the performance overhead of joining tables is to "denormalize" the data. This simply means merging the tables that are participating in the join into a new table. In the previous example, you create a CustomerOrders table that contains all the combined information from the Customers and Orders tables. You can then use the information in this table to satisfy your query without having to perform a join. Denormalization does have a major drawback, so it should be used with care. By denormalizing the data into one table, you are duplicating information and run the risk of having inconsistent information on your database. For example, if the same customer places five orders, the customer's details will appear in five separate rows on your CustomerOrders table. Furthermore when you change a customer's data, you must assure that it's data in the Customers and the CustomerOrders table is changed the same way. By using joins, the customer's details are kept in one row on the Customers table.

The ORDER BY clause should also be used with care. If the columns used in the ORDER BY clause are in the same order as that provided by an index, the query can usually be optimized to use the index. If not, the database server must first select all the required rows and carry out a sort in its cache. Such processing has the potential to consume large amounts of memory. Therefore you should index all columns of database tables when the column is used in a ORDER BY clause of a SELECT statement that potentially returns a large resultset.

SQL Server 7.0 provides a new feature that analyses queries and suggests indexes that may improve query performance. To use this feature—called Query Analyzer —open the SQL Server Enterprise Manager, expand the tree in the left pane and select the database where the analyzed SQL statement is usually executed. To open the SQL Server Query Analyzer choose Tools, SQL Server Query Analyzer from the menu. In the analyzer window enter the SQL statement to analyze (for instance the SQL statement of Listing 21.3). Also make sure that the correct database is chosen from the database select box.

Then select Query and Perform Index Analysis from the menu.

In SQL Server 7.0 the SQL statement you entered is analyzed and a recommended index is suggested (see Figure 21.1).

FIGURE 21.1

Build recommended index (Query Analyzer Index Analysis window).

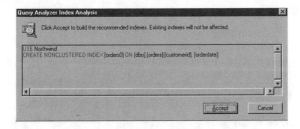

By clicking Accept, the index is built immediately. The previous example shows the suggested index for optimizing the previous query.

On a SQL Server 7.5 database system, the Index Tuning Wizard window appears when choosing Tools, SQL Server Query Analyzer. In the Index Tuning Wizard window click on the Next button to select server and database. Make sure that the items "Keep all

21

existing indexes" and "Add indexed views" are checked. Click on the Next button and
select the SQL statement source in which the index analysis is based, for default the
"Query Analyzer selection" is used, and click on the Next button. Select the tables where
indexes should be analyzed, to analyze all indexes click on the button "Select all tables".
Start the analysis by a click on the Next button.

SQL Server also provides you with a way to see what decisions the Query Optimizer has
made on your behalf. These decisions, called an *execution plan,* enable you to compare
alternative pieces of SQL to determine which is the most efficient. To show the execution
plan in the Query Analyzer window, select Query, Display Estimated Execution Plan
from the menu. This produces a diagram showing the relative cost of each part of the
execution plan (Figure 21.2).

FIGURE 21.2

*Execution plan before
index optimization.*

The two plans in Figure 21.2 and 21.3 show the execution plan before and after an
index—suggested by the Query Analyzer index analysis—is applied.

FIGURE 21.3

*Execution plan after
index optimization.*

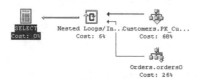

You will notice that the first execution plan has an extra step, as well as a potentially
expensive sort. By adding the suggested index, the optimizer is able to streamline the
execution plan, reducing the overall number of tasks and carrying out the bulk of its
work in the first two tasks.

If you need more detail on any particular part of the execution plan, simply place the
mouse icon over an individual task (see Figure 21.4).

FIGURE 21.4

A detail of the execution plan.

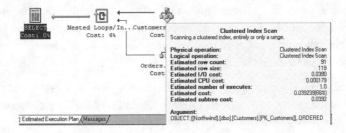

By comparing the estimated subtree cost from the leftmost task (in this case, SELECT), you can determine which statement the Query Optimizer thinks is the most efficient. The subtree cost includes the cost of execution of the task and all tasks below it in the tree.

Another way to compare SQL statements is to use statistical I/O information. To turn on I/O information, in SQL Server Query Analyzer select Query, Current Connection Options from the menu, and check the Show stats I/O box.

When you run a query, a number of lines are displayed after the results detailing the I/O cost. Using these results, you should try to write SQL that minimizes the number of logical reads.

Following is an example of I/O statistics:

```
Table 'Orders'. Scan count 91, logical reads 214, physical reads 0, read-ahead
reads 0.
Table 'Customers'. Scan count 1, logical reads 4, physical reads 0, read-ahead
reads 0.
```

Using Stored Procedures

Stored procedures offer a number of advantages over dynamic SQL. In performance terms, they execute quicker because SQL Server has already determined the execution plan. They can also reduce network traffic by carrying out a series of SQL statements before returning results.

When using stored procedures, you separate all your SQL statements from the database client, and place them where they belongs—on the database server. If you subsequently find a bug in the SQL statements, you can usually change the relevant stored procedure, drop it, and recreate it. If you use dynamic SQL and a compiled language, such as VC++, you have to change the source code of the program, recompile and reinstall it—a much more error-prone and time-consuming task.

21

There are a number of techniques you can use that further improve the performance of stored procedures. First, if a stored procedure returns only one row, the results should be returned as output parameters. This enables you to access the information without using a cursor and its associated overhead.

Finally, you should always try to perform your inserts, updates, and deletes using stored procedures instead of cursors. Cursors have a lot of associated overhead, so they should be used only to loop through a resultset to retrieve information.

Enforcing Connection and Resource Pooling

Connecting to a server can be expensive in performance terms. When you connect to a server, a lot of processing happens on your behalf, including the following:

- Finding and connecting to the server
- Validating the connection information
- Returning a validated connection to the application

The speed of the network also plays a big part in how quickly your connection request is carried out. If you connect using a low bandwidth network, such as a modem, or if the network is carrying a lot of traffic, the speed of your connection request suffers. If you constantly send connection requests across an already heavily loaded network, your requests add to its load, making the network slower.

NEW TERM   Ideally, if you have already successfully connected to a particular server, you would like to reuse the connection. Reusing connections is achieved through a technique called *connection pooling*.

For a long time, programmers had to come up with their own solutions for connection pooling. Version 3.0 of ODBC (included in OLE DB 1.1), finally introduced this long-awaited feature. With the release of MDAC 2.0, OLE DB resource pooling became available, which also provided pooling of connections, although the default pooling mechanism was still ODBC. This changed with MDAC 2.5, which uses OLE DB resource pooling by default over ODBC connection pooling.

If the OLE DB providers and ODBC drivers you use support connection pooling, you automatically benefit from this feature by using ADO.

Investigating ODBC Connection Pooling

Let's take a look at how ODBC handles connection pooling. The first connection request an application makes to a server is passed to ODBC's pooling components. The pooling components store the connection details, provided by you as parameters passed to the

ADO `Connection` object. Then the connection request is passed to the server. In return a live connection is passed to the application. Note that at this stage the live connection has not been added to the pool. The connection can be added to the pool only when the application calls the `Close` methods of the `Connection` and `Recordset` objects. This is a very important point.

NEW TERM If a close is not issued, a problem called *connection creep* can occur. With *connection creep*, the number of open connections on a server keeps growing, potentially leading to resource problems or exceeding the available licenses.

Therefore, it is essential that when you are finished with a recordset and connection, they should be explicitly closed so that the connection can be returned to the pool. Remember to set the recordset's `ActiveConnection` property to `Nothing` when you create a disconnected recordset. Not doing this causes the recordset to remain connected, stopping the release of its related connection to the pool.

When you close the connection, the pooling components of ODBC store the live connection with the already stored connection details and make it available for reuse.

When the next connection request is received, ODBC again passes it to the pooling components. If a connection exists in the pool that has identical connection information (even user ID and password), the associated live connection is returned. If no match can be found in the pool, the connection request is processed as before, with the request being sent to the server. The words "identical connection information" have particular significance. The pooled connection is returned only if the connection string you have passed to the ADO `Connection` object exactly matches the connection string of the pooled connection. For example, the following two connection strings have different UID values. If one was associated with a live connection in the ODBC pool and a connection was opened with the other, the pooled connection would not be returned:

```
"DSN=Northwind;UID=Fred;PWD=;"
```

```
"DSN=Northwind;UID=Shirley;PWD=;"
```

Reusing a connection can also be affected by a difference in dynamic ADO properties. Basically, the simple rule is the following: To reuse a connection from the pool, make sure all the values passed to the ADO `Connection` object are the same before it is opened.

Although ODBC connection pooling can give your applications a significant performance boost, there are a number of issues you need to consider. If you are using SQL Server 6.5 or below, there is the potential for connection pooling to hold onto resources in the temporary database, `TempDB`. This can occur if you are creating temporary stored procedures for prepared SQL statements.

21

When you use connection pooling with these versions of SQL Server, you should disable the creation of temporary stored procedures. To do this, you need to go to the operating system's Control Panel (Windows 95/98 and NT) and open ODBC or 32-bit ODBC. In Windows 2000, you go to Start button, Programs, Administrative Tools, Data Sources (ODBC). This opens the ODBC Data Source Administrator window. You then select the System DSN tab, select the appropriate SQL Server 6.5 data source, and click Configure.

This opens the Microsoft SQL Server DSN Configuration window In the Microsoft SQL Server DSN Configuration window click Next, provide the login ID and password when necessary, and click Next again. Uncheck the Create temporary stored procedures for prepared SQL statements and drop the stored procedures option (see Figure 21.5).

FIGURE 21.5

*Microsoft SQL
Server DSN
Configuration
window.*

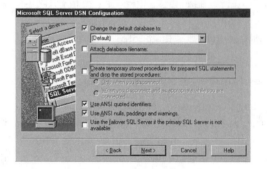

Then click Next and Finish. This option is disabled for data sources using SQL Server 7.0 (or later). In version 7, SQL Server does not create temporary stored procedures when preparing a command.

Another problem that occurs in badly programmed ASP applications is the practice of storing a live, unclosed connection in a session or application variable. Another practice is storing a connection globally and sharing it between threads, causing each call to the global connection to be synchronized. Using either of these practices limits the number of users an application can support. A connection stored or used in such a manner will never be added to the pool. When using session variables to store connections, you also run the risk of exceeding the number of available licenses or slow down your Web server much more than necessary. A better solution is to obtain a new connection on receipt of an HTTP request and only use it as long as necessary, but no longer than until the HTTP response is sent.

Now that you have considered the downside, let's look at how you can control ODBC connection pooling to benefit from its advantages.

You can control ODBC connection pooling in a number of ways, but the simplest method is to use the ODBC Data Source Administrator. In its window select the Connection Pooling tab, which displays a list of the ODBC drivers available (see Figure 21.6).

FIGURE 21.6

Connection Pooling tab in ODBC Data Source Administrator.

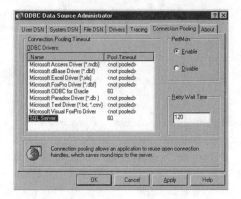

The Enable radio button enables you to monitor pooling performance using the Performance Monitor, at which you will look later today. Note that typically this option should be left disabled unless you are investigating a specific problem, otherwise additional resources are occupied and connection pooling slows down. The retry wait time relates to how ODBC processes dead server connections. If pooling is enabled for a driver and the driver detects that a connection is "dead" (this could be due to network failure or server failure), the connection is marked as dead returned to the pool, and an error is returned to the application. The period specified in the retry wait time is added to the time the connection was returned to the pool, giving the time the next connection attempt should occur. Any requests that retrieve a dead connection from the pool before this wait time has expired receive an error. When a request is received and the wait time has expired, the connection is retried. If a connection request is successful, processing proceeds as normal. If the request was unsuccessful, the wait time is reset and the dead connection returned to the pool. Note that the retry wait time applies to all the ODBC drivers.

To enable ODBC connection pooling double-click on the driver's name in the Connection Pooling tab. The Set Connection Pooling Attributes dialog box is displayed. Then select Pool Connections to this driver, and connection pooling is enabled. You also need to consider how long unused connections should be held before being removed from the pool. The default is sixty seconds. When determining how long you should hold a connection, you must weight the overhead of setting up a new connection against the potential for unused connections to sit in the pool tying up resources. Unfortunately, the only way to determine the appropriate figure is by monitoring your application (by using the Performance Monitor tool.

21

OLE DB Resource Pooling

Resource pooling in OLE DB works in a similar fashion to ODBC's connection pooling, with some subtle but important differences. When OLE DB receives a connection request from ADO, it checks for a resource pool that contains an unused connection with matching connection information. If a suitable connection is found, it is taken from the pool and returned. Otherwise, a new connection is established with the database server. When the connection is released by the using application, it is returned to the pool. Any connection in the pool being continuously unused for longer than the timeout period is automatically removed from the pool and its resources are released.

The way OLE DB manages its pools is very different from ODBC. With ODBC, the number of pools is usually equal to the number of processors, with a single pool potentially containing connections that use different drivers and have different connection information. With OLE DB connection pooling, a certain pool contains connections of the same connection information. Every combination of OLE DB provider and user logon is assigned to its own OLE DB connection pool. This means that OLE DB connection pooling uses more pools than ODBC connection pooling.

Another difference is how OLE DB deals with a retry wait situation. In a similar fashion to ODBC, OLE DB blocks attempts to obtain a connection until a retry wait period has elapsed, with the default being one minute. Then the first retry is attempted. If this is unsuccessful, the next retry happens after two minutes, and then after every five minutes until a valid connection is returned.

Connection creep, wherein the number of connections to a database keeps growing, is the same for OLE DB as it is for ODBC. All the causes of connection creep previously discussed in the ODBC pooling section still apply. It is worth reiterating that the most common cause of connection creep is not explicitly closing the ADO Connection and Recordset objects. Until a close has been issued, the connection cannot be placed in the pool for reuse.

You have three choices for controlling the pooling services of an OLE DB provider:

- Using the Registry
- Setting the connection string
- Using the OLE DB API

Let's examine how you can enable or disable various aspects of OLE DB resource pooling using the Registry. In this example, you disable connection pooling of the OLE DB driver for SQL Server, SQLOLEDB. First, you need to determine the class ID of the driver by running the Registry editor, REGEDT32, and opening the key for HKEY_CLASS-ES_ROOT/SQLOLEDB/CLSID (see Figure 21.7).

FIGURE 21.7

Registry key of SQLOLEDB shown in Regedt32 window.

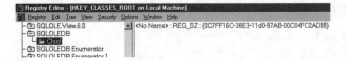

Then open the Registry entry under HKEY_CLASSES_ROOT/CLSID/0C7FF16C-38E3-11d0-97AB-00C04FC2AD98 as shown in Figure 21.8.

FIGURE 21.8

Registry entry of the class id of SQLOLEDB.

The value of OLEDB_SERVICES shows what services are currently being provided. A value of 0xffffffff indicates that all services, including resource pooling, are enabled. If you change this to a value of 0xfffffffc, services except pooling and automatic transaction enlistment are enabled. Table 21.1 shows all the valid settings for each method of control.

TABLE 21.1   OLE DB Service Settings

Default Services Enabled	Registry DWORD Values	Connection String	OLE DB API DBPROP_INIT_OLEDBSERVICES property value
All services	0xffffffff	"OLE DB Services = -1;"	DBPROPVAL_OS_ENABLEALL
All services except pooling and automatic transaction enlistment	0xfffffffc	"OLE DB Services = -4;"	(DBPROPVAL_OS_ENABLEALL & ~DBPROPVAL_OS_TXNENLISTMENT & ~DBPROPVAL_OS_RESOURCEPOOLING)
All services except Client Cursor Engine	0xfffffffb	"OLE DB Services = -5;"	(DBPROPVAL_OS_ENABLEALL & ~DBPROPVAL_OS_CLIENTCURSOR)
All services except pooling, automatic transaction enlistment, and Client Cursor Engine	0xfffffff8	"OLE DB Services = -8;"	(DBPROPVAL_OS_ENABLEALL & ~DBPROPVAL_OS_RESOURCEPOOLING & ~DBPROPVAL_OS_TXNENLISTMENT & ~DBPROPVAL_OS_CLIENTCURSOR)

21

continues

TABLE 21.1   continued

Pooling and automatic transaction enlistment only, session-level aggregation only	0x00000003	"OLE DB Services = 3;"	DBPROPVAL_OS_TXNENLISTMENT & DBPROPVAL_OS_RESOURCEPOOLING
No services	0x00000000	"OLE DB Services = 0;"	DBPROPVAL_OS_DISABLEALL

Locking Data

From a performance standpoint, locking will often give you the most challenges. Locks have three characteristics that impact the throughput and performance of an application:

- Concurrency
- Duration
- Granularity

It is worth delving a bit deeper into how a data provider, such as SQL Server, handles its locking, so you can understand why it is such an issue. SQL Server has the following types of locks:

- Shared (S)
- Intent shared (IS)
- Update (U)
- Exclusive (X)
- Intent exclusive (IX)
- Shared with intent exclusive (SIX)
- Bulk update (BU)
- Intent schema (Sch-S and Sch M)

Let's examine some of these lock types to see how they impact requests from different connections. Before SQL Server carries out an operation on your behalf, it first tries to acquire the necessary locks needed to ensure the integrity of the data. For example, a shared lock is typically obtained on a row before it is selected. While a row has a share lock on it, it can be read by other connections (that is, have other share locks placed on it), but cannot be updated or deleted. This means that an update or delete request will be blocked until the share lock is released.

Update locks are acquired when reading data with the intention of updating, such as when you declare a cursor with pessimistic locking. Only one update lock can be acquired on a piece of data. If another connection also wants to acquire an update lock, it must wait for the first one to be released. However, update locks do not stop share locks from being acquired on the same piece of data by other connections.

Exclusive locks are acquired before updates and deletes. An exclusive lock cannot be acquired on a piece of data if it has any type of lock (including exclusive) already on it. When an exclusive lock has been acquired, no other types of locks can be acquired until it has been released. This means that a row that has an exclusive lock on it is unavailable to other connections.

Intent locks indicate that a share or exclusive lock is to be acquired in the future. For example, an intent exclusive lock indicates the intention to acquire an exclusive lock at a later stage.

The descriptions of the lock types show that you must be very careful when locking to avoid blocking problems. When developing highly scalable systems, you should always try to make the server choose a lock type that enables the row to be used by as many connections concurrently as possible. You can influence the type of lock obtained through the `CursorType` and `LockType` parameters. For example, if you choose a `CursorType` of forward-only and a `LockType` of read-only, only shared locks are acquired, which maximizes the number of connections that can access the row concurrently. If you choose a `CursorType` of dynamic and a `LockType` of pessimistic, update locks are acquired on the rows that were accessed. If you then update or delete a row, the update lock is first upgraded to an intent exclusive lock and then to an exclusive lock, stopping any other connection from accessing the row until the transaction was committed and the lock released.

The next issue you need to consider is the duration a lock is held. The longer a lock is held, the less concurrency an application has. You should always aim to minimize the time a lock is held.

When you use transactions, issuing a commit or rollback releases all locks that have been acquired. If you use the `BeginTrans` method of the `Connection` object, you should make sure that you issue a `CommitTrans` or `RollbackTrans` as soon as practical to release all the locks that have been acquired. Remember that even share locks block updates and deletes. You should never start a transaction, execute a number of SQL

21

statements, and then wait for user input before committing a transaction. This means that the length of time the transaction takes is totally in the hands of the user. If the user decides on a long lunch before responding, you are in a lot of trouble.

Locks can be applied at various levels of database items (granularity). SQL Server 7 supplies the following levels:

- Rows
- Pages
- Keys
- Ranges of keys
- Indexes
- Tables
- Databases

The larger the granularity, the less the concurrency, but the better the execution time. For example, if you wanted to update every row in a 100000-row table, you could either acquire one exclusive table-level lock or 100,000 row-level locks. Because each lock consumes system resources, locking at the table level improves the performance of your SQL statement or database action. On the other hand, if you acquire a table level lock, no other connections will be able to access the table while you perform your update.

For high-volume applications, you typically want to apply locks at the lowest level of granularity possible to maximize concurrency. SQL Server automatically determines the granularity of a lock, using a number of criteria. You can influence its decision by providing so-called hints on SQL statements. For example, the following statement forces SQL Server to take row-level locks while updating the Customers table:

```
UPDATE Customers WITH (ROWLOCK) SET ContactName = 'James Brown'
➡  WHERE CustomerId = 'ALFKI'
```

For maximum concurrency, you should always try to obtain the locks as late as possible, release them as early as possible, and use a lock type and granularity that has the smallest impact on other users of the server.

Employing SQL Server Profiler

Tools such as SQL Server's Server Profiler enable you to see locking activity. To use the Server Profiler, you must have SQL Server 7 installed. From the Tools menu of the console of SQL Server Enterprise Manager, select SQL Server Profiler. In the Server Profiler, first make sure you have access to all the locking events so you can see in the trace what type of locks are being acquired and released. To do this, from the Tools menu select Options and click the radio button All event classes, as shown in Figure 21.9.

FIGURE 21.9

Events and selected radio button All events classes.

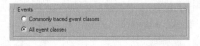

To set the options for the trace, from the File menu select New, Trace. This opens a dialog box that allows you to select the events you want to trace. To trace all locking activity, select the Events tab, select Locks under Available events, and click the Add button, as shown in Figure 21.10.

FIGURE 21.10

Trace window.

So you can determine where and what type of locks are being applied, select the Data Columns tab and add Database Id, Object Id, Transaction Id, and Event Sub Class.

To start tracing, select the General tab, supply a name for the trace, and click OK.

The trace automatically displays any activity on the server when a selected event occurs. By running the trace while you are testing your application, you are able to see locks being acquired and released by SQL Server as it executes your SQL. Figure 21.11 shows the result of running the trace while executing an update on a row using a dynamic, server-side cursor with pessimistic locking.

FIGURE 21.11

Result of running the trace.

21

As previously mentioned, an update lock is acquired when the row is read, followed by intent exclusive and exclusive locks when the update occurs.

To determine what database an event applies to, run the following SQL statement against the master database, using the database ID in the event:

```
SELECT * FROM sysdatabases WHERE dbid = 6
```

This shows the name of the database. To determine the table (or index) being locked, run the following SQL statement against this database using the object ID in the event:

```
SELECT * FROM sysobjects WHERE id = 213575799
```

Dealing with Database Deadlocks

Deadlocks, or as they are sometimes called, "the deadly embrace," are caused by locking problems. Let's assume you have two connections accessing the same database. One connection reads a customer row from the Customers table, obtaining a share lock. The second connection reads an order row from the Orders table for the same customer, obtaining a share lock. The first connection then tries to obtain an exclusive lock on the same order row so that it can change some of the details. However, because the second connection has obtained a share lock on this row, this request must wait. The second connection then attempts to obtain an exclusive lock on the same customer row of the Customers table. In this case, the request must wait because a share lock has already been acquired by the first connection.

Unfortunately, both connections are now in a deadly embrace. Both are effectively blocking each other from completing their work.

Data providers, such as SQL Server, detect a deadlock and force one of the connections to roll back, enabling the other connection to complete its work. However, such a solution is far from ideal.

One method of making sure that deadlocks do not occur in your application is to carry out requests on tables in the same order. In the previous example, if the Customers table would be always accessed before the Orders table, a deadlock would never occur. At worst, a request would be delayed until a lock was released from a row it is trying to read, update, or delete. This sounds like an easy solution to implement. However, in any reasonably sized application, ensuring that all requests are carried out in a specific order becomes very difficult.

Another solution is to focus on the performance rules previously stated on locking. If you maximize the concurrency of your locks and minimize their duration and granularity, you can significantly reduce the chances of a deadlock occurring.

As a last resort, you can give hints to some providers on how to carry out locking. As mentioned previously, SQL Server enables you to provide locking hints with your SQL statements. In fact, you can tell SQL Server not to acquire any locks while reading rows from a table. If you do not acquire any locks, you cannot cause a deadlock. Following is an example of an SQL statement that uses a locking hint to ensure no locks are obtained:

```
SELECT * FROM customers WITH (NOLOCK)
```

Using NOLOCK does have a downside, however. First, it applies only to SELECT statements. Second, because you are not obtaining share locks or honoring exclusive locks, you can potentially read "dirty" data. Dirty data is information that has been changed but is yet to be committed. For example, assume that a request to select a number of rows from your customer table using NOLOCK is issued. While collecting the rows to satisfy this query, SQL Server reads a row from the customer table that has been inserted but has yet to be committed. After the read takes place, the connection that inserted the customer row issues a rollback, removing the row from the table. When you then display the results of your NOLOCK query, you show a customer's details that do not exist in the customer table!

Because of these problems, NOLOCK should be used only as a last resort.

Running ODBC Trace

You can trace all the calls to your ODBC drivers by using the ODBC trace. This reveals all ODBC activity executed and enables you to search for ODBC warnings and errors. To start tracing in Windows 2000, open the ODBC Data Source Administrator: Open Data Sources (ODBC) from Start button, Programs, Administrative Tools. In Windows 95/98 or Windows NT 4.0 open ODBC or 32-bit ODBC instead. Then select the tracing tab, and click Start Tracing Now (see Figure 21.12).

FIGURE 21.12

Tracing in ODBC Data Source Administrator.

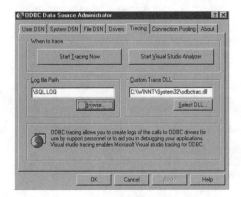

21

A trace of all ODBC calls will be generated to the file specified in the Log file Path text box.

Here is a sample output of tracing:

```
VB6             e4-e3   ENTER SQLAllocConnect
        HENV                038C1238
        HDBC *              0012F0A4

VB6             e4-e3   EXIT  SQLAllocConnect  with return code 0 (SQL_SUCCESS)
        HENV                038C1238
        HDBC *              0x0012F0A4 ( 0x038c12e0)

VB6             e4-e3   ENTER SQLSetConnectAttrW
        SQLHDBC             038C12E0
        SQLINTEGER                  103 <SQL_ATTR_LOGIN_TIMEOUT>
        SQLPOINTER          0x0000000F
        SQLINTEGER                   -6

VB6             e4-e3   EXIT  SQLSetConnectAttrW  with return code 0
(SQL_SUCCESS)
        SQLHDBC             038C12E0
        SQLINTEGER                  103 <SQL_ATTR_LOGIN_TIMEOUT>
        SQLPOINTER          0x0000000F (BADMEM)
        SQLINTEGER                   -6
```

This can be useful as a simple method of determining the activities ODBC is carrying out to service your requests. To analyze ODBC traces, use Visual Studio Analyzer tool. Its documentation can be found in the MSDN Library.

Using Visual Studio Analyzer

Visual Studio Analyzer was first released with version 6 of Visual Studio Enterprise edition. It provides features that enable you to tune and debug your applications. Essentially, it captures events of interest that occur on a machine being monitored and provides powerful tools for analyzing these events. For example, you can capture events that show how your application is interacting with ADO. You can start analyzing your application by following these steps:

1. Create a new project in Visual Studio Analyzer.
2. Connect to the machine(s) running your ADO application.
3. Define a filter that will collect the events of interest.
4. Start collecting the events in the event log.
5. Start the ADO application.

6. Stop collecting events.

7. View the event log.

8. Filter out unwanted events.

When you use the Analyzer Wizard to create a new project, you are led through these steps up to and including the starting of event collection. The events that are collected depend on the filter you have applied. Figure 21.13 shows some of the events you can choose when monitoring ADO.

FIGURE 21.13

Edit new Filter window.

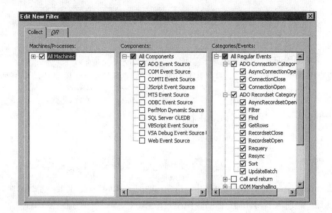

You can also collect events from ODBC, SQLDB, MTS, and so on. You can even collect events from your own application. After your recording filter has been set up and events are being collected, you start running your application. As soon as your application starts, you see events appearing in the event log (unless the recording filter is too restrictive). After you have executed the parts of your application you are interested in, stop the event log and begin to analyze it. Note that you can have as many event logs as you like, but only one can be actively recording at any time. Figure 21.14 shows an event log generated by applying a recording filter that only collected ADO events.

FIGURE 21.14

Event log.

Time	Event	Source Machine	Source Process
23:05:42	ConnectionOpen	DISKOWL01	vb6
23:05:58	ReturnNormal	DISKOWL01	vb6
23:06:34	ConnectionOpen	DISKOWL01	vb6
23:06:35	ReturnNormal	DISKOWL01	vb6
23:06:35	ConnectionOpen	DISKOWL01	vb6
23:06:35	ReturnNormal	DISKOWL01	vb6
23:06:35	QuerySend	DISKOWL01	vb6
23:06:35	ReturnNormal	DISKOWL01	vb6
23:06:35	RecordsetClose	DISKOWL01	vb6
23:06:35	ReturnNormal	DISKOWL01	vb6
23:06:35	ConnectionClose	DISKOWL01	vb6
23:06:35	ReturnNormal	DISKOWL01	vb6
23:06:35	ConnectionOpen	DISKOWL01	vb6
23:06:35	ReturnNormal	DISKOWL01	vb6
23:06:35	QuerySend	DISKOWL01	vb6
23:06:35	ReturnNormal	DISKOWL01	vb6
23:06:35	RecordsetClose	DISKOWL01	vb6
23:06:35	ReturnNormal	DISKOWL01	vb6

21

The information in the event log can be displayed in a number of ways, including a graphical timeline as shown in Figure 21.15.

FIGURE 21.15

Event log displayed as graphical timeline.

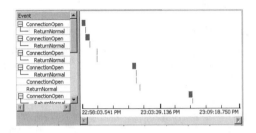

When you come across an event of interest, you can open it to view its details, displaying arguments passed, the duration of the event, the source component name, and so on.

This tool in particular provides you with a way of analyzing your application so that you can then effectively tune and debug it.

Using the Performance Monitor

You can monitor various aspects of an application using the Performance Monitor. In particular, the Performance Monitor enables you to see how ODBC's connection pooling is performing on a machine. First, enable the collection of performance-monitoring counts for ODBC connection pooling as outlined in the section "Investigating ODBC Connection Pooling." Then open the Performance Monitor window by selecting Start, Programs, Administrative Tools (Common), Performance.

To start tracing ODBC connection activity, select Edit, Add to Chart as shown in Figure 21.16.

FIGURE 21.16

Add ODBC Connecting Pooling parameters to Chart.

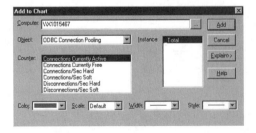

This enables you to select the computer to monitor and the objects and counters to display. For ODBC connection pooling, there is a choice of six counters. To monitor a particular counter, select it and click the Add button.

The counters for ODBC pooling are as follows:

Connections Currently Active being used by applications	The current number of connections
Connections Currently Free available for connection requests	The current number of connections
Connections Sec/Hard data sources per second	The number of connections made to
Connections Sec/Soft pool per second	The number of connections from the
Disconnections Sec/Hard data sources per second	The number of disconnects made to
Disconnections Sec/Soft pool per second	The number of disconnects from the

The Performance Monitor helps determine bottlenecks in your application by monitoring CPU, memory, disk I/O, and disk resource use.

When monitoring servers running Web applications, the Performance Monitor can return information on Active Server Pages, FTP Server, HTTP Server, Gopher Server, Terminal Server, and Internet Information Server (IIS). The Performance Monitor also can be used to see how SQL Server is performing.

All these are available by selecting the appropriate object and counts in the Add to Chart dialog box (Figure 21.16).

When using the Performance Monitor, remember that it should never be left on for a long period of time, because it uses up a remarkable amount of resources and ironically decreases performance of your machine.

Hardware Needs

No matter how much you undertake performance tuning, the hardware is the ultimate limiting factor on how fast an application will run, how many users it will support, and how reliable it is. Just consider the following components in turn:

- Disk subsystem
- CPU and memory
- Network
- Power supply

21

Selecting Disk Subsystem

When choosing the disk subsystem, make sure that its speed and storage capacity is adequate. Also consider the issue of fault tolerance. A server with one disk has a single point of failure. If the disk has a head crash, the entire server will be unavailable. Before choosing a suitable disk subsystem, you need to decide what level of fault tolerance is adequate. That is, you need to weigh the cost of having the server unavailable against the cost of providing some level of fault tolerance.

You can use redundant array of independent disks (RAID) to provide performance and fault tolerance. RAID comes in various levels, with the most common being 0, 1, and 5.

RAID level 0 is performance-oriented, provides no fault tolerance, and is often used on machines running SQL Server. RAID level 0 spreads read/write requests across multiple disks, carrying them out simultaneously. For I/O-intensive applications, such as SQL Server, this usually means a large performance boost.

NEW TERM   The technique of spreading read/write requests across multiple disks is called *disk striping,* with stripes of data being written simultaneously over multiple disks.

RAID level 1 provides fault tolerance. All the information from the primary disk(s) is copied to the mirror disk(s). If the primary disk should have a head crash, the mirror disk can take its place immediately, with no disruption to service. The copying of data to the mirror is carried out by the hardware, and so is very fast. In performance terms, RAID level 1 offers some advantage in reading data and no advantage in writing data over a single SCSI disk.

RAID level 5 provides both performance and fault tolerance. To use it, you must have at least three disks. RAID 5 uses striping, with a technique called *parity,* which provides high levels of performance. If one of the disks should become unavailable, the data it holds is reconstructed from the data contained on the remaining active disks, with only a slight impact on performance.

Considerations About CPU and Memory

When selecting the CPU, you have two choices:

- How fast
- How many

Multiprocessor machines are now commonplace, and are well suited to most server requirements. Products such as SQL Server take full advantage of multiprocessors by distributing work among each processor.

Using a multiprocessor system can double the cost for software licenses. This is logically the fact when a software or component is licensed per CPU.

For server machines, the amount of memory should be carefully considered. If there is too little, the operating system will be forced to constantly write and retrieve the contents of the memory to disk, in a process called *paging and swapping*. Excessive memory demands on the machine can result in a situation called *thrashing,* where the only work being carried out on the machine is paging to satisfy the memory requirements of the applications.

Network

If fault tolerance for a server is an issue, the server should have two network cards and two network connections. The speed of these connections also impact the throughput of the work carried out by the server. For high-speed enterprise servers, you should consider using gigabit Ethernet to maximize throughput.

Power Supply

For enterprise servers, the uninterruptible power supply (UPS) should be able to supply enough power to enable a computer to continue working until backup generators step in. At worst, the UPS should enable the machine to power down in a graceful manner.

Using a Network Load Balancing Cluster

Windows Load Balancing Server for Windows NT 4.0 (WLBS) or Windows Clustering technology (Windows 2000) enables you to spread Internet requests over a number of servers running IIS.

To use WLBS, choose a server that serves as a gateway for requests. When the WLBS server receives a request, it is redirected to one of a cluster of IISs. The method to select the particular machine for receiving the request can be either round-robin (each IIS in turn) or dynamic (based on resource use on the IIS). If a particular server becomes unavailable, WLBS stops forwarding requests to it.

This enables you to provide optimal levels of service with some fault tolerance. However, if the gateway machine should crash, the whole Internet site would be put out of action.

21

Clustering Servers

Microsoft's Server Cluster technology (also known as Windows Clustering) provides a solution for enterprise-level fault tolerance. Windows Clustering enables you to group two servers into a cluster, with each server being referred to as a node. Each of the nodes in the cluster sends the other a signal, indicating it is still active. If one of the nodes fails to detect the other's signal, it immediately performs a number of checks to establish whether its partner is still up and running. If these checks fail, it begins an automated failover process, which transfers all the work being undertaken by the other node to itself.

Using Windows Clustering shields users from the catastrophic failure of one of their servers.

Summary

This day was about performance and tuning of database applications using ADO. You can use the Recordset and Connection objects to influence performance and scalability of an application. By determining lock types of Recordset objects, duration of connection transactions, some special locking hints in SQL statements to determine the behavior and therefore the speed of database processes.

By adding indexes to database tables searching for certain values is speed up. So the execution of SQL statements, as well as accessing data via the Recordset object directly is faster and the application is more scalable.

Connection pooling in ODBC and OLE DB is another issue that implicit speeds up establishing database connection especially in multi user and Web applications.

Of course the overall performance of database clients and servers is also determined by the hardware in use, the band-width of the network, or the network traffic. By using clustering services or network load balancing clusters an application also becomes more scalable and performs faster.

To track performance issues on a certain computer you can use the Performance Monitor tool. It allows you to track certain application parameters and performance counters in graphical displays or log files.

Q&A

Q **My Web application runs smooth without any performance tuning? Why should I invest any effort in tuning a running application?**

A When the number of users of your Web application grows, then bad programming techniques as well as a database without indexes defined on its tables bring your Web application faster to its limit than you might think first. With the number of concurrent users the importance of tuning and measuring performance counters become exponential important.

Workshop

The quiz questions and exercises are provided for your further understanding. See Appendix A, "Answers," for the answers.

Quiz

1. Which technologies of MDAC 2.5 allow connection pooling?
2. What part of a database table influences performance of SQL statements especially when some thousand datasets are stored in the table?
3. What Recordset options can you adjust to gain the best mix of recordset features and performance for your database application?

Exercises

As this is mostly a theory chapter there is no exercises.

21

Week 3

In Review

To review the concepts presented in the previous seven days, let's look at the case study for Repairs Unlimited, a company offering repair services worldwide to the heavy industry (24×7). It does not sell the necessary spare parts itself, but has business partners that do.

The customers of Repairs Unlimited expect that any disruption of their process is as short as possible, and pay large amounts of money for the availability of Repairs Unlimited's support staff and engineers (via service contracts). Therefore, Repairs Unlimited must be in close contact with the business partners that sell the necessary spare parts for each machine at the customers' plants so they can restore operation as soon as possible.

To guarantee fast replacement of machines and the repair of parts, each customer of Repairs Unlimited is inventoried to have a database of machines and its spare parts handy when time is ticking. This database must be available 24 hours a day to every support engineer around the world (this database is accessed via a Windows front end, through dial-up lines to the headquarters). Securing this information is vital so that no customer can see another customer's database.

Repairs Unlimited is linked to its business partners via proprietary data interfaces. These links are used to check for part availability as well as to order any necessary parts. Today, this functionality is implemented in various supplier-specific client applications. To unify the various interfaces, however, it should be moved to the central server where all other information is stored and processed.

With the information you gathered from Repairs Unlimited, you can easily see that it is vital to access both customer information and spare part availability fast. Because only customer information is stored in Repairs Unlimited's data stores, engineers have to query each business partner's databases via its client programs.

To change the situation, you propose that Repairs Unlimited and its business partners agree on a data exchange standard, preferably XML because it would be platform-independent. This data exchange format allows Repairs Unlimited to duplicate essential spare part information into its databases, thus enabling extremely fast search for availability and ordering without the engineers' need to know different front ends for various suppliers.

In addition, you can tighten security on the links to the business partners, because now only the central server needs to communicate with servers at the business partners' locations—for retrieving spare part information and placing orders. No end user needs direct access to these links any more.

This strengthening of security allows you to move Repairs Unlimited's front end from Windows to a Web-based front end. You suggest that the Web server be secured with SSL and client certificates to assure customers that their data is 100% safe from prying eyes.

By standardizing on Internet Explorer as the browser for this Web application, you can put more intelligence on the client, especially enhancing performance for database update and insert tasks. Therefore, you recommend employing RDS with custom data factories, which—in conjunction with SSL and client certificates—allows good security.

Finally, with all security in place, Repairs Unlimited can replace the direct dial-in lines with Internet connectivity through a firewall and standard ISP accounts for its support staff and engineers.

APPENDIX A

Answers

Answers for Day 1

Quiz

1. What do you have to consider when you want to install a newer MDAC than version 2.5 on a Windows 2000 machine?

   You must use a Service Pack for Windows 2000 that contains the newer MDAC version. When running a normal MDAC setup program (`mdac_typ.exe`) that is not part of a service pack, Windows 2000 refuses to delete the old MDAC files. So you cannot install new MDAC files, of course.

2. After you download MDAC 2.5 from the Microsoft Web site you also want to get information about the newest features of ADO 2.5, the syntax of all ADO objects, and the use of various OLE DB providers. What documentation contains all the information you search for?

   All the information about ADO 2.5 objects, their methods, properties, events, collections, syntax information and examples can be found in the Microsoft Platform SDK. The Platform SDK documentation contains extensive information about technologies such as ADO, MDAC, OLE

DB, ODBC, ASP, COM, DCOM, COM+, Indexing Service, and other technologies related to or based on Windows 95/98, Windows NT 4.0, and Windows 2000.

3. You want to find out which ADO version is installed on a Windows 98 machine. What tool can you use that tells you the MDAC and ADO version, as well as the version numbers of all MDAC files installed?

Use the Component Checker tool to identify the current MDAC/ADO version installed on a machine. Furthermore Component Checker lists all the files, libraries, and DLLs related to MDAC that are installed on your computer. It also enables identifying DLL conflicts and removing the current MDAC installation from your machine. The Component Checker tool is available for download from the Microsoft Web site at

`http://www.microsoft.com/data/`

4. Name the basic technologies that are contained in the Microsoft Data Access Components (MDAC) 2.5.

The basic technologies contained in MDAC 2.5 are ADO, OLE DB, and ODBC. This comprises the ADO object libraries, OLE DB provider for various data sources, and ODBC drivers for databases.

Exercise

Today is about theory, so there is no exercise.

Answers for Day 2

Quiz

1. How can you determine how many records a Recordset contains?

The number of records in a Recordset can be retrieved using the `Recordset` object's `RecordCount` property. However, the Recordset must support approximate positioning. This is needed when using a static or keyset cursor.

2. When you have an open connection, how can you find out which ADO version is used?

The ADO version can be retrieved reading the value of the `Version` property of the `Connection` object. You do not have to open the connection. You only have to create the `Connection` object to retrieve the value.

```
1: Dim conn As ADODB.Connection
2: Set conn = CreateObject("ADODB.Connection")
3: ADOVersion = conn.Version
```

3. Given the fact a data source has an OLE DB interface, can it be accessed using ADO?

Any data source, no matter if relational (as a database) or another type of data can be accessed using ADO as long as it has an OLE DB or ODBC interface. ADO is just a thin layer upon OLE DB. OLE DB can access ODBC data sources using the OLE DB Provider for ODBC.

4. What are the four cursor types used in an ADO Recordset?

The four cursor types are forward-only, static, keyset, and dynamic.

5. What characteristic does an empty Recordset have?

An empty Recordset has set both EOF and BOF properties set to the value TRUE.

6. How can you find out if a certain field is allowed to contain NULL values?

The key is to test the field's Attributes property. When the field's Attributes property indicates the value adFldIsNullable, it accepts NULL values.

```
(Recordset("Fieldname").Attributes And adFldIsNullable) > 0
```

However, when the Attributes property indicates the value adFldMayBeNull, it can return NULL values.

```
(Recordset("Fieldname").Attributes And adFldMayBeNull) > 0
```

Exercise

Not only the Connection and the Field objects have a Properties collection. The Recordset object also contains a Properties collection that can provide useful information about the Recordset. Open a Recordset to a data source of your choice using ADO and read all values from the Properties collection of both the Recordset and the Connection object.

A possible solution (which can be run, for instance, in Excel 2000) is presented here. It opens a Connection to the Northwind database and retrieves an empty Recordset from the Products table. Of course it also retrieves all names and value from the Connection and the Recordset objects.

```
1: Dim conn As ADODB.Connection
2: Dim rs As ADODB.Recordset
3:
4: Set conn = CreateObject("ADODB.Connection")
5: Set rs = CreateObject("ADODB.Recordset")
6: conn.Open "Provider=SQLOLEDB;Data Source=BoyScout;" & _
7:    "Initial Catalog=Northwind;User ID=sa;Password=;"
8:
9: Debug.Print "CONNECTION Properties:"
10: For Each Property In conn.Properties
11:    Debug.Print Property.Name & ":" & Property
12: Next
13:
```

```
14: Set rs.ActiveConnection = conn
15: rs.Source = "SELECT ProductID FROM Products WHERE 1 = 0"
16: rs.Open
17:
18: Debug.Print ""
19: Debug.Print "RECORDSET Properties:"
20: For Each Property In rs.Properties
21:    Debug.Print Property.Name & ":" & Property
22: Next
23:
24: rs.Close
25: conn.Close
26: Set rs = Nothing
27: Set conn = Nothing
```

Answers for Day 3

Quiz

1. Is it possible to execute a SQL statement to insert new data into a database?

   The SQL INSERT statement can be used to insert data into a database. It can for instance be executed by using the Execute method of the Connection object.

2. How do you retrieve an Autonumber value from a database?

   You can use a correctly prepared Recordset to insert a new record into a database with the AddNew method. When the Recordset is stored in the database, the field of the Autonumber column in the Recordset is updated. The value can then be retrieved from the Recordset.

3. Which methods do you use to insert BLOB data into a database chunk by chunk?

   You use the AddNew method to add a new record to a Recordset. The BLOB data can be inserted into the database by using the AppendChunk method of the BLOB Field in the Recordset. When the BLOB field should be stored in the database, you use the Update or UpdateBatch method to store the whole Record containing the BLOB in the database. Which one you use depends on the Recordset locking.

4. When using Visual Basic, what possibilities does your application have to retrieve information about an error that occurred?

   When you have enabled error handling, by using the On Error Resume Next statement, you can retrieve information about an error by using the Visual Basic Err object. You can also iterate over the Errors collection of the Connection object involved in the ADO operation.

A

5. How do you delimit date values in an INSERT statement when dealing with Microsoft Access or SQL Server?

   You can use apostrophes to delimit date values in SQL statements for both Access and SQL Server. When using Access you also have the possibility to use pound signs to delimit date values.

Exercise

Write a script that inserts a new customer into the Customers table of the SQL Server Northwind database using an INSERT statement. The definition of the table is shown in Figure 3.13. Add some error handling code to prevent the script from terminating when your INSERT statement contains an error or violates any database rule— for example, the Primary Key constraint of the CustomerID column. When an error occurs, your script should read all errors from the Errors collection and present all properties of each Error object to the user.

Listing 3.11 provides a possible solution. The script is written in Visual Basic and uses the Debug.Print statement for presenting data to the user.

LISTING 3.11 Inserting a New Customer into the Customers Tables Using the INSERT Statement and Error Handling

```
 1: Dim conn As ADODB.Connection
 2: Dim ConnError As ADODB.Error
 3: Dim strSQL As String
 4: Dim strDescription As String
 5: Dim lngNumber As Long
 6: Dim strSource As String
 7:
 8: Set conn = CreateObject("ADODB.Connection")
 9: conn.Open "Provider=SQLOLEDB;Data Source=BoyScout;" & _
10:     "Initial Catalog=Northwind;User ID=sa;Password=;"
11:
12: strSQL = "INSERT Customers (CustomerID, CompanyName, " & _
13:     "ContactName, ContactTitle, Address, City, Region, " & _
14:     "PostalCode, Country, Phone, Fax) " & _
15:     "VALUES ('ALEIN', 'Albert Einstein''s', " & _
16:     "'Albert Einstein', 'Owner', 'Energy Drv 1', " & _
17:     "'Vienna', 'Vienna', '1150', 'Austria', " & _
18:     "'01 1503', '')"
19:
20: Debug.Print strSQL
21:
22: On Error Resume Next
23: conn.Errors.Clear
24:
```

```
25: conn.Execute strSQL
26:
27: If conn.Errors.Count > 0 Then
28:     Debug.Print "The following errors occured:"
29:     Debug.Print
30:     For Each ConnError In conn.Errors
31:         strDescription = ConnError.Description
32:         lngNumber = ConnError.Number
33:         strSource = ConnError.Source
34:         Debug.Print "Description: " & strDescription
35:         Debug.Print "Source: " & strSource
36:         Debug.Print "Error Number" & lngNumber
37:         Debug.Print ""
38:     Next
39: End If
40: On Error GoTo 0
41:
42: conn.Close
43: Set conn = Nothing
```

Answers for Day 4

Quiz

1. When you want to delete all records from the Products table (see Figure 4.5) that contain the `SupplierID=8`, which SQL statement performs this task?

FIGURE A.1

Definition of the Products table.

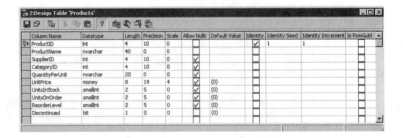

The SQL DELETE statement looks as follows:

```
DELETE FROM Products WHERE SupplierID = 8
```

Note

When you want to execute the DELETE statement against the Northwind database, you will get an error because of the Foreign Relationship defined in the database. You would have to delete all records that have a reference to the products with the SupplierID 8.

2. What are the two locking types that can be used when you want to prepare an updateable Recordset?

The two locking types are optimistic locking (for immediate update mode) and batch optimistic locking (for batch update mode).

3. Design a SQL statement that increases the number of UnitsInStock by 5 for the product ProductID=17. The products are stored in the Products table.

The resulting SQL statement looks as follows:

```
UPDATE Products SET UnitsInStock=UnitsInStock+5 WHERE ProductID=17
```

Exercises

1. Write a script that updates the database record of the Products table with the ProductID 14 so that its UnitsInStock value is set to 25. Use a SQL statement to change the value.

The SQL statement used is the following:

```
UPDATE Products SET UnitsInStock=25 WHERE ProductID=14
```

And a possible solution for the script is presented here:

```
1: Dim conn As ADODB.Connection
2: Dim strSQL As String
3:
4: Set conn = CreateObject("ADODB.Connection")
5: conn.Open "Provider=SQLOLEDB;Data Source=BoyScout;" & _
6:     "Initial Catalog=Northwind;User ID=sa;Password=;"
7:
8: strSQL = "UPDATE Products SET UnitsInStock=25 WHERE ProductID=14"
9:
10: conn.Execute strSQL
11:
12: conn.Close
13: Set conn = Nothing
```

2. Write a script that prepares a Recordset for batch optimistic locking and populates the Recordset with all products from the Products table that have the SupplierID 8. Let the script increase the Unitprice for all products in the Recordset by $2 when the UnitsInStock value is lower than 5 and the value in the column UnitsOnOrder is greater than 10. When more than two product Records are changed, the script should write all pending changes to the database.

The following script is a possible solution:

```
1: Dim conn As ADODB.Connection
2: Dim rs As ADODB.Recordset
3: Dim strSQL As String
```

```
 4: Dim lngRecords As Long
 5:
 6: strSQL = "SELECT * FROM Products WHERE SupplierID=8"
 7:
 8: Set conn = CreateObject("ADODB.Connection")
 9: conn.Open "Provider=SQLOLEDB;Data Source=BoyScout;" & _
10:     "Initial Catalog=Northwind;User ID=sa;Password=;"
11:
12: Set rs = CreateObject("ADODB.Recordset")
13: rs.LockType = adLockBatchOptimistic
14: rs.CursorType = adOpenStatic
15: rs.Open strSQL, conn
16:
17: lngRecords = 0
18: While Not rs.EOF
19:     If rs("UnitsInStock") < 5 And rs("UnitsOnOrder") > 10 Then
20:         rs("Unitprice") = rs("Unitprice") + 2
21:         lngRecords = lngRecords + 1
22:     End If
23:     rs.MoveNext
24: Wend
25:
26: If lngRecords > 2 Then
27:     rs.UpdateBatch
28:     Debug.Print lngRecords & " records have been changed."
29: Else
30:     rs.CancelBatch
31:     Debug.Print "No record has been changed."
32: End If
33:
34: rs.Close
35: conn.Close
36: Set rs = Nothing
37: Set conn = Nothing
```

Answers for Day 5

Quiz

1. Which of the following search strings cannot be used as an argument for the Find method of the recordset?

   ```
   1: "Product = 'Server"
   2: "UserID >= 7"
   3: "Weight < 140"
   4: "ShippingDate = 9/30/1997"
   5: "FirstName like '*ith'"
   6: "LastName like 'Wil*'"
   7: "Title = 'Good Morning Vietnam'"
   ```

In line 1, the closing apostrophe (') for the string value is missing:

```
Wrong:    "Product = 'Server"
Correct: "Product = 'Server'"
```

In line 4, the date must be delimited by pound signs(#):

```
Wrong:    "ShippingDate = 9/30/1997"
Correct: "ShippingDate = #9/30/1997#"
```

In line 5, an asterisk can be used only at the end of the string value or at the beginning and the end of the string value:

```
Wrong:    "FirstName like '*ith'"
Correct: "FirstName like '*ith*'"
```

2. When you apply a filter string to the `Filter` property of the `Recordset` object, which one of the following filter strings is invalid?

```
1: "LastName = 'o'Conner'"
2: "FirstName = '*imson*'"
3: "Title like 'Teach yourself *'"
4: "(Age = 7 OR Age = 28) AND (Name = 'Chris')"
5: "LastName like 'Hom*'"
6: "City > 'Springf'"
```

In line 1, the apostrophe of the string value must be replaced by two apostrophes:

```
Wrong:    "LastName = 'o'Conner'"
Correct: "LastName = 'o''Conner'"
```

In line 2, the equal operator must be replaced by the like operator when you want to search for all values in the column Firstname that contain the string `imson`:

```
Wrong:    "FirstName = '*imson*'"
Correct: "FirstName like '*imson*'"
```

Line 4 cannot be used as in the presented form. The `AND` operator cannot concatenate clauses that contain the `OR` operator. This is a limitation of the `Filter` property:

```
Wrong:    "(Age = 7 OR Age = 28) AND (Name = 'Chris')"
Correct: "(Age = 7 AND Name = 'Chris') OR  (Age = 28 AND Name = 'Chris')"
```

3. You want to use an Array of bookmarks in conjunction with the `Filter` property of the `Recordset` object. The array named `arrA` is defined as a static Visual Basic array with a statement as follows:

```
Dim arrA(20)
```

Assuming that all elements with the array indexes 1–19 contain valid bookmarks, what can you do to filter your recordset using the array named `arrA`?

You can assign an array of bookmarks to the `Filter` property only when all elements of the array contain valid bookmarks. The elements of the array `arrA` with the indexes `0` and `20` do not contain a valid bookmark. Therefore, you have two possibilities.

The first possibility is to build an array that contains all elements with valid book-marks, as in the following line:

```
rs.Filer = Array(arrA(1), arrA(2), arrA(3) ... arrA(19))
```

The other possibility is to assign valid bookmarks that already exist in the array to the elements with the indexes 0 and 20, as shown in the following lines:

```
arrA(0) = arrA(1)
arrA(20) = arrA(1)
rs.Filter = arrA
```

4. You are using the following lines of code in an application to populate a recordset named rs. Then you want to use the Sort property to sort the retrieved recordset. However, using the Sort property results in an error. Please correct the code so that it is possible to use the Sort method:

```
1: strSQL = "SELECT FirstName, LastName, City FROM Employees"
2: Set rs = CreateObject("ADODB.Recordset")
3: rs.CursorLocation = adUseClient
4: rs.LockType = adLockReadOnly
5: rs.CursorType = adOpenStatic
6: Set rs = conn.Execute(strSQL)
7:
8: ' Sorting the Recordset fails ...
9: rs.Sort = "LastName"
```

The Sort property fails because in line 9 the recordset, which is stored in the variable rs, has in fact a server-side cursor. You can use the Sort property only with a client-side cursor!

You might think that you have prepared the recordset in line 3 to use a client-side cursor. That is true, but in line 6 you assign an entirely new Recordset object to the variable rs. This new Recordset object is supplied by the Execute method of the Connection object and has nothing in common with the Recordset object stored in the variable rs in lines 2–5.

The correct code, where the prepared Recordset object is used to hold the Recordset delivered by the SQL statement stored in the variable strSQL, is the following:

```
1: strSQL = "SELECT FirstName, LastName, City FROM Employees"
2: Set rs = CreateObject("ADODB.Recordset")
3: rs.CursorLocation = adUseClient
4: rs.LockType = adLockReadOnly
5: rs.CursorType = adOpenStatic
6: rs.Open strSQL, conn
7:
8: ' Sorting the Recordset succeeds ...
9: rs.Sort = "LastName"
```

Exercise

Write a script that retrieves a recordset with all records from the Employees table of the SQL Server 7.0 Northwind sample database. Let the script filter the recordset using the Filter property with a Filterstring. The filtered recordset should contain all records with a value such as Sales* in the Title column. Then find the first record that contains the value King in the LastName field of the record. Write the values of the following columns of the matching record to the user: Title, LastName, FirstName.

A possible solution, written in Visual Basic for applications, is as follows:

```
 1: Dim conn As ADODB.Connection
 2: Dim rs As ADODB.Recordset
 3: Dim strSQL As String
 4: Dim strSearch As String
 5:
 6: Set conn = CreateObject("ADODB.Connection")
 7: conn.Open "Provider=SQLOLEDB;Data Source=BoyScout;" & _
 8:    "Initial Catalog=Northwind;User ID=sa;Password=;"
 9:
10: Set rs = CreateObject("ADODB.Recordset")
11: strSQL = "SELECT * FROM Employees"
12: rs.CursorLocation = adUseClient
13: rs.Open strSQL, conn
14:
15: rs.Filter = "Title like 'Sales*'"
16: rs.MoveFirst
17: strSearch = "LastName = 'King'"
18: rs.Find strSearch, 0, adSearchForward
19:
20: Debug.Print rs("Title") & " " & rs("LastName") & _
21:      " " & rs("FirstName")
22:
23: rs.Close
24: conn.Close
25: Set rs = Nothing
26: Set conn = Nothing
```

Answers for Day 6

Quiz

1. What properties and methods does the Recordset object provide to enable dividing a recordset into several pages?

Using the PageSize property, you can set the number of records per page (the default value is 10 records per page). You can read the number of the current page or jump to the first record of a page using the `AbsolutePage` property. The number of pages in the recordset can be retrieved from the `PageCount` property. Note that the database provider must support paging when you want to use the built-in paging methods and properties of the recordset.

2. What methods can you use to navigate in a recordset?

    You can use all `Move` methods (`Move`, `MoveFirst`, `MoveLast`, `MoveNext`, and `MovePrevious`) to move the position of the recordset cursor. You can set the ordinal position of a certain record or set the cursor to an ordinal position using the `AbsolutePosition` property. To refer to a certain record, even if the order of the records in the recordset is changed, you can use the `Bookmark` property.

3. What property do you have to use when you want to find a specific record fast?

    Use the `Bookmark` property to store the position of a certain record. To find a certain record, you can use the `Find` method or similar methods and properties.

4. What can happen if you have a filtered recordset and you want to jump to a certain record using the `Bookmark` property?

    You have to consider whether the record is still in the currently visible recordset. The record referred to in the bookmark can be deleted, or the record can be invisible when the recordset is filtered (using the `Filter` property).

5. What does the `AbsolutePosition` property return, and what else can you use the `AbsolutePosition` property for?

    The `AbsolutePosition` property returns the ordinal position of the current record in the visible recordset. If the `AbsolutePosition` returns a number smaller than zero, it indicates that the recordset cursor points to EOF or BOF, or that the recordset cursor's position is unknown.

6. How can you determine the number of records in the current recordset?

    You can read the `RecordCount` property to determine the number of records in the currently visible recordset. When the `RecordCount` property returns -1, the number of records cannot be determined. Note that you should use a static or keyset recordset when you want to use the `RecordCount` property.

Exercise

Rewrite Listing 6.3 (simple paging through a recordset) so that the user can also jump to the first and the last page. In addition, include the feature that enables the user to jump 5 pages forward or backward at once.

A possible solution is provided in the following listing:

```
1: Dim conn As ADODB.Connection
2: Dim rs As ADODB.Recordset
```

```
 3: Dim strSQL As String
 4: Dim lngPageSize As Long
 5: Dim lngCount As Long
 6: Dim lngCurrentPage As Long
 7: Dim strInput As String
 8: Dim lngInput As Long
 9: Dim strPaging As String
10: Dim blnInputOK As Boolean
11: Dim blnPaging As Boolean
12:
13: Set conn = CreateObject("ADODB.Connection")
14: conn.Open "Provider=SQLOLEDB;Data Source=BoyScout;" & _
15:    "Initial Catalog=Northwind;User ID=sa;Password=;"
16:
17: Set rs = CreateObject("ADODB.Recordset")
18: strSQL = "SELECT ProductID, ProductName, SupplierID, CategoryID, " & _
19:    "QuantityPerUnit, UnitPrice, UnitsInStock, UnitsOnOrder, " & _
20:    "ReorderLevel, Discontinued FROM Products ORDER BY ProductID"
21:
22: rs.CursorLocation = adUseServer
23: rs.CursorType = adOpenStatic
24: rs.LockType = adLockReadOnly
25: rs.PageSize = 10
26: rs.CacheSize = 11 'rs.PageSize + 1
27:
28: Set rs.ActiveConnection = conn
29: rs.Open strSQL
30:
31: blnInputOK = False
32: While blnInputOK = False
33:     strInput = InputBox("Records per page (1-100)?" & vbCrLf & _
34:     "(0 = Exit)", "Paging in recordset", "10")
35:     strInput = Trim(strInput)
36:     If strInput = "0" Then Exit Function
37:     If IsNumeric(strInput) Then
38:         lngInput = CLng(strInput)
39:         If lngInput >= 1 And lngInput <= 100 Then
40:             blnInputOK = True
41:         End If
42:     End If
43: Wend
44:
45: rs.PageSize = lngInput
46: rs.CacheSize = rs.PageSize + 1
47:
48: ' Begin Paging
49:
50: strPaging = "first"
51:
52: blnPaging = True
53: While (blnPaging = True)
```

```
54:     Select Case strPaging
55:         Case "first"
56:             lngCurrentPage = 1
57:         Case "last"
58:             lngCurrentPage = rs.PageCount
59:         Case "forward"
60:             lngCurrentPage = lngCurrentPage + 1
61:         Case "backward"
62:             lngCurrentPage = lngCurrentPage - 1
63:         Case "5_backward"
64:             lngCurrentPage = lngCurrentPage - 5
65:         Case "5_forward"
66:             lngCurrentPage = lngCurrentPage + 5
67:     End Select
68:     ' Check range of page number
69:     If lngCurrentPage < 1 Then
70:         lngCurrentPage = 1
71:     ElseIf lngCurrentPage > rs.PageCount Then
72:         lngCurrentPage = rs.PageCount
73:     End If
74:
75:     ' Set page
76:     rs.AbsolutePage = lngCurrentPage
77:
78:     Debug.Print "Current page: " & rs.AbsolutePage & " / " &
➥ rs.PageCount
79:     Debug.Print "Records on page: " & rs.PageSize
80:     Debug.Print
81:
82:     ' Show records of the page
83:     lngCount = 1
84:     Debug.Print "Absolute", "Position", "Pages", "Name"
85:     Debug.Print "Position", "on Page"
86:     While (Not rs.EOF) And (lngCount <= rs.PageSize)
87:         Debug.Print rs.AbsolutePosition, lngCount, _
88:         rs.PageCount, rs("ProductName")
89:
90:         rs.MoveNext
91:         lngCount = lngCount + 1
92:     Wend
93:     Debug.Print "- - - - - - - - - - - - - - - - - - - - - -"
94:     blnInputOK = False
95:     While blnInputOK = False
96:         strInput = InputBox("Navigate in the recordset." & vbCrLf & _
97:         "1: Page backward" & vbCrLf & "2: Page forward" & vbCrLf & _
98:         "4: Go 5 Pages backward" & vbCrLf & "5: Go 5 Pages forward" &_
99:         vbCrLf & _
100:        "7: Go to First Page" & vbCrLf & "8: Go to Last Page" & _
101:        vbCrLf & _
102:        "0: End paging", "Paging in recordset", "2")
103:        strInput = Trim(strInput)
```

```
104:          Select Case strInput
105:             Case "1"
106:                strPaging = "backward"
107:                blnInputOK = True
108:             Case "2"
109:                strPaging = "forward"
110:                blnInputOK = True
111:             Case "4"
112:                strPaging = "5_backward"
113:                blnInputOK = True
114:             Case "5"
115:                strPaging = "5_forward"
116:                blnInputOK = True
117:             Case "7"
118:                strPaging = "first"
119:                blnInputOK = True
120:             Case "8"
121:                strPaging = "last"
122:                blnInputOK = True
123:             Case "0"
124:                blnPaging = False
125:                blnInputOK = True
126:          End Select
127:       Wend
128: Wend
```

Answers for Day 7

Quiz

1. What is characteristic of the name of a variable or parameter in a stored procedure?

   A variable or parameter name begins with an at-sign (@).

2. Can a stored procedure return a recordset?

   A stored procedure can, of course, return one or more recordsets. You just have to call SELECT statements in the stored procedures that build the recordsets.

3. In which language is a stored procedure for a SQL Server database written?

   A stored procedure for a SQL Server database is written in T-SQL (Transact-SQL), the SQL version that is used in SQL Server databases.

4. What kind of data cannot be used as values for stored procedure output parameters?

   You cannot use data of the SQL Server data type text, ntext, or image as values for output parameters.

Exercises

1. Write a script in Visual Basic or VBScript that executes the SQL Server 7.0 stored
    procedure `LastShippingAustria` (see Listing 7.4) and reads its output parameter.

    A possible solution, written in Visual Basic, is as follows:

    ```
     1: Dim conn As ADODB.Connection
     2: Dim cmd As ADODB.Command
     3: Dim Param As ADODB.Parameter
     4:
     5: Set conn = CreateObject("ADODB.Connection")
     6: conn.Open "Provider=SQLOLEDB;Data Source=BoyScout;" & _
     7:    "Initial Catalog=Northwind;User ID=sa;Password=;"
     8:
     9: Set cmd = CreateObject("ADODB.Command")
    10:
    11: cmd.CommandText = "LastShippingAustria"
    12: cmd.CommandType = adCmdStoredProc
    13: Set cmd.ActiveConnection = conn
    14:
    15: Set Param = cmd.CreateParameter("ShippedDate", adDate,
    ➥ adParamOutput, 8)
    16: cmd.Parameters.Append Param
    17:
    18: cmd.Execute
    19:
    20: If Not IsNull(cmd.Parameters("ShippedDate")) Then
    21:    Debug.Print "Date: " & cmd.Parameters("ShippedDate")
    22: Else
    23:    Debug.Print "No Date found."
    24: End If
    25:
    26: conn.Close
    27: Set cmd = Nothing
    28: Set Param = Nothing
    29: Set conn = Nothing
    ```

    When the stored procedure does not find any value in the `ShipCountry` column of
    the `Orders` table with the value `Austria` in the `SELECT` statement, the output para-
    meter contains no valid value (`NULL`). This case is checked in the line 20 of the
    script using the Visual Basic function `IsNull`.

2. Write a stored procedure that uses one input parameter named `@EmployeeID`.
    Return the number of orders from the Northwind `Orders` table in the output para-
    meter `@OrdersTotal` that have the same value in the column `EmployeeID` as the
    value in the parameter `@EmployeeID`. Also return a recordset that contains all the
    records that have the value of the variable `@EmployeeID` in the column `EmployeeID`.
    The data type of the parameter `@EmployeeID` is the same as of the column

EmployeeID in the Orders table (SQL Server data type int). Note that you can use the T-SQL function COUNT to get the number of records:

```
SELECT COUNT(*) WHERE Condition
```

A possible solution for the stored procedure looks as follows:

```
1: CREATE PROCEDURE CountOrders
2:    @EmployeeID int,
3:    @OrdersTotal int OUTPUT
4: AS
5:
6: SELECT @OrdersTotal=COUNT(*) FROM Orders
7:    WHERE EmployeeID=@EmployeeID
8: SELECT * FROM Orders WHERE EmployeeID=@EmployeeID
```

The Visual Basic code to call the stored procedure CountOrders might look as follows:

```
 1: Dim conn As ADODB.Connection
 2: Dim cmd As ADODB.Command
 3: Dim Param As ADODB.Parameter
 4: Dim lngEmpID As Long
 5:
 6: lngEmpID = 4
 7: Set conn = CreateObject("ADODB.Connection")
 8: conn.Open "Provider=SQLOLEDB;Data Source=BoyScout;" & _
 9:    "Initial Catalog=Northwind;User ID=sa;Password=;"
10:
11: Set cmd = CreateObject("ADODB.Command")
12:
13: cmd.CommandText = "CountOrders"
14: cmd.CommandType = adCmdStoredProc
15: Set cmd.ActiveConnection = conn
16:
17: Set Param = cmd.CreateParameter("EmployeeID", adInteger,
➡ adParamInput, 8, lngEmpID)
18: cmd.Parameters.Append Param
19:
20: Set Param = cmd.CreateParameter("TotalOrders", adInteger,
➡ adParamOutput, 8)
21: cmd.Parameters.Append Param
22:
23: cmd.Execute
24:
25: Debug.Print "Number of Orders: " & cmd.Parameters("TotalOrders")
26:
27: conn.Close
28: Set cmd = Nothing
29: Set Param = Nothing
```

Answers for Day 8

Quiz

1. You are using two database connections in a script at the same time. When using methods of only the ADO Connection object, can you enforce a transaction that covers the database tasks executed against both connections?

   It is not possible to include two connections in one transaction using methods of the ADO Connection object. This is clear when you see that calling methods of a Connection object affect only that particular connection.

   However, COM+ supports transactions that span multiple database connections.

2. When using Active Server Pages, how can you easily wrap two different database connections in one transaction?

   Using the TRANSACTION directive in the first line of an Active Server Pages script automatically wraps all objects that support transactions in an ASP page-level transaction. Therefore, all database changes performed by database providers capable of transactions are included in the ASP page-level transaction.

3. Is it possible to enforce a transaction on every data source connection when using the methods of the ADO Connection object?

   It is not possible to enforce transactions on every data source. You can use transactions only against ADO data source providers that can manage transactions, such as the OLE DB Provider for SQL Server, or the OLE DB Provider for Jet (Access database).

Exercises

1. Change Listing 8.6 ("Enforcing Transaction Using T-SQL Statements") so that the first INSERT statement is encapsulated in a SQL Server transaction named InnerTransaction.

   The following script provides a possible solution:

```
 1: Dim conn As ADODB.Connection
 2: Dim rs As ADODB.Recordset
 3: Dim lngOrderID As Long
 4: Dim lngProductID As Long
 5: Dim lngEmployeeID As Long
 6: Dim lngUnits As Long
 7: Dim curUnitPrice As Currency
 8: Dim blnCommit As Boolean
 9:
10: lngEmployeeID = 3
11: lngProductID = 14
```

A

```
12: curUnitPrice = 24.25
13: lngUnits = 5
14: blnCommit = False    ' Set to True to perform updates
15:
16: Set conn = CreateObject("ADODB.Connection")
17: conn.Open "Provider=SQLOLEDB;Data Source=BoyScout;" & _
18:    "Initial Catalog=Northwind;User ID=sa;Password=;"
19:
20: ' Begin transaction
21: conn.Execute "BEGIN TRANSACTION MyTransaction"
22:
23: ' Insert record
24: conn.Execute "BEGIN TRANSACTION InnerTransaction"
25: conn.Execute "INSERT INTO Orders (EmployeeID, OrderDate) " & _
26:    "VALUES(" & lngEmployeeID & ",'" & CStr(Now) & "')"
27: conn.Execute "COMMIT TRANSACTION InnerTransaction"
28:
29: ' Get Identity column value of last insert
30: Set rs = conn.Execute("SELECT @@IDENTITY AS OrderID")
31: lngOrderID = rs("OrderID")
32: rs.Close
33:
34:
35: ' Insert record
36: conn.Execute "INSERT INTO [Order Details] " & _
37:    "(OrderID, ProductID, UnitPrice, Quantity) " & _
38:    "VALUES(" & lngOrderID & "," & lngProductID & "," & _
39:    curUnitPrice & "," & lngUnits & ")"
40:
41: ' Commit or cancel all database changes
42: If blnCommit = True Then
43:    conn.Execute "COMMIT TRANSACTION MyTransaction"
44:    Debug.Print "Order with Order ID = " & lngOrderID & _
45:    " inserted into database."
46: Else
47:    conn.Execute "ROLLBACK TRANSACTION MyTransaction"
48:    Debug.Print "Order with Order ID = " & lngOrderID & _
49:    " was canceled."
50: End If
51:
52: conn.Close
```

2. Write a script that connects to the SQL Server 7.0 Northwind database. In the
   Products table, lower the value in the UnitsInStock field by 105 in the record with
   the ProductID = 6. Retrieve the new value of the field UnitsInStock. When it is
   lower than 20, abort the transaction, cancel all changes, and write a message to the
   user. When the values is 20 at minimum, commit the transaction and save the
   changes.

Here is a possible script:

```
1: Dim conn As ADODB.Connection
2: Dim rs As ADODB.Recordset
3: Dim lngProductID As Long
4: Dim lngUnits As Long
5: Dim blnCommit As Boolean
6:
7: lngProductID = 6
8: lngUnits = -105
9: blnCommit = False
10:
11: Set conn = CreateObject("ADODB.Connection")
12: conn.Open "Provider=SQLOLEDB;Data Source=BoyScout;" & _
13:     "Initial Catalog=Northwind;User ID=sa;Password=;"
14:
15: ' Begin transaction
16: conn.BeginTrans
17:
18: ' Update record
19: On Error Resume Next
20: conn.Execute "UPDATE Products SET UnitsInStock = UnitsInStock + (" & _
21:     CStr(lngUnits) & ") WHERE ProductID = " & lngProductID
22:
23:
24: Set rs = conn.Execute("SELECT UnitsInStock FROM Products " & _
25:     "WHERE ProductID = " & lngProductID)
26:
27: If Not rs.EOF Then
28:     If rs("UnitsInStock") >= 20 Then
29:         blnCommit = True
30:     End If
31: End If
32: rs.Close
33:
34: ' Commit or cancel all database changes
35: If blnCommit = True Then
36:     conn.CommitTrans
37: Else
38:     conn.RollbackTrans
39:     Debug.Print "Database changes are rolled back."
40: End If
41:
42: conn.Close
```

Answers for Day 9

Quiz

1. What do you have to check before you use a connection that was opened asynchronously?

   Before you can use a connection, you have to check whether the connection is fully opened. A Connection object (conn) is opened when its State property returns adStateOpen.

   Check whether the connection conn is open:

   ```
   ...
   If conn.State = adStateOpen Then
      ' Perform actions
      ...
   Else
      ' Raise Error
      ...
   End If
   ...
   ```

   Wait until the connection conn is open:

   ```
   ...
   While conn.State <> adStateOpen
   Wend
   ' Perform actions
   ...
   ```

2. What name do you have to use for the WillConnect event handler subroutine when using the following definitions for the Connection object:Dim conn As New ADODB.

   ```
   Connection Dim WithEvents connEvent As ADODB.Connection
   ```

   Assume that the script uses the Connection object named conn to perform the ADO actions.

   Enable events using a statement as follows:

   ```
   Set connEvents = conn
   ```

   Then you can use the Connection object connEvent to trigger the events for the actions of the Connection object named conn. Therefore, the name for the WillConnect event handler sub of the connection conn is connEvent_WillConnect.

3. Provide the name of the WillChangeField event handler subroutine for the recordset objRs, which is defined as follows:

   ```
   Dim WithEvents objRs as ADODB.Recordset
   ```

   The name for the event handler is objRs_WillChangeField.

4. Listing 9.13 does not execute the event handler subroutine named
    rs_EndOfRecordset. Change the script so that the event handler sub is executed.

LISTING 9.13   No Events Are Triggered

```
 1: Dim rs As New ADODB.Recordset
 2: Dim WithEvents rsEvent As ADODB.Recordset
 3:
 4: Sub NoEvents()
 5:     Dim conn As New ADODB.Connection
 6:
 7:     On Error GoTo NoEventsError
 8:
 9:     conn.Open "Provider=SQLOLEDB;Data Source=BoyScout;" & _
10:     "Initial Catalog=Northwind", "sa", ""
11:
12:     Set rsEvent = rs    ' Enable event handler
13:     Set rs = conn.Execute("SELECT * FROM Customers")
14:
15:     While Not rs.EOF
16:         Debug.Print rs("CustomerID"), rs("CompanyName")
17:         rs.MoveNext
18:     Wend
19:
20:     rs.Close
21:     conn.Close
22:     Set conn = Nothing
23:     Set rs = Nothing
24:     Exit Sub
25:
26: NoEventsError:
27:     Debug.Print err.Description
28:     Debug.Print err.Source
29: End Sub
30:
31: ' Recordset Events:
32: Private Sub rs_EndOfRecordset(fMoreData As Boolean, adStatus As _
33:     ADODB.EventStatusEnum, ByVal pRecordset As ADODB.Recordset)
34:     Debug.Print "> Recordset EndOfRecordset event was triggered."
35: End Sub
```

First, you have to change line 13 of Listing 9.13. In this line, the variable rs is
overwritten with the Recordset object returned by the conn.Execute method; no
more events are enabled because the variable rs refers to another Recordset
object, as in line 12. Change line 13 to the following statement:

```
13:     rs.Open "SELECT * FROM Customers", conn
```

As the connection event object named rsEvent triggers the events, which are
caused by actions performed on the connection conn, the name of the event handler
in line 32 has to be changed to rsEvent_EndOfRecordset.

Exercises

1. Rewrite Listing 9.5 so that only one object named objConn is used instead of the objects named conn and connEvent. Of course, the object objConn should support events so that the function of the code remains the same.

   Listing 9.14 is a possible solution for the rewritten code of Listing 9.5.

LISTING 9.14   ADO Connection Object and Events

```
 1: Option Explicit
 2:
 3: Dim WithEvents objConn As ADODB.Connection
 4:
 5: Sub MyMethodSync()
 6:     ' Enable Error handling
 7:     On Error GoTo MyMethodSyncError
 8:
 9:     Debug.Print "Begin MyClass.MyMethodSync()"
10:     Set objConn = New ADODB.Connection
11:
12:     Debug.Print "Opening connection synchronously..."
13:     ' Open connection synchronously
14:     objConn.Open "MyNorthwind", "admin", ""
15:     ' objConn.Open "Provider=SQLOLEDB;Data Source=BoyScout;" & _
16:       "Initial Catalog=Northwind", "sa", ""
17:     Debug.Print "Connection was opened synchronously..."
18:
19:     ' ...
20:
21:     Debug.Print "Closing Connection..."
22:     objConn.Close                    ' Close Connection
23:     Debug.Print "Connection was closed..."
24:
25:     Debug.Print "End MyClass.MyMethodSync()"
26:     Exit Sub
27: MyMethodSyncError:
28:     Debug.Print "Run-time Error in MyMethodSync!"
29:     Debug.Print err.Description
30:     Debug.Print err.Source
31: End Sub
32:
33: Private Sub objConn_InfoMessage(ByVal pError As ADODB.Error, _
34:   adStatus As ADODB.EventStatusEnum, _
35:   ByVal pConnection As ADODB.Connection)
36:     Debug.Print
37:     Debug.Print "Connection InfoMessage was triggered."
38:     Debug.Print "Error Description: " & pError.Description
39:     Debug.Print "Error Source: " & pError.Source
40:
```

continues

```
41:      Debug.Print "Connection Status Number: " & adStatus
42:      Debug.Print
43: End Sub
44:
45: Private Sub objConn_WillConnect(ConnectionString As String, _
46: UserID As String, Password As String, Options As Long, _
47: adStatus As ADODB.EventStatusEnum, _
48: ByVal pConnection As ADODB.Connection)
49:
50:      Debug.Print "Connection WillConnect event was triggered."
51: End Sub
52:
53: Private Sub objConn_ConnectComplete(ByVal pError As _
54: ADODB.Error, adStatus As ADODB.EventStatusEnum, _
55: ByVal pConnection As ADODB.Connection)
56:      Debug.Print "Connection ConnectComplete event was triggered."
57: End Sub
58:
59: Private Sub objConn_Disconnect(adStatus As _
60: ADODB.EventStatusEnum, ByVal pConnection As ADODB.Connection)
61:      Debug.Print "Connection Disconnect event was triggered."
62: End Sub
```

> **Note**
>
> Pay attention to the fact that you also have to rename the event handler sub names, because the new Connection object that raises the events is named objConn.

2. Write a class module with the method named ADOAction. In the sub named ADOAction, the class module has to retrieve all records from the Employees table from the SQL Server 7.0 Northwind database. Open the connection asynchronously and fetch all records from the Employees table into a recordset named rsEmployees; use the Execute method of the Connection object with an SQL statement and the asynchronous option parameters adAsyncExecute and adAsyncFetch. Also, provide the option parameter adCmdText to indicate that the first parameter of the Execute method is a SQL statement, because this accelerates retrieving the recordset. Then write all values from the FirstName and the LastName field to the user.

   The code for the solution of the exercise, executed as a Visual Basic class module, might look like Listing 9.15.

A

LISTING 9.15 The ADOAction Method

```
 1: Option Explicit
 2:
 3: Sub ADOAction()
 4:     Dim rsEmployees As ADODB.Recordset
 5:     Dim conn As ADODB.Connection
 6:
 7:     ' Enable Error handling
 8:     On Error GoTo ADOActionError
 9:
10:     Set conn = New ADODB.Connection
11:     conn.Open "Provider=SQLOLEDB;Data Source=BoyScout;" & _
12:       "Initial Catalog=Northwind", "sa", "", adAsyncConnect
13:     While (conn.State And adStateOpen) = 0
14:         ' Wait and drink coffee
15:     Wend
16:
17:     ' Performing operations on the ADO connection:
18:     Set rsEmployees = conn.Execute("SELECT * FROM Employees", , _
19:         (adAsyncExecute Or adAsyncFetch Or adCmdText))
20:     While Not (rsEmployees.State = adStateOpen)
21:         ' Drink another coffee
22:     Wend
23:
24:     While Not rsEmployees.EOF
25:         Debug.Print rsEmployees("FirstName"), _
26:             rsEmployees("LastName")
27:         rsEmployees.MoveNext
28:     Wend
29:
30:     rsEmployees.Close
31:     Set rsEmployees = Nothing
32:     conn.close
33:     Set conn = Nothing
34:
35:     Exit Sub
36: ADOActionError:
37:     Debug.Print "Run-time Error in ADOAction!"
38:     Debug.Print err.Description
39:     Debug.Print err.Source
40: End Sub
```

Answers for Chapter 10

Quiz

1. Write down the SHAPE command for relating the Shippers table to the Orders table.

   This one was a bit tricky because the relationship between the Shippers table and the Orders table isn't obvious unless you examine the foreign key relationship—the ShipperID and ShipVia columns are related. Therefore, the SHAPE command has to look like:

   ```
   SHAPE { select * from Shippers }
   APPEND ({ select * from Orders }
   RELATE ShipperID to ShipVia) as rsOrders
   ```

2. When you issue a MovePrevious in the parent rowset of a parameterized hierarchy, will the child Recordset be fetched from the database server or taken from the cache?

   The default behavior for parameterized hierarchies is that, when MovePrevious is issued, the child Recordset's chapter is fetched from the cache, not re-executed at the database server. You can turn off caching by setting the Cache Child Rows property to False.

3. What is the difference between a service provider and a data provider?

   The Data Shaping service provider supplies the data-shaping functionality, whereas the data provider supplies rows of data to populate the shaped recordset.

4. Are the following two NEW statements equal?

   ```
   NEW adChar(20) AS myNewField
   NEW DBTYPE_BSTR(20) AS myNewField
   ```

   No, they are not equal. The ADO data type adChar compares to DBTYPE_STR.

5. Name at least two limitations to reshaping.

   The limitations are that you can only refer to Recordsets created in the same session only, that you cannot modify existing rowsets via an APPEND clause, and that you cannot reshape parameterized rowsets.

6. Why are parameterized hierarchies dependent on an active connection?

   The reason why parameterized rowsets are dependent on an active connection is that the child Recordsets are populated at the time when you move to a new parent row. Therefore, you cannot disconnect parameterized hierarchies from the database.

7. Which refreshing takes more network bandwidth: Requerying or Resynching?

   When you issue a Requery, new data for the child Recordsets (and dependent Recordsets) is requested from the database, which could incur—dependent on the size of the resultsets—quite a network load.

Exercise

Take the SHAPE command from Quiz Question 1 and output all field names and
data types in the Excel worksheet. It should be generalized to work with any level
of nesting.

A possible solution in Excel might look like the following listing:

```
 1: Option Explicit
 2:
 3: Sub ShowShape()
 4: On Error GoTo Err_ShowShape
 5:     Dim strShapeCmd As String, cn As ADODB.Connection, rs As
➥ADODB.Recordset
 6:     Dim nRowInSheet As Integer
 7:
 8:     strShapeCmd = "SHAPE { select * from Shippers } "
 9:     strShapeCmd = strShapeCmd & "APPEND ({ select * from Orders } "
10:     strShapeCmd = strShapeCmd & "RELATE ShipperID to ShipVia) as
➥rsOrders"
11:
12:     ' create the objects, and then open the connection
13:     Set cn = New ADODB.Connection
14:     Set rs = New ADODB.Recordset
15:     cn.Provider = "MSDataShape"
16:     cn.Open "data provider=sqloledb.1;user id=sa;password=;
➥initial catalog=northwind;data source=strangelove"
17:
18:     rs.Open strShapeCmd, cn
19:     ShowFields rs.Fields, nRowInSheet, 0
20:
21:     Exit Sub
22: Err_ShowShape:
23:     MsgBox Err.Description
24:     Exit Sub
25: End Sub
26:
27: Sub ShowFields(ByRef flds As ADODB.Fields, ByRef nRowInSheet As
Integer,
➥ByVal nNestDepth As Integer)
28:     Dim fld As ADODB.Field
29:     For Each fld In flds
30:         ActiveWorkbook.Worksheets(1).Cells(nRowInSheet + 1, nNestDepth
+ 1)
➥ = fld.Name & " " & fld.Type
31:         nRowInSheet = nRowInSheet + 1
32:         If adChapter = fld.Type Then
33:             ShowFields fld.Value.Fields, nRowInSheet, nNestDepth + 1
34:         End If
35:     Next
36: End Sub
```

Answers for Day 11

Quiz

1. What does the acronym *OLTP* stand for?

   OLTP stands for Online Transaction Processing. This is the kind of database used in the day-to-day operations of your business.

2. Which SQL Server 7 service lends itself for filling a data warehouse?

   The Data Transformation Services (DTS) that comes with SQL Server 7 enables easy and yet powerful transformations and data cleansing.

3. How are dimension tables and the fact table linked to each other?

   The fact table's primary key consists of foreign keys from the dimension tables.

4. Where is base data stored for the ROLAP dimensional storage option?

   With ROLAP storage, base data remains in the data mart.

5. Which schemas can you choose to relate facts and dimension tables?

   When you deal with simple dimensional data, you can create a star schema. The snowflake schema comes into the picture when your dimension tables are normalized.

6. When you design storage options, what are your options on deciding about the level of aggregation?

   The aggregation level can be limited either by a storage limit or a certain percentage of performance gain. You also can manually select the gain you want, and therefore limit the level of aggregation.

Answers for Day 12

Quiz

1. In case you omit the slicer specification, what is returned by OLAP Services?

   When you omit the slicer specifications (the WHERE clause), the default measure for the cube you are querying is returned.

2. Are the following two lines of code equal?
   ```
   Measures.MEMBERS ON AXIS(3)
   Measures.MEMBERS ON CHAPTERS
   ```

   Yes, these code lines are equal. AXIS(0) equals COLUMNS, AXIS(1) equals ROWS, AXIS(2) equals PAGES, AXIS(3) equals CHAPTERS, and AXIS(4) equals SECTIONS.

3. When you display the members of the Measures dimension on the COLUMNS axis, are there any obstacles you have to observe?

   There is one thing you have to observe—calculated members are not displayed by default. You have to add them by enclosing `Measures.MEMBERS` in the `ADDCALCU-LATEDMEMBERS()` function.

4. Is the following MDX statement valid?

```
SELECT [Product].[Product Family].MEMBERS ON COLUMNS,
       [Store].Store State.MEMBERS ON ROWS
FROM Sales
WHERE [Measures].[Profit]
```

   No, the MDX statement isn't valid. The square brackets for `Store State` are missing.

5. What are the differences between BDESC and DESC?

   The `BDESC` flag breaks the hierarchy; it arranges members in the set without regard to the hierarchy (descending, of course). The hierarchical ordering represented by `DESC` first arranges members according to their position in the hierarchy, and after that it orders each level.

6. Why would you want to cross-join sets?

   You cross-join sets to keep the dimension down to two, thus being able to present the results in a grid.

7. Do you need to open a `Cellset` object to get at cell data?

   Yes! The object you do not necessarily need is the `Catalog` object. `Cellset` is mandatory.

8. Which service creates the cube when you issue a `CREATE CUBE` statement?

   The PivotTable service is responsible for creating client-side cubes with the `CREATE CUBE` statement.

Exercises

1. Create the MDX expression that allows you to display sales profit as well as the change from month to month for the year of 1997. Hint: Use PREVMEMBER and DESCENDANTS.

   The solution to this exercise is the following:

```
WITH MEMBER [Measures].[Profit Increase] AS
  '[Measures].[Profit]-([Measures].[Profit], [Time].PREVMEMBER)',
  FORMAT_STRING='###,###.00'
SELECT {[Measures].[Profit],[Measures].[Profit Increase]} ON AXIS(0),
       DESCENDANTS([Time].[1997],[Month]) ON ROWS
FROM Sales
```

2. Your boss asks you to create a MDX query for him. He needs to query year to date sales monthly, for each product category in 1997. Hint: Use SUM, YTD and DESCENDANTS.

The solution to this exercise is:

```
WITH MEMBER [Measures].[Y2DateSales] AS
  'SUM(YTD(), [Measures].[Store Sales])',
  FORMAT_STRING='#.00'
SELECT DESCENDANTS([Time].[1997],[Month]) ON COLUMNS,
      Product.[Product Category].MEMBERS ON ROWS
FROM Sales
WHERE ([Measures].[Y2DateSales])
```

Answers for Day 13

Quiz

1. Which provider property do you need to query to obtain information about whether Record objects are supported?

   You must query the Hold Rows property to see whether the provider allows the user to retrieve records or change the position while holding previously retrieved records with pending changes.

2. What permissions do you need to set so users cannot upload script files?

   You must disable the Script source access permission (which is disabled by default).

3. Is the following a valid way to bind a resource to a Record object?
   ```
   cn.Open "URL=http://localhost/WebDAV/
   rec.Open "yourfile.txt", cn
   ```

   Yes, this is a perfectly correct way to open the file yourfile.txt in the directory WebDAV on the local machine.

4. What is the DAV: namespace equivalent for CHAPTERED_CHILDREN?

   There is no such equivalent. ADO provides information about chaptered children via the RecordType property, and access to the chaptered children recordset via the GetChildren method.

5. What is the most severe limitation of the Exchange OLE DB provider?

   You can use the ExOleDb provider only on the machine where the Webstore resides.

6. When searching the Webstore, why would you limit the dav:sql statement to deep traversal?

Doing a deep traversal is actually no limitation—it enables you to search a folder and all its subfolders for messages meeting the search criteria.

7. What `CreateOption` do you need to supply to `Record.Open` when creating a new public folder?

You have to pass `adCreateCollection` as the `CreateOption` parameter when creating a new public folder.

Exercise

Create a program that recursively dumps all files and folders of a Web site branch. Write it in a way so it could be easily used to traverse a public folder structure of an Exchange Web store.

The following is a possible solution to this problem:

```
1: Option Explicit
2:
3: Sub TraverseURLTree(ByVal strURLCurrent As String, _
4:                     ByVal nDepth As Integer, _
5:                     Optional ByRef nRow As Integer)
6:     Dim rec As ADODB.Record, rs As ADODB.Recordset
7:     Set rec = New ADODB.Record
8:
9:     rec.Open strURLCurrent, , adModeRead, adFailIfNotExists
10:     If rec.RecordType = adCollectionRecord Then
11:         Set rs = rec.GetChildren()
12:         While Not rs.EOF
13:             If (True = rs("RESOURCE_ISCOLLECTION")) Then
14:                 nRow = nRow + 1
15:                 Cells(nRow, nDepth) = "(+)" &
➥rs("RESOURCE_DISPLAYNAME")
16:                 TraverseURLTree strURLCurrent & "/" & _
17:                             rs("RESOURCE_PARSENAME"), _
18:                             nDepth + 1, nRow
19:             Else
20:                 nRow = nRow + 1
21:                 Cells(nRow, nDepth) = rs("RESOURCE_DISPLAYNAME")
22:             End If
23:             rs.MoveNext
24:         Wend
25:         Set rs = Nothing
26:     End If
27:     rec.Close
28:     Set rec = Nothing
29: End Sub
30:
31: Sub CallTree4DAV()
32:     Dim nRow As Integer
```

```
33:     Worksheets(1).Activate
34:     Cells.Clear
35:     TraverseURLTree "http://localhost/WebDAV", 1, nRow
36: End Sub
```

Answers for Day 14

Quiz

1. What is the limitation of using OpenSchema?

   With OpenSchema, you can only browse schema definitions—you cannot modify the schema.

2. Does the Jet OLE DB provider support the creation of new catalogs?

   Yes, the Jet OLE DB provider supports the creation of new catalogs. The necessary method call might look like this:

   ```
   cat.Create "Provider=Microsoft.Jet.OLEDB.4.0;Data Source=mydb.mdb"
   ```

3. What are dynamic properties? Why are they used in ADOX, and can you name one?

   Dynamic properties are properties that are specific to a provider. You can access dynamic properties via the Properties collection. A provider-specific property you used is the Autoincrement property which is used to create MS Access Autonumber fields.

4. When creating a primary key index, which important properties do you need to set?

   The properties you need to set for a unique primary key are: PrimaryKey (True), Unique (True) and IndexNulls (adIndexNullsDisallow).

5. What is the advantage of cascaded relational integrity?

   The big advantage is that when the parent column is updated, the child columns automatically receive the new value too, thus keeping the relationship intact.

6. Why do you need to reference the ADODB type library when creating views and procedures?

   The reason why you need to reference the ADODB library is that views and procedures are created with Command objects.

7. What does a connection string look like when you are administering security?

   To administer security, you must be able to access the workgroup database (system database). This security database is specified in the connection string as follows:

   ```
   cat.ActiveConnection = "Provider=Microsoft.Jet.OLEDB.4.0;" & _
       "Data Source=c:\new.mdb;" & _
       "jet oledb:system database=c:\system.mdw"
   ```

Exercise

Create a new catalog named mydb.mdb using the Jet OLE DB provider. Add a new table named "tExercise" to this catalog. This table contains the following columns: ExerciseID (Autonumber), Chapter (Integer), Description (VarChar, 255) and DifficultyLevel (Integer). ExerciseID is a primary key that does not allow Nulls.

To test the database, insert a row with following values: Chapter=14, Description=Create a new catalog, DifficultyLevel=0. Use INSERT INTO for the insert operation.

A possible solution to this problem is presented in the listing shown here:

```
1: Option Explicit
2:
3: Sub Exercise()
4:      Dim cat As ADOX.Catalog
5:      Dim tbl As ADOX.Table
6:      Dim col As ADOX.Column
7:      Dim idx As ADOX.Index
8:
9:      ' create the new catalog
10:     Set cat = New ADOX.Catalog
11:     cat.Create "Provider=Microsoft.Jet.OLEDB.4.0;Data
➥Source=c:\mydb.mdb"
12:
13:     ' create the table
14:     Set tbl = New ADOX.Table
15:     tbl.Name = "tExercise"
16:     cat.Tables.Append tbl
17:
18:     ' create the primary key column
19:     Set col = New ADOX.Column
20:     With col
21:         .Name = "ExerciseID"
22:         .Type = adInteger
23:     End With
24:     Set col.ParentCatalog = cat
25:     col.Properties("Autoincrement") = True
26:     tbl.Columns.Append col
27:
28:     ' create the primary key index
29:     Set idx = New ADOX.Index
30:     With idx
31:         .Name = "PrimaryKey"
32:         .IndexNulls = adIndexNullsDisallow
33:         .PrimaryKey = True
34:         .Unique = True
35:         .Columns.Append "ExerciseID"
36:     End With
```

```
37:        tbl.Indexes.Append idx
38:
39:        ' now add the remaining columns
40:        tbl.Columns.Append "Chapter", adInteger
41:        tbl.Columns.Append "Description", adVarWChar, 255
42:        tbl.Columns.Append "DifficultyLevel", adInteger
43:
44:        ' now try the new database
45:        Dim cn As ADODB.Connection
46:        Set cn = New ADODB.Connection
47:        cn.Open "Provider=Microsoft.Jet.OLEDB.4.0;Data Source=c:\mydb.mdb"
48:        cn.Execute "INSERT INTO
tExercise(Chapter,Description,DifficultyLevel)
➥ " & _
49:             " VALUES(14,'Create a new catalog',0)"
50:        cn.Close
51: End Sub
```

Answers for Chapter 15

Quiz

1. Why would you set the transaction level to Disabled?

   This setting tells COM+ to ignore any transactional requirements a component might have. You use this attribute to enforce compatibility for COM components that are not built for COM+ applications.

2. How do you set the Done bit in your component?

   The following piece of code sets the Done bit to `True` (enabling JIT deactivation of the component):

   `ctxState.SetDeactivateOnReturn True`

3. Which interface implements the `Construct` method that is used to pass the constructor string?

   The `IObjectConstruct` interface implements the `Construct` method.

4. Why should you never use the `Refresh` method on the `Parameters` collection of the `Command` object?

   Calling `Refresh` incurs a roundtrip to the server to fill in the `Parameters` collection. In a high-load scenario, this can easily turn out to be a major bottleneck.

5. What is the primary advantage of stateless components?

   The primary advantage is that stateless components can be reused via the JIT mechanism of COM+. This feature allows an application to serve more requests with the same resources.

6. Which type library do you need to reference in order to be able to use COM+ services?

In order to use COM+, you need to reference the COM+ Services Type Library.

Exercise

Create an entirely new component project named ADO25Exercise. Add a class named Browser, which supports transactions (but does not influence them) and has the following function:

```
GetRecordset(strSQL) As String
```

The String that is returned is the Recordset persisted using the Save function as XML (hint: use the Stream object and its ReadText function).

The connection string is passed via the component's constructor string.

The following code presents a possible solution to the problem:

```
 1: Option Explicit
 2:
 3: Implements IObjectConstruct
 4: Private m_strConnString As String
 5:
 6: Public Function GetRecordset(ByVal strSQL As String) As String
 7: On Error GoTo Err_GetRecordset
 8:     Dim cn As ADODB.Connection
 9:     Dim rs As ADODB.Recordset
10:
11:     Dim objCtx As ObjectContext
12:     Dim ctxState As IContextState
13:
14:     Set cn = New ADODB.Connection
15:     cn.Open m_strConnString
16:
17:     Set rs = New ADODB.Recordset
18:     rs.CursorLocation = adUseClient
19:     rs.LockType = adLockBatchOptimistic
20:     rs.CursorType = adOpenForwardOnly
21:
22:     ' open the recordset
23:     rs.Open strSQL, cn
24:
25:     ' create a new stream object and persist the rs to it
26:     Dim stm As New ADODB.Stream
27:     rs.Save stm, adPersistXML
28:
29:     ' and now read all the text and assign it to return value
30:     GetRecordset = stm.ReadText()
31:
32:     ' because we don't influence transactions, simply deactivate us
```

```
33:    Set objCtx = GetObjectContext()
34:    Set ctxState = objCtx
35:    ctxState.SetDeactivateOnReturn True
36:
37:    Exit Function
38:
39: Err_GetRecordset:
40:    ' same here: only deactivate, don't complain
41:    Set objCtx = GetObjectContext()
42:    Set ctxState = objCtx
43:    ctxState.SetDeactivateOnReturn True
44:
45:    ' tell the client about the error
46:    Err.Raise Err.Number, Err.Source, Err.Description
47: End Function
48:
49: Private Sub IObjectConstruct_Construct(ByVal pCtorObj As Object)
50:    m_strConnString = pCtorObj.ConstructString
51: End Sub
```

Answers for Day 16

Quiz

1. Which statement refreshes the `UnderlyingValues` of the recordset that is stored in the variable `rs`?

   You can refresh the `UnderlyingValues` of a recordset using the `Resync` method:
   ```
   rs.Filter = adFilterNone
   rs.Resync adAffectGroup, adResyncUnderlyingValues
   ```

2. How can ADO detect concurrency problems when you update disconnected record-sets and write them back in the database?

   Each recordset consists of three recordsets: They can be accessed using the `Value`, `OriginalValue`, and `UnderlyingValue` properties of the fields in the recordset. Through the values in the three recordsets, it is possible to check whether a record has been changed or whether the record in the underlying table has been changed or deleted. Through the `Status` property of each record you can also check whether the record was added to the recordset using the `AddNew` method, or whether the recordset could be updated using the `UpdateBatch` method.

3. What cursor type, cursor location, and lock type must a disconnected recordset have?

   A disconnected recordset must have a cursor type of static, its cursor location must be client-side, and its lock type must be batch optimistic locking.

4. What kind of columns should a recordset retrieve from a table when you want to change values in the recordset and write it back to the database?

When you want to write a record from a disconnected (or another client-side) recordset back to the database, it is strongly recommended that you also include all primary key values in the recordset. Otherwise, ADO cannot determine unequivocally to which record in the database table the record belongs, and the update may fail.

5. Which possibilities do you have to obtain a disconnected recordset with or without using a data source?

Without a data source, you can prepare a client-side recordset with a static cursor type and a batch optimistic locking. Then, you declare its fields, open the recordset, and add new records to it.

You can also retrieve a recordset from a database, a text file, or a persistent recordset from a disk. To disconnect the recordset from a database, you set its ActiveConnection property to Nothing.

Exercise

1. Write a script that adds two new records to the Customers table of the SQL 7.0 Northwind database. The two new records should have the values AAAAA and AABBB in the CustomerID column. Note that you also must provide a value in the CompanyName column.

Prepare a disconnected recordset and populate it with all records from the Customers table, where the CustomerID is less than the value ALF. Then disconnect the recordset and write the content and the Status property of each record to the user.

Use SQL statements to delete the record with the CustomerID AAAAA and change the record with the CustomerID AABBB in the database.

Add a new customer record with the CustomerID ALLLL to the disconnected recordset.

Reattach a connection to the disconnected recordset, enable error handling, and write the recordset's content to the database using the UpdateBatch method. When an error occurs during calling of the UpdateBatch method, write the error description to the user.

Set a filter to make only the records with conflicts during the call of the UpdateBatch method visible (the Filter property is set to the adFilterConflictingRecords argument). Write the Status property, the

CustomerID, and the CompanyName of each conflicting record to the user. Set a filter to view only affected records (adFilterAffectedRecords) and write all records that were affected by the call of the UpdateBatch to the user. Then remove the filter (set it to adFilterNone) and show the Status property, the CustomerID, and the CompanyName of all records from the recordset to the user.

Refresh the data of the recordset using the Resync method. Intercept any error that might appear and write all records (and their Status property) that had conflicts during the refresh to the user (use the Filter property with adFilterConflictingRecords). Then show the Status property values and some values of all records affected by the refresh using the Filter property with the argument adFilterAffectedRecords. Show the Status property of all records in the recordset.

Finally, delete the records from the Customers table, where the CustomerID is either AABBB or ALLLL.

Here is a possible solution written in Visual Basic:

```
 1: Dim rs As ADODB.Recordset
 2: Dim conn As ADODB.Connection
 3: Dim strSQL As String
 4:
 5: ' Create and Open Connection
 6: Set conn = CreateObject("ADODB.Connection")
 7: conn.Open "Provider=SQLOLEDB;Data Source=BoyScout;" & _
 8:     "Initial Catalog=Northwind;User ID=sa;Password=;"
 9:
10: ' Delete Customers AAAAA and AABBB if exist
11: conn.Execute "DELETE FROM Customers WHERE CustomerID = 'AAAAA' " & _
12:     "OR CustomerID = 'AABBB' OR CustomerID = 'ALLLL'"
13:
14: ' Insert Records into Table
15: conn.Execute "INSERT INTO Customers (CustomerID, CompanyName) " & _
16:     "VALUES('AAAAA','Alpha Company')"
17: conn.Execute "INSERT INTO Customers (CustomerID, CompanyName) " & _
18:     "VALUES('AABBB','Beta Company')"
19:
20:
21: ' Create Client-Side Recordset
22: Set rs = CreateObject("ADODB.Recordset")
23: rs.CursorLocation = adUseClient
24: rs.CursorType = adOpenStatic
25: rs.LockType = adLockBatchOptimistic
26:
27: ' Populate Fields of the Recordset
28: strSQL = "SELECT * FROM Customers WHERE CustomerID < 'ALF'"
29: rs.Open strSQL, conn
30:
```

A

```
31: ' Disconnect Recordset
32: Set rs.ActiveConnection = Nothing
33:
34: ' Show Recordset Content
35: Debug.Print "Local Recordset:"
36: rs.MoveFirst
37: While Not rs.EOF
38:     Debug.Print "Status Record " & rs.AbsolutePosition & _
39:     ": 0x" & Hex(rs.Status)
40:     Debug.Print rs("CustomerID") & " " & rs("CompanyName")
41:     rs.MoveNext
42: Wend
43: Debug.Print
44:
45: ' Delete Customer AAAAA from Database
46: conn.Execute "DELETE FROM Customers WHERE CustomerID = 'AAAAA'"
47: Debug.Print "Customer AAAAA Deleted from Database."
48: ' Change Customer AABBB in Database
49: conn.Execute "UPDATE Customers SET CompanyName = 'Gamma Company' " & _
50:     "WHERE CustomerID = 'AABBB'"
51: Debug.Print "Customer AABBB Changed in Database."
52: Debug.Print
53:
54: ' Change Customer AABBB in Disconnected Recordset
55: rs.MoveFirst
56: rs.Find "CustomerID = 'AABBB'"
57: If Not (rs.EOF) Then
58:     rs("CompanyName") = "Delta Company"
59:     Debug.Print "Local Customer AABBB changed."
60: End If
61: ' Add Customer ALLLL to Local Recordset
62: rs.AddNew
63: rs("CustomerID") = "ALLLL"
64: rs("CompanyName") = "Lambda Company"
65: Debug.Print "Local Customer ALLLL added."
66: Debug.Print
67:
68: ' Connect Local Recordset to Database and Update
69: rs.ActiveConnection = conn
70: On Error Resume Next
71: rs.UpdateBatch
72: Debug.Print "Update performed."
73:
74: If Err.Number <> 0 Then
75:     ' Error During Update
76:     Debug.Print "Error During Update:"
77:     Debug.Print Err.Description
78:     On Error GoTo 0
79:     Debug.Print
80: Else
81:     On Error GoTo 0
```

```
82: End If
83:
84: ' Show Conflicted Records after Update
85: rs.Filter = adFilterConflictingRecords
86: Debug.Print "Conflicted Records after Update:"
87: While Not rs.EOF
88:     Debug.Print "Status Record " & rs.AbsolutePosition & _
89:     ": 0x" & Hex(rs.Status)
90:     Debug.Print rs("CustomerID") & " " & rs("CompanyName")
91:     rs.MoveNext
92: Wend
93: Debug.Print
94:
95: ' Show Recordset Affected by Update
96: Debug.Print "Records Affected by Update:"
97: rs.Filter = adFilterAffectedRecords
98: While Not rs.EOF
99:     Debug.Print "Status Record " & rs.AbsolutePosition & _
100:     ": 0x" & Hex(rs.Status)
101:     Debug.Print rs("CustomerID") & " " & rs("CompanyName")
102:     rs.MoveNext
103: Wend
104: Debug.Print
105:
106: ' Show Recordset after Update
107: Debug.Print "Recordset after Update:"
108: rs.Filter = adFilterNone
109: While Not rs.EOF
110:     Debug.Print "Status Record " & rs.AbsolutePosition & _
111:     ": 0x" & Hex(rs.Status)
112:     Debug.Print rs("CustomerID") & " " & rs("CompanyName")
113:     rs.MoveNext
114: Wend
115: Debug.Print
116:
117:
118: ' Refresh Recordset
119: On Error Resume Next
120: rs.Resync
121: Debug.Print "Refresh performed."
122: If Err.Number <> 0 Then
123:     Debug.Print "Error during Syncronizing:"
124:     Debug.Print Err.Description
125:     Debug.Print
126:     Err.Number = 0
127: End If
128: On Error GoTo 0
129:
130: ' Show Conflicted Records by Refresh
131: rs.Filter = adFilterConflictingRecords
132: Debug.Print "Conflicted Records by Refresh:"
133: While Not rs.EOF
```

```
134:     Debug.Print "Status Record " & rs.AbsolutePosition & _
135:     ": 0x" & Hex(rs.Status)
136:     rs.MoveNext
137: Wend
138: Debug.Print
139:
140: ' Show Record Affected by Refresh
141: Debug.Print "Records Affected by Refresh:"
142: rs.Filter = adFilterAffectedRecords
143: While Not rs.EOF
144:     Debug.Print "Status Recordset " & rs.AbsolutePosition & _
145:     ": 0x" & Hex(rs.Status)
146:     rs.MoveNext
147: Wend
148: Debug.Print
149:
150: ' Show Recordset after Refresh
151: Debug.Print "Recordset after Refresh:"
152: rs.Filter = adFilterNone
153: While Not rs.EOF
154:     Debug.Print "Status Record " & rs.AbsolutePosition & _
155:     ": 0x" & Hex(rs.Status)
156:     Debug.Print rs("CustomerID") & " " & rs("CompanyName")
157:     rs.MoveNext
158: Wend
159: Debug.Print
160:
161:
162: ' Delete Customer AABBB
163: conn.Execute "DELETE FROM Customers WHERE " & _
164:     "CustomerID = 'AABBB' OR CustomerID = 'ALLLL'"
165:
166: rs.Close
167: Set rs = Nothing
168: conn.Close
169: Set conn = Nothing
```

Answers for Day 17

Quiz

1. What permission do you need to set on the MSADC virtual directory?

   Because RDS relies on an ISAPI application, the permissions must be set to allow Execute.

2. Which registry keys must be changed so the `MSDFMAP.Handler` is the required default handler?

   You must change `HandlerRequired` to 1 and set the `DefaultHandler` value to `MSDFMAP.Handler`.

3. Give some reasons why you would use the MSDFMAP handler.

   The primary reason is that you can hide your database connection string, which must contain the server name, username, and password. Second, you can limit the SQL statements that can be executed to a list of ones you created.

4. What is the name of the client-side RDS component that is used by the DataControl to contact the server's DataFactory?

   The DataSpace component is responsible for contacting the server-side DataFactory. It also caches the response it gets from the DataFactory.

Exercise

Create an RDS page that uses the MSDFMAP handler. It will return all records of the Suppliers table, but display only ten records per page. (In a table, see the DATAPAGESIZE property.) The user must be able to page with the Next and Previous buttons. In addition, display page-of-pages and the RecordCount.

A possible solution is presented in the following listing:

```
1: <html>
 2: <head>
 3:    <title>Exercise: Paging suppliers</title>
 4: </head>
 5: <body bgcolor="#ffffff">
 6:
 7: <OBJECT classid="clsid:BD96C556-65A3-11D0-983A-00C04FC29E33"
 8:    ID="rdsDC" height=0 width=0>
 9: </OBJECT>
10:
11: <h2>Suppliers in the database</h2>
12: <TABLE DATASRC="#rdsDC" DATAPAGESIZE="10" ID="SuppliersTable">
13: <TBODY>
14:    <TR>
15:       <TD><SPAN DATAFLD="CompanyName"></SPAN></TD>
16:      <TD><SPAN DATAFLD="Address"></SPAN></TD>
17:      <TD><SPAN DATAFLD="City"></SPAN></TD>
18:        <TD><SPAN DATAFLD="Country"></SPAN></TD>
19:    </TR>
20: </TBODY>
21: </TABLE>
22: <input type="Button" name="btnPrevious" value=" &lt; ">
23: <input type="Button" name="btnNext" value=" &gt; ">
24:
25: <DIV ID="divPageOfPages">page-of-pages</DIV>
26: <DIV ID="divRecordcount">recordcount</DIV>
27:
28: <SCRIPT LANGUAGE="VBSCRIPT">
29: <!-- #include file="adcvbs.inc" -->
```

A

```
30: ' we always start at the first page
31: m_nCurrentPage = 1
32: ' initially set to zero
33: m_nPageCount = 0
34:
35: Sub window_onload
36:   strHandler = "MSDFMAP.Handler,TysAdo25.ini"
37:   strServer = "http://<%=Request.ServerVariables("SERVER_NAME")%>"
38:   strConnect = "Data Source=NorthwindDatabase"
39:   strSQL = "SuppliersRDS"
40:
41:   rdsDC.Server = strServer
42:   rdsDC.Connect = strConnect
43:   rdsDC.SQL = strSQL
44:   rdsDC.Handler = strHandler
45:   ' open fully synchronous
46:   rdsDC.ExecuteOptions = adcExecSync
47:   rdsDC.FetchOptions = adcFetchUpFront
48:   rdsDC.Refresh
49:
50:   ' get page count, set record count and update buttons
51:   m_nPageCount = GetNumOfPages()
52:   divRecordcount.innerHTML = "Records: " & rdsDC.Recordset.RecordCount
53:   SetPageOfPages
54:   ShowAvailNavButtons
55: End Sub
56:
57: ' retrieve number of pages in recordset
58: Function GetNumOfPages()
59:   GetNumOfPages = rdsDC.Recordset.PageCount
60: End Function
61:
62: ' set the page display
63: Sub SetPageOfPages()
64:   divPageOfPages.innerHTML = "Page " & m_nCurrentPage & _
65:     " of " & m_nPageCount
66: End Sub
67:
68: Sub ShowAvailNavButtons()
69:   ' select when to display the previous button
70:   If 1 = m_nCurrentPage Then
71:     document.all("btnPrevious").style.display = "none"
72:   Else
73:     document.all("btnPrevious").style.display = ""
74:   End If
75:
76:   ' same with the next button
77:   If (m_nPageCount = m_nCurrentPage) Then
78:     document.all("btnNext").style.display = "none"
79:   Else
80:     document.all("btnNext").style.display = ""
```

```
81:    End If
82: End Sub
83:
84: ' move to next page, update page display and button state
85: Sub btnNext_OnClick()
86:    SuppliersTable.nextPage
87:    m_nCurrentPage = m_nCurrentPage + 1
88:    ShowAvailNavButtons
89:    SetPageOfPages
90: End Sub
91:
92: ' move to prev page, update page display and button state
93: Sub btnPrevious_OnClick()
94:    SuppliersTable.previousPage
95:    m_nCurrentPage = m_nCurrentPage - 1
96:    ShowAvailNavButtons
97:    SetPageOfPages
98: End Sub
99:
100: </SCRIPT>
101:
102: </body>
103: </html>
```

Answers for Day 18

Quiz

1. Which three methods must be implemented for the `IDataFactoryHandler` interface?

   The `IDataFactoryHandler` interface sports three methods: `GetRecordset`, `Reconnect`, and `OpenConnection`.

2. Where do you need to mark a custom handler as a safe handler?

   Before a handler can be used from RDS, it must be marked as safe in the registry under the following registry key:
   `HKEY_LOCAL_MACHINE\SOFTWARE\Microsoft\DataFactory\HandlerInfo\SafeHandlerList`.

3. Which security restrictions are in place for custom business objects over RDS?

   By default, you are not allowed to instantiate a custom business object over HTTP using RDS. You first have to assign it launch permission under the `HKEY_LOCAL_MACHINE\SYSTEM\CurrentControlSet\Services\W3SVC\Parameters\ADCLaunch` key.

4. Name the property you have to assign a disconnected recordset to for the `DataControl` to use it for display.

   The disconnected recordset must be assigned the `SourceRecordset` property of the `DataControl` object, for example:

   ```
   Set rdsDC.SourceRecordset = myBusObj.GetSuppliers()
   ```

Exercises

1. Write a custom handler `MyHandler.Exercise` that allows read operations only (`Reconnect` and `OpenConnection` with `lFlags` of `cWriteAccessFlag` should fail). The connection string is a constant; however, the SQL statements are to be honored.

   All you have to do is to modify the `OpenConnection` method of the `Custom.Handler` example that was presented today. The following listing contains the entire source code for the handler that solves the problem presented in the exercise.

   ```
    1: Option Explicit
    2:
    3: Private Const cstrConnStr = "provider=sqloledb.1;user id=sa;
   ➡password=;initial catalog=northwind;data source=strangelove"
    4: Private Const cWriteAccessFlag = 1
    5: Private Const cModifyQueryFlag = 2
    6: Private Const E_ACCESSDENIED = &H80070005
    7:
    8: Implements MSDFHDL.IDataFactoryHandler
    9:
   10: ' get a recordset from the database
   11: Private Function IDataFactoryHandler_GetRecordset(ByVal conn As String,
   ➡ByVal args As String, ByVal query As String) As ADODB.Recordset
   12: On Error GoTo Err_GetRecordset
   13:     Dim cn As ADODB.Connection
   14:     Dim rs As ADODB.Recordset
   15:
   16:     Set cn = IDataFactoryHandler_OpenConnection(conn, args,
   ➡cModifyQueryFlag, query)
   17:
   18:     Set rs = New ADODB.Recordset
   19:     rs.CursorLocation = adUseClient
   20:     rs.CursorType = adOpenStatic
   21:     rs.LockType = adLockBatchOptimistic
   22:     rs.Open query, cn
   23:     Set rs.ActiveConnection = Nothing
   24:
   25:     Set IDataFactoryHandler_GetRecordset = rs
   26:
   27:     Exit Function
   ```

```
28: Err_GetRecordset:
29:     Err.Raise Err.Number, Err.Source, Err.Description, _
30:          Err.HelpFile, Err.HelpContext
31:     Exit Function
32: End Function
33:
34: ' reconnect a disconnected recordset to the database
35: Private Sub IDataFactoryHandler_Reconnect(ByVal conn As String,
➥ByVal args As String, ByVal pRS As ADODB.Recordset)
36: On Error GoTo Err_Reconnect
37:     Dim cn As ADODB.Connection, strQuery As String
38:
39:     Set cn = IDataFactoryHandler_OpenConnection(conn, args,
➥cWriteAccessFlag, strQuery)
40:     pRS.ActiveConnection = cn
41:
42:     Exit Sub
43: Err_Reconnect:
44:     Err.Raise Err.Number, Err.Source, Err.Description, _
45:          Err.HelpFile, Err.HelpContext
46:     Exit Sub
47: End Sub
48:
49: Private Function IDataFactoryHandler_OpenConnection(ByVal conn As
➥String, ByVal args As String, ByVal lFlags As Long, ByRef query As
➥String) As ADODB.Connection
50: On Error GoTo Err_OpenConnection
51:     Dim cn As ADODB.Connection
52:
53:     If (lFlags = cWriteAccessFlag) Then
54:         Err.Raise E_ACCESSDENIED
55:     ElseIf (lFlags = cModifyQueryFlag) Then
56:          ' do not modify query string
57:     End If
58:
59:     Set cn = New ADODB.Connection
60:     cn.Open cstrConnStr
61:
62:     Set IDataFactoryHandler_OpenConnection = cn
63:
64:     Exit Function
65: Err_OpenConnection:
66:     Err.Raise Err.Number, Err.Source, Err.Description, _
67:          Err.HelpFile, Err.HelpContext
68:     Exit Function
69: End Function
```

2. Create a business object named MyBusObj.Exercise that implements one method named Fetch. This method takes as input parameter a string (SQL statement) and returns a recordset. The database connection is the Northwind database.

The following is a possible solution for the business object:

```
 1: Option Explicit
 2:
 3: Private Const cstrConnStr = "provider=sqloledb.1;user id=sa;
➥password=;initial catalog=northwind;data source=strangelove"
 4:
 5: Public Function Fetch(ByVal strSQL As Variant) As ADODB.Recordset
 6: On Error GoTo Err_Fetch
 7:     Dim cn As ADODB.Connection
 8:     Dim rs As ADODB.Recordset
 9:
10:     Set cn = New ADODB.Connection
11:     cn.Open cstrConnStr
12:
13:     Set rs = New ADODB.Recordset
14:     rs.CursorLocation = adUseClient
15:     rs.CursorType = adOpenStatic
16:     rs.LockType = adLockBatchOptimistic
17:     rs.Open strSQL, cn
18:     Set rs.ActiveConnection = Nothing
19:     Set Fetch = rs
20:
21:     Exit Function
22: Err_Fetch:
23:     Err.Raise Err.Number, Err.Source, Err.Description
24:     Exit Function
25: End Function
```

Answers for Day 19

Quiz

1. Which interface must be supported by objects that are passed as first parameter to the Save method of the Recordset object?

   The object you pass as first parameter must support the IStream interface. It is supported by the Stream object as well as the Response object.

2. Can you open persisted recordsets from the local hard disk only, or are other locations also supported?

   You can open persisted recordsets from the local hard disk, any network share you have access to, and an URL (Web page).

3. You have a data island defined. How do you refer to it from within a TABLE tag?

   The TABLE tag has to contain a DATASRC attribute, such as the following referring to a data island named myIsland:

   ```
   <TABLE ID="tblIsland" DATSRC="#myIsland">
   ```

4. How does the data island tag look when your data source is a file named `data.xml`?

   The correct data island tag looks like this:

   ```
   <XML ID="myDataIsland" SRC="data.xml"></XML>
   ```

5. Is it possible to use a raw persisted ADO recordset as source for a data island?

   No, it is not possible to use a raw persisted ADO recordset as a source for a data island. It can take plain XML files as input only.

6. Which attribute do you use in a `TABLE` tag for child elements in a hierarchical data island to be able to enumerate the children?

   You have to set the `DATAFLD` attribute's value to the name of the child elements.

Exercises

1. Create a shaped recordset (relate CustomerID to CustomerID for the Customers and Orders tables) and return it as an XML-persisted recordset to the Web client.

   The following listing presents a possible solution:

   ```
    1: <%
    2: Set conn = CreateObject("ADODB.Connection")
    3: Set rs = CreateObject("ADODB.Recordset")
    4:
    5: conn.Provider = "MSDataShape"
    6: conn.Open "data provider=sqloledb.1;user id=sa;password=;
   ➥initial catalog=northwind;data source=strangelove"
    7:
    8: strSQL = "SHAPE {select * from Customers}"
    9: strSQL = strSQL & " APPEND ("
   10: strSQL = strSQL & "{ select * from Orders } "
   11: strSQL = strSQL & " RELATE CustomerID to CustomerID) as rsOrders"
   12:
   13: rs.Open strSQL, conn
   14: rs.Save Response, 1
   15: %>
   ```

2. Use the XML returned from Exercise 1's ASP page to drive an RDS-enabled Web page.

   The following listing presents a possible solution:

   ```
    1: <html>
    2: <head>
    3:   <title>RDS with hierarchical recordsets</title>
    4: </head>
    5: <body bgcolor="#ffffff">
    6:
    7: <%
    8: strURL = "http://"
    9: strURL = strURL & Request.ServerVariables("SERVER_NAME")
   ```

```
10: strURL = strURL & "/adobook/xml/exercise1.asp"
11: %>
12:
13: <OBJECT classid="clsid:BD96C556-65A3-11D0-983A-00C04FC29E33"
14:   ID="rdsDC" height=0 width=0>
15:     <PARAM NAME="URL" VALUE="<%=strURL%>">
16: </OBJECT>
17:
18: <TABLE DATASRC="#rdsDC" ID="SuppliersTable">
19: <thead>
20: <tr>
21:   <th>Company</th>
22:   <th>Address</th>
23:   <th>City</th>
24:   <th>Country</th>
25:   <th>Order History</th>
26: </tr>
27: </thead>
28: <TBODY>
29:    <TR>
30:   <TD VALIGN="TOP"><SPAN DATAFLD="CompanyName"></SPAN></TD>
31:   <TD VALIGN="TOP"><SPAN DATAFLD="Address"></SPAN></TD>
32:   <TD VALIGN="TOP"><SPAN DATAFLD="City"></SPAN></TD>
33:   <TD VALIGN="TOP"><SPAN DATAFLD="Country"></SPAN></TD>
34:   <TD VALIGN="TOP">
35:   <TABLE DATASRC="#rdsDC" DATAFLD="rsOrders" ID="OrdersTable"
➥width="150">
36:   <thead><tr><th>Order ID</th><th>Order Date</th></tr></thead>
37:   <TR>
38:     <TD><SPAN DATAFLD="OrderId"></SPAN></TD>
39:     <TD><SPAN DATAFLD="OrderDate"></SPAN></TD>
40:   </TR>
41:   </TABLE>
42:   </TD>
43:    </TR>
44: </TBODY>
45: </TABLE>
46:
47: </body>
48: </html>
```

Answers for Day 20

Quiz

1. With ADO 2.5, which database systems allow you to manage users and roles via an ADOX connection?

   In the MDAC 2.5 release, only the OLE DB Provider for Microsoft Jet allows you to use the ADOX objects User and Group. An application can manage users and groups of Access databases when you're using ADOX.

2. When using an SQL Server 7.0 database, is it possible to adjust database permissions on SQL Server so that only selected stored procedures can be called to shield the database data from direct interaction with the user and malicious SQL statements?

In SQL Server 7.0, you can, of course, set user permissions for every SQL Server database object separately according to the intended restrictions of each defined database user. So it is possible to restrict a user to executing selected stored procedures without the possibility of gaining direct access to database tables or views by adjusting permissions for all involved database objects.

3. On which operation system must a database server run to allow Windows NT authentication?

Windows NT authentication can be used only on Windows NT and Windows 2000 operating systems, so the database server and the database client must run on either a Windows NT or a Windows 2000 system.

Exercise

Today is about theory, so there is no exercise.

Answers for Day 21

Quiz

1. Which technologies of MDAC 2.5 allow connection pooling?

Both OLE DB and ODBC allow connection pooling. However, ODBC is using another pooling technique than OLE DB.

2. What part of a database table influences performance of SQL statements especially when some thousand datasets are stored in the table?

Indexes created on certain table columns determine whether table data can be accessed fast or not.

3. What Recordset options can you adjust to gain the best mix of recordset features and performance for your database application?

You can adjust the CursorType, CursorLocation and LockType properties of the Recordset object to gain the optimal performance together with necessary Recordset features.

Exercise

As this is mostly a theory chapter there is no exercise.

APPENDIX B

Technologies, Features, and Release Packages of MDAC and ADO

If you are interested in how ADO evolved over the various versions of OLE DB and MDAC, this appendix is for you. Knowing the history of ADO is especially important when dealing with older ADO versions or related software. However, if you will never have to deal with older versions, you can skip this appendix.

ADO is part of the Microsoft Data Access Components (MDAC). Therefore, the history of ADO is connected with the MDAC history. MDAC comprises technologies such as ADO, OLE DB, ODBC, and other components (drivers, libraries, and so on).

The following summary provides only a general overview of the major releases of MDAC and its predecessors. If you want all the details of the ADO and MDAC history, refer to the Microsoft Platform SDK. Navigate to the technical article titled "MDAC Version History" by searching for the article's title in the Search tab of the Platform SDK Documentation. Double-click on the found

article to view it. You can locate the article in the Platform SDK content by choosing
View, Locate Topic in Contents from the menu in the Platform SDK Documentation win-
dow. The article is located in the content tree under Data Access Services, Microsoft
Data Access Components (MDAC) SDK, Microsoft Data Access Technical Articles,
MDAC General Technical Articles, MDAC Distribution Past and Present, MDAC Version
History.

MDAC 1.0 and 1.1 (OLE DB 1.0 and OLE DB 1.1)

MDAC 1.0 was formerly known as OLE DB 1.0 SDK (August 1996) and OLE DB 1.1
SDK (December 1996).

Release OLE DB 1.0 SDK contained the following components:

- Preview of ADO
- ADOR
- OLE DB 1.0
- OLE DB Provider for ODBC
- OLE DB Software Development Kit
- ODBC 2.5
- ODBC Drivers for Access, Excel, SQL Server, Text files, Paradox, Visual Fox Pro, xBase
- Jet Drivers for Excel, Paradox, Red (now Jet), Text, xBase

Release OLE DB 1.1 SDK contained the following components:

- ADO 1.0
- ADC (Advanced Database Connector, was ADOR)
- OLE DB 1.1
- OLE DB Provider for ODBC
- OLE DB SDK
- ODBC 3.0
- ODBC Drivers
- Jet Drivers

MDAC 1.0 was delivered through various distribution mechanisms. MDAC 1.0 was distributed on the Web and shipped with Active Server Pages (included in IIS 3.0 and Visual InterDev 1.0), Visual Studio 97.

MDAC 1.0/1.1 is now obsolete and no longer generally available.

MDAC 1.5

Microsoft Data Access Components 1.5 had a series of separate releases between September 1997 and March 1998, each including different versions of ODBC 3.5, OLE DB 1.5, RDS Components 1.5 (formerly known as ADC), OLE DB providers, and ODBC drivers.

The most important releases of MDAC 1.5 are the following six:

- MDAC 1.5 (IE 4.0) shipped with Microsoft Internet Explorer 4.0 and Internet Client SDK 4.0.

- MDAC 1.5 (PDC) updated the components shipped with IE 4.0. It was available only on the 1997 Professional Developers Conference CD-ROM.

- MDAC 1.5a was available for download on the Web.

- MDAC 1.5b was available with and integrated in the Microsoft Windows NT 4.0 Option Pack, which contained Internet Information Server (IIS) version 4.0.

- MDAC 1.5c could be downloaded from the Web with the MDAC standalone and a smaller MDAC redistribution setup that installed only the runtime components.

- MDAC 1.5d (final) can be found within Windows 98 and Internet Explorer 4.01 Service Pack 1. Both products contained only an incomplete subset of MDAC components, but the most current set of ADO 1.5 and RDS 1.5d objects.

To summarize, MDAC 1.5 contained the following major components:

- ADO 1.5
- RDS 1.5 (former ADC or ADOR)
- ODBC 3.5
- ODBC drivers—a new Oracle driver is included additionally to the other drivers
- Jet Drivers with the new Exchange and Lotus 1-2-3 drivers
- OLE DB 1.5
- OLE DB Providers—for ODBC and new for Jet (MDAC 1.5c)

MDAC 1.5 is also obsolete and no longer generally available.

MDAC 2.0

The MDAC 2.0 introduces a few new technologies and contains the complete MDAC SDK. The MDAC 2.0 redistribution program is contained in the MDAC 2.0 SDK, which combines and updates the contents of MDAC 1.5, ODBC 3.5 SDK, OLE DB 1.5 SDK, and the OLE DB for OLAP specifications. MDAC 2.0 versions were released during the period of July 1998 and January 1999.

The three important releases of MDAC 2.0 are

- MDAC 2.0.3002.20 (GA), also known as MDAC 2.0
- MDAC 2.0.3002.23, also known as MDAC 2.0 SP1 shipped with Microsoft Windows NT 4 Service Pack 4
- MDAC 2.0.3002.28 (GA), also referred to as MDAC 2.0 SP2

The MDAC 2.0 versions contained the following technologies (or parts of them):

- ADO 2.0
- ADO MD 2.0 (new)
- RDS 2.0
- MDAC SDK
- OLE DB 2.0
- OLE DB Providers—Oracle (new), Jet 3.5 for Access, ODBC, SQL Server
- OLE DB for OLAP (new)
- ODBC 3.51
- ODBC Drivers—for Access, Excel, SQL Server, Oracle, Text files, Visual FoxPro, Paradox, xBase
- Jet Drivers—for Excel, Exchange, Red (Jet or Access), Text files, Lotus 1-2-3, Paradox, xBase

The MDAC 2.0 introduces a redistribution program, which installs all the MDAC components as well as OLE DB providers and ODBC drivers. This avoids most problems that were introduced by separate installations of different versions of previous MDAC versions. Before MDAC 2.0, it was possible that only parts of MDAC were installed on a machine, maybe in various directories. So potential errors were introduced by trying to handle different versions of the same MDAC component at the same time.

MDAC 2.1

Introducing MDAC 2.1 (versions released between November 1998 and July 1999) caused version-naming confusion. The most current MDAC 2.1 version is the generally available MDAC 2.1.2.4202.3.

There are five releases of MDAC 2.1:

- MDAC 2.10.3513.2 (or MDAC 2.1) shipped only with Microsoft SQL Server 6.5 Service Pack 5 and SQL Server 7.0.
- MDAC 2.1 SDK Updater (available on the Microsoft Web site) contained the new Software Development Kit for MDAC 2.1.
- A subset of MDAC 2.1.1.3711.6 was part of the Internet Explorer 5 release. It is also known as MDAC 2.1 SP1 for Microsoft Internet Explorer 5.0.
- MDAC 2.1.1.3711.11 (MDAC 2.1 SP1) was available for download and also shipped with Microsoft Office 2000, Microsoft Back Office 4.5, Microsoft Visual Studio 98 Service Pack 3, and Internet Explorer 5.0a.
- MDAC 2.1.2.4202.3 (MDAC 2.1 SP2) was the final release of MDAC 2.1 and is available for download from the Microsoft Web site.

The following major technologies are part of MDAC 2.1:

- ADO 2.1
- ADO MD 2.1
- ADOX 2.1 (new)
- RDS 2.1
- OLE DB 2.1
- OLE DB Providers for ODBC, SQL Server, and Oracle
- JRO 2.1 (new)
- ODBC 3.51
- ODBC Drivers
- Jet Drivers
- RDO (new)—Remote Data Objects are a thin object layer interface to the ODBC application interface, including RDC (Remote Data Control)—RDO was distributed only in MDAC 2.10.3513.2.

MDAC 2.5

MDAC 2.5—available since February 17, 2000—can be downloaded as Microsoft Data Access Components (MDAC) 2.5 RTM (2.50.4403.12) from the Microsoft Internet site at `http://www.microsoft.com/data/`.

With the release of Windows 2000, MDAC 2.5 is part of the operating system. This has two effects. First, new releases of MDAC will be shipped with service packs for Windows 2000. Second, the ADO 2.5 and MDAC 2.5 documentation is contained in the

Platform SDK and not in the MDAC 2.5 setup program or in Windows 2000. The reason for this fact is, that all documentation about technologies supported by Windows 2000 is contained in the Microsoft Platform SDK and not in the documentation shipping with the operating system or the MDAC 2.5 package.

The first generally available release of MDAC 2.5 is MDAC 2.50.4403.12 (or MDAC 2.5 RTM), which is part of the Windows 2000 operating system and is also available for download to other Microsoft operating systems, such as Windows 95, Windows 98, and Windows NT 4.0 (service pack 4 or higher). New to MDAC 2.5 is that it is available only for x86 platforms, not for Alpha machines. Users of Alpha machines have to use the latest MDAC 2.1 version instead.

The following major technologies are part of MDAC 2.5:

- ADO 2.5
- ADO MD 2.5
- ADOX 2.5
- RDS 2.5
- OLE DB 2.5
- OLE DB Providers—for ODBC Drivers, SQL Server, Site Server Search, Internet Publishing, Jet 4.0 (Access 2000), Oracle, DTS Packages, Microsoft Directory Services, Microsoft Data Shaping Services, OLAP Services, Indexing Services, SQL Server DTS Flat File, OLE DB Simple Provider
- JRO 2.5
- ODBC 3.51
- ODBC Drivers—for Access, SQL Server, Excel, Text, Visual FoxPro, FoxPro VFP, dBase, dBase VFP, Paradox, Oracle
- Jet Drivers (ODBC Desktop Database Drivers)—for Excel, Exchange, Access, Text files, Lotus 1-2-3, Paradox, xBase

APPENDIX C

OLE DB Providers and Services for ADO

The following OLE DB Providers are part of MDAC 2.5 and therefore available for an ADO connection:

- OLE DB Provider for SQL Server—This provider enables ADO to access SQL Server databases on one or more computers running Microsoft SQL Server.

- OLE DB Provider for Jet—This provider allows ADO to connect to Microsoft Access databases.

- OLE DB Provider for ODBC—Through this provider, you can access an ODBC database driver. This is especially useful when only an ODBC driver is available for your database.

- OLE DB Provider for Oracle—Use this provider to connect to Oracle databases.

- OLE DB Provider for Indexing Service—This provider supplies programmatic read-only access to Index Server content and property indexes. Index Server allows fast full-text queries over the content of documents stored on a computer or an Internet server.

- OLE DB Provider for Internet Publishing—Use this provider to access resources served by Microsoft FrontPage or Internet Information Server (IIS) with FrontPage extensions enabled. FrontPage resources can be Web source files (HTML and ASP files) or Windows 2000 Web folders.

- OLE DB Provider for Active Directory Service—This provider allows ADO to connect to heterogeneous directory services through Active Directory Service Interfaces (ADSI). In MDAC 2.5, the provider is limited to read-only access.

- OLE DB Provider for DTS Packages—The provider allows accessing Data Transformation Services (DTS) Packages. Using DTS, you can import, export, and transform data between any OLE DB and ODBC data source or text file format. In MDAC 2.5, the provider is limited to read-only access.

- OLE DB for OLAP Provider—This provider allows ADO to access multidimensional data providers through SQL and multidimensional expression (MDX) statements.

- Data Shaping Services for OLE DB—These services are used in combination with an OLE DB Provider to create relationships between data. Instructions for the provider are executed using the SHAPE language.

- OLE DB Remoting Provider—This provider is used in combination with other OLE DB Providers. The OLE DB Remoting Provider enables your application to access other OLE DB Providers running on separate machines or in a separate process on the same machine. To communicate with other processes, the provider uses named pipes. For network communication, it uses either DCOM (Distributed Component Object Model) protocol or HTTP/HTTPS (Secure Hypertext Transfer Protocol).

- OLE DB Persistence Provider—This provider enables you to save a `Recordset` object directly to a file and later restore the `Recordset` object from the file. All information—such as schema information, data, and pending changes—are preserved. MDAC 2.5 supports two file data formats: the open eXtensible Markup Language (XML) format and Microsoft's proprietary Advanced Data Table Gram (ADTG) format.

- Cursor Service for OLE DB—This Service is automatically invoked for client-side ADO recordsets. This service enhances certain functions, because it allows you to navigate through a recordset forward and backward, enables batch updates, or creates temporary indexes on the recordset data even when the underlying OLE DB Provider does not provide these features. To invoke the Cursor Service for OLE DB, set the `Recordset` or `Connection` object property named `CursorLocation` to the ADO constant `adUseClient`:

- OLE DB Simple Provider—This provider is used to access OLE DB Providers created with the OLE DB Simple Provider (OSP) Toolkit. The OSP Toolkit enables developers to build OLE DB Providers over simple data sources, such as in-memory arrays. You do not have to build an OLE DB Provider from scratch to expose an OLE DB interface to a simple data source. OSP Toolkit is language-neutral and therefore also supports Visual Basic, Visual C++, and Visual J++.

For further details—on such topics as ADO connection strings, features, and limitations—refer to the Microsoft Platform SDK.

C

APPENDIX D

ADO Programming Quick-Reference

ActiveX Data Objects (ADO) can be used in many programming languages[md]for example, in Microsoft Visual Basic, VBScript, Visual C++, Visual J++, JScript, and other languages supporting COM objects.

This appendix enables you to become familiar with using ADO in Visual Basic, VBA (for Microsoft Office applications), and VBScript (for Active Server Pages on Internet Information Server).

This book focuses on using ADO with Visual Basic and VBScript. Developers using other languages, such as Visual C++ or Visual J++ or JScript, will find all the information about using ADO with their language in the Platform SDK documentation.

Using ADO with Visual Basic

In a Visual Basic project, you can use all functions, objects, and constants provided by ADO 2.5.

To use ADO 2.5 in your Visual Basic project, you should reference the ADO 2.5 library. This enables Visual Basic to create and use ADO objects similar to intrinsic Visual Basic objects. When you want to use ADO constants in your project, you also should reference the ADO 2.5 library. ADO constants are often used as arguments for methods and properties of ADO objects to indicate specific options.

Referencing ADO in Visual Basic

To Do: Referencing ADO in Visual Basic

Referencing the ADO 2.5 library in your Visual Basic project is done as follows:

1. In the Visual Basic window, select Project, References from the menu.

2. Select Microsoft ActiveX Data Objects 2.5 Library from the available references list.

3. Verify that at least the following libraries are also selected: Visual Basic for Applications, Visual Basic objects and procedures, Visual Basic runtime objects and procedures, and OLE Automation.

4. Click the OK button and close the window. Now the ADO 2.5 library is referenced to your Visual Basic project.

To create ADO objects in Visual Basic, you can use either a `Dim` or a `CreateObject` statement.

When you reference the ADO library, you can use the autocompletion feature of Visual Basic. Another advantage is that you can use ADO constants in your code without explicitly defining their values. ADO constants are used, for example, to define the data type of a field or the parameter of an object's method, or to set or compare values of ADO object's properties.

Creating an ADO Object Using the `Dim` Statement

When you have referenced the ADO library in your Visual Basic project, creating an ADO object using a `Dim` statement is done as in the following code. Use the keyword `New` in a `Dim` statement to declare and create an ADO object in one step:

```
Dim conn as New ADODB.Connection
```

The variable conn is declared, and an instance of the ADO `Connection` object is created and stored in the variable conn:

```
Dim rs as New ADODB.Recordset
```

The variable `rs` is declared and contains an ADO `Recordset` object.

Declaring and creating an object using a `Dim` statement can also be done in separate steps:

```
Dim conn as ADODB.Connection
Set conn = New ADODB.Connection
```

Creating an ADO Object Using `CreateObject`

When using the `CreateObject` statement, declaration and creation of an ADO object is done in two steps:

```
Dim conn as ADODB.Connection
Set conn = CreateObject("ADODB.Connection")

Dim rs as ADODB.Recordset
Set rs = CreateObject("ADODB.Recordset")
```

When there is no reference to ADO defined for your Visual Basic object, you can also create ADO objects using a `CreateObject` statement:

```
Dim conn as Object
Set conn = CreateObject("ADODB.Connection")

Dim rs as Object
Set rs = CreateObject("ADODB.Recordset")
```

Creating objects using `CreateObject` is usually slower than using a `Dim` statement with the `New` keyword.

Using ADO Objects in Visual Basic

An ADO object can provide properties, methods, collections, and events.

An object's property is an attribute of an object that usually can be read or set.

Methods are routines that an object provides for execution.

In a collection, an object stores related objects of the same kind. The objects in the collection can be accessed through the object's name, the collection name, and the name of the collection object.

After you have created an ADO object and stored it in a variable, you can use the variable to access the object's properties, execute its methods, or access elements in its collections.

The following example provides a schematic overview of how to use properties, methods, and the `Fields` collection of the `Recordset` object.

D

First, declare the object variable and create the object:

```
Dim rs as New ADODB.Recordset
```

Now the variable `rs` contains an instance of the `Recordset` object.

You can write values to the recordset's property (the `LockType` property of the `Recordset` object):

```
rs.LockType = 3
```

To read a value from a recordset's property, do as follows:

```
lngVar = rs.CursorType
```

Executing a method, such as the `Open` method of the `Recordset` object, is done as follows:

```
rs.Open
```

Methods also can take arguments and return values, as in the following example:

```
blnCheck = rs.Supports(adBookmark)
```

To access an element from the `Fields` collection of the `Recordset` object, use a statement as follows:

```
strName = rs.Fields("FieldName").Value
```

Every element of a collection is itself an object and usually provides various properties. In the last line of code, the `Fields` collection element with the name `FieldName` is accessed, and its `Value` property is read and stored in the variable `strName`.

This book features many Visual Basic code examples that make use of various ADO properties, methods, collections, and events.

Using ADO in Visual Basic for Applications

Using ADO in Visual Basic for Application (Microsoft Office applications) is similar to using ADO with Visual Basic.

To Do: Referencing ADO in VBA

You should reference the ADO 2.5 library in your Office project. For instance, when using ADO in a Microsoft Access project, you can reference the ADO 2.5 library as follows:

1. In the Microsoft Visual Basic window, select an element from the VBA Project pane.

▼ 2. Select Tools, References from the menu.

3. Select Microsoft ActiveX Data Objects 2.5 Library from the available references list.

4. Verify that at least the following libraries are also selected: Visual Basic for Applications, OLE Automation, and Microsoft *Application* Object Library (where *Application* stands for Word, Access, Excel, and so on).

▲ 5. Click the OK button and the ADO 2.5 library is referenced to your VBA project.

Referencing the ADO library in your VBA project enables you to create ADO objects using `Dim` statements. You also can use ADO constants without explicitly defining them in your script.

Creating ADO objects using `Dim` or `CreateObject` statements is done in VBA the same way as in Visual Basic.

Using ADO with VBScript

Using ADO with VBScript is similar to using ADO with Visual Basic or VBA. However, because VBScript uses only the `Variant` data type (which can store data of all data types as well as objects), you cannot use the `Dim` statement to assign ADO objects to variables. Furthermore, VBScript does not support using the `New` keyword in `Dim` or `Set` statements.

To create an ADO object in VBScript, use statements such as the following:

```
Dim conn
Set conn = CreateObject("ADODB.Connection")

Dim rs
Set rs = CreateObject("ADODB.Recordset")
```

Because you cannot reference the ADO library in VBScript, you have to define ADO constants explicitly before using them in your script.

ADO provides two files containing definitions for all ADO constants:

- For server-side scripting, such as in Active Server Pages (ASP), use the file `Adovbs.inc`, which is installed in the `<Root>:\Program Files\Common Files\System\ado\` folder for default.

- For client-side scripting, such as VBScript running in Internet Explorer, use the file `Adocvbs.inc`, which can be found in the `<Root>:\Program Files\Common Files\System\msadc\` folder for default.

You have the possibility of copying and pasting ADO constant definitions from these files to your application. If you are doing server-side scripting using ASP, copy the

D

Adovbs.inc file to a folder on your Web site, rename the file to Adovbs.asp for security reasons, and reference the file from your ASP page using the include directive. The include directive must not be surrounded by code delimiters (`<%` and `%>`), and could look like the following:

```
<!--#include File="Adovbs.asp"-->
```

The following are other limitations of using VBScript instead of Visual Basic:

- You cannot use On Error GoTo <Label> statements in your script. Only On Error Resume Next and On Error GoTo 0 are supported.
- VBScript does not support all intrinsic Visual Basic functions. For instance, IsNumeric can be used in VBScript. However, the Format function cannot be used.

When using ASP with an ODBC DSN to access a database, make sure that you are using no User DSN, because Internet Information Services (IIS) are running in their own user context. Therefore, you have to use an ODBC System DSN instead of a User DSN for ADO connections in ASP pages.

INDEX

navigating
large recordsets, 154-166
Recordset object
MoveFirst method, 41-42
MoveLast method, 41-42
MoveNext method, 41-42
MovePrevious method, 41-42
size considerations, 153
nested transactions, 214
enforcing, 220-224
schematic diagram, 219
support for, 219
Netscape Navigator, XSL templates, 563
network cards, performance tuning issues, 621
NEXTMEMBER expression, MDX statements, 338
Northwind database, stored procedures, 181-183
adding, 188-190
calling, 192-195, 201-205
executing (Command object), 195-199
modifying, 191-192

O

object libraries, ADO references, establishing, 29-31
Object Linking and Embedding for Databases, *see* **OLE DB**
objects
collections, 19
COM+ applications, building, 444-447
Command, 17-18
component libraries
ADO 2.5, 15, 20-21
ADO MD, 15, 21-22
ADOX, 15, 20, 22
Connection, 17-18
declarations, 30-31
late binding, 31
Error, 17
Field, 17-18
ownership, assigning, 414-415
Parameter, 17
Property, 17
Record, 17
semistructured data, 360
Recordset, 17-18
Bookmark property, 128-129
Filter, 139-142
Filter property, 142-144
Find method, 129-133
Index property, 133-139
schematic representation, 19

Seek method, 130, 136-139
Sort property, 148-150
Status property, 144-148
semistructured data, 360
ODBC (Open Database Connectivity), 7
call tracing, performance tuning options, 615-616
connection pooling, performance tuning issues, 604-607
data connections not through DSN, 32-33
OLE DB Provider, 32, 683
through DSN, 32
security, tracing tools, 591-592
OLAP (Online Analytical Processing), 299-300
data analysis (Excel), 313-316
OLE DB Provider, 684
versus data warehouse terminology, 302
OLAP Server
axes definition, retrieving (ADO MD), 344-348
cellsets, displaying (ADO MD), 348-350
cube data, retrieving (ADO MD), 342-344

R

RAID (Redundant Array of Inexpensive Disks), 620

RDO (Remote Data Objects), 19

RDS (Remote Data Service), 499
- advantages, 501-502
- business objects
  - build considerations, 545
  - creating, 546-548
  - Excel environment, 550-551
  - extending to Internet, 534-535
  - Internet Explorer environment, 551-552
  - marshaling, 533
  - model, 532
  - proxies, 532
  - registering, 548-549
- client applications, XML recordsets, 560-561
- components, 500-501
- configuring, 502-505
- custom handlers
  - coding, 538-541
  - creating, 535-537
  - implementing, 535-542
  - invoking, 533-534
  - registering, 541-542
- Data Control, populating with XML data, 562-563

data path
- business tier, 500-501
- data tier, 500-501
- presentation tier, 500-501
default handler
- disabling, 506
- installing, 525-527
- script changes, 527-528
- security considerations, 524-525
disadvantages, 502
disconnected recordsets, access protocols, 500
intranet security problems, 589
RDSServer Data Factory, client connections, 542-544
recordset data (MS Remote Provider), 544-545
security
- considerations, 589-590
- default handler, 524-525
- default handler, disabling, 506
- default handler, installing, 525-527
- default handler, script changes, 527-528
Web pages, creating, 507-523

RDS Library (Remote Data Server), 21

RDSServer Data Factory, Excel connections, 542-544

read-only locking, 51

reading BLOB values, GetChunk method (Field object), 89-90

reconfiguring default Web site, MSADC directory (RDS), 502-504

Record object, 17
- database providers, 361-362
- recordset rows, representing, 361-362
- semistructured data, 360
- WebDAV
  - resource connections, 367-368
  - resource properties, 368-371

RecordChangeComplete event, 246

RecordCount property (Recordset object), 54-57, 155

records
- databases
  - deleting, 432-433
  - updating, 434-435
- fields
  - current values, 61
  - defined size determination, 60
  - names, 57-58
  - original values, 60-61
  - properties, 57
  - size determination, 60

Other Related Titles

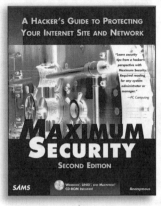

Maximum Security, Second Edition
0-672-31341-3
Anonymous
$49.99 USA/$70.95 CAN

Sams Teach Yourself SQL in 21 Days, Third Edition
0-672-31674-9
Ryan Stephens
$34.99 USA/$52.95 CAN

Sams Teach Yourself SQL in 10 Minutes
0-672-31664-1
Ben Forta
$12.99 USA/$19.95 CAN

Active Server Pages 2.0 Unleashed
0-672-31613-7
Steve Walther
$49.99 USA/$71.95 CAN

Sams Teach Yourself SQL Server 7.0 in 21 Days
0-672-31290-5
Rick Sawtell and Richard Waymire
$39.99 USA/$57.95 CAN

Building Enterprise Solutions with Visual Studio 6
0-672-31489-4
G.A.Sullivan
$49.99 US/$71.95 CAN

Sams Teach Yourself CGI in 24 Hours
0-672-31880-6
Rafe Colburn
$24.99 USA/$37.95 CAN

Microsoft SQL Server 7 DBA Survival Guide
0-672-31226-3
Mark Spenik; Orryn Sledge
$49.99 USA/$74.95 CAN

F. Scott Barker's Microsoft Access 2000 Power Programming
0-672-31506-8
F. Scott Barker
$49.99 USA/$74.95 CAN

Sams Teach Yourself Internet Programming with Visual C++ in 21 Days
0-672-31823-7
William Robison
$39.99 USA/$59.95 CAN

Microsoft Windows 2000 Troubleshooting and Configuration
0-672-31878-4
Robert Reinstein
$49.99 USA/$74.95 CAN

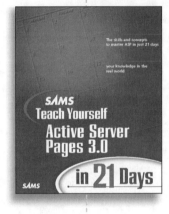

Sams Teach Yourself Active Server Pages 3.0 in 21 Days
0-672-31863-6
Scott Mitchell, James Atkinson
$39.99 US/$59.95 CAN

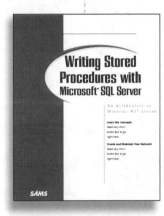

Writing Stored Procedures with Microsoft SQL Server
0-672-31886-5
Matt Shepker
$39.99 US/$59.95 CAN

www.samspublishing.com

All prices are subject to change.

ActiveX Data Objects (ADO) 2.5 Model

Connection

Collections
Errors
Properties

Properties
Attributes
CommandTimeout
ConnectionString
ConnectionTimeout
CursorLocation
DefaultDatabase
IsolationLevel
Mode
Provider
State
Version

Methods
BeginTrans
Cancel
Close
CommitTrans
Execute
Open
OpenSchema
RollbackTrans

Events
BeginTransComplete
CommitTransComplete
ConnectComplete
Disconnect
ExecuteComplete
InfoMessage
RollbackTransComplete
WillConnect
WillExecute

Recordset

Collections
Fields
Properties

Properties
AbsolutePage
AbsolutePosition
ActiveCommand
ActiveConnection
BOF
Bookmark
CacheSize
CursorLocation
CursorType
DataMember
DataSource
EditMode
EOF
Filter
Index
LockType
MarshalOptions
MaxRecords
PageCount
PageSize
RecordCount
Sort
Source
State
Status
StayInSync

Methods
AddNew
Cancel
CancelBatch
CancelUpdate
Clone
Close
CompareBookmarks
Delete
Find
GetRows
GetString
Move
MoveFirst
MoveLast
MoveNext
MovePrevious
NextRecordset
Open
Requery
Resync
Save
Seek
Supports
Update
UpdateBatch

Events
EndOfRecordset
FetchComplete
FetchProgress
FieldChangeComplete
MoveComplete
RecordChangeComplete
RecordsetChangeComplete
WillChangeField
WillChangeRecord
WillChangeRecordset
WillMove